W9-DJQ-760

Children of Parting Parents

Children of
Parting Parents

Lora Heims Tessman, Ph.D.

NEW YORK • JASON ARONSON • LONDON

Tessman, Lora Heims, 1928-
    Children of parting parents.

    Bibliography: p.
    Includes index.
    1. Children of divorced parents. I. Title.
RJ507.D59T47   155.9'2'4   77-94094
ISBN 0-87668-307-3

Manufactured in the United States of America

to my three loves...
Jack,
Debbie, Lisa

PREFACE

This is not a report of a research project. It is a sharing of my experience with many children, adolescents, and adults who came to see me while in the midst of trying to cope with reactions to their parents' parting, because of separation, divorce, or death.

Some were in extended individual psychotherapy, and I came to know them very well; others came for briefer periods of help, focused on the current disruptive changes in their lives; or for an evaluation of their situation, sometimes but certainly not always followed by referral to or collaboration with other resources. Others were referred because of an urgent array of symptoms and not because of their parents' parting. Still others, aware of the potentially disruptive effect of divorce on their children, came just in order to evolve ways of being able to support their children emotionally through the expected period of distress. I was repeatedly impressed with the many parents whose deep caring for their children was reflected in a willingness to remain aware, and to respond to the child's needs as helpfully as possible, even when the parent himself was in considerable turmoil. For divorcing parents, for example, this often involved a willingness to differentiate between his own anger and disappointment in the spouse and the child's continued need to value and long for him, without being pushed to experience this as a conflict of loyalties. This is not an easy task.

In working with the children and parents, I came across a number of reactions in myself: Frequently, I found myself admiring the courage of child or adult who insisted on going to the heart of a matter which pained him greatly but needed to be faced. Often I was profoundly moved by the deep quality of a child's or adult's grief, a final distillation of sadness and unrequited longing. Repeatedly, I was delighted by the essential humanness of the person: namely, the remarkable creativity and innovative potential of the mind when fueled with fervor. I saw inventions in imagination of the most individual ways of cherishing what was once experienced, even if in multitudinous disguise. Such cherishing remained still fresh and lively as central motivating forces in the lives of children and adults, after emerging from its bout with anger, planned revenge, or desolation. Admitting to the impressiveness of computers, satellites, DNA, and other complicated machinery, I find myself still favoring the most complex generator of all; the human being with his fertility of imagination and feeling. Some of this perhaps became most clear in some adults who had been children of the deceased, and who eventually recaptured through a song fragment, or a saying, or the gestures of an arm, a leitmotiv of shared enjoyment still untarnished after supposed burial thirty years earlier. Finally, a reaction in myself with which I frequently had to cope was an unbelievable degree of frustration in some cases, such as some custody disputes, in which an escalation of difficulties for everyone could be predicted but, apparently, not stopped.

Although psychotherapy is one of my central interests in itself, it will not be the focus of this book. Illustrative case material is not presented in its entirety, but is selected in terms of its relevance to parental parting. Precautions to disguise the identity of the individuals have been taken in all cases, and individuals quoted most extensively have been asked for permission to include their material. Of necessity, much had to be omitted.

As I did not have the chance to meet most of the participants in this book before the time of their separation or divorce, impressions about what in their daily interaction had brought the relationship to a definitive halt are post hoc, and will also not be a major focus. I am neither for nor against divorce. It seemed clear, however, that in almost all cases seen the particular divorce was a step in the right direction for the individuals involved, although it caused pain and did not in itself solve the problems in their lives.

It becomes pertinent to ask what factors progressively worked to stretch the discrepancy between what the marital partners wanted and needed of each other, and what they felt possible, either between them or as a family unit. Difficulties in flexibly meeting each other's needs were expressed over and over again in the form of a felt lack of communication or intimacy, lack of respect for each other as individuals, or a need for flight from the ties of marriage or parenthood itself. The divorce was often seen as essentially a need to preserve or develop the self, though at the cost of considerable guilt and anguish. Needless to say, unfulfillable and idealized expectations of the marriage partner, born of wishful fantasies rather than experience in close interaction with others, were bound to come to grief. However, this seems to me, even when true, to be too facile an explanation. It is most certainly rooted in personality; but how have such discrepancies also been promulgated through culturally shared mythologies, which in the past have indelibly marked the growing personality? It is probably harder to walk well if your feet have been bound throughout childhood and are now stunted.

Such interweaving of the influence of the wider human interaction network; the intimate relationship between spouses and between each parent and child; and the complexly developing psyche within the individual confronted with a loss are assumed in the choice of topics for theoretical consideration. Their actual blending occurs only in the behavior, feelings, and images, as described here, of the children and adults themselves.

ACKNOWLEDGMENTS

My warm appreciation goes to those friends and colleagues, recent discussions with whom concerning the issues dealt with in this book have raised new questions in my mind, aroused either doubts or understandings in regard to old questions, or led to a sudden sense of contact with previously elusive notions. I have gained much from such conversations with Dr. Merton Kahne, Dr. Irving Kaufman, Drs. Carola and Leon Eisenberg, Dr. Rochelle Friedman, Dr. Jean Baker Miller, Dr. Robert Weiss, Dr. Mahlka Notman, and others. The lasting influence of valued contact with a number of other individuals beginning during the early years of my clinical experience is also acknowledged with respect and affection. These include Dr. Bessie Sperry, my first clinical supervisor, and Dr. Daniel Levinson, Dr. Stanley Cath, Dr. Paul Myerson, Dr. Benson Snyder, and the late Dr. Henry Wermer.

I also want to thank members of the M.I.T. Psychiatric Service and those therapists, in clinic or private practice, who along with teachers, lawyers, guidance counselors, group activity leaders, and others collaborated in the care and treatment of some of the children and parents.

To the individual children and adults encountered and described here who shared their experiences, and are in this sense participants, go my thanks, my appreciation of them as individuals, my compassion for the sadness in their lives, my enchantment at their inventiveness and perservance, and my best wishes for their future well-being.

Special thanks go also to Gini Egan, who typed and transformed a sometimes unreadable manuscript into readable form, and to Mrs. Jan Blakeslee, whose generous editorial talents were most welcome.

My deepest gratitude is reserved for my husband, Jack, who not only offered the emotional support, revitalizing pleasures, and encouragement which made this work possible, but also translated this into such tangible forms as flexibly shouldering home tasks; and for our daughters, Lisa and Debbie, who resourcefully participated in many ways, such as by taking over all the cookie baking and vegetable planting in the family for the "duration" of this work, and by continuing to be their own delightfully refreshing selves.

CONTENTS

Part I: Theoretical Considerations

CHAPTER 1   THE HUMAN RELATIONSHIP NETWORK: 1
             ITS SUPPORTS AND LACUNAE

The Impact on the Parents During Marriage   5

   Changing interaction between men and women   6

   Changing attitudes toward childrearing   14

   Changing role of the family in history   22

   Changes in ideology and in customs concerning   24
   marriage, divorce and child care

The Human Relationship Network During the Period   30
of Parting

   Supports and lacunae for parents   30

   Supports and lacunae for children   35

   The function of the human support network during   37
   parting: Summary

CHAPTER 2   THE ROLE OF IDENTIFICATION   41
              PROCESSES

Introduction of the Issues   41

Mixtures of Identification and the Quest for   45
the Wanted Person

    Vignette 1: Peter   45

    Vignette 2: Emily   45

    Vignette 3: Linda   46

Some Questions Regarding the Role   48
of Identification

Identification as a Process in Development   50

    In early childhood   50

    In adolescence   60

    In post-adolescence and adulthood   70

Identification as a Mode for Coping with Loss   80

A Note about the Ego Ideal   84

CHAPTER 3   THE QUEST FOR THE WANTED   90
              PERSON

Nature and Function of the Quest   90

Psychic and Behavioral Mechanisms in the Service of the   94
Quest and their Development

    Basis for the quest in the unconscious   97

    Early cognitive models of what makes objects   99
    appear and disappear

    A developmental study of ideas about death   102

    Early experienced interactions and their later re-emergence   104
    in nonverbal forms of the quest

    Some forms of psychic mechanisms in the service   106
    of the quest

        Identification and introjection   107

Searching 107

Remembering 108

Presences 110

The magic re-creation of the person, 111
through gesture or thought

The transitional object and transitional 111
phenomena

Pseudologia and "lying" 116

Denial and negation 118

Magical gestures of imitation vs. trial identification 120
for the purpose of empathy

Fantasy 120

Some empirical findings regarding the quest 121
for the absent person

Comments 128

CHAPTER 4   GRIEVING 131

Grief in Childhood 132

A Component of Adolescence, Analogous to Mourning 140

The Capacity to Bear Painful Affects: Its Relation to 141
Adult Life and to Grieving

Part II: Encounters with Children and Parents

CHAPTER 5   PARENTS DIVIDED AND PARENTS MULTIPLIED: 149
SOME EFFECTS OF MULTIPLE PARENT FIGURES
ON THE IDENTIFICATIONS OF THE CHILD

Psychic Factors and the Human Support System 149

Some Characteristics of the Families 155

Encounters with Children and Parents 162

A reunion fantasy in the absence of actual loss: Jeremy 162

Some initial reactions to separation: Sean,   171
Jenny, Daniel, Craig and Betsy

    Sean   171

    Jenny   174

    Daniel   177

    Craig and Betsy   184

Working through transient disguised symptoms   193
of grief: Mark

Shifts in identification processes over a period   204
of time: Noah

An early identity crisis and incompatible   226
identifications: Jeffrey

Two retrospective views of the effects of early loss   233

    Grief unexplored: some consequences in character   234
    structure: Pam

    Some effects of multiple separations and severe   248
    deprivation: Lou Ann

Defenses against loss and mistrust of   268
remarriage: Robin

Comments on Enrichment of Identifications   271

CHAPTER 6   THE CHILD IN THE ILL-FITTING   277
                 CUSTODY SUIT

The Child Transformed into Enemy: The O'Malleys   281

The Child in the Service of a Father's Conflict: 288
The Knights

Custody Suit Averted: A Disturbed Mother-Child   292
Relationship in Therapy: The Walshes

Custody Renounced and Regained: Four Sets   301
of Circumstances

    Family ties as felt impediment: Rachel Glade   301

    Reluctant abandonment of custody   303

Mrs. Greenwall 303

Estelle Phillips and George 304

Change of custody by mutual agreement: 310
Ernst Martinique

Custody change necessitated by emotional incapacity 311
of one parent: Gerardo and Lucretia Castillo

Gerardo Castillo 311

Comments and Conclusions 319

CHAPTER 7 "THE TRUTH IS A HIT ON THE HEAD WITH A 323
A HAMMER": IMAGES OF THE PARTING
PARENT AND SELF IN PUBESCENCE
AND ADOLESCENCE

Characteristics of the Group 326

The adolescents 326

The parents 330

Further reactions of adolescents and parents 331

Encounters with Adolescents 339

The wish for external stability during times 339
of inner change toward autonomy: Erika

The experience of "truth" about the self and 341
parents and its relationship to future goals

Truth and idealization: Abbey, Carole, Eva 342

Initial acceptance of the devaluation of an 347
absent parent: Karen, Heather

Prolonged denial and negation: Shirley and Eddy 349

Pseudologia and consoling fantasy: Eileen, Linda 354

Restitutive hallucinations and consoling fantasies: 357
Angela

Transitory disbelief and negation: Christopher 358

Protective disengagement: Ralph, Julia 359

Relationships to others during the period of 361
intense stress

Friendships: Jane   361

The "substitute family" Eileen, Linda, Angela   364

Involvement in fulfilling parental needs: Randolph,   371
Sarah, Heather, Karen

Some family styles of coping with stress, and their   375
relationship to the adolescent's development

Impulsive acting out: The Wingers   376

The consoling alliance; postponement of grief   390
and of individuation: Karen, Heather

Hope and despair in the search for truth: images   400
of a new civilization: Eva

CHAPTER 8   "WHEN DEATH DID US PART": THE IMPACT   415
               OF THE DECEASED—A COMPARISON

The human support network   416

Reality sense   418

The quest for the lost, wanted parent   419

Identification processes   421

Encounters with Children, Adolescents and Adults   422

A child: guilt, fear and transfiguration—Vicky   422

Two adolescents: supported grieving—Tod   423
and Peggy

Adults bereaved in childhood   428

Literal clinging to the dead: Mary Ann   428

Identification in the absence of memories: 429
Michael

The displaced beckoning of a lost, loved   440
mother: Alex

Fidelity: "The words I love you forever   445
make me cry": Amy

Discontinuity in the image of a parent: the strength   455
to survive loss and be whole: Natasha

Integration of an enriching identification with the   472
quest for affects shared with a loved father: Wendy

Comments   481

Part III: Toward a Conclusion

CHAPTER 9   WAYS OF COPING WITH PARENTAL PARTING: 490
SOME RELEVANT FACTORS

Age   492

    Under two   492

    Age 2-5   493

    Latency   496

    Adolescence   498

Information about the Causes and Effects of the   500
Divorce or Death

The Personality of the Child at the Time of   506
Parental Parting

The Meeting of Needs for Sustained Caring   509

Parental Modes of Coping with Stress   510

The Relationship with the Absent Parent   512

The Relationship with the Home Parent   516

New Parent Figures and Step-Parents   521

CHAPTER 10   REFLECTIONS ON THERAPY   527

Work Related to the Human Relationship   529
Network Surrounding the Person

The Absence of the Wanted Person   532

The Impact of Personality Organization on Transference,   542
Countertransference, and the Therapy Process

    The neurotic child or child in reactive distress   545

    The impulse-ridden child   547

    The psychotic child   549

CHAPTER 11   TOWARD A CONCLUSION   553

Identifications and the Quest   553

The Human Interaction Network and the Quest   558

Contingencies in the Human Support Network   563

Comments   564

APPENDIX   SOME FAMILIAL CIRCUMSTANCES COMPARED   573

REFERENCES   579

INDEX   595

Part I

Theoretical Considerations

Chapter 1

THE HUMAN RELATIONSHIP NETWORK:
ITS SUPPORTS AND LACUNAE

You are not alone in the world.

Never be a bystander.

—Two slogans originating in
the pre-Soviet agricultural
communes (Ziferstein 1968)

"I guess I'm just like a defector from the war," said fifteen-year-old Andy
after he had run away from the homes of both his separated parents. "I can't
take it anymore. I just have to start thinking of me, myself now and let them
worry about what's happening to them. And I hope I'm never asked in court
which one I want to live with, because no matter what I said I would be
gunning down either my mother or my father and I can't do that". Slowly he
added "the trouble isn't that they're separated. . . . I'm used to that . . . it's that
they're not far enough away from each other to leave each other in peace. I
think I was running. I was kind of looking for a place . . . you know . . . for
people who can live in peace for a while."

The child of parting parents must deal with the loss or drastic alteration of
the relationship to at least one parent, as well as with a new level of exposure
to parental distress or bitterness. This inevitably involves a rupture in the
continuity of caring that he or she experiences. Whatever the quality of the
relationships within the family prior to separation, the rupture leads to
transformations in the images of the self and of the parting parents, associated

with intense feelings about the meaning of the change. Such transformations, occurring in the context of the child's remaining relationships, may have multiple effects on his further development. Children who are partially or totally bereft of the relationship to a previously loved parent need a network of human support in order to work out, rather than to disguise and distort, the grief within them.

Explorations in this book will focus both on the actual human relationships which shape the child's experience, referred to here as the "human relationship network," and on the internal processing of the experience, discussed in terms of the interplay between "identification processes in development and in loss," "the quest for the wanted absent person," and "grieving."

All people are affected by the human interaction network within which they live or to which they become emotionally attached. Even the prisoner in isolation, or the psychotic individual who appears to be inaccessible to human contact, lives in a world of images of others that turns out to be connected to the way he is actually being treated by those around him. The cogent network differs for different ages, individuals, or cultures or subcultures. For example, for the infant the perceived quality of the parent's surrounding arms, face, and body become synchronized into the first perceptions of a human relationship network. Winnicott's (1970) concept, that mutuality experienced within the "holding environment" forms the nexus of the baby's future sense of reliable well-being, speaks to this level of interaction. Yet even this example leads to the examination of wider dimensions of human interaction, so that we might ask, "What kind of human network can support the parent so that he or she can support the child?" Comforting arms, real or symbolic, regain importance for the bereft child or adult.

The broader social network is in part influenced by political, technologic, and other factors. Its function also varies for individuals and for the same person during different periods in life, but generally includes: the provision of available sources of emotional gratifications, through potentially loving relationships; the transmission of standards about attitudes, values, and prohibitions (although these may be replete with contradictory messages), and of ways of implementating them; the conveying of positive and negative reactions about the individual's actual behavior; and often the distribution of actual opportunities for meeting needs or dealing with life tasks, e.g., in the form of work, economic or status rewards, choice of and expectations about participatory roles within the family, the community or among peers.

Comments about the human relationship network here will be arbitrarily selective; I shall focus on features which appeared strongly to affect the parting parents or their children. Most of this appears directly in the individual case material, e.g., the different degree of social support afforded the father who leaves home as opposed to that offered the mother who leaves home; the differences between human support networks desired by the children of the divorced, and those sought the children of the deceased; the devastating repetition of deprivation through loss suffered by some families who remain socially and economically in a marginal position over generations; and the rich human support needed and well used by some children to sustain them through a period of distress which seemed necessary in order for them constructively to integrate the meaning of the changes in their lives and loves.

Less clear in the individual case material are those aspects of the social structure which, often unseen, have become a part of the individual's basic assumptions and expectations about the self in relation to others; these are to various degrees harmonious, illusionary, conflicting or openly discordant with their wishes as well as the actual opportunities available to them. What are the reverberations of inner changes within individuals on such aspects of the human interaction network? For example, in our culture the nuclear family is expected to be the primary source of emotional support, but this expectation has become discrepant with what actually happens for an increasing number of people. For many, both the idea and the experience of the family is changing. We take this as our point of departure.

The Impact on the Parents during Marriage

How often in seeing a troubled marriage do we first think of disturbance in the individual or in the dynamics of a marriage relationship, without adequate awareness of the network of human relationships and its values within which the marriage and the people were expected to function! As M. Kahne (1976) notes, a person who is different or foreign, who has a different approach to life, is more apt to be designated as a source of trouble than his human environment. The surrounding human network is especially crucial in considering the troubles of the child of the divorced or deceased and of his parents. Children who are partially or totally bereft of a previously loved parent need a network of human support in order to work out rather than to disguise and distort the grief within them.

Two time periods become a focus of questions. First, what characterized the human relationship network before the parents parted, during their marriage and earlier formative years, and what bearing does this have on their and the child's current situation? Secondly, what resources are available to or absent for the parents during the period of heightened distress which is usual before, during, and after divorce or death? What supports the parent to enable him or her to support the child?

There are exciting possibilities in the changes of recent times and also some disturbing results of changes. Some of the positive changes grew, in part, out of the desperation of men and women who felt suffocated by what was demanded of them or was forbidden to them by their culture, their families and eventually themselves. They took emotional risks in raising the kinds of questions which forced a reappraisal of the interaction between men and women, women and work, and parents and children. Many gained much, and against considerable and continuing odds. Some who were used to proceeding against odds—for instance, many black people—appeared to integrate the changes with a sense of familiarity. Others, whose parents perhaps had had an overdose of desperation, seemed to throw the proverbial baby out with the bathwater, equating the changes with a freedom from emotional commitment or responsibility toward others. In a search for gratification and for relationships "without strings attached," they present themselves as far from satisfied or fulfilled.

We may fruitfully ponder more upon the impact of changing interaction between men and women; changing attitudes toward childrearing; the changing role of the family over the last few centuries; current changes in people's customs regarding marriage, divorce, and custody; and the impact of all these factors on the social structure within which the parents (of different age groups and subcultures) encountered in this book, and their children, functioned.

The accelerated rates of change in our technology, ideology, and ways of life in themselves not only strain the sense of continuity between one generation and the next but require a new level of individual flexibility as well. As Eisenberg (1972) puts it: "Values now change so rapidly that what a child is taught by his parents may no longer be functional when that child becomes an adolescent, let alone an adult. However wide the range of behaviors man can exhibit—evidenced by the comparison of one society with another—the task of developing adaptive attributes is very different when radically changed behaviors are required within an individual's lifetime rather than over the history of a people. The question now becomes, not how malleable is man, but how much change can a man undergo and still maintain his psychic integration? Here we lack empirical data; there is no precedent for such rapid change."

CHANGING INTERACTION BETWEEN MEN AND WOMEN

Certain features of changes affecting human relations have maintained steady momentum and are becoming integrated or woven into family lives. One of these is the women's liberation movement: the affirmation by women that they are as complete human beings as men, and claim a parallel freedom of choice for personal fulfillment as well as a parallel emotional and monetary validation of their worthiness. The inner as well as the external struggles associated with such liberation have deeply affected women's self-perception, and their relationships to family life and children. Both the positive features and some miscarriages of liberation goals color the changes in family relationships discussed in this book, from the standpoint of the child. Of course, this movement follows many different winding paths: its progress is yet halting and uneven; and what may be contemplated as a giant step in some countries or social circles is already taken for granted elsewhere. This is true not only in the case of women, but also in a variety of other movements based on individual freedom of choice in life style, sexual preference, etc. Thus, one is not surprised to find two news items in close juxtaposition, both involving appeals to the populace through the media (*Boston Globe*, November 2, 1975): One describes a conference of transvestites who declare that a function of their open meeting is to show that they are not afraid to be in public. The second is an interview with Mrs. Anwar Sadat, wife of the president of Egypt, who is considered a feminist, and who is advocating reform of the divorce laws on Egyptian radio. By Muslim law, a married man can still divorce himself by saying three times "I divorce thee." Mrs. Sadat's proposed new laws would make it impossible for a man to obtain a divorce without his wife's knowledge. Along the spectrum between these two, throughout the United States there are currently lively battles over ERA, abortion laws, and paternity as well as maternity leave.

Alongside the new engagements at the legal front, there are many new ways in which men and women relate to each other. The impact of women's liberation is very different for different segments of the population. Among many poor families the "right to work" may be ludicrous in the face of a situation in which they may have never have been able to consider the "right not to work." There is a wide split between feminists whose goal is to enjoy a more equal partnership in their relationships with men, and those who feel moved to fortify themselves in a separatist endeavor which they see as the only feasible way to engage successfully in what they picture as a power struggle with men. Nevertheless, equal pay for equal work, freedom of choice about personal roles within the confines of reality (realistically one cannot be a full-time professional, full-time parent and full-time person of leisure at the same time), and freedom of choice about the use of one's body and about childbearing (with the aid of contraceptives and the possibility of abortion) remain as significant cornerstones of any social structure which is to house the development of women's full personal potential and most rewarding relations to men and to her children. At a personal level, the complicated interplay of women's self-images with those of their husbands or partners and their children will be involved in the explorations in this book.

Men and women are interdependent enough that what happens to one sex also affects the other. One short-term concomitant of the woman's liberation movement has been noted: increased assertiveness on the part of some women has been accompanied by growing numbers of men who complain of feeling sexually inadequate. However, more long-term and subtle effects are beginning to emerge. For example, I find that in working with groups of people who come together to discuss issues of parenting fathers are increasingly often participants who describe a tender and nurturant interaction with their young children; this would have been much less usual even ten to twenty years ago. "I just long so to hold him in my arms again; I didn't know it would be this way!" said a masculine young father of his eighteen-month-old son, who was visiting grandparents for a few days. Similarly, more men openly acknowledge sexual wishes to be fondled, courted, and caressed at times without having always to be the active partner, or the one to hold himself responsible for making each sexual encounter "successful."

The ideologic components of women's liberation can lend themselves either to interpretations which polarize the sexes into two camps of self-defense, or, instead, to social permission for new patterns of genuine mutuality. A value on open communication has shifted from its more adolescent emphasis, a few years ago, on "telling each other everything"—an emphasis which often resulted in the infliction of pain in the name of honesty despite an ideal of "togetherness." Now, more often one hears people value "communication" in terms of wanting to understand and to be responsive to one another's needs; such openness is based on the assumption that both men and women need intimacy and sharing, passion and dependence as well as autonomy, privacy, and emotional elbow-room to pursue individual interests or careers.

This is associated, for fortunate couples, with a flexible division of labor within the home. Degrees of involvement in caring for the children and decisions about who does what in the household are on the basis of individual likes and dislikes rather than on preconceptions of tasks linked to sex roles. Most often, a certain amount of continued friction around the least pleasant or most demanding tasks in such a collaboration is inevitable, although couples now display great variety in the tasks they consider to be demeaning. Women more often continue to feel responsible for the emotional atmosphere of the home and the care of the children. Some like this and some do not.

Because both cohabiting partners are less ashamed and gingerly about the evident range of needs within the other, it appears less likely that the one will need to live vicariously through the other, or will feel cheated by the other's accomplishments or lack of them. With fewer prohibitions about what is considered "unmasculine" or "unfeminine," perhaps men and women can more easily admit the real differences between them and enjoy them. This, of course, does not mean that personal traits in one will not grate on the other, as in any human interaction they sometimes must, but at least it is more of an individual grating, less tied to a priori, sex-role expectations. I must admit to surprise at the speed with which some of these changes are taking place in young couples. About half the parents described in chapter 5 [of children aged one to ten] had divorced and then remarried or sought out a love partner who was more able to relate to them in the ways described above. I mention surprise, because numbers of these parents did not, in their own early childhood, have parental models who could function this way. After a first marriage or love affair in which they felt constrained by sex-role expectations even more stringent than those of their parents, some bent over backwards for a period of time in order not to repeat the pattern. They then worked toward the mixture of autonomy, intimacy, and sharing of child care they wanted; often they succeeded, though numbers experienced pangs of anxiety over the idea of again giving up their independence.

The older generation of parents, who married from seventeen to thirty-five years ago, often found they had to make much more drastic changes in their lives to move in this direction. A number failed, and had also been for many years without social support for resolving personal and marital difficulties. Many eventually built productive lives around new interests in work. Numbers eventually had friendships, love relationships or both, but proportionately fewer than in the younger group. A few of the women and a greater number of men remarried happily, with or without a change of involvement in work or career. During the period their adolescent child was being seen a number of these parents expressed their feeling that they were finding social support, for the first time, for what they had long needed to accomplish.

What kinds of changes then, are reflected in these differences, and what might we expect in the future?

In a perceptive discussion of the dilemmas of contemporary womanhood, Eisenberg (1975) states, "Respect for human's variability demands of us that we attend to individual dispositions and preferences and that we not imprison members of each sex by imposing Platonic ideal types upon them. . . . In a fully human society, the goal of social institutions should be to maximize the possibilities for personal choice for women and men. . . . A freer world would be one in which the economic means might be available and the social encouragement provided to allow women—and men—more rather than fewer choices, to work to the extent that work is fulfilling—to stay at home as house father or house mother when child care is more gratifying—to share working and caring roles when that best meets needs for personal growth as well as child development." He points out that economic stress is a constraint on choice, describing the marked class differences in women's work patterns. "Among middle-income families, the proportion of wives who work tends to decline as husbands' incomes increase. Among low-income families, wages for men must be adequate for family needs before women can "choose" whether to work or not." Although the majority of Americans are now in favor of married women working (and about 50 percent do) in contrast to twenty to thirty years ago, more than half the women who work report that they would prefer not to work, or, at most, part-time. Simultaneously, he notes the progressive loss of status of women over the last two centuries, while family functioning changed from one in which agricultural and other labor was divided among all members of the family, to the recent urban pattern which has isolated the father from the family in his work and relegated the woman to taking care of home and children. Thus, the "allegedly feminine virtues, which until recently have been celebrated in our society are a much more recent invention than most of us are likely to recognize. . . . Society made a virtue of necessity by idealizing a feminine prototype that emphasized passivity, dependency, nurturance and the like."

The emphasis on passivity and dependence as defining and dominating the woman's character, even within her role as wife and mother, involved at the very least a distortion of the very active components of adequate mothering. In fact, most often the earliest identifications of the child are with aspects of such active mothering. Such social perceptions then further influence woman's character, which is strained toward attempting to fulfill the prophecy. Often, a disturbing result has been a severe kind of self-devaluation in women, which inevitably then is expressed toward and experienced in a subtle way by their children.

Miller (1973) suggests that "women have always grown in certain ways despite whatever obstacles were in their path. What is new today is the conscious and explicit search for even further growth by large numbers of women, not only the great or gifted." She continues:

If women aspire to enlarge their own lives and to focus directly on their needs, will they violate some inborn or natural psychological rules. . . . and if so, will these women misguidedly pursue destruction of themselves, men, or children? The great weight of evidence . . . demonstrates that this is a misconception. Although this point may seem a simple one, it has not been a minor misconception. . . . The prevalent conceptions that women should not attend directly to their own needs have been major causes of their problems—and concomitantly, but by different routes, of the problems of men and children. . . . The problem is not that women did not have these strengths, but that they have been encouraged to transform them into something else. . . . the crucial issue here is that the inappropriate transformation has been the prescribed one . . . . Men too are led to inappropriate transformations of themselves, but in different ways.

Eisenberg (1975) and Miller (1973) concur in affirming repeatedly that the liberation of women cannot proceed without the liberation of men. Similarly Linner (1971), describing the climate of change in new family and life styles in Sweden, includes "men's emancipation" as prerequisite to genuine equality between the sexes, while acknowledgement of differences can still exist.

The widening implications of these points of view have become associated with revisions in psychological research theories about the functioning of men and women, and have led to new implications for the practice of psychotherapy. Along with Miller, other clinicians have recently reconsidered the meaning of a variety of symptoms in women, particularly phobias, depression, and other expressions of psychic powerlessness (Symonds, 1973; Seidenberg, 1973). Within this frame of reference, symptoms, as compromise formations, are viewed as expressing a "disguised protest, an attempt to block participation in a prescribed way of life." Therapeutic intervention can then be addressed to the stultifying misfit between what the woman perceives as her prescribed role or as the only way to stay loved, and the renunciations of personal growth and being such a fit involves. Although the parent is the crucial mediating agent for inculcating self-images associated with culturally approved roles, and the individual must still come to terms with values, ego ideals, and prohibitions derived from that interaction (see chapter 2), this is more difficult to do while the rest of the human interaction network continually reinforces these values in word and deed.

In a careful, exhaustive review of research studies to date, Maccoby and Jacklin (1974) find that, contrary even to earlier findings of their own and others (Maccoby, 1966), observations of children's actual behavior and performance do not confirm commonly held myths about sex differences. For example, although teachers and parents rate girls as more compliant, dependent, and passive than boys, observations of actual behavior are contrary to these stereotypes. Although there is a consistent sex difference in that boys are behaviorally more aggressive and inclined to seek dominance in various situations, girls do not in fact respond by compliance. Intellectual differences continue to be found regarding the better early verbal development in girls, and the better spatial organization in boys. In abstract thinking, analytic thinking, creativity and initiative in problem solving, however, consistent sex differences are not demonstrable. Although studies show that girls' self-confidence about intellectual accomplishments is less than that of boys during the college years, similar differences in self-esteem are not found before or after this time. Such new evidence suggests that the nature of the shifts in women's roles must be cast in a slightly different light. It is not that women are struggling to overcome their passivity, low self-esteem, intuitive rather than conceptual thinking, etc., but that they must cope with the breakdown of various mythologies which they, too, believe as adults (e.g., as parents or teachers), but which do not correctly describe them. The bearing of such mythologies upon "power relations" insofar as they involve men and women's roles, however, seems to be complicated by the implications of the continued consistent finding (Maccoby and Jacklin, 1974) that males show greater strivings toward dominance; both in relation to other males and to females.

Not only do sex role stereotypes fail to fit girls' and women's actual behavior, but other studies suggest that women overestimate the degree to which men expect them to have these qualities. McKee and Sheriffs (1960), for example, found that women believed, mistakenly, that men wanted to restrict them to certain "feminine" qualities, while Steinman (1963) noted that college girls greatly overestimated the degree to which their fathers wanted them to be "other-oriented," a characteristic commonly ascribed to the female. An intriguing sidelight of this study, however, was that the fathers perceived their "ideal woman" as highly other-oriented, so that the women may have been correctly responding to perceived wishes in their fathers, rather than to the verbalized expectations. It is unclear, but quite possible, that such perceptions are translated into affective bonds experienced in a sense of shared ego ideal.

Miller's thinking makes a major new contribution to the understanding of identification processes in the child, as these are affected by attitudes of those in the surrounding network. She notes that

> growth for men has tended to be conceptualized as movement away from those attributes identified with women. ... It becomes apparent that when we think of growth we have conceptualized in the image of a man. Psychoanalysts have said that a boy must first renounce early identification with the mother, and then, later renounce sexual attraction to her. He must renounce not only the person, but the process in which she is engaged as well. ... A male baby is supposed to give up identification with certain ideas, ... e.g., passivity. ... He is encouraged to give up identifications with those processes, e.g., the care of human life, which women are doing. Yet this process would probably be salutary for everybody to identify with rather than renounce. ... Underneath it all runs the interdiction of another, even more basic process, which ... seems the most frightening prospect of all: close and direct emotional engagement with another human being who is different—and female. The boy is encouraged to turn to the world of men, where processes are structured to limit direct emotional involvement with anybody, male or female. ... How does this initial renunciation affect one's capacity for direct emotional engagement with all that one subsequently encounters?

Cultural values attached to sex roles affect the parents and children encountered here at many levels. Inequality of opportunity in the job market or in compensation reveal them as real and potent forces. In the words of Nyquist, (1975), "Equality is not when a female Einstein gets promoted to assistant professor; equality is when a female schlemiel moves ahead as fast as a male schlemiel."

Options for women must still broaden in such a way that women who prefer to be single, have no children, or give priority to a career do not feel shame, the need to justify themselves in social situations or "outrageous stereotyping in regard to their ascribed characteristics" Adams, (1971).

Some women express their resentment at having fallen prey to what they have experienced as a new, compelling ideal of womanhood, the ability to combine a demanding career with family life. When such an ideal is promulgated as realistic, yet is felt as difficult or impossible to live up to, it pressures women no less than the older forms of stereotypes (Hopkins, 1976). Freedom to pursue only a career must also become an acceptable choice. Meanwhile, increased options for men are mirroring the arduous but steady progress toward equality of the sexes. For instance, an increasing number of men are awarded custody of their children, proving themselves to be excellent parents.

More subtle but no less potent influences on the lives of children are the qualities of the emotional engagement between men and women. An infinite variety of interactions can enhance the child's growth and provide rich models for identification. Thank goodness, there is no one "right" way because there are so many. However, there are also ways which are clearly not right. When a marriage has never had, or has irretrievably lost, the flexibility that enables each partner to feel self-respect (regardless of whether the cause lies in overwhelming, unresolved conflict in one partner, or stems from the particular interaction), the failure, of necessity, is reflected in the child's view, complicating his own affective interactions and his ability to synthesize his identifications with each parent and their attitudes toward each other. Empirical studies suggest that nothing is gained for the child by parents staying "unhappily" together for his sake (Landis, 1960; Lynn, 1974).

Among the parents encountered, the majority in the younger age group (twenty-thirty-five) and the minority in the older age group (thirty-five-fifty) had sought out and found a variety of groups, social agencies, or friendship networks that supported them before and during the period of transition in their lives. These included "consciousness-raising" groups, family service agencies, singles groups, fathers-for-equal-justice organizations, individual therapy, colleagues, and friends. The parents usually had to take the initiative in finding such support. Most frequently their changed situation catapulted them out of the circle of friends they had previously shared with the spouse. Often, they at first felt rebuffed about this. Numbers of women were especially hurt by a feeling that their still married friends now saw them as a "flirtatious" threat within their own marriages and no longer invited them. After a period of time, many found that their own needs had changed sufficiently so that they had less in common with the preoccupations and way of life of married friends, and found themselves seeking out people in a position more similar to their own, who, they felt, would "understand" more.

Others maintained contacts with two groups of people: their "old" married friends, who provided some continuity of caring relationships, whose children were often friends of the children, and who were also sometimes sought out in hopes of hearing news about the former spouse; and a new group of divorced people, who were sought out to share problems, offer advice, and provide opportunities for new heterosexual relationships. In numbers of cases, no human support network was available to the parent, or was unacceptable to him during periods of intense depression or suspicion of others. Some parents were subjected to a kind of social avoidance by their previous network of relationships. In such cases, there tended to be a social mythology about the reasons that the marriage had terminated. This was difficult to counteract, for example, in cases where mothers left home. It is further described in the clinical chapters. The lack of available human support networks when the divorced or bereaved person needed them tended to deepen depression, confirm images of oneself as being worthless, unlovable and failing, and made it extraordinarily difficult for the parent to give emotional support to the child.

CHANGING ATTITUDES TOWARD CHILDREARING

Parents once again seem to be moving toward trusting themselves to do what is best for their children. For some decades, while a frightening array of evidence regarding the harm which may be done to the developing child by parents was being amassed, the task of childrearing appeared formidable.

Two streams of thought—psychoanalytic discoveries about the enormous powers attributed to the mother by the unconscious of the child, and psychological studies of the devastating developmental and emotional arrests in children who had received inadequate or "rejecting" maternal care— pushed all aspects of the mother's role to the forefront of scrutiny. Enlightened parents, and especially mothers, wanted at all costs to avoid being "rejecting" or inadequate, whatever that might be.

However, the result was often that parents bowed to the "expertise" of others, feeling unsure and guilty about which of their complex feelings were "all right" to express to the child, overburdened with a sense of total responsibility for each aspect of his development, and losing out in the area of spontaneous expression. Their vulnerability to the feeling that as parents they were "flawed" increased the likelihood that they would expect and need to find evidence of flaws in the child—a need children notice, and incorporate into their own attitudes toward themselves.

Of course, many positive changes in attitudes toward children did take place during this time. In fact, childrearing practices in various socioeconomic groups changed greatly. Davis and Havighurst (1947) reported that middle-class parents, often on the advice of experts, instituted strict and early weaning and toilet-training, but that working-class parents were much more permissive in these areas. The United State's Children's Bureau, as recently as 1935, advised that "training of the bowels may be begun as early as the end of the first month. It should always be begun by the third month, and may be completed during the eighth month." The influence of the behaviorist, John B. Watson (1929), who believed in early behavior conditioning, was felt by a generation of very clean uncomforted babies, picked up only at scheduled feeding times, while their parents otherwise tried to numb themselves to their cries. Watson advocated introducing soap suppositories at the time the infant was placed on a potty to accomplish toilet training as a conditioned response. Since then, various favorite pediatricians like Berry Brazelton (1974), along with a host of psychoanalytically oriented clinicians who view toileting as a social habit, have made perfectly clear that the advantages of waiting with bowel and bladder training until the baby's muscles are ready to cooperate, and he can participate and make it his own achievement, are many. Around 1960 Bronfenbrenner (1958) discovered that the middle-class mothers who had previously been more strict than working-class and lower-class mothers were now more permissive. Middle-class mothers now more often allowed self-demand feeding and weaned later from the bottle; they were now instituting bowel and bladder training later than were working- and lower-class mothers. He pointed out that childrearing practices were likely to change more quickly in those segments of society which had closest access and were more receptive to agents of change, such as public media, physicians, clinics, etc. Methods of discipline were also found to differ. While the middle-class parents used more symbolic and manipulative techniques such as reasoning, isolation, and appeals to guilt, working-class parents used more physical punishment and were more oriented toward maintaining order and obedience.

Such differences may be closely linked to the surrounding social support network. Rainwater et al. (1959) suggest that central to the working-class parent's outlook is her underlying conviction that most significant actions originate from the external world, rather than from within. The neighborhood is often seen as chaotic and potentially catastrophic. The mother feels she has little ability to influence events and must live with pervasive anxiety over possible fundamental deprivations. Pavenstedt et al. (1967), working with multiproblem families and their children in nursery school describe similar parental views of the world. Rainwater et al. state (1959) that while the middle-class mothers wanted to give their children "worthwhile experiences" to make them well rounded, working-class mothers were concerned that the child follow rules of authoritative guidance to become moral and upright. Focussing on differences in values, Kohn (1963) points out that working-class parents want their children to exhibit conformity to external proscriptions, middle-class parents want their children ultimately to become self-directed. He lists the life conditions related to these differences as occupation, education, and economic status. Kohn discusses the fact that "middle class occupations are more subject to self direction and getting ahead in them depends more on the individual, where working class occupations are more subject to standardization and direct supervision, and getting ahead in them depends more on the collective action of labor unions." The helplessness to influence the events around one that many working people—both men and women—may feel appears, it seems to me, in subtler but equally pungent form for those parents constrained by the apparent opposite: that is, by a role that prescribes almost total responsibility for doing all the right things for their children, while simultaneously they find themselves in a nexus of social expectations and sometimes a degree of social isolation that undermines their confidence.

Research in child development underwent, and one hopes is still undergoing, growing pains. Several decades ago the devastating and apparently irreversable effects of the lack of adequate parenting on the developing baby were repeatedly demonstrated. Most infants studied, in institutions, were contending with the fact that there was no possibility for them to form a sustaining relationship to a parent figure, rather than with an actual loss. In general, the prolonged absence of a parent figure in the earliest months revealed itself in a failure of both physical and mental development, accompanied by apathy, rather than grief, which would be a later development. Bakwin (1949) summarized these findings as follows: "Infants under six months of age who have been in an institution for some time present a well-defined picture: The outstanding features are listlessness, emaciation and pallor, relative immobility, unresponsiveness to stimuli like a smile or coo, indifferent appetite, failure to gain weight despite the ingestion of diets which in the home are entirely adequate, frequent stools, poor sleep, proneness to febrile episodes, absence of sucking habits, etc." These changes are not observable in the first two to four weeks of life, but can be seen any time thereafter, sometimes within a few days of the baby's separation from the mother. Goldbarb (1943) compared children of similar backgrounds who had been raised in foster homes with those who had been in institutions from birth or shortly thereafter until three years of age before being transferred to a foster home. At around age six, the latter group showed strikingly more behavior difficulties, including hyperactivity, severe mental retardation, difficulties in speech development, etc. Beres and Obers (1950) also described the personality difficulties, particularly in the area of forming relationships, that beset older children who have been deprived of mothering in infancy. However, their children were less drastically affected than those cited by other writers.

The central role of the adult in the intellectual and emotional development of the child was increasingly recognized by researchers. Spitz's (1945, 1946, 1962, 1965, Spitz and Wolf, 1946, 1949) extensive studies of babies compared developmental quotients, personality development, and disturbance, as well as the role of autoerotic activities during the first two years of life, for infants in two European institutions, and for varying types of mother-child relationships within the one. His material also shed light on the differential effects of separation from the mother according to the age of the baby, and the therapeutic importance of making rapid restitution for loss of mothering during babyhood.

Developmental quotients were compared for infants in a "foundling home" and a "nursery". The foundling home provided excellent physical care for the babies, but adult contact and other forms of stimulation were at a minimum after total separation from the mother by the age of three months. There were from eight to twelve babies per nurse. The other institution, the "nursery," was established to care for the newborn babies of delinquent girls in a penal institution. Though comparable to the foundling home in physical facilities, the nursery children were less isolated, had toys, and were usually cared for by their mothers, under the supervision of the nursing staff. During the first four months of life developmental quotients were higher for the foundling children (124 foundling, 101.5 nursery), who were said, on the average to come from "good parental backgrounds." However by the end of the first year the foundling group had dropped to an average quotient of 72, reaching an average of 45 by the end of the second year. Although major improvements in nursing care were made when the babies were fifteen months, they failed to respond to this treatment, the developmental arrest appearing to be permanent. Spitz referred to the condition as "hospitalism." In spite of the good physical care the rate of deaths was extraordinarily high, as was the number of children exhibiting severe withdrawal, immobility, and lack of interest in humans. Concomitantly, autoerotic activities normal for babies could not be found among these children. In the most basic way the children in the foundling home, who had never experienced a sustained caring relationship in the first place, seemed to lack motiviation to live, to invest interest in others or in themselves.

In contrast the children in the nursery maintained their initial average developmental quotient (105 at the end of the first year).

Spitz compared the kinds of autoerotic activities manifested by the babies in the two institutions, with a small comparison group of home-reared infants. He compared absence of autoerotic play, rocking, fecal play (most often with copraphagia), and genital play, relating each, in the order listed, to a different degree of satisfactory mother-child relationship. Particularly interesting is the group exhibiting fecal play, all of them "nursery" children. Their mothers alternated between effusively involved and harshly rejecting behavior, and tended to suffer from depressive episodes. Feces, as akin to transitional objects utilized to deal with loss, will be discussed elsewhere in this book. Although Spitz's findings were theoretical milestones, the lack of a large control sample of normally developing babies probably resulted in skewing the implications of some of the findings, for mothers and mental health workers, in a pathognomic direction. For example, a proportion of well-developing babies who have come to my attention go through a period of fairly active crib-rocking or head-banging within the context of excellent overall development and parent-child relationship.

In a finding relevant to the issue of the loss of a parent, Spitz and Wolf (1946) described a syndrome which occurred in some of the children in the nursery, during the second half of the first year of life after they had made, and then "lost" a relationship to their mother. Spitz called this "anaclitic depression." It included very weepy behavior that took the place of former outgoing friendliness—especially screaming or weeping when an observer approached. After about three months, the weepiness subsided and a frozen rigidity appeared instead:

> The children sat with wide open, expressionless eyes. In conjunction, there was frequently a loss of abilities previously learned, a retardation of reaction to stimuli, slowness of movement, loss of appetite, refusal to eat, loss of weight and insomnia. Along with this syndrome went a physiognomic expression which in the adult would correspond to depression or intense grief. In all the cases which developed the syndrome, the mother had been removed from the child starting somewhere between the time it was six and eight months old for a practically unbroken period of three months. The better the relationship between mother and infant had been before separation, the more likely it was that the depression would ensue. Not all children whose mothers were removed developed the syndrome. The depression disappeared in all its manifestations after the mother was returned, if this took place after not more than about three months. If the separation was longer than this, unless an adequate mother substitute was found, the arrest in developmental quotient was apt to remain even after reunion.

These kinds of data regarding the severe effects of deprivation of parenting during babyhood so shook the mental health field that a super-sensitivity to early separations prevailed for a time. Some of this was felt by parents, in the form of increased guilt over any kind of absences from their child, including those associated with the mother's working.

Over the last decade or two, a more careful and controlled look at the effect of separation on child development forced a reconsideration of exactly which factors were responsible for severe early deprivation. Not only were communal childrearing practices in other cultures scrutinized more closely (Bettelheim, 1969; Bronfenbrenner, 1970) but the effects of institutional living were screened through the variables of the number, kind and consistency of available parent substitutes. It was found that the quality of available care and caretakers make an enormous difference. Skeels (1940, 1942) found experiences after early infancy had major impact. For example, early retardation was not irreversible when young babies (e.g. eleven months) were given to individual, mentally retarded "foster mothers" in a ward in which they could devote themselves fully to their charges. Other studies showed reversal of developmental retardation by increasing social, tactile, and perceptual stimulation of the infant. Children who had remained with their parents until well after the first year and had the opportunity to form emotional bonds reacted differently from those previously studied (Rutter, 1973). More importantly, and in conjunction with the increasing need for day care for children of working mothers, research was focussed on the quality of substitute parent figures and their role in the child's development—not only on its cognitive features, but on the quality of the child's emotional attachments as well. Caldwell (1973) states, "Studies related to the effects of day care on intellectual and cognitive development show that in general children are not harmed by experiences in a day care environment at an early age, as many researchers had feared, and, in fact, many young children benefit significantly from the exposure." She cites the studies of Provence, at the Yale Child Study Center, who observed the psychosocial development of a group of children in a day-care center to discover the way a young child internalizes the social experiences inherent in early group activities and integrates them with other significant social, emotional, and developmental tasks. Caldwell focussed her interest on the reciprocal attachment of children and their own mothers. She compared mother-child pairs who had been involved in a Syracuse day-care program from the time they were about a year old, with mother-child pairs where the children had remained in the exclusive care of their mothers during the same time. She concludes: "Findings of the study should be very reassuring to all persons concerned with infant day care. In terms of the attachment of the children to their own mothers, there were no significant differences between the day care and home-reared infants." Day-care children were just as attached to their own mothers as those who had remained at home. In addition, it appeared that the day-care babies enjoyed interaction with other people more than the home-reared infants, a finding that is consistent with other recent studies. Equally important was the finding that the strength of attachment of the mothers to their children was no less than for the children reared at home. An intriguing additional finding, when day-care and home-reared samples were combined, was that the strength of attachment of a child for his mother was correlated with developmental levels. That is, "Children whose development was most advanced, usually were rated as the most attached to their mothers. Similarly, there was some evidence that the most advanced babies tended to have the most attached mothers." It is important to note that the day-care center involved did not accept infants younger than six months. They adopted this policy in order to permit the essential mother-child attachment to develop before the child was placed in a situation which might conceivably have weakened it.

Others (Skard, 1965) concluded that separation before six months of age is rarely harmful as long as proper care and stimulation are provided, but that between six months and three years, some continuity of care is essential to the development of the capacity for emotional attachments. Wallston (1974), studying the effects of maternal employment on children, cited studies showing that employment per se was a less crucial variable than the absence of supervision vs. the presence of adequate parent substitutes. Yarrow (1961, 1962) found that although maternal employment per se was almost unrelated to childrearing patterns and to the summary measure of adequacy of mothering, a further breakdown of data according to "satisfaction" showed that dissatisfied, nonworking mothers had the least adequate mothering and confidence in childrearing. That personal satisfaction and confidence of the mother constitute variables crucial to the well-being of the child is consistent with the material about children and parents encountered in this book. Rapaport and Rapaport (1969) note the increasing emphasis on partnership in family life among dual-career, professional parents, and the awareness on the part of the families of possible effects on the children.

Inextricably entwined with the re-evaluation of attitudes toward childrearing are the variables chosen for study. Such subtle issues as feelings invoked by the father-infant interaction, sex stereotyping of infants by parents, and the influence of peer relationships in babyhood are making their appearance. Greenberg and Morris (1974) picturesquely describe the impact of the newborn on the father, suggesting that optimal development for "engrossment" ("by which we refer to a sense of absorption, preoccupation, and interest in the infant") may be enhanced by tactile contact between the two during the initial days of life. They suggest that the father, if encouraged to express his engrossment, is "gripped and held by this particular feeling and has a desire to look at, hold and touch the infant." They question current hospital practices which discourage such contact, making the fathers feel inadequate or unwanted. They hypothesize that there may be a "critical period" in the father's entry into the psychological world of the child which, if frustrated, may be difficult to recapture in positive quality and intensity.

Sex stereotyping of infants by parents was studied by Rubin, Provenzano, and Luria (1974). They asked whether the sex of the infant determined how the parents organized their perception to a wide variety of attributes, ranging from size, to activity, attractiveness, even future potential, in the infant. They concluded, "The data indicate that parents—especially fathers—differentially label their infants, as a function of the infant's gender. These results are particularly striking in light of the fact that our sample of male and female infants did *not* differ in birth, length, weight or apgar scores." Mothers rated both sexes closer on the adjective pairs than did fathers, but both parents agreed on the direction of sex differences. However, "mothers" it appears "rated sons as cuddlier than daughters, while fathers rated daughters as cuddlier than sons." Ah, how much begins that way?

Apolloni and Cooke (1975) studied peer behavior as a variable influencing infant and toddler development, shifting from the much more usual emphasis on parent-child interaction. Toddlers in our culture have often been described as exhibiting parallel play, but not yet interacting with each other in significant ways, although children reared in the kibbutz or in institutions have been noted for their attachment to each other. Studies quoted by Apolloni and Cooke, however, conclude that peer interaction is an important variable furthering the social functioning of the preschool child. The most constructive situations, evocative of progressively cooperative social interactions, developed in the specific situation in which the same toddler peers were consistently paired for periods of play over a sustained period of time, and developed a friendship. Although it is a new way to look at it, this is not inconsistent with the notion that a sustained dyadic relationship provides the soil from which sprout the seeds of lifelong affective themes, both within the individual and in the form of readiness to be engaged with others.

Now that we are reopening those questions about childhood development which perhaps were prematurely foreclosed by the almost exclusive stress laid on the early mother-child interaction for which the mother was held solely responsible, we may hope that mothers will be less constricted by guilt, that human beings will acknowledge that they share responsibility for enriching the growth of the young, and that parents will feel renewed confidence about what they have to offer, as a couple, or if necessary, separately. We must hope, too, that our preoccupation with cognitive strides and competence in children (also an area recently much investigated) will not obscure the perhaps life-long yield that early, mutually enjoyed and sustained relationships will nourish in the child. As a colleague opined, perhaps the best preventive measure against vulnerability to severe depression in adulthood is "to have once been unambivalently loved as a child" (Leon Eisenberg: personal communication).

THE CHANGING ROLE OF THE FAMILY IN HISTORY

A large body of thinking has revolved around the changes brought about by the increasing industrialization of the Western world, including the shift from the supportive emotional atmosphere of the extended family of the past to the isolation from support suffered by the modern, so-called nuclear family. Lasch (1975) describes this sociological conception of the family as follows:

> In identifying the distinctive features of the modern family as its isolation from larger kinship structures, sociology implies that the history of the family should be seen as the decline of the large, extended, patriarchal family and the rise of the nuclear family. According to this interpretation, the small family is ideally adapted to the requirements of industrial society. As a result of the growing specialization of social and economic functions that has affected every institution, the family has lost its economic, protective and educational functions and has come to specialize in emotional services. Where kinship served as the unifying principle of earlier forms of society, the modern social order rests on impersonal rational and "universalistic" forms of solidarity. In a competitive and highly mobile society, the extended family had no place. The nuclear family, on the other hand serves industrial society as a necessary refuge. It provides adults with an escape from the competitive pressures of the market place while at the same time it equips the young with the inner resources to master those pressures.

As Lasch makes clear, this view of the family raises as many historical questions as it answers. The extent to which industrialization has affected kinship ties; the antiquity of the nuclear family; whether the extended family molds personality structures radically different from those produced by the nuclear family: all these and many other questions remain topics of considerable debate. Also at issue, and very relevant to the focus of this book, is the child's relationship and identification with the parents in the modern nuclear family. Lasch considers the heart of the issue, focussing on the affective components involved: "What mattered was the emotional intensification of the family life, which strengthened the child's identification with his parents. This at once sharpened the struggle necessary to achieve autonomy and gave it a stronger basis by forcing the individual to develop inner resources instead of relying on external direction." He concluded that the family isolation "gave the relations between parents and children a new intensity which enabled the young to become more fully autonomous than before, even as it increased the psychic cost of socialization. It was not so much the internal structure of the family that changed, as its relation to the outside world. As an institution, defined above all as a refuge, a private retreat, the family became the center of a new kind of emotional life, a new intimacy and inwardness." However, there is an evident disadvantage:

If the emotional intensity of bourgeois family life encourages the child's identification with his parents, the father's withdrawal into the world of work created conditions that weakened this identification in the long run. The significance of a father training his children for work, in societies where the family still serves as a center of productions, is that it tempers the child's fantasies with practical experience, softening the early impression of an omnipotent, wrathful and punitive father. ... the modern father finds it difficult to provide this information. Such skills as he possesses are likely to become technologically obsolete in his own lifetime and there would be little point in transmitting them to his children even if there were an opportunity to do so.

He concludes that "the weakening of parental care in the long run makes it more difficult than ever for the child to become an autonomous adult.... The child no longer wishes to succeed the father, he merely wishes to enjoy life without his interference. "Feeling that the child retains an exaggerated idea of the power of authority because he cannot test his ideas against everyday reality, he fears that the child will continue to see the world as starkly divided between power and impotence. "Questions of morality get reduced to questions of strength. He remains in a pre-oedipal phase. He has little incentive to grow up."

Some of the conditions that Lasch so incisively analyzes seemed to have stirred men and women toward an inner revolution against them, as well as a resolution to take hold of the direction of their lives, in the ways described earlier. Their future is not yet written. However, many of the parents of children encountered in this book are people who have suffered from the strains described by Lasch, resulting in an untenably conflicted human relationship network; they are struggling to find a better way to live.

CHANGES IN IDEOLOGY AND IN CUSTOMS
CONCERNING MARRIAGE, DIVORCE AND CHILD CARE

Ideology

Judging by the trends in ideology within the United States, both men and women are increasingly expected to make choices regarding their life style, the quality of their relationship to each other, and the degree of their involvement in work and in caring for children. A recent national opinion survey (Market Opinion Research, 1975) showed the majority of women over eighteen say that they now favor the "woman's movement." Almost half the married women stated that if divorce or separation should come, custody of the children should depend on circumstances, while only 17 percent felt children should automatically be given over to the mother. Forty-two percent said that a woman should pay her exhusband alimony if his circumstances required it. Reports based on another detailed mail survey (Sullivan, 1975), indicate that the majority of both men and women believe that both marriage partners should have a career, and that the wife should take time for her career to bear and raise children. A few do not want children to disrupt their lives, but most want one or two. A great number believe that if husband and wife work, they should share bills, housework, and childcare. As sampling methods were not detailed, the representative nature of the data is in question, as is the relationship between the voicing or writing of an opinion and actual behavior. Nevertheless, if seems clear that the ideologic emphasis on greater equality in sex roles and the associated favoring of wider choices within these roles is growing in acceptance. As such choices seem ever more desirable, however, there comes with them a sense of individual responsibility that may result in a variety of strains, quite different from those which were previously experienced as the consequences of constraints in choice. Some of the new strains arise from inner conflicts over different, sometimes contradictory components of the new ideal image of the self; others from the recognized or unrecognized discrepancies between the ideology (e.g., of equal opportunity or equal pay) and the current realities (e.g., of various inequities in pay); and others still from the insufficent leeway in social institutions and programs to provide the necessary support system for practical implementation of the changing ideals. Finally, there are also conflicting directions within the ideology itself, most strikingly in the area of loving relationships. While the search for intimacy and for more open expressions of loving is cherished, a commitment to permanence in a relationship is often seen as potentially damaging, rather than as allowing for the ripening of fulfillment within that relationship. The emotional ties involved in marriage and in sustained caring for children are often pictured simultaneously in these contradictory ways.

Women frequently describe awareness of a conflict between their desire for a deep emotional commitment to a mate, and the value they place on independent self-realization, currently pictured by many as centered outside the home. For many women childrearing remains, much of the time, a deeply rewarding and fulfilling part of life, which nothing else can exactly duplicate in its emotional satisfactions. There is not yet adequate data about the growing numbers of young women who have made an irreversible decision, while still in their twenties, to forfeit childbearing (for example, the growing number who seek hysterectomies as a form of contraception). How will they fare in their later years?

Recently numbers of women have clearly articulated the difficulties experienced in trying to live up to a new, idealized version of simultaneous pursuit of a demanding career and family life (Hopkins, 1976; Smith, 1976). Hopkins, a scientist who eventually gave up family and opted to focus on her successful career, writes: "Those of us who went through Radcliffe in the 60s all emerged with at least a mild case of the . . . superwoman-brainwash (successful career woman, mother of several children, husband optional). A few months in a laboratory were sufficient to convince me that someone was putting me on, but I was amazed at my tenth reunion to discover how many Radcliffe graduates felt they were failures because they had not lived the myth. One of these failures bitterly described this myth to me as 'the most pernicious influence in western civilization.' " Smith, a recent law school graduate, married and with two children, stated in a commencement address

I bring you bad news: It will be a long time before the needs of family and career will be comfortably wed. Childraising is important. It has its moments of unequaled joy. It is also difficult and time consuming. You will be working with men and women without family commitments, who will expect you to work long hours with them. You will want to work those hours. If you cannot, you may not be hired or you may lose a promotion or be fired. If you do work the long hours, you will have guilt feelings. You should have guilt feelings. The professions are filled with men who do not see enough of their children; to imitate them is no solution. . . . Part time work is another solution. There are not and will not be many part time jobs with adequate compensation, responsibility, and status as long as part time work is women's work only. I look forward to the day when men will share not only vacuuming but childraising, when career patterns will be flexible enough to accommodate people who want to spend their time with their families. What I fear is that, like our mothers and grandmothers, we will become two kinds of women— women with children and women with careers. . . . If my own experience means anything, I cannot overstate how difficult it is to do justice to both children and career. It is a constant battle. It *does* have its rewards.

In both these descriptions the ideal career model adhered to was one which required full-time energies to be successful. Quantity of work involvement was inseparable from quality. However the meaning of such success may be based on the traditional "masculine" model of work, supported by traditional institutional rewards and models. As Miller (1976), Eisenberg (1975), H. Kahne (1976), Light (1976), Rapoport (1969), and Rowe (1976), explore these issues further they concur in proposing that dual-career families may, and often do, function in a different and more flexible fashion, with a different distribution of emotional rewards for work and for child care for both partners, if institutional support for such functioning is present. Some women (Rivers, 1975) write of their pleasure in having happily, if not smoothly worked out such a state of affairs. As ideology concerning sex roles continues to change, it will be important that new possibilities do not turn into the tyranny of new demands for conformity, which would undermine the necessary respect for individual variations in the kinds of satisfaction that is sought.

Customs

Changing marriage customs, alternate life styles, different views of divorce, childbearing and caring, and work patterns are a reality, independent of anyone's conjectures. The extent of the change is extraordinarily variable in different countries, and within different social, economic, or educational outlooks within the United States.

In 1975, Katz (1976) reported another four percent increase in divorces in the United States, pushing the annual number over the million mark for the first time in history. This was more than twice as many as in 1966, when the upward trend began to rise sharply. Katz compared the numbers of divorces registered for each hundred registered marriages in twenty-five countries (1973, 1974), ranging from a high of sixty in Sweden and forty-four in the U.S.A. to a low of 10 in Japan and France. He concluded that divorce has risen most in those countries with liberal divorce laws, decreasing church influence, and large numbers of employed women who can frequently become financially independent. Countries in which the Catholic church remains influential still rank low. In countries with a rising divorce rate there is now greater social acceptance of divorce as a means of resolving marriages which are considered unworkable by husbands and wives, both among the prestigious and prominent, and among working people in lower socioeconomic circumstances.

The laws are beginning to reflect these changing attitudes. For many years, while categories such as "cruel and abusive treatment" had to be the grounds for a majority of divorces, it was a widely accepted practice for couples and attorneys to fabricate incidents to provide grounds for divorce. For example, in Massachusetts where the category of "irretrievable breakdown" as grounds for divorce was finally added in 1975, 90 percent of divorces had previously been under the "cruel and abusive" treatment category (Wheeler, 1975).

Freed (1974), detailing recent changes in divorce laws, described liberalizing changes in twenty-six states between the years 1972 and 1974 alone. By 1974 there remained only five states "where marital misconduct is the sole basis for divorce, but in all of these states reform is in the wind." She summarized the trends discernable from a comparison of the laws in 1974 and 1972: "A growing number of states have opted for the sole ground of irretrievable breakdown and in an increasing number of those with more conservative legislators, irretrievable breakdown has been tacked to existing grounds. Many states have abolished all or some traditional defenses. In a number of jurisdictions where divorce is predicated upon living apart, the length of time of the separation has been decreased, notably in Vermont, where a six month period is the shortest in any jurisdiction. Recognition that marital breakdown may and does occur without fault on the part of either spouse appears to be the clear blueprint of the future for marriage dissolution in this country." As the divorce laws themselves gradually enter a more enlightened era, post-divorce obligations and their enforcement are becoming an area of focus for reform.

Alternate life styles, including various forms of cohabitation without marriage, homosexual liasons, communal living (Rothchild and Wolf, 1976) have also all risen in registered frequency and are more openly accepted. U.S. census data show that during the sixties there was over an eightfold increase in the number of men and women living together in the United States without being married (Sullivan, 1975). There is also a growing proportion of women in the United States who are single or divorced and not remarried. In 1975, for example, almost 40 percent of women aged twenty to twenty-four were single, compared to 24 percent in 1950 (Schneider, 1975). Between 1960 and 1974 the number of unmarried women in this age group rose by one third (Kahne, 1976).

The incidence of remarriage is also high, suggesting that most divorced people have found a particular marriage untenable, but are not turning against marriage per se. Weiss (1975a) reports:

The likelihood of remarriage is greater for younger people but remains high even for individuals who divorce in their forties. For example in the 1960s, among those aged between thirty-five and forty-five at the time of their divorce, almost 60 percent of the men and about 40 percent of the women had remarried within four years. At the present time it appears about five-sixths of divorced men and about three-fourths of divorced women eventually remarry, and the rate has been going up steadily. Most of those who separate and proceed to divorce can, therefore, look forward to eventual remarriage.

The birthrate continues to decline. In 1975, for the fourth consecutive year, the nation's birthrate reached a record low, despite an increase in the number of women of childbearing age (Katz, 1976). The steepest decline in childbearing appears among college graduates. For example, Belin (1976) points out that while according to the U.S. Bureau of Census reports the proportion of married women between the ages of 25 and 29 who are childless was nationally 17.4 percent in February, 1975, the proportion of childless women five years after graduation from Radcliffe was 86 percent. Simmons and Wellesley figures about their graduates were similar, though not quite as extreme. Five years after graduation the Simmons graduate had 0.32 of a baby, Wellesley only 0.07. Belin stated that the comparison for the classes ten years out of college was less dramatic, but here too the rate of births had dropped by close to 50 percent. H. Kahne (1976) reported that the fertility rate of the average American family had fallen from 3.7 children per family in 1960 to 1.9 in 1974.

Another social phenomenon visibly on the incline is that of wives leaving home. Articles regarding the increase are common in the media (Adams, 1972; Beeles, 1976; Bralove, 1975; O'Brien, 1976; Sklar, 1976). Bralove cited the statistics of the nation's largest private investigative agency, specializing in finding missing persons. Fifteen years ago the ratio of runaway husbands to runaway wives sought by clients was 300 to 1. In 1974, the New-York-based agency handled 1,136 cases of runaway wives and 989 cases of runaway husbands. During the early part of 1975, the agency indicated that twice as many wives as husbands were being sought after they had run away from home. The president of the agency pointed out that many of the women did not wish to stay away permanently, but wanted to renegotiate the basis of their role in the family. A Chicago attorney commented that the number of women opting out of marriage and giving up custody of their children represented "definitely a new trend" over the past five years. A judge noted that "many of the women who never would have dreamed giving up financial security ten years ago ... are leaving marriage now determined to strike out on their own. They are going back to college, getting jobs, and even spurning alimony." O'Brian stated, "No one goes so far as to predict women will exit from marriage. But a number of experts concerned with the rapidly rising divorce rate warn of the importance of two danger signals: the woman desparately in search of an identity beyond marriage and the man who ignores her needs and his own feelings until it is too late." The diverse fragments of the trends cited above lack substantial documentation; however, as a sampling from many more examples, they are too consistent to be ignored. (Leaving the family and renouncing custody will be discussed in chapter 6.)

The customs of child custody are also again in transition. As Baum (1976) pointed out, the rule of awarding a mother custody of her children when there is a divorce is a relatively recent tradition. Toward the turn of the last century, for example, according to New York law "the father of a legitimate unmarried minor was entitled to its custody." Once the importance of the mother in the early psychological development of children was stressed, for example in psychological research and literature, the father began to lose his superior right, and custody began to be based on the "tender years doctrine" which held that "other things being equal" the mother was best suited to care for the child. Now increasingly men were discriminated against in custody suits, even though in 1923 the New York statute was rewritten to read: "In all cases there shall be no prima facie right to the custody of the child in either parent." For some decades custody disputes were resolved by the necessity of having to prove in court that one of the parents was "unfit" for the care of the children, a kind of social condemnation, which (as discussed in chapter 6) has farreaching implications for the child. Currently there is a movement in custody disputes parallel to the movement toward "no fault" divorce. The stigma of "unfitness" is decreasingly necessary, and a new emphasis is being placed on awarding custody to the parent best able to meet the emotional and other needs of the child, though both may be "fit" for example, Judge Riboudo, who awarded custody to the father in the Salk case (1975), stated: "both parties have exhibited love and affection for their children, but the father better serves their emotional and cultural needs." This is in line with the emphasis on the "best interest of the child" (Goldstein, Freud, and Solnit, 1973). Although custody is awarded to the mother in the great majority of cases Finkelstein (1975) reported that between 1970 and 1974 the percentage of children under six years of age living with a divorced father was increasing faster than the percentage of children under six living with a divorced mother. A number of organizations, such as Fathers for Equal Justice, are concerned with bringing both the rights and the capabilities of fathers as parents into more public view. Joint custody has also become a more frequent option (Baum, 1976).

In an important paper H. Kahne (1976) linked current trends of social change to perspectives for the future, as well as to social policy recommendations. Documenting such changes as the increasingly pervasive absorption of women into the labor force, the postponement of and decrease in childbearing, the rising divorce rate, the increasing educational level of women, the greater freedom accorded to such alternate life styles as communes, open marriage, sequential relationships, and the sharply rising numbers of single-parent households, she outlined the impact on children. She pointed out, for example, that "the largest increase of working mothers in the past five years has been in that group who are female heads of families. It is children of these mothers who most often must cope with twin problems of the absence of a parent and poverty status." She stated that "fewer siblings, working mothers, single parents are all likely characteristics of children's future environment. If marital disruptions continue to occur at their present rate ... it is estimated that between 34 percent and 46 percent of children under 18 will be affected (most frequently by divorce) for a substantial (average five years) period during growing. Children have become a part of the social change that is the new world of adults."

Kahne emphasized the close relationship between family functions and relationships and prevailing family structure. In the most prevalent family form in the United States today, the dual-worker family, growing emphasis is placed on symmetry of function and flexibility of sex roles. Such symmetry is encountered already in a number of social classes and a number of countries. A twleve-country survey, cited by Kahne, found an unmistakable trend toward a family structure with decisions and task allocations made through cooperative coordination of roles, not linked to sex.

In her discussion of changing family patterns, Kahne sensitively underlined the problems of "a sense of anomie, isolation, and a non-supportive emotional environment for meeting the inevitable traumas of life" in a culture where impermanence in caring relationships has become so much more prevalent. Summarizing the crucial provisions for social support that she advocated, she commented that the future for children "will be both more complicated because of the flux of family life and tensions attendant on changing norms of behavior, and at the same time will be eased by the social awareness of themselves as persons and the social concern that other persons have for their welfare."

No one can predict with certainty at what rate the current changes will continue to take place, nor what will lead them in directions perhaps unforeseen. Nevertheless, for better or worse, these changes indicate how large a segment of our population is either a partner or a child of a parting parent, and is not usually spared the accompanying pain. It would be desirable if our social policies allowed economic and work realities, provisions for flexible sex-role involvements and for sustaining care of children to accelerate in accordance with the need.

The Human Relationship Network
During the Period of Parting

SUPPORTS AND LACUNAE FOR PARENTS

During the period of heightened distress which is usual before, during, and after the parting of parents, the need for a human support network is greatest, and the individual without it most vulnerable. Although the support of others can neither change nor undo whatever degree of pain is associated with the parting, its presence, like symbolic comforting arms, may help to make the pain bearable enough to be experienced as such, rather than disguised or distorted into forms which in the long run may be more debilitating to the individual.

As the parents and children described here were not generally seen prior to the parting, material regarding support during that time is retrospective and sketchy. However, judging from experience with other couples and individuals who had marital problems that did not culminate in divorce, relationships to friends, colleagues, neighbors, support groups—whether "couples," "parenting," "awareness," or "hiking" groups—or individual therapists were often important for the individual as a sounding board, as a way of getting feedback about the effect of their own behavior on the marriage, and in providing a sense that they were not alone in the issues they faced. Currently, the number of such couples who have their own parents in the vicinity and emotionally supportive appears to be in the minority.

The parents who separated, with some exceptions, appear to have made less use of such social support and to have experienced a greater sense of isolation prior to the breakup of the family. As with the intact families, those who had available parents or other extended family to whom they felt they could turn were in the minority. In cases where family help did exist, most often the resumption of a relationship with the family in which the parent in some way became dependent once more (e.g., lived with family members), though temporarily helpful, in the long run was usually ambivalent. Eventually the parent felt a need to live independently again.

A significant number of parents who did have a dependable circle of friends, colleagues, neighbors, or support groups first became aware through this contact that others saw them as a different sort of person than did the spouse. This realization began to give them enough confidence to attempt to alter their interaction within the marriage. Individual therapy sometimes also stimulated this. In such cases, the decision to separate was eventually reached if one or both partners felt that what was essential to them now could not be forthcoming in the marriage. Although many times the decision was mutual, most often one parent wished it more than the other. In spite of agreement about the need to separate, I saw no separation or divorce unaccompanied by feelings of rebuff in one or both spouses, or partners. Separation is not to be undertaken lightly.

A large number of parents had felt quite isolated at the time they were considering separation. Some were in a network of social relationships and values which actively advised against separation, at least until the children grew up. When such advice was reinforced by "experts" (such as child guidance clinics) as well as relatives it was indeed difficult to buck. When it happened to be the wrong advice, it could result in increased bitterness in the marriage over the years prior to separation and increased disturbance in children, by then adolescent, who had witnessed and borne the brunt of the bitterness.

More extreme were a very few cases in which a parent seemed to see no way out of an extraordinarily unhappy social isolation. For example, in two families a promotion for the father led to a move into a more affluent neighborhood, replete with values, vocabularies, and ways of spending time which left the new family feeling different and isolated, bereft of previously easy access to neighborhood sociability. In one such family, the mother died as a consequence of a severe alcoholism that had not been a problem in her life before the move. The other mother, who had considered divorce in spite of the consequent religious excommunication that she feared, instead committed suicide one evening after an argument with her husband which had culminated in an unheeded plea from her that he take her to visit either an old friend or her mother. Although it is impossible for any one person or group to be always at the right spot at the needed time, a progressive pattern of isolation from previously important social supports greatly increases vulnerability.

In some other cases, particularly when the individual was about to be admitted to a hospital for psychiatric care, internal changes had taken place that made him unable to avail himself of previous sources of social support, e.g., increased suspiciousness or a need to maintain emotional distance sufficient to preserve essential defenses against catastrophically overwhelming feelings or the possibility of catastrophic acts.

Once separation had occured the kind of social support needed seemed to change. The majority of parents (though not all) struggled with feelings of depression, guilt, or doubt about whether they were making the right decision. They strongly wished for someone else to validate their own perception of the situation. Parents who were not struggling with depression were usually those who already had another relationship for which they were leaving the marriage, and hence already had such validation. If the new relationship had been sought primarily for consolation, or to assuage the parent's doubts about his sexual adequacy, desirability, or other aspects of personal worth, it tended not to last, but eventually to be replaced by more suitable ones. Emotional support from a previous friendship circle is a complicated issue, well described in great detail by Weiss (1975a), and will not be further elaborated here. Within the group of parents I encountered, the women most often complained initially about those of their previous friends who, they felt, were now avoiding them, or simply not "inviting" them any more, while the men were still invited by previous friends, but felt to varying degrees that it was impossible to communicate to their peers and colleagues at work the distress they were undergoing. Some described their time at work as "unreal" to them because of the discrepancy between what they felt and what they did; others felt helped by keeping their work life in a separate sphere, in which they could continue to function as much as possible as before. Numbers of working women also appreciated this feature. Some sex-related differences were notable in social responses to the single parent with young children. While many women did not find extra offers of help with child care, unless they actively sought these out, men who were caring alone for their young children were considered unusual, and had uninvited offers of extra attention for themselves and for their children. At the same time, men who sought custody often experienced bias against them, not only in court, but even from friends.

Two kinds of resources that provide extraordinarily supportive interventions at a crucial time have recently come to my attention. Weiss (1975a, b, 1976) describes his (and coworkers) groups in "seminars" for the separated" and "seminars for the bereaved." The format of the groups includes an emphasis on providing information—about issues ranging from the many practical problems associated with living without one's spouse, to compassionate descriptions of the usual variety and sequence of emotional reactions one can expect in oneself, from the time of separation or loss until one begins to orient oneself toward new or resumed life goals. For many of the parents I encountered, such openly offered information, which leaves the individual feeling less different and guilty about the contradictory array of feelings experienced, had been unavailable and would have been most helpful. The second process in the seminars consisted of a discussion format in which the participants could express, compare, and gain support from each other about, their individual reactions. Weiss's comments about some differences he found between groups of the separated and groups of the bereaved parallel similar differences expressed by children of the divorced and the bereaved, to be compared in chapter 8. He stated (1976), "The nature of their loss caused the bereaved to view themselves differently than the divorced or separated. The separated tend to define themselves as misunderstood, betrayed, stigmatized and perhaps personally flawed. The bereaved are more likely to view themselves as both victim and survivor, perhaps illegitimately so, in relation to their spouse. . . . Compared with the separated, the bereaved appear less self-doubting, more hurt; in consequence they more quickly resent awkward or clumsy attempts to help."

In the form of divorce counseling, a second, quite different aid has been organized as a research project by Wallerstein and Kelley (1976) for divorcing families; for both parents and children, first during the period of separation, and then for later follow-up. They found that in the divorcing period itself stress-heightened anxiety and shifting relationships enhance the chances of effecting beneficial changes. This is also a time when there are many decisions with long-range consequences regarding the postdivorce structure of the relationships, including visitation, custody, etc. Wallerstein and Kelley convincingly demonstrated the important role of their service to divorcing families in general. Those found to be in need of further therapy were seen or referred for this beyond the planned intervention period of six weeks. Wallerstein and Kelly focussed on the divorce experience within a "normal" population and did not accept children with a history of psychological difficulty, or those whose general social or intellectual functioning fell significantly below the developmentally appropriate norms. In this way, their population differed from the children and parents encountered here, some of whom came without a history of psychological disturbance, while many others did show signs of prior difficulties. Nevertheless, I find many similarities between the reactions of children discussed in their material and the children encountered here.

Descriptions such as those by Weiss and Wallerstein and Kelley leave no room for doubt that similar resources should be made available in communities where none such yet exist.

Parting parents often sought out individual psychotherapy. Weiss (1975a) cited Gurin's finding that 22 percent of separated and divorced men and 40 percent of separated and divorced women, around 1960, had sought professional help for personal problems. Others consult physicians because of physical symptoms, such as insomnia, vague headaches, depressive fatigue, etc., which have emotional bases. Among parents who had had psychotherapy before or during the period of their divorce, a number reported to me that this process had not dealt with questions of helping their children through the divorce and its aftermath. It was not clear whether this question had not been relevant for them before, or had simply been neglected. In numbers of cases, a parent commented that he would have tried to support his child in a different way if he had only known earlier what the child was really going through.

A similar gap in available resources appeared in a number of cases in which a family could have profited from attention to the child's readjustment to a parent returning from a hospitalization for serious physical or mental illness, although a program of aftercare for the parent had usually been planned. After I had worked with such a parent-child pair, one psychiatric hospital began to refer similar situations when discharge from the hospital was being planned. It appears to me that a service within which both child and parents would have the chance to explore and work through anxieties obscuring the parent's re-entry into the family, would provide a useful adjunct to aftercare programs.

The role of the court was an unpredictable one, and will be discussed in greater detail in chapter 6 in connection with custody suits. Although the court is potentially an important resource for affiliating itself with divorce and postdivorce counseling services, or divorce-mediation centers its adversary components, intrinsic to the current processes of litigation, at times unfortunately worked to the detriment of all members of a divorcing family.

SUPPORTS AND LACUNAE FOR CHILDREN

The degree to which a human support network was available to the children described here varied enormously. For all the younger children and to a lesser degree for the adolescents, the degree of emotional support which the home parent was able to offer was of primary importance. Almost equally significant for many children of divorce was the support of continued interest, visitation, or access to the absent parent as long as this benefit was not overridden by unmanageably harmful hostilities between the parents. If the absent parent was seriously devalued by either the home parent, or by the social interaction network surrounding the child, this constituted a further loss to the child—of the value of the parent and the value of aspects of the self. When both parents were able to maintain a caring interest and some contact with the child, the nucleus of the human support network had remained intact.

Children seemed best able to cope with the distress about parental death or separation when other meaningful relationships could remain undisrupted. For young children, this meant that it was usually worthwhile to keep the same babysitters, nursery school, or day-care arrangements, contacts with extended family or neighbors as before. When possible, it was helpful to the child not to have to move out of a familiar home and surroundings simultaneously with the parents' separation. However, a number of children did adapt to this kind of change when necessary, as long as the important relationships were maintained. In numbers of cases, special efforts were made by the families to avert an immediate move—e.g., the family of a ten-year-old who was quite attached to his house waited until a year after remarriage to move, and then considered only houses within the neighborhood, so that he would still have his friends within walking distance. In other cases, involving a custody change, parents rather than the children changed their domicile. Sometimes this was not possible, either because of financial factors, job opportunities elsewhere, or the refusal or emotional inability of a parent to move himself. Thus, several mothers had to move elsewhere with their children in order to effect a separation.

When grandparents and other relatives were in the vicinity, they often played an important role. Often they were less ambivalent toward the grandchild than toward their own grown son and daughter. However, the parents of one spouse sometimes struggled over whether maintaining a "civil attitude" toward the other spouse constituted a form of disloyalty toward their own child. In a few cases, the original grandparents not only functioned in a supportive role to the child after divorce, but when a parent remarried the new set of grandparents (some children had three or four sets) could themselves become important figures for support and enriching identifications.

Schoolteachers and guidance counselors were almost universally helpful when they were consulted about a particular child's needs. Sometimes very individual prescriptions were needed. For example, one teacher was able to shift her attitude toward a boy she had previously suspended after she discussed with me her humiliation about his making a "fool" out of her in front of others. She was told that this was not a "personal" attack, that he might have done this with any teacher, since he was testing whether he could make his worst fears about being thrown out (like his father) come true. Realizing that he was in some distress, she could then be firm without being frightened by him. Another child, who was acutely afraid her mother would die while she was in school and had become school-phobic, needed to be greeted each morning in an individual, two-minute conversation before she could settle into a work routine. She was upset by "new" papers before finishing the old ones ("old" stood for her past relationships and family life) and for a time needed the reassurance that she could finish her "old" papers first and that they would be kept in a safe place and not thrown away. She also needed to be called by her "old name" (her father's last name). The teacher cooperated in establishing a predictable ritual involving such symbolic reassurances about loss in easing the child's re-entry into school. On the whole, it was helpful for teachers to know that a death or divorce had occurred. Most teachers spontaneously responded by being sure they did not withdraw interest and support from the child at this time, and became aware of the significance of the child's sometimes puzzling behavior. Teachers were sometimes reassured by knowing that although extra understanding might be needed, it was important that the child not be treated as "different" from classmates in regard to various "ground rules" at school. For numbers of adolescents, for instance, programs were set up (in collaboration with the adolescent) to make it impossible for him or her to cut classes without being noticed.

Continuity of some friendships was particularly important to older children and adolescents. Some children went through many vicissitudes of feeling toward a number of friends who remained stable in their lives. Others changed friends, or became newly capable of having friends, as they themselves changed. In early and mid-adolescence, friendships became most volatile, but also often expanded their influence to include the friend's family or other adults associated with friends' activities. Some children between the ages of nine and eighteen found it impossible to confide about parental parting to any peer for a prolonged period of time.

Continued attendance at church or temple, scouts, drama class, or the particular school with which the child had a positive involvement also proved supportive. For example, a remarried couple, expecting to bring their stepson into the family, arranged for him to finish the year in the familiar school near his mother's home, while at the same time encouraging neighborhood friendships with a view to his changing school the following year. Many children, of both divorced and deceased parents, were highly sensitive to what was being said about their absent parent by those in the social network who had known that parent. The opinion of someone who knew the absent parent counted for more, and could be a more meaningful support to the child, than the opinion of a stranger.

Numbers of children could have profited from a group in which their experiences and reactions could have been shared, and information provided about what they might expect from themselves and their parents at present and in the future. That the intensity of distress is not expected to last in parent or child forever is something good for the children to know (this is discussed in greater length in chapter 9). One boy, while in the process of terminating his individual psychotherapy, organized and led such a group in his school.

Children and parents knew they could call me between sessions when there was a sudden difficulty. This is not something I generally encourage with patients, other than during periods of overwhelming anxiety, unusual stress, or the likelihood of "acting out" in a way that might have negative consequences for them.

However, because the problems of dealing with intense feelings about a person who was now missing from their daily lives were part of the trauma they had undergone, it deemed unwise at first for the therapist also to be totally unreachable between sessions. The complications and limitations of confronting loss within the therapy relationship are further discussed in chapter 10.

Those parents who knew that under stress they would feel tempted to accuse their children of being "just like" the absent parent in a derogatory way were also invited to let me know this over the phone if necessary, rather than derogating the child.

THE FUNCTION OF THE HUMAN SUPPORT NETWORK
DURING PARTING: SUMMARY

This book describes a series of individuals subjected to a disruption of their relationship with a primary attachment figure—a parent. The disruption is not of their own choosing, but occurs because of their parents' need to part, or because of death. The child must deal with this disruption—which may range from complete loss of the parent, e.g., if there is a suicide, desertion, or a complete withdrawal from the child, to a transformation of the nature of the relationship—by coming to terms with the pain which separation from a loved person in itself induces.

The experience of the separation is affected not only by the quality of the previous relationship and the inner developmental stage of the child, but also varies in important ways according to the meaning the child attributes to that loss. In turn, the meaning of the loss has a major impact on how the child views himself, e.g., as worthwhile, or as someone to be discarded, as useless and blameworthy, or as still a potential source of joy to himself and others. The meaning of the loss is intricately tied not only to the changed relationship but also to the meaning it has been given within the human network surrounding the child. This means that the child will be deeply affected by the parent's own response to the separation and to the image of the missing or partially missing parent conveyed to him explicitly, implicitly, or with some discrepancy between conscious and unconscious messages, by the remaining or custodial parent. The parent, of course, is equally affected by the combination of personal distress about his or her own loss and the meaning of that loss. One aspect of that meaning is reflected by the social network surrounding the parent.

For both the child and the parent, the presence of human support networks becomes a crucial issue at the time of separation or divorce. Even when both partners wish and agree to the separation, the process is usually accompanied by a painful period for the parent, highlighting awareness of confusingly "missed" aspects of the relationship, and bringing to the fore previously unknown recesses of the inner experiences of loneliness, pockets of self-blame, self-doubt and rage at the partner, depression or its equivalent in the form of physical symptoms. The presence of the child in some cases is experienced as another demand or reminder of the spouse, arousing additional ambivalence. In many others, parents described the child as "what really kept me going" during the period of greatest difficulty.

In recent years, there have been major changes not only in the growing incidence of divorce and separation, but also in the aura of social acceptance surrounding such separations. In the Western world, an increasing number of people believe that both men and women should have the option of many different roles. There is, fortunately, less social pressure toward making one's marital status an a priori definition of respectability or worthiness disgrace or failure. Nevertheless, there are innumerable instances in which, for a variety of reasons an individual simultaneously loses a spouse and the previously known human support network. In the first place, many social events are still so "couple-oriented" that the single adult is perceived or perceives him- or herself as somehow out of place and no longer sharing common interests with a previously known set of family-oriented friends. At other times, the single adult is hurt by what he or she perceives as increasing distance from previous friends as though the divorced person's presence threatens intact, but insecure marriages by bringing discord to light.

The most extreme cases of "social shunning" which have come to my attention are those in which a woman has lost custody of her children, or has decided, for a variety of reasons to be discussed later, to leave her home and children. This kind of shunning, e.g., extreme avoidance by previous friends attending the same PTA meeting, has an aura of the dread of contact within it. It is not clear whether the avoidance by the previous friends revolves around a fear of contagion, i.e., that at moments they, too, might be tempted to leave their children, or arises from unresolved feelings over their own childhood dread of abandonment, which makes them ambivalent toward any parent who would carry out this act. In effect, this type of shunning creates a rent in the human support network which opens the way for a disastrous fall in self-esteem for the parent.

In any case, most often child and parent are simultaneously dealing with the loss of or transformation in a relationship to a previously loved person and a previously reliable human support network. In this chapter, the focus has been on this support network, as embodied in the broad social structure and culture within which the family functions and which is intimately related to the parents' and child's sense of himself among others and his capacity for coping with loss.

Chapter 2

IDENTIFICATION PROCESSES
IN DEVELOPMENT AND IN LOSS

When I am a man, then I shall be a hunter
When I am a man, then I shall be a harpooner
When I am a man, then I shall be a canoe-builder
When I am a man, then I shall be a carpenter
When I am a man, then I shall be an artisan
Oh Father! ya ha ha ha

—Kwakiutl Indian quotation
from E. Steichen, *The Family of Man.*

Introduction of the Issues

Given the social nature of the human being, identification with others colors growth with multiple hues. But identifications are only one of several aspects of an individual's sense of identity. Whom one loves may be another.

The process of identification has a central role in the development of the child, as well as special functions in his attempts to ameliorate the partial or total loss of a loved person. The dynamics of identification are reflected in transformations in the image of the person identified with, as well as transformations in the image of the self. The location of the perceived attributes also changes: it may be experienced primarily as residing in the parent, the self, the external world at large, or in newly wanted or feared persons.

A number of questions come to mind, and will be explored in this and the following chapter: What is the fate of the image of the person identified with, when that person more or less exits from the actual life of the child? Does the child's vision of a wanted, absent person as reappearing in the external world fade, as identification with aspects of that person is intensified? Or, one might put it this way: Can identification with a person whom one has wanted, but lost, function to preserve components of the relationship, and yet coexist with an active quest for the lost person in reality?

The clinical material to be presented suggests that identifications play an important part in enhancing the personality of the child who has totally or partially lost a parent through divorce or death. It allows him or her to preserve the relationship psychically and continue to make use of whatever mixture of affection and guidance emanated from that parent. By the time a child is eighteen months old, he has already committed a part of himself to the wish to be "like" each parent in some ways. Giving up the parent, and the associated wish for likeness then, would also involve giving up the part of the sense of self identified with that parent.

As Erikson (1959) has pointed out, eventual ego identity is "more than the sum of the childhood identifications. It is the accrued experience of the ego's ability to integrate these identifications with the vicissitudes of the libido, with the aptitudes developed out of endowment and with the opportunities offered in social roles."

Healthy identifications are evolved at different developmental levels, within the context of a continuing relationship. The natural course is for such identifications to become more realistic and selective, because constant reality testing, within the limitations of the child's ego development, remains a part of the process. Although at first magically powerful, idealized, and destructively feared images of parent figures are a natural component of the child's dependence on his love objects, these more archaic qualities recede as the child evolves a separate identity that is derived in part from the internalized attributes of both parent figures. As the early experiences of identification with the parent figures also have components of intensely satisfying intimacy at preverbal, physiologic, and affective levels, the affective component of the sense of togetherness achieved in that period may remain at an unconscious level as a chord which resounds with an immediate sense of well-being, or of dread, in shaping the later sounds of life experience. These deep-seated ties to a sense of goodness or anguish will also constitute a substratum in the child's ego ideal, or his image of the person he would like to become.

In discussing early identification processes, we must distinguish two types of identification. The first is derived from the wish to be at one with the loved person, to experience intimacy through sharing. This is ordinarily involved in the infant's first "imitations" of affect, gesture, etc., which reflect those of the caretaking person. Brody (1956), for instance, noted that infants whose mothers stare into space during early feedings are also most apt to turn their gaze in a similar direction, though they often stare at a light. It seems they identify with the avoidance of eye contact by learning not to look at the face of the parent, yet displace the wish for visual stimulation by turning to another light in their young lives! The second type of identification can come into play only after there is some beginning discrimination of the self from the caretaking person. In order to involve the caretaker, the child then also begins to identify with those who are the center of the caretaker's interest, including the spouse and siblings. This involves the sense of being *different* from the mothering one, but *like* those whom the mother loves or to whom she directs attention.

Disturbances can occur in either of these two components of identification. The process of identification, which assumes the need to be like someone who is valued, involves fantasies which have libidinous but also competitive components from the child's point of view. These components are deeply enmeshed with the adult's own motivation concerning such reflections of him- or herself. The child, rather than the adult, may choose to make this explicit, by displaying an identification with the implicitly expressed affective messages from the adult, even when these are contradicted by the adult's manifest ideology or rules of conduct. A most common example used to be that of the sexually active young adolescent girl whose mother had from so early warned her not to "whore" around that the girl had sensed and acted on a preoccupation of her mother rather than one originating in herself.

Identification with the parent has been presented so far as a component necessary to the young child's growth and the progressive stabilization of his identity. Simultaneously, however, the growth and sense of continuity of his identity demands a core of recognized self-images, which do not depend on identifications with others. Hence, the child's differences from those around him must also become valid and valued aspects of his self-image. As long as his own sense of identity is primarily bound to identifications with only one or two others, he remains vulnerable to sudden loss of self-esteem, or, more seriously, loss of a sense of his own identity, when there are disruptions in his relationships to the identification figures. In the long run, identification figures also become most valuable to him as their attributes are selectively internalized and become a part of his own character structure, synchronized with aspects of his character *unlike* those of his identification figures but recognized by himself as his own. Such independence, however, occurs only partially in childhood; it is, indeed, an open question how far it is completed during adult development. For example, these issues often reemerge in late middle age, when a sense of their own mortality and the passage of time may drive individuals once again to concern themselves with inner development and may lead to further growth.

If the process of identification becomes the overriding mechanism by which the child ensures a sense of closeness or access to those he needs, it can interfere in the development of an acceptable, individual sense of identity. The broadening of the child's social circle, which normally occurs when he plays with other children, and even more so at the time he enters school and becomes aware of the diversity of values among peers, teachers, and family members, often helps him to recognize qualities in himself from a fresh perspective. In two-parent families, real but compatible differences between parents contribute. So does a new parent figure who becomes meaningful in his life. In single-parent families, identification figures outside the family may have special importance.

Early identification with parent figures might be seen as the center of gravity around which the child's later affective experience, goals in life, and sense of his own distinct identity revolve. When such identifications have helped the child both to experience gratification and to tolerate the sense of separateness derived from bearable doses of disappointments in the idealized parents, the process of identification becomes more realistic, selective, and increasingly under the control of the individual. It has been postulated that the propensity for empathic understanding and behavior toward another individual involves not only the ability to identify temporarily with another's affective experience but also to reorganize that identification into the context of one's own personality structure. For example, pleasurable and successful caring for an infant may require some capacity to empathize and identify with dependent infantile needs, but if the parent became lost in that identification and began to act like the baby, the parent's ego would have regressed to a chaotic state and the baby would be without care. (Benedek 1959).

The interweaving between identification as an ego mechanism and the building of a secure identity brings to the fore those aspects of identification which foster, not identity growth, but defense against the inner pain of experiencing loss. Identification can serve that function even when there is no actual disruption of relationships, but when the individual fears that aspects of his own growth invite loss of love from the adults; he needs to cling to identifications at the expense of further differentiation of himself. These disturbances in the identification process are not, however, the focus of this book and will not be further detailed.

In psychoanalytic thinking, the concept of identification has been central to a vast array of functions within the personality. In the discussion here, knowing that much is omitted and oversimplified, we limit ourselves arbitrarily to considering identification as a developmental process, and as a defense against loss.

Mixtures of Identification
and the Quest for the Wanted Person

In attempting to sort out the place of identification in the clinical phenomena encountered, I was struck in particular by the repeated indications that identifications with the lost wanted parent, acquired both developmentally and to help deal with loss, seem to coexist with a quest, still externally directed, for that parent. Although many transformations in the image of the lost parent take place, and will be described within a variety of personality structures and familial and social dynamic interaction networks, the quest for the presence of the absent other frequently persists in harmonious or discordant form. This quest may be linked to the interaction as experienced by the child rather than to the image of the person per se. It may appear, many years later, in surprisingly concrete forms of repetition. Three vignettes illustrate different mixtures of identifications and quests and precede the more theoretical review of the problem.

VIGNETTE 1: PETER

Peter was three-and-a-half when his mother left home to pursue a career in law. His father had been quite willing to take custody of Peter and his two-and-a-half-year-old sister, devoting himself to child care after working hours, and able to maintain continuity in supportive relationships by keeping the children in the same day-care center where they had been before their mother left. Peter had been told that mommy missed the children, but lived too far away now to be able to visit. After a period of regression to babyish behavior and clinging to father and his favorite day-care worker, he seemed to accept the situation "well." At day care, he was described as taking a new sudden interest in cooking and in feeding the dolls. In playing house, he persistently now chose the role of "mommy," rather than "daddy," a contrast to the period before she left home. At home, he declared that he wanted to be the one to "cook for daddy" and insisted on making "saghetti," which was the favorite food his mother had often made for him. Several months after she left, when out for a walk with his father, he was apt suddenly to shout, "Get away, Daddy," push his father away, and run down the street toward an approaching woman, calling, "Mommy, Mommy." It was only after the repeated discovery that the distant woman was not "Mommy" that Peter would rush back into his father's arms, sobbing. This was the point at which his open grieving for the mother began.

VIGNETTE 2: EMILY

A touching example of a reunion fantasy was evident in the psychic life of Emily, a graduate student in her twenties, who had been adopted as a baby.

She was periodically troubled by being compelled to cut her arm or leg, which was always precipitated by a disappointment in a potentially mothering person that Emily perceived as an indication that this person did not want her to live. Secretly, in a paper bag, which she took great effort to conceal in her clothing, she carried a much used and partly mutilated soft, stuffed fur kitten, which she assumed had been given to her by her mother when she left the child at the adoption agency. Possible separation from the kitten gave rise to panic reactions. This young woman continued to hope each birthday that her mother, whom she had never seen, would somehow find and visit her for a birthday celebration, recognizing her daughter by recognition of the toy kitten. The week after her birthday, she was always deeply depressed.

As Emily had no "real" experience with her biologic mother (although she did with both adoptive parents), her loss was not one for which, through memory, she could grieve. Yet much feeling was focused on her birthday, the only day in her past on which she could know for sure that she and her mother must have been together. One aspect of her quest for her mother was condensed in the kitten, which, used as a transitional object, comforted her when she held it and from which separation caused anxiety. In fantasy, the kitten not only represented the concrete expression of her mother's love or gift to her as a baby, but was also endowed with the enduring print of her babyhood self: to provide the means by which her mother would recognize and therefore want to be reunited with her.

VIGNETTE 3: LINDA

Linda, the middle of three children, had a distant relationship to her mother throughout childhood, but experienced warmth and tender handling by the father. He took over the bathing and much of the physical care of the baby Linda, who suffered from eczema, while her mother was repulsed by her appearance and avoided handling her more than necessary. He continued bathing her until she was ten, and later she vividly recalled his gentle touch. In her preschool years, she had followed her father around, avidly wishing to participate in whatever he did. In nursery school, she had refused ever to part with the fireman's hat father had given her, declaring that she was not *playing* that she was a boy, but insisting that she really was a boy. She and he often played firemen together. By the second grade, she accepted, unusually late in development, that being a boy was makebelieve. When she was eleven the parents divorced; the father suffered a psychosis with a hospitalization that was followed by a remarriage and many changes in behavior toward Linda. She was referred for treatment at age fourteen, plagued by depression and inability to concentrate in school or make friends. After much adolescent turmoil, involving both her identification with her father and her reactions to his beating her in a fit of rage on a visit at age seventeen, she mourned the loss of the loving, but also all-powerful image of him to which she had clung. She evolved a more realistic conception of her father and felt less vulnerable to his influence in shattering her self-esteem. She worked out enough of her anger toward her mother to evolve and enjoy a more feminine identification. Her mother became more supportive of her in important ways. With graduation from high school, she also finished treatment and left the area to attend college.

When she was twenty-five, she came back to see me with a fear which puzzled her. After some years in which she made fairly masochistic choices of love partners, she had finally established a stable relationship with a young man she cared about, who returned her feelings, and who was considerate of her. She described herself as happy with him, but she feared that she might do something to disrupt the relationship. It turned out that she felt a compelling attraction to another man, whose eyes, at a social gathering, she met across the room. He had been talking excitedly about the music conductor, Arthur Fiedler, who was known to love following fire engines to reach the scene of a fire. Cliff and Linda shared their admiration for Fiedler's verve in carrying this through, even when he had to interrupt whatever else he was doing. They did not say much more to each other, but she began to fantasy about Cliff. When Don, with whom she was living, was away for a week, she looked up the other man. She had not felt that she wanted an affair with him, but rather that she wanted to be wherever he was, and do whatever he did. Yet she said she did not really "like" him. I finally said, "Your description reminds me of what you used to tell me when you were a little kid and shadowed your father all over the place with your firehat on." She blushed and answered, "That really freaks me out to hear you say that . . . because the night when he and I were together while Don was out of town for that week, . . . we went to a Halloween party dressed up as the fire brigade . . . and then we came home and took a shower together . . . but I didn't want to go any further than that . . . and I haven't seen him since. But I am afraid I might go see him again. It's not really that I like him—he's too macho—but I think we understand each other without words. I had forgotten all about that firehat I always had. Now I remember, too, when my mother was mad at us, like on a Saturday, Daddy used to take me to the firehouse and the firemen would let us climb all over, and slide down the pole. Daddy would always say not to tell mother about the pole because she would think that was dangerous."

Remnants of both the early identification with and quest for the lost beloved father seemed to coexist. The stress precipitating their re-emergence in action—that is, an imminent decision about whether to marry Don—had revived fears about her parents's unhappy marriage and her own childhood and adjustment to feeling that only her father cared about her. Although she consciously wanted to marry Don, unconscious fears about repeating her parents' relationship revitalized the still active, though long latent, quest for earlier joys and sorrows.

In each of the cases briefly sketched above, the child had to make a different, difficult acceptance of the loss of a parent figure, and the implications this had for the image of the self. For Linda, the loss involved a drastically altered relationship with father; for Peter a real desertion by his mother; and for Emily the loss of a dearly held belief that her mother had loved and wanted her.

Some differences in the ways such different "realities" are perceived will be dealt with in later chapters. Separation from the wanted person involves the slow and painful decathexis of the inner psychic representations of that person. It is these psychic representations, emanating at times from unconscious and nonverbal organizations of perceptions once experienced, which seem to remain ready to be externalized and reapproached in the external world. When the experiences have been at least intermittently good, they perhaps sculpt the form of hope eternal. What Peter, Emily, and Linda had in common was that they had not given up hope that they could make their wish come true.

Some Questions Regarding the Role of Identification

When one views the lives of children of parting parents, the crucial role of the interplay of identification processes with continued or future relationships with others brings the following questions to the fore:

1. What identifications are enriching rather than debilitating to the developing personality?

2. What identifications become alien to the child's conscious concept of the self and yet make their appearance in distorted forms (e.g., as symptoms, or "negative" identity [Erikson]; suicide attempts, etc.)? How do they get pushed into this role within the child's inner reality?

3. When identification is with a missing, wanted person, and is utilized as a defense against loss, does it take the place of the person, or coexist with a variety of forms of reunion wishes? Such reunion wishes may emerge in a variety of states of consciousness, e.g., dreams, daydreams involving "presences," fantasy, transitional object phenomena, psychic attempts at recreation of the person, unconscious anticipations (e.g., eternally searching the mailbox for news from far away), suicidal fantasies, acting out, the patterned repetition of affectively charged components of the lost relationship with others that one comes to care about, or the search for precious intimacy achieved by shared emotional experience whose major impetus is the pleasure

in shared reality (inner or external) rather than the mastery gained by identification.

4. How are identifications and images of the wanted person transformed during the process of grieving or longing and how do these transformations affect the image of the self or newly wanted persons? When such grieving does not or cannot occur for inner or external reasons (e.g., immaturity, lack of support in family members; identification with other modes of dealing with tensions or grief in the family), what happens to the image of the wanted person and the self?

5. If reality testing of the transformations in identification patterns and images of the missing wanted person and the self continues to be possible— clearly, if the parent has died or disappeared, it is not—what effect does this have? What factors in the family and social network make possible—or preclude—effective reality testing about the parent?

To deal with the clinical complexity of identifications as these emerge in the children's lives, it seems necessary to take into consideration the following:

1. Developmental changes in the nature of the identifications made, ranging from the wish to merge with the wanted person, to the wish to be the same as, or merely like, the wanted person. Using Jacobson's (1964), Anna Freud's (1952) and Schafer's (1968) delineations of this developmental process, we will also trace its cognitive counterparts in the work of early childhood. The work of Piaget (1954), Blos (1962), Erikson (1959), and Fraiberg (1969) will be referred to in tracing developmental changes through adolescence, with the work of Kohlberg and Gilligan (1971) and others providing the parallel framework in cognitive and moral or ethical development. Comments on continued development in identifications in adults include references to the work of Erikson (1956), Benedek (1959), Miller (1973), Levinson et al. (1974), Cath (1965) and others.

2. Identification as a way of dealing with loss. Starting with Freud's formulation regarding mourning, identification as a defense against threatened loss will be examined.

3. Identification with the wanted person may be expressed in a variety of ways, including emphasis on shared affective states, identification with ego modes (e.g., denial) or impulses (e.g., aggression); identification with affecto-motor states; identification with specific mental content; or with perpetuated prohibitions or ideals, e.g., identification with a "shared" ego ideal.

4. Identification and rivalry with a third person who is desired by that person one wants, i.e., the wish to be like that object. This may involve being different from rather than similar to the wanted person, e.g., like the fantasied "mistress" of one's father.

Identification as a Process in Development

IN EARLY CHILDHOOD

Jacobson describes the developmental changes in the process of identification, as the child matures.

The earliest kinds of identifications represent "fusions of self and object images." Jacobson (1954, 1964) stated that at first the infant can probably hardly discriminate between his own pleasurable sensations and the objects from which they are derived. Only when the perceptive functions have sufficiently matured can gratifications or frustrations become associated with the object. As unpleasurable or frustrating experiences are repeated (such as the wait for hunger pangs to be satisfied) and associated with separation from the love object, fantasies of total incorporation of the gratifying object begin to arise, expressive of the wish to re-establish the lost unity. Jacobson opined that "this desire probably never ceases to play a part in our emotional life. Even normally, the experience of physical merging and of an 'identity' of pleasure in the sexual act may harbor elements of happiness derived from the feeling of return to the lost, original union with the mother. . . . These earliest wishful fantasies of merging and being one with the mother are certainly the foundation on which all object relations as well as all future types of identifications are built." She stated that the adult ego will make extensive use of introjective and projective mechanisms, based on such fusions between self and object images, for the special purpose of establishing feeling and fantasy identification at any level, not only with love objects, but with the whole environment. "Our empathic understanding of others, especially those we love, depends on such temporary—either short-lived or more long lasting— identifications." She was careful to point out that in contrast to the earliest stages of identification, such temporary fusions induced in the service of the ego do not normally weaken the boundaries between the images of self and object, whereas in the early infantile stage such firm boundaries have not yet been established. She concluded that as long as those fantasy and feeling identifications coexist and collaborate with mature personal relations and firmly established ego and superego identifications, they will not in any way affect a person's feelings of identity. She added that child analysts seem to agree that up to the age of three conscious fantasies of merging with love objects are within the margin of normal development.

During a second stage in the development of the identification process, a more active type of primitive identification develops from the child's increasing efforts to imitate the love object. Observations of infants show abundantly that the baby begins to perceive and to imitate the gestures, the inflections of voice and other visible affective manifestations of the mother. Brody's (1956) description of the correlation between the mother's and infant's gaze while the infant is nursing has been mentioned. The infant's interest in the mother's facial expression has been described in detail by Spitz (1955) and a number of other writers. Lowenstein (1954) stated that "during the first year, one can clearly observe a very specific learning process, namely the infant's attempt to understand what the mother feels and thinks." He described an infant whom he observed at the age of six weeks to display facial expressions which exactly imitated his mother's at the moment, while he watched her intently with an expression which, in an older child or adult, could be described as "drinking her in with his eyes." Lowenstein believed that children try to learn very early what adults feel by this specific form of identification.

Piaget and Buhler noticed, too, that this type of exact imitation precedes a reciprocal response or relationship. Buhler (1930), in her observations of children at the Vienna Institute, found that at first the infant repeats whatever expression is on the face of the adult—he smiles when the adult smiles and frowns when the adult frowns. Slightly later, the child has a reciprocal reaction. For example, if the adult continues to frown, the baby cries. I must say I have seen many babies who do not corroborate this observation. Fenichel (1945) described the close connection and interrelations between the still predominantly receptive infantile fantasies of this period and the imitations of the love object which begin in the first year of life but already require the participation of the motor apparatus. Jacobson (1964) commented that since these imitations originate in the close empathic tie between mother and child, they probably emerge from what may be called primitive affective identifications. She stated, "Early reciprocal affecto-motor identifications between mother and child precede and usher in the child's imitations of the parents' functional activities."

Jacobson's concept of "affecto-motor identifications" helps clarify a number of clinical phenomena encountered in the children of parting parents. In a number of the youngest children brought to treatment the "symptom" was in the form of affective or motor behavior, which eluded explanation unless seen as reflecting an ego-alien identification with a missing parent. Its "symptomatic" nature generally meant that it comprised an aspect of the lost, wanted parent which the child prized, but the spouse did not. Hence its more open expression, in the form of "being like" the parent, or in fantasy, would have been at the risk of disapproval from the custodial parent. In older children and young adults, ego-alien fragments of such identifications also erupt to puzzle the patient and pay tribute to the strength of his or her early ties.

Jacobson appears to date the affecto-motor stage of identifications as occurring roughly during the latter half of the first years, when the infant's reality testing has increased sufficiently for him to perceive the differences between himself and his parents, and as self and object images become established and differentiated. She saw these types of identifications as achieved through projection and introjection, based on fantasies of incorporation. They are characterized by total rather than partial identifications, achieved by magic rather than real alterations in the ego. However, they lay the foundations for self-esteem and a future sense of well-being.

During the next developmental stage of identifications, after the age of two, the desire for a complete union with the parent begins to give way to strivings to become only "like" the parent. Jacobson called these the beginnings of "ego identifications." They depend on the ability to perceive single mental characteristics in the love object and to effect appropriate changes in the self-representation and in the ego in accord with objective reality.

Jacobson dated the period when "the advanced forms of identifications predominate" to the resolution of the oedipus complex and the establishment of the superego. At this time, she describes the identifications as *largely independent of the ongoing relationships with the love object*, and integrated into the total functioning of the personality, enriching it in the forms of character traits, ego activities, and sublimations.

This aspect of Jacobson's developmental theory is a problematic one, when viewed in light of the clinical material. Although the children seen clearly demonstrated the shifting nature of maturing forms of identification, as she described it, three features repeatedly made their appearance: (1) Those aspects of identification most distressing to the child had to do with earlier rather than later levels of identifications. (2) Symptoms involving ego-alien identification could *not* be predicted from the overall personality maturity, or even the age of the child. Rather, they were more closely correlated with the particular ego processes utilized by the parents to handle stress, and the degree of support or prohibition regarding grief for the missing, wanted parent. (3) For none of the children or adults seen were the identifications "largely independent of the ongoing relationship with the love object."

Transformations in identification patterns occurred in response to current interactions with the parent and the spouse; current interactions or lacunae in the human support network; and the current social meanings ascribed to the early identifications by the individual, his parents, spouse or lover, therapist, or human support network at large. For example, it proved possible to transform the function within the child's personality of a degraded part of the self, identified with a parent who had been declared "unfit" in a custody suit, once it was forcefully clarified by family, court, therapist, or community that this did not mean she or he was a worthless person. Thus, the validation of a valued identification by still actively influential human forces appeared deeply to affect children and parents into maturity.

One finds a most thorough delineation of differences in the use of the concept of identification in the writings of Roy Schafer (1960, 1968). His clarifications of the theoretical confusion resulting from the diverse assumptions underlying the notion of identification as both a process and a result also led to formulations consistent with the clinical material that points to the simultaneous existence of identification as a way of dealing with loss, and the continued psychic presence of the lost, loved one in the external psychological world of the individual.

Schafer defined identifications in the following way:

> In its fullest sense the process of identifying with an object is unconscious, though it may have prominent and significant conscious and pre-conscious components; in this process the subject modifies his motives and behavior patterns, and the self representations corresponding to them in such a way as to experience being like, the same as, and merged with one or more representations of that object; through identification, the subject both represents as his own one or more regulatory influences or characteristics of the object that have become important to him and continues his tie to the object. The subject may wish to bring about this change for various reasons; an identification may acquire relative autonomy from its origins in the subject's relations with dynamically significant objects.

> Identifications, once established, are not necessarily static; they may be generalized, pruned, tapered, revised in their detail, and coordinated with other identifications.

> Identification takes place not with a person, but with one or more representations of that person. The subject's conception and experience of that person is only one possible version of him. This version is determined by the subject's pressing needs and intentions, his mood, his projection, his limited experience with or immature comprehension of that person, and other selective and distorting factors, as well as by the nature and extent of his objective appraisal of that person. The proportion of influences exerted by each factor varies with each object and with the subject's developmental level at the time and with the situation.

Schafer followed Jacobson fairly close in recognizing the continuum of levels of identification and of the subjective aims and experiences associated with them. However, he emphasized the *simultaneous* participation of these levels in identification in general. He summarized these levels as follows:

1. Trying to be like another person is an endeavor defined primarily by the secondary process mode or function. It implies that the subject clearly recognized his separateness from the object. It implies a stable conception of that other person as a model and as a basis for comparison. The endeavor is likely to be cast in and to be tolerant of relative terms, that is, to aim for approximate resemblance and not identity. Typically, it is concerned with one or a few characteristics of an object whose complexity is appreciated. And rather than being intended to replace the separate object, it usually carries with it a wish to be recognized and rewarded by the object for the resemblance that is cultivated, for, to a significant extent, it is in the service of the subject's interest in relation with external objects. In these ways, the striving to be like the object is relatively neutralized, objective, and ego-syntonic. It indicates a significant advance beyond early infantile modes of function.

2. Trying to be the same as another person involves significant primary-process features. Its aim is psychological identity, which can only be illusionary and magical in nature. It is likely to include a substitutive aspect, i.e., to aim to replace the external object relations with the identification. The peg on which the sameness is hung may be only trivial, through actual, physical, or attitudinal features of the object, but the inner experience of "sameness" will have larger implications, bearing for example on the strength or sensuality or guilt of the object. This type of identification presupposes fluid and magically transformable self-representations as well as significant restrictions of reality testing. The subject need not aim at identity of overt action; he may emphasize mainly fantasied identity with the object.

3. Merging with another person is essentially a primary-process phenomenon. It condenses representations of the total subjective self and the object. In the subject's experience, it is as if there were only one person, not two, though flux in this experience may remind him that there is not actual unity or, at least will confuse him. Merging may be represented consciously, though ordinarily it is an unconscious experience. For example, it may be conscious in dreams, daydreams, passionate and ecstatic states, psychotic and drug states, and the state which Winnicott calls "primary maternal preoccupation." These examples make it clear that an altered state of consciousness—outside the range of ordinary waking consciousness is involved in conscious merging. Typically, incorporative wishes and fantasies are involved in it; the hypothetical prototype here being the infant's fusion of rudimentary self and object images in the nursing situation. Approaches to complete merging of subjective self and object are evidenced by a high degree of fluidity or ambiguity in localizing attributes and experiences in the

subjective self or the object; as if self and object substitute freely for each other; as if interest in individuation has been pretty much suspended, and, as if, ultimately, it is differentiated unity that is experienced or sought rather than the relation of one person to another.

Schafer regards the three aims and experiences delineated above as concurrent aspects of most identifications. Typically, all three levels are included, but one or another will be most prominently represented and occasion most conflict. This assumption opens the way for further understanding and differentiation of a variety of psychic mechanisms which contribute to the identificatory process or stem from its interaction with other processes but are associated with different underlying capacities, aims, and results.

For example, Schafer pointed to the role of infantile forms of identifications in some highly mature ego states: the capacity for the highest level of empathy, termed by Schafer "generative empathy," involves a mixture of "merging" as one component along with others ("sameness" and "likeness") of a more articulated and sophisticated kind. On the level of generative empathy, the subject, as far as his own experience goes, feels that he is one with the object, he feels what the object feels; and yet, above all, out of self-interest as well as interest in the object, he maintains his individuality and perspective at the same time. This ability to maintain an empathic stance with the feelings of parting parents was strikingly evident in a number of the children seen throughout the period when the identification processes in general lost some of their defensive, unconscious and primitive functions, and grew to be more articulated and selective.

Empathy, as an ego mechanism, has also been discussed by Paul Myerson (1963) in a perceptive and fresh consideration of the modes of assimilation of unconscious material during psychoanalysis. He pointed to the usual sequence he observed in the patient's reactions to stressful events, from the initial employment of primitive defenses to the utilization of increasingly more autonomous appraisals of the situation. He raised the question "at what point are we able to delineate thought processes as an aspect of assimilation rather than defense?" and answered it in terms of the point at which there is instituted a delay which permits a shift from a primitive, mostly passive mode of reaction to a more integrated and active one. He concluded that "the Anlage for such a shift occurs in childhood when the anxious child, temporarily helpless in dealing with a stressful situation, is able to identify with his parent's more supportive attitude and begin to search for more 'realistic' aspects of the traumatic events which have rendered him helpless. It is the child's at least partial internalization of his parent's aim—to understand, to tolerate and to master a threat—that forms the model for the process of assimilation." He followed this formulation with examples in which his own analytic role helped the patient to identify with these ego-strengthening modes of assimilation, which can have defensive functions, e.g., to deal with the threat of loss by identifying with the mental state of the disappointing love object; and yet be adaptive at a high level of ego integration.

Schafer commented that "the optimum for general personal development appears to be a balance (within wide limits) between identification and continuing object relation. This is so because, despite all the hazards of external dependence on other persons, and all temptations to develop a splendid and objectively productive self sufficiency, the ultimate pleasure possibilities are greater, the ultimate sense of mastery more secure, and the ultimate growth more luxuriant, when object relations are combined with identifications." The conflicts of many contemporary women, described in chapters 1 and 5, revolve around the balance between the intensity of relatedness to others, and their assumption that this would imply a diminution of the independence which our culture now increasingly values.

In the foregoing discussion, identification in childhood, that is, the wish to be like the parent, has been viewed as growing out of the emotional attachment to the loved person. It involves, or results from the ability to give up the wish and need to possess that person totally, a wish the child finds impossible in reality. The good sense of closeness to the parent, however, is maintained in the parent's absence partly by becoming "like him." The effect of such childhood identifications on the person's later relatedness depends on the quality of the relationship. For instance, when the child's experience with the caretaking parent is primarily frustrating or discomforting, the identification with the parent may be defensive in nature. Internalization is usually incomplete and the child does not show the gains in adaptive capacity which normally accrue from positive identifications. The child's experience of pain, when this occurs in relation to such a parent, makes the parent at least partially dangerous. As a resilt, the child, at a very basic level, is not receptive to the parent, but rather needs to ward off and keep the parent at a safe distance. That is, when internalization proceeds by way of a predominantly positive tie to a loved person, it is much more likely to proceed to completion—if not disrupted by loss—than the kind of internalization that develops from predominantly aggressive ties.

Receptivity to later identifications is apt to follow these early patterns of positive identification, while an early pattern of the opposite type—that is, "identification with the aggressor"—may be used as a way of becoming an adult in order, among other things, to protect oneself from expected harm. Nevertheless, as is evident from work with children and adults whose suspiciousness or violence toward others is part of such an identification, surrender of an identification based on an ambivalently regarded love tie is also accompanied by a profound sense of loss or a feeling of not being "oneself" when this has been the major relationship to a parent during childhood. Some dramatic examples of this phenomenon were witnessed repeatedly by mental health workers who, twenty or thirty years ago, with the best of intentions, would place an aggressive, delinquent adolescent into a "loving" foster home in order to attempt to make restitution for all the deprivations or cruelties the child had suffered. It was not uncommon to find that by the third day the foster parents would call in despair because the child had vandalized the furniture, run away, or torn up the new clothes, only later exclaiming in bewilderment that he or she would have to be "not me" living in a loving home, or that "even my own mother wouldn't know me" without bruises or defiance.

In other persons, the expectation that closeness will be destructive in some way leads to much more subtle attempts to fend off or control new wishes for identification or constrict the choice of acceptable identification figures to those whose protective armor in this area is bright.

Ego Modes, Content, and Synthesis of Identifications

Identification may occur both with the ego modes, including skills and ways of problem solving, and with the mental content of the person with whom one identifies. Myerson's (1963) description of the mechanism of empathy fostered by the ego modes experienced and identified with during the process of psychoanalysis provided an example. Johnson (1949), Pavenstedt (1967), Tessman and Kaufman (1963), and many others have described the impulsive antisocial behavior of certain children as representing simultaneously an identification with the ego modes of tension discharged by impulsive action, and the content of unconscious wishes of the parent, who condones the behavior, although he may simultaneously appear to punish it. The concept of "identification with the aggressor" points to the defensive function such identifications may have.

Another striking example can be found in the recent demonstration (Bellak and Antell, 1974) that children in playgrounds of different countries displayed vastly differing amounts of physical aggression with the intent to harm, and that the amount of aggression was highly correlated with such aggression directed toward them by the adults. On the playground German adults hurt German children, and German children hurt each other, over five times as often as Italian or Danish adults and children. The authors comment: "The dramatically greater aggressiveness of the treatment of German children shown in this experiment fits the notion widely held by Germans themselves that German culture is *kinderfeindlich*, or hostile to children. A West German poll showed recently that up to 60 percent of parents believe in beating, not slapping or spanking, but beating their children. Munich psychologist Rolf Luckert has said 'We beat our children dumb in this nation.' " The authors are careful to note that the study can draw no conclusions about causation, but "simply describes some apparent relationship between aggression endured and aggression meted out." This study, and others discerning quite different patterns of ideologic content (Adelson, 1971) in different countries (Germany, England, and the United States) lead us to conjecture to what degree individual identifications, and their derivatives as expressed in ideology and behavior coincide with the culturally shared values with which the parents and their children have lived.

However, Adelson points out that within countries also "there are profound individual differences in political cathexis. We can venture some generalizations about those youngsters intense about politics and strivings toward ideology. The most apparent common denominator is their origin in families which are politically active and for whom politics are morally passionate. The youngster takes not only the direction of political thought from his parent, but also their moral intensity. We find this on both the left and the right."

The way in which the parent approaches the world, masters challenges, solves or avoids problems, interacts with others, and copes with potential anxiety or depression profoundly affects the child's view of what is possible. In addition, he repeatedly experiences the parent's approval or disapproval concerning his own attempts at mastery. Although this is true for all problem-solving, parental ego modes for dealing with loss often became central issues for the children encountered here and will be discussed in greater detail in the clinical chapters.

The child's image of the parents with whom he identifies may be distorted in accordance with his particular needs and developmental level. Frequently the conscious image is simplified in a way which emphasizes certain characteristics at the expense of denying the presence of others. For example, a nine-year-old girl whose birthday parties had always been held at restaurants rather than at home explained to me "my mother doesn't know how to make a birthday cake herself because she is a nurse!" At that moment she preferred concentrating on her mother's achievement to dealing with her sense of deprivation about her mother's difficulty in directly meeting the child's dependency needs. Usually, as the child develops into adolescence, and frequently much earlier these days, there are rapid vacillations in the image of the previously idealized parent, often with a denigration of the very same characteristics which were previously admired. A piquant display of conflict about the identification figure can be seen in those adolescents who are adept at mimicking their parents, attempting to minimize the influence of the identification by exaggerating it into caricature. The role of illusion about the parent, the self and the nature of the world is deeply entwined with such vacillations and will be discussed in later chapters.

Schafer pointed out that "another relevant aspect of the parents' characters is their inclusiveness and degree of synthesis. For example, a sharp polarization of 'masculinity" and 'femininity,' or activity and passivity, between the father and mother respectively (or vice versa) indicates a weakness of synthesis on each parent's part. This polarization provides models for identification that will make it hard for the son to integrate his own masculinity and femininity or his active and passive tendencies. He will be split internally as his parents are externally—or, more exactly, he will take over both his father's intense internal struggle against feminine identification and his mother's against masculine identifications." His identifications will thus "resist synthesis." In chapter 1, I discussed the historical and cultural roadblocks for such synthesis, and chapter 7 contains illustrations from adolescents.

Analogously, separating or divorcing parents tend to polarize or exaggerate the differences in personality characteristics between them, often with sex-linked meanings. This may be a necessary, defensive maneuver by the parent who is trying to extrude those components of identification with the past partner which make the separation more difficult. The attempt to extrude the identification is also an act of anger, mobilizing the aggression necessary to sharpen ego boundaries and delineate one's own life as separate from that of the former spouse. The complications for the child are not only that he feels that the "extruded" qualities, with which he has also identified, are now devalued aspects of himself, but that it is common for parents unconsciously to re-establish the balance of previously established and identified-with characteristics by projecting them onto the child. This mechanism occurred most frequently in extreme form within the population seen, in a number of cases in which a mother, separating from father during her daughter's pubescence, bombarded the daughter with implicit and explicit messages about how much the daughter was like the father. This tended to create a highly ambivalent but also seductive tie to the mother.

As the child reacts to the identifications made manifest by the parents, the parent reacts to identifications manifested by the child. The extent to which the parent needs to view the child as a reflection of himself, rather than as a separate person, colors the intensity of the parent's reaction with anxiety, as well as with pride. Frequently the parent's view of himself as he would like to be is imposed on the child, in the form of identifications to be striven for. However, simultaneously often the ego-alien, unconscious, feared, and rejected components of the parent's self-image are communicated with equal force in the parent-child relationship. Because of their unconscious and therefore unnegotiable nature, these components erupt in the form of anxiety about what may be "wrong" with the child. Some parents, low in self-acceptance, cannot believe that anything coming out of them, that is, a child, can really be any good. Others convey their vigilance about whatever components of their own development were insufficiently resolved in relation to their own parents. The conflicts are restimulated in the parents when the child approaches the developmental issues which embody them. Because of the parent's continuing preoccupation and disproportionately upset, angry, or controlling reaction, the child not only senses the parent's anxiety about the particular impulse or behavior (for example, signs of messiness, out-of-control aggression, homosexuality, direct emotional expressions such as crying rather than "toughness," failure in various achievements, etc.), but frequently feels that the parent really "expects" him to "turn out" like the embodiment of the conveyed fears. This conveyed expectation expresses the parent's fear that the unacceptable aspects of the self, which had been so laboriously hidden or repressed, will after all emerge to be exposed to public view through the behavior of the child, resulting in the parent being blamed. The positive aspect of the re-emergence of the parent's old conflicts in the parent-child relationship is the new opportunity for working through in a different way. The pleasure in this process can mitigate old deprivations in the parent, enhancing the parent's sense of mastery and inner freedom. For the child, the libidinous aspects of the parent's reactions to certain identifications may anchor these as self-images in the ego ideal. This will be discussed in a later section.

When two parents are bitterly separated and polarized about what attributes can be valued, the kind of projection described above is frequently shifted to the feared notion that the child will turn out to be like the spouse. Simultaneously the parent may more intensely look to the child to be the embodiment of cherished hopes and ambitions, as a way to assuage the disillusionment and the assaults on self-esteem incurred or felt to be confirmed in relation to the spouse. Different mixtures of such expectations may be projected onto different children within the same family. Although complicated and often contradictory attitudes toward the child's identifications are common, the child becomes more vulnerable to them in a one-parent family, in which they cannot be balanced or given perspective through the simultaneous presence of a second adult with different attitudes toward the child's identifications. In such cases, identification figures outside the family become especially important.

IN ADOLESCENCE

During pubescence and adolescence rapid transformations in the image of the self and of the parents occur as cognitive, affective, and sexual energies kaleidoscope in new combinations and intensities. Although the picture of the "difficult years" of adolescence in our culture has been heavily stressed, it is also a period when renewed opportunities for inner growth can open the way toward a positive reworking of constricting or negative childhood identifications, as well as ways of relating to others. Hartmann, Kris, and Loewenstein (1946) opined that the potential for new developments after the first five years of life, and into adolescence has been underrated in past psychoanalytic thinking. Blos (1962) pointed out that sometimes a more fruitful re-engagement of past problems at this time is "not in spite of, but rather because of emotional turmoil" and commented on the important role of new identifications and counteridentifications at this time. Erikson (1956) noted the simultaneous presence of increased conflict and a "high growth potential" during adolescence. He described the period as "characterized by an abundance of available energy, which, to be sure, revives dormant anxiety and arouses new conflict, but also supports new and expanded ego functions in the searching and playful engagement of new opportunities and associations." He described an increasing sense of identity as being experienced "preconsciously by a sense of psychosocial well-being. Its most obvious concomitants are a feeling of being at home in one's body, a sense of 'knowing where one is going' and an inner assuredness of anticipated recognition from those who count. Such a sense of identity, however, is never gained nor maintained once and for all. Like a 'good conscience' it is constantly lost and regained, although more lasting and economical methods of maintenance and restoration are evolved and fortified in late adolescence." Both Blos and Erikson richly documented various forms of miscarriage as well as "normal" adolescent development. In viewing the lives of the adolescents encountered here, we shall return to the implications for identity formation when the "anticipated recognition from those who count" has been rudely disrupted, and to the relationship of such disruption to the sudden loss of "knowing where one is going," the loss of life goals or drastic renunciation of ego ideals, previously held dear. The clinical material suggests that these aspects of adolescent development which depend on the increasing independence from the image of the parent figures as these were internalized in childhood, can be seriously arrested, postponed or distorted when actual loss of the parent or of his value (in the eyes of the spouse or community as well as in the eyes of the adolescent) makes the inner loss entailed in demystifying his image too risky or catastrophic. Cognitive and libidinal advances and the possibilities for progressive synthesis of earlier identifications are affected. In contrast, when an absent parent is still available for testing the reality of the adolescent's perceptions of him and his reaction, inner transformations in the image, contributing to both identification and individuation in the adolescent, can be more easily dared. Such reality assessment can occur not only through contact with the actual parent but also in the active engagement of the reactions of valued others to the notions about the absent parent expressed (or not expressed—for example, when unconsciously known, but denied) by the adolescent.

Descriptions of adolescence from developmental, normative, or clinical vantage points are abundant and will not be reviewed here. However, some features of adolescent individuation, accompanied by moods analogous to those of mourning; changes in emotional ties to parents and peers; changes in the conception of truth and reality, and the ego ideal (discussed in a later section) are arbitrarily selected for brief comment, as they bear on points stressed in later chapters.

Blos (1962) succinctly summarized the way in which "adolescent individuation is accompanied by feelings of isolation, loneliness and confusion. Individuation brings some of the dearest megalomanic dreams of childhood to an irrevocable end. They must now be relegated entirely to fantasy. Their fulfillment can never again be considered seriously." He spoke of the adolescent's mourning for a "sense of deep losses" which have to do both with taking leave of the aggrandized image of those beloved in childhood, and the parallel image of the idealized self. However, this is necessary before new love relationships with realistic expectations and satisfactions can become meaningfully invested. Let us raise some doubts about what happens to these "dreams of childhood" associated with past, disrupted love towards the parental image, in children of parting parents. When the loss has been traumatic, so that the feelings of mourning associated with it would have been shattering to the individual if faced directly or all at once, both pain and passion may remain intensely associated with it. The "dreams of childhood" tied to the image may be neither available for conscious fantasy nor given up in the realm of "serious consideration" for fulfillment. When the child has experienced such dreams as part of the imagery associated with an affective interchange with a loved and then lost parent, the usual demystification of such images may not take place, and other solutions to the discrepancy between image and reality must be sought. Meanwhile energy available for more mature or for different models of emotional investment in others may remain in limbo.

Recent studies make clear, however, that a fair proportion of adolescents continue consciously to model themselves after a parent, and this parent is not necessarily of the same sex. Douvan and Adelson (1966) report, in fact, that adolescent girls chose their father as a model more often than adolescent boys. At age fourteen 31 percent of boys and 35 percent of girls chose father as their model; by age 16 only 18 percent of boys but 30 percent of girls still did. This is not incongruent with Kohlberg and Kramer's (1969) view that an idealized love relationship with the father prods girls to reach a particular stage of moral development (the "good girl-good boy stage") earlier than the boy, but also to remain in it longer, (often to adulthood) rather than progressing beyond it. Kohlberg (1966) believed that both sexes define themselves in terms of the father's acceptance and approval, and that identification with the role complementary to that of the father is more important to the girl's development than is identification with the role complementary to the mother for the boy, while Sears (1965) suggested that gender roles are highly influenced by the kind of contact experienced with each parent and that the father's affectional intrusion into the girl's rearing tends to "masculinize" her. These studies, again, demonstrate the complicated interplay of identifications, the quality of the continued relationship, and the ego ideal.

The capacity to develop meaningful new love relationships is held by Helene Deutsch (1944) to be central to adolescence. "The task of adolescence is above all to develop from the phase of intensified narcissism to that of object-love and to achieve in this a favorable unification of the affections and instinctual drives." Freud (1910) long ago pointed to one of the difficulties encountered: "The results of the infantile object selection reach into the later period; they are either preserved as such or are refreshed at the time of puberty. . . . The object selection of pubescence must renounce the infantile objects and begin anew as a sensuous stream. The fact that the two streams do not concur often enough results in the fact that one of the ideals of the sexual life, namely, the union of all desires in one object, cannot be attained." The conflict between the push toward new objects and the pull toward the old ones is discussed further by Deutsch: "The fact that shortly before new objects are found, the rising instinctual drives turn for a time to the old objects, creates a characteristic difficulty of adolescence. Affective struggles take place between an intense desire to 'get away' and an equally intense urge to 'go back,' and this backward movement, which is now endowed with sexual force, actually arises from the reestablishment of the situation which existed before the latency period." A frantic drive for new "object-finding" becomes a normal component of this struggle.

Frequently, the young person will first tend to isolate himself from the family "and live with them as though with strangers" (Freud, 1946). His level of instinctual anxiety is now once more heightened, for in giving up the parents as love objects, the child must also alienate himself from his superego, which represented the incorporated image of the parents. Not only does the adolescent need a new love, but a new model as well. This may be in the form of passionate friendships with age mates, or be attachments to older models. The importance of the "best friend" through early adolescence has also been stressed by Sullivan (1940), Blos (1962), Deutsch (1944) and others. Sullivan (1929-33) found the history of such a friendship prognostic of the adult's capacity for relationships. The adolescent strives toward attaining the qualities of the beloved friend or idol of the moment.

Sigmund Freud (1914) distinguished between the "anaclitic" type of object choice, chosen because it provokes associations about another or original object of the past—usually the parent of the opposite sex, sometimes the parent of the same sex, siblings, or other persons from the infantile environment—and the "narcissistic" type of choice, in which an object is chosen because it represents some characteristic of the person's own personality. Both types, the anaclitic and narcissistic, may operate in a number of ways. They may function in a positive way; that is, the object chosen is similar to the past object or to one's own ego. When they operate in a negative way, the object chosen is the opposite of the past object or of one's own ego. Finally, they may operate in the "ideal way," in which the object chosen represents what one once wished the past object or one's own ego might be. Freud concluded that the human male has just two sexual objects: himself and the woman who tends him. Where Freud found the anaclitic type of object choice is more characteristic of men, he saw women as more prone to narcissistic object love and thus tending to fuse identification with her other love needs. Jung's (1934, 1961) conception of the anima and animus, representing archetypical images of feminine and masculine components of the personality, lends itself more easily to the understanding of those types of love relationships based on the complementarity of needs having the potential for reciprocal satisfaction as well as the evolvement of aspects of a shared identification which may be more "complete" and productive than either partner could be alone. The labeling of these components as a-priori "masculine" and "feminine" may be a disservice to the self-image of both men and women.

The first type of love to which the adolescent frequently turns after the phase of intensified self-absorption represents an "ideal object choice" to take the place of the parent, who is now to some extent devalued. The relationship may be in the form of a "crush" or "hero worship" of a teacher, camp counselor, group leader, or older friend. Blos (1941) stated:

> the crush, with its highly charged emotional content, is basically different from more mature forms of relationships. The adolescent tends to develop crushes on older persons, initiating relationships with a sudden violence. These friendships are broken off as abruptly as they were begun and the old attachments are readily replaced by new objects of adoration. On the adult level such conduct would be considered faithless. But the adolescent is in the process of orienting himself to adults outside the family and must experiment with his relationships to parent substitutes. His affections, which he could formerly express directly in the family, are released explosively upon adults whom he can worship and imitate.

A disappointment in such a love object around whom the ego ideal is molded may lead far beyond the devaluation of the object itself, and result in total disintegration of the ego ideal, just as the earlier disillusionment about the parent produced the superego alienation from the ego. Gitelson (1948) stressed the importance of the ego ideal in the character synthesis of the adolescent:

> The adolescent, psychically on his own after his emancipatory strivings away from parental direction once again uses more primitive mechanisms of defense and control which must substitute for the lost internalized representation of parental example. These defenses include the magic of thought and act and, conspicuously, the magic of identification. The latter operates as a means of borrowing, without acknowledgment and without discrimination or assimilation, the strength of those who appear strong. It is as though the adolescent, having finally arrived at a disillusionment in his parental ideal, will not again let himself in for such an injury to his security and self-esteem. The transient identifications which characterize the even normal adolescent appear to be a constant flight from disillusionment and constant quest for certainty.

The adolescent is disillusioned not only in the parental ideal, but also with the failure to reach the compensatory goals with which these ideals have been replaced. The paramount importance of the peer group at this age derives from the chance it provides for the adolescent to recover and preserve his self-regard.

When conscious identifications with the parents have been given up, the child may continue to act in accordance with the parents' image of him, or in accordance with the unconscious needs of the parent. As Johnson (1949) first pointed out, the delinquency of an adolescent may be a response to unconscious wishes in the parent, who gains vicarious satisfaction through the child's expression while simultaneously consciously rejecting the behavior in both himself and the child.

While the withdrawal of cathexis from parent and parent surrogates proceeds, it is usually invested in the peer group, varying in its degree of sexualization. Zachrey (1940) stated "in adolescence there is a great value in the close association with the gang. Through it the youngsters strengthen their identification with people of their own sex, establish greater self-adequacy, and, at the same time, a growing capacity to feel with and give to others. The responsibility and loyalty to the gang gradually broadens to include larger and more heterogeneous groups, e.g., the community and society." The element of identification with peers is manifested in the fact that friends within it have been found to be similar in age, background, and such factors as intelligence and interests. As adolescents grow older the degree of similarity in physical maturity is increasingly correlated for both boys and girls, while social status becomes more important in girls' friendships only. In line with this, sociometrically measured, adolescent girls are less democratic than the boys and tend toward more exclusive cliques (Krech and Crutchfield, 1948). The girls tend to be less likely to express aggression directly against their peers, but find an outlet for this in a willingness to be highly rejecting and exclusive of other girls, when the gaining of social status may be involved. These types of friendships, based on an "extension of the self" tend to disintegrate when dissatisfaction with the self-image is acute (Jones, 1948).

Symonds (1945) commented that in adolescent fantasies, as measured by the thematic apperception test, love toward members of the family is found much less frequently than aggression. No stories were given showing love, as such, for the parent of the opposite sex. He concludes that "apparently the incestuous barrier is closed by a stricter censor than are aggressive tendencies." Meanwhile, increased heterosexual interest was found, long ago, to be correlated with physiologic indicators of adolescence, rather than chronological age, for both boys and girls (Sollenberger, 1940; Stone and Barker, 1939).

Jacobson (1961) pointed to the ironic need of the adolescent to identify with an adult, who allows him to loosen the role of the identification. This process is difficult for those parents whose identification with their children is in turn threatened when the child chooses to ally himself with "different" figures— e.g., of a different religion or social class. She stated "The development of a Weltanschauung rests on the establishment of identification with parental figures who grant not only instinctual and emotional freedom but also freedom of thought and action. This freedom of thought has a dual effect on the further remodeling of the psychic system; it both supports the integration of and achieves a further reduction of the role of identifications."

Changes in the image of self and of parents in the adolescent involve both cognitive and emotional factors, just as in childhood development. Piaget (1969) traced the cognitive changes; his work is matched by parallel studies of changes in moral development and its underlying assumptions by Kohlberg and Gilligan (1971). Piaget stated

Now the great novelty that characterizes adolescent thought and that starts at the age of 11 or 12, but does not reach its point of equilibrium until the age of 14 or 15—this novelty consists in detaching the concrete logic from the objects themselves, so that it can function on verbal or symbolic statements without other support—the result consists in the possibility of manipulating ideas in themselves and no longer in merely manipulating symbols. In a word, the adolescent is capable of building or understanding ideal concepts or theories. The child does not build theories. The adolescent is capable of projects for the future, of nonpresent interests, etc. He has the capacity of reasoning on hypotheses.

In the view of Inhelder and Piaget (1958) the most important general property of the formal-operational thought of which the adolescent is capable concerns the real versus the possible. Unlike the child, the adolescent begins his consideration of the problem at hand by trying to envisage all the possible relations which could hold true in the data, and then attempts, through a combination of experimentation and logical analysis, to find out which of these possible relations in fact do hold true. Reality is thus conceived as a special subset within the totality of things which the data would admit as hypotheses; it is seen as the "is" portion of a "might be" totality, the portion it is the subject's job to discover. For the adolescents discussed here, a progressive striving to sense the "real" versus the "possible" fostered useful reality testing about the parting parents. However, as the image of the "possible" derived not only from inner wishes, but also from affective interchanges which had really been experienced in the past, the fate of the "possible" remained tied to the young person's views of what would be possible for him to experience in the future.

In Piaget's view, stages of mental development are not direct reflections of the child's external world, though they depend on opportunity for their formation. This opportunity consists of the interaction between the child's readiness and external experience, which then leads to a restructuring of the child's mental organization. It must be kept in mind that the age at which the potential adolescent development in logical and epistemological thinking occurs is extremely variable, and that in fact, for many people, according to a number of studies, it does not occur at all (Kohlberg and Gilligan, 1971).

Changes in puberty, affecting concomitant cognitive assumptions, have been studied by others. For example, Ellinwood (1969) cited by Kohlberg and Gilligan (1971), found that "prior to adolescence emotions were experienced as objective concomitants of activities and objects. The child experienced anger because events or persons were bad; he experienced affection because persons were good and giving; he felt excitement because activities were exciting or fun. At adolescence, however, emotions are experienced as a result of states of the self rather than as the direct correlate of external events." Associated with the discovery of subjective feelings and moods is the discovery of ambivalence of feeling, e.g., feeling hate and love for the same person, enjoying sadness or feeling sad about pleasure. In the cognitive area, when adolescents are able to think about thoughts, to create thought systems or hypothetico-deductive theories, this process involves the logical construction of all possibilities, that is the awareness of the observed as only one subset of what may be logically possible. This implies "the notion that a belief or proposition is not an immediate truth, but a hypothesis whose truth consists in the truth of the concrete propositions derivable from it." This means a different conception of truth and reality. For example, in the child's attainment of the stage of concrete operations (which for Piaget occurs around the age of eight or nine) he is led to differentiate subjective and objective, or "appearance" and "reality." At this level, reality is equated with the physical and external, e.g., the child can now identify the dream as something which does not threaten him once he wakes up because he can define it as an inner mental event, and hence "subjective" and "not real."

In adolescence, the development of "formal operations," however, leads to a new view of the external and physical; that is, the external and physical are only one set of many possibilities of a subjective experience. The external is no longer the "real" or "objective" and the internal the "unreal." Often the adolescent, in fact, has the notion that the most real thing is the self. This discovery can be an esthetic experience—a kind of celebration of the self "as the self enters into a union with the self's counterpart outside."

The interface between the "self" and the counterpart, in the form of the parent as an identification figure, is central to the issue of how the adolescent copes with the loss of a parent figure at this time, and emphasizes the importance of the nuances of social meaning or value given to the missing parent by others in the human network surrounding him. It is hypothesized here that a devaluation in the image of the lost parent reaches the pubescent or adolescent at a point of particular vulnerability on the one hand, and creative potential on the other. When new conceptions of truth about a parent are experienced as an assault on the image of self, as in the cases of some of the adolescents discussed in chapter 7, what is suddenly experienced as "real" and what is "possible" once again become fused, either remaining as an impasse to further inquiry, or surmounted in a variety of ways there described.

Kohlberg and Gilligan (1971) defined six stages of moral development, organized on three major levels: preconventional, conventional, and postconventional. They viewed them as stages, in the sense that a more advanced stage cannot be reached without the individual's having traversed the earlier one; however, once he has reached a "higher" stage, there may be regressions and recoveries in flux with the individual's emotional life, e.g., as he goes through a transitional state of "identity crisis" for a time. As the stages have their counterparts in the thinking of the children under discussion, they are here recounted in some detail:

1. *Preconventional:* While the preconventional child is often well-behaved and is responsive to cultural levels of good and bad, he interprets these levels in terms of their physical consequences (punishment, reward, exchange of favors) or in terms of the physical power of those who enunciate the rules and labels of good and bad. In the middle class, this level usually comprises children aged four to ten and includes two stages.

2. *Conventional:* The conventional level usually becomes dominant in preadolescence. Maintaining the expectations and rules of the individual's family, group or nation is perceived as valuable in its own right. (This level also has two stages.)

3. *Postconventional:* The postconventional level is first evident in adolescence and is characterized by a major thrust toward autonomous moral principles which have validity and application apart from the authority of the groups or persons who hold them and apart from the individual's identification with those groups or persons.

This level includes three stages:

a. A social-contract orientation, generally with legalistic and utilitarian overtones.

b. Orientation to internal decisions of conscience, but without clear rational or universal principles.

c. Orientation toward ethical principles appealing to logical comprehensiveness, universality, and consistency. These principles are abstract and ethical (e.g., the Golden Rule); they are not concrete moral rules like the Ten Commandments. Instead they are universal principles of justice, of the reciprocity and equality of human rights, and of respect for the dignity of human beings as individual persons.

The rejection of conventional moral reasoning begins with the perception of relativism, the awareness that any given society's definition of right and wrong, however legitimate, is only one among many, both in fact and in theory. It is precisely this relativism, in the form of the adolescent's questioning of rules at school, the meaning of parent's behavior with each other, etc., that for a number of young people I saw created a "shock," a period of disbelief or an introduction to depression, when viewed in the light of a personal history that they suddenly perceived differently. Although Kohlberg tended to pinpoint individuals in terms of the particular stage at which they function, the clinical material about the adolescent's self- and world perceptions, viewed under the stress of either personal loss, or of a loss which is both a personal one and a loss of the moral value attributed by society to an identification figure, suggests that individuals may function simultaneously at a number of stages. In particular, losses at this time may impede the free development of postconventional moral judgments when conventional or preconventional judgments about the missing parent are imposed on his or her image by the surrounding human network. As we shall see, Eddy's image of father was at a preconventional level. Even those individuals like Eva, later discussed, who developed to a high level of postconventional morality, simultaneously maintained early and powerfully influential conventional levels of self-evaluation, tied up with usually unconscious, only partly accessible images of unlovability or self-condemnation.

How is the lowering of self-esteem connected to the sense of loss or distance from the just synthesized ego ideal? According to Blos (1962):

> The ego ideal gradually takes over some super-ego functions. This change takes place in its most dramatic form during adolescence. . . . Identifications of the adolescent period play a major part in giving the ego ideal additional content and specific direction. Normally, they lack in the irrationality characteristic of the super-ego and are, by definition, ego-syntonic. . . .
>
> Any discrepancy between ego ideal and self-representation is felt as a lowering of self-esteem; this state can assume intolerable proportions. In the adolescent we often observe a self-image formation with "paranoid" reactions caused by a hostile identification with a degraded parent image. This state is followed by a narcissistic restitution of the depreciated self; and only in this way are certain adolescents able to counteract the self-criticism and negative environmental reactions which incessantly pound at him.

We might ask: under what circumstances is moral and cognitive development seriously disrupted by the loss of a previously valued parent figure during adolescence? What is the relationship between such disruption and the high frequency with which school failure, inability to concentrate, etc., accompanied the disturbance in the adolescent with such experience regardless of intelligence or previous interest in learning? (According to Kohlberg and Gilligan [1971] the correlations between the attainment of cognitive levels, as defined by Piaget, and IQ are only around 50.) What effect does the particular loss have on the individual's perception of "truth" and sense of reality? And, finally, are there some connections between the range of perceptions of "truth" and "reality" and the range of identification and person-quest patterns in the individual?

IN POST-ADOLESCENCE AND ADULTHOOD

Adulthood, as a period of continued development has not received its share of attention in psychological thinking, particularly within our culture. Adulthood and aging are given extraordinarily different positions within the life cycle by different cultures. Whereas old people are frequently viewed and treated as useless encumbrances in the United States, in Japan, with its gerontocratic emphasis, the older a person becomes the more respect he is accorded, congruently with the assumed increase in wisdom and spiritual essence. A compliment commonly paid to the older Japanese is "For him the process of becoming human is complete" (Rohlen, 1976).

The changing role of identifications, the continued need for "models" which inspire, and the place of love relationships, as these affect adult development, concern us here.

Post-adolescent experimentation in love relationships in our culture usually gives way to a more or less permanent choice of a partner, either within or without marriage. The age at which the first serious choice is made, again, varies on the average in accordance with subcultural norms and socioeconomic factors, opportunities for prolonged education, etc. However, in most of modern western society, a state of being in love is everywhere recognized as both universal and unique. Being in love is unlike anything else in life in its power to excite soaring happiness or abject sorrow, or to stimulate yearnings which are so compelling that all or other considerations temporarily seem unimportant. A love relationship consummated in deeply pleasurable ways gives the individual the knowledge, ever after, of the altered state of the self, in abandon to loving. Sensual, affective, and ideational components of the self are temporarily synthesized and conflict-free in the imagery. New energies, previously bound in defense, become available, in an expansive sense of well-being, accompanying sexual fulfillment with the loved person. While mourning over losses entails the painful renunciation of an anticipated future, the future is always present during love. At this time one cannot imagine one's love ever ceasing; hence the increased vulnerability to the response of the beloved, combined with the joy. The feeling of being in love involves a celebration of an ironic sense that one has finally "recognized" or "found" the person who one would have loved all along, combined with the conviction that the reality of love returned is gratifying beyond all expectations, much better than one could have, or had fantasied. In this sense one is gratified that the loved person behaves differently from the way one could have imagined, that in fact his own and different reality has swept away and altered the form of love yearnings from the past. Because the person could not be conceived in imagination one feels freed from the shadow of attachments in the past. Although one can endlessly describe the person one loves, the choice of beloved is not explicable beyond a certain point, it is beyond the realm of the rational, and may feel as though out of one's control. Though one frequently encounters the overestimation of the other when one is in love, such sexual love itself is not overestimated, for it forms one later bedrock of the inner sense that life is worthwhile; it is only the expectation that nothing will change that runs counter to the experience that enduring loving relationships are dynamic, like the rest of life, and that neither time, nor ambivalence, nor the encroachment of some frustrating, shared realities and choices can be held at bay. The timeless quality of consummated passion resists change in the imagination, in line with the inability of the unconscious to acknowledge or picture an "absence" of a wanted person once he or she is felt to be present. This component will be discussed in chapter 3.

Unlike mutual love, unrequited love is known by its pain rather than joyous celebration. It cannot lend itself to the pleasurable alteration of one's wishful fantasies by the refreshing reality of the other person. Hence it remains in the realm of fantasy frustrated. Past, insufficiently resolved love attachments of childhood, now disguised as well as changed by different sexual energies are frequently adhered to in this painful fashion. In adolescence unrequited love has an important function in protecting the individual from re-experiencing the old love ties directly, but the fantasied love relationship often includes restitution for hurts and rebuffs suffered in past loving with new sexual energy. The repetition of past traumas in new love relationships which are not unrequited, but instead are a living out or self-fulfilling prophesy of the individual's worst fears about loving, will be discussed in a later section. Many times a commitment to an enduring relationship, such as marriage, is made not primarily because of the qualities one loves in the partner, but because of the compelling need for distance from other, unresolved relationships, e.g., to establish independence from a mother. However, when the individual is emotionally free enough to be realistically selective about his choice, the beloved person usually represents a mixture of perceived ideal characteristics and the attachment to someone who is seen as potentially fulfilling one's erotic, intellectual, playful, dependent and other needs while ready to accept such fulfillment himself. To varying degrees the ideal components, as well as those perceived as libidinally exciting and gratifying, also derive from real or idealized images of persons loved in the past. Dormant components of past attachments may fuel expectations of an intensely loving and gratifying interchange. This may give the individual the confidence to be open to the new love he experiences in a way which leaves room for "risk-taking." That is, the person may allow his love to deepen and be refreshed by an openness to perceive the partner as he is (including the changes in him over the years and consequent changes in the relationship), even when that image becomes to some extent transformed (as it inevitably will) from the original image which drew the partners together.

If the force of the idealized image of people loved in the past still exerts too compelling an influence; or the outcome of previous rejections and unmet needs has created a self-image of being unlovable; or the needs themselves embody the wish for a parent rather than for a mature love partner, then the image of the love partner tends to be cast into a relatively rigid mold. Occasionally, the mold fits, and all is well. However, often discrepancies between the original image and the reality become sources of disappointment and irritation, proof of having "failed" in some unspoken or uncommunicated test one has set for oneself, or proof of not being worth loving. The originally felt love, together with the wished-for mold, may then be broken and may be seen as irreparable.

Early in an enduring love relationship or marriage, the sense of identity is affected in three major ways. First, an important new component of one's identity, perhaps previously fantasied about, is the reality of being a fulfilling love partner, as well as a new security about being loved. One is changed by the fact that continued caring about the well-being of the partner has become a part of one. Secondly, with the gratification of being loved, the image of the gratifying partner is internalized to some extent, leading to changes in, or enhancement of one's identifications. This may involve a closer approximation to valued components of the ego ideal than could be lived out previously. Disillusionment about the partner in this area can, in turn, create a marital crisis. A third aspect of identity change revolves around the mutual identification between partners in a couple as having in common various shared realities and mutually determined goals, with the feeling of "struggling together" toward the attainment of goals. In the context of the secure relationship with an anticipated future, it becomes tolerable to postpone gratifications for greater long-range rewards, to recognize limitations in the self and the mate, and to prepare for being attuned to changing needs. For many individuals, becoming parents may be emotionally the most important of these next steps into adulthood. For others it is irrelevant. More peripherally, there comes into being a new identification as a partner in a particular couple, recognized by oneself as well as others as having a distinctive style of working and playing, relating to friends and community, establishing priorities among values, etc. A uniquely shared sense of humor, felt to be irreplaceable with anyone else, may express such identification at a deeper level. When major renunciations, disguises, or distortions of crucial components of one's identity are made by one partner in a couple in order to adapt to what is perceived as necessary to function as a couple, or later as a family, the seeds of trouble are sown. Similarly one or both partners' need to cling to the interaction and image of the mate as experienced initially may undermine the continued growth of the relationship, as its stability is rocked by the changes occurring in later stages of adult life. For many couples such changes lead to a change or marriage partner, rather than change within the relationship.

An enduring love relationship allows for the development of a fluid interplay between relatedness and enhancing identifications referred to earlier. Great strains, however, are put on the relationship when one of the individuals relies too heavily on the other for a figure for identification, living vicariously through his or her accomplishments. This pattern, so common in our culture for women in the past, is presently no longer so tenable as previously. Women in general now have more support for self-development.

Under these conditions, those women who have relied on a dependent role in marriage as the nexus of their identity are having problems which they might have avoided thirty years ago.

In recent years, I have seen numbers of previously highly dependent women in their forties who suffered an exacerbation of symptoms when they were not only faced with the individuation of their adolescent children but also found themselves feeling acutely inferior and excluded by the majority of former female friends who were developing new interests of their own, with an initiative these women did not feel able to muster. These women felt that the changes accompanying the women's liberation movement imposed disruptively demanding standards of independence on their lives.

Another impediment to enhancing identification in marriage occurs when one partner is deeply critical of, or dissatisfied with the other. Old doubts about adequacy are reinvoked, with the feeling that no matter what one does, one cannot satisfy the spouse. This is one reason why often marriages in which the motive of one partner is to "rescue" the other come to grief. The person who feels intensely unloved and unlovable invites rescuing through love; however, such feelings stem from early experiences of deprivation and anger in the parent-child relationship, and usually cannot be undone by mature heterosexual love; and inevitably recriminations are directed to the spouse for disappointing the person. (Anthony and Benedek 1970)

Ironically, many individuals choose love partners with whom they willy-nilly repeat the unhappiest parts of their relationships with parent figures from whom they have tried to get some distance. On the surface, this seems silly and contradictory. However, individuals are prone to repeat in adult life relationships or experiences which have been traumatically overwhelming in childhood. This has several features: the childhood trauma may not be consciously remembered until the nature of the pattern is pointed out repeatedly by someone else; in fact, acting out the experience may ward off the greater danger of having to remember. In addition, the person is in an active rather than helpless position in the new relationship. Repeating painful rejection with a new loved person is less catastrophic to the person, because he is now not a helpless child, but mature enough not to be totally dependent on the new person, who matters less than the original parent. Usually, the rejection has been actively provoked, or brought about rather than suffered passively. Most common is the picking of a love object who is either rejecting, promiscuous, sadistic, or restrictive in some previously experienced, resented way; or the parent who suffered from being abandoned or abused as a child repeats this with his or her own children by physically or emotionally deserting or abusing them. When such acting out of old trauma characterizes the major life pattern of the individual, sympathetic support for the victim in relation to the hurtful partner (that is, expressing sympathy with the person who has a "mean" spouse) is no help because it cannot budge the situation.

Instead, it tends to confirm the person in his need to be victimized in order to maintain support. However, the important role of the involved feelings in the life of the person must be acknowledged, in addition to their painful consequences. Eventually, the whole pattern and the individual's role in actively bringing it about must be brought to awareness before it can be shifted. Frequently old griefs over rejection in childhood, postponed because they would have been overwhelming at the time, first emerge in relation to feelings of loss regarding the new loved person. Thus, the need to complete earlier, unfinished grieving may be the driving force behind a particular choice of beloved.

A shift in identifications is again experienced when an individual becomes a parent. Benedek (1959) points out that pregnancy and parenthood are, in a sense, developmental stages, when old conflicts with parent figures may be either reactivated or resolved in a new way by the final shift from considering oneself as "son" or "daughter" to becoming mother or father. Much of a woman's capacity to nurture her baby and relax enough to empathize with his or her needs, or her response to each of the growing child's developmental stages, will be subtly colored by the degree to which she felt that her own mother responded with acceptance or threat to these impulses in her. Similarly, the mixture of tenderness or "toughness" which a man experienced from his own father is apt to make its appearance in the degree to which he treats his son with tenderness or "toughness." For each parent, again, the reality of successfully or pleasurably living through a particular developmental stage with a child is a renewed opportunity for repairing old wounds in the image of the self. Often impulses seen previously as unacceptable in the self can be integrated as part of a positive identification, once they have been experienced harmoniously in relation to one's child. In contrast, unresolved problems with one's parents may haunt each new stage of a child's growth, in the parents' dread of having to re-expose issues which took much psychic energy to repress.

It is worthwhile to note that many fathers today who freely enjoy a tender, playful, caring relationship with both their sons and daughters appear to have integrated an identification which includes the diminishing taboo, in our culture, on tenderness in men, even though their own fathers had treated them quite differently. Although of course the wish and resolution to behave toward a child differently from one's parents (e.g., less harshly) is also a strongly motivating force, it is rarely as conflict-free as some of the current trends in fathering appear to be. It would be sad, however, if the new freedoms in parenting, given positive momentum by greater equality between the sexes led to the interpretation that fathers and mothers should function identically toward their children. A mother's and father's differences in relating to the child are valuable to him, broadening identification possibilities and anticipated adult relationships.

In adult life the love partner has been seen as pivotal for the individual's self-image and constructive functioning within the family and community. Less attention has been paid to the role of a loved or admired figure in contributing, to some degree, to the fusion of pleasure and work. This bears on my later discussion of adolescents who found themselves transiently unable to work or learn once the wanted parent was absent. Furthermore, it underlines crucial ways in which adult men and women continue to be supported or frustrated by the surrounding human network, its dominant values, and the possibilities for individual relationships that it offers. When for instance, models of power, status, and efficiency underlie the conscious social values expressed in a work situation, human interaction becomes devalued as a motivating force, and must then be relegated to the realm of ego-alien fantasies or viewed in other ways as a distracting disturbance. As suggested by Miller (1973), this may constrict both men and women to stereotyped and unnatural roles.

The role of identifications as well as relations to loved others in the process of creative activity is relevant to our topic. Although some, but not others of the children of parting parents demonstrated actual creative talents, that is not the point. What is relevant is that the absence or loss of a previously loved parent seemed frequently to stimulate a psychically creative act in which attempted restitution for the loss was made by the creation of a new and initially unconscious, disguised representation of that parent, to which, I would postulate, the libidinal bond remained. Working creatively or working at all was valued in relation to the image of that person. I believe that the conflict generated by the awareness of such connections, particularly for some of the adolescents, led to a secondary defense—they had to turn against their own creative activities for periods of time—as well as interfering in the ability to concentrate on school work. This will be further detailed in chapter 7. However, the point to be made here and discussed later in this chapter and the next, is that apparently, even when identification is the major defense utilized to cope with the loss, not only are components of the object relationship also preserved in the psyche, but these components may maintain their libidinal connections rather than become neutralized.

In the studies to be mentioned, concurrent components of identification and object relatedness (in reality or fantasy) make their appearance. Snyder and Tessman (1965) commented on a common theme found among a number of creative adolescents and scientists: "the close relationship with an older man who encouraged and sustained the creative one at a crucial period." They spoke of "the search for this kind of relationship as part of the establishment of an identity through identification with an ego ideal, much as it appears in adolescence."

Loomie, Rosen, and Stein (1958), in their research on gifted adolescents in analysis, spoke about the close connection between libidinal excitement and the fantasy of "the benign attitude of the patron." Annie Reich (1958) commented, "It could be that the singular aliveness of the creative artist—which has to do with libidinal excitement—is specifically related to the element of paternal approval and participation in the budding artist's or scientist's infantile sexual activity." Helene Deutsch (1944) commented on the role of the man in creativity among women. She stated that "women are frequently enthusiastic partisans of ideas that apparently have been given to them by others. But closer observation reveals that such ideas were previously conceived and developed in their own fantasy. Creative women frequently cannot value their own ideas until they receive them from someone else." She related this to the "deep-rooted need of women to be fecundated from outside in order to be creative." This is not inconsistent with Jacobson's (1954) observation that the ego ideal in women tends to remain enmeshed or is prone to be re-enmeshed in the vicissitudes of her object relations.

Sublimation has been considered as a form of desexualization, in which the instinctual impulses (of pregenital levels of development), instead of requiring control by constant defense, are deflected into such acceptable channels as curiosity and learning, creative activity, work, etc. Freud postulated (1946) that civilization evolved at the sacrifice of man's direct instinctual satisfaction, and was heir to the same energies. This was accomplished through the sublimation of the instinctual aims, which involves the desexualization or "neutralization" of instinctual energy. However, Ernst Kris (1951) soon pointed to the direct role of the instinctual life and associated unconscious and primary-process thinking in creative activity, such as art. In successful creative activity there is a "regression in the service of the ego" to these primitive ways of functioning, which are then subjected to the more "rational" scrutiny of secondary process thinking.

Analyzing the growing body of clinical material, Kris (1955), Greenacre (1959a, b), and others (Loomie, Rosen, and Stein 1958) have reformulated the concepts of sublimation. They were struck by the frequent proximity of the highest mental process to instinctual satisfaction, usually symbolic and aim-inhibited, but sometimes with direct sexual or aggressive discharge (e.g., the mathematician whose solution of a problem was accompanied by an orgasm). Feverish excitement frequently accompanied creative activity. Kris (1955) presented the hypothesis that it is not after all the distance from the original conflict or libidinal aim which makes the creative act possible, but perhaps the speed of transformation of energy from primary-process to secondary-process thinking. Such excitement suggests unconscious connections with images of others. Kris (Loomie, Rosen, Stein, 1958) pointed to the inevitable link, in his experience, between a creative act and an identification.

Greenacre spoke of the creative person as being involved in a "love affair with the world," and stated "it is unlikely that the creative product is ever undertaken for the gratification of the self, but rather that there is always some fantasy of a collective audience or recipient, whether this is the real audience, as for the stage, or the unseen audience of the writer or painter; whether this be a contemporary or extended into the limitless future. The artistic product has rather universally the character of a love gift, to be brought as near perfection as possible and to be presented with pride and misgivings."

Others have underlined the role of a supporting and inspiring older figure in fostering continued growth in adulthood. For example, Levinson et al. (1972) described the intense relationship between mentor and disciple in a study of adult men in various occupational roles.

> The presence or absence of the mentor is an important component of the life course during the twenties and thirties. The absence of mentors is associated with various kinds of developmental impairments and with the problems of individuation in mid-life. . . . The mentor is ordinarily 8 to 15 years older than the mentee [Levinson's term]. He is enough older to represent greater wisdom, authority and paternal qualities, but near enough in age or attitude to be in some respects a peer or older brother than in the image of the wise old man or distant father. He may be teacher, boss, editor or experienced coworker. He takes the younger man under his wing, invites him into a new occupational world, imparts his wisdom, cares, sponsors, criticizes and bestows his blessing. The teaching and sponsoring have their value but the blessing is the crucial element. The younger man, in turn, feels appreciation, admiration, respect, gratitude, love and identification. Their relationship is lovely for a time, then ends in separation due to a quarrel, death or change in circumstances. Following the separation, the processes of internalization are enhanced . . . and the personality of the mentee is enriched as he makes the valued aspects of the mentor more fully part of himself. When the relationship ends, the pair may form a more modest friendship after a cooling off period. It may take a peaceful form with gradual loss of involvement. More often, however, and especially during the thirties, termination is brought about by increasing conflict or forced separation and brings in its wake intense feelings of bitterness, rancor, grief, abandonment and rejuvenation in the mentee. The mentor relationship is given up as part of 'becoming one's own man.' The person who was so formerly loved and admired, and who was experienced as giving so much, comes now to be seen as hypocritical, oppressingly controlling, seeking to make one over in his own image rather than fostering one's own independence and individuality; in short as a tyrannical and

egocentric father rather than a loving, enabling mentor. It is probably impossible to become a mentor without having been a mentee.

This description invites reformulation, also alluded to earlier, of the continued role of valued emulation figures in young adulthood, well beyond the period of adolescence during which they are generally considered crucial. Although Levinson did not study women during this period of their lives, my experience with adult patients in their twenties and thirties corroborates an analogous phenomenon. The presence of a caring, supportive, and emulated figure may make a crucial difference in whether new goals, as an aspect of ego identity seeking fuller self-development, are successfully achieved even against considerable practical odds, or are relinquished as too distant from goals which could be shared with earlier identification figures. Although this kind of development is often experienced in the context of the women's liberation movement, in the individuals I have seen the encouraging "mentor" may be either male or female. Frequently for the woman there is some discontinuity between the self-image of which she was aware during adolescence and her early twenties, and those characteristics (e.g., competence, potential for independence, etc.) which are developed later in relation to a new identification figure, often identified by the woman as valuing "different" aspects of herself than at least one of her parents did. The task is often to integrate these with earlier aspects of feminine identification. It is my impression, however, that the successful utilization of such a relationship is based on a revitalization of a vibrant, affective link with a person loved earlier during development, though he may have been a quite different sort of person. For a number of women the changed identification could not be integrated into an existing marriage relationship, and led eventually to disruption of the marriage.

Cath (1965) has questioned whether the common assumption that the old person "disengages" his energies from the world of cared-about people is valid. He states that "with middle life, a myriad of experience with significant others and the world at large have resulted in a substantial body of feedback that has had a significant role in determining one's image of the self as significantly helpful or detrimental to the life of others, as good or bad parental images. That this reflection of the self is one serious and important source of adult ego strength that helps determine the capacity to cope with loss and depletion [in later life] seems to me without doubt." Cath states that in old age the need for feedback for positive aspects of the self from others does not cease; on the contrary it becomes more important to outweigh the inevitable constant internal and external loss and to counteract subsequent grief. "The ability to permit strengthening of the self by the nonself may be crucial in old age."

Erikson (1976), long a profound thinker about the life cycle, characterized maturity as a stage of identity involving the polarities of generativity vs self-absorption. Extending adult development into old age, he described identity as culminating in a sense of integrity or despair and disgust. Integrity, requiring an element of hope first acquired in infancy, leads to the possibility of the development of "wisdom." Hope "emerges from the earliest experiences of abandonment as well as of closeness, and throughout life, must rely on the power of unconscious processes as well as on some confirmation by fate and by faith." He defined hope as "the enduring belief in the attainability of primal wishes, in spite of the dark urges and rages which mark the beginning of existence. Hope, then, is the ontogenetic basis of what in adulthood becomes faith; it is nourished in childhood by the parental faith which pervades patterns of care."

Erikson then, brings us full circle in linking the fruits of old age to the seeds of affective interaction in childhood. Indeed it was apparent that for the children of parting parents the affective features of past relationships remained as powerful links to hopes and despairs about one's future. The fate of these links in the total or partial absence of the parent was partly in the hands of the remaining human relationship network, and did not cease to be affected by it after childhood had passed.

Identification as a Mode for Coping with Loss

Conscious or unconscious signs of increased identification with the absent parent constituted one of the most frequent findings in encounters with the children of the divorced or deceased. One way of attempting to maintain a sense of intimacy with the parent, guarding against feelings of loss, was to become more like him as he was perceived by the child and the surrounding human network. Identifications with the lost person differed in the degree to which they were ego-syntonic (an accepted part of the self) or ego-alien (an extruded, defended-against part of the self, which aroused anxiety); in the degree to which they were invited or rejected by the remaining parent; the degree to which they reflected positive components (e.g., valued traits, vibrant affect) or negative (e.g., deadness, feared sadism) of the absent parent; and the degree to which they enriched or constricted the child's further development.

Freud (1940) saw the process of identification as intrinsically linked to the "abandonment" of the cathexis to the person in external reality. He stated: "A portion of the external world has, at least partially, been abandoned as an object and has instead, by identification been taken into the ego and thus become an integral part of the internal world. This new psychical agency continues to carry on the functions which have hitherto been performed by people in the external world. Therefore, perhaps, the defensive nature and the urgency of the identification may rigidify it, and the transformations in the image, once internalized must proceed through different routes." Elsewhere he stated (1927), "It may even be that this identification is the sole condition under which the id can give up its objects." And, (1927): "The character of the ego is a precipitate of abandoned object cathexes and it contains a record of past object choices."

Freud also took into consideration "the case of simultaneous object-cathexis and identifications, i.e., in which the alteration in character occurs before the object has been given up. In such a case the alteration in character would be able to survive the object-relation and in a certain sense to conserve it." He stated that the transformation of libido which takes place during identification "obviously implies an abandonment of sexual aims, a process of desexualization; it is consequently a kind of sublimation." I would take issue with the inevitability of desexualizing the tie to the object when identification proceeds. The clinical material suggests that libidinal strivings may continue either toward unconscious images of the lost person, which are then again projected into the external world to be rediscovered there, or in the form of an assimilation to the ego ideal, which becomes imbued with a libidinous vitality that includes pleasure in approximating ideals which are unrelated to the maintenance of self-esteem by accession to the prohibitions of conscience (superego prohibitions). The ego ideal will be the focus of a later section of this chapter. The postulate that the object relationship sought may not be desexualized when it coincides with identification to deal with loss, is not inconsistent with the reformulated view of sublimation discussed earlier. The underlying presence of such continued libidinal strivings has altered implications for the treatment of either difficulties in working, in loving, or in the integration of identifications that are manifested by some children of parting parents.

As mentioned previously, Jacobson (1954), Deutsch (1944), and others observed a tendency in women to enmesh their ideology, ego ideal or work in which they become invested with images of loved persons. Miller (1973) noted that cultural pressures teach the growing boy to separate his identifications from both the object and the process of direct emotional engagement. The question of the extent to which such differences exist is probably unanswerable, if they exist. Nor, probably, can we determine the degree to which nature of culture is responsible, whether they are optimal or constricting conditions for different people and different periods in life, or what complicated social consequences would ensue from different models. Is it perhaps a one-sided view, that the temptations of Eve weakened rather than enhanced Adam's judgment, and only in this way brought about changes that led to a lot of work?

In looking at identifications as a developmental process from childhood through adulthood, we have come to question whether identification substitutes rather than coexists with continued affective and libidinal interchange with some wanted person. In the face of loss, however, the possibility for fluid interplay of the inner image with the changing reactions that one perceives in the wanted person has been intercepted. Therefore perhaps the defensive nature and the urgency of the identification may rigidify it, and the transformations in the image, once internalized, must proceed through different routes.

In distinguishing "mourning" and "melancholia" Freud (1917) states that melancholia is in some way related to an unconscious loss of a love object; in mourning, on the other hand, there is nothing unconscious about the loss. He pointed out that if one listens patiently to the self-accusations of the melancholic, one cannot avoid the impression that the "most violent of them are hardly at all applicable to the patient himself, but that . . . they do fit someone else, some person whom the patient loves, has loved, ought to love." The key to the clinical picture: "the self-reproaches are reproaches against a loved object which have been shifted on to the patient's own ego." As Freud reconstructs it, there existed an object choice which was undermined by real injury or disappointment. Instead of a normal withdrawal of libido and transference of the energy to another person, the free libido was withdrawn into the ego. "It served simply to establish an identification of the ego with the abandoned object. Thus the shadow of the object fell upon the ego, so that the latter could henceforth be criticized by a special mental faculty like an object, the forsaken object. In this way the loss of the object becomes transformed into a loss in the ego and the conflict between the ego and loved person transformed into a cleavage between the criticizing faculty of the ego and the ego as altered by identification."

Since Freud's time, the accuracy of his insight into the structure of self-criticisms based on defensive identification has been repeatedly documented, but empirically is not limited to the condition of melancholia. To a greater or lesser extent, identification with the lost person is a common reaction, rather than one based primarily or only on the extreme of pre-existing ambivalence. From Lindemann (1944) to Lifton (1976), those who have studied mourning reactions following disasters and have postulated the "survivors' syndrome," as well as individual clinicians dealing with mourning, have discovered self-blame based on remnants of intertwined guilt, identification, and/or magical thinking.

In the children encountered here, identification with negative or debilitating components of the absent parent also had sources other than the degree of ambivalence in the prior relationship between the parent and child. Of course, at times guilt over ambivalence stemming from past deprivation, combined with a propensity toward a lingering but compelling wish for fusion of identities, resulted in either an identification with deadness or persistent suicidal preoccupations. Other times, suicidal fantasies were based on a particular sense of reality—which included the belief that there was no place in the world for someone who loved and identified with two, bitterly incompatible parents, whose love was still needed. One could not be oneself (knowing that one cannot give up the love for either) and, therefore, one could not exist.

More frequently, deep self-criticism occurred as a reaction to those aspects of the personality which were partial and selective identifications with the absent parent. In cases of divorce in which hostilities between the parents were felt as overwhelming or just unalterable, the child identified with the rejection by one parent of the quality identified with in the other parent. In adolescents, this was seen most clearly in the combination of depressed affect and the inability to begin a synthesis of affectional and task-oriented energies. In younger children, it was more often encountered in the form of ego-alien symptoms which were troubling to the home parent, but embodied the child's fidelity to the absent parent. The problems of identification with a devalued component of the absent parent were compounded when the wider human network surrounding the child confirmed the custodial parent's devaluation.

Once such fragments of identification were brought to light, it became possible to re-examine them in light of the human network (with its frequent tendency to stereotype); the remaining family; and the child himself. Debilitating identifications were often combined with conscious, overidealized images of the parent; or defended against by the child's denying all connection with the absent parent while continuing to act out a caricature of the image of his presence.

In cases where realistic limitations in the absent parent's ability to care about the child were present, these had to be faced in a way which did not leave the child with the burden of responsibility for feeling he had "failed" in the relationship. Devaluations which had their roots in the parents' disappointments in each other were accepted as valid from their point of view, but not for the child. Where the parent might wish to "lose" the spouse for good reason, often the child did not, and hence had to be freed from the fear that acceptance by one parent was conditional on his renouncing the other. Unfortunately that fear sometimes reflected an unalterable reality. Finally, in other cases, negative aspects of identifications with an absent parent were based on distortions in the image of that parent. For example, adopted children for various reasons often assume that they were the unwanted child of a "prostitute," an assumption that either propels them to produce unwanted children or fuels a fantasy of being a prostitute who deserves no sustained relationships. Such fantasies do not grow out of an actually experienced relationship, and hence identification in fantasy (which may be lived out by the adolescent) is sometimes the only kind of closeness pictured as possible. Other kinds of distortions abound when the affects surrounding the

separation and divorce—usually a mixture of expressed anger and distress—
are assimilated to the young child's perception of causation. A sense of guilt
may be expressed, connected either with having done something wrong (more
common among the youngest children) or with *not* having done something
right, which would have stopped the parting (common among older children
as well). This often involves identification with the supposed magical power of
the parent to make things go as they should. Negative identifications were
most often ameliorated during the process of grieving for the wanted parent or
for the lost anticipation of a sustained and permanent relationship with that
parent. Such grieving is the topic of chapter 4.

Growth-enhancing identifications with the absent parent also occurred in
generous profusion, in different ways for children of the divorced and
deceased. Such identifications were fostered by an affectively rich relationship
with the parent who has now left, combined with a remaining parent and
human support network which could still to some degree value the
characteristics. For children of the deceased, such identifications in some
cases remained for many years, becoming a central component of adult
character structure, which for the individual was still linked with a sense of
contact with the absent parent. For children of divorce, who continued to
have access to the absent parent, a fluid interplay between identification and
relatedness tended to transform the image of the parent, progressively
loosening the defensive identifications and replacing them somewhat more
selectively. Although such children also grieved, once they again externalized
aspects of the image of the absent parent, the grieving tended to be followed by
a reaffirmation of the depth of their feelings for the original parent,
accompanied by a new openness to other identifications as well.

A Note About the Ego Ideal

The children of parting parents had to make peace with the image of the
absent parent in order to have energies fully available to continue their own
development and to invest in new relationships. Previously unfinished
components of grieving were usually a prerequisite, along with transformations in the image of the self and the parent. Frequently a sign of such inner
peace, which accompanied the shift of energy from constricting identifications or from a still active quest for the parent as he was before the loss, was
the expressed feeling "He (or she) would have liked the person I've become!"
The pleasure accompanying this notion belongs to the sense of contact with an
ego ideal, once felt as shared. For this reason, the ego ideal, as a depository for
affect-laden derivatives of images of the self and parent, is selected for
discussion here, and compared to the role of the superego. It might also be

mentioned, that when ego-ideal components of identifications had been gratifying to the child at one time, these components appeared to endure (even when suspended for a time) with a flexibility which allowed their content to be later enriched by new and satisfying relationships to others he admired. In those children and adults in whom a core of vibrant determination about ego-ideal aspirations resurfaced after they had surmounted their losses, I believe that libidinal forerunners had remained linked with the ego ideal.

Psychoanalytic thinking has concentrated more heavily on superego development and pathology, which will not be reviewed here. The harsh, punitive powers of the superego, when based on archaic images of powerful parents, are well known. There is still debate about the timing of superego formation, whether it occurs in conjunction with the identifications which are heir to the resolution of the oedipal conflict, or is based on much earlier and primitive forms of introjection. However, it is generally agreed that during development, with reality testing, the superego normally becomes less harsh and unyielding as its judgmental functions are progressively taken over by the ego, and it becomes attuned to changing realities. For instance, the adult may allow himself to do things that were forbidden to him as a child, without suffering self-recrimination. Turning against superego prohibitions, as an attempt to separate oneself from the internalized images of prohibiting parents, is also a well-known phenomenon of adolescence, and will not be further discussed here. We note that a feeling of goodness and virtuous self-esteem which occurs when one abides by the particular prescriptions of one's superego is generally not accompanied by intense pleasure, happiness, or joi de vivre. I believe the latter affects are reserved for a sense of contact with one's ego ideal. Such feelings may remain dormant for many years or forever.

The concept of the ego ideal has also been subject to controversy. Jacobson (1954) describes the ego ideal as an identificatory precursor to the superego, less differentiated and developed than the moral prohibitions stemming from the period of superego development. Reich (1954) concurs as to its early origins. Hartmann and Loewenstein (1962) consider it part of the superego system, differentiating it from earlier idealizations. Mackinnon (1949) reserves the term to describe the qualities which the individual values and which are derived from later ego identifications, in contrast to the earlier internalizations of the parents' negative prohibitions, which result in the superego. Jacobson's (1964) delineations, however, do not preclude ego-ideal modifications throughout adolescence and adulthood; these would be difficult to achieve if the ego ideal was solidified at developmentally early levels, and consequently archaic, magical, and rigid. It appears clinically clear that, as Jacobson notes, an affective quality derived from the earliest identifications with the love object continues to color the life experience and expectations of the child, and to contribute to a profound sense of pleasure when the image of the self nears that of the ego ideal. This goes beyond the meeting of obligations to the superego, in that it includes some affective components of "loving" the idealized other. The partially illusionary quality of this does not seem to spoil the pleasure, for the ego ideal is never seen as currently fulfilled, but rather as continually motivating inspiration. Jacobson states (1954) "The prominent, strange, and precious quality of the ego ideal is its unreality and its distance from the real self, of which we are normally perfectly aware, and yet its tremendous influence on our realistic achievement."

Blos (1974) addresses himself to a developmental understanding of the ego ideal, synthesizing divergent views by differentiating a primitive ego ideal, which originates in the early stages of overvaluation of the parent and the self, from the mature ego ideal, consolidated at the end of adolescence. He comments that "in its adaptive aspects the ego ideal counteracts regression, shapes adult commitments and gives them continuity and constancy." He views the ego ideal as taking over functions that had previously been joined to the superego, and able to assimilate content through ego identifications. Eventually the ego ideal "becomes an aspect of an individual's identity." Levinson (1974), in an interesting study of men in their middle years, makes reference to the past adolescent "dream," an ego ideal of adolescence by which men still measure themselves in mid-life.

Blos (1974), Bibring (1964), Nunberg (1932), and Lampl-de Groot (1962) all emphasize the positive libidinal strivings as an impetus to ego-ideal formation, in contrast to the superego. Bibring contrasts the libidinal strivings which give strength to the ego ideal, with the aggressive energies which maintain the need for the superego. Blos points out that while the superego is "an agency of prohibition, the ego ideal is an agency of aspiration." Lampl-de Groot notes that ego ideal and superego "serve opposite ends: The ego ideal serves wish fulfillment and is a gratifying agency. The conscience (superego in the narrow sense) is a restricting and prohibiting agency." He comments that "the ego ideal content 'I am like the parents' implies taking over parental ideals and ethics. The super-ego's content 'I have to do what the parents require of me' implies taking over parental restrictions and prohibitions." Both institutions are marked by identification with the parents and the parental images.

Gratification and libidinal origins are also attributed to the ego ideal by Nunberg, who states "the ego ideal pursues the pleasure principle. . . . the ego ideal is an image of the loved objects in the ego and the superego is an image of the hated and feared objects. . . . the love however is not sensual, for when object libido changes into ego libido, desexualization occurs, which may be followed by sublimation." I would concur that the concept of the ego ideal connotes pleasurable, loved and variously idealized aspects of others linked with self (and in this way is quite different from simply aggrandized self-images, also prominent in adolescence), but I would take issue with the notion that the content is necessarily "not sensual," just as I question the inevitability of desexualization of energy as a part of sublimation. Instead, I would postulate that the ego ideal is linked to memory traces of sensual, libidinal affect experienced in interaction with a particular loved or emulated person, and that these memory traces fuel later strivings toward associated ego ideals. The qualities cherished by the ego ideal, to be described in the clinical material, ranged from childish forms of magic with concrete derivatives, to living up to highly ethical aspirations, for example, from Mark's shared joyous boisterousness with his father, symbolized by noisy "boom booms" (his feces) released for celebrations (chapter 5); to Eddy's emulation of strength and cruel power (chapter 7); to Noah's view of himself as a responsible leader of his people (chapter 5); to Wendy's combination of integrity with emotional forthrightness (chapter 8). The pathway to each of these ego ideals had been danced in a pas de deux.

When the child was quite young or otherwise psychically immature when the relationship was disrupted, the images of the parent were still imbued with highly exaggerated potential power to gratify or to deprive, reflected in the content of the ego ideal. Again, during pubescence, the child seemed to be particularly vulnerable to the idealization of an absent parent. Normally some devaluation of the parent takes place at that time, as a part of achieving enough distance from the childhood emotional ties to achieve autonomy and to redirect the now intensely sexualized needs for love to people outside the family, but the image of the parent can usually again be invested with some affection once this is more or less accomplished. However, when the loss of an idealized parent image occurs because of external trauma, rather than gradual inner detachment, it may become so threatening that it is defended against by a split in the ego ideal: the child continues to idealize the absent parent, either consciously or unconsciously, while devaluing the self.

In the children and adults encountered, ego-ideal strivings were frequently lost, shattered, or turned against (in more extreme ways than usual in adolescence) as aggressive energies, at times induced by the pervasiveness of the trauma of loss, gained ascendancy over libidinous forces. Simultaneously pleasure, a sense of contact with the person previously linked to the ego ideal, and strivings toward a better future were in limbo.

Chapter 3

THE QUEST FOR THE WANTED ABSENT PERSON

I will walk forever till I find you
It is too long the sun takes to rise
and fill the earth with warm and fragrant light

Meet me on the path
from the depth of my spirit I call to you
Come with the rising sun.

—Linda

Nature and Function of the Quest

Freud provided a well-known example of a displaced version of the quest for the wanted person in the description of his grandson, then eighteen months old. When the little boy's mother was absent from the house for some hours, the child invented a game which consisted of throwing a toy, attached to a string, under the bed, and retrieving it repeatedly. As he threw the toy he would repeat the word "fort" (gone) and then undo that state of affairs by bringing it back. By substituting the toy for the mother he could not control, he played out the power be wished for over her comings and goings.

The children and adults described here have convinced me that a quest for the missing wanted person goes on at many levels and in many guises, and that it frequently coexists with the mechanism of identifications as a means of coping with loss.

Reunion wishes and fantasies are a mainstay of all separated lovers, and have been documented in relation to the bereaved (Parkes, 1972; Deutsch, 1937; Rochlin, 1965; Jacobson, 1964), as well as the divorced (Weiss, 1975a) and their children (Wallerstein and Kelly, 1976a, b). In the children and adults with whom I worked, such reunion fantasies provided a fertile field for richly conceived expectations of recreating those aspects of the past, wanted relationship which were most exquisitely laden with affective pleasure or pain. Depending upon the nature of the past relationship, and the developmental level of libidinal wishes of the child at the time the loss was experienced, attempts at such recreation could occur through the medium of ideation, motor behavior, affective, or somatic experience, or be evident in the later choice of loved persons. Although sometimes obvious, the meaning of the phenomenon as linked to a quest was at other times far from obvious or apparent. The diverse expressions of the quest included the following: searching; anticipations or reappearance, or of messages or letters; a sense of the presence of the person; daydreaming involving disguised fragments of the quest; pseudologia or lying in the service of inner integrity; use of transitional objects and transitional phenomena; magical gestures meant to recreate the lost relationship; acting out to defend against painful memory; hyperactivity, motor restlessness, wandering, cutting classes, some types of stealing; suicidal wishes and attempts; repeating and holding onto painful affects focussed on the disruption of relationships or on the choice of loved persons in later life. When the form of the quest is recognized and becomes focussed instead on memories, mourning, and associated alterations in the image of the wanted person to accord with reality, the person has begun to accept what was lost and can turn more fully toward what might still be.

What is the function of the quest and why is it so often secret?

There seem to be three reasons why the quest so often has to be secret: (1) It conflicts with what the individual "knows" is rational; (2) it may jeopardize the security of other relationships by being "disloyal" to them; (3) it may arouse more pain and longing than the individual can cope with at the time. Simultaneously, however, a continuation of the "quest" defends against the deeper grief of coming to terms with a permanent "absence" of the lost person, or permanent major alteration in the relationship. The presence of the quest may function to limit what is invested in other relationships and in inner experience. Yet the quest and its representation may be imbued with either the most precious and individual vitality of the individual, (e.g., stimulating creativity) or the most stultifying renunciations and self-destructiveness. Quests that are either secret or unconscious tend to surface in therapy in preparation for grief.

Returning to the issue of the function of the quest, it might be said that the quest is a precursor of grief, which, however, is valuable in itself as a way of preserving a distillation of the affectively charged images of the self and other which the individual treasures.

The search for a lost person may be carried out quite consciously and literally. In some cases, with adopted children and those whose parents died while they were infants, the search is not driven by the actual loss of a known relationship, but may still represent an essential missing link in the individual's reality sense, as this is related to ego continuity and identity. For children of the divorced or deceased, such searching may be an equally potent restitution of their reality sense, on the basis of the inner knowledge that a real experience that they have had cannot totally disappear.

The quest for the wanted person can be expressed in a great variety of forms, to be explored briefly in this chapter. A series of mental processes, including those of a highly inventive and creative nature, can be fueled by the unconscious assumption that they will bring one in contact with the wanted person again. Creativity itself can be associated with the fervent wish to recreate the lost person in new form. Although once the person is lost, this process is autistic rather than mutual and based on reality testing, the "reality sense" of the individual continues to pay tribute to what can no longer be seen in the external world. That is, it may involve the validation of a perception of a joyous mutuality that the individual once experienced. Components of an interaction once shared on a level of affecto-motor and sensual interaction provide affective themes which give form to the creative expression and may result in a creative product. Many of the individuals, children, adolescents, and adults described here were creative in imagination, in one of the arts or in writing (because of the ease of identification from writings, only occasional fragments are included here). More often, original versions of seemingly impossible reunions were generated in the individual's fantasy life. The striking point about these productions is that they tended to be true to the early affective themes between the individual and the lost wanted person even though they were often also heavily influenced by the quality of relationship to the other, remaining parent as well. For instance, when transitional objects involved fantasies regarding a lost father, the earlier relationship to the mother had been "good" enough to favor their development. In some cases the fantasies were conceived of as a gift, or a way of staying "true" to that person.

The other major area for the unconscious expression of the quest was in "living out" or acting out in later life components of the past interaction with the wanted person, without awareness of their influence.

Identification and the quest may not only exist side by side, but may also emerge during different periods of time. In psychotherapy, one has to differentiate between the acting out of an identification, and acting out which constitutes a component of the quest, for the implications for the individual are different. For example, Linda (whose poem was quoted in the epigraph) had a "nervous breakdown" at age seventeen. This included acting on a suicidal fantasy as well as the conviction that her mother might stab her with a knife. Among other meanings, this episode involved living out an identification with the psychotic episode for which her father had been hospitalized years earlier, following the divorce. She felt at that time that she was identical to him in a variety of ways and knew the rest of her family considered her as the most similar to father. This was identification. It seemed, therefore, important at that point in her development to treat her differently from her father, if *possible,* in order to avoid confirming this sense of being identical. *Not* to hospitalize her, which was manageable in her case because a supportive human network could be mobilized quickly, was one way of attempting to do this. She remained in therapy another year and then left home for college. Years later, when she returned for a consultation in her twenties, she described being irresistably attracted to a man she did not otherwise like, but who was excited with her about dressing up as firemen to attend a Halloween party. Only after it was brought to her attention did she recall that she and her father had tirelessly played "fireman" during her early years, incurring her mother's disapproval. This episode, then was a quest for re-experiencing that joyful, exciting part of the interaction. Another time, when a man she cared for left her, she found herself on the floor whimpering, "Daddy, daddy." This, too, was part of the quest and involved repeating painful affects experienced in relation to father's sudden leaving home.

Holding onto painful affects as a way of repeating the earlier traumas, without conscious awareness of the relationship between the self-fulfilling prophesies and the earlier loss, was a highly common form of the quest, occurring in the children of both the divorced and the deceased. Among the children of divorce this often did not appear as a pattern until their twenties, and was quite different from their reactions in adolescence. It was especially noticeable in girls who had at one time felt intense, positive ties to their fathers, turned vehemently against these ties in adolescence, but were repeatedly devastated by the loss of a man friend in their early twenties. Several adult men, bereaved in childhood, also became aware of a pattern of intense longing, always disrupted by separation and pain before culmination. (Alex, discussed in chapter 8, illustrated this.)

Holding onto the painful affects must be differentiated from a different pattern in which painful affects also occur, but may not be a motivating force in themselves. For example, girls who have grown up in households in which the mother devalues the father, and in this sense have been deprived of permission to enjoy his positive influence, often begin their serious love relationships with an older or married man. Although the experience usually ends in grief, it may be enriching for them by providing for the acceptance of positive feelings toward a father figure previously denied them (Blos, 1963).

Another form of unconscious quest is even more difficult to differentiate from identification. It belongs in the realm of "magic gesture," which will be described later in this chapter as consisting of the assumption that if one repeats a gesture which previously was followed by the appearance of the wanted person, such reunion will occur again. However, unlike in Piaget's example, the actions or gestures have become assimilated to the current image of the parent, and are based on the process of mutual imitation as an interaction. For instance, adolescent Jane, shocked suddenly by being told years after a divorce that her father had been "immoral" sexually, shortly afterwards engaged in sexual activity herself. This was clearly an identification, acted out after his precipitious loss of esteem in her eyes, although separation from him had occurred much earlier. However, another, and initially less clear, element was her feeling that he would somehow now approve of her again, and that although letter-writing had been disrupted some years before, father and daughter would now resume it.

Searching for the lost parent was often an unconscious component of motor restlessness, the need to move and wander, to absent oneself from class in order to seek some undefined gratification in relationship to someone who is "out there somewhere." Only very young children sometimes verbalized these goals: they would not sit still because they were looking all over the house until the parent would reappear. Sometimes they called for the parent as they searched. Not finding the parent immediately caused intense distress in some young children for whom the concept of object constancy was still shaky. This was intensified when the separation from the parent coincided with a move from home. For example, Nicky, at seventeen months, saw his toys and other things in the new apartment where he would live with mother, now that his parents had separated. He cried, kept running to the door and urging her to leave with him. Father had delivered them to the new apartment and then left. He then looked for his father everywhere—in the bathroom, under beds, etc.—in spite of being told that daddy would continue to live at the house and that Nicky would visit with him. The next morning, he would not leave the apartment with mother, but continued to look for his father, calling him ceaselessly. This pattern repeated itself for the whole first week. As soon as he came into the apartment (e.g., after shopping) he would cry and try to leave, then searched restlessly, but the next day would refuse to go out, clinging to mother while she patiently explained that she would stay with him and they would return. Although he visited father several days during that week at the old house, saw, and was told repeatedly that father would continue to live there, Nicky continued to search for him in every crevice of the apartment where the parents had said goodbye to each other. Father had been

Nicky's primary caretaker during his first year of life. Later in this chapter, we return to the developmental phenomenon in which the child continues to look for the lost object at the spot where it disappeared, even if he has seen it being transported elsewhere. Psychically, the trauma associated with the separation may, later in development, "fix" the place or other components of the interaction as a scenario which must be undone.

In older children who have lost a series of persons, restless hyperactivity is a common symptom, sometimes in conjunction with stealing—either forbidden objects or experiences. The child is often disillusioned by the feeling that the stolen object is not after all what he wanted (is not the missing parent) and then throws it away in disgust. Kaufman and Heims (1958) point to some parallels of this behavior with the content and vector of the children's perceptual sequences, e.g., in the Rorschach test. There is a tendency to move from a percept of inner emptiness, to the outer edge of the Rorschach inkblot where something is then seen that can be grasped or is gratifying. The process involves dealing with inner feelings of loss that are too painful by turning to the outer environment for quick gratification. Unfortunately, the gratification obtained in this manner is often disappointing to the child, turning out not to be what he needs. Kaufman described the cluster of feelings that delinquent children who have suffered loss of parenting defend against as the "pre-depressive nucleus." Only a small proportion of the children described in this book were so deprived as characteristically to handle feelings of loss in this manner of quest. LouAnn and Pam (chapter 5) are among them. However, their proportion is much larger in families brought to the attention of the court and other social agencies.

Psychic and Behavioral Mechanisms in the Service of the Quest and Their Development

Let us consider some variations in the way the "quest" is experienced by different individuals; some bases for the quest in the unconscious; the relationship of the forms of quest to early developmental processes, including early cognitive models of the way objects appear and disappear (Piaget); a developmental study of children's changing conceptions of death (Nagy) and formulations about personality development prerequisite to the achievement of the concept of object constancy (in psychoanalytic thinking). Some empirical observations on "searching" will then be presented. Finally, some mental mechanisms which were invoked by some of the children and adults encountered will be discussed.

Judging from the clinical material of children and adults still yearning for a lost, wanted person or for the affective interaction associated with that person, there is often a regression to early modes of thinking and problem-solving associated with the quest. I believe that the regression can occur in this isolated area of functioning, which may have been relegated to limbo in the psyche at the time of loss. The level of development of involved ego mechanisms is not always parallel to that attained by the person in his general functioning, but is a reaction to the traumatic nature of the loss itself. This is unlike the more generalized regression of ego functions that is often recognized by clinicians as a "danger sign" in individuals with prepsychotic or borderline personalities.

Ordinarily, one differentiates, in diagnostic evaluation or therapy, the regression or fixation belonging to the drives (e.g., after a psychic trauma the individual may regress to the relative safety of earlier drives), from that of ego mechanisms, as expressed in a tendency toward severe somatizations, regressive evaluations of current danger, psychotic transference, etc. One worries about such regressions in the ego and hopes to gear treatment to support rather than to undermine necessary defenses against overwhelming anxiety.

In the case of reactions to the loss of a person wanted in childhood, I believe some regression in ego mechanisms can be associated *either* with (1) overwhelming anxiety, which threatens the intactness of the personality and further development or (2) regression in the service of the ego. When used in this way, the regression may occur within a flexible ego structure and be associated with a tolerance for affect and fantasy which lessens the need for energic dissipation through greater extremes of defense. Some degree of tolerance for anxiety and affect appear necessary for the individual eventually also to tolerate unfinished grieving. Zetzel (1970) pointed to the development of the capacity for tolerating anxiety and depression, in turn, as part of the "capacity for emotional growth."

The quest for the wanted, lost person, in the context of such a personality, was still associated with components of magical thinking, in ways to be described. However, it was then also sometimes touched by an emotional exuberance, or wholeheartedness, which one more commonly finds refreshingly undisguised in young children who have not yet learned to withhold love, and which imbued the individual with emotional vibrancy. Individuals discussed here who exhibited such vitality, often combined with rich imagination, tended to have experienced this quality in their early affective interactions. Of course, making this useful in adult life required the repeated permutations involved in integrating libidinous and aggressive wishes, as these developed and changed, with the early experience. Frequently, the later wishes became assimilated to the memory traces of the early affective interaction, producing conflict and a thrust toward necessary transformations of the wanted person and the self. Conflicts about the need to transform earlier images of the wanted person, particularly in his absence, frequently were expressed in the form of symptoms.

One must raise the question of the degree to which the preoccupation with such a quest is paid for in inhibitions about investing fully in new and potentially satisfying relationships. For many of the more fortunate participants in this book, the quest was recognized as such, and appropriate grieving occurred for the person who was absent and who was to be renounced, at least in the form in which he was wished for; a meaningful reinvestment of loving energies in available, satisfying relationships was then possible. This was perhaps most often and most quickly true of those younger children who were allowed to grieve, and then, at the right time, had a substitute figure available as well; and perhaps for those adults who had lost a parent in childhood through death and could eventually relinquish the defenses which previously guarded against feelings of loss, in order to be able to complete the work of grief.

Genuine searching for the wanted person involves an image of persons and the achievement of some degree of "object constancy"—that is, the conviction that a person can continue to exist when out of one's sight.

When repeated loss of a parent associated with severe deprivation occurs prior to the time when the concept of object constancy is established, nurturance, and the bodily states associated with it, may be sought rather than the maintenance of a particular image of the lost parent. This is not purely a matter of the age at which the loss occurs (although age limits the ego mechanisms available to deal with loss) but a matter of the quality of relationships as perceived and experienced by the bereft. Grief appears more difficult to work out when the person has had insufficient good experiences to deal with the image, rather than the psychosomatic process of the wished-for care. However, even in such cases, there may be an expectation that if one waits long enough, "lady luck" or fate will appear to make things better. The ego modes associated with this kind of perception, in the absence of active attempts to bring about good fortune, are reminiscent of the earliest stage of a baby's expectations. Emily's wishes (chapter 1) involved such expectations, as do those of many who suffer from deep and constricting depressions associated with a sense of helplessness about ameliorating one's deprivation.

For example, by the time her mother died when she was eleven, Mary Ann had already suffered multiple losses. The child had jumped into the grave with her mother and was forcibly pried away from her mother's corpse. Multiple changes of foster home placements intensified her sense of deprivation and loss. For the rest of her life, she ceaselessly searched for mother figures and nurturance, but almost any mother would do. When she was an adult, her adolescent daughter functioned as her most attentive mother figure, but even she could not diminish Mary Ann's need for constant nurturing supplies such as alcohol, excessive food, or presents stolen for her by others. She encouraged her daughter toward incest, viewing her as the mother of the family.

The pattern of expecting "rescue" from the environment can have other sources not discussed here.

Let us state some theoretical underpinnings for the discussion:

BASIS FOR THE QUEST IN THE UNCONSCIOUS

Schafer (1968) has coined the apt term "the immortal object." He develops "the thesis that in psychic reality the object is immortal, and that therefore it makes more psychological sense to speak of the various fates of the immortal object than to speak of object loss pure and simple." He reminds us that "there is no (No) in primary-process ideation in the unconscious. Death, as nonbeing, is a varient of (No) and in this respect it cannot be conceived." It is only in secondary-process thinking that concepts such as "No," death or loss are recognized. Even so, negation of the loss may occur. Schafer makes clear that tranformation in the meaning of the object to the person can, of course, be observed or inferred. "The object losses or gains importance; it takes on new hostile or loving significance, or becomes more neutral. . . . it disappears or reappears in the mental life of the person. . . . it is replaced by a substitute and may later replace its replacement; it is either swallowed up by, or swallows up the subjective self, or both, object relationships thereby being transformed into a unity which, however, remains a unity of two-in-one, and not one-unto-itself—hence the subjective bliss and terror it occasions." Although the object of the primary process does change in these ways, it nevertheless appears to retain a fundamental sameness that reflects the subject's unchanging, fundamental, wishful tie to the object.

In the secondary or conceptual organization of memories, the person may be aware of memories of the lost other, "while recognizing them as memories." The mortality of the wanted other stems from this conceptual mode. In contrast, his immortality "stems from the drive organization of memories," which are usually unconscious. However, "in the drive organization memories are not memories, but realities." In this way, early experiences of the wanted person may remain a psychic reality as long as they are remembered or imagined objects of the child's wishes. In chapter 8, I shall discuss the duality of these two kinds of "knowledge" as they impinge on the "reality sense" of the individual, in contrast to "reality testing," which occurs in relation to the external world. Schafer also pays attention to the "drive organization of anticipations," that is, the conscious or unconscious fantasies involving expectations of wish-fulfillment or punishment. "In these unconscious anticipations the lost person is not someone who will, it is hoped, return in the future. He is someone who still exists, though he may be out of sight, touch, hearing, behind a wall, shattered, and so forth."

Schafer concludes that "the child can no more give up or lose an object entirely than he can entirely give up or lose his subjective self." He delineates three fates of lost objects: (1) "their being established as introjects and other primary-process presences;" (2) "their being transformed into identifications which to a degree may take on the character of impersonalized systemic regulations;" (3) "the object being preserved as such, that is, with their index of being external to the subjective self."

Schafer does not see the three fates as mutually exclusive. On the contrary, "the object who is externally preserved will also be represented to some degree and on some level of functioning both as a presence and an identification." He summarizes the impact of this balance succinctly and thoughtfully:

> The individual cannot attempt to control his external objects with absolute confidence of success. Through internalization, he seeks, among many other things, to minimize his vulnerability to objects and to maximize his control over them. That his internalization may ultimately benefit his overall personality development does not argue against this defensively security-seeking function of internalization.
>
> Also, the subject who allows external objects a major place in his world of experience takes his chance not simply with them, but also with himself, that is, with his effectiveness in utilizing his inner resources to cope with these objects. These resources include his capacity for delay, his anxiety and frustration tolerance, his ability to test reality while he is under stress, his ability to manage ambivalence and defeat and so forth. . . .
>
> The child's capacity to live in a world of securely external objects seems to depend in large part on his having experienced continuity and satisfaction in relation to his first objects. On the basis of this experience he can afford to develop and maintain significant object relations alongside his various internalizations and in interaction with them. He can dare to keep open his world of self and object representations. And he will be able to enhance and use the products of internalization in an active, adaptive manner.

Throughout this book, we will return to the interplay of meaningful interactions with persons outside the self, growth-enhancing identifications with the original and with later identification figures, and the interface with the human network that may foster or impede their integration.

The assumption of the continued existence of a lost person has also been described by Jones (1913): "This narcissistic conviction of personality extends to persons loved or respected by the ego, so that when such a person disappears it is assumed that it can only be for a time and that he will surely be seen again, either in this world or the next."

EARLY COGNITIVE MODELS OF WHAT MAKES OBJECTS
APPEAR AND DISAPPEAR

The development of the child's perception of the wanted person as separate and differentiated from himself is treated in detail in chapter 2. Such capacity to perceive a person one wants, and later the development of a sense of "object constancy" about the person when he is not in one's sight, precede the proclivity to link a sense of loss and need to the image of the wanted other.

When a baby with a sound attachment to the parent who cares for him begins to develop the well-known "stranger anxiety," usually by around eight months or earlier, he may protest when attempts are made to take him from the arms of his parent by anyone of whom he is less fond. Frequently, he had adapted to such changes earlier without protest. No one doubts that the baby has now developed and recognizes the "image" of the parent to whom he is attached. He seems less secure, however, that, once relinquished, the parent will return, especially when the baby is prodded by overeager smiles from other strange faces. Though the parent is surely recognized, there remains a question: "Can his image be conjured up at will?"

Fraiberg (1969) has pointed to some confusion in the psychoanalytic use of the term "object constancy." Anna Freud (1960) employed the term "object constancy" to represent the libidinal attachment to the mother, at the time when "the image of a cathected person can be maintained internally" but did not extend this to its cognitive implications. In the literature, "object constancy" is variously attributed to early and later phases of development. Fraiberg clarifies this difference as due to the failure to distinguish between recognition memory and evocative memory, not demonstrated until about eighteen months of age, although before this time there is increasingly fine perceptual memory. The actual age may be open to dispute and may vary (I knew a baby who crooned, "Ma-ma, ma-ma" in a "dream" in her sleep at eleven months, and was not in the habit of calling any other person by that name.). However, the notion of an evocative image as a complicated achievement is relevant to the varieties of quest that will be described. Fraiberg defines evocative memory as "the production of a mental image that has relative autonomy from the stimuli of exteroceptive experience and the stimuli of force and need states."

What are the psychic processes, different from adult assumptions, which make an object appear or disappear for the infant? Piaget's detailed scrutiny concerns nonhuman objects, less exciting and needed by the infant than humans, but providing clues to developing cognitive models. Fragments of such cognitive models reappear in later forms of the quest for wanted persons.

Piaget (1954) concerns himself with how the idea of an object is built up in the developing infant, and the development of an "object concept" as it relates to the perception of reality and causality. He states:

A world composed of permanent objects constitutes not only a spatial universe but also a world obeying the principles of causality in the form of relationships between things, and regulated in time, without continuous annihilation and resurrection. Hence it is a universe both stable and external, relatively distinct from the internal world and one in which the subject places himself as one particular term among all the other terms. A universe without objects, on the other hand, is a world in which space does not constitute a solid environment but is limited to structuring the subject's very acts; it is a world of pictures each one of which can be known, but which disappear and re-appear capriciously. From the point of view of causality, it is a world in which the connections between things are masked by the relation between action and its desired results; hence, the subject's activity is conceived as being the primary and almost the sole motive power.

Piaget states that "observation and experimentation combined seem to show that the object concept, far from being innate or given ready-made by experience, is constructed little by little." He distinguishes various stages, corresponding to intellectual development in general, and culminating at the age of about fifteen or sixteen months in a period when the object "is conceived as remaining identical to itself. Thus, it is only when the object becomes detached from the activity of the child, that objects in motion become real objects independent of the self and persisting in their substantial identity."

Although major changes in the perception of the object also take place after the age of two, we note a number of special features which characterize the baby's capacity to perceive and to refind an "object" prior to the age of about sixteen months:

1. There is no "object constancy" in the experience of the little baby, but rather a continual sense of annihilation and resurrection of the object. Other writers have noted this, in relation not only to intellectual capacity, but also to the drives or tensions within the child. Schilder (1951) speaks of the "dissolution and reconstruction" of the body image of the self and others; Hoffer (1953) feels that the earliest object is perceived by the child purely as a "need-satisfying" object, which psychologically disappears whenever the need ceases, i.e., the object has no characteristics of its own except its tension-reducing quality, and hence no stability. Hartmann (1952) and Sechehaye (1951) assume that aggressive energy must be neutralized to a certain degree before object constancy can be achieved. Anna Freud (1946, 1952) speaks of the development of the fear of loss of the object's love, as compared to the more primitive fear of the total loss of the love object (which, it is believed, no longer exists) as a function of the decrease in the urgency of drives. In all these points of view, the psychic persistence of the loved person is not a given.

Rather, it is a concomitant of the development of the child, from a period when undifferentiated, direct and urgent physiological tensions are dominant, to a stage in which modes leading to gratification have become more predictable and secure, and tension is less overwhelming.

Questions regarding the relationship between the quality of interaction with the first "wanted object," that is, the parent, and the nature of the image of self and others, of course, must be raised. Further, we would want to ask whether, under conditions of stress, such as the loss of the wanted parent, early aspects of the modes of perceiving as well as attempting to "refind" the object are again stimulated.

2. Another aspect of the early mental processes described by Piaget is that for the young baby the presence or absence of the object is related to his own actions. He attempts to produce the lost object through a repetition of certain actions. In other words, he attempts to "create" the wanted object. In counterpart, he may believe that his actions have "destroyed" the object, and may attempt to learn what actions "vanish" the object—that is, lead to its withdrawal. Thus, later anxieties may logically become attached to those impulses in the context of which the child painfully experienced the loss of wanted persons. Also inherent in this stage of mental processes is the use of active rather than passive modes (the use of eyes, hands, total body, etc.) in attempts to regain the lost object.

3. Piaget discovered the tendency to search for an object in both the place and the manner in which it was last experienced, even after changes in relation to it have occurred. This is especially important as a regressive maneuver in the face of threatened loss. For instance, it may recur when the child is disappointed that methods later acquired for refinding the lost object have failed. This mechanism may be paralleled by the later tendency of the child, when threatened with loss, to seek to re-establish the early kind of relationship that he experienced prior to the threat of loss.

4. As Piaget has pointed out, the tactile image has an earlier permanence than the visual image. In line with the regressive impact discussed above, one might expect that this would mean the establishment of the more "primitive" reality of the object, which is tied to direct sensory "contact" experiences rather than to such later modes as vision or verbalization alone. Thus, even though direct tactile closeness may be associated with various anxieties, the need to rediscover an object that has been felt to be lost may impel the child toward such closeness in spite of the anxieties.

It is likely that approximately at the same time that the baby can conceive of a person or object with autonomous qualities of its own, he develops an awareness of himself as an entity capable of experiencing various things, and of symbolizing these experiences in visual imagery and eventually verbal representations. It is also this point in ego development that is marked by an increased acquisition of language, an interest in the naming of known objects, the ability to identify the self in a mirror (Stutsman, 1931), etc. Such representations pre-suppose development of some abstractive capacity, called by Kubie (1953) the symbolic function. Kubie states that "once the capacity for symbolic process has been attained, man's ability to isolate fragments of his experience and to represent them separately makes it possible subsequently to synthesize new psychological concepts out of fragments of earlier sensory events. Each such construction implies, however, a symbolic representation both of the prior percepts and of their synthetic abstractions. Such syntheses of new conceptualizations out of memories of earlier percepts make use of all the devices which are characteristic of the primary process." Rapaport (1951) refers to this "primary process" as the "drive organization" rather than the "conceptual organization" of thought processes. Schafer's conclusions about the "immortality of the object" also belong with this mode of thought. Kubie points out that "early in its formative process every concept and its symbolic representatives develop two points of reference, one internal with respect to the boundaries of the body and one external. This is the key to an understanding of the process by which psychological tensions and experiences can acquire somatic representations."

Having traced some aspects of early development of ideas about the way objects appear and disappear, including changing ideas about what one can do to *make* them return, we now turn to somewhat older children, and their changing notions about the meaning of death.

A DEVELOPMENTAL STUDY OF IDEAS ABOUT DEATH

Nagy (1948) studied children's conscious theories about death, finding that there are several stages in the development of a realistic conception. The earlier ideas may remain in the unconscious later, even when the child or adult intellectually knows or is able to "explain" the realities of the death process. Nagy did not yet concern himself with the effects of emotional support, information, and education about death on the development of the children's ideas, as others have since. Nagy discussed death with 378 children, ranging in age from three to ten. She described three stages of development:

In the first stage, normally from age three to six, death is denied as a regular or final process. Death is seen as a departure or as sleep. It may be associated with peaceful sleep. For instance, one child said, "At funerals, you are not allowed to sing, just talk, because otherwise the dead person couldn't sleep peacefully."

On the other hand, several children expressed anxiety about such confining sleep. For example, one four-year-old stated that the dead person, "cries under the earth because he is afraid for himself." Another child spoke of the dead person's attempt to climb out of the coffin to "scratch the earth to come up, to get a little air." Still another child spoke of the difference between death and sleep, saying that in death the person is put into the coffin and the worms eat him. The examiner asked him if there weren't sand, could he get out? The child replied that he certainly could if he wasn't badly hurt. "He would get his hand out of the sand and dig. That shows he still *wants* to live."

Other children stressed death's relation to a departure. For example, a nine-year-old boy told of hearing of a death when he was six. He said, "I didn't see her anymore."

After the age of six, these kinds of explanations of death usually disappear from consciousness, even though remnants of them can certainly be seen in the common usage of such terms as "the dear departed," or the "sleep of death." The child of five or six to nine years of age most often held an animistic conception. For example, death was personified as a "death man," outside the person, rather than being considered a process. Also, death still is seen as happening only to those whom some agency—"death"—selects to carry off. Only around nine years of age does death begin to be seen as a process which eventually takes place in everyone, a process whose result is admittedly dissolution of bodily life.

The continued unconscious connections between death and sleep, both representative of the wish for a merger or fusion of body boundaries, can be given impetus by either libidinal or overwhelmingly aggressive wishes. Though suicidal preoccupations or attempts may result from either, there are different meanings, and different implications for treatment, according to the preponderant, underlying driving force. One form of wished-for reunion with the person who is lost, in reality or psychically because ambivalence has become too threatening, is contained in the fantasy of blissfully being asleep or dead together. Some theories regarding the experiential basis for this fantasy are reviewed in the next section.

A different kind of fantasy underlies instances in which the individual has identified with a devalued or hated aspect of a wanted person, and wishes to get rid of or "kill off" that aspect of the self, so that the rest of the self may be free to love again. Here, too, there is often a fantasy of what would happen *after* such a death; often, it is believed that all will be forgiven. During or after unfinished grief work, the individual sometimes becomes aware that his "concept of death" has changed somehow, so that it no longer exerts such magnetic force. The wished-for "forgiveness" has in those cases usually occurred during the grief work. The quest for the wanted person through suicide is mentioned because it occurred as a frequent reaction in some of the individuals described here, particularly in chapters 7 and 8. It most often involved situations in which a parent had died (chapter 8) or in which the absent wanted parent was simultaneously identified with by the adolescent, and deeply devalued by the remaining spouse and the human network impinging on the individual. This form of reunion is the least practical, involving total renunciation of the self.

EARLY EXPERIENCED INTERACTIONS AND THEIR LATER
RE-EMERGENCE IN NONVERBAL FORMS OF QUEST

Cogent descriptions of some aspects of early experienced interactions are offered in the work of Lewin (1950) Spitz (1955), and others. These concern us here because of their re-emergence in nonverbal form during certain varieties of the wish for reunion.

Well before the forming of the first visual percept, the infant engages in contact perception, which Spitz refers to as "primal perception." The organs which participate most directly in this are the inside of the mouth, the hand, the labyrinth, and the outer surface of the skin. A readiness for response to stimulation can be demonstrated in and around the mouth from birth on and even before this (Hooker, 1942). However, stimulation of the inside of the infant's mouth evokes a more reliable, consistent response than outer stimulation; this area is considered most highly sensitized. It is probable that in contact with the inside of the child's mouth the breast or nipple forms the child's first "contact" percept and is the first "object" that is eventually recognized as outside the self. This has implications for the later use of the thumb and the transitional objects, to be described.

In addition to the mouth, the involvement of hand movements and outer skin contact are an evident part of the nursing act. Activity of the labyrinth is present as well. It can be shown that one of the earliest "conditioned" responses in the newborn is a change of equilibrium. Spitz states "the sensations of the three organs of perception—hand, labyrinth, and skin cover—combine and unite with the intra-oral sensations. We do not postulate any memory traces, be they even unconscious. But many weeks later these self-same experiences will merge with the first visual imagery, remaining attached to it in the first unconscious and later conscious imagery. In the course of maturation, a modality other than contact perception occurs— namely distance perception. However, what is seen with the eye is still not distinguished from what he feels with his mouth." The bearing of these descriptions on forms of the quest is particularly cogent in the use of transitional objects which combine the aforementioned sensations with memory traces, accrued much later, of loving interaction with a lost parent (e.g., the case of Amy).

Some meanings of fantasies of death and sleep, and the origins of these in the infant's experience have been most thoroughly described by Lewin (1950), who described what he calls "the oral triad of wishes . . . the wish to eat, to be eaten, and to sleep or die."

The need to eat or drink is an observable fact of infant life. The distortions of derivatives of this need, in the form of wishes to incorporate others on a concrete level, that is, cannibalistic wishes, have long been accepted as a prominent ego mechanism (Harnick, 1932; Freud 1917; and Mattie, 1941), as a point of libidinal fixation (Abraham, 1924) or of a focus of guilt (Schilder, 1951) in the depressive disorders. However, as Lewin has pointed out, the passive counterpart of this need—that is, the wish to be eaten—has received much less attention. It emerges out of sensations experienced at a preverbal, presymbolic level, which are only later reconstructed and given the fantasy content of being eaten, or of sleeping or death. Lewin locates this wish in the period toward the end of the act of sucking, with the gradual approach of sleep. Certain perceptions and experiences of yielding, relaxing and falling leave a strong memory impression. The individual is adumbrated by the sensation of being engulfed, or of being supported by the parent during the relaxation preceding sleep. Later, these may be symbolized as falling, drowning, etc. Similarly, in the predormant phenomena reported by Isakower (1938) "the sleeper feels large masses being stuffed into his mouth as he falls asleep; at the same time there is a sense of being enveloped or wrapped into the breast symbol, as if the individual were being swallowed by it. In dreams, sinking into soft yielding masses, such as snow or bodies of water, or more figuratively into dense forests or into a crowd, repeats this sense of being swallowed and put to sleep." In psychoanalytic therapy, the wish or fantasy of being warmly surrounded in a claustrum (or the fear of it, as in claustrophobia) has been commonly assumed to represent a wish to "return to the womb." Lewin suggests that one does not need to assume a memory of prenascent comfort, that the fantasy can be accounted for by the nursing situation, with a shift downward from the breast to the abdomen. It is a fantasy of the baby who already stands, which Bateson and Mead (1949) call the "knee baby," as distinguished from the younger "lap baby." The knee baby does in fantasy what the lap baby did in reality during nursing, but at a lower altitude.

The libidinal components of the wish to merge boundaries with the wanted person are mentioned here to provide a context for those aspects of suicidal fantasies which symbolize a reunion. Other aspects, such as identification with the "deadness" of a lost, wanted person, or the internalization of hostility in lieu of mourning, that also result in suicidal fantasies of a different nature are taken up in the chapters 2 and 4.

The capacity of the individual to deal with an image of the lost person rather than reacting to the loss with "not only a mental but an unknown psychosomatic process" (Jacobson 1953) has been dealt with by numbers of clinicians (Greenacre, 1941; Schur, 1953, 1955) and has important implications for treatment. Descriptions of the somatically experienced aspects of loss are many. The majority trace these reactions to the functioning of the introjected lost object, but some consider them to involve wishes directed to the wanted other person. Many years ago, Ferenczi (1926) related the symptom of dizziness at the end of psychoanalytic sessions to the unwillingness of the patient to give up the gratification of feeling himself cared for by the analyst. French (1929) confirmed Ferenczi's observation and related this further to the desire of the patient to be carried around in his mother's arms. The patient became dizzy only when he began actively to reject his passive tendencies. I believe this observation to be important, for it implies that defenses against the image of the wished-for person unconsciously associated with aspects or care may induce the regressive somatization.

A number of theorists have been grappling with the issue of reversibility vs. permanent vulnerability to regressive ego modes. These studies bear only indirectly on our topic. However, one must ask whether during grief work one can observe shifts from somatic to other expressions, involving memory, images of the wanted person, and associated affect (e.g., the case of Pam in chapter 5).

An empirical comparison of "depth of regression" in the face of separation was made by Brewster (1952). He described the reaction of six psychiatric patients to a month's vacation from their common therapist. Three of the patients had neuroses and three had psychosomatic difficulties. He found that the reaction to separation of the neurotic patients bore semblance to the grief of "normals." It consisted of subjective feelings of loss, irritability, preoccupation with the image of the missing therapist, etc. The reaction was much more severe with the three patients who had psychosomatic illnesses. They became "withdrawn and schizoid," could not work or speak to anyone easily. These patients apparently were preoccupied with fantasies of a somatic interaction or unity with the therapist, rather than a real relation. For example, one patient with ulcerative colitis felt the therapist to be inside of her and talked to him tenderly every night. Yet in later actual interviews, when she was faced with the possibility of experiencing a real relationship with him, she felt as though she had somehow lost him. She stated that he seemed different and she felt "broken up and crippled, my mind and my intestines."

SOME FORMS OF PSYCHIC MECHANISMS IN THE SERVICE OF THE QUEST

Brief comments are made about some forms of psychic mechanisms which appeared transiently during the process of coping with feelings about the lost, wanted person, or became a part of the character structure, in the service of the quest.

Although the identical mechanisms are of course frequently encountered in other contexts, they are discussed here only in relation to the attempted recreation or preservation of the tie to the wanted person. A number of them reflect fragments of their origins in the normative developmental processes, as described by Piaget, Lewin, Spitz, and others. The order in which they are listed reflects neither their developmental origins nor their usefulness to the personality.

a. Identification and introjection
b. Searching, wandering and cutting classes
c. Remembering
d. Presences
e. Magic re-creation of the person
f. Transitional objects and transitional phenomena
g. Pseudologia and "lying"
h. Denial and negation
i. Magical gestures vs. empathy
j. Fantasy

The particular mechanisms and forms of the quest had important bearing on the reality sense of the individual. A fantasy of reunion underlay all except (a).

Identification and introjection. Identification and its more limited and concrete precursor, "introjection," are central mechanisms for preserving the tie to a wanted person, and are discussed in chapter 2. Their reference point is perceived as within the individual rather than "out there." They may, however, be projected and become a "presence." In many of the cases presented here, identification is combined with a quest for the person outside the self. For example, many of the younger children, who experienced their identification with an aspect of the absent parent in the form of an ego-alien symptom (such as fugue states, encopresis) because it aroused anxiety about maintaining the love of the remaining parent, simultaneously expressed their restless searching for the absent parent in the form of motor restlessness whenever they "changed hands" between parents before and after visiting days. In adolescents, the frequently encountered cutting of classes, when associated with an absent parent elsewhere, often had similar meanings.

In older individuals, an eventual balance of ego-integrated identifications with selected positive traits and attitudes of the lost wanted parent, with some continued quest for affects shared with the lost parent, tended to augur well for the richness of personality, and the capacity to tolerate anxiety, grief and joy.

Searching. Searching has already been mentioned. It frequently appeared consciously but transiently for the bereaved, who expected to still "see" the person suddenly. Searching also occurred in several individuals who had never known one of their parents (i.e., adopted children) and in these cases was not associated with grief. Instead, the missing parent was sought because of his significance for the establishment of one's ego identity and sense of worth, which had been shaken by being abandoned. In addition, some children sensed the home parent's continued emotional involvement with the image of the absent parent, as he or she existed in reality (e.g. mother of Jeremy, chapter 5) or in fantasy only (e.g. mother of Pam, chapter 5). The content of the child's fantasies about the missing parent, in such cases, reflected aspects of the home parent's feeling about him or her. Among the children of divorce, searching occurred most frequently among the very young (e.g., Nicky, aged seventeen months), who literally and repeatedly searched their abode for the absent parent, even when they had "seen" that the parent lived elsewhere. Such behavior tended to be intense at first, and accompanied by calling, loud crying, or quiet weeping. Later it occurred only intermittently, with less crying and with greater tendency for the child to allow the home parent to console him. In diminished intensity it tended to recur after visits with the absent parent. "Unconscious searching" in a variety of forms was frequently evident in the behavior of older children, adolescents and adults. Once the meanings of such behavior became conscious, it tended to stop or lessen and to be replaced by previously undone mourning.

It is the searching component of the grief reaction which gives the bereaved person the tendency toward a hyperactive restlessness. This has been previously described by Lindemann (1944): "The activity throughout the day of the severely bereaved person shows remarkable changes. There is no retardation of action and speech; quite to the contrary, there is a rush of speech, especially when talking about the deceased. There is restlessness, inability to sit still, moving about in an aimless fashion, continually searching for something to do. There is, however, at the same time, a painful lack of capacity to initiate and maintain normal patterns of activity."

A common but unconscious type of "searching" occurred in the form of motor restlessness and cutting classes when this had not been part of the child's pattern prior to loss. This will be commented on in greater detail in the section on pseudologia and lying.

Remembering. Remembering the missing, wanted parent was an important aspect of the child's and adult's capacity to deal constructively with the sense of loss. As earlier mentioned, developmentally, the ability for "recognition" memory precedes "evocative" memory, but once some degree of object constancy has been achieved, evocative memory is normally used by the child.

Remembering the missing parent was made easier when people, who had meaning to the child, such as the remaining parent, could share his memories. At times this was needed at the level of "recognition" memory. In the young children, memories most often occurred initially when the child was engaging in activities which had been shared with the wanted parent, both "special," such as picnics, etc., and routine occurrences. In particular, the routines in which a parent had participated, such as bathing the child, putting him to bed, reading stories, etc., were fraught with bitter-sweet mixtures of longing and remembrance for the young child. At times the child showed resistance to having the remaining parent "take over" the routine previously shared with the missing parent, until the remaining parent could assure him of permission to think about or "play" about the activity as shared with the missing parent. In therapy, the very young children frequently led the therapist into the activity once shared with the missing parent, and were then most vividly able to recall him or her in that context (e.g. Jeffrey, chapter 5). Such sharing did not usually occur instantly, but only after the relationship to the therapist had become meaningful for the child. The capacity for evocative memory was usually demonstrated by the same children, after the initial period of affecto-motor sharing of memories, greeted by the child's "recognition," had been gone through. This seemed necessary to validate the child's reality sense about the real, shared experiences with the parent.

Among the older children, "remembering" was conveyed by words, images, and feelings as such, both in therapy and at home, to the extent that the child felt this was not disloyal to the other parent. Even for the older child, though, the memory of those shared activities or moments with the missing parent which carried a sense of precious intimacy often first appeared in nonverbal ways, e.g., as associations to dreams, or aspects of daydreams which the child himself labeled as "made up," or affect connected with fragments or motor behavior (e.g. Gerardo, chapter 6) etc. Although often such memories had not occurred literally as events, they correctly represented a memory of an affective theme between themselves and that parent. Children whose personality structures or familial lack of support made "remembering" especially difficult tended to have greater difficulty in the entire mourning process.

The very act of conjuring up the wanted parent in memory seemed at times to be a part of the notion of the continued existence of the wanted parent. As Schafer (1968) put it, "For a long time, young children who are in the process of discovering, conceptualizing . . . that they can remember, that they do have a memory, display a kind of self-conscious wonder and pleasure in this capacity. These feelings may reinforce ideals of the object's permanence; persons and events that are not part of the perceived present can nevertheless be re-experienced—and the child seems to feel almost as if he is recreating them on the spot." This kind of belief in the ability to create the object the child desires is akin to the confidence of the child, in Winnicott's terms, that he can create aspects of the parent-child mutuality by himself, unchallenged as to the origin of the creation in self or parent. This will be discussed in another section.

Presences. A number of children and adults described feeling themselves in the "presence" of the wanted, lost person in some way. He might always be watching (e.g., Amy, in chapter 8) or suddenly in the room (Natasha, in chapter 8), or always in the background in a way which gave life its direction (Linda, in chapter 7). This was more common for children of the deceased than the divorced, and was apt to appear transiently, especially during grief work itself, at a moment when long-buried memories had been revitalized. Schafer (1968) considered such "presences" as introjects who are daydream figures, "who upon the subject's suspending the reflective self-representation that he is day-dreaming, are experienced by him as objectively present and reacted to as such; however, the temporary oscillating nature of the suspension of the reflective self-representation, together with the intactness of other ego functions, may, and often do, enable the subject to experience the introject as a felt presence that is somehow not an 'objective' presence, that is, not a full-fledged or sustained hallucination." He terms this experience the "primary-process presence." As is true for dream figures, presences may be characterized by being inside, outside, or "there," in some undetermined way; or they may be present in some shifting combination or alternation of these ideas. And like dream figures, the summoning up of these presences may represent wishes of every kind. In the absence of reflective self-representations concerning the act of day-dreaming, "a split in the waking ego organization" may occur, "with a regression to primary process thinking in one segment." The presence may then appear in an altered state of consciousness that is something like dreaming while awake" (e.g., Vicky in chapter 8 and Jenny in chapter 5).

The magic re-creation of the person, through gesture or thought. After a loss has occurred, an imitation of isolated aspects of the interaction may be continued in an attempt to reproduce the earlier experience, thereby also reproducing what has been lost. Among the clearest examples of this process, in relation to nonhuman objects, are some of the early descriptions of Piaget (1954) e.g., "Another seven month old baby reacts with distress after dropping a toy he had been swinging. However, instead of looking to the floor he repeatedly brings his hand to his face, opens it and looks disappointed; he then begins to swing his hand again in the identical manner and looks at it once more." Piaget comments, "For anyone who has seen this act and the child's expression it is impossible not to interpret it in an attempt to make the object come back".

At this stage a child is able to associate a part of an object with the totality. For example, he recognizes his bottle no matter what part is visible, even if only a small part of it is shown behind a screen, or he is presented with the wrong end of the bottle. If the child sees the nipple he brings it to his mouth, whereas if he does not see it he makes no attempt to turn the bottle over.

Nevertheless, he expects the nipple to appear and, evidently in this hope, sucks the wrong end of the bottle assiduously! (A few weeks later, of course, he regularly turns the bottle over, knowing how to find the right end).

Derivatives of this psychic process were manifested by some children of parting parents, who were involved in an imitation or repetition of the affecto-motor behavior experienced just prior to the loved one's disappearance, as though the magic of the repeated motion would make the object reappear. Ferenczi (1950) described the same stage in the development of the sense of reality, after the infant has relinquished the attempt to attain satisfaction merely through insistent wishing. Disappointment, in the form of the nonappearance of the wished-for satisfaction, leads him to abandon the attempt at satisfaction by hallucination and makes him turn to picturing what is real in order to alter reality. During the early attempts to alter reality, before the baby has any realistic knowledge of cause and effect, he enters a period of "omnipotence by the help of magic gestures," that is, a belief in the power of the repetition of gestures which have been associated in the past in time and place with the appearance of the satisfying object (Emily, chapter 1, illustrates this process).

The transitional object and transitional phenomena. In 1953, Winnicott introduced the terms "transitional object" and "transitional phenomena" to designate the first "not me" possession for the infant, the "intermediate area of experience" between the thumb and the teddy bear, between "oral eroticism and true object relationship." He stated that this intermediate area is necessary for the initiation of the relationship between the child and the world, and is made possible by "good enough mothering" at the early critical phase of infancy to allow the baby *the illusion that what he creates really exists.* He states that the transitional object antedates established reality testing and is based on illusion, that it stands for the breast or the object of the first relationship, but differs from a symbol in that it is an actual possession, partly under the control of the child. The object must survive the infant's displays of loving and hating, yet it must seem to the child to have warmth or movement or some vitality or life of its own. The child feels magically safe and comforted in the presence of the transitional object, and may in fact require it, e.g., to go to sleep. It does not have to be literally an object, but may appear in such forms as a tune or particular sound crooned ritualistically to the self before sleep.

Ordinarily the child's transitional object becomes gradually decathected, though it may remain in pathologic forms, such as in fetish, stealing, pseudologia, etc. However, the decathexis involves a necessary process of disillusionment, which is also the mother's task. Thus, Winnicott describes the "good enough mother" as one who makes an active, complete adaptation to the infant's needs at the beginning (thus making the child's illusion possible) but then lessens that adaptation gradually, according to the infant's growing ability to account for failure of adaptation and to tolerate the results of frustration. This helps the child to grow up to cope with necessary limitations in himself and in reality.

Being gradually decathected over the course of years, the transitional objects become not so much forgotten as "relegated to limbo." By this Winnicott means that "in health, the transitional object does not 'go inside,' nor does the feeling about it necessarily undergo repression. It is not forgotten and it is not mourned. Rather, it loses its meaning, and this is because transitional phenomena have become diffused, spread out over the whole intermediate territory between 'inner psychic reality' and "the external world as perceived by two persons in common." He adds, "It is assumed here that the task of reality-acceptance is never completed, that no human being is free from the strains of relating inner and outer reality, and that relief from this strain is provided by an intermediate area of experience which is not challenged in respect to belonging to inner or external (shared) reality and which throughout its life is retained in the intense experiencing that belongs to imaginative living and to creative scientific work." A positive value is thus attached to there derivatives of illusion, including the associated feelings of sharing.

Stevenson (1954) studied the use of transitional objects by obtaining descriptions from mothers of their babies' treasured toys, blankets, etc. She came to the conclusion that transitional objects are an entirely healthy and normal manifestation of the beginnings of the reconciliation between reality and fantasy. In normal children, they finally lose importance as interests and awareness of the outside world grow. She points out that one cannot jump to conclusions about apparently "object-less" children, as these children may psychically have a "hidden sequence" unobservable to or unobserved by their mothers. However, in two examples of children without transitional objects, she pointed to excessive harshness in the mother-child relationship of one, and excessive gratification in the other. Stevenson described the development from "primary" to "secondary" transitional objects, namely "the personification of the object and the projection onto it of human emotions." In our case material, for example, Mark (chapter 5) and Amy (chapter 8) exemplify the former, Noah (chapter 5) the latter. Amy also utilized transitional phenomena, an advance from transitional object. Stevenson commented that the continued need for a transitional object later in childhood suggests that what begins as a progressive phenomenon may in later years become a regressive manifestation.

Kahne (1967) enriched the questions and implications surrounding the fate of the transitional object. He points out that Winnicott "sees in transitional objects and the phenomena associated with them the earliest means through which the individual is provided with those healthy illusions which, when shared with others, give meaning and continuity to life."

In addition to raising questions regarding the diagnostic implications of transitional phenomena in adult life, as well as the possibility of their recurrence under stress even in situations in which there were no initial disturbances in the maturational sequence, Kahne asked: "Do residues of these events play a regular part in the psychology of loss, mourning and pathological responses to such an event? . . . It seems difficult to understand how an object having such crucial importance in psychic development can undergo a process of decathexis without mourning even if only in fleeting, wistful memories, suddenly appearing in consciousness. And if an object has been decathected, by what means does recathexis take place? If a former object has been relegated to the id, what tag of its former identity remains to aid in the retrieval process? Where—for all its piquant expressiveness—are we to place "limbo" in the structure of the mind?" Describing three clinical cases where transitional phenomena emerged in the adult life of the patient, Kahne, utilized sensitively attuned modifications in technique in response to the patient's special needs in the relationship with the analyst. He concluded that,

> The most unequivocal features of the phenomena in the above cases have been their revival under circumstances in which there was a threat to the ego of separation from an important contemporary object. It would also seem that existence of derivatives of such phenomena in adult life is not per se any index of seriousness of social handicap not photognomic of any particular neurosis or psychosis. The fact of persistence of unmodified transitional phenomena may, however, signal the existence of serious disturbances in object relations and reality sense in such persons and alert the clinician to special parameters which may be required for their successful resolution.

Modell (1968) has described "the transitional object relationship" in some detail, in cases where the therapist is treated like a transitional object.

> There is a magical dependence on the therapist to gratify and to protect the self from inner impulse and outer environment; there is a readiness for rage at the object when it fails to meet expectation; there is a need to control the object and shape it in accordance with one's own image; there is an intense ambivalent wish for fusion and the denial of separateness from the object. ⁻A readiness to move toward a more mature or cooperative relationship would be indicated by the patient's beginning to develop a sense of identity as mostly separate and lovable; some faith in his own impulse control; the ability to give up some so the omnipotent

wishes and magical thinking; and a move toward accepting the "real" qualities . . . and limitations . . . of the love object and the self.

Occasionally, one encounters an adolescent or adult who initially is willing to relate to the external world only through the medium of a transitional object. Magical thinking has usually become a major, necessary defense— e.g., an adolescent who had lived in her room in complete isolation from humans for many weeks spoke and related only to her dog, whom she treated like a transitional object while protecting herself from contact with family members with a knife. The dog of course was brought to her therapy hours. In treating such individuals I became interested in the process by which they were able to relinquish such an object sufficiently to reinvest in an interaction with the world of people (Tessman, 1969). Paying attention to the transitional object seemed especially fruitful at two stages in therapy. First, to make an initial contact and express one's caring for the patient, at a time when the object is presented primarily in terms of self-representations but is simultaneously the only external object to which the patient relates. One does not at that time raise any question about the importance of the object to the patient, but is grateful for its presence to comfort the patient when he needs to regress from turbulence in the relationship to the therapist or others in his world.

However, later in therapy, when the individual is ready for a different way of relating, I believe an examination of his relationship to the transitional object—be it therapist, family, dog, or good luck charm—can be extremely fruitful in bringing the issues of magic, omnipotence, and denial of separateness to the fore, so that reality testing can proceed. This may be a painful process in which the person feels abandoned by needed protectors. However, as the sharing of the intermediate experience of the transitional phenomena (as in art or in play) is the basis on which some of the decathexis can take place, the therapist can ally himself with the patient in a mutual appreciation of the object (when this is true) in spite of now open agreement about the "make-believe" character of its original attributes. Eventually, the real characteristics of the object must be differentiated from those the patient has attributed to it. However, important feelings that went into the creation of the transitional object, e.g., humor, creative productions, musical, artistic or nature related feelings, etc., can remain as a source of creativity and pleasure for him.

The concomitant changes in the sense of identity as separate and in the process of developing relationships with others in such cases are not discussed here, because they do not relate to the functions which the transitional object served for the children encountered here. Tolpin (1971) opined that the transitional object is neither mourned or repressed, because it is not really lost. Instead its functions (of soothing) become internalized, so that eventually the child can rely on his own mental processes to "calm himself down." She agreed that the transitional object assists the infant in the work of the separation process. Busch (1974), basing his concepts on empirical observations, differentiated the attachment to a first transitional object, seen between six months and a year, from the kind of attachment to a transitional object made around age two, during the individuation phase. Intrinsic to the first attachment are: the absence of the parent at bedtime and the regressive experience involved in going to sleep. The comforting transitional object invariably had the quality of softness (no plastic or rubber was ever used), familiarity, and the mode of relating to it was through contact perception, especially including the oral cavity of the mouth. Busch also differentiated between transitional objects and transitional phenomena (such as tunes), suggesting that the difference in perceptual mode associated with each would lead to different sets of soothing qualities. He stated that his own records contained no examples of transitional phenomena, and questioned their importance in childhood.

Transitional objects and transitional phenomena were ingeniously created, in the form of treasured components of past intimacy with the longed-for, absent parent, by a number of children and were recalled by adults described here. Where one child (Noah) was conscious of the father-son roles he attributed to himself with his transitional object, in others (e.g., Mark, Amy) the relationship between the chosen object or phenomenon and the lost person was initially quite unconscious. For another child (Lucy, chapter 6) the new use of a transitional object evolved through the therapy relationship and replaced her previous crying while asleep. Transitional objects have been generally associated with the task of mastering separation from the mother. However in several children they were here utilized at a later age in coping with the separation from father, and were clearly marked with the stamp of the child's earlier interaction with him. This included the range from the contact perception associated with first transitional objects, with soothing sensations within the oral cavity, to the distal perception involved in transitional phenomena, sometimes in the same individual. For example, Amy who in latency years, after her father's death, soothed herself at night with an edge of sheet pushed into her mouth, and clearly associated this with father's shirt and skin, also regularly sang to herself before sleep, having taken over the father's earlier bedtime singing. All the individuals seen who made use of transitional objects or phenomena in relation to the absence of the father, had had the experience of receiving "good enough parenting" in babyhood to set the precedent. The one child who first developed an attachment to a transitional object while both she and her mother were in therapy (Lucy, age 4) was probably experiencing a sense of mutality with her mother for the first time.

Although the issues of magical thinking and control were important, in various ways, for the individuals involved, the quality of the relationships they established, to me and to others, had advanced well beyond the "transitional object relationship." The transitional objects and phenomena were an isolated aspect of their functioning, profoundly important as a link to the wanted, absent parent. The decathexis of the specific transitional objects occurred (e.g., in Mark and Noah) when the need for control of or responsibility for the absent parent could be relinquished in favor of more ego-integrated ways of relating to him.

Pseudologia and "lying." Fenichel (1945) described pseudologia as "an intermediate stage between the screen memory, the reality of which is believed in by the subject and the usual fantasy which is strictly distinguished from reality. . . . The formula may be phrased, if it is possible to make people believe that unreal things are real, it is also possible that real things, the very memory of which is menacing, are unreal.'"

Fenichel (1945) cited Helene Deutsch's discussion of pseudologias as consisting of screen stories of something that actually happened. They are compared to national myths, based on historical facts, but falsified by wishes. Fenichel commented: "At first glance one sees that a lie covers up the truth. Helene Deutsch showed that it nevertheless betrays the truth. To this it has been added that the manner of this betrayal anchors the denial."

Although outright denial of loss occurred much more often with the younger children, (e.g., my daddy *is* coming back), pseudologia, and what the parents referred to as "lying," was a frequent feature among the adolescents of divorce. I believe this differed from the kind of "lie" children usually tell; either early, when reality and fantasy are not firmly separated, or later when they hope to avoid the punishment connected to the "truth." The pseudologia or lying often appeared to be in the service of the child's inner integrity. It also involved a reproach to a parent for being untruthful to the child in some way. The child reacted in kind.

Among many of the adolescents, the sense of reality included some convictions about the absent parent which were taboo to express in the home. Where the children of the deceased often had an unconscious conviction leading to contradictory "knowledge" that the person could not be entirely gone, but still existed somewhere, the child who continued to have contact with a divorced parent lived with a duality of "truths" about the parents. Often a parent who was consciously criticized or bitterly argued with still evoked enormous idealization and loyalty. The "lies" were often in the service of the child's own integrity: he stayed true to his own reality sense about that parent, no matter what he had been told. Frequently, the adolescent felt he was lied to now, and had allowed himself to be duped by what he formerly believed about the parents and their relationship to each other. In numbers of cases, the "untruthfulness" was also seen by the child, as a simultaneous revenge for and identification with a "broken promise" which he experienced as a breach of faith. In adolescents in whom "lying" was a referral symptom, the fact of having been lied to emerged rather rapidly as a complaint toward a parent. The "lie" might be implicit, e.g., the promise that if one had always been there, one would continue to be there in the future. One form of dishonesty which appeared frequently was lying about one's whereabouts while "cutting classes" and managing to get away with it, until promotion or graduation, etc., were suddenly in serious jeopardy (e.g. Shirley, Eileen, Eddy, Jane, and others, chapter 7). Some adolescents were conscious of the connection between their father being "absent" from the school scene which he had earlier frequented and their own "absenting" of themselves. Often there was anxiety attached to the idea that it was possible for a previously secure relationship to a parent to be lost out of the family; and one needed, therefore, to test if the rest of the human support network would let one get "lost" too. Some children put cutting classes in terms of "ruining themselves," but being unable to help it. An additional feature of the need to "get out of there" was of course intolerance for the passivity in the classroom, which threatened to bring depressive thoughts to the fore. This was then combined with an assumption that gratification was "out there somewhere." None of the adolescents consciously identified his restlessness in class, and wish to "search" for more fun, with hoping to find the absent parent.

For those adolescents who experienced a fair amount of support in coming to grips with their behavior, cutting classes tended to diminish rapidly, once the child had been seen. In cases where the emotional interest of both parents had been seriously withdrawn, so that the child felt confirmation that his "absence" would not be noted (that his lies were as good as the truth), it was important to set up, together with the school, a program in which an "absence" was quickly observed and reacted to as a problem. Simultaneously, stronger links between the child and school were important, e.g., regular brief appointments between the child and a guidance counselor who each week received data from all teachers involved with the child, and could discuss this; or the importation of a tutor to help the child catch up on areas previously missed. The method of engineering this was always discussed with the adolescent, and there was none who did not consent to this kind of plan. Some adolescents handled it well on their own, with support from me only. For instance, Eileen's problems with "cutting" were clarified for her when she brought her companion in "cutting" to therapy. Jointly, they dated their own absences from school to the leaving of a school principal who had known each of them by name and liked them. Now, no one noticed. (Eileen's mother had comitted suicide, her father had lost interest in her after remarriage.) Eileen took the initiative by going to the principal and helping to set up a program for her friend, making it clear to the principal that the friend had lied (thrown away notices from school before her mother had a chance to read them) because she felt so neglected and "nobody knew." A plan was then worked out between her and the principal, in which he stated clearly that he did not want her to run off, but preferred having her at school even if she did get into trouble there once in a while. Pseudologias, manifested by Eileen, are discussed in chapter 7.

Often "lies" occurred about forbidden activities involving sex, drugs, etc., which the child usually pictured or identified with the parent's indulging in also. This did not mean that the parent was indulging in the identical acitvity, but had done something forbidden and had disillusioned the child in a way that fostered the types of identifications previously discussed.

Often it was not until after the activity that the child "lied" about ceased, that the material about the forms of dishonesty perceived in the parent became conscious. However, it was often possible to take some short-cuts in this route by suggesting to the adolescent that perhaps his "lies" were a way of attempting to bring into the open something he had felt had been done to him—that an important truth had been withheld or distorted. Such attempts to hasten the process were especially indicated if the adolescent's behavior had consequences which could be destructive to his future development.

Denial and negation. As has been stated elsewhere, the tendency to deny painful sensations and facts is as old as the feeling of pain itself. In little children, a wish-fulfilling denial of unpleasant realities is very common (Fenichel 1945). The pervasive use of denial decreases in inverse relation to the development of reality testing, that is, the more the person is able to take reality into account, the less he is able to deny unpleasant facts. However, when an individual is faced with a traumatic or overwhelmingly painful reality, some degree of denial normally makes its appearance again. Individuals who are dying ordinarily deny this painful fact part of the time, in an adaptive manner. Alternating phases of denial and the intrusion of reality usually occur in "stress-response syndromes", as an initial reaction to trauma (Horowitz, 1976). In a similar fashion, to be illustrated in detail in chapters 7 and 8, the trauma of parental death or parting, especially when associated with perceived loss of value or a parent, is commonly first greeted with some degree of denial or disbelief. As in the stress-response syndromes, such denial is disrupted by the intermittent intrusion of intensely disturbing thoughts and feelings regarding the reality of what is happening.

The tendency to deny unpleasant parts of reality is an outgrowth of the inner "hallucinatory wish fulfillment" which has been described by Ferenczi. Anna Freud (1937) called this type of denial of external reality a "pre-stage of defense." It is different from the later denial of certain inner impulses or feelings, which leads to the use of repression. Although denial must be reduced to cope with oneself in the world, some tendencies toward denial remain, in attenuated form. For example, the negation of a painful perception may function as a compromise between consciousness of the data given by the perception and the tendency to deny it (S. Freud, 1925). That is, the "subject matter of a repressed image or thought can make its way into consciousness on condition that it is denied." Among the children encountered, a particular form of this compromise appeared as "premonitions" of painful realities to come, which were actually based on perceptions, preconscious rather than unconscious, and then countered by the child's attempt to reassure himself that they would not come about; that, on the contrary, "everything would stay the same" (e.g. Shirley, chapter 7). Later, the child tended to feel guilty about the content of such premonitions, because he knew he had known what was to come.

There may occur a continuing struggle between denial, and the painful experiences and memories which also push for validation lest the reality sense necessary to a feeling of ego continuity in the individual be violated. Feelings or memories which are consciously denied may nevertheless be acted out repetitively in the individual's behavior, preserving the duality between the denied and the known. Fenichel (1945) referred to acting out as "that special form of remembering in which an old memory is re-enacted, bars the memory from awareness and thus renders it inaccessible to tranformatory interventions emanating from without or within." An additional impetus for denial seen in the children of divorce stems not from the need for inner defense against the feelings about the absent, wanted parent, but from the externally imposed sense of disloyalty toward the remaining the parent that they fear such feelings would involve.

As previously suggested, some tendency toward denial usually remains throughout life as an adaptive way of dealing with stress, or feelings of helplessness, failure or frustration; it provides an impetus for the enrichment of personality through fantasy. Some degree of denial is intrinsic to all forms of the quest for the wanted vanished person. Adaptively, however, denial is usually relegated to a part of the personality only. Otherwise, judgment about the consequences of one's actions would be impaired.

In children of four and five, already, the objectionable truths are often denied effectively in play and fantasy, while simultaneously the child recognizes the truth and the playful or fantastic character of the denial. Some of this denial in fantasy remains in the normal adult, who, knowing an unpleasant truth, nevertheless (or rather, therefore) may enjoy daydreams that deny this truth.

When daydreams about the wanted absent person were possible, especially in combination with memories, the individual was usually at an advanced stage of dealing directly with his loss.

Magical gestures of imitation vs. trial identification for the purpose of empathy. Magical gestures and empathy were both encountered as ways of preserving a tie to the wanted person, although they often appeared at opposite extremes in their effectiveness. Both involved the transient taking on of characteristics of the other person, but used different mental mechanisms to achieve this.

The anticipation that a particular gesture will restore the presence of a lost, wanted person was described above under the heading "magic recreation of the person through gesture or thought." The gesture was the one engaged in during the moments prior to the wanted object's disappearance. Frequently a piece of repetitive behavior in the individuals seen turned out to be behavior which had been shared with the wanted parent prior to his absence (e.g., Linda and her father playing "firemen"). Surprise and acute disappointment tended to follow the realization that the response desired was not forthcoming.

Reik (1936) described the magical gesture under the heading of anticipation, and differentiated it from the developmentally later potential for identification and empathy. He stated that a person behaves as he wants the object to behave, impelled by the magical expectations that the sight of his gesture will force the object to imitate it. Actually, the magical gesture is not an anticipation of what the object is going to do, but of what one wishes the object might do. Clearly, the magical gesture is different from objective empathy, which consists of a temporary identification with a person for the purpose of anticipating what the person is going to do, or how he feels. Trial identifications for the purpose of empathy play a basic part in human relationships. Empathy involves first an identification with the other person, followed by an awareness of one's own feelings after the identification, and in this way produces awareness of the other person's feelings. Many of the children, adolescents, and adults demonstrated heightened empathy in their dealings with the parting parents, eventually integrating this process as an enduring character trait and an asset in their later dealings with others.

Fantasy. As Schafer (1968) puts it, "in fantasying, he [the individual] aims to disregard the actual, at least in some respects, in order to represent something wished for." He substitutes a wishful set for a veridical one. Fantasying is further defined by "the subject's sense of immediately participating in the imaginary situation," unlike most other cognitive processes. Although originally fantasy (like dreams) was viewed as primarily wish-fulfilling, other needs and perceptions may dominate the fantasy life. Thus, for example, a number of children of parting parents had repeated fantasies of painful goodbyes, of being forgotten or discarded by one parent or the other, etc. When this was the case, the fantasy life, painful as it was, occurred in more manageable doses, being in the control of the child, than the more overwhelming pain of the loss they originally felt. Usually such fantasies slowly changed (with support from remaining family members and therapists) in content and outcome, so that a solution utilizing the child's capacity for mastery could be worked out.

Fantasies about reunion of the child with the wanted parent and of reunion between the two separated parents occurred in the great majority of children seen. They tended to be intense, expressed in action and conscious expectations at first, and then were gradually renounced. However, even in the best of circumstances, with both parents happily remarried and the child happy too, there were moments when such fantasies resurfaced (e.g. Mark, chapter 5). Often the child then recognized that these were unrealistic, or modified them to go only as far as having the parents be able to face each other without hatred.

The fantasy life of many of the children of parting parents, when taken seriously as having valid meaning, but not defining reality, was often a most useful and picturesque indicator to the child himself of the pain, depression, and anger, as well as the quintessence of joy that was part of his quest for the wanted parent.

SOME EMPIRICAL FINDINGS REGARDING THE QUEST
FOR THE ABSENT PERSON

A. Freud and Burlingham (1939-1945), Bowlby (1960), Spitz and Wolf (1946), Jacobson (1971), Rochlin (1965), Lewin (1950), Parkes (1972) and Weiss (1975a), have all documented aspects of the continuing quest for the wanted person, following loss. As the nature of the losses varied in important ways, the long-term implications of the reactions vary. For example, Bowlby concentrated on short-term separations between toddlers and parents; while Parkes (1972) dealt with bereavement and Weiss (1975a) with marital separation as well as bereavement. They are discussed together in this section only because each of them discovered the tendency to search for the lost person as a way of reconstituting the attachment still felt to the other, shortly following separation.

Anna Freud and Dorothy Burlingham first brought this phenomenon to our attention in their descriptions of toddlers separated from their parents and sometimes orphaned during World War II and living at the Hampstead Nurseries.

They commented:

For our resident children it seemed comparatively easy on leaving home to accept the separation from their fathers, and even their fathers' leaving England for service overseas. In striking contrast to this comparative indifference was their complete inability to accept the fact of the father's death when it occurred. All our orphaned children talk about their dead fathers as if they were alive, or, when they have grasped the fact of death, try to deny it in the form of fantasies about rebirth or return from heaven. In some cases, this happens under the direct influence of mothers who hide the truth from the child to spare him pain! In other cases, fantasies of an identical nature are the child's spontaneous production.

They discussed also the children's fantasies about those fathers who in reality visited infrequently and did little to keep up a connection with the child. "Out of the meager and in many ways disappointing reality, he fashioned the fantasy of a father to whom he formed the most passionate loving and admiring relationship." In this particular case (a boy aged four) the mother had died, so father was the sole surviving parent. Freud and Burlingham discussed the coexistence of the overidealized, fantasy father with intense hostile reactions, e.g., complaints of the father hurting him or refusing to use his power to prevent the mother's death. Freud's children reacted quite differently to separation from mother than to separation from father. There was prolonged and desolate crying for mothers after separation, but not for fathers. I would be curious to know whether such a degree of difference still exists thirty-five years later.

The response to recent separation from the mother in children between the ages of 12-17 months and 18-24 months has been studied by research teams associated with Bowlby in London and Paris David, Nicolas, Roudinesco, Robertson, and Bowlby, (1952). The children were observed in various settings—an institution for healthy children (e.g., during an illness of their mother), in hospitals and in a sanitorium. The younger group usually returned to their homes in less than fifteen days. Acute somatic reactions, regressions in motor behavior, weight loss, stereotyped and impoverished behavior predominated in the younger group, along with initial signs of acute distress.

Acute somatic reactions no longer seemed to predominate for the separated child of 18-24 months. Instead a predictable sequence of psychological phases is described in terms of a progression through: protest, despair and denial. During the phase of protest, which may last from a few hours to several days, the child feels acutely anxious about having lost his mother, cries loudly and looks eagerly toward any sight or sound which might prove to be his mother. He may actively search for her, expecting her to respond to his cries, in spite of being told she is not in the building. This is followed by a quieter stage of despair and mourning, characterized by a conscious need of mother coupled with increased hopelessness. Crying is monotononous and intermittent. The child in this phase may repetitively ask for the mother's whereabouts under his breath, intersperse her name in nursery rhymes, or even develop tics which represent an aspect of fantasied reunion with the mother. (Because the child cannot tolerate the intensity of his conscious distress for long, he enters the phase of denial, either denying the need for his own mother or for all mothering.)

It is worthwhile to note that in both Freud's and Bowlby's described sequence of responses, active protest and search preceded a despairing phase. It was after this that the denial of need for the mother or mothering occurred. Freud, Bowlby and others referred to in chapter 2 have linked early losses, when not ameliorated by rapid substitution of a nurturant person, to subsequent difficulties in making attachments to others.

Bowlby's meaning of "denial" of need differs from the mental mechanism of "denial" of the possibility of loss, though both function to numb pain.

Spitz (1945, 1946) has done a variety of studies of the effect of separation from parents on the development of the baby, coining the term "anaclytic depression" to characterize the bereft child. However, in relation to the focus of this chapter, the study which concerns us is one comparing various autoerotic activities in a group of 170 children observed during their first year of life (1949, 1962). Spitz related the form of autoerotic activity to the mother-child relationship. Some children limited themselves to rocking or head-banging, others used fecal play, some genital exploration, and others showed no form of autoerotic activity. In particular, sixteen children who predominantly engaged in fecal play and copraphagia had had a long enough period with their mothers to react to the separation as to a genuine loss. None was under eight months of age. Eleven of the mothers showed clinical symptoms of depression (as well as extreme alternations in intense loving and harsh handling of their babies), while ten of the children themselves had depressive phases, without, however the extreme withdrawal of anaclitic depression. When depressed they continued to wish to ingest feces, while when not depressed they also tried to feed feces to others. These infants showed greater interest and ability to deal with environmental objects (as measured by infant tests) than infants who remained fixated in rocking behavior. The copraphagic children's behavior involved dealing with an object which was separate from the body, yet produced by expulsive sensations emanating from the body. They seemed to be struggling with the psychological problems of separateness or with attempts to reincorporate or reunite with the objects. In these instances, the feces seemed to be precursors of the use of transitional objects, which have been discussed.

Heinicke (1965) observed normal two-year-olds placed in a residential nursery while their mothers were in hospital having a second baby. He noted that favorite objects brought from home were clutched and treated affectionately the first three days, then treated ambivalently, and after about 12 days of separation were discarded, and not touched again until the moment of reunion. Unlike the children observed by Freud, these children did cry for their fathers at the end of visits, having difficulty separating. However, Heinicke's conclusions suggested that no lasting difficulty resulted from the separations which they did not exceed the two-week period, that the children "soon reassumed the previous level of affectionate interchange and ego development." There were active attempts to meet the children's needs and expression of their feelings was encouraged in doll play sessions. Heinicke concludes that for those children separated no longer than two weeks "in so far as the conflict relating to the absent parent could be dealt with without involving considerable repression of affects related to these conflicts, the child could more readily and quickly resume the previous level of affectionate interchange with his parents as well as the degree of ego development associated with such a relationship." Children separated longer than this period suffered longer periods of interference with affectionate interchange with both father and mother. It was not until after these affects were restored between parent and child, that the previous developmental level 'e.g. language use, sphincter control, identification with parents) was also restored, and sleep disturbances diminished.

Robertson and Robertson (1971) challenged their own earlier thinking (1952, with David et al.; 1953), by changing a crucial variable during the young child's experience with separation, namely the quality of available human support. Noting that previous observationial studies had been limited to children placed in groups and away from home, they studied four toddlers (aged eighteen months to two-and-a-half) one at a time as their own temporary "foster children" as well as nine others, cared for in their own homes by relatives while their mothers were in the hospital for ten to twenty-seven days. Elaborate plans for the child's sense of continuity were made by instituting close contact between the caretaker and the child's family both before and after the period of separation, by bringing the child's belongings as well as a photograph of the mother to the Robertson's home, using known foods, unaltered toilet demands, reassurance about reunion, willingness of the caretaker to talk about parents and previous life, etc. The "fully available substitute mother" devoted plenty of time and warmth to the interaction with the separated child. Fathers visited. Under these conditions none of the children responded with protest, denial and despair, and all were able to use the substitute for the absent mother. Although there were signs of distress, these were qualitatively different from despair, and were assuagable. All children responded with increased hostility toward mother for a time after reunion. Variations in response among the children were related to "levels of ego maturity and object constancy." Two of the youngest children seemed to shift their attachment temporarily to the foster mother without any signs of conflict. Some two-year-olds showed initial reserve with substitute mother and seemed to experience conflict as their need for intimacy with the foster mother increased. For example, one child, sidling up to climb on Joyce Robertson's lap, said at the same time "don't kiss me, my mummy kisses me." Such conflict is highly reminiscent of that shown by many of the younger children in this book. It was often first directed toward the home parent, when that parent took over the routines which the child had previously shared with the absent parent. This was, however, temporary. The conflict often reappeared in more prolonged fashion at the point at which the child also became fond of a prospective new parent figure or step-parent in the house, feeling disloyal to the absent parent about the divided affection.

The Robertsons challange Bowlby's (1960) generalizations that "acute distress is a usual response of young children (between six months and three to four years) to separation from the mother, regardless of circumstances and quality of substitute care, and, that the stress shown is the same in content and manifestation as the mourning of bereaved adults". The Robertson study is particularly important in relation to the children of the divorced or deceased because it underlines the major impact of the human support system on the child's experience with separation. A temporary separation, of course, presents the child with different inner tasks than does a relationship permanently altered, as through divorce or death. Some children in the Robertson study sought direct support for maintaining the image of the absent parent by asking the substitute family to share it. For example, a child of two years, four months "cuddled his mother's photo under his arm and then asked to have it pinned on the wall and told us all to look at it."

Let us return to the more direct forms of searching:

Jacobson (1971) discussed a "specific response" to early object loss, which she felt played a decisive role in the propensity for states of depression.

The predominant feature in their (patients') reaction to the early object loss was their stubborn refusal ever to accept the reality of the actual events. They remained doubtful about them, distorted them or even denied them altogether. They carried their denial to the point of unconsciously or at times even consciously expecting that one day the lost parent would reappear. Their fantasies and expectation of the return of the lost parent were mostly coupled or alternated with daydreams of the familiar family romance type. In the minds of all these patients this actual or supposed desertion had not been the fault of the lost parent, who they were sure had been a wonderful person. It had been caused by the surviving parent's intolerable character or moral worthlessness.

Her examples include several "varieties" of absence, compared in impact in this book. One person had suffered the death of a mother; a second, adopted child had intermittent, unreliable visits from both parents. A third whose father died prior to his birth had reunion fantasies which could not have been associated with grief (like Jeremy and Emily among cases here).

Lewin (1937) also described the way some individuals glorify the lost parent; unconsciously they believe that he did not die, and this may be combined with a particularly intense ambivalence conflict with the surviving parent.

Rochlin (1965) commented that "Children who are orphaned, young children, who, after their parents' divorce, rarely or in some instances never see the absent parent again, or young children who suffer the death of a parent have, among many reactions in common, one in particular. For years afterward, they find themselves searching strange faces. They hope to find a sign of recognition which will restore the lost one. The search for a lost parent and fantasies about the eventual reunion are common. The restitution of someone loved and believed lost is a timeless theme."

Stengel (1939, 1943) described "wandering fugues" in adulthood as a form of search for parents lost in childhood.

Parkes's studies of widows (1972), referred to in greater detail in chapter 4, underlined the normality—indeed, the almost ubiquitous character—of the continued quest for the lost, wanted person in a variety of forms. These reactions occurred after an initial period of "numbing" or "blunting" alternating with periods of extreme distress, and lasting from several hours to several days. Other signs of affective distress, somatic disturbance and what Parkes calls a "state of alarm" often continued, along with searching. With rich illustrative material, he defined various aspects of such quest. Searching, he pointed out, is "a restless activity in which one moves toward possible locations of a lost object. The person who is searching has to select places in which to look, move towards them, and scan them; he must also select what to see." All perception is selective (Krech and Crutchfield, 1948), but the searcher selects an anticipated perception. The components of the searching behavior are many, including "1. alarm, tension, and a high state of arousal; 2. restless movement; 3. preoccupation with thoughts of the lost person; 4. development of a perceptual set for that person; 5. loss of interest in personal appearance and other matters which normally occupy attention; 6. direction of attention toward those parts of the environment in which the lost person is likely to be; 7. calling for the lost person." Parkes postulated that "maintaining a clear visual memory of the lost person facilitates the search, by making it more likely that the missing person will be located, if, in fact, he is to be found somewhere within the field of search."

The widows' memories, not only visual, but also of the husband's voice or touch, were often remarkably clear. Illusions of having seen or heard the recently dead spouse were common, and usually involved the misinterpretation of some existing sight or sound. Some widows actively tried to recapture fragments of the lost experience, e.g., feeling drawn toward places associated with the husband, or by continued feeling of the husband's clothes. One widow remarked that his smell lingered most strongly here, and she found this evocative of his presence.

Memories were not uniformly painful, and if recollections in the early stages of bereavement gave pain, happier memories often came to replace them. Memories of an ill spouse might be replaced by pictures of him when "he was normal." Parkes stated, "To the griever, the only happening that seems important is the return of the one who is lost and in social animals, from their earliest years, the principal behavior pattern evoked by loss is searching."

In another study of widows and widowers which is quoted by Parkes, about 40 percent of the subjects had a "sense of the presence" of the dead spouse at some time, while a much smaller number had had hallucinations of the dead person's presence. Those who experienced such a "presence" reported more lonliness than those who had no such illusions; they were also aware of "missing" the dead person more, of having more thoughts and dreams about him or her. However, the majority felt "helped" by their illusions and had significantly less sleep disturbance than the rest.

Parkes commented: "The world of the bereaved is in chaos. Because he is striving to find what cannot be found he ignores what can be found. He feels as if the most central important aspect of himself is gone and all that is left is meaningless and irrelevant . . . hence the world itself has become meaningless and irrelevant. In his heart of hearts he often believes that the dead do not return, but he is committed to the task of recovering one who is dead. It is no wonder that he feels that the world has lost its purpose and no longer makes sense."

Another set of beautiful empirical descriptions of aspects of the urge toward reunion in the recently divorced or separated appeared in the work of Weiss (1975a). His theoretical framework, like that of Parkes, was linked to that of Bowlby and centered on the nuances of human beings' attachment to one another. He states that:

> Once developed, attachment seems to persist. Even when marriages turn bad and the other components of love fade or turn into their opposites, attachment is likely to remain. The spouses resemble battered children in their feelings. They may be angry, even furious with each other; they may hate one another for past injuries and fear one another's next outburst of rage. . . . But when they actually consider leaving their marriage they become almost paralyzed with fear. . . . In most marriages headed for separations the partners seem not to relinquish their attachment for one another. . . . They attempt to hide their attachment behind a mask of

indifference. Yearning for the other may nevertheless at times break through and result in a declaration of need if not love, which may in turn lead to a temporary and grudging reconciliation. Or there may be quarrels in which anger is fueled by feelings of rejection, and in which an undertone to bitter accusations is a plea that the other change and become loving.

He gave many examples of couples yearning for an excuse for contact with each other, even when in the guise of disputes, necessary meetings for arrangements or just daydreams which may seem irrational or shameful to the separated individual. He comments on the persistent quality of attachment: "Once a certain other has been accepted as an attachment figure that person can again elicit attachment feelings, at least until he or she is understood as having become intrinsically different. At that point, the individual may be able to say, as did a single parent who claimed that she no longer had any feelings for her former husband, 'I loved him once, but he was a different person then."

Weiss implied that the important turning point in being able to renounce the attachment is the perception that the person loved in the past is now "different." For the children of the divorced and the bereaved there is a parallel turning point. It is different in that they are children, still developing, and that the parting usually has not been caused by a change of feelings between parent and child; there are also differences in the degree of reunciation of the tie necessary for the children of the divorced and the deceased. What is parallel is that the capacity of the child to disengage from those aspects of the former attachment which may hamper his further personal development or his ability to invest deeply in new, available relationships is dependent on transformations in the image of the lost, wanted parent, which are then also reflected in transformations in the image of the self. The tie in some form is preserved, but the child is not restrictively bound.

COMMENTS

The role of the quest for the wanted parent within the total personality cannot be easily or summarily described. It can absorb precious life energies in individuals who might use these energies in other ways. At the same time, it may encompass the very qualities of precious intimacy and vitality which the individual experiences as the essence of himself.

It seems that a balance can be brought about regarding the experience with the lost, wanted person. This seems to happen when areas of quests and identifications are transformed into memories, available both for reality testing (what the person was or is really like) and for making connections between this external reality and the individual's "reality sense" about the meaning of his experience with the wanted person at the time it occurred, and when it was "lost." Continued reality testing is most possible for the fortunate among the children of divorce. It occurs unimpeded in those situations in which both parent figures continue to care about the child, and give him or her the opportunity to experience a relationship without overwhelming prejudice. In other cases, or for the children of the deceased, reality testing must have the extra support of others who can validate perceptions or share with a child a rich array of memories, both positive and negative, about the realities of the lost parent. When there have been actual, serious limitations on the lost parent's ability to love the child, this fact—and the reasons for it—must also be shared with the child, who has sensed it, but often needs to deny it. The reasons must be clarified in such a way that the child is not left with the burden for the "failure" of the relationship. The major impact of the human interaction network as a potential source of support while the child deals with the image of the absent parent has been eloquently documented by the Robertsons (1971) and can no longer be doubted.

Once reality testing begins, it becomes more possible for the child or adult to proceed with grief. Only then does he usually allow himself selectively to identify with those characteristics of the lost person which he still values, while continuing to some degree with the quest for bringing the past, positive, affective themes shared with the wanted person into his new relationships. It is then that the continued "reality sense" of having truly loved and then lost a wanted person includes the perception that his own contribution to that mutuality, his own loving feelings, are still within him, and can set him free to love again.

Chapter 4

GRIEVING

Some griefs are med'cinable.

—William Shakespeare,
Cymbeline, Act III, Sc. 2.

Mourning, grieving and their ramifications are an unavoidable part of life for child and adult alike. They may be shattering to the individual or the impetus for new development. They can occur not only in reaction to the loss of a wanted person, but in a variety of other contexts as well, e.g., the loss of an illusion, the loss of anticipated pleasures, or the loss of a previously intact body part or function. Here, I shall focus on the mourning which follows the partial or total loss of a wanted person, and which involves painful and repeated goodbyes to the images of the lost person encountered in memories, in new experiences which would in the past have been shared, but now will not be, and in hopes for the future. Such mourning may involve intense feelings of sadness and anguish, hurt and anger.

I shall, in addition, comment briefly on the components of mourning that are a usual developmental aspect of the adolescent's attempt to separate and gain some independence from the previously internalized image of the parent, in addition to the actual parent. They are relevant only because, for the adolescents encountered here, this usual period of inner distancing from parents often coincided with the actual loss of the parent.

Grief in Childhood

A wide spectrum of opinion exists about whether a child before adolescence can engage in the mourning process. Some state that mourning cannot be accomplished until adulthood, until after detachment from parental figures has taken place (Wolfenstein, 1966, 1969; Nagera, 1970); and some find mourning is possible for children after early latency (Rochlin, 1953, 1965; Scharl, 1961); others designate the attainment of the phallic level of development as a prerequisite (E. Furman, 1974; R. Furman, 1964b), and still others (Bowlby, 1960, 1963; Deutsch, 1937, 1965; A. Freud, 1960; Jacobson, 1971) show that normal mourning is not found in very young children. Anna Freud believes the achievement of object constancy is necessary to mourning. Bowlby, in earlier works, proposed that grief and mourning occur in infancy whenever the responses mediating attachment behavior are activated and the mother figure continues to be unavailable. Finally, a number of people suggest that the age at which a child becomes capable of expressing his mourning depends also on supportive forces in the environment (Barnes, 1964; E. Furman, 1974; R. Furman, 1964a).

There are a number of sources for confusion in the data, and the theoretical orientations toward mourning. Various studies have drawn on reactions to different kinds and degrees of losses. For instance, where Bowlby's observations primarily concern children temporarily separated from parents and later reunited, Nagera, Furman, Scharl, and Wolfenstein are dealing with the death of a parent. Divorce involves a permanent loss, but a partial one. Others have discussed mourning for a loss of a limb, loss of ego ideal, etc. The long-range implications for the child of these different situations are different. Some theorists derive their data from observations of behavior, e.g., searching, crying, somatic symptoms, etc., while others are based on psychoanalytic material revealing underling thought processes as well. Again, this is an important difference for my subject: during the period following parental parting, numbers of very young children (between eighteen months and three years) engaged in repeated periods of sadness and crying, at times associated with active searching for the absent parent. However, we do not know whether during such periods of grieving the child cried out because of the painfulness of longing for the person who, he hoped, would reappear, although he had not done so yet; or whether the tears were a part of a mourning process during which the fact of having lost the wanted person is gradually faced, and the pain is part of renouncing the still existing wish for the person. In this discussion, the term "mourning" will be used to designate the process during which the person perceives the loss and in one way or another confronts the pain associated with the discrepancy he experiences between the gratification he desires with the absent person, and the impossibility of attaining it. The perception of loss is an essential component. Freud (1917) suggested that the most important factor inducing the bereaved to detach from his love object is the confrontation with reality. Similarly, Klein (1940) commented on the testing of reality as an essential part of mourning, though her reference point is a developmental process. There is some consensus that mourning takes a considerable period of time and is accompanied by a whole series of defenses.

"Grieving" will be used to denote the affective state of sadness, pain, and desolation when unrequited longing for the absent person is paramount; it may occur without perception or acceptance of the loss as permanent. The distinction between these terms, which are differently used by different writers, is arbitrary, but may be useful in separating the meaning of observable, long periods of sadness and weeping in young children from behavior that is similar but is more clearly associated with the decathexis of the image of a wanted person.

In 1937, Helene Deutsch first fully described the "absence of grief" in childhood and its consequences for the adult. She pointed out that in adult life "unmanifested grief will be found expressed to the full in some way or other." She commented on "the phenomenon of indifference which children so often display following the death of a loved person. Two explanations have been given for this so-called heartless behavior; intellectual inability to grasp the reality of death and inadequate formation of object relationship. My hypothesis is that the ego of the child is not sufficiently developed to bear the strain of the work of mourning and that it therefore utilizes mechanisms of narcissistic self-protection to circumvent the process." She added, "Observers note that the ego is rent asunder in those children who do not employ the usual defenses and who mourn as an adult does." She traced the consequences of unfulfilled grief to later life. In one case, a five-year-old boy showed no grief after the death of his mother, to whom he was fondly attached. In pubescence he began to have unmotivated depressions, and tended to break off friendships and love relationships with amazing ease, without feeling regret or pain. Deutsch accounted for this in terms of a displacement in time and dynamic distribution of mourning. In another case, a man incapable of emotion at the funeral of his mother reproached himself for not having mourned. In this case, the unconscious identification with the mother made the mourning dangerous, so that when the affects were revived in analysis, there was a danger of suicide. Another case Deutsch cited is that of a woman who involved herself vicariously in the grief of others, rather than experiencing her own. Her loss had occurred through the divorce of her parents. Deutsch concluded,

the process of mourning as a reaction to the real loss of a loved person must be carried to completion. As long as the early libidinal or aggressive attachment persists, the painful affects continue to flourish and vice versa, the attachments are unresolved as long as the affective process of mourning has not been accomplished.

She postulates a

striving for realization of mourning. This striving to live out the emotions may be so strong as to have an effect analogous to the mechanism which we see in criminal behavior from feelings of guilt, where a crime is committed to satisfy unconscious guilt feelings, which preceded the crime instead of following it. Analogously suppression following a loss seeks realization subsequently.

She concluded "probably the inner rejection of painful experience is always active, especially in childhood. One might assume that the tendency to 'unmotivated' depressions is the subsequent expression of emotional reactions which were once withheld and have since remained in latent readiness for discharge." In the clinical material described here, there are many instances of children who, with adequate emotional support, were able to sustain intense, though finally relieving, experiences of mourning. But notably, though most often the pain of longing for the wanted person could be acknowledged, the finality of the loss, be it through death or divorce, tended to be denied or negated in aspects of behavior related to unconscious fantasies. I have raised the question whether such finality is recognized even in the adult, or whether the lost, wanted person is still eternally sought in disguised forms. I question, for instance, whether the ego ideal is not always tied to unconscious percepts of once treasured moments of mutual intimacy with a wanted person.

Nagera (1970) suggested that mourning is not possible until detachment from parental figures has taken place in adolescence. He distinguished, in the overt manifestations of the child's reaction, between those that are the result of the developmental disturbance introduced by the object loss and the true mourning reaction to that loss. He postulated that only from the stage of object constancy onward do conditions exist that make it possible to observe some aspects of mourning in children. He found that most latency children deal with serious losses through death with massive denial, including denial and sometimes reversal of affect. However, the child usually cathects a fantasy life where the lost object may be seen as alive and at times as ideal. The adolescent has the preconditions for mourning, but responds differently from the adult, in that he is still tied to infantile images, so that sudden loss of objects creates developmental stress, as in younger children. In general, Nagera's cases demonstrated the following: short sadness span, incapacity to sustain mourning, massive use of denial and reversal of affect, search for substitutes, simultaneous symptom formation and character distortion, and the fear of contamination causing their own death, often side by side with fantasies of reunion.

Neubauer (1960) presented clinical material culled from the literature regarding ten patients who were without one parent during the oedipal period. He pointed out that the absence of a parent at this time has pathogenic potentialities for the future sexual identification and superego formation of the child. He found that fantasy objects—immensely idealized or endowed with terribly sadistic attributes—replacing the absent parent were nearly ubiquitous in otherwise very different situations. The remaining parent was often seen as the preoedipal seducer of the child. The child remained with a developmental deficiency which stemmed from not having lived through and mastered the oedipal conflict. When the parent is absent, there is a lack of "oedipal reality." The absent parent becomes endowed with magical power either to gratify or punish, and aggression against him, and the remaining parent as well, becomes repressed.

A number of authors describe a range of mechanisms utilized by children to cope with loss: Scharl (1961) presented case studies of two sisters, five and eight, who witnessed the father's violent death by decapitation in a car accident. "Both children showed processes of regression and restitution although the older girl, being in a later phase of development, was able to support a constructive restitution of her loss and did not succumb to regression to the same extent as her sister. In fact, the trauma enhanced and even promoted the course of her psychic development."

Wolfenstein (1969) wrote:

Mourning of the death of a parent does not take place in children and adolescents. Feelings of protracted grief are avoided, the finality of the loss is denied. The representations of the lost parent remain intensely cathected and there are fantasies of his return. While such expectations exist, there is also an acknowledgment of the fact that the parent has died. Acknowledgment and denial can co-exist without being mutually confronted, constituting what Freud called a splitting of the ego. Often there is a persistent quest for the lost parent; rage rather than grief; the repetition of disappointments; and the vindictive determination that no one can help.

These conclusions are consistent with the reactions of those children I have encountered whose unresolved bitterness about the loss of the parent surmounts the positive attachment to memories of pleasant interaction, but differs from the reactions of others. Wolfenstein (1966) pointed out that "in the favorable instances of adaptive reaction to such a loss, the process differed from mourning. There was an immediate transfer of freed libido to an available parent substitute." Again, this is somewhat at variance with the reactions I observed, especially in children aged two and a half or older. Although some of the children were apt to cling to a parent substitute when they were ready for this, more often the new person served as a catalyst for the beginnings of grief reactions, rather than as a substitute for the parent. A number of the children were particularly "touchy" about any attempt on the part of the new parent figure literally to act as though he was taking the place of the lost, loved person. In the younger children (age two and a half to five), in several instances, the new person was not allowed to sit in "daddy's chair," or share routines the child had previously shared with the absent parent. In the older children this was expressed by conflict about or rejection of calling the new person "daddy" or "mommy" and by articulated refusals to allow the new parent figure to "tell me what to do," as the original parent did. Just one eighteen-month-old girl who had had a very ambivalent relationship with her mother and whose stepmother and father were particularly warm did immediately call the substitute "mommy." Simultaneously, she remained closely attached to her nurturant father. A boy of two years and eleven months who had, however, never met his father referred to the fathering adult in his home as "like a daddy." In those families where older children immediately took to the new parent as a substitute, without expressing conflict about this, the children had conscious reasons for rejecting the lost parent.

Wolfenstein (1969) also found that "another adaptation to the loss is by identifying in a constructive way with the lost parent, thereby replacing the lost parent." She pointed to the problems in this mechanism: the child may not be far enough developed to do this and the image of illness and death may blot out living and constructive aspects of the image of the parent. She reminded us that for immature individuals the loss of a parent is an intolerable injury to fantasied omnipotence, and concluded that the repeated, self-induced suffering of further losses represents an unsuccessful effort to reassert this omnipotence.

Alpert (1964) further described regression as a reaction to the anxiety mobilized for the child by a death, even when this is not a personal loss. She described excerpts from the therapy sessions of four boys, aged four-and-a-half to six-and-a-half, after the assassination of John Kennedy. All the boys were in the "phallic oedipal stage." All of them reacted to the assassination as though they felt implicated and were out to prove their innocence. All renounced their phallic strivings and each in his own way moved back to earlier libidinal positions. She pointed to the developmental confirmation of hypotheses regarding superego formation, in that only the oldest child showed clear superego anxiety in terms of guilt.

Alpert's material reminded me of the reaction of a little girl, age five, whose parents had separated two months earlier, but who had previously been acquainted with grief. The father's increasing alcoholism had been a recent, though secondary difficulty in the marriage. Cheryl was aware of it as connected with his having to move to another apartment. Cheryl had often attempted to be a peacemaker between the parents, and had wanted to bring her father "hot coffee," which she had learned was a step in the sobering-up process. She had been told that she was too young to carry it without getting burned, but could when she was older. When I saw Cheryl the day of the Kennedy assassination, she burst into the room crying, telling me with hurt and indignation: "but I didn't even get to bring him (Kennedy) coffee yet!" She followed this by fears that her father might die without anyone to take care of him. Her next visit to him was preceded by nightmares of "fire burning me up." Her continued attachment to him was expressed in a variety of ways, including intense disappointment in not being big enough to take care of him, an identification with him in suffering the effects of abandonment (her mother had withdrawn emotional supplies from Cheryl at this time, just as from her father), and an association between her inner sexualized excitement during intensely stimulating visits to him (e.g., he took her on rides at night, at times wearing no clothes beneath his bathrobe), and punishment by burning to death if she were to try really playing the role of a mate old enough to bring hot, burning coffee.

When father made and forgot promises to call or have her visit, which he tended to do, in part because mother made these times so unpleasant for him, Cheryl's usual response was to go to bed crying; she made clear in her therapy that the crying occurred particularly whenever she became aware that some anticipated pleasure of togetherness had been lost. This was the reminder to her that the family was now apart, and nothing she could do could change that. In that sense, it involved "anticipatory grief" as well as a realistic perception of the permanence of her loss, and therefore a part of "mourning."

This example has been given in some detail to point to the complex nuances involved in various aspects of the grieving process. It is not surprising that conceptual clarity about whether the child does or does not mourn is difficult to achieve. In reviewing some further discussions we need also to keep in mind the potential semantic confusion regarding the presence of mourning, or depression as experienced by the adult; and the existence of other reactions associated with loss, such as denial, searching, identification, and displacement to substitutes; and the presence or a condition one might call "depression" in childhood, regardless of its immediate association with loss.

Bowlby (1960) proposed that grief and mourning occur in infancy whenever the responses mediating attachment behavior are activated and the mother figure continues to be unavailable. He postulated that the reason for the high pathogenic potential of loss of the mother figure during the period between six months and three to four years is that the process of mourning to which it habitually gives rise all too readily takes a course unfavorable to future development. He likened the responses he had observed in young children to those of adults. These responses include: thought and behavior still directed toward the lost object; hostility; appeals for help; despair, withdrawal regression and disorganization; reorganization of behavior directed toward a new object. Bowlby's studies of children's reactions to actual separation from the parent (e.g., during periods of hospitalization) have been described in chapter 3, along with the doubts raised by the Robertson's (1971) study about the inevitability of such separation reactions if the child is given adequate emotional support during the period of longing for the parent.

Rochlin (1953) discussed the analysis of a child who sustained repeated separations from his mother early in life. Relative absence of the mothering process very early established social isolation of the child. Subject to the trauma of repeated loss and separation, the child attempted to convert objects that seemed animated, changing and unpredictable to a lifeless state, so that he might be able to exert some control over them. Cathexes were shifted from live objects to immobile and lifeless ones. In this way he attempted to stabilize the environment and restore the lost objects. Rochlin's case description is not unrelated to the use of transitional objects and phenomena, which have been discussed.

In a more general view, Rochlin (1965) stated, "The immediate loss of a loved or central and important object, or even an abstraction like liberty or an image of oneself, is often followed by grief or mourning and in some cases by melancholia. Although this is true for adults, there seems to be some question as to what effect such a misfortune has upon children." Like Anna Freud and Dorothy Burlingame, who described some of the effects of separation or object loss during World War II when children were evacuated from London, he believed that regression is the central characteristic. "Regression occurs while the child is passing through the no-man's land of affection, i.e., during the time the old object has been given up and before the new one has been found." Rochlin confirmed that "regression is a constant finding in both young and old and occurs far more often than is generally recognized." He felt that the "young child's frailty is compensated in defending itself against object loss by the swiftness with which it can institute a replacement." Another typical phenomenon, "not so easily observed as regression, is identification with the lost object." Rochlin dated the onset of typical depression and melancholia to adolescence. He stated that "sadness, grief or even temporary depressive episodes occur in childhood, but children do not become elated, just as they do not become depressed in the clinical sense." He stressed the potential for psychological growth which may be catalyzed by loss. he commented, "when losses occur it is generally believed that a balance is restored by the final acceptance of reality. Insufficient attention has been given to the judgment of reality that impels men to attempt to alter it."

Gauthier (1965) described the "mourning reaction" of a ten-and-a-half-year-old boy, who had been in analysis eighteen months prior to the death of his father. The boy went through three phases. First, he attempted to reunite with the lost one at almost any cost. However, such efforts at identification soon were seen to be an aggressive incorporation of the power of the ambivalently lost father. The splitting of the father image into the idealization of the good father and the depreciation of the bad analyst were the main defenses against such aggressive urges. Finally, when the splitting was interpreted, they boy could then abandon the omnipotent, idealized object of identification and turn toward the tasks of the future.

Over the past decade, a number of clinical studies have suggested that the remaining family members and the rest of the environment are a crucial determinant of the child's capacity for mourning. These include Barnes (1964), Robert Furman (1964a, b) and the recent, superbly detailed accounts to be found in *A Child's Parent Dies* (1974), by Erna Furman, describing bereaved children in treatment with a number of analysts. She discussed those features of the remaining familial life which suggested a good rather than poor prognosis for the children. These writers consider it very important that the remaining parent be able to participate in the child's grief. He or she must be able to tolerate his own grief and to convey to the child that he has permission to grieve or long for the dead parent and must share those memories of the dead parent which are appropriate for the child's age and experience.

Barnes (1964) discussed the reactions of two sisters, aged four and two and a half, to the death of their mother. The older girl dealt with her loss through identification, or the defenses against this: she would repeatedly play games in which she would fall down dead and would either rise or stay down. The younger sister showed the strongest denial, and would not talk about her sadness, her mother, or death. Only after nine months did she begin to verbalize her feelings. Barnes attributed this change to various factors in the child's environment which facilitated it: the child's grandmother was giving in to a deep, delayed mourning at that time and the mother substitutes and teachers were receiving extensive consultation to help them support the child through this phase. In a similar manner, R. Furman (1964b) described the mourning of a six-year-old boy whose mother died while he was in analysis. The boy's mourning "unfolded in two distinct phases; the painful acceptance of the reality loss and beginning painful decathexis of the inner world representations." There was a relative absence of denial during both phases. Furman indicates that "work with the father was included since it was essential for the boy that the father allow himself to mourn fully." In another article, R. Furman (1964a) raised the questions: "When is the child capable of the painful internal decathexis of the lost object that is the essence of mourning? What are the factors responsible for the child's inability to mourn or which interfere with his capacity for mourning?" He followed Anna Freud's lead in pointing to the developmental capacities necessary to comprehend death and deal with loss. He made suggestions for ways in which young children can be sustained and supported during mourning: He concluded that two-to-three-year-olds can master the concept of death; three-and-a-half or four-year-olds can mourn; and that these precious abilities can be made unavailable to a child by unfavorable circumstances. He would encourage parents to convey the sense of death as a part of life to two-, three- and four-year-olds and recommended professional support to parents of small children who have suffered an important loss. From my own experience I would agree that three-and-a-half to four-year-olds can mourn. Children two years old and under can grieve intensely.

In the clinical accounts of children in the following chapters, attempts will be made to relate the quality of grief or mourning to the combination of inner resources and external supports available.

A Component of Adolescence, Analogous to Mourning

Blos (1962) reminded us that "the object loss which adolescents experience in relation to the parent of their childhood, that is, in relation to the parent image, contains features of mourning. This adolescent loss is more final and irrevocable than the one which occurs at the end of the oedipal phase."

Root (1957) spoke of the work of mourning as an important psychological task in the period of adolescence, accounting in part for the depressive states of adolescence, as well as for their grief reaction as a postponement of affect. To complete the normal work of mourning required time and repetition. In the course of this work there is a profound difference according to whether the mourned image of the childhood parent can be transformed gradually into a more reality-scaled image of a still existing real parent, or whether these transformations must be accomplished in fantasy alone, as in the case of a dead, entirely absent or massively degraded parent. The different courses of these types of mourning will be explored in chapter 7, and the sections dealing with reaction to the death of a parent. At times, regressed states of adolescence, when they are in the service of mourning, presage the development of a strong and enriched personality.

The loss of a sense of identity which many adolescents describe as feelings of depersonalization, e.g., "this is not me," or "I feel nothing," follows the withdrawal of emotional investment in the parent figures. Blos (1962) commented that "this state is aggravated when the emotional relationship was one on which the sense of identity almost exclusively depended for regulation and maintenance. The rupture of such an object tie necessarily involves, more or less seriously, a loss of sense of identity or a fragmentation."

Laufer (1966) considered how the death of a parent during adolescence can interfere with normal development by preventing the necessary internal changes from taking place. He stated: "The detachment from the oedipal object is a normal developmental task in adolescence, which may be greatly complicated by the actual loss of the object. The oedipal ambivalence to the object which is normally re-experienced in adolescence may then be kept under repression by the idealization of the loss object. This idealization becomes an insurmountable obstacle to the relinquishment of the object, resulting in further compromise formation, defensive measures and ego or character deviations."

Much work has focused on the depression that is part of early adolescence, when children are loosening their ties to the parents; it should be mentioned that parents also feel that they are beginning to lose their children at this time, and a sense of emptiness and an absence of earlier goals often pervades and is part of a grief reaction. This can be intensified by separation or divorce of the parents, putting additional real distance between parent and child. There may be an attempt to recapture the lost child, either through becoming an adolescent playmate, or by overprotecting him, or by a role reversal in which the child is asked to meet the parents' needs for support. For better or worse for the parent, such efforts in the long run generally backfire or are doomed, and meanwhile can interfere with the child's optimal development. Recently, parents are perhaps put to a more severe test than previously: within a rapidly changing world their children often appear—from hair to ideology to technical knowledge—so unlike the parents' ideal image of themselves that parents come to feel that their own biological and emotional link to the future—in the form of their children—is no longer assured.

However, those parents who go through this grieflike period and yet are able to support their child's separation and individuation into an adult, are often surprised at the close new relationship, as between two adults, that then becomes possible. Parents and child may discover not only persisting happy memories about each other, but mutual interests and points of view at a time when they can again bear to admit their identificatory links.

The Capacity to Bear Painful Affects:
Its Relation to Adult Life and to Grieving

Anxiety and depressive affect are natural responses to the perception of the discrepancy between one's wishes and what is possible in reality. If painful affects are experienced as potentially so traumatic or overwhelming that they must be avoided, additional defensive maneuvers are needed to avoid either awareness of one's wishes or the limitations of reality. These can seriously constrict emotional relationships, work involvement, or the enjoyment of pleasures. Ironically, they can also function to stimulate rather than avoid depressive disturbance. One limitation of reality consists in what one is able to do and be. If a fantasy of invulnerability is chronically invoked in association with the avoidance of anxiety and depressive affect, the person is in fact more vulnerable to being shattered when it becomes impossible to maintain such a magical self-image of strength and power. For individuals in therapy, a slowly increasing tolerance for anxiety and depressive affects may be a prerequisite to constructive coping with unfinished, long postponed mourning. For the children of the divorced and deceased, ways of coping with loss have significance beyond their effect on the recovery of developmental and identificatory strides at the time. A major aim in enabling the child to experience his grief in manageable doses is to support his long-range capacity to tolerate painful affects, so that he will not, in the future, fear them as inducing panic, overwhelming helplessness or a shattering of the self. Although developing this capacity requires certain inner resources, the clinical material regarding the children shows that this may be less a matter of age than of the presence of individuals in a supportive environment—most importantly, the remaining parent—who participate by emotionally "holding" the child through the period of grief. My one disagreement with the most recent work of Richard Gardner (1976), whose approach to children is generally imaginative and unstereotyped, is a kind of "short-circuiting" of the period of grief for the absent parent, designed to propel the child more quickly toward the otherwise important, available people in his environment. I do not know what happens to the child's long-range capacity for anxiety and grieving, and the internalized images of the absent parent which impinge on later identification patterns, when work is geared toward such rapid decathexis.

Greenacre (1941), Shur (1953, 1955) and Zetzel (1949) all emphasized differences in adult personality determined by the way the individual experiences anxiety. Greenacre arrived at a series of factors in infancy and early life which lead to a basic, and in her view relatively unalterable, predisposition to overwhelming anxiety. She differentiated this from other clinical conditions, based on developmentally later or less severe difficulties, and associated with what has been called by various theorists secondary, contained, or signal anxiety. Whereas in the first type the capacity to bear anxiety is significantly reduced, in the latter type of disturbance anxiety is associated with areas in which intrapsychic defenses have been erected, but can be experienced in a contained way. Schur made similar distinctions between contained anxiety, which does not exceed the individual's capacity to bear it, and the more overwhelming anxiety that leads to regression, not only in mental content, but also in ego mechanisms and the degree of differentiation vs. fusion in self and object representations. He cautioned against letting such regression go unchecked until it becomes of psychotic proportions, but does not seem to conclude that it is an unalterable predisposition.

Zetzel (1970) included a tolerance for both anxiety and depression as an essential component of the "capacity for emotional growth." In its development, she pointed to the importance of the child's early establishment of "more than one essentially dyadic relationship. In brief, the child who will later become a potentially healthy adult has established successful one-to-one relationships with both parents before the onset of the genital oedipal triangular situation. ... Each parent, in other words, will have been experienced both as a love object and as an object for identification during the pre-oedipal years." When this has been the case, she suggested, "genuine intrapsychic conflict fosters the capacity to distinguish between internal and external reality," and to tolerate contained anxiety and depressive affects. She further related the impact of developed inner resources to ways of coping with depression later in life. "Whatever the precipitating cause of the depression, the quality and stability of previous object relations, the capacity to renounce an omnipotent self-image, and the acceptance of reality appear to be decisive areas. Depression in an individual whose development in these areas has been satisfactory seldom reaches psychotic proportions. Persons whose object relations have been highly ambivalent, whose self-esteem has been dependent either on successful performance or excessive gratification, appear, on the other hand, to be highly vulnerable."

The task of developing tolerance and mastery of depression involves two components. One is tolerating the experience of being unable to modify certain painful, existing realities, that is, allowing oneself to feel helpless about doing anything immediately to get rid of the attendant pain, or sadness. Equally important, however, is the subsequent coping with the disappointing reality by mobilizing one's resources to reinvest oneself in areas of gratification or achievement which *are* possible. Sometimes, difficulty in tolerating the first phase of this process may lead to an overdevelopment of the second. In such cases, passivity becomes so heavily defended against that, although the individual may function in an apparently highly successful fashion, he remains vulnerable when having to deal with loss and disappointment (Zetzel, 1970).

There were some interesting differences in the parents of adolescents and of some of the young children encountered here. I believe these had to do, not only with their earliest predispositions (e.g., tolerance not only for depression but also active mastery), but also with the values espoused in the human support network in which they functioned. More of the mothers of adolescents (some of whom are now in their twenties) were living their young adulthood and bringing up their children before the women's liberation movement and its ideology had reached them in a meaningful way (about twenty to thirty-five years ago). More of them had suffered from years of depression and dissatisfaction, with variations in the degree to which they allowed themselves to be aware of this. However, fewer felt supported in initiating active efforts to make changes in their life situations. For many mothers, by the time the children were adolescents and they did in fact make such changes, the realistic opportunities available to them had narrowed, or their hopes by then were too strained and too great to make palatable what could be had. Nevertheless, usually after some years of struggle, these women became more able to assert themselves in meeting their needs. While their children were young, however, they seem more often to have exaggerated their dependence and helplessness and underrated their capacities for coping. Among the mothers of the younger children, a period of depression and anger was also a prominent feature for many (often not for those who were leaving the marriage after already forming an attachment to a new partner). However, the sense of helplessness about altering their reality was not as pervasive, and many had sought or found some social support for the moves they were making. This difference was reflected in the children's attitudes toward the possibility of constructive change.

Bibring (1953) approached the problem of depression from an ego-psychological point of view, as an affective "state of the ego," be it a "normal," "neurotic" or "(probably) also what is called psychotic depression." He focused on the crucial role of helplessness: "Depression can be defined as the emotional expression (indication) of a state of helplessness and powerlessness of the ego, irrespective of what may have caused the breakdown of the mechanisms which established self-esteem." He distinguished between types of persistent aspirations, and the different tensions between those aspirations and the ego's awareness of the person's inability to achieve them. Self-esteem may collapse if the person feels unable to live up to the ego ideal or superego aspirations while they are strongly maintained. Or, in instances of actual loss of a love object, tension exists between the longing for the object and the wish to retrieve it, and the awareness that one does not have the power to undo the loss. Bibring alerted us to the implication of the "helplessness" for the therapy of depression; its reversal serves as restitution. He stated that generally the depression subsides either: (a) when the narcissistically important goals and objects appear again to be within reach; (b) when they become sufficiently modified or reduced to become realizable; (c) when they are relinquished altogether; (d) when the ego recovers from the narcissistic shock of retaining its self-esteem with the help of a variety of recovery mechanisms (with or without change of object or goal); or finally (e) defense can be directed against the affective depression as such (e.g., through either apathy or hypomania). For the children encountered here, most often modification of the image of the absent parent was instrumental in their capacity both to grieve and to recover from grief. Only very rarely did the child entirely surrender the parent as someone who was still loved and wanted in some way.

Nonetheless, the child had somehow to recognize the change in relationship wrought by the divorce, or the loss of an actual relationship with a deceased parent. Major transformations had to occur in the internal image of that parent or relationship. An exaggeration or idealization of the parents' power to gratify or punish, possess or discard the bereft child had to give way to a more realistic view. The continued, compelling attachment to the wanted, absent parent could indeed render the child helpless when that attachment could not be brought to light, or remembered and re-experienced in bitter-sweet grief.

The bitter-sweet but eventually relieving nature of grief seemed to stem from the alternation, during grieving, between tender, happy memories of the absent person with the self and the repeated recognition that the experience could not be looked forward to again. Children remembered both the past and the wished-for future with the absent parent, reacting to the same image, which first evoked pleasure and then pain.

Parkes (1972), working with the bereaved, noted that "the most characteristic feature of grief is not prolonged depression but acute and episodic 'pangs.' A pang of grief is an episode of severe anxiety and psychological pain. At such times, the lost person is strongly missed and the survivor sobs or cries aloud for him." He described such pangs of grief as beginning a few hours or days after bereavement (after some initial numbing or denial) and usually reaching a peak of severity within five to fourteen days. "At first they are very frequent, but as time passes they become less frequent and take place only when something occurs that brings the loss to mind, e.g., finding a photograph in a drawer, meeting a mutual friend of the lost person, or waking up alone in a double bed."

Jacobson (1957) commented on the difference between the experience of sadness and depression. She stated that "the suffering that promotes sadness always seems to be caused by experiences—or fantasies—of loss or deprivation, such as by loss of gratification, either previously gained or expected, by loss of love, by separation, or, in the course of mourning, by loss of a love object. . . . Even though sadness develops from the experiences of loss and deprivation, which tend to provoke aggression, its qualities hint at the involvement of predominantly libidinal cathexes. Angry and sad moods, for example, commonly exclude each other, although it frequently happens that aggression is used as a defense against a painful experience of sadness. In other words, unlike depression, sadness as such does not involve an aggressive conflict, either with external reality or endopsychically. . . . Practically, of course, states of sadness frequently show depressive features and in depressed states feelings of sadness prevail. But clinical observations suggest that sadness predominates in depression only as long as the libidinal investment in the object world can be maintained by the veering of aggression to the self."

Jacobson's formulations in this area are consistent with the observations made here of both children and adults (most clearly adults bereaved in childhood) that the experience of delayed grief for the absent person was associated with the feeling of mutual "forgiveness" (e.g., in the case of Natasha), which in turn ameliorated the harshness of self-criticism, that is, aggression directed against the self. However, the libidinal longing for the absent person was in itself frequently not re-experienced until some rage, also withheld from the absent person or his image, had been expressed. Already, after the expression of the rage, the child or adult often felt less helpless in his attachment.

For the children of the deceased who had been unable to grieve sufficiently, the wishful fantasies still persisted in disguised quests, or aspects of libidinal energy were bound to a greater or lesser extent by identifications with the lost person. For both the children of the deceased and those of the divorced (for whom the relationship still existed partly in reality, but was changed), it might be said that wishful fantasies were rarely totally renounced. Instead, as the child reinvested his energies in new life goals and relationships, the wishes were transformed by compromises, in accordance with the "reality" of how much continued gratification he could still expect in the actual relationship with the person, and how much had been permanently lost. Simultaneously, the wishful fantasies retained their importance, within the reality sense of the child or adolescent, as evidence of the precious intimacy or love he had once shared with the wanted absent parent in reality, and which now remained within him as "real" to remember or, with others in a different way, to renew. At this point an openness to new identification figures, as well as modifications in the ego ideal, tended to make their appearance. This was often accompanied by a rush of new energies, a self-confidence about having weathered an inner storm, and a remembering—with some sense of distance—of an earlier self, as filled with pangs of nostalgia.

Part II

Encounters with Children
and Parents

Chapter 5

PARENTS DIVIDED AND PARENTS MULTIPLIED: SOME EFFECTS OF MULTIPLE PARENT FIGURES ON THE IDENTIFICATIONS OF THE CHILD

> Love is more thicker than forget
> more thinner than recall
> more seldom than a wave is wet
> more frequent than to fail
>
> —e. e. cummings, *50 Poems*

Psychic Factors and the Human Support System

"I have a new little frog," announced Jeffrey the week after his father, with whom he lived, remarried, "and all the children were at the wedding." Asked how he felt about it, he said "I was glad about it, if they didn't get married I would only have my dada and now I have Joan—she lets me go way high on the swing—and we have a dog and some good new brothers who sleep in the basement and even a cat." Jeffrey's father and stepmother agreed the following week that things were going surprisingly well with the six children they now shared, since the remarriage. "Of course," she added, "we prepared ourselves for the fact that we have more tears and tantrums than the Brady Bunch would." (The Brady Bunch is a TV family comedy about six children and their remarried parents.) Jeffrey is five, and we will return to his history later.

This chapter concerns those children who have had to devise ways of coping with a parental separation or divorce that is followed by a recoupling or remarriage of one or both parent figures. Some of the effects of such multiple parenting on the evolving identification patterns in the child will be explored. I have been impressed by the variety of responses in children, ranging from an enrichment of identity development to severe impairment. I shall attempt to explore those features which appear to augur well for the continued thriving of the child and to differentiate them from patterns which appear to herald increasing difficulty. In order to focus on the development of identifications at a time in the child's life when these comprise a major part of his growth, I shall in this chapter deal with children who were younger than eleven years old when I first saw them (prepubescent), and who have some continued contact with both the original, as well as at least one, and often two, "new" parent figures. This excludes children who have experienced the death of a parent, or whose parent so totally rejected or severed contact with them that the child faced in reality a total loss of that parent (I shall consider aspects of such problems later).

What seem to be the prerequisites for the child's working toward the kinds of identifications with others that are strengthening rather than debilitating to the developing personality? In chapters 2 and 3 questions were raised about the delicately shifting dynamics affecting the forms of identification which appear to coexist with varieties of quests for the absent, wanted parent. It became clear that the human relationship network was one crucial factor. Enduring the inner work and pain of partially losing a parent seemed most possible when certain kinds of emotional support surrounded the child's effort. There are a number of parameters involved here.

In the first place, the children needed direct assurance that their basic needs for physical and emotional care would continue to be met by parent figures while they were trying to work through the partial loss. When this was not done or was not possible, anxiety over losing the remaining parent and having no one to take care of them dependably seemed to remain paramount.

This kind of assurance often involved the active building or maintenance of a supportive human and social network. Rather than working only with the child or the child and family, I found it useful also to do special planning, when possible, with schools, courts, and a variety of individuals important in the life of the child, such as teachers, peers, siblings, housekeepers, therapists of other family members, and the new parent, in order to maintain as much continuity as possible for the child and to attempt to work out ways for him to function in sustaining relationships. Because marital breakup and the inevitable emotional stress are so often accompanied by major financial and other social changes (for example, the home parent may now be going to work for the first time), these changes may add to the child's anxiety and sense of loss. The facing of complicated legal-social issues may be a part of this planning, and will be discussed in chapter 6.

It is equally essential that the parents allow the child to express his feelings about the loss when he is ready for it, and they may need support here. This may be complicated by the habitual defense structure of the parent—e.g., his or her characteristic way of handling anxiety and feeling may be by running into activity, cheerfulness, or "keeping a stiff upper lip"—as well as by the difference in feeling between the parent and the child toward the former spouse. Even if the parent has the kind of personality which makes it possible to face grief and anxiety when it is appropriate, this may still not be easy. The parent may also be feeling bereft, distressed, and irritable, often more than he or she expected, but is still having to cope actively with a difficult life situation meanwhile. It is not easy in that situation to empathize with the child's grief, while feeling one has to control one's own. Conversely, if the parent is relieved to be free of a spouse who he or she feels made life miserable, supporting the child's longing for that spouse becomes more difficult.

The parent is often faced with the contradictory-seeming emotional task of having to mobilize his or her own bitterness and anger against the former spouse in order to disengage from the relationship as a mate, while at the same time supporting the child's continued engagement with the former spouse as a parent.

Yet an enriched or optimal adjustment for the child seems to be fostered by each original parent conveying emotional permission to continue to care about all the new parent figures involved. Eventually, even young children may be able to attain a compassionate appreciation of the original parents' differences and difficulties and be well able to cope with spending periods of time with each person. In my experience, however, the young child's security may be threatened unless he can consider one or the other parental abodes as basically "home base."

Some derivatives of a grief process seem to precede the child's ability to work out these kinds of shifts comfortably. These derivatives often include: (1) transient symptoms which become understandable only if viewed as a disguised identification with the partially absent parent; (2) the maintenance, consciously or unconsciously, of the fantasy of the family reunited without the previous hostilities, or of disguised and transformed aspects of this image; (3) conscious as well as unconscious concern and guilt about the well-being of the absent parent, particularly if that parent is alone or deprived; this may be coupled with the fear of being discarded just like that parent (the child's degree of distress in this process may reflect the degree to which he perceives the parent as distressed); (4) anxiety about being abandoned by the remaining parent, about being helpless and uncared for in a way that is not directly based on identification with the wanted absent parent, but on the fear that, if one can lose one parent, it is just as possible to lose the other. The degree of this will vary in accordance with the child's previous relationship to the home parent.

However, even when this relationship has been good, the child's fear of abandonment by the home parent appears heightened for a period of time. For the child it is frequently associated with the inevitable escalation of anger he sees between the parents, and his experiences and fears that anger will erupt more easily between himself and the home parent as well. His own increased dependency on the parent makes the child feel all the more vulnerable. The case examples dealing with initial reactions to separation will illustrate this.

In addition to the children's hyperacuity about whether they were allowed to miss the absent parent, their coming to terms with the separation seemed to be fostered by the availability of a new parent figure who was willing and able to support the child through the difficult period of sadness, while not at the same time demanding his immediate loyalty or attempting to take the place of the parent. I saw no child for whom the new parent figure replaced the original one entirely, with the exception of one little boy whose father had never seen him and who hence had no real memory of his biologic parent. I have included material about this little boy (Jeremy) to exemplify the existence of fantasies of reunion with a biologic parent in a situation where no "real" loss occurred, in contrast to the losses suffered by the children who are the focus of this chapter.

Often the child who was concerned about the well-being of the absent parent needed either some assurance that this parent would be O.K., or a frank, albeit simplified, explanation when this was not possible. For example, when that parent suffered from continued unhappiness or loneliness, or when he or she was suffering from a serious disturbance, such as a psychosis, the child needed to know that there were helping people available to that parent before his sense of guilt or responsibility concerning that parent could be alleviated.

One might say, then, that the child seems best able to go through the stages of reworking his identification, including some sadness and yearning, when he can solidly rely on his remaining relationship, both physically and emotionally. Among children brought to treatment were those who, for various reasons of family dynamics, or because of major gaps in the human support network available to them and their families, had to abort the inner yearning and substitute a symptom of disguised, ego-alien identification. With children who felt conflicting loyalties—and this was true to a greater or lesser extent with all of them—the initially unconscious nature of such a symptom of identification protected the remaining parent from awareness of the child's need for the other. For example, Jenny's symptoms occurred in an altered state of consciousness, as sleepwalking; Noah was unaware that his behavior was linked to his ideas about his father's expulsion from the house. In such cases, the therapist's simple recognition with the child that he or she might be trying to remember the parent by copying him tended to shift the initial symptom quickly, but this shift usually represented only the very beginning of recognizing and dealing with the process.

Some children, with emotional support, proceeded to express affect and often painful yearnings for the parent who was not with them. Others could not begin this until there was some restitution of activity identical to that which they remembered sharing with the absent parent. For example, Jeffrey had enjoyed pasting sticker pictures with his mother, and he could not discuss his feelings toward her until he requested me to do this with him. This mode was most apt to occur either with quite young children or when there were strongly negative and feared memories to be faced as well. The shared activity seemed a concrete reminder that the tie to the parent would not be destroyed by the negative feelings expressed.

Once the feeling of yearning became tolerated and open, younger children tended both to see some positive and negative features of the parent in a more realistic way, and steadily to make use of the new parent figures as models for identification, as well as accepting interactions with them which had previously been reserved for and experienced with the absent parent. Many children needed initially to reject the new adult as a "replacement" for the parent. For example, Jeffrey's housekeeper came to talk with me at a time when she felt ready to quit her job in frustration over Jeffrey's rejection of her friendly overtures and way of doing things. It was not, however, difficult to convey to her her importance to him and some understanding of why he needed to resist her, and she was able to use her understanding in a highly constructive way with him. Noah said, of his new father figure, "I thought of Steve falling over a cliff every day at first." For the older children conflicts about interests, attitudes, and moral values also preceded acceptance of the enriched possibilities with the new parent. Once a new parent figure began to be accepted, the child often recounted either features of the parent's personality which impinged on him in a constructive way, or the discovery of new shared activity and interests which he enjoyed. Thus, Jeffrey, in his description of the wedding quoted at the beginning of this chapter, pointed out that his stepmother let him go high on the swing and liked him to learn to swim at day camp, while his own mother was highly overprotective and fearful; Noah described Steve's safer driving, and the fact that family activities, such as a museum trip, were new and fun, compared to the older pattern that he had previously longed and wept for, in which the children did things with just one parent at a time. His mother had, in fact, first dared to introduce Steve to Noah after Noah had expressed a wish to learn a certain kind of handcraft in which Steve happened to be skilled.

For the child a time of increasing conflict often coincided with the period when the new parent figure became loved and valued too—often surprising the parent who had been gratified by the child's finally seeming to accept the new partner. But increasing attraction to the new parent figure often came into conflict with the remaining attachment to the absent parent. In therapy at this time, the child often constantly compared old and new parent figure; old memories and wishes toward the absent parent revived with renewed intensity. In several cases this occurred at the point where the child for the first time reported dreaming of the new parent figure. At this time it seemed that the child faced not only his memories but, in coming to terms with the new realities, he also had to renounce future plans and prospective dreams shared with the absent parent; for example, giving up the fishing trips they never had taken but always said they would. Sometimes this meant dealing with old, shared fantasies—for instance, that the father would be cheering the son from the sidelines once he was old enough to play football—and it often became important to arrange for the absent parent's participation in events planned long ago, like bar mitzvahs or graduations.

At this time, too, the absent parent might feel he was losing his child to a rival and attempt to intensify the promises of closeness. For example, Noah's father told him at this time "you and I are the only ones who think on the same wavelength." Jeffrey and Gwen's mother became wrathful if the children mentioned any fun at home, and prepared renewed litigation for custody. In general those parents whose own lives were reasonably happy and fulfilled had a much easier time with it all, and often demonstrated amazing capacity to accept and appreciate the advice that, as much as possible, previous bitterness toward the absent parent should be dealt with directly between the adults, but must not be expressed through the child. At some time or other it tended to become clear in discussion with the parents seen that the child in part identified the absent parent with aspects of himself, and that if that parent was thoroughly devalued by the former spouse, the child would have no choice but to devalue or hide that aspect of himself, rigidifying the aspect of the tie based on low self-esteem, rather than working it through. The parents also tended to become aware that, however it might seem now, their child would probably not thank them in the long run if they needed to denigrate the absent parent to him. In other words, what the former spouse meant to the parent had to be created as a separate issue; many parents had very valid reasons for their bitterness and needed to recognize them for their own well-being. It was made clear to the parents, however, that they certainly should not hide their own anger or disappointment about the former spouse or cover up realistic limitations, when the child needed in fact to recognize these. In particular in those cases (in the minority) in which the absent parent was indeed rejecting of the child, it was necessary to aid in making clear to the child that the loss or rejection was part of the parent's difficulty rather than a failure on the part of the child.

Some Characteristics of the Families

The families considered in this chapter differ to a certain extent from those discussed in later chapters and may also differ from those of other populations of children of divorce. Most of the material in this chapter derives from twenty-four children who were between the ages of one and a half and ten when they first came to my attention, and who came from eighteen different families. There were other children in these families whom I either did not see or about whom material was too skimpy to include. All the children had had a solid enough relationship to their parents to be able to perceive and react to their loss in some way when the parents separated. I have also included retrospective material about two other children who were seen at pubescence, although the initial family separation had taken place at age three for both. These two girls were seen about twenty years ago, and the social climate surrounding their parents' separations is that which existed thirty to thirty-five years ago, in contrast to all the other, current, cases discussed. My purpose here is to explore some of the later effects on character structure of the early separations. In addition, as earlier mentioned, I have included one child who has never seen his father.

A summary of some aspects of the familial circumstances are tabulated in the appendix and compared to the same features in the families of the adolescents (chapter 6). Some relevant differences emerged in living arrangements for the child; patterns of new heterosexual relationships for both parents, and in working pattern of mothers. Most of the children described in this chapter lived with their mothers after the separation (79 percent), so that the father was most often the absent parent. However, 21 percent lived with their fathers; and 17 percent shifted homes within two years of the divorce or spent equal amounts of time with each parent. In contrast, only 58 percent of the adolescents lived with their mothers after separation, and 42 percent lived with fathers; 27 percent shifted homes. In the two retrospective cases, the father was absent in one, the child shifted back and forth between parents in the other.

On the whole the fathers of the young children (or the younger generation of fathers) were less apt than the mothers to establish a new stable relationship with a partner in the first or second year following the separation, although there were exceptions. Remarriage or stabilized living with a man was true of 42 percent of the women, but only 21 percent of the men. The situation is reversed, and with a greater degree of difference, for the fathers and mothers of the adolescents, where only 19 percent of the women were remarried and none stably living with a man, while 50 percent of fathers had remarried, and 12 percent more were stably living with a woman. The majority of fathers of the young children, however, were involved in either serial or transient relationships with a number of women. Only 8 percent of fathers and 17 percent of mothers had had no known heterosexual relationships since the separation or divorce. Mothers who were living with a love partner in a new stable relationship tended to be conflicted about the permanence of the commitment.

Of the retrospective cases, one mother remained unmarried and did not date for the nine years after her husband left; the other remarried a person who was away from home most of the time, and lived with the mother of her first husband even after her divorce and remarriage.

There were also notable differences for the two age groups, in the proportion of mothers working or obtaining advanced education while their children were young. A great majority of the mothers of children aged one to ten were working full- or part-time, or furthering their education (83 percent of under fives, 92 percent of five-to-ten-year-olds). Several began to work or changed from volunteer activities to paid work during the time the child was being seen; one changed from working to not working. Of the retrospective cases, one mother worked, one did not.

Among the mothers of adolescents, only 19 percent had worked when the child was under age five, and 27 percent were working by the time the child was ten. By the time the child was seen during adolescence 62 percent were working, or returning to further education. The shift, in a number of cases, was related as an impetus or consequence of the separation or divorce.

Several other features are relevant to the children's situations: in several cases where a marriage broke up during the first two years after the child's birth, there tended to be a pattern of drastic shift in the relationship between the marriage partners once they approached parenthood (this includes Susan, Daniel, Mark, Jenny, Jeremy, and Robin). In these cases the fathers had actively withheld emotional support from the wife when she was about to be or had just become a mother; and had also actively and sometimes dramatically withheld interest in the infant. For example, one of the fathers had suggested an abortion when his wife became pregnant and later, while considering separation, proposed that the child be adopted by someone else. A second father chronically put wax in his ears or walked out of the house when the infant cried. A third father immediately began to have a series of affairs, leaving his wife alone with the infant. Later, most of these fathers became able to relate to their small children. For example, the father who had suggested the baby be put up for adoption before the couple separated slowly but steadily became more responsible about his son's visiting schedule after the divorce.

Most of these mothers experienced an initial sense of shock about the father's rejection of mother and infant; in a number of cases this contrasted with his earlier attentiveness. The withdrawal of the father tended to be associated, for the mothers, with varying degrees of depression, which in turn affected their relationship to the child. One such mother remembered her sense of delight and satisfaction in her infant son, but became increasingly depressed when he was around six months old at the realization that she, together with her little son, were steadily being excluded by the husband. For various and differing reasons these fathers seemed particularly unready for a responsible, emotional commitment to fatherhood. This, however, did not turn out to be irreversible.

Interestingly it was frequently within this group of women that the mother, after a period of depression, began to discover inner resources in herself that she did not know she possessed. These included "getting over" the sense of failure about believing herself rejected, conquering fears of aloneness and lack of protection or of inability to manage the mechanical and financial aspects of running a household, and the kind of soul-searching and renewed social contacts that led them to further self-development. A number of them undertook career training, or experienced a shift in the degree of responsibility and commitment they felt to a career. In a more profound way, they had begun to re-examine their capacities for satisfaction in their roles as women and as fully functioning human beings. These women tended to be in their twenties or early thirties. Two young mothers, who had initiated the separation because of their despair about the lack of emotional communication between themselves and their husbands, were similarly involved in further self-development. None of these particular mothers (who had kept their children) withdrew emotionally from their children during this period of self-development, even though they all suffered from bouts of exhaustion and the conflicting pulls of their work, love life, and mothering on their energies. A number of them commented at one time or another that during the period when they had been most depressed it was in fact the presence of the child which had "pulled me through."

A number of these women were specifically conflicted between the preservation of their newly found and enjoyed autonomy and binding love ties to a mate. Though involved in stable love relationships, they valued the sense of being able to function independently, if need be. Yet feeling themselves more able to love fully than before, they struggled between an ideal of interdependent partnership without strings attached; and the urge to "give themselves" fully to a new love partner, coupled with the fear of being again disappointed and vulnerable. Working out a life style within their marriage or love relationship that included some "space" for their private and autonomous selves was an important issue for all of them. For example, Sean's mother came for a follow-up interview a year after Sean was seen. She had now been living with her lover for close to two years and reported, "We are so happy that it frightens me still." She said, "I think we both feel freer to express our feelings to each other than I ever thought possible in life. But at the same time I need to know I could live independently if I had to, that I could be a complete person, even away from him." She planned to accept a summer position in a different city, which would involve living just with Sean and away from her lover. She thought once she had proven to herself she could do this that they would probably get married "in the long run." She was not at the moment sure whether formalizing their relationship would be mostly to "please his parents" or involved an additional level of commitment between the lovers.

Daniel's mother, now secure in her career, had lived with the man with whom she was involved for two years, aware of his difficulties about committing himself, especially to being a parent to Daniel. She thought resolutely ahead to the possibility that they would break up and that she might have a number of stable but not permanent love relationships in her life. She wanted to prepare herself to face the question of how this might affect her child.

Mark's mother, in love with the man with whom she had been living, worked through remnants of her depression and established herself in training for a new career, wanting to feel sure that it was not dependence, but involvement with an able and giving person that brought her to new marriage vows. She then married the man with whom she had been living.

Jeremy's mother brought up her son by herself until he was two and a half. At this point a man entered her life. Although aware of how long she had waited to again express the giving and loving aspects of her nature with a man, she was equally aware of the need to plan for periods of personal space and autonomy in working out the living arrangement and emotional expectations between herself, Scott, and Jeremy.

These kinds of issues do not differ in substance from the fabric of mutual expectations out of which an increasing number of marriages are sewn. But these women had in each case developed increased self-confidence after severe self-doubts stemming from childhood patterns of relationships, and heavily influenced by their first marriages. They had endured periods of depression during which they felt trapped in a devalued role, not only in their marriages but in their own eyes as well. Their new self-development was mirrored by a parallel care about providing their children with a positive self-image, and a particular sensitivity to the child's need for supporting love relationships so that, in the long run, he would develop autonomy. These mothers were able to derive some satisfaction from periods of "play" or undistracted focusing on the child's needs, and willingly built this into their daily routine whenever possible. In spite of the complicated demands on their energies, none of these mothers regretted having a child or considered it a liability.

The children in turn seemed to perceive this welcome and, in spite of some anxious bouts over irritability, exhaustion, or depression which colored aspects of their mothers' relationships to them, they seemed possessed of a basic self-confidence about achieving enjoyable contacts with the world. Each of these particular children seems to this point to have developed well. It is too early however, with Jeremy and Daniel in particular, to gauge their future expectations in triadic relationships. A little boy who "outlasts" other men in the household must use different ways of renouncing the idea that he comes first with his mother than does the child who becomes used to the ongoing relationship between his two parent figures.

These women differed from those women who try to solve their fears of being ensnared in a dependent or devalued role by averting all binding intimacies. The mothers discussed showed their enjoyment of intimacy both with their child and with their lovers or husbands but had learned to maintain those options which protected them from the depression and helplessness which they had experienced in their first marriages, and which they now felt had not done them justice as individuals.

In all the cases just referred to, and in the majority of others, the parent encouraged the child to maintain a relationship to the absent parent. On the whole it seemed that the greater the parent's own sense of well-being, the easier it was for that parent not to feel threatened by the child's coexisting attachment to the other parent. However, even in the best of circumstances there were a number of complicating issues apparent. For example, numbers of parents were aware of the quite different treatment of the child in the two households. Most often the home parent, who felt that he or she must carry the larger share of the discipline and guidance, expressed resentment, seeing the "overindulgent" weekend parent as ready to give the child everything and allowing him to do anything. They felt the absent parent would in this way reap an unfair share of the child's love and none of his anger. This was often underscored by the tension that tended to develop after the visit to the absent parent: in the young children hyperactivity, demandingness, temper tantrums, whining, or crying were standard behaviors that made the home parent feel rejected. Differences in life style and behavior toward the child were often unnegotiable between the separated parents, although the home parent tended to make efforts in that direction. When these efforts were ignored by the absent parent, as they often were, past resentment over having been ignored by that parent during the marriage often resurfaced in a way which clarified its earlier effects.

Often it was the child himself who, in the long run, ameliorated the home parents' sense of being cheated, by making clear in some way that he did not equate the absent parent's indulgence with love. For example, one child told his mother of the various presents he was given by his daddy and added rather sadly how daddy told him to go and play with his "new toys" repeatedly, because daddy seemed to be busy a lot in the study lately and didn't have much time to play with the child. The mother was then able to value the preciousness of her romp in the park with her child, in the absence of "new toys."

Other complicated issues arise for both parents viewing the child's integration of the values of two households. At times the parent sees the value system promulgated in the other household as antithetical to his or her own, and is concerned with the nature of the values the child will identify with in the long run. These range from issues of fastidious order in one household versus jumbled disorder in the other, to more abstract concerns over the preference for humanistic over materialistic values or differences in the intellectual or cultural atmosphere. How these children, as adults, will integrate such different value systems remains to be seen. There is no intrinsic reason to believe that the process will differ greatly from the inevitable apperception of different importance attached to values within the intact family. Actually, the existence of such differences, to some degree, between any set of two parents is one of the valuable aspects of growing up with two different adults, a practicing, in microcosm, of the integration of points of view to be met outside the home, in the broader social context through which the child will also continue his development. Most parents tried valiantly to differentiate these differences in values or childrearing practices from their own strong reactions to any "evidence" that the other parent was a bad influence on the child. For example, one mother who felt that the father was more "materialistic" than she, and showered the child with gifts, wished her child to grow up to be an unselfish rather than "possessive" person. This mother had a difficult time when her little girl underwent a period of healthy assertiveness, and absolutely refused to share her toys with others. The mother was particularly sensitive to the possible reactions of the other children's mothers, fearing that they would view her little girl's selfishness as a reflection of herself. Whenever the child would not share her favorite toy with a playmate the mother was tempted to deprive her of something. However, she was able to allow the little girl to decide for herself with whom she would share her favorite possessions, once she recognized the developmental meaning of this possessiveness for the child and had differentiated this behavior from the hated "materialism" of the father as well as from her own assumptions that her neighbors would disapprove—both these factors had rigidified her adult standards of altruism for the child.

In the area of values the most unfavorable results seemed to occur when the parent identified a particular behavior or characteristic of the child as "belonging" to the other parent's value system, and then attacked it in such a way that the child had no choice but to either defend it, develop a symptom around it, or attack it in himself, with associated self-devaluation. If the parent dealt more directly with the value or behavior exhibited by the child, explaining it as something that the present parent either did or did not like, approve, or forbid, the child tended to experience less conflict and was able to deal with the parent's attitude directly in return.

Almost all parents were initially ambivalent about the child's expressed longing for the other parent; they experienced this in part as a rejection of themselves and as an undermining of their own attempt to cope with the separation. There were, however, enormous differences in capacity and willingness to deal with this issue. Even when there was a very willing decision to separate, many parents at times missed or longed for their past spouses in a way which they saw as irrational. Sometimes they experienced this as "jealousy" of the child who was taken to the zoo or ice cream parlor, while their own needs for special attention from the ex-spouse had not been met during marriage. Most parents tended at first to reject awareness of such "jealousies" in themselves, and often handled the eruption of such old longings through contacts in which they expressed resentment over more "justifiable" complaints.

For many parents, contacts after the separation were dominated by bickering over finances and visiting hours, and criticisms about each other's way of life. In several cases minor incidents flared unexpectedly into physical violence, which was new to the couple. Other material suggests that the continued "fighting" was often a way of maintaining contact, often more desired by one partner than the other, an expression of the ambivalence about not being together anymore, in the absence of overt grief. These parents, just like their children, needed to come to terms with the cohabitation of old, unfulfilled wishes and hopeful fantasies which drove them toward continued contact, with the more conscious, irrefutable decision they had made to separate. The children seemed to understand this meaning in their recurrent fantasies of the parents' reunion, often adding quite promptly "but I know that they can't without fighting."

While dealing with the stresses of separation for themselves and the child, most parents had to deal simultaneously with other abrupt changes or adjustments. In about half the cases meeting the economic requirements of two households proved difficult. A number of mothers worked for the first time in order "to make ends meet," rather than because they wished to develop themselves in new ways. Many were realistically much overburdened by the combination of and care of house and children. Fathers who had moved out of their homes, in particular, tended to stress the barrenness of their new living quarters, as a visible sign of their feelings of deprivation. The house as a symbol of former security did not become a central issue for most of the parents reviewed in this chapter (although its continuity was important to many of the children), but became a hotbed of dispute for some of the more disturbed situations described in later chapters. In a number of those cases the fathers remained in the house while the mother or mother and children had to move in order to separate at all. For the children, moving out of their home, in addition to the divorce, was an added trauma.

In spite of the major adjustments around economic difficulties and the realistic overburdening of energies, numbers of parents found themselves emotionally more serene after the separation, and felt renewed energy and interest in their children. They expressed a realization, which did not come about until after the parting, of the amount of previous energy that had gone into the intense, mutual bitterness between the parents at a point where differences were clearly irreconcilable but they were still living together, and the restraining or inhibiting effect of having geared their lives to the schedule or values of a spouse from whom they were already emotionally alienated. Thus they expressed a new freedom and spontaneity in being able to plan their days around their own and their children's needs.

In several cases in which young children of both sexes remained with the mother as the home parent, the boy appeared more disturbed than the girl. In these cases the girl saw herself as "coping," in league with her mother, while the boy seemed more heavily identified as the extruded and deprived child. In one of these cases the parents themselves described how they had "neglected" the boy most in the intensity of their anger with each other. In another, the birth of the boy was seen as the welding force necessitating the marriage of two already ambivalent partners, and was blamed by both parents for this. In both of these cases the boy was the older child, seriously disturbed, in contrast to a mildly disturbed younger sister. In neither case was the bitterness between parents near resolution at the time the children were seen; and in each case the mother's disappointment with her husband for one reason or another was most heavily visited upon the son. In other cases in which there were two boys, or in which a mother had been particularly close to the eldest son, this pattern did not exist.

Encounters with Children and Parents

Some excerpts from encounters with children and their parents follow. In order to relate these experiences to some of the questions raised in previous chapters, they will be examined from particular vantage points:

1. *A reunion fantasy in the absence of actual loss: Jeremy.* The case of Jeremy illustrates the presence of fantasies about a biologic parent the child had never known, and hence has not lost as a real relationship. Although fantasies about his father had an important function for Jeremy, there was no grief invested in memories, and no conflict of loyalties in his ambivalence toward the new father figure in his life.

2. *Initial reactions to separation: Sean, Jenny, Daniel, Craig and Betsy.* Brief vignettes of children's reactions early in the separation will be reviewed, along with the children's attempts to cope with their reactions.

3. *Working through transient, disguised symptoms of grief: Mark.* A year of therapy with Mark, who maintained a stable contact with four parent figures, will be briefly summarized.

4. *Shifts in identification processes over a period of time: Noah.* Therapy material with Noah will be followed in some detail, beginning shortly after his parents separated and extending through his mother's remarriage and the birth of a new sibling.

5. *An early identity crisis: Jeffrey.* Jeffrey's situation provides an example of a child caught in incompatible identifications and attempting simultaneously to live out two separate selves.

6. *Grief unexplored: Pam.* Retrospective case material from work with Pam, an adopted child seen between ages thirteen and seventeen, will be used to illustrate defenses against grief by the time they have become an aspect of character structure. The need for modification of treatment techniques is illustrated.

7. *Some effects of multiple separation and severe deprivation: Lou Ann.* Material from the therapy of Lou Ann, treated between the ages of twelve and sixteen, will illustrate the kind of severe deprivation and multiple separations which make the terror of abandonment so overwhelming that the development of a firm sense of separate ego boundaries remains in limbo, as does reality testing. Therapy techniques needed to be adapted to her character structure, her intensity of need, and her family situation.

8. *Anxieties about trusting a new parent figure: Robin.* A child's fears about loss, resulting in concerted efforts to complicate the mother's remarriage are described.

9. *Comments on enrichment of identifications: Mark, Noah, Gwen, and Jeffrey.* Aspects of identifications enriched by the relationship to a supportive new parent figure, as well as components of the new, extended family will be discussed.

A REUNION FANTASY
IN THE ABSENCE OF ACTUAL LOSS: JEREMY

Jeremy was a bright, articulate, engaging little boy of two years, eleven months when I saw him. His mother first consulted me when he was two and a half and she expected that he would begin to ask questions about his father, whom he had never seen. Beth, Jeremy's mother, clearly cherished her little son.

Beth was a young woman who had maintained a relationship with a man which she had known would involve considerable inherent anguish and renunciation, in order to preserve those aspects which were intimately loving and precious to her. In spite of her bitterness and disappointment about the unfeeling manner in which Pierre had ended the relationship, she yearned for some sign from him that he was pleased about having this son.

Beth and Pierre had decided, for various reasons, against marriage. They had been sexually intimate for a number of years, although they did not live together. Nevertheless, Beth wanted to have a baby by him, not only because of her wish for a child, but clearly as a concrete expression of the feelings she perceived between them. Pierre ended the relationship abruptly in her third month of pregnancy, though she felt that they still loved each other in some way. When she tried to contact him again, he was adamant about not having anything further to do with Beth or with Jeremy. Beth's sense of aloneness around the time of Jeremy's birth was further intensified by the rejecting attitude of her own father, who would not visit her in the hospital. Eventually, she became aware that her willingness to endure so much aloofness from Pierre in return for the intermittent periods in which she felt loved contained collusive elements: she had expectations of disappointments, which she had repeatedly experienced from her father earlier in life. She was surprised and grateful that her mother and friends rallied around her during Jeremy's infancy.

For Beth, as for numbers of other mothers, the image of the absent, but once beloved father of the child remained as an undercurrent of whatever bitterness and disappointment she experienced. For example, in the first interview she could talk easily about her feelings of desertion and anger about having to go through the pregnancy, childbirth, making a living, and caring for her baby on her own, although she had never regretted having the child. Her own, unmet, need to depend on someone, about which she had always been gingerly, emerged in her comments about how tired she was of having people praise her for her remarkable "strength" and "courage" in bringing up Jeremy alone—as though they never recognized how difficult and overwhelming it was at times. I asked what the most difficult moments had been for her. At this her eyes filled with tears. She told me that the most painful time of all was when she had just given birth to Jeremy and was unable to "share the incredible joy" of the baby's birth with the man she still loved. While she was realistically and sensitively concerned with how to deal with Jeremy's never having seen his father, once his questions about this would begin, she continued to daydream about a meeting between the two, about showing the man the child they had created, and having him recognize this child with joy. Remnants of the daydream persisted, in the form of fantasies of arranging to have the two meet accidentally, or of calling Pierre on the phone; she did not, however, carry these out, and they in no way interfered with her later establishment of a new, mutually loving relationship. She knew that in "reality" her feelings for Pierre were over.

When Jeremy was about two, Beth had shown him pictures of his father, telling the child his first name. The child showed no obvious interest in the pictures at the time, but shortly afterwards Beth found him singing his father's name in lilting intonations over and over again. Unlike the children of divorce, who had actually known and continued some contact with both parents, this little boy did not seem to experience any initial conflicts of loyalties.

In spite of the usual struggle with exhaustion, occasional depression, and impatience, Jeremy and Beth continued to have a primarily tender relationship with each other. When Jeremy was two and a half, Beth met Scott, they came to care about one another, and Scott eventually moved in to live with them. Jeremy at first reacted very positively to the new attention both he and his mother were receiving from Scott.

However, after a couple of months he began to show, in graphic fashion, ambivalence about having to share his mother while gaining a father figure. One day, when Scott was coming home later than usual, he asked incessantly when Scott was coming home for dinner, running to the door in excited anticipation whenever footsteps sounded down the hall of the apartment building. Finally his mother asked him, "Is it that you want your dinner or that you want to see Scott?" Without hesitation he replied, "I want to see Scott!" When Scott walked in the door two minutes later, Jeremy ran up and hit Scott as hard as he could, then grasped his mother tightly, shouting, "No, no, she's mine, all mine!"

During this period he asked to see again the pictures of his "daddy" that he had been previously shown and to which he had seemed to pay no attention, but had sung his name, "Pierre." He began to ask Beth where their daddy was, and other questions about him. Beth had replied honestly, as best she could. It seemed very improbable that Pierre would ever function as a "daddy" to Jeremy—although that was the word which had been applied to the picture—while in effect Scott was becoming a reliable father figure. I suggested to Beth that in this situation Jeremy might at least want to refer to Scott as "daddy Scott" in contrast to "daddy Pierre" and that she talk with him about the various things that daddys like to do with their boys, things which Scott was currently doing with him. It seemed important to begin to counteract his feeling of being a fatherless boy (a feeling which still pained Beth) with the realities of the fathering he was actually receiving. For the child of divorcing parents, unlike for Jeremy, the suggestion that the new parent figure be called "daddy" is often counterindicated, and may be vehemently rejected by the child as a sign of disloyalty. Other children, especially if, like Jeremy, they have little or no contact with their biologic, absent parent, and need to feel themselves a member of an intact family again, may welcome it.

When Jeremy came to see me when he was nearly three, there were no overt signs of disturbance, and hence no explanation had been necessary, other than being told by his mother that he was now coming to talk and play with me. He separated from his mother without any difficulty.

t: "I'm glad you came. I've met your mommy before but I didn't know you."

Jeremy: "I'm Jeremy Michael Forest—can I see the toys?"

t: "Sure."

Clearly he had a ready sense of who he was. While he was looking at the puppets, one by one, I asked him about the people who lived with him.

Jeremy: "I have Beth and Scott with me."

He picked up a toy kitten, held and looked intently at it, calling it "kitty."

t: "Tell me about the kitty."

Jeremy: "She's happy."

t: "What's making her happy."

Jeremy: "Me!" He pointed to himself with a smile. Again he exuded the sense of knowing he was welcome in this world. He told me about having a kitty at home. She was happy if "I'm gladder to have it." I reminded him that he told me about having Scott and asked if he was gladder to have him or not.

Jeremy: "I'm gladder to have Scott there, not just mommy and me." He was rumaging through the puzzles and puppets, picked up a crocodile puppet, lifted it open-mouthed and stopped in mid-air.

Jeremy: "Where is the daddy?"

t: "You are wondering where the daddy is?" I meanwhile found and handed him the father puppet.

Jeremy: "My other daddy Pierre, he doesn't know us."

t: "How come?"

Jeremy: "Because he doesn't *want* to know me, he doesn't want to know us." Jeremy now picked up the "devil" puppet and said, "He is mad, I don't like him, so I put him back." He put him face down, back into the drawer.

t: "Then you won't see him when he's mad?"

Jeremy: "Yup."

t: "And you said your daddy Pierre doesn't want to see you?"

Jeremy: "But *I want* to see him—I have a picture of him."

t: "How does he look on that picture?"

Jeremy: "Like a big man."

He waited, motionless, not exploring any more of the play material at the moment. The last thing he had handled was the puppet he thought looked "mad." Had this issue led to a play disruption?

t: "Jeremy, can you tell me how things are when someone gets mad at your house?"

Jeremy: "When my mommy is mad she slaps me."

t: "And then what?"

Jeremy: "Then I slap her and she slaps too and Scott slaps me too." He now picked up two handfuls of assorted puppets and "slapped" one handful with the other.

t: "What makes them most mad, I mean when do they slap you?"

Jeremy: "When I do things naughty."

t: "Like what?"

Jeremy: "Like when I slap her."

t: "How do you feel, what do you think when there's slapping like that?"

Jeremy: "I don't like it anymore."

t: "Anything else?"

Jeremy: *"When I slapped Pierre and he doesn't want to see me anymore!"*

t: "Jeremy, I know you didn't *really* slap Pierre, because Pierre moved to a different house before you were born. Maybe you think you slapped him— you know why?"

Jeremy: "Why?"

t: "You told me this one [pointing to the "mad" puppet he had put face down in the drawer] looks mad, so you didn't want to see him anymore? Remember? Sometimes *you* get mad, everybody does—mommy and Scott too—and then there's slapping and you don't like it. You want to get away from it. Maybe you think Pierre wanted to get away like that—when you feel mad—like about his not coming to see you. But that's not why Pierre went away. Pierre had never learned to do daddy things, he didn't know how to be a real daddy to you. So before you were born, Pierre went away from mommy and you never hurt him any way at all. He was going away from mommy, he *wasn't* going away from you. He left a picture, so you can see what he looked like. Poor Pierre never had a chance to get to know you at all! If he did know you, I'm sure he would like you, even if you got mad at him sometimes. Do you wish that about him sometimes?"

Jeremy: "Yup, that he would come."

t: "And then?"

Jeremy: "And then when mommy slaps me, I wish I were big and she were little."

t: "What would you do then?"

Jeremy: "If I were big and mommy and Scott were little I would put them to bed."

t: "Can you show me with the puppets?"

Jeremy put man and woman puppets lying close to each other on the chair. "I would put them in the same bed, Beth and Scott."

t: "Is that how they sleep now?"

Jeremy: "Yes—and then I would put me to bed in my bed." His interest in being "big" seems so far not associated with displacing Scott in any way, but rather with having better control of his current living situation by dispelling anger (it was his reaction to being slapped) and securing the stability of his mother's relationship with Scott. He reverted to both of their first names again in describing this, somehow allowing her an additional identity in relation to Scott, in addition to being his "mommy."

Jeremy continued talking as he arranged the boy puppet in "bed" in another chair. "Maybe I'll grow up and be a daddy or a doctor—a daddy first and then a doctor."

t: "A daddy is what you want to be first—and then—you *could* maybe do both at the same time."

Jeremy: "Oh no, I couldn't do that!"

He picked up the father and the baby boy puppet again and propelled the baby toward the father.

Jeremy: "He eats the daddy and then he has the daddy inside him—and that's why he ate him."

t: "So that the daddy can't go away from him, he thinks he has to eat him to keep him?"

Jeremy: "Yup." He giggled and played at eating the daddy puppet some more. I was not sure which "daddy" he was talking about.

t: "Scott likes being a daddy with you and you won't have to try to *make* him stay a daddy."

Jeremy: "My daddy and mommy are Scott and Beth, Scott is just like a daddy."

t: "I think you like having them—the way it is now—except the part about getting mad sometimes bothers you. Maybe you have been wanting to see your first daddy Pierre to see if he likes you too?"

Jeremy: "And he would want me to live with him?"

t: "Is that what you wish?"

Jeremy: "I will live with mommy and Scott."

t: "That's right. Daddy Pierre is *not* coming to live with you, he doesn't know how to do daddy things with you. Mommy and daddy Scott both want you to live with them together. Mommy will live with you until you are big, like a big man. She told me that. Should we invite your mommy into the room and tell her what you've been thinking about your daddy Pierre, so she'll know when you want to ask her more things?"

Jeremy: "Okay—what does invite mean?"

t: "Invite means to say 'come in.'"

We proceed to do so.

t: "Jeremy, do you want to tell mommy what we talked and played about?"

Jeremy: "Yes." He showed her the puzzles he did, the toy kitty and the puppets. He told her, "If Pierre came back he would like you and Scott and me and we could all live together!"

t: "We know that that's what Jeremy sometimes wished, but we know too that Pierre is *not* coming back. Poor Pierre is missing out on a lot of fun, because if he had had the chance to know Jeremy, I think he would have liked him very much."

Jeremy: "Mommy, first I want to be a daddy and then a doctor and then I want to be a mommy. And when I grow up I want to take care of you and Scott and put you to bed." He handed the man puppet to his mother, and holding the boy, played at having the man and boy hugging each other.

Jeremy's problems differ from those of other children discussed in this chapter, in that his absent father has never known him, and will probably continue to reject his existence. Jeremy's longing for him is in fantasy only, and contains no affect-laden memories of shared experience. Nevertheless, Jeremy must come to terms with the reason the father has deserted them and free himself of the sense of failure. He knows from a picture that father looks like a "big man," like Jeremy wants to be when he grows up.

At age two, the little boy seems to catch the intensity of his mother's feeling toward the picture of "daddy" who is called "Pierre." His lilting repetition of the name is used, almost like a momentary transitional phenomenon, shared first with the mother and then perpetuated by him, as something to be treasured. We do not know what his concept of a "daddy" was at the time, though he had had experience with affectionate adults, both men and women, and must have heard children calling their fathers "daddy." When Scott first entered the family, Jeremy first reacted with positive feeling, and then became ambivalent—reversing the sequence of reactions toward a new parent figure by the majority of the young children who have lost a parent through divorce. His ambivalence to Scott seems normal for any little boy, especially as it involves having to share his mother so steadily for the first time. All in all, the ambivalence is at present well offset by the growing affection between Scott and Jeremy.

In the interview, two fantasies about the absent father emerged:

1. That Jeremy slapped Pierre and he therefore left home because he didn't want to see him anymore, and

2. That Jeremy and Pierre would be reunited, either by Jeremy's going to see him, by eating and thereby keeping him, or by Pierre's return to live with them all. The last alternative in this fantasy, though clarified as being untrue in the interview, was revived as soon as the mother returned to the scene and he recounted the situation to her.

Jeremy's first idea here (the slapping fantasy) belongs solidly within his stage of cognitive and emotional development. Thoughts are not as yet firmly delineated from deeds. Magic through gestures is still a component of cause and effect. The self is seen as central to making events happen. Jeremy explained the situation to himself by assimilating Pierre's leaving to what was most real in his current life. That is, he loves his mommy and Scott, but sometimes anger and slapping make them not feel like "seeing each other."

Avoidance or its opposite through visual contact (to see or not to see) is mentioned frequently by the younger children as an instant way of coping with the unpleasant. In older children and adults, more frequently denial or repression become the cognitive equivalents of "not seeing." However, the idea of seeing somebody again, as a sign of the continued existence of the relationship, simultaneously may have an infinite time perspective, consciously or unconsciously, for both young and old.

When Jeremy's reunion fantasy was countered by the news that Pierre had never known him, Jeremy first shifted to ideas about filling that void. He would grow up and be daddy and a doctor himself, able to cope with mommy and Scott. He then regressed to the idea of eating a daddy and having him inside to keep. Such playful eating and "keeping" of people who are not under one's control is common in the play of children of Jeremy's age. It is usually associated with ideas of first having, and then becoming what you eat.

Eventually, he appeared to settle down contentedly to the notion of having mommy and Scott as his parents, with the assurance that they wished to stay with him without his forcing them (by eating them) and that his mother did not plan to desert him. Moments later, in his mother's presence, he reversed this acceptance and once again brought up the wish for Pierre to return to live with them all. It is not clear how much the strength of this wish was affected by his earlier probable perception, prior to the advent of Scott, that his mother sometimes wished it too.

The transformations of Jeremy's image of his biologic father and their effect on his own future identifications are still in the future. It seemed important that he be helped to begin the process of viewing his father's departure not as a personal failure (he had slapped him away), but rather because of the current incapacity of the father to love the child. It was made clear that the father was missing "fun" by his inability to avail himself of the pleasure of knowing his son. As there is very little hope that this child will ever know his father, he must disengage sufficiently in his quest for the wanted parent to invest his loving energy in those who indeed will care for him. His clearly stated, and flexibly shifting (as is usual at his age) aspirations to be a "daddy, a doctor, and a mommy" suggest that he is open to those identifications he deems worthwhile; for instance, although he thinks he has "lost" a father, he does not identify this with the ability to be a father, but instead looks forward to growing up to be one. Some months later Scott and Beth were married.

SOME INITIAL REACTIONS TO SEPARATION:
SEAN, DANIEL, CRAIG AND BETSY

The reactions to be exemplified in these five children took place within a year of their father's departure from home. In all but Jenny's case, the mother had wanted the separation. Jenny's mother was conflicted about it, and later tried an unsuccessful reconciliation. Sean's and Daniel's mothers were living with men they cared about and the mothers of the other three had begun to date.

Sean

Sean, age four, was referred because he had lost his "sunny disposition." He now had frequent temper tantrums, cried much more than he had done, and clung to mother when she tried to leave him with the sitter he had previously liked, while she went to work as an architect. In addition, Sean repeatedly threatened to hurt himself and insisted, "I wish I were blind." His mother had let me know that she had separated from her husband about five months before and that he was still unhappy, while her own relationship with a friend, Al, had ripened into love. She told me that shortly before Sean's symptoms became acute, Sean's father "was having a tantrum in front of Sean when he saw me and Al together." Sean was prepared for his visit with me by being told that children come to talk and play with me about things that bother them.

When Sean met me, he clung to his mother, silently hiding his face in her coat and resisting her leaving the room. I commented that when children are worried here about their mommy's leaving, they sometimes like to keep something of mommy's with them while they play here and mommy waits in the waiting room. I assured him that she would not leave the waiting room, and that if he needed to, he could visit whenever he wanted. Although, in general, I prefer not to push toward separating mother and child in the therapy room before the child is ready, I find that especially when time is very limited, children with separation problems can often manage the anxiety about this during an interview when offered a comforting object, in the form of something belonging to their mother. They differ widely in what they choose. Sean's wishes about injury to himself made me feel that his problems would involve some kind of guilt, which would be more difficult to communicate in the presence of his mother; hence I tried to hasten the process.

Sean and his mother went back to the waiting room and a moment later he marched into the room by himself, wearing his mother's boots. He quite literally lived out the notion that if he were in his mother's shoes, she could, of course, not leave him. His free speech and movements were a contrast to moments before.

Sean: "My uncle is going to take the place of my daddy 'cause my daddy moved."

t: "Tell me about it."

Sean: "He went away—that's the only thing, my uncle is much better and my daddy is sort of good. My uncle takes me to the store where the ice cream popsicle and pushup things are. There's chocolate and 'nilla and my uncle lets me pick all by myself."

t: "You like to pick by yourself?"

Sean: "Yea. Daddy doesn't do it like that. In New York, it's sort of gicky now."

t: "Is that where daddy is?"

Sean: "Yea. My mommy's happy sometimes."

t: "How is it then?"

Sean: "She went and got a frisbee for my uncle and me and we all played with it." Sean then told of his father's unexpected visit one day when his mother and Uncle Al were in the bedroom. Daddy had screamed, "I don't like to see you and Al together," and there was a fight. Daddy cried. I asked Sean what bothered him most when he saw that. Sean thought he might get hurt too. I said, "Then you didn't want to see mommy and Al together either, you had liked it playing frisbee, but sometimes you hated it too." He said, "I wished I was blind." His fear of "getting hurt" had turned into the feeling that he *ought* to be hurt, that he was guilty of enjoying himself with his mother and Al, too, while father screamed and cried. However, another kind of impulse also led him to identify with the father in wishing *not* to see mommy and Al together. After he had said he wished he were blind, I asked him, "And then what would you wish?" He said, "When mommy gets mad sometimes . . . I want mommy to stay in her room all her life and then I could go and slip under the door, and she won't see me and I'll slip pancakes under the door and she wouldn't go to work. I really like her not to go to work, that's the only problem." He continued a fantasy of being able to slip under the door because then she couldn't see him then and he would be with her all the time. He showed me with puppets how he would do it, eyes closed. He had assumed that if he were blind he would be invisible too, and therefore could be with her even when she was "mad" and wanted to be without him, or with Al. I commented that his seeing everything that had happened at home, like daddy's leaving and being upset, and mommy's and Al's having fun together must have made him very scared that mommy might leave him too— especially when she's mad at him or he's upset with her. I let him know that mommy had told me that this would not happen, that she wants him to live with her until he is grown up, even if they sometimes get mad at each other and when she is at work; so he would not need to force her by keeping her in her room. Daddy's upset was not Sean's fault, nor mommy's either, so Sean needn't punish or hurt himself about it. Daddy felt unhappy now, he would have to find ways of being happier again, but that did not mean that Sean had to be unhappy too. Maybe Sean was unhappy about seeing Daddy like that too. He said thoughtfully, "Daddy didn't used to be gicky, not like in New York. When I went he cried and made me cry." Sean ended the topic by telling me about his babysitter's child, "my terrible friend who gets to scream at her mommy, but her mommy never gets too mad." He picked out a puppet and tried having her scream at her mommy.

Since this was the babysitter he has been reluctant to stay with lately, he might have been afraid of being tempted to be "terrible" too if she allowed it, but at the moment he seemed to be considering how aggression could be absorbed in the mother-child relationship without excessive guilt.

Sean's fantasy of being blind patently brings to mind the classical oedipal myth, in which Oedipus blinds himself once he sees that he has replaced his father in his intimacy with mother. Some writers have pointed out that the classical notion of the oedipus complex, revolving around the boy's guilt over wanting to replace the father in his sexual possession of the mother, leaves out the original transgression of the father who, in the myth, had rejected and abandoned his son as a potential rival. In Sean's case, the particular meaning of the blindness, however, included more immediately relevant components. If he did not "see" anything, he would not have to face his identification with the father as the excluded and injured party although he would in fact be the injured one in his blindness. (His own impulses toward his mother led him to fear that the same might also happen to him as a punishment.) Moreover, his own impulse to possess her totally would become invisible and unseen. This was a regression, since it would entail his giving up his visible self to blend into her existence, limited to the confines of her room—a sacrifice indeed for a little boy who has pleasure in mastery over frisbees and ice cream cones. He also appeared in guilty conflict over his actual, increasing attachment to Al, whom he had compared favorably to father, and who gave him the kind of ego support (e.g., the mastery of picking his own flavor of ice cream) important to a child who needs as much as possible to affect his sometimes unpredictable environment. Sean's symptoms abated after the single interview, with the help of his mother.

Sean's mother was an able and personable young woman, in the midst of evolving a fuller awareness of her own potential and of the emotional interchange with a new man friend. She had moved out of a marriage in which both partners had felt great difficulties in experiencing or sharing feelings.

Her new friend did indeed release a kind of happiness in her—well described by Sean in the form of a frisbee—in which she had not previously indulged. Although distressed by Sean's recent behavior, alternatively angry and clinging, she was delighted by many of his characteristics, and responsive to his needs. She easily understood his conflict of loyalties, and the idea that he was afraid of losing her as well. Since she was not a rigidly controlling person, she did not perceive his attempts to control her as entirely hostile, and hence was able to work out ways of continuing to reassure him about her living with him (even if she did need to leave daily), while giving him a maximum measure of control at times of necessary separation, e.g., in the form of preparing him verbally, letting him plan what toys to take along, etc. For the following one and a half years, she reported that he dealt better with times when he was leaving her, e.g., to go to kindergarten, than when he was the one left behind. He seemed to continue to have an intuitive understanding of what it felt like to want someone all to oneself. For example, when his father, whom he continued to visit at least every two weeks, had a steady woman friend, Sean became fond of her and announced that his daddy had been right to get mad at Sean one day because, "I was paying more attention to Mary than to Daddy." Sean has the choice of going with father or not and usually chooses to go, being affectionate with both father and Al. At age six he is described as outgoing, warmhearted, and sometimes "stubborn."

At times when mother comes to pick him up at the sitter's (and "terrible friend's") house, he asserts his independence, saying "What a dumb reason to come home, just because you're here." Since it is only a few houses from home, she allows him to stay longer at such times, and he likes coming home on his own. She seems able to accept such comments with a grain of salt, having experienced that a certain amount of verbal bravado bolsters his security enough so that when he does come home on his own, or has a choice of what he wears, etc., he is "full of his sunny disposition again."

In mother's life, the emotional commitment to Al has deepened, and she expresses feeling a happiness with him that is so surprising it frightens her. Particularly the free expression of feeling is new to her, though Al and she still have some difficulty about telling each other when they are angry with each other. Since the relationship to Al is "more than she ever expected" in her life, she is cautious about tempting emotional surrender.

Like a number of other young women described, she experiences a conflict between permanent commitment to the new, satisfying relationship, and her wish to establish, in her own mind, whether she could manage independently if she had to. Before feeling fully secure and satisfied with herself, she needs to test whether she could withstand losing, without feeling lost, and whether she could be as competent as her love partner. For example, she contemplates an offered summer job in a distant city, taking Sean but leaving Al for several months. She suspects that having passed that test she will feel ready to remarry.

Jenny

Jenny, also aged four, was seen because of episodes of sleepwalking and night terrors from which she could not be awakened. For over an hour at a time, she wandered the house, kicking the furniture, hurtling herself against the walls and crying out. Attempts to hold or console her were futile. The first such episode took place while the mother was out for the evening and Jenny was in the care of a new sitter. In the following two weeks, there were four similar episodes when mother was home.

Jenny's mother felt she had married to escape an intolerable home situation: she experienced her mother as cold and critical, her father as "very violent-tempered" and promiscuous. The man she married responded to the birth of their first baby, Jenny's older brother, by drinking heavily and having an affair. Mother became depressed and the little boy showed early and chronic signs of disturbance. Jenny, in contrast, had always seemed outgoing, friendly, and well adjusted. Eventually, mother gathered her courage to separate from the husband, who continually disappointed her in ways that echoed her childhood disappointments, and moved with the children to another city. It was not until then that Jenny became visibly upset.

Jenny stood quietly in the play therapy room, an astute look on her pert, inquisitive face as she surveyed the play material. I told her that her mother had come to talk with me because she thought that Jenny was having some scary times at night lately. Jenny said, "I always have scary nights. Some things mommy says not to tell anyone." I told her that it was okay with mommy even if she told secret things here, because it might have something to do with how scared she got, and I wanted to help her with that.

Jenny: "My babysitter doesn't know about me."

t: "Doesn't know what about you?"

Jenny: "That my mommy goes for overnights with her friend, sometimes she gets sick upset and wants to be away from us for a few overnights."

t: "What do you think makes her feel sick upset?"

Jenny: "Me and my brother—I mean my daddy."

t: "Tell me about him."

Jenny: "He used to like to kick all the furniture, and onced he hit mommy too and onced he did it again and again."

t: "And then what happened?"

Jenny: "My auntie, she got a divorcement and they kicked out all the children out of the house."

t: "Were you afraid that mommy might do that too?" She didn't answer. "Do you remember the scary night times?"

Jenny: "Onced mommy wasn't there and she never told me she was going and I kicked all the things away."

t: "Maybe you thought if you were the kicker, no one else could *kick you* out." She looks straight at me, sadly. "You said your daddy kicks things, can you show me what else you think about him?"

Jenny: "I don't think about him, mommy left him in Chicago."

t: "Are you afraid mommy doesn't want you to think about him? Here are some doll house people. Maybe you can show me about them." Jenny smiled and began to hum while arranging doll house furniture. She began to play with the doll family, naming each and calling the girl doll "Jenny." She then suddenly dropped the girl and called the baby doll "Jenny" instead. The father doll carried the Jenny doll tenderly, gave her a bottle and sang to her, while the mother doll walked around saying "What's wrong with the kids, they are acting up again," and planned to go "on a few overnights to get away from everybody."

As she continued to play, the tender wishes toward, or memories of, the absent father took lyrical shape, in contrast to her initial characterization of him, in word and deed, as the one who kicks and hits others. Although father had been described clearly as the one who kicks, the underlying anxiety about being thrown out or left out by her mother were evident. Sleepwalking did not recur. In a second interview, she reported that she hadn't gone to "kick things away" anymore, but was having "night dreams of monsters coming to get me by the throat." She added touchingly, "You see, I can handle little monsters, but not the big ones; the trouble is they run fast and I only run slow." In again recalling "fights of hitting mommy" before the separation, she demonstrated her experience of the difficulty of having to cope with witnessing aggression in people so much bigger than herself and yet perceiving herself as an inevitable participant, stimulatd to aggression too.

In her previous identification with the aggressor, while sleepwalking and kicking, she had countered the frightening handicaps of only "running slow" when in danger. The following week she had a daytime temper tantrum, following mother's refusal to play a game with her. Mother had put her in her room for forty-five minutes. When she emerged she seemed serene, but said directly to her mother, "When you get mad at me it scares me." She then asked if her daddy was ever coming back, and her mother discussed the situation with her as fully as she could, including a gentle assurance of her own love for Jenny and an open discussion of her own and daddy's "upsets" not being the fault of the children.

One of the referral questions which arose about Jenny had been whether her out-of-control night episodes, about which she was said to have complete amnesia, involved an organic component, such as would be the case with an epileptic seizure equivalent. This possible diagnosis was counterindicated by the nature of the fantasies which emerged, the fact that she did after all remember the content (rather than being amnesic about her episodes), and the rapid shift in symptomatology from the night kicking episodes to nightmares she remembered, and a daytime temper tantrum, followed by more direct communication with her mother about her fears of anger. She had identified with the father in the angry, kicking episodes which preceded the separation, and had also kept secret her longing for the tender moments of "baby Jenny" being held, sung to, and loved by her father.

With the outcome of their situation still highly unpredictable, Jenny's mother, brother Timmy, and Jenny were all ready to avail themselves of referrals for therapy, and did so. A follow-up call a year and a half later indicated that after an attempted, tumultuous reconciliation with the father had failed, the parents separated again. Mother meanwhile had been working well with her therapist, felt much less irritable and depressed and more able to cope with the separation, determined not to let it ruin her life. She began to go to college. Jenny reportedly was doing well, though she expressed distress and sadness about the father's departure. Timmy, who had been described as chronically disturbed, in contrast to Jenny's sudden acute symptoms at the time she was seen for evaluation, became seriously depressed, making suicidal-sounding comments, and was admitted to a residential treatment center for a time. A pattern of the raising and dashing of hopes seems particularly difficult for the child to bear.

Daniel

Daniel's mother, Carla, was a brilliant and forthright young woman in her late twenties, who came because she wanted to help her two-and-a-half-year-old son, as best she could, to deal with the separation from his father, and her own reinvolvement with another man. Her own realization of having felt unloved by her parents as a child had been a fairly recent and painful one, but she knew in the long run that it had contributed to her having risked leaving a "bad marriage" with the determination not to settle for less than a fulfilling life.

She had been brought up in a strict household, and had considered her mother's constant criticism of her as justified. A strong tendency to devalue herself remained. She had lived with Bob during college, but both sets of parents were so shocked that the couple decided to marry, in spite of some doubts about each other. When Carla became pregnant after six years of marriage, Bob suggested an abortion. She was repelled and hurt—she wanted the baby. For a long time she tried to talk herself out of feeling depressed after his birth, telling herself she had a beautiful house, handsome husband, beautiful child, and had no reason to feel so miserable. Bob's critical attitude and stereotyped image of her as a wife became clearer to her, for they contrasted sharply with the admiration of her colleagues, the positive response she evoked in other social relationships, and the nature of the professional promotions she was offered. As she put it, "It was always his career and my job." As she involved herself in more professional responsibilities, he finally said, "You either pick me or the job." She went away by herself for a month and then returned to choose her child and her career.

She described again feeling shocked, when in a discussion of the separation Bob suggested that the simplest solution for Daniel might be to have someone else adopt him. She felt that his insensitivity to the needs of the child mirrored his insensitivity to her. However, during the actual period of separation, Daniel's father cried a lot, appearing stunned by the turn of events, while Carla's depression lifted. At this point, father showed a new interest in Daniel, really playing with him in a new way and looking forward to having him on weekends.

After his father left home (when Daniel was a little over two), whenever male visitors came into the house, Daniel ran to sit in his father's chair and would not allow himself to be budged until they left. This sometimes went to the point of his falling asleep, still sitting in the chair. Only when Daddy came to visit was he willing to sit in his usual chair.

Within a few months he reacted to weekend visits to his father with increased signs of tension. Before the weekend he asked incessantly, "Is it Sunday now?" and cried with impatience when it was not. On Monday mornings after the visit he would ask, "Is today the day I see Daddy?" and usually cried for half an hour when told it was not. When he talked to his father over the phone during the week, he often told him, "Don't cry a lot!"

At this time, his father had explained to him, "Mommy and I don't love each other any more," and the question, "Do you love me?" became obsessive with Daniel. He habitually ran to the milkman and mailman, as well as up to complete strangers, in order to ask them, "Do you love me?" During these months, whenever any man approached mother, even simply to say hello to her, Daniel became tense. However, he told father at this time, "You have to be nice to Mommy." During this time he continued willingly to spend days with the babysitter, whom he had known since he was a year old.

After some months, he began to make tentative, friendly overtures to a man the mother was dating, and who later moved in with Carla and Daniel. Mother was careful not to overlook Daniel's needs in her new relationship with Martin. For example, she waited many months after the onset of intimacies before being ready to have Martin move in with them. By this time, Daniel was always glad to see Martin come, no longer clung to his father's chair, but tended to compete with Martin for mother's attention. When he was about three, he had a period of long night waking and was particularly insistent about trying to get into bed between mother and Martin. Carla was not only exhausted by this, but was aware of Martin's growing impatience with Daniel. At this time, when he visited his father, and a woman friend was there, he usually had a tantrum. In my discussion with Carla she was clear about realizing the importance for Daniel of dealing with his anxiety over loss of love. We discussed his night waking and wanting to come into her bed as an indication that he probably needed some secure extra time with mother. She readily decided to set aside such times with him, especially after work and before his bedtime, rather than allowing him to spent part of the night in her bed, which appeared to overstimulate him, exhausted her, and made Martin increasingly a rival of Daniel.

Daniel's relationship with Martin slowly improved, especially since Martin became more willing to do individual projects with him, spending some time alone with the little boy, uncontaminated with issues of rivalry for Carla's attention. As his affection for Martin increased, he now showed signs of anxiety about "being bad" in some way associated with visits to father. Carla was aware of the discrepancy between the kinds of expectations of discipline at "home" and Bob's laissez-faire attitude during weekend visits, and the child's apparent ability to adjust to these differences. The father was less depressed. One Monday, when it was not a day to see daddy, Daniel explained this as, "Maybe he doesn't want to see me in short pants." The issues of being "short" or "long," little boy or big man, were coming to a head for him. For a time he developed intense anxiety about urination, desperately wanting to go to the bathroom all the time. He repeatedly called out, "Mommy, mommy, it's coming," and rushed to the toilet to urinate a drop or two, only to repeat the performance a few minutes later. He had seen his father urinate "a lot of pee-pee." This anxiety about sensations in his penis, which are characteristic for his age, seemed linked to the notion of daddy's rejection of or anger at him and also to conflicts about being like the father (who pee-pees a lot and is big, while he, in contrast, has short pants or penis). Since he saw daddy as having been ousted and left crying like himself, but also as having "stopped loving" the person who ousted him, his conflict is fraught with considerable anxiety and guilt about the consequences of being manly and peeing freely. The distinction between being a little boy, who only makes a little pee-pee, and the father—a normal developmental crisis for a three-and-a-half-year-old—differs from the behavior of a year preceding, when Daniel acted as though he could be the father, sitting in father's chair and crying both before leaving the house and after returning, like daddy did. This particular anxiety seemed to occur at a time when he had also come to love the new parenting figure in his life. He must have assumed that the parents would reject him for sharing his love ("daddy doesn't want to see me"), much as he had previously felt angry and rivalrous with any intruder. However, the anxiety at this time remained focused on the issue of urination, while he was generally developing well, enjoying himself with children in nursery school and with mother and Martin and home. He seemed to feel secure enough so that one day when his father called to cancel, he answered with aplomb, "It's okay, I have two daddys now." He successfully inveigled Martin into spending the afternoon with him.

At the height of his anxiety about urination, he sounded like this (he had stayed overnight with his father and mother had picked him up a few minutes prior to the session):

Daniel: "I just came from daddy. He plays with me and watches TV and lives in a new house now." Picking up a dart gun, he told me, "I can never use one because it can go in your eyes. Mommy told me it would hurt me."

t: "It's okay to try here, because we'll keep it on a safe target, we won't let you get hurt . . . you can show me what you think with it."

Daniel: "I want to play the gun with mommy, but I can when I'm five and bigger."

t: "How will it be when you are bigger?"

Daniel: "I wanna make a boat." He picked out of a bag of wood pieces a big and a little boat bottom and cylinder shapes, long and short, but "the same amount of fat," while I got out the glue. His perception was correct, the pieces were of identical diameter. ("same amount of fat")

Daniel: "This is the up one, the up thing—it's tall and skinny and it can go up, with bullets in it, with gun powder. It'll shoot at everyone, it'll shoot the mean people."

t: "And then what?"

Daniel: "And then they'll shoot me. I want the puppets now. I hate the daddy puppet, I love the bear one and the crocodile. The bear will beat the policeman, the crocodile has the sharpest teeth." He put the crocodile on his hand. "I bited the mommy and she got all dead and nothing happens to me. Ha, ha, ha. Now I want to go hug my mommy." He went to the waiting room and returned after a hug.

t: "I bet you wanted to make sure she was still there to hug you after you played at biting her. You wanted to make sure that nothing would happen to you too, after you thought about hating the daddy puppet and getting shot back. Thinking and playing things like that, about biting and shooting can't really make it happen. Maybe you can show me what worries you about the up thing and what it might do."

Daniel: "I want to glue it on." He used glue to secure smoke stacks to two boats. "This is a pipe for water and smoke to come out."

t: "Water comes out too? A lot or just a little bit?"

Daniel: "A lot of water comes out. The big one has the big pipe, but both boats are very fast. Water comes out fast too."

t: "Does the little one want to be the fastest sometimes?"

Daniel: "It always does."

t: "And you?"

Daniel: "I'd love to be a giant, I would beat people up. I would beat up everyone except my friend giants. If I shooted one he would get alive again."

t: "And then what?"

Daniel: "There would be no more school, except only for my giant friends." He now took the little pipe off the little boat, which hadn't yet dried, and instead put on a "big pipe." "If the glue comes off it will break—or if the big boat bumps it hard."

t: "It's a good strong boat, and the pipe doesn't have to break at all, and your pee-pee won't break either, even when you touch it and when you want it to be big. You told me about wanting to have your friend giants with you, but getting rid of mean people, remember?"

Daniel nodded, while we were still busy meanwhile securing the pipes to the boats with rubber bands while the glue dried.

t: "I think it must have been hard for you to know sometimes who would be your friend giant and who might get mean. Like Martin used to get mad at you, and now he is like your friend giant most of the time and you have fun together."

Daniel: "He runs with me and I don't get in that bed anymore."

t: "And your daddy?"

Daniel: "He cried with me, now he doesn't cry anymore and I just crieded once more."

He was very clear about the past issues he is trying to put behind him now—the wish to share mother's and Martin's bed, which had made Martin angry, and his and father's crying—a memory belonging to when he was "little" and father was separating from them. He had earlier told his father "Don't cry a lot." He and I discussed times when he wished the men away, when people were upset and "mean" at home, so in his mind he wanted to be big and shoot them away. But it wasn't Daniel who made anyone go away. Someday he would be big as a man, but that would take a while. Right now, he was a boy. He could make all the pee-pee he wanted without ever hurting anyone, because it never hurt people for him to make it.

When after his session he went to the waiting room he "raced" the two boats for his mother and I told her how important it was for Daniel to be sure about the "pipe" not breaking on the little boat, even when it wanted to go fast. The anxiety about urination disappeared after that day, but the following months he was still mildly concerned about getting his hands "sticky." Though this concern occurs mildly among a fair proportion of nursery-school-aged children, it may have been more directly related to "touching" for him.

Reassurances about the continued role of the "giant friends" in his life could not be given, since Carla and Martin had not as yet made a permanent decision about whether to marry or separate. Carla felt that Martin's own losses earlier in his life still made emotional commitment a difficult enough issue between them so that they could not foreclose the likelihood of separating.

Several months later, Carla and Martin separated, each feeling that it was the right decision for them. They saw each other still in a fond fashion. Martin also visited to play with Daniel. Carla and Daniel were about to move to another part of the country where Carla had accepted a responsible professional position. Daniel appeared both subdued and restless in his interview. The restless quality conveyed a "searching" for people left behind. He played with the toy airplane, saying, "I will fly to California, but there is nothing there, I will fly to Mexico but there is nothing there." In reality, it had been arranged that he would fly back to visit his father. I asked how he felt about going to live in New York, without daddy or Martin being there. He answered simply, "I'm sad about Martin and about daddy—daddy more. All my toys will come and I will put them in a box and they will be there."

t: "What else would you like to take along?"

Daniel: "You, I wish I would put you in the suitcase, in the box." He smiles a little, knowing it won't be so. "Can I visit you when I come to see my daddy?"

t: "I don't know if you can, if daddy would bring you. But it would be fine with me if he could. I do know missing people feels sad. What else do you think about it?"

Daniel lay down in a soft chair, curling up on the cushion, as though wanting to be held for comfort. I sit on the floor, close to the chair. He discussed if daddy or Martin would forget him if he forgot them.

Daniel: "Somebody on the Electric Company [a TV program for children] was singing."

t: "Singing what?"

Daniel: "Oh Spider man—where are you coming from? Nobody knows who you are."

t: "Does that song make you think of anyone?

Daniel told me that he thought mother would forget daddy and Martin, but that Daniel would not. He stated that he wished that mommy and Martin had gotten married. Asked what he thought of when he wanted to remember them, he told me of a "scary thing" he saw in the night last night, but "I still didn't cry."

Daniel: "There was a man and some children and he said, 'Go to sleep and I'll kill you!' The man had a brown shirt and yellow hair."

t: "Who has a brown shirt and yellow hair?"

Daniel: "I do, but that man was bigger." He added, "If they were doing it on purpose, I would still want to go with them—even when they forget me." We tried to untangle what he means.

It turned out that being told to go to sleep was like being forgotten and left behind for him, and the idea of killing came up in association to Martin "doing that on purpose" to him. Again we needed to review the separation of Martin from mother, not Daniel. He feared retribution by Martin, whom he once wanted to replace, when he wouldn't go to sleep while mommy and Martin were in bed together. Now Martin will indeed be gone, and Daniel realizes that he will miss him and still wants to be with him. I try to make clear to him, as well as to Carla, that Daniel and daddy and Daniel and Martin don't have to forget about each other, even if mommy feels like doing that herself.

Daniel has lost two important fathering people and is valiantly trying to integrate, rather than to deny or belittle their meaning to him. The combination of his mother's forthrightness with her sensitive caring about him I expect will make her able to carry this through, even though she needs to leave her own past attachment to them behind.

Initially, Daniel's identification with his father was expressed on an affecto-motor level. He placed himself in father's chair, and shared his tearfulness. Although it is not clear how much the crying expressed his own distress or was also an identification with the father's, he was aware enough of his father's need for comfort to tell him on the phone, "Don't cry a lot." Mother was able to be supportive of him and consistently respected his wish for contact with the father, even though she felt "put upon" by what she felt was the father's laxness in setting limits. Daniel's crying expressed grieving rather than mourning. It was intensified before and after visits to father, times when he had just had or expected contact with him.

His relationship to Martin was difficult at first. Martin was not initially able to focus emotionally on the little boy and often resented his presence. Rivalry from both sides was prominent and Daniel tried to interrupt the relationship by his mid-bedmanship. Such attempts are usual for little children, but because of the circumstances aroused more than the usual amount of anxiety (i.e., his later dream of "Go to sleep and I'll kill you"). Slowly, the relationship with Martin improved and by the time Carla and Martin separated, the man and child liked each other a lot.

Nearing age four, and at the height of awareness of genital sensations and excitement, he developed anxiety about his penis, and felt constantly that he must urinate, but could not. In his play about smoke stacks, guns, crocodiles and water pipes, he confused fantasies about penile sensations with the squirting of water, biting, and killing. He wanted his penis to be big and make water fast, but he did not want to have it broken in retribution. He pictured that if he were a giant he would shoot everyone except his friend giants. His mixed experience with the two men in his life, who have been alternately loving, rivalrous, and rejecting of him (father in his infancy and babyhood) made it more difficult for him to define whether they were friend or foe.

However, when a separation between mother and Martin was definite, he was openly "sad" about missing daddy and Martin, although he was assured that he will visit by airplane. He was generally attuned to, and tolerated his sense of loss in this session, expressing the yearning through a restless searching (by toy airplane) and "not finding," asking to take me along in his suitcase, curling up in the chair for comfort. His nightmare of being told to "Go to sleep and I'll kill you" was probably connected to the ambivalence about Martin. However, he indicated that he identified with this figure too, since Daniel was the one who had the brown shirt and yellow hair, like the man in the dream. Eventually, he worked out something important to him, that perhaps indeed mother will want to forget daddy and Martin, but that does not mean Daniel will have to, also. The role of a beloved man in Carla's and Daniel's lives continues to be crucial for each, but in different ways.

Craig and Betsy

Let us look at the reactions of two children, Craig and Betsy, to the separation of their parents, at a time when the future is still highly unsettled for them.

Robert and Sally, the parents, both of strict Catholic background, had married very young after knowing each other briefly. For both, it was the first venture into a love relationship, and in retrospect both felt that they had been too immature and knew little of what to expect from each other as marriage partners or parents of children. The marriage became full of constant, resentful bickering, and with the birth of Craig this increased. Robert, then a graduate student, came to question many of his former religious beliefs and was drawn to experimenting with a variety of philosophies of living. He was preoccupied with issues of his personal growth, felt alienated from his wife, and regularly greeted her with a barrage of criticism about details of her housekeeping, mending, and care of the children. Although consciously he was trying to free himself from the "strictness" by which he felt confined in childhood, he seemed unaware of the punitive nature of the perfectionist and critical standards he imposed on his wife, and later, when she was managing a job as well as the household, seemed impervious to how overwhelming her daily tasks were for her.

Sally experienced her husband as stingy, angry, and uninterested in her needs. When Craig was six and Betsy four, she became "very, very" depressed; she left home to visit friends for a couple of months, and then returned, suggesting a separation. For a time, Robert moved his bed to a different part of the house, and then moved out, but saw the children regularly. When I saw Craig and Betsy about a year later, the divorce was still unsettled. Sally was working; had made a continuing relationship with one or two men; was doing her best to manage the household and children but still was often feeling overwhelmed. However, she also felt she was coping with things on her own for the first time in her life, and this gave her new pleasure and self-confidence.

Robert was meanwhile trying to work out his relationships to women, and beginning to do some soul-searching about the repetitive difficulties he encountered. He continued to make a point of never disappointing the children in the promised regular visits, especially since he felt Craig in particular had been ignored a great deal by both parents between the ages of two and five. This was when Betsy was born, when Robert had become increasingly engrossed in his own pursuits and critical of Sally, and the parents began to face the problems between them more directly. However, he had not felt welcome in the household since Sally had begun to spend time with another man.

Eight-year-old Craig was brought for an evaluation because his school became concerned over the degree to which he daydreamed in class, was inattentive, did not complete work, and was a "loner" in relation to other children. Father added that he seemed to want to get himself punished; mother reported "strange" behavior, like his standing out in the rain for an hour, not responding to being called in. He was encrusted with mud by the time he came home; this was shortly after father had moved out of the house.

Craig was a handsome, sad-faced little boy who sat more quietly in his chair than most eight-year-olds would, without attempts to explore the play material in the room. When asked about himself and his family, Craig first described his sister as someone who "doesn't let me in her room—like when I play with her—she doesn't let me in her room and I have to wait outside."

He said that his mother and father were fighting all the time. Then mother went away and after a while she came back and explained that Daddy was going to live in Nahant "but still take me places." I asked what he thought the fights were about and he said, "That my mother didn't have a job and so she asked him for money and then he would get mad." I asked if he thought that she needed the money, and he said: "Yes, she had to ask him to get some food or there would be no food."

Currently, parents are living apart and father has continued to take him places, which he likes. Mother is sometimes nice, like when she bakes cookies, and other times gets mad at him and yells. When her boyfriend comes she wants him to be very good because if the boyfriend gets tired of having kids around he will leave. However, his sister won't let him in at the time and if he could wish for one thing being different at home it would be that his sister would let him in and play with him more.

When I asked if he felt sad and lonely about the things he'd been telling me, he said, "Yes, most of the time." I asked what he thought about then and he indicated that he liked to think about stories and plays, in fact at school he often didn't listen and was making up things instead, and sometimes that made him feel better. He often started his daydreams by watching a play on TV and thinking about changing it day after day. I asked what kind of stuff he daydreams about and he said, "If I were a magician I would stick the knife in the rock and only the real king could pull it out. There is a slave boy who has to carry heavy water and if he does something wrong he gets whipped. Then one day he goes and can pull the knife out and then when he is king the richer people who were his masters—he gets even richer than them and then he becomes king." When asked about the characters in the story, he described the chores he himself had to do around the house and said he had daydreams then, too. He then made up a play with the puppets, using the witch and the devil whispering to each other to steal something. "Then they hire a pet alligator to scare everybody in the house, including the baby's teddy bear, until they get all the money and rush out till the policeman gets them. Then they go to jail and get out in two years. They don't try to leave because they knew they would get caught again."

On a sentence completion test, Craig was overwhelmingly concerned about the issue of food and being hungry. Out of a total of 30 sentences, 20 dealt with food or hunger for him. Examples are, "He looked for—food"; "He most disliked—being hungry"; "When he was sad he—was hungry"; "He wants to become—someone with bits of food." When I asked about his feeling hungry he indicated that he is always hungry in school, that he only has a little toast for breakfast and sometimes is so late getting up in the morning and mother tells him he has to go without it. (I later spoke directly with the mother advising other methods than withholding food to motivate him to get up in the morning; e.g., spending a few morning moments with him herself, to support him with the relationship while he bridged the chasm from sleep to facing another day.) As he clearly indicated, the meaning of his preoccupation with such basic supplies as food and money was complicated by his perception of father's anger at the mother's need for money to buy the family food and other basic supplies. He indicated also that thinking of food, like daydreaming, had the function for him of covering his wish for emotional contact (not to be "shut out," as he put it) and dealing with feelings of anger and frustration (e.g., "When the boss was unfair he—got even hungrier," etc.).

He mentioned as the good things in his life three friends who sometimes play football with him; a lot of the time, though, he does not feel like seeing them. He commented about his father, "He always used to take us some place but he still does now."

Craig was a youngster with a clearly depressive reaction to family stresses he has experienced. He saw himself as adding to the burden of his parents, who were having their own struggles with each other in such a way as to leave him with a limited sense of basic emotional support. Though consciously aware of his sense of sadness, expressed also in his face, he also handled his anxiety by a regression to a preoccupation about food and a feeling of eternal hunger. At the same time, he preserved hope in the form of such daydreams as he recounted in which the "slave boy," who was unappreciated in spite of all the chores he did, became magically strong, rich, and kingly. In general, he denied anger and seemed to expect punishment for more assertive behavior. However, he appeared open and eager for supportive relationships.

Clearly the parents needed some help in meeting their own basic needs sufficiently so that being supportive to this youngster would not be so difficult for them. In addition, the boy needed some therapeutic help with the depression as well as with his self-punitive perception of his own role in the parents' difficulties.

Craig's sister, Betsy, was a beautiful six-year-old with facial features similar to her brother but without the sadness which characterized his face. She readily accepted the explanation that children come to talk and play here about whatever bothers or worries them. She first talked about her brother. "He fights me, pulls my hair, and jumps on me. He likes to lock me up in the sleeping bag. When I get in he holds the top shut so I can't get out." I asked what that was about and she said, "I think he wants to kill me because he doesn't like me because sometimes I want to play with my friends and I guess he plays with me sometimes too."

When she goes to school, she said, he runs ahead of her, staying in her way, and doesn't want her to go ahead or talk to a friend. Sometimes she runs behind a car to sneak away from him. Asked what she does about that, she said that she tells her mother and every time he does something bad he has to go to bed right after supper. Once he took his hat and left it in the rain so it would get all wet and he had to get to bed early over that. She sounded quite satisfied about Craig being in the position of the culprit.

When I asked about her mother and father, she said, "My mother and father fight." Asked what it was about, she said, "When it's breakfast time sometimes no food was ready and whenever Daddy came back home from work no supper was ready and he would yell about not having any food ready and so they kept fighting." She indicated her father moved away because the food was never ready. Asked what she thought about that, she said, "Well he could have moved down in the cellar and made his own breakfast. My mother is so busy that she doesn't wake up sometimes so I make my own breakfast a lot of times. Sometimes I have to or there isn't any lunch ready." She stated that she was not given any explanation about his moving. We discussed the reality of the situation in some detail and she indicated that she wished sometimes mommy and daddy were living together again, if they knew how not to fight each other. She indicated that mother had had two boyfriends; sometimes they were nice to the kids, playing games or on her birthday taking her to a restaurant. When the boyfriend was over, mother let the children do things they couldn't do other times, because she didn't notice much. I asked what kind of things and she answered, "Like letting us play outside in the rain without our rain hats or anything on."

"Daddy used to come regularly when he was in his first apartment, but since he moved he comes about twice in a while," which meant to her that often she did not know whether he was coming or not. She knew when mother would be home, because mother was working in the department store and she knew she wouldn't be home till after that. Meanwhile, they were taken care of by a lady named Mary, who is sometimes nice and sometimes yells at them, "Go out, go out, it's a nice day." Betsy mimicked her very adeptly and giggled. I complimented her ability to show me how Mary sounds. We talked of how Betsy sometimes tries to keep people from hurting her feelings by making fun of them. She confides that she makes fun of Craig, and sometimes Daddy, but she did not tell them, and "feels sorry" when she did it about Daddy.

In a sentence completion test and in general, her responses were much less depressed, constricted, or food-preoccupied than those of her brother. Although there was concern about maintaining good relations with her mother, again she showed less frustration of dependency needs than Craig's test did. Related to these issues with her mother are sentences like, "Women should—be nice to their children"; "She is—a good girl—she helps her mother"; "She becomes very angry when—she doesn't do what she is told— her girl doesn't"; "She most dislikes—when she gets mad (who?) mother gets mad"; "When she didn't know how to get out of a difficult situation she— called up her mother." At the same time, she states "She most admired—her father was nice and good."

Material on a less conscious level emerged in the puppet play she then put on. The grandmother puppet was strangling the witch because the witch wanted to kill her. The grandmother just whispered in her ear and was only faking because she really planned to strangle her. After this, the grandmother turned into the nurse and offered the witch a cup of tea so that the aggression between the two female figures was followed by the shift to nurturing. At this point, Betsy helped herself to the candy available to her in a bowl, says, "Oh, I just love this kind." At the end of the hour, she indicated her play was not finished, and wanted to come back. She asked if the candy would be gone, if other children ate it or if there would be some next time. I assured her there would be some here.

Although many similar themes emerged with Betsy as with brother Craig (the parents fighting over the issue of basic supplies, symbolized by food; the attempt not to provoke the mother's anger as a way of insuring some stability, the issues about being told to go outside when a parent figure is engrossed in her own needs, etc.), on the whole, Betsy presents many fewer initial signs of guilt, depression, and withdrawal. She seems to see herself as more satisfactory to the mother than Craig and though she is aware of considerable strain in herself, seems to be coping rather well at the moment.

There are features that both children share, but their image of themselves and their roles within the family are different. Both children wish that their parents were living together, but "happy," not "fighting." Both children are aware of the anger in their parents and its vague relationship to immaturity, that is, the frustration of dependency needs directed toward each other. Craig puts it in terms of fighting over money, which the family, however, needed for food. Betsy describes it in relation to the food itself, which was not "ready" for father. Craig presents himself as eternally hungry and thinking about food; while Betsy proposes that father could have cooked his own food, a solution she has adopted herself to cope with her own and the family's needs.

Craig draws a picture of family members, but all are looking in different directions; Betsy draws the same family, calls it "When we were still a family," but makes herself bigger in the picture than her mother and her older brother Craig.

Craig's ambition over the past four years has been to become a chef when he grows up. In reality, all four members of the family feel they are not being taken care of as they wish—that is, that a source of nurture is acutely missing.

A piece of the drama between the parents seems to be being lived out between the two children. Craig's most consciously bitter complaint is about his sister's shutting him out of her room and at times turning to other friends. He actively tries to do something about this, "locking" her in her sleeping bag, blocking her from running ahead of him to school, getting up in the middle of the night to play with her friend. While Betsy at first complained that he does these things because "he doesn't like me," by the second interview she was quite clear that it was because "I don't like him, and that's why he wants to kill me sometimes." She added with satisfaction that every time he did something bad he had to go to bed right after supper, leaving her mother and herself together. Or, if he did something really bad like "squirting us with his watering can in our bed or drawers, he won't be able to watch TV for a month or year." In spite of getting himself identified as the culprit, it is easier for Craig to cope actively with his exclusion by Betsy, toward whom his deepest dependency is not directed, and who does not, after all, have the power to shut him out forever. In relationship to his parents and at school, he lives out a different aspect of his identifications. Let us look both at his behavior and his fantasies.

Father is currently "absent" most of the time, and no longer feels "welcome" in the house. In school, Craig is described as literally having an "absent" stare and excluding himself from interaction with others. At home, he lives this out more graphically by standing outside the house in the rain and mud as though he does not belong inside, not allowing himself to respond to calls. He confirms this by throwing out into the rain a hat he likes until it is ruined, knowing that directly he will be punished. This piece of his behavior gains significance from Betsy's description of times when her mother is preoccupied with her man friend, so that she does not notice, or lets the children do things they aren't ordinarily allowed, e.g., "to go out in the rain without a rainhat or anything." Going out in the rain becomes a way of making clear the feeling of exclusion by the mother (which he shares with father), while she turns to someone else. When this is not sanctioned by her, however, it also makes him a target of her anger. Although he does not directly express anger to her, Craig frequently frustrates the mother, because he will not cooperate in household tasks (again like father), even when this is at the expense of not getting what he wants most, e.g., dressing so slowly that he does not get breakfast. Meanwhile, he feels, "sad, lonely and hungry" much of the time. His terror, about being unwanted, is reinforced when he is told to stop making a nuisance of himself when the mother's man friend is visiting, or the man will not like "them" (mother and children) and unhappy consequences will follow.

Now to look at the fantasies with which Craig consoles himself: he describes a slave boy who has to do all the chores and gets whipped when he does something wrong. However, he secretly harbors the magic strength to pull out a knife, which proves he is really a king, in the long run richer than his masters. He relates the idea of the "slave boy" to the chores around the house, the chores he shares with mother. He sees his father as the punitive critic about chores, though mother makes him carry them out. "Slaving" over housework is an image his mother has suffered from, and from which she wishes to free herself. She too has been denied money by the "stingy" father (king) and treated like a slave, and she talks of taking matters into her own hands now, no longer letting her former husband lord it over her. She now has a job, earns her own money. In fantasy, Craig both identifies with and extrudes her past role, by being the slave boy about to become king. In a similar fantasy of obtaining what is needed, he uses a witch and devil puppet until they have learned their deed will inevitably be punished.

Behaviorally, then, Craig lives out some of his identification with the father as "absent," unwanted, extruded from the house, and as unable to please the mother who, he feels, has turned her attentions elsewhere. In miniature, he replicates this with Betsy, with whom he dares more actively to try to capture and express his masculinity, e.g., by squirting in her bed and drawers. At the same time, he sees himself "used" as an unappreciated slave (as mother saw herself by father) and harbors secret fantasies of revenge by taking over the "king's" riches. He does not risk expressing his feelings openly to either parent, or to his teachers at school, but instead withdraws from his impossible plight to sadness and a sense of resignation. We don't know exactly why he sees so little hope of altering his situation in relation to his parents, but have a clue in the father's comments that Craig, who represented to them tangible evidence that the marriage both parents regretted could not easily be dissolved, had been mostly ignored between the ages of two and five, after the birth of Betsy. These are the years during which the child's sense of autonomy normally develops and needs to be supported by active feedback: he must know that the ways he tries to grow like his parents by copying them, as well as to master manageable doses of his environment on his own, are good. Craig's parents, during these years, were bitter toward each other and his presence did not help; this is what he shows us he learned. We see in him not only a clinging to negative aspects of each parent's view of the other, but also the risk that the development of his own assertiveness may involve further loss (if he is not nice, mother's boyfriend will not like him). The mother, having long been devalued by the father, could not help reject this likeness of him.

Although he shows us complicated perceptions of people's relationships to each other, we see in him a regression of the level of ego functioning and his own identification with others. As is common during a state of depression, he is desperately preoccupied with people as "need-fulfilling" or deserting, feeling bereft of the most basic sources of sustenance. Thus, as he made clear, he is eternally hungry.

Betsy has coped with the same parental difficulties in a somewhat different way. In the first interview particularly, she presents herself as the good and helpful child, occasionally Craig's victim, in contrast to Craig, who does naughty things. Although she, too, makes a reference to being unwanted (she describes her babysitter as sometimes nice and sometimes yelling "go out, go out, it's a nice day"), this feeling is much less prominent in her fantasies and behavior than for Craig. Betsy appears to handle her own dependency needs by being helpful enough to stay in her mother's good graces, and at times, reversing roles with her mother. Thus, she not only "fixes breakfast," like she says daddy ought to have done for himself, but when mother is not feeling good, she makes a sandwich for mother as well as for herself and Craig. She is aware of missing father when she states that he now only comes "twice in a while." However, she allows mother's boyfriends to be nice to her and likes their presence. Some insecurity about mother is clear in her statement, "My mother is so busy she doesn't wake up sometimes." Her deep need not to provoke the mother's anger is indicated by the sentence completion test, and her play with puppets. ("She is a good girl—she helps her mother"; "She most disliked when—she gets mad at mother"; "Women should—be nice to their children.")

In her puppet play a female figure was strangling the witch because the witch wanted to kill her. After this, the witch disappears and the female figure turns to the nurse and offers her a cup of tea. In a similar way, Betsy smooths over potential trouble at home between herself and mother by becoming the nurturing one.

In the two interviews she also changed the way she presented herself: the first time, she showed her charming, helpful self in a variety of ways, e.g., when the phone rang in my office she answered it so quickly and automatically that I did not have time to let her know that I take care of it. By the next interview, however, she allowed me to see her pleasure in planning to exclude Craig, or in seeing him punished, and her careful avoidance of putting herself in the same position. In a number of ways, she was able to see herself as satisfying to the mother. First of all, she identified with the mother's current attempts to cope with her previous depression, by developing her own resources and getting pleasure out of being able to cope with a difficult situation, which had previously left her helpless and feeling used. That is, Betsy also took matters into her hands, answered the phone and prepared food when it was needed. She mirrored her mother's anger toward dependent or demanding men, by excluding and devaluing her older brother, Craig, and making clear father could have cooked his own food. In addition, she directly met her mother's dependency needs by taking care of her. This was summarized in her picture of "when we were a family" in which she was bigger than mother or Craig. She described the picture in terms of making herself "grownup like a mother and big enough to beat up Craig." Though currently she is described as a social and happy little girl most of the time, she will probably have difficulty if, in her adolescence, her security in being acceptable remains tied into her need to mother her mother. She does not show the regression to the overwhelming importance of basic supplies, such as food, that preoccupies Craig, nor the withdrawal and inability to "take in" in the form of learning, but only a hint of the kind of disruptions of relationships that affect such ego functions as the development of a sense of time. In this area, she speaks like a younger child of father visiting "twice in a while" and brother being deprived of TV "for a month or a year." She relates the arbitrary sense of time to the unpredictable comings and goings of people. Like the young child's rhythm of the urgency and fulfillment of needs, which as they become more predictable form the underpinnings of a stable sense of passage of time once the child is cognitively ready for it, some of the events in Betsy's life are still defined by their inner rather than conventionally external measure of time. Yet, as evidenced by her picture, she plans for a future.

The differences in Craig's and Betsy's sense of their own worth reflect an unwitting dynamic in the parents' handling of the stress between them. Mother was aware that during Betsy's earliest years she had felt close to and protective of the little girl, whom she saw first as helpless and compliant, like herself, and then as an ally who could cope resourcefully enough to counter and disprove the criticisms of the man who had hurt and devalued her. Meanwhile, Craig, who was an active toddler during Betsy's infancy, not only added to the mess and chaos her husband was constantly complaining about, but also came to be seen as an intruder whose demands interrupted her relationships to a new group of friends she was attempting to make on her own. In both ways, he became a reminder of her husband's attitude toward her, and she often experienced an inexplicable harshness toward him. Both children seem to have taken in different aspects of her attitude toward herself and toward them, in their earliest identifications. Betsy saw herself as somebody who was basically worthwhile and cared about, and had resources to cope with stress when necessary; Craig saw himself as someone to be extruded, as unsuccessfully interrupting relationships he intruded upon (like his sister's and friends'). At the same time, he fantasized about being the unappreciated slave, the role which mother had compliantly but resentfully carried out in relation to father for some years. Like mother, he became "very depressed." On this was superimposed the dramatic identification with the father during the time of separation, both in regard to ungratified dependency needs ("father left because food was never ready"—Craig was always thinking of food), lack of welcome in the house (standing out in the rain) and guilt—by putting himself in the position of the culprit whom the females had gathered their strength to blame in order to regain their own self-esteem.

As yet, this family has not worked out ways of establishing secure continuity in their own lives, nor agreement about the care of the children, but their potential for this is better since they have learned to care about themselves and have become aware of the sensitive reactions of the children. Craig's increasing difficulty startled them into a recognition of the consequences of their style of discord; and they have committed themselves to attempting to work out their problems. Individual treatment, in addition, has been recommended for Craig. Craig and Betsy are well aware of the difficulties in the past and the parents' current efforts to do something about them; they have as yet either to reap the benefits or to be in a situation where they can enrich their past identifications through rewarding, additional parent figures.

WORKING THROUGH TRANSIENT
DISGUISED SYMPTOMS OF GRIEF: MARK

A summary of a year of treatment of four-year-old-Mark follows. Mark's parents separated in his second year of life, when children very generally use a comforting transitional object to help them cope with more transient separations. However, his attachment to his boom-booms (feces) was a complicated one, representing not only his attempts to reconstruct aspects of his relationship to the wanted father when he was not with him, but also embodying an area of difference in attitudes he sensed between his parents.

Mark at age four was referred for encopresis. His mother and his nursery-school teacher were also concerned because he seemed so babyish and clinging and unable to approach or play with other children. He spent much time at nursery school by himself, sucking his thumb. When he did make a bowel movement in his pants, at home or school, he usually became highly anxious, "jumping up and down, yelling and aggressive." At the time he was described as "disgusted with it—wants to make sure he doesn't get his finger in it." Yet he had steadfastly resisted depositing it in the toilet. When I saw Mark, each parent had a steady new relationship, both of which later eventuated in marriages. Mark spent a week each month with his father and the woman with whom he lived, while the other three weeks he lived in another city with mother and Frank, his prospective stepfather.

Mark managed to separate from his mother during his first interview after having her come into the playroom with him, where he asked her to touch various toys and puppets he would use later in the hour, and then to hold his "blanky" (which he always carried with him) for him in the waiting room until he returned. When he saw a toy cannon in the room, he told the story of Babar, the King of Elephants, who was so happy to have children born that he announced their birth with "booms" of the cannon to the whole country. Mark mentioned that he made "boom-booms" (his word for bowel movements) himself only when he wanted to, but kids at nursery school called him a baby for making them in his pants. He wondered if Babar could make babies if he wanted, or first had to ask Celeste, the Queen of Elephants in the Babar story. Thus he introduced the being and making of babies as immediate and closely related concerns.

Mark: "I think I was a baby once but I wasn't really a baby."

t: "Tell me about it?"

Mark: "I was in my mommy's breast, I was a baby maybe, but I fell out. I would open up Mommy's tummy and put a baby in there, but it's too fat to stuff in there."

Taking a cue from his holding and touching behavior, while separating from mother, and his insistence on having his "blanky," a transitional object, "held" by mother, as well as from what he said, I commented, "Did you feel like you were dropped, not held close enough when you still wanted to be a 'real' baby?—that you 'fell out' like you told me, before you were ready?" Later I added that he might want to ask mommy or me more about how babies really get made. During the same hour he told me:

Mark: "Mommy hates loud noises and tells me to keep quiet when she is tired a lot, but sometimes I make noises anyway and then she gets mad at me and tells me to go away. But daddy likes to laugh loud."

After picking up a squirt gun and shooting tentatively into a bowl, he laughed loudly (like he had just described his daddy doing) then ran anxiously into the waiting room to "see if mommy waited" and asked her directly, to her surprise, "How do babies get made?"

Mark seemed to identify his "boom-booms" with the loud noise and expansiveness which he knew his father enjoyed, but which was also an aggressive intrusion on his mother's quieter, more self-controlled nature. What was "stuffed" inside and could fall out was also related to the making of babies. Later he made clear a number of other meanings as well, particularly the attachment to the feces as a restitutional mechanism for dealing with his fears of loss. He had had considerable earlier separation from his mother. This occurred when mother, going through a difficult period of her life, had times of mild depression which made it hard for her not to feel distant from Mark. The pants full of feces functioned as a kind of transitional object; in part a kind of reminder of the outgoing gladness of the elephant king becoming a father (and his father did think he was a delight); and in addition an object, perceived as partly himself and partly not, which he could hold on to for company when he dreaded being abandoned by the mother during her depressed moods. In their interaction, having to clean him up mobilized the mother's anger and sense of helplessness about feeling controlled by him, but revitalized the relationship for Mark, albeit in a negative way. This component of the symptom became the initial focus of treatment, for it had such negative repercussions in the mother-child relationship, but with its amelioration, identification conflicts became central.

As Mark began to work out his problems, the assertive, aggressive, and exuberant sides of himself were increasingly brought into the open, not only with me, but with his mother as well. It seemed to me that an important part of his progress was related to the fact that his mother, in spite of having had periods when she felt depressed, controlling of him, and angry at his attempts to control her in turn, also had an abiding connection with a kind of elan de vie, which she described as having been characteristic of her own father, whom she had greatly loved in early childhood and who then disappointed her and her family by having an affair. As Mark began to improve, and particularly after she no longer had to contend with the bowel problem, she could reciprocate his exuberance tenderly, while coping with his direct aggression more comfortably than before. Mark had a spontaneity about him which led him rapidly to try out various notions underlying his inhibitions.

Mark dealt with a number of issues related to the imagery he associated with bowel movements—babies, food, liquids, and emptiness. By his second session, I had added for him to the usual play material in the therapy room an ample amount of peanut butter clay, and a small toilet. His mother had reported that the week after his first session he had seemed conflicted about his bowels, telling her, "I feel a boom-boom coming, and I don't want it to go in my pants and not in the toilet." Another day he started jokes about another child going to the "boom-boom school" (his nursery school) and putting the boom-boom all over laughing hugely at this idea. When he came into the therapy room he headed for the squirt gun, started to pick it up and withdrew his hand.

t: "Last week you were upset after you squirted, and had to check if mommy was still there." He nodded and went over to the mound of clay. I told

him that it was made of peanut butter, so he could do what he wanted with it.
He molded a number of balls. He asked about the toilet. I said it was here so
that children could play about boom-booms or pee-pee and show what their
worries were. I told him that if he wanted to put some in the toilet, we would
not flush it, we could save it here or take it out again. With that, he entered
into a rollicking game of throwing hunks of peanut butter clay into the toilet
with good aim, and then immediately retrieving them. Holding onto the clay,
he turned back to the gun and said,

Mark: "I had a dream of that gun last night. I can shoot it into the other
room (the adult therapy room, to which the connecting door was open)."

t: "I bet you could. Was that in your dream too?"

Mark: "No, I dreamed I put this (the stopper which kept the water in the
gun) back in the gun so something would be in it; it would never get empty."

t: "You might be worried about people getting empty."

Mark: "I'm hungry now."

He helped himself to a cookie from the available bowl.

Mark: "I'm fuller now."

He said there was a plastic candy man, all filled with little balls of candy. He
would like to be a "candy man."

t: "What then?"

Mark: "I would be full and I could even give some to mommy."

t: "Are you trying to tell me that both mommy and you feel like you need
filling up sometimes, and that makes it harder to let the boom-booms out?"

Mark: "And if they come out then I could shoot you and mommy?" Using
the dart gun now, instead of the "milder" one with the plastic bullets or water,
he plays at shooting me and goes to the waiting room to shoot mommy.
Though the darts are rubber-tipped, they can still cause injury, and ground
rules have to be quickly established about shooting the puppets rather than
really shooting mommy with the dart. While lugging puppets with him to the
waiting room, I let him know that letting boom-booms out does not really
hurt mommy, even though sometimes he wants to hurt her, and then is afraid
she might go away, or leave him feeling empty. He said quietly, "I get mad
when I always have to wait nor her."

The following week he told his stepfather-to-be, "I want to be a baby that
walks and talks and goes to the bathroom." At nursery school, he played
"being baby" with a group of little girls, one of whom became his first and
steady playmate there for a few months before she moved away. He still
avoided any rough and tumble play with boys. In therapy, he complained
about one of the boys.

Mark: "He hits me and I scream at him."

t: "Can you tell him to stop, that you don't like that?"

Mark: "I don't know."

Another week, he reported that the boy hit him and he said, "Get your boom-boom face out of here, get your silly face out of here or I'll squeeze boom-boom all over your face." Both boys started laughing together and then played with cars. However, he still hesitated about the idea of asking a school child to come home to lunch with him, " 'cause I'm not sure if he'll be nice to me."

Mark made clear in many ways that he treasured times of good feeling between himself and his mother and dreaded the sense of emptiness connected with earlier depression. While we were dealing with the intrapsychic issues connected with the bowel problem, I suggested to the mother that there be as little interplay as possible about the boom-booms when he made them in his pants (e.g., that she not become involved in cleaning him up, but to leave it to him, even if he ended up a little messier. This was difficult for her, but she tried it). She should, however, let him know she was ready for a celebration time with him when he was ready to make them in the toilet (King Babar, a kind of "ego ideal," had been inclined toward celebrations). During his third hour, we had talked about his feelings while "waiting for mommy." Mark had said, "And I don't have my blanky all the time and I like to feel my boom-booms there." Like his blanket, they were a warm and comforting presence when mother was unavailable. In his play therapy, he spent much time with the peanut butter clay as well as the water gun. He ate the clay, threw it in the toilet, took it out. Whenever he emptied the squirt gun, he said, "I'm hungry now," and went for a cookie. He repeatedly set a whole row of puppets up in front of the toilet and shot them with the dart gun. "All these people are dead and the last one will be deadest and then I'll shoot mommy."

When he was able to ask, "Does mommy get mad at me like I get mad?" we talked more fully about how it was not his fault that mommy had times of feeling sad and angry, that all people—he and mommy too—get angry, but that he was afraid to let his anger show, because he knew mommy had gone away from dada and he was scared that she would go away from him too. He couldn't stand feeling empty and alone, so he kept his boom-booms and was afraid to lose them or anything more. Sometimes the boom-booms seemed angry at mommy to him and sometimes they reminded him of dada making a nice noise; sometimes they kept him company when he wanted to be cozy like a baby or to have a baby. But now he knew that they would not be used up, he could always make more another day; and that they turned out with nothing bad about them, even though mommy had made faces when she had to clean him. Now, he could have people to keep him company instead, and could show them when he felt angry or sad or in a silly mood. He poignantly showed me (by mimicking her face) how mommy used to look at his boom-booms with disgust because he didn't want her to look in his face when she was mad; he told me that if he had been a "candy man" so full "that a little spilled out on her," she might have smiled instead. That week, he asked his mother in the park, "When you were a baby, did you go boom-boom in your pants?" and she was able to discuss it with him.

When, in the fourth week, Mark did begin to make bowel movements in the toilet, he and his mother celebrated by getting a toy at the five and dime store. Mother found that she resented the idea of having to "give" him something in return, as this felt to her like bribery, and we clarified that the "celebration" did not have to be in the form of an object. An extra time at the park, or reading an extra story became a satisfactory solution for both.

One day in therapy, he did not stay within the "safety rules," aiming the dart gun directly at his mother, and had to be physically stopped by me. He was terribly angry, screamed at me in the waiting room, "Now I'll never come and play with you again," and then burst into tears. After this, we could relate his fears not only to others having left him, but to his own wish to get rid of people when they stopped or disappointed him in what he wanted; and then his fear that that would make it really happen. The reality of shifting parent figures every month turned out to mean to him at that time that he could make one set of parent figures disappear while he was with the other. He told me he had only "done" this when he was "mad."

Once the toileting problem was over, and Mark had lived through the process of getting very angry at me without destroying our relationship, he turned his attention more and more to the issue of having two sets of parent figures. In therapy, he would herald this theme by building two airports out of large blocks, and zooming, airplane in hand and with appropriate noises, from one to the other. He told me the various things that daddy is good and "best" at, and I indicated that he was growing bigger and more able to do a lot of things, too. He had a period of great interest in being big and skilled, e.g., as he was building his airport, he said to me, "This might be taller than you." He pleaded for a bike instead of a trike, learned avidly, and was gleeful about showing his skill to the other kids on the block. He reportedly played with the boys at school now, though he did not like to share his toys.

At home, mother reported he was much more affectionate toward her, with a lot of spontaneous hugging. At the same time, he showed his possessiveness about her more openly to his mother's fiance. "I don't want to sit next to you, I want to be with mommy." When he was angry at his mother, he was less apt to cling to her as before. Occasionally, in a bout of anger, he would mimic mother's characteristic saying "Oh for Christ's sake, why don't you leave me alone," in such a funny way that she could not help but laugh, but more often now he stated, "Okay, I'll do it by myself."

His interest in being big and admired (a usual one of his age, compared to the clinging to anal concerns) was also accompanied by some anxiety. He suddenly wanted to be "private" in the bathroom, but asked mother to wait outside because, "I'm afraid of robbers." In therapy, he built enormously high block constructions "to make sure the robbers don't get in." When he used a gun in therapy, it was now the "pop-up-ping-pong ball one." Although he was now able to hold his own well with his best boyfriend and in school, he crumpled under criticism from mother's fiance. One day while in the bathtub he put a big paint brush under his penis and called mother, "Look what a big penis I have!" We discussed, in therapy, how his penis would grow and what it would be able to do. No one would rob him of it, even when he wanted such a big one. In therapy, he pictured Frank (mother's fiance) as his rival rather than father, but not to such a degree that he did not fully experience the tenderness toward mother. When she asked him what he wanted for Christmas, he replied with playful confidence, "I wish you and I'm going to get you!"

Until the time of his mother's remarriage, he dealt, in and out of therapy, with the theme of what was possible between the two of them, and what he might have to renounce. He told me that his dada wouldn't "mind if I got mommy, he doesn't need her because he has Joyce." This statement is similar to a feeling expressed by a number of children of parted parents; the father is not experienced as the actual and successful rival for the affection of the mother, and anger and love toward the father centers on the desertion more often than the usual rivalry, which must be dealt with in a different fashion. Mark's mother reported a conversation,

Mark: "Mommy I want to have a baby with you!"

Mother: "No, little boys cannot have babies with their mommies."

Mark: "When I grow up I will be a man and have a baby with you."

Mother: "No, mothers never have a baby with their sons, even when they grow up."

Mark: "Oh, okay, then, I guess I'll marry Susie and have a baby with her."

Mother's remarriage was taking place the following month.

His mother reported, "At the wedding, he had a very good time. All his friends were there, and of course we gave him a part in it." After marriage, somehow the hostility toward Frank seemed to disappear; he ran to him now when he came home and hugged him. She described him as "happy and loose" these days, no longer shy about going to visit other people's houses, etc. Simultaneously, for the first time, he was sometimes harsh and rejecting of his mother's company and generally more independent of her, preferring to ally himself with Frank. He loved working together with Frank on things requiring tools, repairing his toys, etc., and sometimes said to mother, "You don't know how to do that, Frank knows better." It was at this point that he allowed Frank to become a major additional identification figure for him. Mother experienced some sadness about his "sudden male chauvinism," a feeling of losing her tender little boy after they had lived through so much together and had arrived at mutual tenderness after some painful soul-searching. Although this is a type of renouncing every mother goes through as her child becomes more independent, it was felt deeply by a number of those mothers whose relationships to their children became more treasured than their marriages, even when they also contained elements of ambivalence. The changing or loosening of the bond with the child, which often occurs at remarriage or committed recoupling, is then accompanied by a tender, nostalgic kind of grief which can form the basis of a later compassionate understanding between mother and child. The parent at this moment is often aware—usually with some trepidations, which are recognized as echoes of the former disappointing marriage—of the depth of emotional commitment to the new love partner. For the parent to be clear about this seems to help the child to accept the reality, to deal with the remaining magical wishes and fears about the home parent, and to settle more comfortably into the role of being the child.

Mark, too, dealt with the remaining wish to have a baby within his home and family—and the fantasies of his own babyhood which he had always linked with this wish. He told me,

Mark: "When I grow up, I don't want a baby because we might not have room in my house and it might be scared of my kitty cat. My mother had a baby with my dada—I guessed that. My first guess was that mommy made a baby with my dada, but there was no room in the same house. But I'm going to make something by magic."

t: "No room in the house, what does that mean?"

Mark: "No, mommy and daddy kept fighting, like Joey and I do, they couldn't get along sometimes. Once the other day mommy was crying in the morning, but she doesn't do that any more much, because she and Frank don't do that."

t: "How come?"

Mark: "Because I always know they always make up again."

t: "Then you can count on them being your mommy and Frank, even if someone gets sad or mad for a little while, they will stay your family, and you can grow up without worrying about that?"

That day, during his therapy hour, Mark hammered together and painted a large wooden sign on which he put the names of "all my people." These included both sets of parent figures, me, his best friend, Joey, and his cat. He wanted to plant it in the garden outside my office, so we took it outside and staked it firmly in the earth. I did not take up whatever unconscious connection between planting and babies growing he might still have had. He mentioned that he had a lot of new friends at nursery school now, but they didn't have to be on the sign, because it was his best friend that he would keep even when school was over. Next week he was going to visit his father.

t: "Will that make you miss mommy?"

Mark: "No, it doesn't. It makes me glad to see daddy again and miss mommy too. I want to go on the roof with daddy, we both like to do that, we both like to go way up high and we can shout and make a lot of noise." He has adapted to making loud noises with his father, without having to have the concrete evidence of a "boom" at home to remind him of this shared pleasure.

Mark: "Joyce never wants to go up there, so just daddy and I do, but I like that because then she makes cookies and hot chocolate for us when we come down."

Termination, with all patients, brings up old anxieties in spite of highlighting new areas of mastery. When I first brought termination up with Mark, he gave no verbal response, but simply continued to show me all the things that he could now do; he had been demonstrating them. He would not discuss how he felt about this, but at the end of the hour said, "When I get to be six, I go here one more time, and when I am seven, one more time." He pointed to his name on his drawer. (It is my habit to give each child in therapy a drawer of his or her own, with his first name on it, in which to keep half-done pictures, projects, a special piece of wood, or half-cookie safely from one session to the next. The drawer belongs to that child only, and is protected from assaults by other children. Issues of sibling rivalries often come up around the drawers.)

Mark pointed to his name on the drawer and asked: "How long will you keep this?" For several weeks, termination was a major topic, reviving issues of anger and rejection with guilt over his own impulses. However, he also made clear that he was able to remember and "keep" people, even when he could not see them all the time.

At his last regular appointment, he was sitting close to mother in the waiting room. He said, "I forgot what I did last time here, I even forgot where the guns and blocks are."

t: "Did you think I will forget you and you tried to forget our time together, too?"

He said he remembered now, and came into the therapy room. I gave him a goodbye present of an airplane that can be flown high and we went outside to try it. He stood at a distance, and flew it to me, and I to him while we waved at each other. He laughed with delight at how high it goes. Once he launched it, then ran toward me, both he and the airplane landing together, in the grass at my feet.

Mark: "And can I come visit you a different year?"

t: "Of course!"

Mark: "And can I come and visit when I am a man, and even if I have a little boy?"

t: "If you want to—and meanwhile, I will think of you sometimes, too, okay?"

Mark: "Okay."

A follow-up visit was planned for the following year.

In chapter 10, dealing with adaptations in the therapy process, altered termination procedures will be more fully discussed. However, with children of parting parents I do not turn down requests for follow-up visits, unless I believe them to be unrealistic (e.g., the family is moving far away or the parent would not support it). The sustained wish for creating a baby, apparent in Mark's material and, later in this chapter, in Noah's, which is a normal, though often unconscious, aspect of a boy's development, has additional significance in these cases (both Mark and Noah utilized transitional objects and were creative people, albeit at different developmental stages), as an assurance about the continuity of the self. Mark wanted to undo the baby for whom "there was no room in the house" by the wanted baby. Earlier, he would not discard his "boom-booms" even when there was no room. Both boys share with some other boys in the sample a period of having lived fatherless with their mothers. This strengthened both some aspects of their identification and their sense of reciprocity with their mothers. In both these boys the notion of making something viable to give the mother to make her happy coexisted with the idea of making something which would be an eternal source of supplies for the self and under the child's own control, when nurturance from mother (and later erotic response) was not available to them. Their love for the wanted, missing parent, and practice of creating his image during his absence, in both cases was experienced among other ways also in the form of transitional objects and remained as an enriching confidence in attributing a reality to their creations.

At age six, Mark continued to live with his mother and stepfather Frank, and to visit his own father and Joyce regularly. He made the regular plane trip on his own, was proud of this accomplishment, and did not seem to be anxious about the transition, that is, before or after his trips. Somewhere in the future is the plan for him to spend a year with his father, if they both wish it. Probably that would be in his adolescence. At present, his need for security with his mother is still too important. Mark came for a follow-up visit, while his mother continued to come in for a session every few months for a year to discuss issues which came up between Mark and the rest of the family.

Mother is a perceptive, very likeable person, with a rich range of emotional resources available to her, in relation to her family and in her work. Happy in her marriage and with Mark, she seems to have less need to be controlling with the little boy, and the instances of joyous times together are many. The memory of the difficult years remains vivid, often restimulated by some interaction regarding Mark and his father. For example, when Mark reported excitedly that "dada" had invited him to spend a year, not knowing if this meant right now or later, she battled silently against her feelings of rejection by Mark and also recognized that the father should have discussed the issue with her first. She recalled the difference in father's fantasies about "having a son" years ago, and his actual withdrawal from her and the baby when the reality of caring for Mark was at hand. Similarly, she feared that the idea of a year with him was the kind of castle in the sand that would not yet work out. I asked her what, she felt, had made it possible for her not to interfere with Mark's abiding affection for his father, in spite of her own different feelings. She said, "Whatever else went on, both of us have been deeply committed to not putting Mark in the middle. I never resent his love for his father—even though I'm sometimes bothered by the idealized version of that. What I still feel sadness about is that in his second year of life, I was so depressed and angry much of the time—I really didn't know how to get hold on what had happened to me—but feel that he just didn't have a secure environment during that time. He really lost both me and his dada that year and the next—you know how he was when I first brought him to you. I still sometimes wonder about whether he will always be especially vulnerable to depression or losses—and wish I could have given him all he needed then."

It was clear to me that she had given him all she could, considering the stress over her own sense of loss and rejection at the time; and indeed the lingering awareness of how these issues felt to her has enriched her empathy and supportive tie to him. However, the fact that the current lives of all four parent figures are full and happy, on the whole, provides the fertile ground for his continued growth.

Mark, meanwhile is described as "generally happy," playing readily with other children in school and around the neighborhood, and "less shy" about initiating interactions. He still has his "moments of stress," when he is irritable or resorts to going off and sucking his thumb. Exploration of such moments revealed their connection with times of frustration, which result from his making "big plans" and then having to face the fact that he cannot carry them through. For example, while carrying a half-completed craft project home from school, his imagination will lift it to new heights, his excitement increases, but once he is home he cannot get it to conform to his wishes. Then he becomes angry and rejects the whole project impatiently. He might then suck his thumb and "sulk." Such high hopes dashed by reality testing can be looked at from a number of dimensions. They contain remnants of his previous attachment to transitional objects, which symbolized the precious intimacy with father (boom-booms for spontaneous boisterousness, or "sand-castles," in mother's words) but also, at a less conscious level, the then dormant and now often open elan de vie between himself and his mother, who believes that this was the quality she got from her own father. Such imaginative flights and impatience with the limitations of reality are also an aspect of creativity, which may stand him in good stead in the future.

His rejection of his accomplishments, however, appears sporadic, while his pleasure in new mastery as well as creative activity predominates. For example, he has recently found special joy in participating in a pottery class, where he is delighted about "not only getting his hands into the clay, but making such beautiful things, too." As beauty is partly in the eye of the beholder, he is assured of a more welcome reception for his current creations, than for his creative "boom-booms" long ago.

Mark retains the capacity to enjoy and emulate aspects of all four parent figures, being clear about what he likes doing with each of them, and simultaneously having learned to live with the moments of sadness about not being able to have all four of them together. One day, he said to his mother,

Mark: "It makes me sad when I am at dada's and I really miss you there."

Mother: "But then you can look forward to coming home."

Mark: "No, that doesn't work—because when I am home, then I miss dada!"

Although it has been a long time since he verbalized the hope of mother and father reuniting, and recognizes this to be impossible, remnants of the wish still appear in an attenuated form: he puts a distance between the accepted current reality and the wish, in time:

Mark: "You know, I really wish that in ten years daddy and all of us would live together sometimes—that would be really nice!"

SHIFTS IN IDENTIFICATION PROCESSES
OVER A PERIOD OF TIME: NOAH

Noah is a boy who is not only in touch with much of his inner experience, but also has the ability to communicate and often to reappraise the meanings of his experience. I knew him from a time shortly after his parents separated, when his father became depressed; through a period of obvious mutual bitterness between the parents; through his mother's involvement with and eventual remarriage to another man; and finally through the birth of a new baby sister.

Reversing my usual procedure, I shall reserve presentation of the case material until after a more general analysis; the complex implications of the dreams especially are, I believe, better understood in that context.

Noah illustrates the mixture of developmental levels of identifications discussed earlier, displaying observable shifts in the level most prominently related to each of the three major parent figures involved. We see first the behavioral, unconscious and affecto-motor aspects of his identification with the partially absent father, followed by a long period during which he vacillated about renunciation of certain aspects of his growth. For a time, he attempted to feel totally like the father, in order not to lose the sense of contact and intimacy with him. The ego mechanisms he utilized to deal with this identification included the use of a transitional object, stemming from an early period of development, and the use of his highly developed capacity for empathy, reflecting aspects of a much later level of ego organization. Aspects of his early idealization of the father, as well as of himself, were components of an ego ideal which had been fostered by the combination of his parents' and grandparents' high expectations and loving investment in him. Slowly, he was able increasingly to differentiate himself from his father, to perceive his father in a more realistic, though still loving fashion, and to limit the degree to which he renounced his own autonomous development. For the first time, there was a lifting of a previous inhibition of aggression and rivalry in his relationships to his father and to his boyfriends.

In spite of strong initial resistance to the growing role that his mother's fiance, and then husband, would have in the family's life, aspects of emulation and identification with Steve appeared increasingly in the material, mixed with the normal rivalry that Noah had not faced in early childhood. During this stressful period, aspects of identification with all three parent figures emerged at different levels of consciousness and there was a shaking up and revision of fragments of early representations of himself. His house, a symbol of security, was clung to for a time like a transitional object. These early images related not only to the fear of loss, which plagued him when he felt most ambivalent about his parents, but also to the potential loss of his role in providing them with needed emotional supplies. This was part of the early ego ideal of mutual enhancement which has been an important driving force in his life. Simultaneously, selective ego identifications with traits of parent figures became the predominant level.

After his mother's remarriage and during her pregnancy, Noah experienced intense conflict between his growing identification and rivalry with his stepfather. In reality, he was no longer first in his mother's life and felt betrayed. Again, we see a range of levels of identification: in his dreams these included the wish to re-establish the preambivalent unity with the mother by being either mother or baby, with a simultaneous dream perception that this state of affairs could not survive. In his symptomatology, he first denied and then accepted with relief the role of the stepfather in the pregnancy and new family organization. He made a kind of peace with three different parent figures, and finally directed his major interest to pleasurable activities with his age mates. He further integrated and enriched his identifications with selective attributes of three sets of grandparents, each with different personal, cultural, and religious heritages.

Throughout the period of therapy, the ego ideal of mutual enhancement, referred to above, remained as an affective possibility in all his relationships, even when his more grandiose view of his own and his parents' powers gave way to increased reality testing and some acceptance of his own as well as their limitations. Similarly, his delightful humor, his capacity for appreciating nuances in his perceptions (except when he was quite depressed) and his tolerance for periods of anxiety and depression were impressive. In his ability to endure anxiety and depression, he belonged with those individuals (described by Zetzel, 1970), who exemplify the capacity for emotional growth. I found him to be an immensely rich human being. I attribute this richness both to his own potential as a person, and to the strong, caring and satisfying emotional interchange which both parents had with the boy at the time when the rudiments of identificatory experience are laid, and which I believe influenced the positive quality of certain affective features of his ego ideal in a way that survived the shedding of the more archaic, magical images of people also associated with it for him; a shedding that was necessary before he could value himself realistically, within his own skin.

At various times in this process, the external changes in his family situation stirred up new impulses and conflicts which resulted in regression or new, transient symptoms before he could begin to resolve them. Simultaneously, changes in his ego organization made it possible for him to rework aspects of emotional growth which he had bypassed prior to his parents' separation, and which had resulted in mild symptoms of separation anxiety and phobias throughout his latency years, prior to treatment.

Because of the emotional distance between his parents for some years before their separation, while each of them was highly involved with him (he also had a brother, Kenny), Noah's normal sexual and aggressive impulses had been both stimulated and deflected from the parent figures, and became for Noah too dangerous, since they could put him in the place of the rival parent. Although this role was desired at one level, at another it would deprive him of the security of being a child, which he needed. The earlier symptoms, which will not be discussed in detail here, appeared related to defenses against awareness of such impulses.

It is important to note that although Noah intensified his attempts at total identification when he felt threatened by loss, these identifications did not replace the actual relationships, but cohabited with them while changes in his perception of and wishes toward his parent figures took place.

In order to glimpse Noah's ability to develop a differentiated view of the parent figures involved, as well as his reactions to them, I will begin his story with his description of the adults and himself about two months prior to his mother's remarriage, and then progress backwards to the initial interview with him.

Two months before his mother's remarriage, he commented:

Noah: "I know I feel more safe about driving in the car with Steve and have more fun with him now, but I don't feel as good as with my father, because I care more about my father. My father says we think on the same wave length. I feel sad without my father, but I wouldn't feel sad without Steve. But I also like Steve to be around because my mother doesn't get mad at me and Kenny as much when he is there. With my father, when he is depressed, I know seeing me makes him feel better—I mean like the other night, doing something with us instead of just standing around feeling sad. I *like* the feeling of helping him feel better, but I *don't like* his feeling sad in the first place; that still makes me feel like crying."

Noah was first seen in therapy at the age of ten, when there was a sudden threat of his suspension from school. Previously, he had always been an excellent student, relating well to both teachers and friends, although, as mentioned above, he had a history of some mild phobias, nightmares, and separation anxiety during his early school years.

The parents had separated after considerable turmoil a few months before I saw Noah. His mother, Brenda, had become angrily clear that her marriage would not change for the better and that by maintaining the marriage she was renouncing her chances for a better life. However, she had considerable guilt about the harm the separation might do to her husband, toward whom she had felt increasingly cold over a period of years, and about her overclose companionship with Noah during her marriage, sometimes to the emotional exclusion of her husband.

After the separation, the father suffered from periods of incapacitating depression, alternating with restless, hypomanic times. He had been in treatment for some time. The week preceding Noah's school difficulties, father had been making the rounds of the family friends (with Noah and Kenny in tow), barraging them with humiliating, ridiculing, and angry comments about mother's behavior. The following week, Noah began to lead a group of boys in school in openly ridiculing his teacher in front of the class, perceptively pointing out every hypocritical detail of her behavior, in contrast to her statements about what she expected from the children. She happened to be vulnerable to his derision. For example, when the boys spied on her during recess, they found her plucking her eyebrows, while talking out loud to herself about them. The boys then "told on her" to the rest of the class the next time they were chided for being preoccupied and not paying attention to her. (Mother used to chide father for not communicating or paying attention to her.) She first sent Noah to the principal, but when this did not stem his derision, she finally pushed him bodily out the door, slammed it behind him, and said she would have him suspended until he apologized. He said he would not return anyway. Concurrently, Noah's father had been banned by mother from coming into the house. Noah would not talk to the school psychologist and told me when I saw him that this was because he was afraid he might cry and then could not face his schoolmates. I said, t: "I know kids get teased by the other guys if they cry in front of them, and that makes for a tough situation. It must have been quite a job for you not to, especially if there were other things lately that you have been feeling like crying about too. From what I've seen of kids whose parents are separating— even when they are a lot older than you—I know there are lots of upset feelings of all sorts."

Noah: "I guess I've been upset about my parents' separating and sometimes I cry secretly at night. I don't let mother hear me. I just wish my parents would make up and that things were like before."

He then showed me the troll-like figure, which he secretly kept in his pocket, named "Alfie." Sometimes he consoled himself by talking to Alfie or pretending that he was Alfie's father and was about to take him to a baseball game. His actual father had to pick him up down the block now because he was not allowed in the house. Noah readily accepted my statement that getting himself pushed out the door at school might have something to do with his father being pushed out of the house these days; and that he might want to deal with his feelings about this in other ways than getting himself pushed out, even if his judgment of the teacher were correct.

He repeated that his teacher *was* a hypocrite and I did not dispute it. Instead, I commented that I was not surprised he felt like crying sometimes, that it must be hard for him when he knew that he wished his parents would make up, and that his father would be okay, but felt helpless because he had no way to make that really come true. I offered to try to help him understand more about what he wished and feared, and about what was actually happening with his parents, so that he might feel less helpless about what to expect from them and himself. He asked to return. He added, "Maybe if I went back to school, I could get along with the teacher if she found someone else to pick on instead. I might still think she's a hypocrite, but I could keep it to myself or tell you. That way, I would still be with my friends."

Then he said, "I don't think my mother should always put blame on my father. She has a thing in her which exaggerates time, and whenever he forgets to do something—a lot of time he forgets—she makes him feel crummy. I try to remind him before she can get mad."

In beginning to structure the therapy situation for him, I purposefully focused on two aspects of what he had presented. One was the sense of helplessness about accomplishing restitution in the family. This was inferred from his characterization of his crying and transitional object as secret, something he was ashamed of exposing to others, and yet necessary to him in his attempt to bridge the gap between his wish for the parents to make up and the reality he perceived. Simultaneously, I proposed relating his perceptions to the real, ongoing changes in his parents' relationship to each other and to him. Although the latter is certainly not a standard procedure in structuring therapy with a child, I have often found it useful with children of parting parents. Frequently, the child is so overburdened with notions of what he should be able to do about his parents' situation that constantly appraising his reality situation in addition to his inner life supports the child's eventual ability to accept a self-image consistent with his size. Of course, this cannot occur unless the parents are able, also, eventually, to free the child from being a primary source of emotional support. During the first several months of Noah's therapy, I also saw the mother at regular intervals; father was already in treatment. Communication with the school and teacher was also established. Father was seen occasionally around issues affecting his son.

Noah's wishful fantasy about the parents reuniting appears in early interviews with almost all of the children, though a number of them clearly state that they know this cannot happen, or at least not without a resumption of fighting, or "not getting along." However, Noah's revelation of his use of the transitional object "Alfie" occurred in association with the loss of his fantasy of reuniting the family. Interestingly, he not only pictured Alfie as a companion, but also, reversing the father-son roles, identified himself as the father who took Alfie places and made him happy, while making the transitional object his son. He correctly pictured their interaction as fairly conflict-free in the absence of mother, and at this point blamed some "hypocrisy" as the cause of trouble. This theme will reappear. Meanwhile, provoking expulsion from school had served also to express his anger toward his mother in a way he shared with father, but led to another loss ("I won't be with my friends.").

Noah's wish to hide his crying from his classmates is a normal and adaptive maneuver, since he would most likely be ostracized for behavior which, given our current cultural attitudes, is considered a kind of weakness among ten-year-old boys, who generally are struggling to renounce their own dependent wishes, which for them often include the intimacy of "expressing emotions."

However, he also hid his tears from his mother. Her attitude toward his grief was complicated by the fact that, throughout her own history, grief reactions about important losses had remained unresolved. At the death of her father, to whom she had been extraordinarily attached in childhood, she did not mourn. She didn't feel much of anything except that she was now free to separate from her husband without fear of hurting her father or destroying his "illusions" about her marriage. The two men had been extremely close to each other. Brenda's father's death had an impact on the timing of the separation, which preceded the husband's acute depression. His loss as an important father figure affected Noah's father, and also had bearing on the relationship he sought with his son. However, the ramifications of this are too complex to be detailed here.

Another death for Brenda, that of a younger brother, had occurred when she was twelve. Again she "could not cry" and did not remember thinking about the brother much afterwards. However, she told me that when her canary died about a year later, "I sobbed my heart out." This kind of displaced grief reaction has been discussed in a previous chapter. This mother, for whom grieving over a loved one was difficult to experience or witness, had to face and attempt to deal with this process in her son. She did her best to do this because of her strong wish to support her son emotionally, but it was not an easy task for her.

During the next session, Noah told me of a long, complicated dream which involved father, his brother, Kenny, and himself traveling, while a decision was being made about who should be the president for making peace between Israel and Egypt. Egyptian "mummies" (to which he associated mommies) were involved. Suddenly, Noah realized in the dream that he might be too late to get back home, which was an old castle, before it closed for the night. They all ran, but only Noah got in before the big gate closed behind him, leaving father and Kenny outside. He awoke, feeling "bad" about their being left out. He recalled that in his dream the president looked like he had "my mother's father's face" but a different body, and had announced that he wanted to find a special place no one had been before and he knew where it was. The outline of the map had the shape of one side of Noah's school. "When everybody else got locked out and only I got through, I felt so bad about it, I tried to scream and to help them get through but I couldn't."

This theme of being "in" while others, such as the father, were excluded, was a centeral one for Noah at this time. Simultaneously, it had to be faced in a different way by the mother, who had to change her expectations of Noah's role in her life. Mother remembered that during Noah's babyhood, at times when she felt acutely lonely and depressed about her disappointment in her marriage, she occasionally found herself thinking about Noah: "This is the only person I love." This was before Kenny was born, and became important to her too.

Noah reported a couple of incidents during the preceding week that the dream reminded him of. Kenny had confided to him for the first time "that he thought I wouldn't mind if he died and he thought mother wanted him to die."

Noah: "He hates it when I sing loud and thinks I do that just to tease him, to get him to go out of the room."

He felt "bad" about Kenny's communication, well aware that he does sometimes wish him out of the way. Meanwhile, Noah had been reinstated at school and had been chosen by his classmates to play the part of God in a play. Maternal grandmother (wife of the dead grandfather, who appeared in the dream) was coming to see him in the play and "always tells me how proud she is of me." Needless to say, the issues that hour included Noah's guilt about being allowed in, when the father wasn't; the role of the grandfather in having kept the family together; and the question of having to "play God" as the way of making both himself and his family proud.

I suggested that he encourage Kenny to share his despair with mother, who did not know of it and thought Kenny to be "the least affected by it all," so that Noah would not be the only one having to cope with Kenny's distress. I raised the question of Noah's own underlying fears of being deserted and excluded, like the others, if he fell short of his own and his parents' expectations. With humor in his eyes, he responded by writing, "God spelled backwards = dog." The degree of significance of these alternatives for him did not become clear until much later, when it became apparent that Ophelia, his female dog, represented issues of having babies and being born; that mother was eager to get rid of the dog because she felt unable to train it, but restrained herself from doing so; and that father currently referred to mother as a bitch. However, the two contrasting identificatory figures of God and dog did indicate conflicts around the early stages of ego ideal and identification development, represented by extreme and partial symbolizations of power.

Noah's yearning for his father, whom he actually saw at least twice a week most of the time, was intensely expressed over a period of months, often with a moving degree of affect. Simultaneously, he grappled with the following issues:

1. Sadness and guilt about his father's being left out by mother and an identification with father's bereft state.

2. Intense libidinous wishes toward the mother, with feared fantasies of being "cut off" or burned while he was in such a state of excitement (e.g., in dreams of being encouraged to put his finger into a hot and dangerous electric socket in a special round box). His first reactions to these impulses and anxieties were regressive ones; that is, his imagery would shift to symbolizations of mother-baby (or bitch-puppy) closeness. However, these were associated with different dangers.

3. Anger at the mother for various "hypocrisies," and the presentation of different versions of the "truth" than he heard from father. Feeling fooled by mother was related to his continuing wish to make the teacher look like a fool.

4. Sobbing, grief, and anger at mother for wanting no further contact with paternal grandparents, who had also played an important role in his life.

5. Attempts to make everything up to his father by giving him things, and assuring him frequently that he loved him. This also had components of a feminine identification of wanting to give father what mother wouldn't.

6. A concomitant inhibition (which he had to some extent throughout his latency years) of the competitive and angry aspects of his otherwise solid and richly companionable relationships to other boys.

These issues will be illustrated only briefly, as they reflect his shifting ego organization but preceded the more definitive fluctuations in identification patterns which are the focus of this chapter. Comments on illustrative dream material will also be abbreviated, omitting much.

Early in treatment one day, Noah was discussing his paternal grandparents, with admiration for the grandfather doing the best woodworking in the world, and grandmother liking to cook and bake more than his mother did. Bursting into tears and then sobbing, he said, "and last week mother said she never wants to see my father's parents again." They had insulted her. He was pained by the sense of loss of the grandparents, with whom he had a close relationship, as well as empathically experiencing the rejection they must be feeling. He faced his fear that his mother shut people out of her life completely if she was angry at them—his own anger might result in her loss. We tried to separate the reality components of this, in the losses he witnessed, from his expectations of magical retaliation for his angry feelings. A series of routine events as well as special occasions brought memories of the absent father's role, and each time he experienced this as a loss. E.g., when the family celebrated the Seder, "My aunt said Kenny and I made the whole Seder—but I felt I wanted my father there and it just wasn't as good without him . . . I would rather have stayed home myself than not have him be there."

A series of dreams revolved around his libidinous and sexual feelings toward mother, and the dangers associated with these for him.

Noah: "I dreamt I was sleeping and woke up and looked around me—and there was a silver thing and I could open it and a cup and coke were in it and I drank it and got another. Then I found out that they were filming 'Good Times' and I had discovered something that nobody knew and then they decided to film the same script and add my discovery. Then it was cub scouts and my father's friend—he's a shrimpy little guy but he's the leader—came in at midnight and I was asleep already in the dream. I woke up and was watching 'Good Times'—only it was different than I thought and I realized that I would have to wait till next week to see what was filmed."

The discovery of "something nobody knew" is reminiscent of his earlier dream of finding a place "where nobody had ever been before." His own associations included the following.

Noah: "The silver box in the wall was like a fuse cabinet, except a fuse cabinet sticks out and this was *built in*. Also, my father's father is making a box—then I think of not a box, but I made a pocketbook that size for my mother out of a pair of jeans. I did it during the Martin Luther King show because I didn't want to see the bad part about his getting killed. If I think of the drink, it's the kind I like. My mother's father always liked Dr. Pepper, but when I tried it it wasn't so good. I like coca cola, cherry soda best."

Nothing came to mind about "watching 'Good Times'" but he commented that sometimes lately when he is upset he "waits till next week" for his therapy hour, and then gets a "picture" of what is bothering him. His multiple levels of being observer and participant in the dream accurately reflect his ego capacity to observe or reflect on his own behavior without the sense of depersonalization which sometimes is found in obsessional individuals who use isolation to defend against affect. We might also note that he can picture obtaining gratification from the box (or mother's jeans-pocketbook) and watching 'Good Times' in order also not to see the "bad part about Martin Luther King getting killed." Instead of the president of the country, it is this time the "king," a champion of nonviolence, who has come to grief.

During the same hour, he described mixed feelings about being the "man of the house" now.

Noah: "When we went someplace, my father used to bring in the suitcases and hang them in the car. I did it last week and mother was proud of me. I remember a long time ago when father left and went someplace and I told mother how to set up the sprinkler and she told everyone how proud she was because I was the real man of the house."

We discussed how uncomfortable this made him when her pride in him involved a "put down" of father.

Noah: "Once when my whole family was all mad at each other—and at my little brother, too, when I was little—it seemed like a chain reaction but I didn't like it. So I made a ribbon that said, 'First Prize for the Best Father' and gave it to him, and then father said, 'I just love Noah!' "

Clearly, Noah, too, has been a champion of peace.

The next week he reported a "bad dream" the night after his last session.

Noah: "During our clarinet lesson these guys were trying to take away my clarinet secretly, but I saw them. They were trying to take all the kids away too. Fifty people were protesting in front of our house, they got in the house, tried to fight me and got me down—my mother didn't want to be bothered, then my father came in and I woke up.

"One guy tried to take my finger and put it in a plug—looked a little like our old family room, the tiny den we used to have—and it looked a little like, you know some refrigerators that you open the door with a little handle. The worst guy who was wrestling with me—in real life he was the one who worked in the kitchen at camp. The kids used to call him Tommy Jelly-Nose. In the dream, he thought I didn't want him to come in—that I closed the door because I didn't want him in and so he forced the door open and put my finger in the plug where it could get a shock or explode."

For the first time, he discusses some of his sexual anxieties directly. He mentions, "I've been neglecting Alfie lately, for playing with Ophelia instead."

Recently, Ophelia tried to lick his penis, which felt funny.

We discuss his perception of the guy outside the door; how in past dreams he has been aware of feeling "bad" for people left out, but now he is bringing up the thought of the guy wanting revenge about Noah not *wanting* him in. With anxious laughter, he brings up the possibility that "Jelly Nose" might have wanted to turn Noah into "jelly fingers" by forcing his finger into the electric plug. We discuss this not only as it relates to fears about his penis, but also in terms of his guilty fantasies about being "man of the house" and excluding his father. Again, the realities of the marital difficulties are clarified as having to do with the parents' problems with each other, independently of what Noah has wished or done. He cannot and does not have to be "man of the house," because he is a kid, but there is no reason for him to have "jelly fingers" either, because he has everything it takes—and in good shape—so that when he grows up and is ready he can be the man of the house if he wishes with a family of his own in it.

After the parents' divorce became final and some months later, mother began slowly to introduce the children to Steve. Noah's first reaction was, "I never want to see him, I wouldn't want anyone else to do anything with me except my father."

When Steve visited, Noah stayed in his room, though Kenny and Steve played together. Noah stated emphatically, "Mom doesn't want to see grandfather any more because he is so rude to her, so it's not fair if she expects me to see Steve when I don't want to." The next month he reported,

Noah: "Steve really likes Ophelia a lot and I think I'm a little bit jealous; what if she comes to like him better than me? I must admit though he's a good cook and he brought us all some chocolate cake he made."

The following week, he announces:

"I had a really weird dream. It was the last day of school. I punched Mrs. O. (teacher) in the face and said some swears to her, so she sent me to the principal. My mother and father came down the hall and I sat on my mother's lap disguised as a baby—my father disappeared. Then I was riding in my father's car with Mr. K (the principal) dressed as a policeman. I lay on the bottom of the car so no one would see me. Father said we had to go to a banquet with men and ladies and I said, 'Did you ever see *It Pays to Be Ignorant* on TV?"

In reality, he had recently volunteered to take the blame when another boy had called the teacher a "swear" and had been sent to the principal, but not punished. He became aware that his willingness to take the blame was related to the kind of guilt and "looking for punishment" discussed in relation to earlier dreams. In this dream, we see a regression from the intensely stimulated and feared sexual fantasies of the previous dreams to the wish to be a baby on mother's lap, "disguised" so that no one will know who he really is or what he knows ("It pays to be ignorant"). Perceptive as he is, he has had a lot to see (including his parents' divorce and mother's man friend) and deal with, and wishes at least in his dream to retreat to the less conflicted days of babyhood. Meanwhile, in his behavior creative sublimations and enjoyable activities with his friends continued as an important part of his life. He and a friend jointly invented a comic strip, featuring caricatures of people drawn with humor and talent; he put on a magic show; won an athletic prize in school; and learned to horseback-ride with his father. He told me about this,

Noah: "When he's around the house he's sad and doesn't talk, but when we're doing something like riding, he's okay."

Two weeks later, he recounted another dream,

Noah: "It was the last day of school and we were going to have a party. The leader of our group didn't really tell us what we were supposed to bring. I didn't have anything to bring and mother was working and the party was going to be over at six—and I still couldn't find anything to bring. Before that, I went outside and in a shed was a little dog ... my dog ... a little thing with big triangles. The triangles were its babies but it had died. One pup was still alive and it was almost as big as the mother—all the others were dead. I got all sad because they died. Then mother came home the second part of the dream and the mother of that pup came. (Noah is meanwhile constructing and gluing together a person out of wooden sticks.) And suddenly Ophelia was jumping into the flames and the flames were the same size and shape as the pups—I just thought of that—I was screaming and couldn't scream—something held me back from screaming. My clarinet was standing there and sometimes I lay it down. I pushed my clarinet on Ophelia to put out—to smother the flames. Mother came in and asked what happened and I told her it was okay, but I thought the slightest push would make the whole house on fire and I was afraid and then I finally went to sleep. My mother was there and the baby pup. The mother dog had had babies but I told my mother that there was no one around to give her a baby, but she said that you can have babies by this funny way of twisting youself, putting your mouth a certain way. I knew that isn't really true." He drew a detailed picture of the "mother dog," the "dead baby," and the "live baby sleeping" with its boundary contiguous with the mother. He recalled that when he was small, maybe three or four he had always wanted a baby sister (shortly after his brother was born); he did not know whether it would be mother's or his.

The night before the dream, Ophelia had run away. Noah had gone looking for her on his bike, but it started getting dark. He thought she might be lost and started to cry; because he could not stop crying and it was raining he could hardly see. Mother finally called Steve, who came over and helped to find Ophelia. Before Ophelia got lost, he had been watching "Mannix" on TV, and Mannix's car had caught on fire. In regard to the clarinet there had been a dispute, with father supporting Noah's continued lessons, which he wanted, while mother preferred the piano which made less noise. The ramifications of this dream are so numerous, that only a small selection of implications (and of the ideas Noah linked with it) can be taken up here. It seemed clear that Ophelia's running away had reinvoked Noah's fears of losing his mother at a variety of levels. Mother's absence meant he had nothing to offer and if he had nothing to offer he could not come to the party. (This relates to aspects of his ego ideal, discussed earlier. However, giving something was also a long-standing defense as well as substitute wish for giving himself.) The lost mother dog makes its reappearance with a baby—dead and alive. (Noah's actual first separation from mother was when his baby brother was born.) The mother dog jumps into the flames "that were the same size and shape as the pups," thus merging with them in the heat of the flames, as well as in Noah's drawing of them. Ego boundaries have dissolved (as in sleep) and Noah cannot scream. The standing clarinet, which in previous dreams had represented the penis, is pushed on the mother dog to put out the flames (a vivid symbolization of his heterosexual wishes), but the dream then reverts to an oral explanation which does not necessarily require a separate partner for the production of a baby (he had reported Ophelia's trying to lick his penis). He remembers the period of wanting a baby without distinguishing its origin in mother or in him.

The dream is commented on with this degree of detail for two reasons: (1) it represents his symbolization of an early level of identification, including the wish for merging with the mother at both an infantile and later sexual (flaming car, etc.) level. This identification surfaced at the time that he faced some actual losses of mother: the real man of the house, the father, had been discarded in Noah's eyes, and he feared he might be next; and the man mother was going to marry had been introduced to him, so that Noah was losing his position as the one with whom mother was most involved. Meanwhile, he had become more aware of his libidinous wishes toward her, in the light of his defense of the father. (2) The dream was a forerunner of new conflicts he would face when his mother actually married and became pregnant.

Progressively, as mother was happier and became more able to restrain her anger at father, Noah became more able to be critical of father without overwhelming guilt. For example, he had repeatedly experienced that when his father was in a "high mood," he could not really relate to Noah in the sense of talking or doing things with him in a relaxed way, but instead made a frantic round of visiting friends, taking Noah and Kenny with him. He would promise the boys that he was only dropping in for five minutes, but this often turned into an hour. Father would talk at a rapid pace to the friends, while Noah and Kenny felt neglected and were relegated to watching TV until father was ready to continue the same thing at another friend's. Noah began to object to such trips, told his father he didn't like it on "his" time, and sometimes now refused to go along. He was no longer preoccupied with feeling sad, but instead spent more energy in active adventures with peers, e.g., an all-day bike exploration; the joint editorship of a comic strip, already mentioned, etc.

We will skip some months in order to pick up the material prior to remarriage, to illustrate the reactivation of identification conflicts, and the new opportunity for a different working through. A component of Noah's sadness still lay dormant and unresolved; for it tended to be reactivated by other changes or partial losses in his life, e.g., the decision to move to another house when mother and Steve were to marry; a rebuff by a close friend at summer camp and the change from his familiar elementary school to the larger, more anonymous Junior high school.

As mentioned previously, when Steve was first introduced to Noah, he wanted nothing to do with him. As he once said, "I used to think of him falling over a cliff every day." Steve responded with understanding and respect for what was going on, did not push himself toward Noah, but was available and helpful to him. (He would come by in the morning to make breakfast for the boys or give them a ride to school.) Shortly after this, at camp that summer, away from parents and therapy, knowing that mother and Steve were home together, Noah became upset and "homesick" after a rebuff from a close boyfriend, re-experiencing an intense feeling of sadness whenever he was away from his mother or father. It was during this period, until the remarriage, that it became possible to begin to differentiate the nature and source of his grief from those of his father, who was suffering from a depression.

This process was complicated by the fact that the mother, previously very understanding of Noah's conflict, became frightened that the boy's tears and sudden apathy meant that he had inherited his father's difficulties, and tried to provide him with a list of cheerful thoughts and activities to invoke whenever he felt a sad mood coming upon him. During the first couple of days of junior high, Noah felt lost, separated from former friends, and could not stay in school lest he burst out weeping.

I immediately got in touch with an extremely helpful school guidance counselor, so that together we might work out a way to maintain a human support network for Noah in the new unfamiliar junior high. It was not the moment for him to have to endure additional losses, and his friendships had always been important for him. Furthermore, his fear of overwhelming weepiness needed to be dealt with in a way which would not compromise his current peer relationships.

He was quickly shifted to another class where he would be together with his two best friends; and he was assured that if he felt he had to cry, he could leave the classroom and go to the counselor's office until he felt okay again. Knowing he could leave, he did not have to make use of this, and soon reported liking school very much, especially the greater freedom and variety it offered than elementary school had. During the rest of that first week of junior high school, he needed also to call me on the phone several times between appointments and felt okay about doing this.

In October, the first dream involving Steve appeared:

Noah: "Father and me and Kenny went on a canoe trip with the camp; we started to get in rough waters—a storm—everybody else tipped over and we hadn't yet. Then the dream blacked out and Steve was there instead of my father—and it was like the Planet of the Apes, the apes tried to capture the humans, and the only people who really wanted to get free were Steve and Kenny and I. Everybody was human then, but the slaves were scared of the people in charge, but somehow we weren't. We finally escaped while no one was looking, and then all the other slaves saw that we could and then they also weren't scared and escaped."

Among his associations about slaves and people in charge were: "I'm worried about my father. He says that grandma treats him like he is a child, but he is not a child; it's like she is in charge of him still."

In this way, he tells us for the first time about the possibility of identifying with Steve as someone who "was not scared of those in charge," wanted to get free and did so, thereby giving courage to other slaves who watched. At the same time, father's dependence or "scaredness" is now viewed as a childlike characteristic, rather than totally the result of abandonment by mother. In Noah's behavior, increased assertiveness with friends (telling the class bully off in straightforward but not mean fashion) and reported enjoyment of the freedom allowed him at school were prominent. At the same time, he increasingly enjoyed sharing constructive activities with Steve, and stated that he knew Steve cared about him and Kenny as well as Mother "when he does things like build a 'run' for Ophelia so she won't get lost again or skating with us." The same session, he reported another dream in which his father reappeared, and then gave a comparison of his feelings about Steve and his father, quoted earlier. He added, "I know now that I like having Steve around—for my mother too—I want him around so that my mother will be happy—I think also my mother can then let my father be happy."

For the first time, too, the impulse to give something to father is tempered: "Last week, I had two dollars and saw a flower store. I wanted to give my father something, but I only spent one dollar on him, not the whole thing."

He was told that he could continue to give important things to father without giving all of himself or having to be like him exactly. He could keep for himself those things he decided in the long run he liked best about the way father was, but need not feel he had to be those things which made father suffer.

Noah: "My father involves me in everything; he tells me all his troubles and I don't want to be involved in all that so much any more."

The following week, he stated:

"A couple of times in the morning this week, I got another sad feeling for no reason."

t: "Tell me about it."

Noah: "I sort of feel guilty or sad—and it goes away at school—it's like I still feel homesick in my dreams and sad and wake up wanting to be home with mother and father."

t: "You mean like before they separated?"

Noah: "Yes, but we actually never did things like other families—and now with Steve we might—but I used to tell myself all the time, someday we'll do things like other families. I think I was kidding myself. Now I know we *won't* with my father, ever."

t: "When you planned things to be different, you longed for how you wanted it to be with mother and father—and then you think of how it is, what's really possible and what isn't."

Noah: "Yes, that's how it is, I didn't think of it that way, but it's *disappointed that everything that's going on is going on* ... Sometimes, I wonder if my father is going to continue feeling bad—I mean for always—and whether that would mean that I will too."

His "disappointed" refers to the grief for renounced future dreams that I commented upon earlier. We discussed his fear that if his father felt bad that would mean he would too. I reminded him (as we had talked about this previously) that there was no reason to believe that his father would not work out his problems and feel better, too; that it was usual for divorcing adults to have a long period of distress and loneliness, mixed up with anger, but eventually they would begin to work out a new life for themselves. Though we knew his father had been badly shaken up and had not wanted to separate, he was now trying to work on his own problems so that he might have a better life in the future. Noah's feeling bad, in any case, would not help father, and I wondered if he was again trying to "make up" for some other feelings he had toward his father.

Noah: "Sunday morning when they said if my father didn't come they would take us to the museum, I secretly hoped that father would come Monday instead, because I thought I would have more fun with Steve and mom—I think it's because they are feeling better about themselves. I hope we won't move far away when we move, because I still really want to be where my friends are."

t: "Your mother and I talked about this, that when you move to a new house it is important if possible that you can still reach your friends."

Noah: "My father said it's not good to have everything done for you—he said his mother always fixed things for him and now that he's older, he has no one to fix it. I felt weird when he said that. I didn't know if it would be bad for me when I grew up—like for my father. I hope that when I get married I don't get divorced. You know, I don't know what he feels when he feels sad, I now think *it's a different feeling than mine.*"

The following week, a phone call from mother informed me that she had broken the news to father about her wedding date next month. She found it harder to tell him about getting remarried than she thought—he had been feeling better so he was in a reasonable mood, which made it harder, because it was more like old times. In fact, he had guessed why she called, and she cried when she told him, surprising herself. It was then possible, with her, to relate this to Noah's feelings—that his tears were not evidence that he has "inherited" father's difficulties, but were part of the pain of letting go old affectionate memories and hopes.

Noah came in reporting he was happy and excited about the wedding, and then added in a puzzled voice, "Something different is happening with Alfie (the transitional object troll he used to keep in his pocket)."

Noah: "I mean I don't do things like that much any more—they sort of stopped after I started coming here last winter—now I don't know what to do about it. Any object, a pencil, napkin or eraser, it seemed to me they were feeling sad, so I took them near my bed to comfort them, and it's really stupid because they couldn't have any feelings—it must be really me or my father that's feeling that. But if I neglect them, don't take care of that object, like the Kleenex, I'm afraid people might do the same—I don't know what I should do with them, my room is all cluttered up."

t: "What would you like to do?"

Noah: "Get rid of them."

We discuss again, as many times before, that the job of feeling responsible for his father is too big for a kid, that his father's doctor and others will help him with that; but that Noah is still grappling with fears of being deserted himself, fears we know come from a long time ago, and happen now when mother pays attention to Steve.

Noah: "I'm sort of telling Alfie that I'm neglecting him but that I'll do something about it. When he's lying down his eyeballs fall back—you see he can never stand upright without someone holding him—so I gave him an operation so he could stay upright on his own. My pompom dogs have magnets on them, so I took them off and glued them to the bottom of Alfie so he would stay upright—and elevated his back with a rubber band so he could go to sleep if he wanted. I treat him special now. I fixed a bunch of Kleenex and put them all together so they can talk and won't be alone."

Noah, aware of his increasing attachment to Steve, experiences this guiltily as neglect of the father, with whom his identification is now more selective. He seeks to maintain the positive aspects, while distancing himself from some of the disturbance and repeatedly questioning how identical or different similar feelings are in the two of them. His mother is allowing this differentiation to take place increasingly, as she herself finds herself tearful in telling father of her remarriage and saying goodbye, and can understand Noah in these terms as well. Noah touchingly tries to repair his neglect in his fathering of Alfie, who could not stand upright (like the father in depressed times), by giving him an operation which will make a man of him, that is, make him able to stand upright and still have someone to talk to. Standing upright is related to the clarinet "standing upright" as a sign of manhood. Noah also knew that father's contacts with women friends (who he had met) had turned up no enduring prospects as yet.

The next week, Noah told me that Ophelia by mistake had chewed up Alfie, and said, "I really know it makes no difference to him." He then uncluttered his room of all these objects.

The week after the wedding, there was one more, although different, reference to tears.

Noah: "The wedding was a good one. Steve and I went to bake the cake Saturday, and Mom's friend Margie helped, and while it was in the oven, I went to play basketball with the kids." He tells of the presence of his own friends and relatives and Steve's, and feeling good about their being there. "But at the wedding—for a minute it made me cry because of the fancy words."

t: "What fancy words?"

Noah: "The words about loving each other—it didn't feel sad-sad, but it felt really happy-sad, and I never felt that before."

Life went well for Noah during the period after his mother's remarriage. Most noticeably, he became more able to utilize some appropriate aggression in his relationships to others, and not feel as threatened when it was directed toward him. Both erotic and angry feelings were more directly expressed toward me, e.g., when he fantasied I preferred another patient (an adult male) to him. When his mother again fought over the phone with father, he told her directly that she should try to stop that because it made things so much harder for him and Kenny. The previous summer, Noah had felt very easily "hurt" when a friend—or his father—criticized him in any way. Now he has a couple of fights in school, and then befriends a bully by facing him directly with the consequences of his behavior.

Noah: "Everybody hates Bobby because he hits people whenever they don't pay attention to him, but I still like him . . . so I told him to cut it out or I will hit back, that he should cut it out because the guys won't pay attention to that way anyway." When we discussed his own anger and previous fear of ever hurting anyone, he made an important differentiation of his potential victims.

Noah: "I wasn't afraid of hurting Bobby because he can take it—even though a lot of kids hate him. But if someone *can't* take it, then I'm careful not to hurt them." He added, "My mother and father didn't have a fight for a long time, but a couple of days ago father called and mother hung up mad, but I didn't feel sad or bothered—because I thought they could handle it."

He said there was still one kind of time when he has a sad feeling:

Noah: "It's when I wake up in the morning and no one else is awake . . . it feels like I want to stay home with my mother and she doesn't want me to feel that way."

t: "Is it still hard for you to see her giving attention to Steve?"

Noah: "Yea, like the other night, she wouldn't do anything with Kenny or me—just with Steve."

t: "And you still miss her then?"

Noah: "Yea, but Steve does a lot more with us now. He showed us how to sail and let us do it, and fooled around with fixing the stereo. He's good at that and I felt kind of proud of him. But I don't let any of the kids call him my father; I don't want to call him stepfather because that would mean my father is dead, so I call him Steve and technically my mother's husband. It's funny, but I kind of wish my father's girl friend—I mean the trouble is I don't think she really cares enough about him."

Noah remained actively involved in doing a variety of things with each of the three parent figures, but more of his total energy was devoted to activities with his friends. The day he talked about the feeling of "wanting to stay home with my mother" he also said that actually, he had a better time at school or at friends' houses than at home now.

The first Christmas after mother's remarriage he gave a glowing account of the three sets of grandparents; not only did he have two Chanukahs, as he was used to, but an added Christmas celebration with Steve's parents. Steve had planned this carefully to come past the actual Christmas day in order to avoid stirring up a conflict of loyalties for Noah and Kenny and the cultural heritage shared with their parents.

Remnants of intense conflict appeared once more as his mother's pregnancy progressed. Noah graphically expressed feelings found in many children whose mothers felt distance enough from their husbands over a period of time so that the son's attachment was reciprocated in a way which made the boy feel that he had a special and central role in her affections. Normally, a little boy with the same wishes renounces them to some degree as he discovers that the most special, sexual, and intimate relationship is between the parents. Noah had not yet renounced these wishes, though he suffered from the guilt of having outdone his father as a rival in mother's eyes. The cost of not working this out previously for him is seen in his combination of high expectations of himself and inhibition of his feelings of rivalry toward males whom he, at the same times, loved. He spun out at length his concept of his mother as a hypocrite, a person who had betrayed him and broken promises. After a time, he differentiated the ways in which he felt his father had been betrayed from the unspoken "broken promise" that became evident in her pregnancy by Steve.

During the last few months of the pregnancy, Noah became increasingly hostile toward his mother, accusing her of not doing anything for him anymore (like driving him to a friend's house, getting his favorite cereal, or craft material he needed for school projects) and threatening to hit her (much like his bully friend, Bobby, who according to Noah hit people who didn't pay attention to him). He made endless demands and complaints. Mother, shaken by this new behavior, one day locked him out of her room and in an angry moment told him that maybe he should go live with his father.

Noah dreamed: "I was dropped off at the opening of camp, that camp last year I didn't like, that mother promised I wouldn't have to go back to. I didn't know who dropped me off because I was asleep, I couldn't see, not even the car. There were mosquitoes all over my legs and I was trying to hit them. Then my mother came and told me that father had been the one to drop me off, that he had driven wild and had a girl friend with him. But I know he wouldn't actually do that. He has told me if I ever need him to call, and he would come no matter what else he had to do, and I don't think that's true of my mother. By the way, there is a new rule at home, from now on I have to cook my own breakfast and buy my own mittens so that if I don't like what I get I won't have anyone to complain to."

He resisted any discipline from Steve, telling him, "I'm only going to do what my mother says." In his hour, he discussed being able to accept Steve as a person but not as a father. His mother told him he will be punished if he does not obey Steve; that she and Steve "weren't two separate people," that they agreed on everything. Noah stated, "I feel outnumbered."

Meanwhile, he continued to be aware of new reactions to his father:

Noah: "Lately, I don't really know how he feels—I mean sad or not. I usually ask him now. Last week he said, 'it was a great week,' but he didn't look so good. Usually, he says, 'not so good.' I realize now I can't tell anyway if he feels sad or not, because that week he went on good dates and made a lot of money at work. I guess I mean I realize now there is no reason why I should feel sad every time he does. I tell him more often about things that are important to me, too."

t: "Like what?"

Noah: "Well, like about wanting him and my mother to both help plan my bar mitzvah—I know that's still over a year away—and he didn't know how it would be at a party with his family and mother's mother too—and maybe Steve's family. I told him the good thing about divorced parents is that you get Chanukah on both sides and get to do a little bit of Christmas too. I let him know I had fun with Steve's parents, and found out a lot I'd been curious about. My new grandma is like me; she loves animals and doesn't like to see them get hurt. But I still liked grandma and grandpa just as much. So he laughed and said, 'ok'. "

Thus, Noah is able to add important figures in his life, without feeling that he must make a choice.

In his dreams, the sense of desertion by mother continues.

Noah: "I came home from Hebrew School and no one was there except Ophelia—I wanted to pick up the phone to call mother across the street—but it wasn't working; and then I saw the water was coming out of the dishwasher all over the floor and I couldn't do anything."

The helplessness about reaching mother when he needed her brought back memories of his early phobias and nightmares. When frightened by these, when he was little, he recalled that he would quietly sneak into his parents' bedroom, lying down next to father and going back to his own room before they woke up "so mother wouldn't know and get mad."

At a conscious level, he denied any misgivings about the coming baby at this time, saying only that he hoped it might be twins. However, as Noah's mother became near term, his verbal attacks continued, alternating with periods in which he had a transient new symptom. He developed an eye tic. He states,

Noah: "I can't really control it, and my mother got really mad at me and said 'cut it out or I'll throw you out of my room.' Things used to be different."

t: "What do you mean?"

Noah: "I think she used to love me in a different way."

He dreamed of a black vulture that was "about the size of a baby" and "was going to peck and eat me up. But then I saw it was following us and turned out to be a nice one, not mean. I wanted to let it come inside and Steve wouldn't let me, but it was sort of crying outside. I went to pet it because it was sort of lonely, and sad but I still wasn't allowed to bring it in. All I remember is that my new grandma (Steve's mother) came up, and we were in a play where she was nice to it."

When most angry at his mother, Noah called her "Rosemary" with venom, telling her that the baby would be deformed or a monster. In an anxiety-laden session, he told me that he knew he could get mother upset by calling her this. He recounted the story of the movie *Rosemary's baby*. Rosemary got pregnant and had the devil's son, which had webbed feet, yellow eyes, and green skin like a monster.

Noah: "One night the devil came right into her bed and she thought it was a nightmare, but the next morning woke up upset. The witches had talked to her husband and told him it would be a great thing for her to have the devil's son, so he tries to calm her."

In Noah's complicated series of feelings about this story, it became clear that he was trying to deny and not "see" the husband's role in the pregnancy, and that the devil was perceived at one level as Steve but at another as himself.

The monster baby was the embodiment of punishment for the infidelity and betrayal by mother, Steve, and most of all the guilt over his intense, ambivalent wishes toward the mother. At another level, the monster was also himself, deformed by his blinking eye and open anger (monster), both of which the mother rejected. This was pictured in his aggressive vulture "about the size of a baby," who turned out to be lonely and crying until the grandmother was nice to it.

Because of the resurgence of Noah's fears of abandonment, the coming of the baby, and the mutually ambivalent and guilty relationship between mother and son at the moment, it seemed important to support each of them as much as possible prior to the birth. A session had been held with the mother, and now mother, Steve, and Noah were seen together. He was tearfully able to express to them his sense of rejection underlying some of the current wave of hostility and she was able to acknowledge the shifts in their life in practical as well as emotional terms, and to separate this from her caring about him. Steve made clear his active support about sharing in meeting Noah's needs (like giving him rides), but also in enforcing the ground rules (e.g., about Noah's not hitting mother) when necessary.

When the baby arrived, Noah was not neglected. Steve's mother made a welcome cake featuring the names of each member of the family. Mother "made up" even with father's parents. Noah reported that he and his mother were getting along well. "She's very tired, but it doesn't bother me." He proudly brought a picture of the baby and as we looked at it I commented that he wasn't blinking any more. He confirmed that he "doesn't do that anymore" and added, with a grin, that "the baby is really cute, not at all like a monster or anything." He said, "Sometimes I like to hold and feed her too . . . but lately I've been very busy with homework and my friends." Soon afterwards, he told me one day: "You know, I haven't felt scared for a long time like I used to. Like when I had to have that shot in my behind the other day, I realized it was the first time no one had to hold me down, and I really didn't mind. And now when my father says, 'tell mother this' and vice versa, I tell him 'no, you tell her yourself, you're as big as she is.'"

Thus, he was attempting to encourage his father to identify with him at this point and not to be "afraid" anymore. When his stated well-being had persisted for a time, I asked what he thought accounted for his feeling so good lately. He gave a number of answers pertaining to his inner state, but then added: "Remember when I told you that actually our family never did things together like other families did, but I always kind of pretended that we did. Well, now I don't have to pretend anymore, because now I think we really do."

A couple of months later, Noah himself initiated a discussion of termination, by saying that he less often felt the need to come here now, and likening it to not having felt that "homesick" feeling for a long time. "It seems like everything is going fine and things are settled down at our house." We jointly went over the kinds of things he had accomplished here. He first talked of the time when he let himself "be sad here with you" without having to keep that a secret between himself and Alfie. He laughed at his memory that Alfie had been "almost real" to him. However, he thought the biggest change in him had been, "Whenever I'm mad at somebody, I just say so now and I don't get as scared of things."

The following session, Noah described a close friend of his whose parents had just separated and who is "having trouble like I had about being afraid I'd get kicked out of the house. We're their allies and he comes to our house whenever he runs away from his house. That happened last night when his mother went out for a date for the first time. He reminds me of what I went through, so I think it helps him to see me now . . . though sometimes I don't think that's fair because he never helped me when I had trouble. Remember when I had problems with my mother too, and when I used to think it was all my mother's fault?" I remembered.

Noah: "I think it helps him really, because I also feel *it's not me anymore*— what I mean is that I can look back and see how it happens to him and help him because it doesn't happen to me anymore."

Thus, retaining his compassion and empathy, Noah was able to differentiate his identity from his self-perception in his own past. It was at this point that I felt free to tell him that I was trying to understand how children feel about and cope with separating parents and asked how he would feel about my sharing some of his thoughts, and dreams and experiences about that, in writing, with others. He grinned and said, "Well, you know I'm a show-off—so I'd like that a lot!" We will return to Noah later in this chapter, and in chapter 11.

AN EARLY IDENTITY CRISIS
AND INCOMPATIBLE IDENTIFICATIONS: JEFFREY

Loss of the sense of self is usually associated with more serious disturbance than are the symptoms arising out of conflicts of identifications. Yet in the context of parental conflict, acute identity disturbance may occur as an outgrowth of the need to maintain two incompatible identifications.

Freud (1927) long ago suggested that when identifications "become unduly intense and incompatible with one another a pathological outcome will not be far off. It may come to a disruption of the ego in consequence of the individual identifications becoming cut off from one another by resistances. Perhaps the secret of the cases of so called multiple personality is that the various identifications seize possession of consciousness in turn." Such identifications include not only the personal attributes of the identification figures, but also their view of the world and perception of reality, as the child experiences them in accordance with his own developmental level. At times, children of parents who have suffered psychoses feel estranged from their own identity when they enter a social system with a reality view different from that which was learned at home—for instance, at the time of entrance into school. Often they feel compelled to choose between the truth they learned at home and the truth as the rest of the world perceives it. Although such children in consequence sometimes refuse to go to school, and may be labeled as having a "school phobia," their difficulties are not properly described as a phobia, with its more usual underlying separation anxiety and the displacement of unconscious hostility from the parent-child to the school-child interaction. Neurotic, school-phobic children show little identity disturbance; in contrast the children I refer to experience a frightening "loss of self" in an environment that operates under assumptions different from those held in their home.

Jeffrey, the little boy quoted at the beginning of this chapter, had the inner resources and the family support to avert the sense of "loss of self" when his custody changed from his mother to father. He had two parents who presented him with widely divergent, incompatible views of what the world was like, and handled him very differently. He dealt with this split by attempting simultaneously to live out being two separate selves, but his two selves stopped short of becoming "multiple personalities." I think him remarkable in his ingenious temporary solution. Each of the two selves was in the image of the relationship to one of the parents.

Although children of his age often invent an "imaginary companion," who, they insist, is certainly real enough to have a place set for him at the table, this tends to have a different function. The imaginary companion is usually an animation of a particular impulse the child rejects in himself or is way to control that impulse; or it takes the place of a transitional object. For example, the imaginary companion may be blamed for misdeeds of the child, at a time when rudiments of conscience or fear of punishment make the child wish to "extrude" the naughty deed, while knowing it has some relationship to him; or the companion is protective ("like a fierce lion who only obeys me and chases robbers away"). Or he assuages loneliness, and is talked to much like the somewhat older child will talk to his or her pet cat. However, the imaginary companion is invariably under the control of the child and its aims are always friendly toward him.

Jeffrey's other "self," in contrast, was not under his control, nor friendly toward him. It was considered "bad" by him but couldn't go away. His two selves, each at odds with the other, represented how he experienced himself in relationship to his two divorced parents. He needed both as long as he was insufficiently secure about his future with his father. The incompatible nature of his identification figures made growth-promoting identifications impossible. This situation is quite different from those of children whose parents' attitudes and personalities are quite unlike each other, but who present a similar perception of external reality. Such differences between parents are in fact often enriching for the child, who has wider options for identifications and becomes aware of the fact that one does not have to be a certain way in order to become adult. Over a period of time, Jeffrey was able to relive both the frightening and the positive aspects of his earlier relationship to his mother. He needed to establish the positive features first, as a kind of reassurance to himself that he would not destroy his inner image of her when he re-encountered and did battle with the more frightening remembrances.

Jeffrey's father had gained custody of his four children after about a year of parental separation. While living alone with mother, who had had a psychiatric hospitalization when Jeffrey was between the ages of one and two, Jeffrey and his siblings were warned by her about the father's "dangerousness" until they became fearful of even talking to him on the telephone. She was suspicious of the neighbors and cautioned the children not to mingle with them. Although there were some areas of appropriate mothering, others were clearly pathological. Jeffrey experienced a range of interactions with mother. These included her sleeping with him at times, and at other times locking him in his room for long periods of time. Later, a large box of dried feces, dating back to that year, was found in his closet. When she lost her temper she tended to claw the children with her fingernails.

When first seen, Jeffrey was clinging, fearful of going outside to play, and, in father's woman friend's later words, "like a caged animal, so tense and hard to handle." In therapy Jeffrey would initially relate events about his mother only after being allowed to engage with the therapist in one activity he mentioned having enjoyed with mother. I agreed to making "sticker pictures" with him, like mother used to. His aim seemed to be to hold onto the positive aspects of the relationship to her while facing his fears. Jeffrey played out, with puppets, his wish that he could have both parents happily together, and his awareness that outside help was needed for dealing with impulse control and with "hurts in the family."

Jeffrey: "This could be the mother and father (Jeffrey is using the witch and the devil puppets); this is what we need for the family, a happy family—the mother and father and a policeman and a girl and a pet."

t: "Where's the boy?"

Jeffrey: "There he is (Jeffrey uses baby instead of boy puppet) and a nurse. First, the boy growed and they both lived happily together. Then their mother growed and they all three lived together (Jeffrey has them hug) and then the sister grew and they were happy together and then their pet grew and went to the family. And then the nurse and policeman grew and got in the family and helped them with all the cuts and robberies in the family."

"Cuts and robberies" was an understatement of what the mother felt she had suffered and wished to inflict on the father, neighbors, etc., in turn. Father, however, attempted not to undermine the positive aspects of the children's remaining contact with her, in spite of being sorely provoked.

One of Jeffrey's symptoms was that in his room he urinated on the floor by the closet door. He soon reported that it was not he, himself, who did this, that there were two people living in his room. One was Jeffrey.

Jeffrey: "The other is a bad boy who has a closet in his room that's a bathroom; he has no friends and isn't allowed to have any; he has a baby brother, but it got squished (mother told him about a miscarriage prior to his birth). The boy does not like his mommy anymore, but his daddy is dead, he has been dead for a year. Onced he wished his mommy were dead, but he had to visit her. He knows it's wrong to make on the floor, but he has to do it. He has to stay there all the time even if I don't want him to. Sometimes I'm not there—not anywhere at all—and he's there all by himself."

Meanwhile, Jeffrey, the "other" boy, began actually to play with children in the neighborhood and made a beginning, though tenuous friendship to the housekeeper. He refused to sleep in his old bed. "The other boy sleeps in my old bed." He reported terrible dreams of monsters coming to take him away.

Needless to say, Jeffrey was still frightened that abandoning his former self might mean total abandonment, and needed considerable reassurance about the fact that the court (like the policeman and nurse in his puppet story) had decided that the best place for him to grow up was now living with his father, and that no monsters or people would be allowed to take him away. The urinary symptom disappeared, while he continued to reject his old bed (with his old self) and liked sleeping on a mattress in a tent he and his father had set up for play in his room. He accepted more kinds of food prepared by the housekeeper. He was able to tell me one day that his daddy promised to keep him, and that it is he, not the other boy who doesn't like to visit mommy anymore. It was then finally he could say with relief that the other boy had gone away; and that now he could always find himself.

Jeffrey instead now brought to therapy, for several sessions in a row, a large hopping toad in a cage. He indicated that the toad had "bad dreams" about being "locked in his cage" and wanted to explore. Freed in the office, the toad unfortunately preferred hiding under the radiator to adventure, but this allowed Jeffrey to discuss the toad's worries, while building him "houses to visit" out of blocks. Jeffrey now enjoyed playing outside with neighborhood friends, but did not always obey the housekeeper or father when called to come in.

The use of the toad suggested that he was now able to isolate the identification as the scared, locked-up boy to a smaller, more manageable island of his ego, while he himself was freer to function in accordance with his new environment. Once the permanence of his relationship with father was settled in his mind by father's promise, he accepted the attitudes of the "bad boy" (not wanting to visit mommy) as within himself, and no longer had to preserve the locked-up-urinating-by-the-closet boy who belonged to mother, in toto. At the same time, he acted toward the toad as his father acted toward him, letting him out of the cage to visit other houses, and talking about his worries. It was also during this time that he was able to bring up a mixture of feelings about his mother. This included lonesome moments of missing her "when she's nice to me," fears about her intense contacts (e.g., "she kissed me all the time and I couldn't get down") and her unpredictable anger (and this led him to thoughts of the squished dead baby brother). He tried to repeat some of this with father (e.g., asking father to sleep with him and bite his "pee-pee") but accepted father's refusals with apparent relief. For a time he was reluctant to go with his mother on visiting days, but seemed to have less anxiety about this once Joan, a divorced woman with two sons of her own, became a regular participant in the household.

Jeffrey continued to work out his ideas about a safer kind of autonomy. For example, he used his therapy time for building "strong boats," "harbors," and "hitching posts" out of wood, glue, and nails, and connecting them to each other by a thin string. He made the boats go on "long trips on their own" and "never get lost" as long as they knew where their hitching post was. Thus, the boats were neither alone, nor constrained in their movements. Meanwhile, father and Joan were approving of his wanting to go to day camp like a boy down the street and learn how to swim, which he did. If his father had to go on an actual trip, overnight, which was rare, Jeffrey seemed to like a symbolic reassurance of their belonging together, such as a picture of himself and his father which had been given to him.

Father reported at this time that his behavior on Mondays (after Sunday visits to mother) was characterized by wildness, inability to play quietly or amuse himself, compulsive running in circles in the house, with an inability to stop even when disciplined, a regression to babytalk and complaints of headaches, starting Sunday nights and continuing through Mondays. By Monday evening, at bedtime, he would typically calm down. Again, on Saturdays, he would begin to become fretful and sometimes verbalized that he wished he did not have to go on Sunday. Meanwhile, there were no more references to "the other boy" in his room, and he had asked to have the "old bed" removed; he had previously not allowed this. In the fall, he entered happily into kindergarten activities, and was described as being very bright and zestful in his play with other children. When his father remarried, he became particularly fond of his new big brothers, and his vision of bliss was to be worthy enough to be included in their baseball games. In turn, Joan reported her surprise about how tender and tolerant her sons were with their new young siblings, saying that this was a side of their personality which she had never seen before. All six children occasionally shared some outing with Joan's former husband, with whom, as they could see, she was quite comfortable, in contrast to the continuing controversy between Jeffrey's mother and father. It was important for Jeffrey and his siblings to participate also in this model of parental parting.

As Jeffrey became more secure about the affectionate interactions and comfortable ways of settling disputes within his new family, he tried to deal with the incompatible images of reality presented by his mother and the relations of these images to the person he was.

Mother's communications, about which he now asked many questions, had to do with the image of the world as hostile and fraught with dangers. If his contact with it was too close, he would get contaminated or "poisoned" by it, and his destruction would follow. One image of this brought up by Jeffrey, was that he would get squished like a rotten egg and be like his dead "baby brother" (the miscarriage). He reported that mother let him know Jeffrey's new family and the neighbors of whom he was fond were part of the contagious danger, but alliance with the powers of mother could protect him. This view was contradicted by and was "incompatible" with the reality of his current experiences.

For example, Jeffrey said he had told mother about going to a neighbor's house and playing with the little girl, "but they don't even have one brother." He was glad that he had brothers at home now. Mother told him it was just as well that Mrs. W. didn't have a son, because of the bad things she did, like cheating, lying, and stealing what mother had. She had pretended to be mother's friend, too, and then she lied and tried to hurt mother and Jeffrey. Jeffrey asked how, and mother said that she lied so that daddy would get everything. According to Jeffrey, she added that "people like you and me get hurt, so it is not good to have friends who lie." She then told him that she loved him with all her heart, and he should be a good boy and not tell anybody about their conversation. She told him she had the power to make people do what she wanted, but that it might take some time.

The comments about getting hurt reminded him of mother's having told him that he had had a baby brother, who got squished. He had asked his mother about this and reported that she said that the baby was no good anyway, it was like a rotten egg. At times when she had held on to him and kissed him, and wouldn't let him get down when he wanted, he was afraid if he weren't a good boy like she wanted, he too would get "squished" by her like the rotten egg.

She warned him not to get close to other people because "there is a lot of polio around," and if he catches this, he would not be able to move. This, of course, reminded him of being locked up, and having to pee-pee by the closet, because it would make mother too mad if he wanted to get out. When he told her he had for the first time at home tried "mushroom sauce" on his hamburger, she let him know that many mushrooms are poisonous. She frequently told him that daddy was trying to "poison" him against her, though in reality the father did not do this.

Work with Jeffrey was complicated by the continuing emotional pressure from his mother to choose to "belong" to her by rejecting his father and new family; and the implication that dangers would befall him if he did not do so. However, he progressively tested out the two kinds of reality presented to him, and chose to trust the validity of his own perceptions, now no longer housed in the bodies of two different boys.

Gwen, Jeffrey's ten-year-old sister, was initially upset at being taken away from her mother, felt it was an unfair conspiracy, since she and mother had been so close. Like her mother, she felt she did not get proper recognition in school, scouts, or drama club; she was "robbed" of the prize that should have been hers by some imposter. Of all the children reviewed in this chapter, her initial identification with her mother was most attitudinal, and least expressed in ego-alien behavior. She spoke freely about missing her mother terribly, and was described as "crying over the least little thing" at home. These at first were small slights directed either at her or by implication at her mother. She worked some of these out in the arena of triadic friendships with girls of her age, with more than the usual mixture of possessiveness, exclusiveness, and disloyalties. A turning point in differentiating herself from her mother came when a friend let her know quite directly that she did, in fact, like Gwen, but would not want her friendship if Gwen got mad each time she related to someone else as well, like her mother did. Although Gwen's sorrow for her mother appeared early in the picture, it was only after she had somewhat solidified her friendships, slowly began to trust me, and could count on Joan as a part of her future, that she brought up her fear of not agreeing with mother on everything. As she put it, "I don't want her to say things about me like she says about my father." There were then a host of painful memories of mother's wrath and what Gwen called "weirdness" before her psychiatric hospitalization, and Gwen's own sense of desolation, anger, and helplessness at the time. With compassion similar to Noah's, she spoke of mother's quirks as not surprising, in view of mother's upbringing. She had had to contend with grandmother's "weirdness." Gwen was increasingly open about not wanting to share in it herself. Although more competitive with the two big brothers than Jeffrey (mostly for Joan's attention), she too was glad of their presence, said she never had as much fun at home before, and asked directly for aid in countering her mother's pressure for promises of loyalty. She slowly became guilty about what she felt she owed her mother (e.g., when mother told Gwen on the phone, "You were born of my belly, so it is only justice for me to get more of you than your father," Gwen hung up the phone).

Jeffrey's and Gwen's father and new stepmother strikingly demonstrated to me the effect of an emotionally rich and supportive new family structure in ameliorating a potentially serious disturbance of identification in the child. For good personal reasons there was nothing more important to either of them than the emotional well-being of each individual involved, and they spent an enormous amount of time and energy with the children. This seemed to make it possible for them to withstand endless provocation from the children's thoroughly bereft and vindictively embittered mother, without countering this by devaluing her in the eyes of the children. Whenever the mother's behavior toward the children was positive, they supported it warmly. More often, they needed to walk the fragile tightrope of helping the children to see that their mother could not help some of the frightening things she did, because she had so much difficulty in having ever allowed herself to feel loved, that her behavior did not mean that the children were at fault; and finally, that they need not feel guilty when they were furious with her. Although this mother could not restrain her continued angry and critical tirades at father, stepmother, and the children who were no longer living with her, the new family constellation became the center of gravity for the children's identifications. Only within this secure context could they maintain an open mind about the question of reestablishing an increased relationship with their mother, on a less disturbed basis, at some time tin the future.

TWO RETROSPECTIVE VIEWS OF THE EFFECTS OF EARLY LOSS

Pam and Lou Ann* are described to illustrate the role of parental separation in subsequent character formation, in cases in which the home parent was unable to support the child emotionally through a period of grieving. Because of difficulties of their own, Pam's and Lou Ann's mothers also could not meet the children's intensified needs for nurturance from them. Lou Ann suffered greater extremes of deprivation and subsequent interference with her emotional development. The descriptions of these children will be retrospective, in the sense that parental separation occurred before the child was four years old in both cases, but the material presented here is from therapy begun, respectively, when Pam was close to thirteen, Lou Ann was twelve and a half.

*I had the opportunity to treat Pam and Lou Ann within the delinquency research unit of the Judge Baker Guidance Center, made possible by a research grant (M286) from the National Institute of Mental Health, U.S. Public Health Service, 1955-1960. I wish to express my appreciation for the stimulating collaboration with Kaufman, M.D., project director, and research team members, Joan Zilbach, M.D., David Reiser, M.D., Harry Durkin, M.D., Chester d'Autremont, M.D., Elizabeth Makkay, M.D., Beatrice Simcox Reiner, S.W., Edward Stone, S.W., and Dorothea Jones, S.W.

Grief Unexplored: Some Consequences in Character Structure: Pam

Pam illustrates the meshing of a number of issues discussed in previous chapters. Pam's mother did not think her daughter grieved at age three and a half when father left. "She just became wilder." One way Pam handled the loss of her father was to identify with the behavioral qualities of his "delinquent" behavior, for which her mother could not forgive him, and which alienated mother from Pam as well. There was also an identification with her fantasy of her biologic mother, who had been the first in her life not to "want" her. Neither of these identifications was initially conscious, although her wish to be free and independent of those who would disappoint her was clear.

Initially, Pam's tolerance for anxiety and affect were low, resulting in difficulties relating to people, in controlling impulses and in having enough conflict-free energy available for the mastery involved in learning at a level in line with her intelligence. Her self-sufficiency defended against the close, dependent attachments she craved and feared. Treatment with her was geared initially toward helping her tolerate a relationship with me, in which she would feel sufficiently in control not to be overwhelmed with affective experience before she could tolerate it; and yet would know that she could not control me either. This was necessary while she was still in the period in which "acting out" her impulses was her predominant way of handling tension. After we both survived this period, she showed great interest in how I lived, and was drawn toward the possibility of an adult life that included "college," etc., and wanted realistic support and assistance in exploring these issues.

As is characteristic of children who have long defended against a "depressive nucleus" by acting out, as well as by utilizing activity in contrast to passive wishes, once she had made a relationship, she presented the first signs of feeling "hurt" and in need of care through physical symptoms, associated with bodily experiences related to early stages of development (Lewin, 1950), e.g., difficulties in eating or "nausea" when someone was nice to her, dizziness and sensations of heat (which also had sexual components). The affective components of her longing for her absent father and the memory of associated grief did not emerge fully until she had been in treatment about three or four years, after a period in which she gave indications of wanting to identify with me in various ways. The shifts in her perception of herself and father and mother are reflected in her changing relationships to peers, her interest in learning and future plans, and a new tolerance for dealing with inner stress.

Pam's spunkiness and engaging repartees made her especially fun to work with, though at the same time her personality initially induced a kind of countervigilance in me, for I knew that if I allowed her to outmaneuver me, she would become so frightened of her impulses that I would no longer be counted on as a protection and hence would be of no use to her as a therapist.

Work with Pam also differed from that with children previously described in this chapter in the approach to identification processes. Because she had not had the chance to identify in a positive fashion with either parent, but alternated between the characteristics of the "delinquent" father and the feared identification with the "weak and nervous" mother, she needed to evolve an identification with me or someone else before she felt secure enough to deal with her feelings about the past. Her problems had prevented her from growing through identification with teachers or peers. Her ambivalence about this identification process—with me or anyone else—was demonstrated in her initial provocativeness, which she assumed would disrupt the relationship, and later the somatic aspects related to ideas about taking in (eating problems), extruding (vomiting), or sustaining the tensions aroused by making close relationships (how quickly things are consumed by fire!).

Pam was in therapy for close to five years. She was referred at age twelve and a half because of stealing, running away, disruptive behavior in boarding school, rebelliousness toward her mother and other adults, and difficulties in learning. She had had a previous brief contact with a child guidance clinic at age seven, when she threw rocks at other children, used "bad language," and was unmanageably disobedient at home. The recommendations for treatment, however, was not carried out at that time, and instead she was sent to boarding school by age nine.

Pam had been adopted in infancy. Her adoptive mother was a submissive woman, who described herself as always having been "mousy" and fearful. However, in interviews with a social worker, it was evident that she was preoccupied with sexual, including homosexual, behavior on the part of others, as well as with the violence which she fantasized Pam might do someday. She described Pam as such an active, colicky, but demanding baby and toddler that mother felt continually run ragged by her. Later, she had increasingly feared that Pam would grow up and kill someone, or that she might be a lesbian. She seemed intimidated by her, felt rejected by her and was unable to set normal limits for her. Until she began therapy with the social worker, mother had acted as an obedient little girl toward her own mother and father, in whose house she eventually lived after the adoptive father had deserted the family. She seemed unaware of the constricting depression which had made the relationships to her husband and child seem like such demanding impositions of her. Unlike some of the mothers described early in this chapter (who were seen about twenty years later), she had no "consciousness" of options for doing something about her unhappy life, nor any social support for risking initiation of change.

The adoptive father had run away with, and later married, his secretary when Pam was three and a half. He was viewed by Pam's mother as "delinquent" in a variety of ways. These included "lying," some drinking (which did not sound excessive), as well as the "immoral" act of running away with the woman with whom he was having an affair. Mother had not realized that anything was wrong in the marriage, and the act had caught her by surprise. She had not enjoyed sexual relations with father, nor physical intimacy with Pam. She recalled having always called Pam "daddy's girl," because the two were so close and especially involved in a lot of roughhousing and other physical contact. Their favorite game had been playing "horse," with Pam riding high on father's shoulders. She had often chided them for making "spectacles of themselves" in their play together. Since father left the family and moved to another state, he sees Pam only very occasionally, but usually sends a birthday present with a letter. Mother is often angered by the letters, which apparently include such phrases as "don't tell mother."

After father left, Pam and mother lived for a time with an aunt, until Pam's unruly behavior made it impossible for them to stay. Thereafter, the mother moved in with her own parents, and went to work, leaving Pam in the grandparents' hands during part of the day, until she was sent to boarding school. Occasionally, during vacation, mother sent Pam to stay with the paternal grandparents, in spite of her assertion that they would be a bad influence on the child.

Pam was a spunky, vivacious girl, and in initial interviews was vivid and dramatic in her verbalizations, often in a provocative or sexualized way, as though to make sure she would get some reaction from adults. When told she would have some psychological tests, she said she expected that she would lie on a couch in a dark room and have pictures of nudes flashed on the ceiling for her to talk about. She was disappointed in this expectation. Testing showed her to be a very bright girl, with a superior IQ in spite of her failing grades. She showed an ego structure which lacked flexible mechanisms for dealing with tension and indicated alternations between impulsive action or affect outbursts, and periods of withdrawal from people and rigid control over her feelings about them. A strong depressive undertone was noted. She seemed to present her identification problems in a nutshell when she answered a question about what she would *most* and *least* want to be by stating that she wanted to be a "wild stallion because then I could be wild and free and not obey anyone nor have a care in the world." She least of all wanted to be "a chicken because then you have to live with a bunch of other old hens and end up making a meal for somebody."

In therapy, Pam seemed to go through a number of phases, with a different kind of relationship both to me and to other people in her environment, and with different types of defense organizations and anxieties coming to the fore during each.

Phase I: Acting Out. During the first phase of treatment, Pam structured the relationship with me, as well as every outside relationship, into either a fight or a sexualized situation. At boarding school, she went out of her way to break the rules. She spoke freely of her pleasure in trying to shock the teachers because she could always get a rise out of them. For example, while the other girls might say "good morning, teacher" with a smile, as they were supposed to, she would say "go fuck your boyfriend," with the identical smile and then watch for the reaction. Or she might run through the school naked, except for purple underpants, and then indignantly accuse the teachers of staring at her like men. She had had intermittent sex play with boys for some years, and later with an older man. She could not get along with girls her age, but concentrated her interest on either the adults or much younger children. However, she was also known to withdraw and stay by herself in the library at school, not reading, for many hours at a time. When reprimanded at school, she would laugh or say she did not care. Since she had not responded to discipline, nor to encouragement or affection, the staff of the school felt unable to "reach her" and had considered recommending sending her somewhere else. However, they were quite willing to continue with her if this could be important for her, and to work collaboratively with the therapist, even when informed that change was unlikely to be quick or smooth.

In therapy, Pam initially often came late or skipped appointments. She boasted freely about a number of delinquencies, asserting that what she liked best was getting teachers mad at her. She briefly described her mother as "frail, weak, and nervous" but could not discuss anything else about her feeling about either parent initially. She classified all the people she knew according to how powerful they were, admiring the unafraid—among whom she included her father—and was contemptuous of any sign of weakness or fear in herself or others. She warned me by the third interview that anyone who had ever gotten to know her—which was rare anyway—regretted it later, and expressed almost angry amazement that I had not been scared away by her already. In her initial interview, in wich she was more verbal than in the series which followed it, she gave a kind of preview of later recurrent themes.

Pam was telling me about sex play with a boy last summer which had stopped short of intercourse. They had joked about his wearing a "safe" or not and he told her it would be no fun that way, "like going swimming with your rubbers on." She decided she didn't like him. Anyway, she would rather have a baby than a boy friend. She has always thought that if she ran away and "started a baby," nobody could stop her.

Pam: "The only thing which has stopped me so far is wondering how much it hurts to have a baby, because someone said once to me that something hurts 'worse than having a baby.' I always think that if I don't have a husband, I would leave it in a basket for some nuns because I know they wouldn't throw it out."

t: (purposefully ignoring at this point the likelihood that she fantasized that she herself had been born and "thrown away" by being given up for adoption by her own mother, because I did not have enough of a relationship with her to deal with this yet) "kids often think that having a baby would solve things about being lonely and having trouble with mothers, but then they find out it doesn't solve those things after all—but instead makes stuff harder for them. Having a baby when you're grown up is quite different. It sounds to me like the question of getting thrown out is an important one to you. You know, I think we should find out what you really need—instead of a baby—right now."

Pam: "One thing I can't stand is when anyone is nice to me, like if the teachers get mushy or call me honey. There's this girl named June down the hall—she's younger than me and gets crushes on women—I think she must be crazy."

t: "No, that doesn't mean she's crazy. . . ."

Pam: "A long time ago, I kind of liked Miss Lynn, too, but not any more."

t: "What did you mean about getting crushes?"

Pam: "I meant that that's the wrong kind of love. That's probably why Miss Lynn throws me out if I ever come into her room after school."

t: "Is that what you think drives her away?"

Pam: "I know it is."

She then talked of how she could not stand being touched by any of the teachers. Some of the teachers, when they hurt your feelings, try to make it up by a kiss. Pam can't stand that and feels much safer kissing boys. She hates to be called "honey" because it makes her feel like a baby. She hates to be babied. It's funny though, when she hears a teacher calling another girl "honey" she gets so mad she could kill them. She'd like to, in fact. She thinks it's all right for babies to be taken care of, and knows that nuns would take care of a baby. She then said she "had thought about solving the baby by having a problem. I smiled at the slip she had made and took up how hard she tries to prove to herself that she doesn't want any care, that she can "solve the baby." She answered, immediately, "If I had a baby, no one could say I was one!"

In the next few months Pam was either seductive or angry in her interviews. For example, she would put her feet on the desk, a position which lifted her skirts, exposing her underwear. Or, at times she would invite me to touch her, e.g., to feel her new permanent, and when I would not do this, she furiously spoke of loathing a boy who once spent two whole hours with her without making a pass at her. Whenever I had to be away, Pam generally said she was glad, as she didn't like to come and this was her last time anyway. At one point, she said she would come only if the teachers said she had to. Working together with the school made it possible to give her this external support (the teachers said she had to), which then relieved her. If she came on the basis of wanting to, she felt this was a weakness. She always kept some bullets in her pocket and showed these to me.

During this time, it seemed important to proceed very slowly. Although Pam could be very articulate, it was necessary to avoid pressing for background or associations, as one might be tempted to do, because at this stage acting out was her first way of dealing with rising tensions that she could not tolerate. Techniques used in working with children like Noah would have undermined her need for ego-building.

The sexual preoccupations were dealt with by taking them up in more general terms (including the transference feelings) so that she could experience the relationship as safe and could begin to feel it was all right to identify with me or with others, without the sexualization which she feared so much as overwhelming. The sexualization, among other meanings, was felt to be a component of the early organization of the libido, in which the energy available for making identifications has not as yet become neutralized enough for comfort, or differentiated from sexual and aggressive impulses. In response to such behavior as exposing herself while at the same time expressing loathing for "woman love" and her intent to run away, I believed it best to deal with Pam's anxiety by simple statements that I wouldn't let her do anything here that would frighten her, so she didn't really have to run away. Because sympathetic or warm feelings toward her were so frightening to Pam, I needed to use self-restraint about these, and light, apparently joking approaches at times seemed most called for, in conjunction with consistent, repeated reminders that she couldn't control me entirely, and that I did not intend to be drawn into her attempt to act out being rejected and abandoned by me.

Phase II: Somatic Experiencing of Distress, with Predepressive Components. The first reference in therapy to somatic sensations, and then somatic symptoms themselves, began nine months after the beginning of treatment. They occurred together, or perhaps as a defense against a vague beginning feeling of depression associated with an amelioration of the provocative delinquent behavior in school. During this period, there were vacillations in the defenses. Acting out would recur, particularly when the inner tension regarding her growing awareness of herself became too great.

In the fall, Pam first mentioned having the "blues" and also said that she had stopped "acting up" in school and had recently gotten a good grade in conduct. She explained this change as, "I must be getting sick or something." She began to come on time or early for her sessions. One day she complained that she got hot when she was here with me, and was "roasting." She added that opening a window would do no good because she always got hot when she talked to me. She then yelled angrily that she was stubborn and had a temper and would get mad, so didn't I want her to leave immediately? When I again said I would take the risk because I wouldn't let her do anything here she'd be sorry about, she grinned in spite of herself and said with admiration, "You sure got crust." She complained that she didn't know how to sit still and talk, she never had, she always got jittery. She would rather go horsebackriding with me.

The following session, she again became anxious, saying she was hot and couldn't we leave now. She was really sweaty and would rather walk and not talk. I said sure, we could do that. (I had suggested this once myself during the early summer but she had turned it down at that time.) I said it was natural for her to feel uncomfortable, that other kids did too when they talked about some of these things. This seemed to relieve her so that she then settled down again, not wanting to walk but telling me about her roommate. She then said that she would be impossible to live with. No one could stand her very long. Anybody would need a lot of patience. Probably, I would have a character with not much patience. She was not waiting around to find out. She said Christmas, only until then. Then she was leaving. At this point, she held her lighted cigarette to the wrapping, watching for my reaction and repeating that she was difficult and impossible. I sat back and said, "It must be quite a job to *have to prove* that you are stubborn or difficult." She immediately rose up indignantly and said, "I *don't have to*; I *want to*."

t: "Why?"

Pam: "To make you mad and test you out. What if I start to light fires? What would you do?" She began to set the piece of paper on fire with the cigarette. I said I would want to find a safe place for her fire and said that there was a sink right behind her chair. She did this for just a moment longer and then blew it out herself. She sat quietly for a moment and then said: "I know what would really make you mad."

t: "What?"

Pam: "If I called you Lora."

t: "Why should that make me so mad?"

She burst out with a great deal of feeling, "Because you're my psychologist, not my friend. You wouldn't have anything to do with me except here. The only reason you can stand me here at all is because you even see worse people and that's your job and you get used to it. That's the only reason you let me come."

I told her it was true this was different from being friends, because we mainly talked about her, but that didn't mean that I did not think she was the kind of person that I would enjoy or value as a friend. She then said, very quietly, "I guess I can call you by your last name, the way I have been." She then said she thought my secretary was just beautiful. She wished she could look like that. She told me of an incident that had happened that week, about somebody in school whom Miss Lynn threw out of the room because she called her a name and was disrespectful. She began to make a little fire in the ashtray now, saying "It's funny how a flame can burn up everything in a minute."

t: "Even what's been built up for a long time?"

Pam: "Oh, you psychologists with your ideas. You're probably thinking what am I afraid of building up, if it can get destroyed by fire in a minute."

t: "That wasn't my thought but I think it is a good one."

She smiled. She said when she was coming up to the clinic today there were a lot of people downtown talking about Republicans and Democrats. The people for Ike looked like they were ready to fight the others. She herself was for Ike and wondered who I was for. I smiled and said, "Going to see if we can start a fight?" She said sometimes at school she had a feeling that she had to start a fight right away. She then said she wondered why. I said I wondered, too.

During this period, Pam began to talk of her wish to know about her past. She implied that her adoptive father had done many things she couldn't talk about but was tempted to tell me. However, thinking about the past "makes me sick and would make you sick, too." I told her hearing about it wouldn't make me too nervous.

The session after mentioning these memories from the past for the first time, Pam came with heavy make up, jewelry, and seductively dressed. She brought with her a picture of her favorite teacher at school Miss Lynn, kissed the picture and stated that this teacher was just the same height as the therapist. She then immediately announced that she was going to leave early today—and would I please tell her when half the time is up—because she was going to the South End to pick up men. I told her "no," I would not do that, and she should stay instead, which she did. In this and following sessions, she revealed her fantasied future as a prostitute. She stated that she wanted something "off a man," any man, a night of fun with a lot of men and then never to see them again. She did not want to even know them.

Pam associated her needing what she calls "man love" to the teachers' now expecting her to be a "goodie goodie" (as she has behaved better this fall) and being "mushy" with her. She reminded me that father was certainly not a goodie goodie.

I said that maybe the time had come for us to look at what being a goodie goodie meant to her, and why she had to protect herself so hard from being that. It now slowly became possible to lay the groundwork for recognizing that she had a pattern of admiring the rambunctious ones, who managed to outsmart the righteous-sounding goodie goodies, though sometimes at a cost to themselves. These patterns of behavior were tied to her perceptions of the father, in contrast to the mother. Her identification with her image of the father was valued by her as an ego ideal, and simultaneously stimulated and then devalued by mother. This was complicated by the fact that "caring" left one vulnerable to being deserted. To have interpreted these identificatory links too early would have interfered with those components of her defense structure which utilized "strength" and "being in control" as necessary ways of preventing a regression to experiencing her dependent wishes with overwhelming intensity.

There were also opportunities to face her with reappraisal of her perception of her character traits. As her defiance and "stubborness" had been cast in negative terms most of her life, and since she had been deserted in reality, she saw herself as basically "impossible to live with" and did not appreciate the positive components in her "stubborness," which had been necessary to cope with her losses (both father and mother) as well as she did.

For example, one day she said she didn't mind a change in appointment time because she wasn't quite as fussy as last year. Did I think she was impossibly fussy last year or just plain stubborn? I laughed and said I thought of it as neither. She said in amazement, "Pam not stubborn?" I said, "Nope, Pam keeping things under control." She said, "oh," in a relieved way and said it was okay to change the appointment time.

Pam's sense of humor and enjoyment of her rule-breaking adventures were also a positive part of the ego ideal, established in the early loving contacts with her father, which mother had described in terms of "making a spectacle of himself." For an example of this period, here is part of one session following the one in which she had planned to pick up men (a plan she didn't carry through).

Pam always had cigarettes, not allowed at school, because she hid hers in a hole made in her pillow, while teachers only looked in drawers and clothes. This day she told me of an incident that happened on the streeetcar home last week. Pam was sitting there smoking her cigarette and an old lady sat next to her. The old lady started talking about how terrible today's teenagers are, smoking and everything. She was surprised nice people would have anything to do with them, etc., and then asked Pam to put out her cigarette. Pam told her if she didn't like it she could goddamn well move. The old lady got up in a huff and went to the conductor, who came to speak with her at the next stop. Pam said that he was a nice, fatherly—and then quickly changed it to "grandfatherly"—man. He came over to Pam and asked her to put out the cigarette. At this point, she pretended that she could only speak German and said "ach?" in a puzzled way. He put his arm around her, pointed to her cigarette and shaking his head, said "nein." She put it out and the conductor then scolded the little old lady for having said all those things about the "little girl" who didn't understand what she was saying. I grinned and said that she sure had been bent on getting the best of the goodie goodie old lady, and Pam went into a gambit of disdain for goodie goodies, and especially squealers, like a girl at school who threatened to tell on Pam for smoking. She started talking for the first time about when she was a little girl, about six years old, and was "left home alone." She used to throw rocks and call children names, telling them they were full of shit. Her aim was pretty good, and often she hit the children. They would squeal on her and then she would get punished. This was the same period when she and her mother had lived with the aunt, who also worked. I said,

t: "Home alone?"

Pam: "Oh yes, my mother was much too busy—I mean she worked and couldn't take care of me—besides I was too tough to take care of."

t: "Who took care of you?"

She silently pointed to herself. I said very quietly, "Maybe you felt thrown out yourself. No wonder you felt like throwing things then!" After a moment, I added that she had mentioned some other people, like father, who weren't goodie goodies either. She immediately answered by saying that her father would have taken her to any beer parlor but she had already told me she couldn't tell me about that. As she said this, her voice was angry. I said that maybe that was one reason she had such trouble liking herself unless she was acting up. I continued that she sounded like she thought I would disapprove of her father, and I wondered why. She went back to talking about the teachers, and of how wrong she felt it was to get attached to any one person. She would never again really care about anybody. I said, "Because they let you down or go away?" She then told me about the three girls who had run away from school, who she had mentioned last session, but had said she couldn't tell me about. One of them was now pregnant and had a disease from using dirty safes. Another, sent to reform school, had committed suicide (the suicide was true). I said, "What do you think she did that for?" Pam said, "because the boy she loved left and after that she went with just anybody and her mother didn't want to see her any more anyway and now she's ruined herself. She just wanted any man after that." I said "To forget who she loved?" and Pam nodded silently. It was the end of the hour and Pam asked if I would have the same office next year, if I was staying. I said, "Yes, I'll be here next year, same person, same place."

Following this period, Pam often looked pale and depressed. She talked haltingly and felt tired. One session, she asked for some paper, saying she felt not like drawing but just doodling. She said she was a lot less nervous than before. She never could relax before. At this point, she began to smoke a cigarette. She said she could now even tell me that she liked me. In fact that she liked me all the time she said that she didn't. I said, yes, before she had acted as though she thought she was going to be a nuisance to people she wanted to be with. She said, like Miss Lynn? She suddenly looked extremely pale and said she felt sick and dizzy. She looked really sick within a minute and was also perspiring profusely. I asked her what would make it better, some fresh air, or a place to rest her head?" I mentioned the fresh air because I wanted to give her a chance for the defense of gettting out of the room and walking if she needed it. However, she said" "a place for my head," and put her head down. She sighed deeply and said she thought she was never really relaxed unless she was asleep. Otherwise she was always jittery. I said maybe she always felt that she would have to be ready to get herself together and pick up and go at any time and that would make it hard to relax. She kept her head down and said sometimes she knew she was supposed to pick up and go.

She began to make more references to having to grow up without a father, she couldn't stand being with her mother because it made mother nervous to have Pam around. Otherwise, why would she have had grandmother take care of her, after her aunt had thrown mother out because of Pam? Why would she be at boarding school? Pam stated that recently she felt like crying much of the time, especially when someone was nice to her. She wouldn't be caught dead crying in front of the teacher and would have to run out of the room. Sometimes, she felt dizzy, like lying down, and just closing her eyes. She also had been having "eating troubles" lately. She looked at breakfast; but it made her sick and she had to run out of the room even though "all the time I was starving inside." Pam began to come very early to her hours and asked for my attention more directly than she could tolerate at first. She occasionally now reported dreams. She dreamed of rejected fat girls and Eloise (who is a "demon" character in a book, and whose parents separated because of her). We were able to discuss her fantasies and the reality of her parents' divorce. She wondered why she had to act up whenever there was someone around who acted righteous or goodie goodie, but did not feel much inclined to in other circumstances. For some months, she had intermittent rashes and a continual lower backpain, with negative medical findings.

At this time, Pam had some relationships to other girls her age. These were with only one girl at a time and included intense jealousies about any competitors. She again spoke of wanting to kill the favorite student of her favorite teacher, but now felt tearful about this reaction instead. At school, the teacher reported Pam now had temper outbursts when not given her way, but seemed to respond well to limits, like a little child needing to be told what to do, but then responding positively, unlike her earlier behavior. The teacher felt better about her because she could "reach" her. Pam spent little time with her mother on weekends home, but instead tended to the illegitimate children of a promiscuous woman across the street. She stated that she no longer wanted an illegitimate baby because it could never "respect its mother or itself." I commented that Pam's own (biologic) mother might have been a nice person and have cared for Pam. Only now did Pam begin freely to discuss her assumptions (a topic she previously tabooed) that her own mother had her as a teenager and didn't want her. She had somehow assumed her own fate had to be similar, but as she said, had never "thought about it." We discussed this a great deal. Pam had both wanted to "find" her mother by sharing her assumed life as a prostitute and having an illegitimate baby, and to punish her adoptive mother by living out her expectation of Pam being "immoral." This discussion seemed to represent a turning point for Pam. She began to explore other identity possibilities and found herself for the first time unable to commit delinquent acts. At first she described this inability as "losing my nerve" and became angry and frightened at the thought that she might be losing her "will-power," that is, to be "bad" if she wanted to.

During the next period in treatment, Pam asked a great deal about the therapist's way of living. Sessions were taken up discussing hairdos, how college girls decorated their rooms (these she asked about), etc. She arranged her room at school to look like the therapy room, managing to find identical curtains. She decided she wanted to be a nurse or schoolteacher and asked the therapist's help in getting her a volunteer job. She wanted the therapist to accompany her to places where she could find out about career opportunities, and I did this. She began to study hard, though she complained of difficulties concentrating. She joined a young people's church group to which she became devoted, but said that a problem was that the other girls thought her boy-crazy, when actually she didn't want to do something "bad" with a boy, but just wanted affection and had an easier time talking with the boys than with the girls. She discussed the book *Peyton Place,* in which the daughter just wanted to be friends with a boy or look at a sunset, but the mother imagined all kinds of things going on, till the daughter practically couldn't do anything else. We could now take up her anger "when mother expects the worst of me," and her real underlying wish to please her mother. Pam discussed not liking herself sometimes and raised the question of why she told lies.

In her third year of therapy, Pam began to want to find her own mother and wanted me to do this for her, fearing it would hurt her mother's feelings. Instead, she was finally able, with encouragement from the mother, who had made sufficient progress herself in treatment, to talk with her mother about this, and began to establish a comfortable communication with her mother. The two discussed *Peyton Place* and its meaning with each other, after Pam had discussed this in therapy. For the first time, she said that she liked going home for weekends.

Phase III: Mourning. Approximately a year later, Pam began to work out some of the unresolved childhood grief, and now experienced this in terms of memories and affect, rather than primarily in terms of somatic symptoms and ego-alien depression. Painfully, she remembered in detail the discord between the parents before her father's leaving and his broken promise to be back "soon." She did not know what the word "soon" meant. She remembered thinking that "words" and thoughts were useless, it was better to *do* things.

She remembered that just after her father left, she was placed with another family for a few days. This family took her to a merrygoround, and when it came time to get off she wouldn't but clung to the horse's tail and mane while it whirled around, crying and screaming. She could never cry after that, until now.

I reminded her that she had liked playing "horse" with her father. Now, she began to sob each time she tried to say the words which she finally gulped out, "I guess I loved my father."

With anguish, now more limited to her therapy hours than extending into her school life, she recalled the many times of "feeling so hurt" when she thought of her father "having fun" with someone else. She became aware that the small role her father played in her current life was not a fair measure of his rejection of her, but had to do with his awareness of the mother's reluctance about their contact in the past, and even the birthday letters. She wrote her father a long letter (she generally had not answered his before), telling him of some of her feelings. He promptly responded by deciding to drive down to spend a birthday with Pam so the two could talk and clear up any past misunderstandings. Both Pam and father braved adoptive mother's discomfort about the visit, while mother's social worker emphasized with her that Pam's need for this did not imply rejection of mother.

In therapy, Pam could now begin to tolerate the image of herself as a child who had felt rebuffed by her mother and deserted by the father who used to console, enjoy, and romp with her. She sensed also that his behavior "needled" but excited her mother, and was unsure what this had to do with his being "thrown out." She had wanted to be like him because she had had the most "fun" with him, but her anger at both parents also made her take on "with a vengeance" whatever negative qualities she thought mother attributed to him. In this way, she could at least get mother (and later, teachers) excited and mad, which was better than nothing, even though it led to punishment. In this way, she tried not only to take his place, but also the biologic mother's in her adoptive mother's mind, because her adoptive mother gave so many warnings about the bad things others might do. Sex was foremost among these. Pam expressed relief that she had not actually gotten pregnant "just to show my mother."

Phase IV: Growth Renewed. During the following few months, the school reported some changes in Pam's behavior. She seemed eager to learn, and did especially well in extra reports or projects. She was apt to take on too much work: instead of four major subjects she took five, and flunked one in the fall. However, this was additional and she was maintaining her requirements for the teaching college curriculum. For the first time, she was meeting homework deadlines and passing tests. She was placed with two roommates this year; the teachers stated this would have been impossible previously. She was involved with, and liked by her peer group at this time, and seemed much less interested in the adult teachers. Although she no longer attacked the other girls sarcastically or carried a "chip on her shoulder," her problem was now that she was oversensitive to any rebuff, having her feelings hurt easily.

In therapy, Pam brought less vivid material to her sessions, and appeared less driven to provoke some variety of intense interaction between herself and me. Before exams or other times of heavy school schedule, she cancelled sessions, and then resumed them. Her materials dealt primarily with current problems of boy- and girlfriends, and her future plans. Where she had earlier once introduced me to a peer as "my psychologist, she works with the worst cases," she now introduced me to a different friend as "my psychologist—she is helping me plan my future." She liked both roommates, though one was more of a goodie goodie than the other. Her idea was that she now got along with her mother because she had "grown up." When asked how this happened, she once said that she finally decided—when she was still a kid a couple of years ago—that I didn't just see patients because I *had* to (as Pam had insisted earlier)—because "probably you don't get paid that much"—but maybe because I liked to. Then she got to thinking that maybe her own mother hadn't given her away because she didn't like her either—that there must have been other reasons—and her adoptive mother now probably wanted her too, only Pam hadn't given her a chance to show it. Pam now wanted to be a teacher or medical missionary, perhaps in the jungle or some place where they really needed it, with the idea that if she came all that way to help, the people would really know she wanted to, and this would make them want to get better. (This fantasy has also other aspects with the fantasied, uncivilized component representing her own impulses, with which she was trying to deal). Pam stated that the problem she now wanted to work on was that of knowing that married men "send" her more than the boys her own age; she was afraid that if her feelings were hurt about something that was where she would turn. In regard to her own previous delinquent behavior, she utilized some reaction formation, e.g., complaining about girls who swear, but enjoyed breaking minor rules, like staying up "after lights out." She especially made herself available to other girls with "problems," asserting that more important than studies or than just fun was not pushing away someone who needed a person to count on to talk to. She stated that people should neither have to crawl for attention nor have to steal it. I agreed. During her termination year, I commented in my notes:

"It is difficult to evaluate how Pam will continue to deal with the issues of growing up. During the years of treatment, she had had the continuing support of school as well as eventually mother and father, each more able to relate to her than previously. It is likely that each future loss, e.g., of the school when she is eighteen, of her favorite teacher who is leaving the school, etc., will reactivate to some extent the original traumas and her reactions to them and that she should continue to have available to her some therapeutic resources."

About ten years after termination, when Pam was in her late twenties, I heard from her again. She had finished college successfully, and enjoyed her work as a teacher. She was described as having especially good rapport with the adolescent kids, and was both liked and respected by her colleagues, though she tended to make "snippety" remarks to the female principal. She had married four years earlier and described the first year of marriage as difficult at times. However, her husband had been patient with her when she was "childish" or "sulked"; without "humoring me, he really listened" and she felt increasingly that they cared deeply about each other. She said that she wouldn't have believed she would be so happy, all settled down with one person and married, and wanted me to know that the time had really finally come when she felt ready to be a parent and wanted a child of her own. I silently recalled her plan to a have a baby, as divulged during her first therapy session, and knew she had come a long way since then.

She laughed, "I bet you never expected that from that impossible brat I was!" I laughed too, and said, "So we still disagree about you having been impossible! I never did go for that idea, you know. As a matter of fact, I really liked working with you and, by the way, I bet at this point you'll make a really good parent, too."

*Some Effects of Multiple Separations and Severe Deprivation: Lou Ann.**

Lou Ann was referred by a child guidance clinic after she was found stealing pocketbooks.

Lou Ann's childhood had consisted of periods of extreme deprivation and abandonment, alternating with occasional indulgence. Her family characteristically handled stress through impulsive action and repetitively acted out their problems about loss.

Lou Ann's mother, Mary Anne, was born when maternal grandmother was fourteen years old. Maternal grandmother then married a much older man, leaving Mary Ann with great-grandmother, who was often cruel to the child. However, Mary Ann's mother was in and out of the household, and affectionate to Mary Ann, who became very attached to her. When Mary Anne was eleven, her mother died. Mary Anne had a memory of jumping into

---

*A brief summary of the case material and its relationship to character type, family experience, and implications for treatment were discussed in Tessman and Kaufman, 1969. Other excerpts from the material were presented in 1958, at the American Orthopsychiatric Societies meetings: Workshop: "Individual and Community Oriented Therapy with Two Delinquent Sisters and their Mother," with Irving Kaufman, M.D., Project Director, Beatrice Simcox Reiner, S.W. (treatment of mother), Joan Zilbach, M.D. (treatment of Betty), and Corinne Carr, Boston Children's Services (group work with Lou Ann).

the grave with her mother, being forcibly pried apart from the corpse and having her ankles broken in the process. She described being "in shock" for two weeks after this, unable to move. There may be distortions in the memory. As troubles with great-grandmother continued, Lou Ann's mother was placed in a home for dependent children by the time she was twelve. After a series of temporary living situations in adolescence, she married Lou Ann's father on brief acquaintance, feeling that she would like his mother a lot.

Lou Ann's parents separated when Lou Ann was three. Her mother moved in with the paternal grandmother, expressing her own continued need for a mother. She gave Lou Ann to the father, who remarried a woman who was promiscuous. While this stepmother entertained men, Lou Ann was locked in a closet and tied with ropes. Years later, Lou Ann remembered the combination of noises in the room, her own hunger, and her fear of crying out lest she be punished. At age seven, she was found to be suffering from severe malnutrition and was losing her hair. At that time, custody was returned, after intervention by the Society for the Prevention of Cruelty to Children, to her mother, now alcoholic, and married to a seafaring man who only returned home occasionally. Between the ages of eight and twelve, Lou Ann became highly competent in the care of her mother and siblings. She did much of the housework and cooking. In order to buy milk for the children, she took charge of the finances, at times hiding money from her mother who, she knew, would spend it on drink. The mother, on occasion, bought great quantities of cake and candy; at other times there was famine. Mother had told everyone she wanted another baby to keep her from being lonely, and at times played with the children's dolls. When Lou Ann was thirteen, her own father returned to move in with his mother, downstairs from his former family, after the failure of a third marriage. He had found this wife in bed with his brother. Although mother later admitted she knew that he began making passes at Lou Ann, she left them alone for long periods, e.g., going off for a weekend, and a sexual relationship started between the father and Lou Ann. Like other girls who have experienced incest, Lou Ann tended to see herself as the adult in the family and felt responsible for providing the father and mother with care. Because she was aware of complying with the mother's unconscious wishes for parenting, which included pushing her toward the incestuous relationship, she did not experience guilt about the act itself. However, the exposure of the incest relationship resulted in further separation and loss, that is, imprisonment of the father. This final family disruption, rather than the incest itself, was experienced as a source of guilt and further trauma.

Treatment must be long-term and intensive with children like Lou Ann who have suffered such severe deprivation and whose own identification figures are involved in chronic, severe acting out of their own deprivations and losses. The open search for parent figures, though often coupled with a deep distrust and need to flee from all contacts, makes possible the initial stage of treatment, geared primarily toward establishing a relationship that is not judgmental about the past behavior and supportively available to deal with the intensity of current stress.

In Lou Ann's case, this involved attempts to stabilize her human support network. Her mother was seen in treatment, although she tended to flee from this contact throughout most of the first year, accepting it gradually by the second year. The social worker made home visits to her when initially she would not come in. Contacts were maintained with the children's school, money was found for winter coats and other necessities. Lou Ann's therapy appointments were increased to twice a week when she seemed to need this, and then, for a time, to three times a week. In her second year of treatment, a special afternoon club was organized around her, to help her with peer relations, with a variety of normal group activities she had missed out on in younger years, and later with group explorations in visiting and talking with people with various vocations (airline hostesses, hairdressers, and other vocations which appealed to her). Although placement from home was considered a number of times for Lou Ann, when it had been tried twice, earlier, she had simply run away back home unable to be away from her mother. On the basis of similar experience with other children whose problems were not too different from hers, we felt that there was initially very little likelihood that she could tolerate this separation without either running away again back to her home, or acting out her problems in the new setting in such a way that she would be extruded and thereby perpetuate her cycles of loss.

A. Psychodiagnostic evaluation. When Lou Ann first came to the clinic, she was a scrawny little girl, wearing a crumpled, soiled cotton dress which was too thin for winter. Her blonde hair was long and disheveled. Her wide gray eyes searched restlessly. For her second session, she wore a ribbon around her hair, saying she had just washed her hair because she wanted to "come clean."

During the diagnostic interviews and the psychological testing sessions, she presented herself very evidently as a waif whose burdens and losses far exceeded her years. She expressed the wish for someone who would magically solve her problems by providing for her many unmet needs.

In her reaction to the testing process, Lou Ann revealed the fluidity of her ego boundaries and the intensity of her needs. She not only dealt with the test material verbally in a very personal way, but simultaneously expressed, through action, the fantasied solutions to the anxieties stimulated by the testing. Her reliance on action to deal with emotional threats indicated the level of ego development at which she was functioning. Lou Ann consistently attempted to draw me into her activity, thereby communicating to me that being left alone with the test materials—or with her own thoughts—was intolerable to her, and that she needed the reassurance of maintaining an interaction with another person.

Throughout the testing, Lou Ann conveyed by her behavior that she pictured the world as a place made up primarily of mothers and babies. She expressed bewilderment about which of the two roles should be hers and what each must provide for the other. Repeatedly, the babies had unfilled needs, and the mother was unable to take care of them because she herself was so fearful and deprived that she could react to the child only as though it were a comforting toy or a mother to her. At first, tentatively, and then more openly, Lou Ann interspersed her test responses with efforts to test what I was going to do about her needs and especially to determine how long the relationship with me could last. As is characteristic of this type of delinquent child, who manifests an oral-erotic orientation and only partial object differentiation, for Lou Ann the anxiety became focused on the separation which she assumed or had learned follows a close relationship, rather than on the content of the relationship itself.

The following examples illustrate the features discussed above:

In the testing room, Lou Ann first noticed the baby doll in the crib. She jumped to get it and during the rest of the time either hugged it to her or set it on the table next to the test material. She said she had only one good doll which she took to school to keep in her "drawers." She hoped the teacher wouldn't find out or she might steal it. Asked if she thought the teacher needed her doll, Lou Ann answered that her mother loved to play with dolls and babies and Lou Ann wanted to make her a yarn baby doll for her birthday. Apparently, she felt that she owed mother a baby or doll. She wanted to know whether I would take good care of the doll, feed her, dress her, or let the doll starve. I answered that we were here at the clinic to help people with understanding what they need,, and that I could see she needed care. I was cautious, not yet knowing whether I would be her therapist or if therapy would be carried through at all. In a few minutes, she began asking directly how long she could stay, could she work here when she grew up, could she come back when probation was over, etc. She offered to keep the doll house in order and run errands if she could. After she had told two Thematic Apperception Test stories in which the mothers died, she suddenly said that the doll's name was Lucy-Ann Jones and that she was my two-month-old baby who was sick and I was bringing her to the doctor to find out what the trouble was. Lou Ann was the doctor and explained that the baby had a "heart and a hole in her stomach." She said the milk went in all right but went right through so the baby never got full. She wrote the remedy on a piece of paper: "A bottle of iron pills, and warm up." The baby should be brought to the clinic at the same time every week. The iron pills were to make her strong, she said, and added, "She has to get stronger than her mother, doesn't she, in case her mother gets sick?"

Throughout the testing, Lou Ann spoke of mother's illnesses and fears as readily as of her own: she said that mother was too sick to come to the clinic much because she doesn't like to walk, then said mother was scared because she had a black pimple growing under her bosom and was afraid someone would see it. (In fact, mother had come with Lou Ann but was waiting for her across the street instead of keeping her own appointment at the clinic.) Lou Ann told me mother was knocked down by lightning when she was a child and now wanted to keep out of storms. In fact, when it rained mother cried, and kept Lou Ann home from school to console her. Lou Ann would like to come here to make pretty things like jewelry for her mother to wear or put on her handbag; mother had a big bag but it's pretty old and there wasn't much in it. (The items Lou Ann had stolen were handbags.)

As Lou Ann pictured it, for both mother and child the depression was centered upon the sense of emptiness that Lou Ann symbolized by the mother's empty bag, her doll stolen out of her drawers, and the baby's "heart and a hole" in her stomach. Viewing the problem as an inner emptiness or a loss of body substance would indicate that she had experienced enough of a relationship to wish to incorporate a love object as a way of holding onto it, as well as having experienced the trauma of loss of relationships. She symbolized the loss in a manner consistent with this level of development: she felt that something inside her had been taken away. Her restitutive wish was to fill up the emptiness in her mother and herself.

Summary of test findings: On the Wechsler Bellevue Intelligence Scale for Children, Lou Ann earned an IQ score of 91. The concrete quality of some of her thought processes was particularly noticeable, as was her low tolerance for tension and hyperactive distractibility. Her lowest scores were in tasks requiring any abstraction or planning ability. However, a possible organic impairment which might be suspected from her subtest scatter was later counterindicated, for when she was retested after two years, she had gained enough in these areas so that, for example, abstraction became one of her better abilities.

In the projective tests, Lou Ann appeared as a youngster who was far more comfortable dealing with external realities than with her inner tensions. Her most integrated responses were given to the Thematic Apperception Test, which provideds a stimulus that is more structured than the Rorschach and maintains the support of picturing real-looking people. However, her stories tended to adhere closely to the realities of her own life situation. Lou Ann's Rorschach protocol showed a general ego disturbance that included some distortion of reality, strong impulsivity, and a great investment in kinesthetic, temperature, and other sensations associated with the oral period of development. Further, there seemed to be little in her perceptual world that was not seen in motion, either in flight, excitement, or pursuit; either attacking or being attacked. The most repetitive response sequence in the Rorschach was expressed by images of being burned up with tension at a time when she was isolated from the needed love object. Her reference to fire seemed to represent this kind of primary oral tension rather than more focal sexual excitement. Her restitutional attempt would be to form a fantasied oral union either by eating or being eaten by someone, thereby becoming inseparable from him or her.

The following example illustrates such images in her response to the Rorschach test: She described the whole second card of the Rorschach as looking like the fire they had in a store near her. On the next card, which is frequently seen as two separate people, she fused the percept into one creature and described it as follows.

Lou Ann: "Ooh! A monster in space. Here's his arms and nose and eyes and hair and this is his bones—like he was a human being once and turned into a monster. Mother says when a person goes into space he turns into an ugly creature—Ooh! here's the blood—and then his bones showed and he had no flesh and all he ate was human flesh, when they came to this planet and he was under the control of an ugly queen named Jessa—no put down Carol." Here the separation from mother earth is very literally equated with the loss of flesh that must be restored cannibalistically in relation to the powerful queen.

In her TAT stories, Lou Ann pictured the mother figure as a frightened and damaged little girl who is mourning her own losses and is also looking for a mother. For example, she told a story of a woman who marries a man so that she can live with his mother. Even when the man kills someone and is put in jail she will take him back to keep her mother-in-law from running away because she is so scared of being alone. Fifty percent of her stories dealt with someone having a baby. At times, the baby was named "Donald" like Lou Ann's father.

The baby with father's name was described as, for example, "the cutest little rascal you ever saw" and it functioned in the stories to make amends to mother and temporarily to alleviate her depression. Nevertheless, most of the babies in her stories eventually died of neglect. Amends to mother were necessary because Lou Ann thought that her own demandingness was hurting her mother further, and might result in losing her entirely. For example, in one story the doctor told the children that if they made the sick mother get up again to fix their supper it would put her in bed forever.

Another aspect of Lou Ann's relation to her father was identification and empathy with him. She saw him, like herself, as having turned into a monster or criminal as a result of having been cast out by an unfaithful woman.

Repeatedly in her stories, she tried to prove that the criminals in jail turned out to be good after all—either because they reformed or caught other criminals—and were forgiven by their wives so that another baby could be born. At a deeply unconscious level, Lou Ann was allied with the father in her resentment toward the woman and in his plea for absolution.

Finally, Lou Ann dwelt at length on her image of a magically good mother figure. For example, she told a story of a rich lady who took in a little boy who had holes in his clothes and no food and holes in his house. He had no parents. The lady took care of him and never made him work and gave him $10 a week for the rest of his life.

It was evident from the diagnostic material that Lou Ann was eager for help. The therapeutic problem was to gear the treatment toward providing her with enough support, both in the environment and within herself, so that she would be able to tolerate the intensity of need which a new relationship would evoke without further threat to so vulnerable an armor.

B. First Year of Treatment with Lou Ann. Lou Ann arrived early for her first treatment session. Since she didn't find me in my office, she left a note until her appointment time. It said "God bless this food for Jesus sake and bless us all—Amen." Thus, she communicated her first concept of treatment as a feeding. When she did see me, however, she explained that she had just been practicing her writing.

During this session, Lou Ann assured me that her mother was awfully good to them, not at all a mean mother. When I asked her what a mean mother would be like, she said a friend of hers had one. There were three children and the mother used to buy whiskey and beer with all the money instead of clothes for the children; she was afraid someone would find out. The youngest two children were tough like fresh teenagers, but the oldest couldn't be because she had to do the work. She took care of her mother when she was sick and tried to save out money for milk for her brother and for the other bills, but her mother beat her when she found out there was some money left and wanted to drink more. When I said the oldest girl must have had a hard time, she quickly said that she, Lou Ann, felt sorry for her and used to take her to the movies. Lou Ann suddenly said she would fight anyone who would call her mother a name. It was as though Lou Ann was giving me fair warning not to interfere with the mother-child pathologic tie by allowing her to recognize as her own feeling the deprivation and anger she had described. It was necessary to respect this defense, especially during the early stages of treatment, before she had established enough of a relationship to help her tolerate the anxieties associated with weakening or losing the tie to the mother.

The following session she immediately began to play that we were being attacked by Russia. "It's lucky I got here just before the explosion. The

Russians don't have enough to eat and want to control the whole world. We better hide under the table and make sure there is enough food for the dogs and babies." She would be able to save us. Thus, she seemed to describe her need for protection from the onslaught of her own impulses as well as what she saw as the deprived, explosive, powerful mother. In treatment, Lou Ann communicated many ideas about magical and omnipotent control and destruction. She showed that she needed to think of herself, too, as all-powerful and responsible both for the mother's welfare and her misfortunes and hurts. She repeatedly brought up the idea that babies must be stronger than their mothers, for mothers would only keep babies who can provide the mother with medicine and care. I felt that it would not be helpful at that point to try to reassure her (as one would with some other children) that she was not responsible for her mother's fate, for she still needed such omnipotence concepts as a defense against being overwhelmed by her feelings of helplessness. Instead, I told her that from what she said, I believed that such scary things had happened to her when she was little that she needed to think people could make all kinds of things happen, good and bad, like magic. We would talk about what things can really happen so she would feel safer.

During the next two months, Lou Ann began hesitantly to bring out some resentment toward family members. She hinted at how much work she did at home and how Betty and Don took her things. She complained about how slowly mother walked, making Lou Ann wait for her when Lou Ann liked to skip and walk fast. However, she always reasserted her readiness to fight anybody who said mother was not nice, and she actually did have such fights in school sometimes. I let her know that I knew mother had some troubles that made things hard for Lou Ann and that Mrs. Reiner [her mother's therapist] wanted to help mother with these.

One day, she brought a picture of herself as a baby seven days old and asked me to keep it. I said that I enjoyed seeing it but that I wouldn't need to keep it because I could see her and liked her the age she was. I did this for several reasons. I wanted to support Lou Ann's concept of herself as a person in her own right rather than in the role of an infant or mother. Also, during this initial phase of treatment, I did not want to stir up either the awareness of more painful memories than she could manage or a too-regressive transference before more channels for handling such feelings were available to her.

When her birthday approached, Lou Ann wanted to go shopping with me for her present and very quickly picked out a doll. She alternately called the doll by her own name and by my name, saying her mother said she could. She said all the dolls in the stores needed someone to "love them up," and explained to the salesgirl that the doll was to help her be less lonesome. In later interviews, she told me she sang the doll to sleep every night and then fell asleep herself. During this time, she sometimes referred to herself as "little L" and to me as "big L" and played at imitating me. She said she wanted to be a lady like me when she grew up, and named her dog "Lady Fluffy" while her mother's dog was named "Baby Helen."

One of the themes that came up frequently was her joking about wanting to steal something from me. However, she seemed more aware than most delinquent children that what she really wanted was the relationship, which she visualized achieving by stealing. For example, once she told me to close my eyes and pretended to put a big beach ball into her paper bag. When I said something like, "I know you don't really want me to close my eyes to your wanting to take things," and added that I thought we'd better find out what she really needed, she then asked if she could come twice a week. We agreed that she would, in the fall, as soon as my schedule allowed. She seemed satisfied with this but often asked when it would start. She began increasingly to ask for many reality contacts with me—to go to a show with her, to go swimming, etc. She brought up a lot of feeling about the clinic closing in August. For example, she brought a stray dog to the clinic and wanted me to take him home over the summer. When I couldn't she reported the next week that he had gotten killed. We talked of how she was showing me how hurt she felt whenever she was shut out and how afraid she was of people leaving her when she needed them. Together, we marked on the calendar the day the clinic would reopen and she would come to see me again. She asked me to write to her and then failed to show up for her last appointment before vacation, leaving before being left.

In the fall, on a twice-weekly schedule, we seemed to enter a new phase. During the first two sessions she managed to scold me indirectly for the summer desertion by again playing doctor and telling me that the dolls looked like they had been neglected for weeks and now had all kinds of scratches and cuts. I said I was sorry to hear it because I did not want them to hurt themselves even when I could not be with them. Perhaps they could tell me about their feeling mad at me instead. She said, "Yes, if I hadn't brought them to the doctor now it would have been too late." She knew a boy who used to bite his own hand, and then they had to cut it off. Almost invariably, feelings about separation were described by Lou Ann in terms of consequent injuries or death.

Lou Ann continued to bring up material centered upon wanting to steal, and then asked me to go looking at things in the stores with her. She also had complained of not liking to stay inside a room so long. She got a queer feeling, like wanting to jump. During this session, we began to go out walking through the stores. Meanwhile, Lou Ann consumed large quantities of food. Working in this way, within her defense structure, utilizing oral supplies and motility, seemed to make it more possible for her to deal with her frightening memories.

She often gave her most significant or anxiety-provoking material while walking fast or filling her mouth. Yet she was never able directly to verbalize her wish for food. She would write down her request for food and then want a written answer, always adding to her note, "not out loud." Bit by bit and haltingly she recalled when she was very little and lived with her father and his second wife, father would be away and the wife would tie Lou Ann up in the closet and once put pepper in her mouth when she started to scream out loud. Lou Ann was to keep quiet while lots of men visited the wife in the bedroom. She remembered the dark closet and strange noises and long periods of hunger, for the wife sometimes went out while Lou Ann waited, still tied. When her hair began to fall out, and she got sick from lack of food, some doctors had looked at her, and then mother took her back.

An ever-present issue for Lou Ann was what I would give to her for herself or for mother. In a way, it was a difficult decision whether one should accompany this very deprived child into the tempting stores where she wanted so much to take everything. Yet from her excellent knowledge of the layout of various stores, it became evident that she wandered through them by herself anyway. It seemed that she was asking for the external control of a needed relationship while she was in the stores, thereby perhaps lessening momentarily the impulse to steal. She had shown me previously that what she was trying to steal was a relationship to a mother. She needed the unmet experience of being with the mother in a different role than that which stimulated delinquency. We settled on an allowance of 25¢ a week for her to spend as she liked in addition to food. She gained a great deal of weight at this time. She frequently would ask what I had had for lunch and wanted the identical food for herself, in this way attempting to incorporate the therapist's identity with food. For a time she gave up cokes for tea after I had once ordered this when with her. I felt the allowance had to be separate from the food, for otherwise the oral need would be too great to leave her any choice. I wanted her to learn to count on a predictable supply, in contrast to the feast or famine pattern she had experienced. The money became a very important issue, in the sense that around it were played out her attempts and also fears of being able to control me. All in all, she seemed relieved when she knew she could gladly have her quarter but couldn't force more out of me. For example, she once tried to pay the bill at the meal and short-changed me. I grinned and said, "So far so good, and now where's the rest," and she laughed and said she just wanted to know if I was on the ball. At first, she always picked out something that was too expensive, thereby showing her need to feel deprived, but eventually she was able to save up for several weeks to buy a wallet. Showing her she couldn't control me seemed important for two reasons. Because of her incorporative impulses, she thought if she were in control she could literally use me up and thereby lose me. In addition, if she were the "stronger" she would have the disappointment of again having to be adult without having a parent.

During the fall, Lou Ann began to menstruate, and also to express many anxieties about growing up. Mother had told her that Lou Ann was named for mother's own mother, Lou Ann, who had conceived the mother at Lou Ann's age of thirteen. She reported that mother had told her she was old enough to do whatever she wanted to do, like having her ears pierced by her stepfather. She experienced this sexual reference as a loss of protection from the mother and a pressure to act out what mother's mother had done. Her own father was back in town and making a bid for her affection. She desperately tried to get mother to come to the clinic regularly to see the social worker and now seemed relieved at the thought that other maternal figures were concerned. Once she even told her mother she was taking her shopping and then announced they were really on their way to the clinic.

There now came a period when Lou Ann expressed the wish for a more total relationship with me, in the context of her experiencing more fully the fear of her own depression and frightening inner feelings. For the first time, she spoke of feeling anxiety or having the blues, rather than describing external frightening events and injuries. One day she wrote on the black board, "Little L loves Big L. I just have to belong to somebody or I'll belong to the devil." Although she had talked before about not listening to the devil, as an external bad influence, she now identified "devil feelings" in herself. These consisted, for example, of thinking of her family as dead. She began to have what she called "hateful" nightmares in which mother would be in a coffin and brother hanging from a rope in the bathroom with his eyes bulging out and stepfather and Betty with blood all over them. We took this up in terms of when she was little: sometimes the family had been as good as dead to her when she needed them, and now her "hateful" and hurt feelings were a way of reminding herself of those times. She brought up some bizarre memories: that mother had thrown Donald out the window into the garbage can that had rotten tomatoes in it. (This may have been a screen memory of a miscarriage or a reference to menstural blood.) She experienced fury about what she saw as her mother's throwing her out as a baby herself, although she knew, as she said, "that mother couldn't help it." Lou Ann found my home address in the phone book and would appear on my doorstep with Betty or Donald for a drink, or to go to the bathroom, on Sunday mornings after the children had gone to church together. She commented on how easy it would be to cook for me if she lived with me.

Toward the end of the year, she began asking such questions as, "This isn't me, but if there was a girl you had seen regularly and she didn't have a good life and wanted to move away from her mother, what would you say?" We talked about the need to work out with such a girl what would be best for her. I said that unfortunately I couldn't have her staying with me because I thought it was important for kids to be taken care of, and being at work all day, I wouldn't be able to do that. I said I was sure the girl would feel let down and mad at me if she thought I might and then didn't. Lou Ann nodded and said, "She sure would!" It seemed important at this time for me to clarify that I was not the all-giving mother for whom she wished; this obviously could not be carried through and might have resulted in more intense disappointment and anger in Lou Ann later. After this, she would explain to Don and Betty that no child lived in my apartment because I wouldn't want them to stay lonesome when I went to work. Once in a while, she would remind herself, saying, "So you can't have anyone, can you?" but added that my place would be so much easier to keep clean than mother's. While discussing other placement possibilities (which we seriously considered but knew had been unsuccessful before and she and mother vehemently resisted), and all her mixed feelings about this, I also recognized with her that her requests for more reality contacts with me and her complaints of lacking friends or fun except at the clinic meant that she did need something more; there were people who could help with this, and I would be glad to help her find them.

A Children's Services Club seemed especially suited for a variety of reasons. Lou Ann was at a point when the memory of early desertions, together with more internalized depression and anxiety, made her need for the reassurance of interaction with people especially great. Her difficulties included the constriction of her emotional involvements almost totally to within the family, so that she had no normal peer relationships to provide either identification figures or less emotionally loaded relationships than those with adults. Finally, her capacity to use activity as well as relationships to bind her tensions made a therapeutically oriented club group seem especially helpful in leading her toward discovering and trying out acceptable ways of finding satisfactions. With this in mind, she was referred for group work in addition to continued therapy.

C. Second year of treatment. During the second year of treatment, Lou Ann and her family were in one or another crisis most of the time. At the beginning of the year, she was continuing to appear on my doorstep, often with her sister, Betty. Once Betty had fallen and was dripping wet and cold, with a scraped knee. Another time, Betty needed a drink of water, on the way home from church, though my home was quite a distance from the route home for them.

A difficulty with her visiting me was that when it was time to leave she repeatedly felt rejected. For example, she would convey these feelings by comments about her mean school nurse who wouldn't want kids to dirty up her car, etc. When these conflicts became evident, I said I knew she was having trouble about coming to my house because she felt hurt when she had to leave. This was her way of reminding herself how shut out from mother she felt as a little girl, and I did not want to see her repeat that hurt to herself. She answered simply, "But I always hurt when I'm not with you." In speaking of her total self as hurt, Lou Ann was describing the pain she had experienced as the abandoned child who was still dependent on the actual presence of the parent for satisfaction of her needs. Because of the intensity of her awareness of her needs at this time and because of her tendency to deal with the pressure of such awareness by acting out, I offered her a third hour each week at the clinic. She eagerly accepted and continued three times a week throughout that year. Yet she still occasionally appeared at my house and inevitably I, too, became in her fantasy, in part, the rejecting mother who shut her out. She could express resentment to my only in threats said in a joking tone; for example, if she asked me if I would be at the clinic when she came for her next hour and I said, "Sure, I'm not running out on you," she would say, "You better not run out on me or I'll kill you." At other times, she threatened to get a hammer and break all the clocks to bits so that her hour would never "run out."

Certain expressions used by Lou Ann were analogous to her reporting screen incidents. They involved a condensation of traumas as experienced by her, and the ego processes she utilized partially to deal with the associated anxiety. For example, the phrase about a needed object or substance "running out on" her was only of these multiply determined ideas. At various times, it referred to the loss of parental support when a mother figure deserted by literally "running away" from her, the body-image loss of inner substance, and her attempt to cope with the trauma through a repetition compulsion. The repetition compulsion included an identification with the activity of the lost object, so that hyperactively, she, too, "ran" after it or its symbolic equivalent in an effort to destroy or regain it.

At this stage of treatment, it seemed helpful to utilize such condensations in her own terms and to relate them symbolically to other, less pathological experiences and ego mechanisms. For example, she seemed to find relief in hearing over and over again that I would not, and did not want to, "run out" on her.

Hyperactivity and references to running out were Lou Ann's ways of conveying her experiences of object loss. The therapy at this time was geared toward helping her become aware and acknowledging with her that there was a "running-out" problem, as a step toward dealing with the detailed, affective meanings of her traumas and losses. This was prior to so-called "insight therapy," which could not be utilized until much later.

At about this time, father, between jobs and at the end of his third marriage, came to visit his mother as well as his children. He was particularly nice to Lou

Ann and she told me about him. At first, Lou Ann complained that he had never given her mother a good thing, not even a $5.00 handbag. He used to beat mother. The first day, Lou Ann called father a big fat pig and didn't let him near her. However, mother was afraid of her anger toward him and went to bed with a headache, so Lou Ann was left alone with him. He told her all about the "bitch" he was married to last, whom he found in bed with his own brother. He called himself a "loser" whom everyone left in the lurch.

Lou Ann was aware that father's turning toward her was because of his own deprivation. She told of the time when her mother had gone out dressed "fit to kill' and father was left crying on the doorstep like a baby until Lou Ann hugged and consoled him. She was pleased now by father's taking her to the movies and buying her a watch and remembered that when she was little she used to love him though "he never did give mother a thing." Now, he said that when he died he would leave Lou Ann his insurance and with that she could take care of mother the rest of her life. Again, the relationship to father included a way of making restitution to mother. Meanwhile, mother decided suddenly to go away on a trip for several days, leaving the children and father home. She wanted to visit her own mother's grave in an adjacent state. She did *not* inform her social worker or me about the trip.

On her return, after several days, mother made an emergency call to me at home to say that Lou Ann's father had "done it to her." Mother had also called the police and told them they better come and get him or she would kill him with the kitchen knife. During the next few days, either mother's social worker or I were almost constantly with the family during the court proceedings. Betty and Donald were preoccupied with playing hangman. They brightened and became cheerful at lunch time. Lou Ann had had a pregnancy test, and she and mother were convinced she would have father's baby. Lou Ann had just described to me how her urine had been put in the refrigerator. When she was told that the results of the test were negative, her face dropped with disappointment. She said indignantly, "They shouldn't have froze it in the refrigerator!" as though they had frozen the baby out of her. She spoke of it almost as though it were a toy or doll, telling me later that her mother had made her promise that Lou Ann would give "the little rascal" to mother to bring up. Mother continued to feel murderous rage at father, and it became evident that her anger revolved around his interfering with the tie between mother and Lou Ann, as well as between mother and father's mother. In court, she told Lou Ann to "shut up," then slapped her between the legs, leaving her hand in Lou Ann's genital region, as though the right to Lou Ann's body was hers alone.

When father left the court room, she lunged at him and police restrained her. She paced outside the door, then, mumbling she would wait till they brought him out so she could kill him. Her body trembled, her eyes rolled up, and she seemed out of contact. Lou Ann clung to me, crying for me not to let mother near father for fear she really would kill him. I finally put my hand firmly on mother's shoulder saying that she was needed now with Lou Ann. She had to collect her fee for court appearance and then go to see Mrs. Reiner at the clinic. My intent was to convey to her that the other relationships still existed. She responded docilely to being led down the hall. It seemed incongruous that within a few minutes, mother and daugher looked like carefree children, laughing and joking when they received the three-dollar court fee and had lunch afterward. Later that weekend, Lou Ann brought paternal grandmother to see me, pleading with me again not to let mother kill father. Paternal grandmother told me that she and mother had called each other names over this but would make up because they were like mother and daughter themselves and if any man came between them they would either want to die or kill someone. Mother had talked the other night of killing herself and the children, but said she blacked out instead. She had previously had such blackout states (with no neurological findings) when extremely angry. The paternal grandmother told me some of Lou Ann's father's history, including the fact that father had tried to kill his brother for sleeping with his wife; she mentioned several situations of promiscuity and incest in the family.

After the fight, mother and paternal grandmother became friends with each other again and decided to handle the relationship to father by "burying the hatchet in him." She was expressing the concept that she too needed to have a mother before she could be one. Lou Ann commented that day that she thought I liked her better than anyone else liked her, because she was still Lou Ann to me. Thus she expressed awareness that mother didn't perceive her as a person, but as a way of getting a baby and making friends with paternal grandmother again. Later in treatment, Lou Ann explored this idea about her identity: that a person could be more than something to fill another's needs.

Like a number of other children, Lou Ann manifested no guilt about the incest relationship. She thought that this was what her parents wanted of her. However, she did feel grieved and upset about the fate of her father, whom she now was losing to jail. Finally, she seemed to work out to some degree that perhaps this would be a place where he would be assured of care and would not be repeatedly deserted. However, this was not "promised" as a reassurance, since realistically we could not affect his situation. She knew his need for care and that his problems about desertion had led him into so much trouble all his life. She also began to express grief over the many times she had lost her father, as well as her identification with him. She always felt sorry for his deprivation and his need to be hostile. Although her family needed to think of her as an innocent victim of an attack, Lou Ann knew that it takes two people to make incest and that her own resentment of women (including me) as well as her wish for this baby and her responses to his attention had made her receptive to incest with him. She saw no reason to turn down his invitation. After a while, however, she concealed these feelings, began verbalizing attitudes similar to those of her mother—that "he's rotten through and through"—and did not want to mention him. Nevertheless, she made one more attempt to join him symbolically. She stole a wallet from a clinic secretary, as though to send herself to jail, too. As far as we know, this was the only recurrence of the initial symptoms of stealing while Lou Ann was in treatment.

During the late fall, mother stayed away from the clinic. Lou Ann came in one day and said, "Well here I am back from the hospital with my baby." In her arms, she carried a puppy so realistically bundled in a blanket that people in the street had, according to her, commented about it. She told me that mother had to have all her insides out and had told Lou Ann that she could never have a baby any more, so that if they were to have one in the family, it would have to be Lou Ann's. Lou Ann had been forbidden to tell me this, because mother knew from Mrs. Reiner that she was not supposed to say things like that to Lou Ann. I checked, and found out that mother was not having a hysterectomy but a bladder operation, explaining the difference to Lou Ann. I told Lou Ann very directly and repeatedly that I knew mother thought she wanted a baby, but what she really wanted was a mother, and having a baby wouldn't help one bit because it wouldn't bring a mother. Mrs. Reiner was busy trying to help mother with what she *really* needed. Lou Ann broke into tears, saying she had always tried to be a mother to her own, as she was named for her grandmother. Lou Ann's identity problem included her belief that she was the person to make restitution for her mother's needs by getting pregnant; I indicated that this would not in reality meet mother's needs nor would it enable her to be a person in her own right. At this point, I could say that this was not her job, because she was worth something just as herself, and didn't owe her life to anyone. Although she previously had needed to verbalize responsibility for her mother's fate, she now at times accepted this interpretation.

Lou Ann brought both siblings with her to the interviews. All three children reported that mother was saying she would die in the operation. We all went to the cafeteria, where Lou Ann often had a meal during the therapy hour. The children were tense and quiet at first, but seemed able to discuss their anxiety after they had eaten. Lou Ann said that when an old woman is left alone in the desert she burns up and evaporates; no one ever sees her again. She was terrified this might happen to mother if they left her. For Lou Ann, separation still meant burning up with tension. Betty said that mother knew she was going to die because she had a feeling of the life going out of her; that was just how she had felt, she said, before her own mother died when she was eleven. She asked the children to promise to stay close by her. Again, I talked very directly to the children, telling them that people do not usually die in the operation mother was going to have; the doctors wouldn't do it if they thought she would. Mother was feeling the sadness of missing her own mother and it made her want to keep her mother company in her imagination, by thinking about having the life go out of her. This seemed to make sense to the children, for mother had recently been talking at home about how her own mother had always wanted to keep her, only grandmother stole her away. Betty said hesitantly, that she, too, had been told not to talk at the clinic about mother's thoughts of death or of her own mother. After Mrs. Reiner saw mother and took up some of these issues, the anxiety seemed to abate.

Since the incest had occurred, Lou Ann frequently spoke again of being empty, and fantasied incorporating something phallic. She joked about dogs turning into hot dogs, and she asked me in written notes whether there was meat in the ice box because her "belly" was not filled. I began to talk with her about the way she sometimes ate food when what she really wanted was nice company to enjoy; maybe we could use some of our time talking about her wishes and fears about getting to know people. She brought up many of her difficulties at school with "kids who call me a big fat slob," and others who would walk off with her boyfriend. Her usual response was either to withdraw or threaten to knock their faces in. It had been apparent that one of her ways of making contact with new peers was through aggression, and that her experiences in the club relationships were very new to her, as was the sense that she was not going to meet rejection and hence could consider a different approach to people.

Around Christmas, Lou Ann asked more insistently about when Betty, who now often accompanied her, could have a therapist of her own. We agreed that they each needed someone all their own, and a therapist was assigned to Betty, too.

D. *Third year of treatment.* After the second year of treatment, there seemed to be fewer external crises for Lou Ann, and I shall comment on the third year only briefly. It was in this year that Lou Ann began to show some shift in her ego structure that made it possible to begin using therapeutic techniques with her that resembled those used with a neurotic child while at the same time the realities of her environment had to stay in focus. These shifts showed up most clearly when she was retested. In the intelligence test, her pattern shifted so that the capacity for abstractions doubled, and motor activity was no longer her best ability. Her chief gains, in addition to abstraction, were in tests of information, comprehension, and social judgment; she lost points in speed of visual motor coordination. Her total IQ score increased, but not enormously. In the projective tests, too, the impulsive and bizarre features decreased, and in their place more self-controlled and compulsive defenses appeared. The solution of having a baby gave way, to some extent, to the wish to achieve some success and pleasure in life through a variety of possible roles. Separation anxiety, of course, was still very prominent.

Here are some comparative examples of stories she told in response to the same Thematic Apperception Test Cards at ages twelve and a half and fourteen and seven months:

Picture of middle-aged woman peering into a room (Card V)

Age 12.5: "Well, this is a mother and her husband, I mean someone whose name was Tom and he was arrested for killing a person so he broke out and they got scared and when he did he went to his house and broke in and the mother screamed and the neighbors screamed and she was going to have a baby and they called the police and they came but then so, they let him go free because he did good while he was in prison. And so then they had a baby named Tommy. Stories do end sad."

t: "Sad?"

"Well, the baby got sick and died and nobody took care of him."

Age 14.7: "This is a mother, her daughter had her boyfriend come over to the house. Mother got curious and she opened the door. They were kissing. She didn't like it. Mother asked what was he doing. Boy said he was kissing her goodnight. So he went to leave and she picked up a bookend and went to hit him with it and daughter got in the way. The doctor found out that the mother was a little mentally sick so they put mother in a rest home and the younger couple got married."

*Picture of boy in foreground, man on an operating table,
with men bending over him, in background (Card VIII)*

Age 12.5: "It's an operation. That's a little boy. It shows someone, his father having an operation. And one day father got cancer and died. My aunt had cancer once. So then the hospital asks for some special stuff against cancer, they ask the doctor. But the doctor says, 'We don't have any for you' so then the boy went home, tried to mix some, some chemical to make him get clean and never get cancer. But then he got hit by electricity coming home from school."

t: "Can you tell me about the electricity?"

"It was thundering and a branch hit him on the head and that's what happened to my mother when she was eight years old. She always gets scared of electricity. Once when she came home from school she was unconscious for fifteen hours from it."

Age 14.7: "This boy is dreaming of becoming a famous doctor. One day, he goes to see his father operate. He sees all it takes, the guts. He sees how interesting it could be. When he grows up his father sends him to college, and when he grew up and graduated he became the best doctor in town."

In these stories, several shifts are evident. Foremost, perhaps, is that the unmitigated catastrophes portrayed during the initial testing are no longer so pervasive nor uncontrollable. There is less impulsivity and emphasis on constant action. In the later story, card five, the girl differentiated herself from the mother's outburst by defining it as "a little mentally sick" and by putting her in a "rest home," while the daughter separated and lived a different life. In the earlier story, the child's, mother's, aunt's and father's experiences were mingled and almost interchangeable with each other. A subtle reference to the lack of environmental support and social rejection to which this kind of family is often subjected occurs in the early story eight, in which the doctor turns down the request for medicine, "We don't have any for you."

The later story eight involves delayed action, ambitious future plans, and a successful father as a model. There are still some signs of unrepressed, condensed-thought processes, that is, primary-process thinking, e.g., her comment that the boy "sees all it takes, the guts" is probably a condensation of "guts" as courage, and the "guts" which can be seen in the operation. Unlike in the earlier stories, however, the main characters initiate and carry through participation in a form of life they choose. Lou Ann's actual ambition at this point was not to become a doctor, though she indeed had a chance to admire and relate to the doctors at the rest home where she now worked. Instead, she wanted to fnish high school and become a hair dresser, and was on her way to doing this, when I last heard from her several years later.

In school, at almost fifteen, she began to show noticeable improvement both in her work and care of appearance.

This shift in defenses of an ego structure more capable of organization was manifested in her therapy and was concomitant with her beginning efforts to deal with the issues of differentiation from her mother.

Where previously she had assumed that she and her mother shared the same ideas and feelings, she now questioned the necessity for this identification. For example, she wanted to know why it was that when her mother was given a flu shot, Lou Ann felt the pain in her own arm. She thought about wanting to lose weight, while previously she had said she couldn't because she and her mother were just alike.

Although previously we had talked about the fact that her life did not have to turn out just like mother's or grandmother Lou Ann's, the separation implicit in this had been too threatening for her to really believe it. Now she sometimes said with relief, "I'm glad I won't have to go through all that," and described this in terms of various occupational choices available to her when she grew up. Her visits and talks with the club members to people in various occupations were very meaningful to her in this context, because she saw people enjoying themselves in various ways.

In the spring and summer, Lou Ann began to deal with her identity in terms of her feelings about the kind of man who appealed to her. She first chose a delinquent boy (also being seen at the clinic) and began to provoke him by teasing. She said she felt sorry for his doctor, and invited him to walk her to the streetcar after the hour. His response was to say he wanted her to know how he treated his girls, and to slap her hard across the face. She beamed and confided in me that "now she knew he really liked her." (Lou Ann's mother had often said she felt father loved her most when he beat her.) For a time, the two made sexualized, fighting approaches to each other. The boy's therapist and I referred to ourselves as bodyguards to protect them, and spent some time with the two of them together telling them there were other ways to get acquainted, played ball with them, etc.

During the summer, when Lou Ann went to a coeducational camp, she insisted on having long pajamas, rather than shorties, so that she would be "warm in bed without company." In the fall, she described a schizophrenic boy who stared at her in the clinic, and a drunk on the subway, as people for whom she would have felt sorry in the past. She would have had to console them, but now she was afraid of them. There seemed to be less compulsion to identify with the totally deprived.

During this year also, Lou Ann began to work steadily every afternoon as a volunteer in an old people's home. She was considered especially reliable and sweet with the old ladies. For Lou Ann, this more sublimated activity not only fulfilled the need for more structured activities but also her old wish of establishing a relationship with a cared-for and a caring one.

Treatment now consisted in dealing at a more verbal level with her conflicts, which she was now able to identify as relating to different aspects of herself, rather than as existing totally between herself and the environment. One example was a discussion of the movie, *The Three Faces of Eve*, where she described to me how there had been a good Eve who had always done what people wanted of her; a spiteful Eve who was hateful to her husband and didn't like her mother; and, when the psychiatrist put them together, there was suddenly a new and real Eve who was just herself. Lou Ann said she too now wanted to be "just herself" and felt safer being that, that she no longer "lived life to please mother."

Perhaps, in summary, her own identification and the shift in her image of the possibilities for relating to another, wanted person are best conveyed by a comparison of her responses to the Rorschach inkblot at the time of initial evaluation and about two years later: "Looks like two people—like they were sculptured. I can see the shaped heads and they're wearing high heels. Both women are drinking tea."

DEFENSES AGAINST LOSS AND MISTRUST OF REMARRIAGE: ROBIN

Jessica and Alan were a vivacious, engaging couple, married just a few months, and clearly in love. They fondled each other with their eyes during pauses in the two interviews. Their problem was about Robin, Jessica's ten-year-old daughter, who was intensely jealous of, and provocative with, Alan. Alan had spent the previous weekend toying with the idea of "splitting" from the marriage because the amount of "hassle" with Robin was successfully spoiling his relationship with his new wife to the point where he was not sure it is "worth it." During a spat between the three that weekend, Alan for the first time became aware of the deep sense of commitment Jessica felt toward her daughter and felt left out. He had married young, been once divorced and then had a series of relationships with "no strings attached." However, once he got involved with Jessica, he knew he wanted to marry her, and described her as "the most interesting woman I know," although he was well aware of disliking the idea of having the sudden responsibility as a father, having made an earlier decision not to have children.

Jessica's own parents had divorced when she was seven years old. They had "always fought," as long as she could remember. First the children lived with mother. Father would set up appointments to see them, and then not "show." She remembered her little sister's crying and being disappointed, while her role was to try to cheer them up by distracting them, since she came not to believe his promises anyway. Later there was a custody suit in which Jessica's mother was declared "unfit" to care for the children because she was living and traveling with another man, and Jessica and her sisters went to live with the father. However, after a time, father turned them over to the grandparents. Jessica remembers phone calls with her mother in which the latter said, "How I wish we could live together!" while Jessica felt guilty. She finally stopped feeling guilty at age sixteen or seventeen, when she suggested that mother move near them so they could really see more of each other. Mother had replied instantly with a list of objections in terms of the "lousy weather" and other trivialities. She felt at that time "as a revelation" that mother had not really cared to be with her, and had been making her feel guilty for nothing. She vowed not to repeat this with a child of her own.

Not long after this, she became pregnant with Robin, married Robin's father, and remained with him until the child was two. They were not happy together, their reproaches including the fact that "we didn't really choose each other," but felt pressured to marry because of the pregnancy. However, Jessica felt that her first husband was basically a kind man, unlike her father, with whom she has had a great deal of conflict. After the divorce, Jessica moved, with Robin, to live with paternal grandmother and grandfather. She felt this was not an anxious period for Robin. The grandparents provided a warm support system, both for her and the child, and Robin seemed quite secure. Meanwhile, Jessica took the initiative to obtain more advanced education, making her current, interesting occupation possible. She too had a series of relationships. Her relationship to Robin, in which she consistently invested time and energy (unlike her own mother), "outlasted" all other relationships. Jessica appeared to me to have had extraordinary resilience, in view of her own past losses, in providing her child with a deep, caring love, expressed in spending time and in sharing an array of age-appropriate experiences with her. She did not turn to her child for mothering.

Robin's father had remarried and when the child visited him he was extremely attentive to her, but frequently made invitations which he did not follow through. Some years before, Robin had blamed her mother for the separation, saying "my father doesn't live with us because of you," but since his remarriage no longer did this.

Robin's current behavior seemed at first glance to be aimed totally at disrupting her mother's relationship with Alan. She teased and insulted him perceptively in just those areas in which he felt vulnerable. She could not tolerate seeing Jessica and Alan being intimate with each other (on the bed, watching TV, holding hands) without plopping herself in their midst, so that their hands literally separated. However, she then would casually drape a leg over Alan herself. She pleaded with them, "Don't do it tonight" and had moved her mattress to the end of her room, furthest away from Alan and Jessica's bed in the adjacent room.

Times that Jessica and Alan planned together when Robin was out were interrupted by "emergency calls"—she had forgotten and needed to be brought her sneakers or her lunch. For the first time, Robin frequently questioned how much her mother cared for her, for example, saying last weekend, "If I died, you either wouldn't notice or you would say 'Oh, she's dead—why don't you get her out of the way, now.'" Nevertheless, Jessica conveyed that she understood how Robin must feel, and that there was basically a strong and workable bond between them. However, this shouldn't be at the expense of her relationship to Alan.

As the description of Robin continued, it became clear that this was a bright, vigilant little girl who functioned well in many areas, was extremely independent in many ways, covering much of her wish for nurturance and attention with provocativeness, but also making all kinds of not very disguised overtures to Alan to act in a protective and fatherly way toward her. For example, though she declared herself unafraid, she was distressed to the point of tears about the plight of her pet cat, who was up a tree and "must be so scared." She begged Alan to help her rescue it. While they did this, she lost her baseball cap. Alan, slightly cat-scratched and feeling his heroic rescue should at least entitle him to some relaxation with Jessica, instead heared Robin imploring him to help her retrieve the cap, now admitting that she did not like to go out by herself in the dark. In these ways of enlisting his aid in retrievals, she seemed to ask him to restore something valuable she had lost, but was determined not to give up.

During the initial interview with Jessica and Alan, some attention was focused on Robin's apparent vigilance about new fathering figures. Since she had no reason to "trust" in the permanence of fathers in her life, she was defending against further feelings of loss by constructing most challenging, and sometimes infuriating initiation rites for Alan's entrance into the family. Generally, she had felt some security in Jessica's bond to her, and was not about to let go of it lightly. However, if they survived the current storm with each other, there were indications that Robin not only wished for both a mother and father, but that some of her defensive feistiness might at least give way to the point of being just a readiness for challenge, a quality Alan and Jessica both liked. It was suggested that the couple try having sexual activity while Robin was out, as the sound was too unbearably stimulating for her; and that Alan send up a trial balloon in the form of offering to do some things with Robin alone, to begin building up a relationship out of the context of the triangle and at times when it was not a necessary rescue operation.

During the second session, the couple reported that things were somewhat better, although not yet running smoothly. Alan had attended Little League practice with Robin, and couldn't help but admire the way she stood up to the teasing from the boys. He had found that taking some special time to focus on her and her needs had made Robin much more friendly to him. We discussed the issue of "splitting," which he had always kept in the back of his mind as a possible way out, e.g., in high school, when he demonstrated very superior intelligence, but disdained to complete assignments, etc. Now, however, he felt strongly that if things could be worked out between Robin and Jessica and him, he would much prefer that, to leaving the marriage.

The point of this vignette is this: an extremely common issue for the children of divorce as well as for their parents is the degree to which they can trust themselves to love again. Robin, like many of the children, does her best to hold onto what she has, and to extrude the intruder. She would rather not love and lose again. However, at second glance her underlying wish for a fathering figure is equally clear. For children who have lived alone with one parent for several years, sharing the parent again in a "permanent" way is difficult itself, even though it may be better for them in the long run. Jealousies about the parent's intimate relationship, looks, touches, serving of food, etc., to the new partner are often made clear, in a very hostile fashion, by both boys and girls. This may become more extreme in pubescence and adolescence.

However, the adults, too, have often been shaken in trusting themselves and their judgment in loving and being loved again. Jessica must have been disillusioned in consistent caring relationships early in life, and yet had managed to transform these experiences into an empathic understanding of her daughter. I watched her sit without flinching or anger while her new husband talked about "splitting" and wondered what had made her able to face such a possibility again. It occurred to me that although she had known loss, she had also known her resourcefulness in such a way that she knew, once she had chosen (as she had chosen not to desert her daughter and now had chosen Alan), she lived by her choice.

Alan and Jessica demonstrated another quality: the capacity to laugh at themselves and accept each other and their foibles with Robin, and the flexibility to try again. Some humor, acceptance, and flexibility in the face of astounding circumstances may be valuable assets in those who embark with their children on a new marriage, still wary about how far to commit themselves to new loving.

Comments on Enrichment of Identifications

All the children described in this chapter were potentially open to the influence of identification figures other than those who had helped to shape their earliest experiences. However, a prerequisite to being able to utilize new identification figures in an enriching way appeared to be some degree of working through the meanings of their loss and the integration of the identification with the partially missing parent. The initial defenses against the intrusion of a new figure, before the child had worked this out, were clearly indicated in a number of cases; e.g., by Daniel when he sat in his father's chair so that no other man could literally "take his place"; by Noah in his initial hostility to stepfather; by Sean in his symptom of wishing himself blind so he would not "see" the new man in mother's life; by Jeffrey in refusing foods from the housekeeper and insisting on an activity shared with mother to be participated in by the therapist before allowing a discussion of his mother. A minority of children showed immediate interest in a new parent figure, when that parent was responsive to him or her. Thus, Betsy seemed receptive to her mother's friend's attention and presents, although she devalued rather than depended on them, as did Jeremy, who had never seen his father and later became more ambivalent. Gwen liked her stepmother right away, but she had already felt "duped" by her mother in a number of ways when stepmother Joan came into the picture.

The two children described retrospectively, Pam and Lou Ann, had suffered a disturbance in the identification process per se, and had no possibility for a healthy identification with either parent. The developmental lag in the ego mechanisms utilized for identification and the concomitant effect on the character structure, was much more severe for Lou Ann than Pam. However, in both cases a period which included some identification with the therapist, as well as expressed wishes to be her child, preceded the girls' broadening of identification figures in adolescence. Certain aspects of identifications with the therapist could also not occur until the girls made clear the dangers they had previously experienced in this process. In each case, when the child was ready, additional adults were introduced into the treatment program in a planned fashion: a group leader for Lou Ann, someone to explain vocational choices for Pam, and a social workers to work with the mothers of both girls. When a therapist is not involved, foster parents, teachers, tutors, and others in the environment may have a similar role as long as the child's anxiety does not drive him to attempt a disruption of the relationship.

However, once the grieving process for the partially missing parent had been set into motion, many children's appreciations of the new identification figures grew. We see this clearly for example in the case of Noah, who deeply loved his father but came to see him for a time as someone who had remained too dependent "to stand on his own two feet" and hence seemed weak and vulnerable. Steve was increasingly pictured as a figure who managed not to be "scared" of coping with other people and the external world, and in his dreams Noah began to picture him as a leader. Coping with his own aggression had been a problem for Noah and, although this was an area which would have emerged to be worked with in therapy in any case, the additional model of a man less afraid of aggression in his dealings with others and with Noah was helpful to him. Interestingly, while Noah began more often to quote Steve's attitudes about various things, as well as to share his interests, he simultaneously maintained his appreciation of his father, as well as the strong affectional tie based on their earlier experience together. He, however, refused to intervene for his father, thus relinquishing the reversal of roles, and instead allowed himself to turn his energy increasingly to being a "kid" instead of an adult with his peers. This was more possible for him, also, because, as he said, "my father hasn't been badly depressed for quite a while now." Once he felt he had permission from all parent figures involved, he took special pleasure in having an extra set of interested grandparents with different values from either of the others. He developed what sounded in therapy like a very personal philosophy of enriched cultural relativism, while pointing to the tangible benefits of celebrating extra holidays.

Mark also was helped in the ego integration of various impulses by the permission that he increasingly felt to relate fully to his four parent figures. Although the two home parents became his center of security, he continued to express joy about contacts with father and Joyce. He came to view the two households in terms of his sharing two ways of life, both good and valuable.

He was able to adapt to behaving somewhat differently in the two settings, recognizing the positive features and limitations in each of the relationships. Thus, he reserved a certain kind of boisterous jubilation to share with his father, who, like Mark, enjoyed "going up on the roof to shout loud"; yet he recognized that there was a limit to how much time his father would take away from his work to be with him, and he did not rely on his father as he did on the home parents. With his mother, his best moments were of a more tender enthusiasm, which she identified with her own beloved father's elan de vie, while he knew that when he was highly distressed or aggressive it would be upsetting to her. Yet he was secure enough so that he could describe his visit to father as periods when he "liked seeing daddy and missing mommy." Meanwhile, at home, he increasingly identified with Frank as "knowing how to fix things better than mommy."

Gwen and Jeffrey experienced first a liberating contrast between their own mother's suspiciousness of others and Joan's warmth, supportive behavior, and love of their father. Gwen first evinced her wish to be like Joan when she wanted to copy her hairstyle, follow her taste in clothes, etc. Increasingly, her attitudes toward others reflected Joan's patience, tendency to give others the "benefit of the doubt," etc., personality characteristics diametrically opposed to the attitudes she first presented, and which had been like her mother's, that is, the feeling of being disliked, plotted or discriminated against, unfairly missing out on prizes in various events. In addition, Joan's sons, the oldest in the family of shared children, added an enriching influence which ranged from baseball and friendly pillow fights to ways of settling squabbles. Joan noticed that the contact with the younger children, and especially with the two-year-old, brought out a tenderness in her sons she had not guessed they possessed. For Gwen and Jeffrey, an additional, important aspect of enrichment occurred in witnessing and participating in their new brother's relationship to their own father, divorced from Joan. As the relationship between Joan and her former husband was a good one, fairly free from strain about the children, Gwen and Jeffrey could see that parting parents did not need to be vindictive toward each other, and that the child's love for one did not preclude the possibility of love for the other. Gwen, in particular, was a child who was attuned to considering all eventualities in life. She spoke of the possibility that if, when she grew up and fell in love and got married, something went wrong in the marriage even though she and her husband would try their hardest to avoid it, then at least she would make sure that she would not take it out on her kids, by making them feel bad about it. She would want to stay friends, like Joan and her former husband.

The most striking component of enriched identification, which I have not previously mentioned, seems to occur in those children whose central or home parent has undergone a change from being primarily unhappy to being primarily happy—a change with which the child ultimately identifies. All of the children aged three or over seemed aware that before or during the initial period of separation, at least one of the parents was upset, sad, tired, mad, or "wanting to get away from me" a fair amount of the time. The child's preoccupation with loss seemed to stem not only from the loss of the partially missing parent, but also from the depression or withdrawal and heightened aggression of the home parent at the time of greatest stress. This was true even for children who were in the center of their parents' emotional life, in the sense that the parents had turned to them for love which they felt they could not share with their mates. I have mentioned emotional support and "permission" for the child to grieve, or still to love the absent parent or enjoy life after the parents had parted. At the deepest level, the child seems to feel this permission when he or she perceives that the parent feels worthwhile and is moving toward a full life. It is then that he, too, feels entitled to weave a rich variety of threads of identification into the fabric of his still developing self.

Let this chapter be closed with Noah's thoughts and coping with a new "loss" when he was twelve and a half. He had gone through his first experience of liking a girl a lot, walking home from school with her, the two of them making endless phone calls to each other. He was elated and confident. Then "one day she called me and said she didn't like me as a boyfriend any more and I was pretty sad. My mother said maybe she is not worth being interested in, but I know I really still like her." Devaluing the disappointing female, like he and his father had done two years earlier, was not his response now, even when "suggested" by the mother. "The next day, I hear she called up Nick, one of my best friends, and it turned out he was going to take her to the dance. Then I started to hate her for not paying any attention to me, anymore, but I wanted Nick to know I knew about it . . . I didn't want to give him up for a friend either, but I was really mad at him too."

After a few weeks, during which he sometimes felt miserable when he saw them together, and sometimes felt he didn't care too much, she let him know that she had found out that she liked him best after all. He was happy that "we like each other like before," while also making overtures to Nick, letting him know he was still considered a friend.

He now discussed his family and his views about marriage and divorce: "I think it was the right solution now about my mother and father getting divorced. At the same time there are still moments when I wish they could be together; I think my bar mitzvah is important to me that way, to see that they can stand each other at least enough to get together on that. But I know that I would never want my mother to divorce Steve and remarry my father—what in the world would happen to the baby? Also, I think they are really right with each other."

"My father is seeing a new woman. I don't like her as much as Nina, but I'm not saying anything because he has to find out for himself who he can get along with best. He has been feeling better for about a year now, and that's meant I haven't had to think about cheering him up when I'm with him."

"About my own life—I don't think I would like to get married until I'm sure I wouldn't get divorced—and I don't want to start having children until I'm sure about that. *It's not just that it's hard on the kids, but hard on the parents, too.* The thing is, I don't know what clues I would use to *know* we—I mean whoever I love and I—won't change toward each other. Except, like I think Steve and mother will never get divorced. I know I don't *want* them to—and I used to want them to, I guess, most of last year. Probably my best bet is to ask myself if I really feel pretty grown up, before going ahead and trusting myself to get married."

Chapter 6

THE CHILD IN THE ILL-FITTING CUSTODY SUIT

And the king [Solomon] said, "Divide the living child in two,
and give half to the one and half to the other."

Then spake the woman whose the living child was unto
the king, for her bowels yearned upon her son,
and she said, "O my lord, give her the living child,
and in no wise slay it."

But the other said, "Let it be neither mine nor thine,
but divide it."

Then the king answered and said, "Give her the living
child, and in no wise slay it: she is the mother
thereof."

—Alleged proceedings in an early
custody suit [I Kings 3]

"Why is my father suing for custody," asked ten-year-old Rick, "when he
doesn't even want to see me?" Kevin, aged eleven, put his dilemma a different
way: "I can't be myself anymore when I'm with mother," he said, "but I'm
afraid to tell her because then she'll hate me like she hates my father."
The plight of the child who finds himself between his parents in a custody

A shortened version of this chapter was presented at the meeting of the American
Orthopsychiatric Association, 1976.

suit used to be a relatively rare one. Recently it seems to occur with increasing frequency, and is accompanied by strains for the child which go beyond those more usually encountered within the growing number of divorces or shifts in partners for parents. Recent estimates are that well over one million children in the United States experience the divorce of their parents annually, and that custody has been agreed upon before the case comes to court in only 85 percent of these cases.

Among parents who agree about the custody of their children there are a growing number who work out either legal joint custody or its practical equivalent. This works well for the minority of parents who still manage to get along well with each other. The more common pattern of the child's spending a limited amount of time with the absent parent (weekends, vacation, etc.) may involve long periods of separation, but does not usually evoke the feeling that one is forfeiting one's relationship as a parent. Custody litigation, however, almost always brings this issue to the fore.

This discussion deals with some of the features that seem to make the custody suit particularly ill-fitted to the needs of the child who must integrate the meaning of his parents' divorce in some constructive fashion. Using clinical material, I shall focus on motivations leading to attempted conflict resolution through a custody suit, the way the process is experienced by parent and child, and the child's later attempt to cope with this traumatic experience.

Some questions will be raised regarding the role of the court, judge, and lawyers as well as mental-health professionals in the custody suit. Judge David Bazelon has pointed out (Derdeyn, 1975) that in such adversary procedures "adversity is supplied not by the process, but by the parties to the conflict." I think the truth of this is painfully felt by all who are involved with a custody suit and exposed to the conflicting needs of individual parents and the child. Nevertheless, there may be a significant interplay between the parties and the process that may unwittingly undermine the well-being of the child and that should be looked at as well.

When parents part in bitter, unresolved conflict over who shall have custody of the children, regularly occurring difficulties seem to include the following:

1. The suing parent has a strong need to establish publicly that the other parent is at fault and is incompetent as a parent and a human being. This attitude, particularly when "validated" by the court, has serious implications for the child's attempts to identify with the positive features of the disgraced parent. In the cases of the O'Malleys and Knights, below, this need was acted out in the court proceedings; such acting out was averted in the case of the Walshes, Martiniques, and Castillos.

2. The suing parent frequently expresses an identification with the child as hurt or neglected by the spouse, and also expresses the need to repair the sense of hurt through care and attention from the child. The child feels strongly pressured to be parent rather than child, and especially may be expected to shore up his parent's self-esteem. This is sometimes complicated by a past history in which one parent was temporarily emotionally incapacitated, so that the other parent had to take over the physical and emotional care of the child for a time.

3. In a number of cases, once the custody suit is over and it becomes clear that the child cannot fulfill the emotional needs of the parent, he or she may rapidly lose interest in the child, who must cope with the sequence of first being the object of the patient's expressed avid desire and then being rejected. For example, in one case a young mother felt her reputation was restored when she won custody of her four children, but a few months later decided she wanted to be "free" of their care and shipped them to the father who had tried to prove her incompetent. In another case a father, who had hotly fought for custody of his son and lost, repeatedly rejected the son's attempt to make weekend or summer plans to see the father. In a third case the parent informed her children that she intended to regain custody, but told them when they phoned her, "Don't call me mother anymore, I have my own life to live."

The children cope in various ways with what is first an intense conflict of loyalties and then appears to include a deep sense of mutual rejection with at least one parent. When one of the parents has been psychotic during a period prior to the custody suit, there often remains an area of distorted reality testing as an identificatory link to that parent. It may be dormant until issues of the child's identity in relation to the losses he has incurred, and the arbitrarily imposed choice of relationships, can be brought to the fore and reworked. One obstruction to such necessary reworking may be the custody suit itself, which defines the "deserving" and "undeserving" parent not only in the psychic sense but also in the social network surrounding the child and parent. Unfortunately, the social ostracism which is still often associated with losing custody of one's children surrounds defeat with a further destructive reality for that parent. Before exemplifying with case descriptions I would like to allude briefly to several features of the legal system which augur particularly poorly for the child's interest.

First, the parents in custody proceedings are represented by lawyers, while the child either has no independent representation, or at best a "guardian ad litem" appointed by the judge and having the right of conducting an impartial investigation. However, as Derdeyn (1975) has stated,

> Even when he pursues his task with vigor, the guardian ad litem is not the
> equal of the lawyers of the parents or other parties petitioning for child

custody. The contending parties have the choice of legal criteria to be applied, choice of settlement and choice to apply various delaying tactics in the interests of their employers. The guardian ad litem has none of these prerogatives. When a clinician is engaged by a particular parent or his lawyer, two factors will work to limit the usefulness of the evaluation. One, the opposing parent will likely refuse to be interviewed. Two, the consultant recommendations may not find their way to court. The consultant's evaluation can be used only if, in the opinion of the attorney it will advance his client's case; it will be disregarded if it does not.

Whereas it is the role of the investigator to bring all relevant facts to light, it is, ironically, the responsibility of the parents' lawyers to hide any evidence which might be detrimental to their client. The child's guardian ad litem, unlike the lawyer, has no power to instigate action or appeals.

Secondly, adversary court proceedings may be psychologically significant; they may become a powerful ally or enemy of the parent, and thus contribute to maintaining or facilitating a distorted view of reality. Particularly with suspicious, litigious individuals, court proceedings can support wishes for omnipotence which in the long run are destructive to the emotional health of the parent as well as to the likelihood that he or she can maintain a constructive relationship to the child. The O'Malleys exemplify this point.

Thirdly, the time involved in the settlement of custody may extend over a period of years and seriously undermine the child's basic need for a secure continuity of central relationships.

The proposition that the custody suit is ill-fitted to the needs of the child does not imply that there are not some situations in which such legal action must still function, either to protect the welfare of a child, or as a necessary, reality-based limit-setting for a parent unable to function adequately. An attempt to ameliorate the child's helplessness by involving him actively in the decision of the court may become complicated by his guilt over the knowledge that he will be partly responsible for defeating one parent or the other. Thus one eight-year-old child who was angry after "wasting a morning in court" when her expressed wish to stay with her mother went unheeded expressed great relief about the decision six months later when she had discovered it was not true that her mother could not get along without her. She was terrified to hear that mother was renewing custody litigation, and pleaded not to have to admit in court that she was happy with her father and his new wife and children, being certain that she would thereby let her mother down and incur her wrath.

Let us look at some summaries of case material in the following situations and consider the implications for the child and parents.

1. The child transformed into enemy: The O'Malleys
2. The child in service of a father's conflict over dependency needs: The Knights
3. Custody suit averted—a disturbed mother-child relationship in therapy: The Walshes
4. Custody renounced and parenting regained: (i) Rachel Glade; (ii) Mrs. Greenwall, Estelle Phillips and George; (iii) Ernst Martinique; (iv) Gerardo Castillo

The Child Transformed into Enemy: The O'Malleys

In the case of the O'Malleys, extended custody litigation occurred, to the detriment of both children and each of the parents. Maintained by one parent, who needed to rectify a wounded self-image, and assuage the deep sense of being unloved from which she had suffered all her life, the continued litigation alienated the children who had previously cared about her. Although the father and a variety of mental-health professionals tried to assist the mother in maintaining a positive tie to her children, in the long run she needed to see them, like others in her world, as her enemies.

For the father, who was remarkably responsive to the children's need for security, the litigation continued to undermine his ability to assure himself and the children of the continuity of their life together, drained him of financial resources, and activated a sense of helplessness about his ability to direct his fate, rather than forever remain in the power of his exwife, her well-financed lawyers, and the court.

Kevin, ten, and Mimi, aged four when custody litigation began, were children capable of having a meaningful relationship to each parent in spite of the chaotic features of their early upbringing. However, they needed assurance that their new security and happiness in being with their father and stepmother would not be capriciously disrupted. The mother's particular problems and the action of the legal system unwittingly colluded to polarize their emotional choice in a way which cast the mother, who was previously viewed ambivalently, totally in the role of a feared enemy. There were consequences for the children's identification patterns. Having once also loved this "enemy," they had internalized aspects of her functioning, which they now feared within themselves and needed to extrude. By ages six and twelve, when final custody was still unsettled, their earlier touching faith in the protective power of police, judges and authorities had given way to a precocious cynicism in which legal authorities, previously trusted, became unreliable for them. No longer was little Mimi piping up with, "But judges are smart, they know better than to make us ever go back." Their emotional health was meanwhile fostered by their new, vibrant, and sensitively attuned family life.

Mrs. O'Malley was a highly intelligent research chemist who achieved well when she worked in isolation. Her professional success was marred only by recurrent antagonisms toward colleagues by whom she felt unappreciated and cheated of the special recognition she felt should be hers. In childhood she had had to adjust to her mother's preoccupation with her father's periodic hospitalizations for paranoid schizophrenic episodes, and the effect of her own ambivalent attachment to him. She had always felt taken advantage of, neglected, and unloved as a child, and when she married, as a wife. She also had always feared becoming like her father. After the births of Kevin and Mimi, and while her husband's parents were ill and required special attention, she felt increasingly neglected, and was given to rage reactions and panic. In a psychotic decompensation she asked her husband to call the police to bring her to a psychiatric hospital. She was discharged some months later, but the marital difficulties continued, and she angrily terminated treatment with the psychiatrist and increased her vitriolic attacks on her husband. He at that time attempted to appease her, but to no avail. She began to view him as dangerous to herself and the children, alleging that a psychiatrist had told her that Mr. O'Malley was endangering her life. The psychiatrist clarified to her lawyer that this was totally a distortion, that at no time had he implied or considered this to be the case. The couple separated, with father experiencing relief at being out of the marriage, but also concern for the welfare of his children. On the phone the children sounded frightened and uncommunicative to him. At this time he first consulted me with a request to evaluate the children and consider psychotherapy if it was indicated. However, once the parents had separated, the mother did not allow him to see the children and told them that he might kill them all. She tended to keep the children in the house, telling them that they would not be liked by the neighbors. During this period of their stay with her, the children received chaotic care, probably reflecting the mother's conflicted view of herself and the world. There were periods of kindness and effusive affection in shared play, which was later remembered by the children. These alternated with times when distortions of reality, rages, or the use of the children for direct expression of the mother's needs reigned unpredictably. For example, at times she engaged in sexual play with Mimi. Other times punishments were unpredictably cruel and unrelated to verbal guidelines for the children's behavior. For example, Kevin recalled that she gave Mimi permission to cut a design out of some cloth remnants, then went to sleep, leaving Kevin to put Mimi to bed. In the middle of the night, she shook both children awake, hitting them hard, enraged at the sight of the cut cloth and completely denying her previous permission. Mimi was often locked in her room for long periods of time. Occasionally baby sitters reported that the house was impossibly filthy and smelled.

Father first went to the court to establish visitation rights and to counter the mother's accusations of his dangerousness. The judge appointed a guardian ad litem, who submitted an extensive report that concluded that there was no reason for the father not to have access to the children, and raised questions about whether the mother was emotionally stable enough to be given permanent custody. At the time of the divorce custody was granted to the father, who then again contacted me to see the children and help with this transition in their lives.

After they came to live with the father the children did well, continuing to see their mother regularly. Although there were major changes in their view of the world, themselves and their parents, these did not disrupt their remaining sense of attachment to their mother. Both children were seen for a period of psychotherapy, and regular meetings held with father, occasionally the housekeeper and eventually a stepmother. Mother refused all invitations to talk with me or anyone else about the children, but told them she was coming back to take custody and make the father leave. She kept her address and phone number a secret, always letting the children off a block away from the house.

Over the next few months Kevin and Mimi began to flourish under the care of their father and housekeeper, and eventually with their stepmother and new baby brother. Kevin had been particularly close to mother, as her confidant and, at times, caretaker. He told me that he wept when mother left, that he missed the long talks she had with him about people who had been mean to her, and that she should not have been sent away. He was worried whether she would have anyone to listen to her, as they no longer saw former friends or neighbors, and even their favorite sitter had not come anymore lately, as her parents wouldn't let her. Mother said that was because they were afraid father might come, so he guessed that must be it. He did not know what to believe about father; mother said that he wanted to drive them all over a cliff, but father had been nice all week. Today he had been helping take all the locks out of the bedroom doors because Mimi had kept asking when she would be locked up, and father had said it was not good to have to worry about that. He thought mother and he "understood" each other because kids at school were mean to him sometimes too, and talked behind his back about how to keep him from getting the math prize.

In therapy Kevin began to see his mother in a different light, as he became aware of her distorted view of the "hostile" nature of the real world, by which he had been influenced. He continued to be compassionate about his mother, in terms of her loneliness and loveless childhood. Aware of his grandfather's "craziness," he felt his mother had never had a proper chance at life. Simultaneously he now felt he had been duped by her repeatedly and was particularly bitter about her distorted warnings about father. He recalled bizarre incidents when her words and deeds were contradictory prior to her hospitalization and afterwards, when she was the only parent in the house. He was on the way to working out the mixed meanings of her behavior to him, separating his own view of human relations from hers, and having some sense of mastery over his response on visiting days.

Mimi struggled for a time with a set of symptoms which represented an attempt to maintain a sense of closeness with both parents. Compulsive masturbation meant, among other things, being "mommy's little girl," a reminder of when the two had played in bed. She tried to join her father in bed, and to take his hand to her genitals. He refused, taking her gently to her own bed, where he sat by her side singing songs until she fell asleep. Hyperactivity initially masked her anxieties about loss and hurt. Her symptoms abated, she became outgoing and affectionate instead of hyperactive and fearful, and delighted in sharing activities with the father, e.g., together they designed a dollhouse he built for her, in which each child had a room and bed of her own, but the child could reach the parent through the hallway whenever she needed to. Of course there would be no locks. She, too, related frightening incidents of mother's quick and out-of-control mood changes. Though she did not view her mother's behavior as understandable in the way that Kevin did, she planned ways of trying to cope with her mother if trouble arose (e.g., she knew she could phone father). Meanwhile she went quite willingly on the visits.

Trouble snowballed as Kevin and Mimi became obviously happy with their new life. Mother could not control her rage if the children mentioned any fun they had at home, repeatedly accused father of poisoning their minds against her; she began relentlessly to criticise every aspect of their behavior and appearance and vowed that she would regain custody. In different ways both children became frightened and began to resist further contact with her, but were afraid to tell their mother why. Kevin told me he repeatedly tried to tell mother he did not want custody changed; she simply could not hear this, but continued to talk of how nice it would be when she once again had custody, as though he had never said it.

It seemed important that Kevin's message be clearly stated in a form which would be available to all involved, and would not lend itself to misinterpretation. As Mrs. O'Malley had not availed herself of invitations to come to the clinic to talk about her children, and still kept her phone number a secret, I wrote a letter with copies for father and his lawyer, and mother via her lawyer's address. It expressed my concern that Kevin was seemingly shouldering a feeling of responsibility for his mother's welfare that no boy of eleven could manage without high psychic cost, and stated that this issue might alienate mother and son more than necessary in the long run. I flatly stated that the adults involved should relieve Kevin of this pressure by establishing some "ground rules" between them, so that he and Mimi would not be used in the controversy between the adults. I described Kevin's despair at concluding that telling mother that he did not want to be put in the middle had been of no use. I suggested that Kevin did care about his mother and her welfare, and that it would probably be in her best interest if she wished to establish a long-range, positive relationship with the children, to work these issues out in a different way. I again stated that if she wished, I would be glad to cooperate in either seeing her about the children or helping to make a referral. Such attempts by me and by one of the lawyers to spell out the need for "ground rules" in a way which would not put the children into an impossible position in the middle were not heeded. As the children became increasingly terrified at mother's anger, now refusing to go with her at all, not only did her vindictiveness increase, but she also followed them home, called them on the phone pretending she was a different relative before switching to her own voice, etc. Both children suffered a recurrence of night terrors related to these incidents.

Most upsetting to Kevin, after a week of refusing contact with her, was one incident when he was called to the phone for a supposed long-distance call from another relative, only to find that the voice changed into his mother's, with the usual accusations. He now began to have nightmares in which he ran, terrified, through a hall while one, another and yet another and another arm of his mother reached out of dark rooms to grasp him.

Kevin also wrote a letter, for use with the judge, mother, or court, stating some of what he could not tell her directly.

He wrote that he was afraid of his mother, and listed a series of things that had happened between them. His fear had less to do with the simple fact of outbursts of rage at him, which he felt he could have adjusted to. More germane were the quicksilver changes in his mother's mood and behavior, and especially the contrast between the way she treated him—"sweet as honey"— in front of other people, and the eruption of "mean" accusations when she was alone with him and Mimi. He wrote that she had warned him that she wanted to hurt him, but that she couldn't because people might be watching her while she was fighting for custody. Kevin wrote that he could no longer be himself when with his mother, that he could never talk to her because she did not know how to listen. He wrote of his mother's hatred for his father, stepmother, new siblings and even the animals; Kevin loved them all and wanted to stay with them. He complained, in his letter, of her attempts to trick him in various ways, and his fear of the power she said she has had to change everything, like custody.

With adequate financial resources to sustain prolonged litigation, Mrs. O'Malley now began a series of contempt-of-court complaints against the father, and as well appealed the whole custody decision, alleging a judicial error. A series of different judges with different attitudes were involved in the contempt charges. Although mother had been threatening Mimi for some months that she would call the police to make her come, Mimi at first did not believe her. One judge appointed a guardian ad litem again, and during his investigation, in a joint interview between Kevin and mother, she tried to convince him that Kevin must be "mentally ill" to say the things he did about her, thus again projecting and externalizing her difficulties.

Kevin was intensely upset, after this interview, about a number of issues that he later discussed with me. One was the fear that he might indeed turn out to be "mentally ill" if it could "run in the family, like Mom and Grandpa," that he probably would be so now, if he had continued to share the ideas about the world which he had held when he and his mother lived together. He also recognized that he identified his own thoughts of "getting even" with her, when she tricked him, as crazy thoughts of misrepresenting reality to her. When he had written in his letter that "I can't be me when I'm with her," he meant that she did not allow communication with anyone who did not agree with her, and that in fact "my own self now" can no longer pretend to agree. He cried as he described how his mother had denied Kevin's description of her behavior and tried to convince the court psychiatrist that Kevin was crazy. The reality of Kevin's perceptions had been disputed many times before, but he now finally trusted his own judgment of what was true. We discussed Kevin's reaction to all of this, his mother's disturbance and her need to see all the trouble as coming from outside herself rather than from within. I stated clearly that I knew Kevin was not crazy, and he recalled the various views of the world he had shared with mother in earlier years and now felt differently about. His second area of distress was clearly that there was as yet no legal assurance that the mother's power "to talk so reasonable and sugar sweet when she wants to" would not convince the court that she was right, and threaten his life with his new family. He no longer showed concern about her any more, for obvious reasons now needing to dissociate himself, his future identification and his life from her. He said simply "I just can't care about her any more—I'd rather not see her in my whole life again."

When the case was continued, a different judge was assigned; he refused to hear any witnesses and stated, about Mimi, that he could not understand how "any five-year-old would not want to see her mother." He concluded that visitation must continue and that father would be liable to a prison term if he did not comply. This implicit condoning by the court of the mother's "rightness" and the father's "wrongness" was followed by increasingly extreme behavior on her part over the next two weeks. Not only did she yell at the children that she would get their daddy "locked up in jail" if they did not come with her, but she actually called the police to appear at their door with her on visitation day. Fortunately the police witnessed the children's panic, told the mother to go home and refused to enforce the visitation order. Mimi, her terror of her earlier experiences of being "locked up" restimulated, had to be seen for an emergency appointment. Eventually, after a series of further hearings, the contempt-of-court order was rescinded, although litigation about permanent custody was still awaiting appeal.

This mother seemed driven to maintain contact with a family she could not tolerate losing. She did this through a characteristic way of experiencing impulses or wounded self-esteem in an externalized and projected form. Thus she explained the situation in terms of external enemies. First her exhusband and eventually, ironically, her children came to be seen either as "mentally ill" when they criticized her or as enemies who must be controlled by the police. In this instance the court played into her fantasies. Although police had been used as protection against her own impulses at one point in her life (when she requested their presence to take her to the hospital) she now saw the situation as one in which she could marshal allies to control the children and "lock up" her exhusband. The children in turn came to perceive that the mother's claim of "loving" them was vested only in a form to which they could no longer mold themselves. Such legitimization of omnipotent hostile fantasies was, I believe, antitherapeutic for her, encouraged her pursuit of further litigation, and led to increased alienation between herself and the children to whom, at some level, she wanted to be a good mother. Mrs. O'Malley had the financial resources for extensive litigation and choice of experts (when some psychiatrists would refuse to testify for her in court, she could find others who would). She, too, deserved more protection from herself than she got.

For the children, the harmful consequences of the period of enforced visitation, as well as continued doubt about whether their custody with father was in jeopardy, were obvious. Fortunately their father's assurance that he would not let this happen, and would go to any extreme necessary to prevent it, gave them considerable security. Less obvious, but equally important, was the artificial polarization of the qualities of the two parents in their minds. This interfered with the process of coming to terms with the loss of their mother, to whom they had once been close, by short-circuiting the initial attempts both children had made to integrate rather than repress and extrude components of an earlier identification with her. Kevin was able to bring the shadow of the fear of "craziness" to light, but still felt haunted by it as the remnant of his mother's "curse" of him, while Mimi, planning tit for tat, consoled herself with the thought that if her mother were to grab her while she was on the neighbor's bike, which was clearly not mother's property (like Mimi was not her property), she too, would be justified in calling the police.

For both children, meanwhile, the reassuring daily reality of their family life is the center of gravity for their solid growth.

There is no doubt that individual treatment of persons described as "litigious" is as a general rule fraught with difficulties. A low tolerance for experiencing rejected impulses as one's own underlies the need to handle inner tension by projecting it onto external hostile forces. The sense of injustice is real, and indeed tends to be based on earlier real experience. However, the need either to distort reality or to provoke its collusion in a hostile interaction in order to cling to the image of the past, including the only "self" that is known, is usually unconscious. Also unconscious may be the overestimation of potential power, needed, in fantasy, to subdue (or protect oneself from) the unjust enemy. In either individual treatment or necessary intervention by a social institution, such as place of work, college, etc., an important first step toward defusing and de-escalating hostile interaction based on this dynamic is persistently and openly to face the individual with reality correction of the perceived interaction, as well as to clarify the limits of action and consequences of transgression. This is not primarily the therapist's job, but must be carried out by the social network with which the individual comes into contact—e.g., work supervisor, college dean, campus patrol, etc. The individual often perceives the failure to make such clarifications as proof of the correctness of his ideational system. Because such individuals are often highly controlled, persuasive, and rational-sounding, the area of distortion may be difficult to perceive without extensive knowledge of their behavior.

In the case of the O'Malleys and others like it, I believe court action unwittingly meshed with the particular difficulties from which the mother suffered, resulting in an escalated and prolonged acting out of the mother-child disturbance in a way which was deleterious to the welfare of both. Although a guardian ad litem had been appointed, congruent with the "best interests" of the children, he was powerless either to instigate more rapid action or to insist on having needed evidence.

It is, then, the more encouraging to report that in this case court intervention did finally provide a solution. In the course of a last, protracted litigation, a different judge, perceptive and undaunted by complexities, pursued a detailed investigation of the children's situation. After this they could be assured that their custody would remain with father and forced visitation was a thing of the past.

The Child in the Service of a Father's Conflict: The Knights

In the following case the impetus for a custody suit resulted from the fears upon which the marriage had crumbled. Mr. Knight, the father of ten-year-old Rick and four children in late adolescence or older, wanted custody of his young son in order to keep him from becoming "weak" and "sissified" while being brought up by a woman.

Max Knight had been a surgeon, first in the army and then in civilian life. He had regaled his children throughout their childhood with tales of Army life as the happiest period in his memory. He did not speak to them of his childhood. His father had died when he was nine years old. The youngest among several siblings, he was the only one boarded out after his father's death, to a woman who sometimes beat him. He assumed this was because he was the least liked in the family. In adolescence he had been teased about his small size, and felt that he never was quite accepted then or in adulthood as "one of the boys."

Mrs. Knight, a shy and compliant young woman, interrupted college to marry Max. She described the early years of the marriage as "superficially successful" although her husband had told her he was "disappointed" in marriage shortly after the wedding. She assumed that it must have been her fault. However, raising five children, adding to the house, teaching the children how to repair cars and do carpentry projects became shared sources of family pride. When her youngest went to school, Mrs. Knight began working part-time as a tutor, reviving the interest she had renounced when she married in becoming a teacher. Exposed to warm human relationships at work, she became increasingly aware of the lack of communication between herself and her husband. The distance between them was augmented when she suffered a series of physical illnesses, involving surgery and leaving her with some scars. Her husband was increasingly critical and disgusted with her and their already limited sex life ceased. Mrs. Knight began to seek some emotional intimacy with him, in the form of talking. He made it clear that he abhorred anything so "emotional," and that marriage to him was just a "financial contract." He became abusive, threatening physical harm and telling the children that he hated their mother and had for the last fifteen years, that their relationship "sucks." She became afraid of his threats and upon the advice of a lawyer sought a court injunction against his presence in the house. Having decided "I need communication with my husband and don't consider it a weakness any more," she now wanted a divorce. He returned from the court hearing in which he was asked to "stop harassing his wife" enraged and humiliated. The following day a worried call to a clinic by the oldest son, Joseph, indicated that his father had been talking suicide or murder, vowing to destroy or get even with his wife in some way. He was seen in a clinic for an emergency appointment, began and abruptly terminated treatment with a psychiatrist and consulted a series of lawyers. Although at this point he agreed to divorce, he would not consider a settlement without having custody at least six months of the year of his youngest son. He did not consider whether this might be disruptive to the boy, nor did he ask his wishes.

His philosophy, that women are not fit to bring up boys, recapitulated the tragedy of his own childhood, when the death of his father resulted in his being further ousted by his mother, and left him to the care of a rejecting, punitive woman. The dissolution of the marriage occurred when he felt pressured to participate in "emotion" and to deal intimately with a "scarred" body, both of which were signs, to him, of an "unmanliness" which he had both rejected and feared in himself in his attempts to survive a troubled adolescence. His own dependency wishes catastrophically shattered when he was nine, he turned against them with violent finality. Not surprisingly his reaction to separation from his family was associated with thoughts of death.

Although father changed lawyers a number of times, both Mr. and Mrs. Knight's lawyers were astute individuals who were well aware of some of the underlying issues and their interpersonal consequences. For example, Mrs. Knight's lawyer made the wise suggestion that, in order to minimize the dangerous humiliation Max Knight might feel if he were in the passive position, she allow him to be the one to file for divorce. She did this, able to steel herself for the fifteen minutes of demeaning insults he leveled at her in court. The judge did not cut him short.

Mr. Knight told his older children that he wanted them to testify in court for him and was "ashamed of them" for not taking sides. They reacted in a variety of ways. Joseph answered that if he went to court he would have to testify that things were going well at the house. After this he suffered considerable anxiety about letting father down; this surfaced in the form of sudden examination anxiety in college—a problem he had never had. The notion of success, which at the moment meant a competitive defeat of the father, was fraught with conflict.

A younger son, Robert, who physically pushed his father out of the house when Max tried to hit his wife, broke down in tears after this act, describing his identification with father's lack of trust in people.

All the older children seemed attuned to Rick's need to have them around more and be taken along to various activities. Ten-year-old Rick was the most attached to his father and was bewildered by the turn of events. Although he did not want to live with him, he seemed especially pleased that father wanted him and made the most requests to see him. He was hurt by the frequency with which the father forgot his promise to see Rick or found himself too busy. After the divorce took place and custody was awarded to the mother, he was upset at hearing Max yell at Martha on the phone "And I don't care what happens to Rick." It was at this point he finally said, "Why does he ask for custody if he doesn't even want to see me?"

In the following months Dr. Knight vowed that he would rather lose all his money than share it with his wife. He tried to enlist the children's aid to get "justice" in court. He stopped financial support for all the older children, and one son had to leave in the middle of his senior year in college, until he earned enough on his own to return. He wrote a letter asking the children to help him fight the injustice of a legal system which required him to pay alimony. He stated that brave men and brave children must stand ready to defy these values at any cost. Dr. Knight continued his struggle with repeated court appeals against "unfair" aspects of the financial settlement, winning a number of decisions, although his former wife was in spartan circumstances compared to his own.

Progressively engaged with the court, and continuing to function satisfactorily at work, he progressively disengaged himself as a father, seeing Rick at most once every two or three months. Rick, still hurt, made clear that he now felt his father didn't care for him and eventually made a close attachment to a basketball coach who had been enlisted to spend extra time with him.

About three years after the initial divorce action, Max Knight moved to another state, where he had been offered a particularly responsible position. He came to say goodbye, telling his oldest son "I think I will miss all the court fights—they were some of the most fun I ever had." Eventually he struck up a correspondence with this boy, based on the agreement that Joseph should not address him as "dad," but call him by first name like "equals." Joseph participated, but reported that he could not remember the days when he felt he had a "dad," that he felt like he was writing to a stranger with whom he had only a little in common. Rick did not write.

In contrast to the O'Malleys, the Knight children were not subjected to actual shifts in caretakers, nor were their early developmental experiences as chaotic. However, through the custody suit Rick, in particular, came to the painful awareness that his father's wish for him was motivated by forces which had nothing to do with him. Progressively he was, and felt, deeply rebuffed as his father's son. In this case the competence of the lawyers in the area of disturbed human relationships, and their awareness of the vulnerability of this outwardly enraged man, may well have played a role in averting the acting out of a more dramatic tragedy.

For Max Knight, childhood emotional dependence had been interrupted by catastrophic loss, and by an attempt to banish all feeling and anxiety in order to assure himself of "manliness." Although he could not tolerate emotional intimacy as a husband, and later even as a father, he eventually attempted to undo a piece of his traumatic adolescence. He requested no longer to be a dad to his oldest son, but to be accepted as just "one of the boys," on a first-name basis. A custody suit, and Rick's needs, were ill-fitted for attaining this end. However, it is quite possible that, as the distress about the divorce and its meaning recedes for Max Knight, he will re-establish a more interested, fathering role with this son and with his other children.

Custody Suit Averted—A Disturbed
Mother-Child Relationship in Therapy: The Walshes

When I met Lucy she had just turned four. Hilary Walsh, her mother, was referred to me a week after release from a psychiatric hospital where she had been for six months. She told me "Ever since Lucy was born I have had trouble with her—I committed myself because I was afraid I would destroy myself or Lucy. The last few months before I went to the hospital she would wake up at night screaming, and I would go in and beat her." She was ashamed of herself, but unable either to control or understand her behavior, while fearing she might actually go further and kill the child. She added "I am also in the middle of a divorce, and I do still have custody, but Bart wants to declare me unfit and get custody. While I was in the hospital his parents and he took care of the kids. Now they have beautiful table manners, but seem like robots to me." She told me she very much wanted to be a good mother to her children, but still feared her loss of control. I saw Lucy in psychotherapy and simultaneously worked with the mother, particularly on issues related to Lucy. After first seeing Lucy I met with the father, a successful engineer, who was bitterly disillusioned about his wife in a variety of ways. We attempted to separate his feelings about his wife, and why, inevitably—given his expectations—his marriage had not worked, from his concerns about the child's future. I took the point of view with both parents, that in Lucy's interest, it was too early to foreclose the issue of custody permanently. The parents' lives were still very much in transition, and the child attached to both of them in important ways.

Because of the strength of their underlying longing for each other and the willingness of both mother and daughter to deal with the painful feelings of their recent past, their relationship was highly amenable to treatment.

Hilary Walsh had grown up in a constricting household in which she was kept in a childlike dependence. She learned to mistrust her own impulses and judgment, becoming highly vulnerable to the feeling that she was a bad person whenever she felt like offending those she most needed to please. During her adolescence her mother began to suffer from arthritis and a chronic heart condition. Hilary was repeatedly told that she must not upset her mother in anyway, for the result might kill her. She did not allow herself to express anger at her mother's increasing criticism of her as she began to have some heterosexual interests; both parents stringently tabooed her interest in a boy who was not Catholic. Mother regularly went through her drawers and purse and read her letters. One day Hilary had talked on the phone with a Jewish boy she had secretly seen. Her mother eavesdropped on the conversation, and then could be heard falling down a flight of steps. Hilary, in terror, at first did not even go to look at her, because she was convinced she had indeed killed her mother in this way. She had not. However, Hilary never saw the boy again. Not long after this she married a Catholic boy, Bart, of whom both parents approved. This young man turned out to be constricting and critical of her in many ways, like her mother; e.g., he was upset at her wanting to wear slacks around the house rather than dresses, and forbade her ever to smoke or drink, indicating that she was not turning out to be the "nice girl" he wanted for a wife. Two months after the marriage Mrs. Walsh's mother died; a month later Lucy was conceived. For Mrs. Walsh the child cemented the marriage and she began to feel desperately trapped.

Mrs. Walsh indicated that she felt enormously inadequate as a mother from the beginning. Lucy had eaten and slept poorly since infancy. Lucy made her feel like a helpless child, and she resented it. When she cried, or "screamed" at Mrs. Walsh (Mrs. Walsh, as a child, was not allowed to do this because it might upset and kill her mother), Mrs. Walsh alternated between feeling her own wish to scream in rage, and facing what she felt as Lucy's accusation that she was a bad mother—equivalent to being an unlovable, bad girl. Having lived under the threat that she would cause her mother's death if she was bad, she now had periods of knowing she wished her child to die (in order for the crying and "screaming" to go away).

In work with Mrs. Walsh, a distorted view of her baby quickly emerged, and made it possible to begin sorting out the image of her child from that of her mother, who "tried to run my life and humiliate me whenever she could." Mrs. Walsh had seen her baby as bigger and stronger than she was, with the power to run and ruin her life. When her husband would tell her she was treating the infant too harshly, she felt he was siding with Lucy, preferring Lucy as a female to her. She described seeing a frozen smile on Lucy's face when the child was two, when the parents had argued. Whereas Lucy probably did this in an attempt to deny and master her anxiety, mother saw it as proof that Lucy was gloating in her victory over mother. More and more she saw Lucy in a reversal of roles, as the gloating, powerful mother who accused her of being bad and successfully squelched any expressions of anger or sexual rivalry. In her mind it was Lucy, transformed into this mother, whom she had to get rid of in order to grow up and be a woman herself; her own death through suicide had been her other frightening alternative.

Mrs. Walsh's motivation for child abuse occurs in a minority of such cases; it involved an isolated area of distorted perception. The dynamics differ from the more common picture of the parent who has been physically abused and neglected herself in childhood and retains a low frustration tolerance as well as the need to handle the earlier anxiety about being abused by changing from the passively experienced assault to an active one. Identifying with the aggressor, the abusing parent, especially when under stressful circumstances which thwart his own dependency needs—which have been thwarted so many times before—attacks the dependent child. Most such parents live in chronically depriving circumstances, often without adequate financial or emotional support. In both types of child abuse there is a tendency toward role reversal in the parent's expectations of the child. Mrs. Walsh was neither physically abused or neglected, but was overprotected and not allowed to grow up without feeling that her independence would kill her mother. Until after her hsopitalization she had felt no choice but to give in to her mother's influence at her own expense. She married a man who continued her mother's criticisms and moralistic standards. Her image of Lucy, especially at night, when ego defenses are more permeable—she did not beat her during the day, though she "spanked"—underwent a delusional transformation in which Lucy became the powerful, accusing mother instead of a baby; and at times the rejected "self" who screamed in a way which had been defined as dangerous and bad by the mother. What sounded like "screaming" to mother was heard as ordinary crying by others.

Work with the mother centered on: (1) differentiation of herself from the blurred identifications with her mother and her daughter; (2) support of her growing capacities for actually mothering Lucy and of the new pleasure she experienced in allowing herself freer communication and the spontaneous expression of a variety of feelings between them, including both love and anger; (3) consideration of her own growth as a person. This included both the relationship to a man friend, very different from Bart, who, she felt, liked her for herself, and was also willing to take an active, warm, and yet firm interest in Lucy; and her wish to develop a career choice which she had renounced long ago.

When Mrs. Walsh's mother had been dying, she was not informed; after the death she said she wanted to see her, but father insisted the coffin be closed, because he didn't "want any hysteria." Mrs. Walsh now felt angry with her father for interfering with the chance to say goodbye to her mother and for not allowing that death to become more of a reality, because of his need to keep all feelings under control. She decided for the first time to call him "Dad" instead of "Daddy" and to cut down his daily phone calls to her, which were usually full of unwanted advice, to once a week. She reported "Yesterday was the fifth anniversary of my mother's death. I decided to sell my mother's jewelry— *without telling my father*——I didn't go to the cemetery—I sold the jewelry and with the money I went to buy Lucy a dog." In many ways she described a shift in emotional investment from mother and death to Lucy and life.

She became a sensitive, playful, giving, and appropriately restraining mother, although she remained conflicted about how much of her energy was spent on bringing up her child at a period in her life when she felt she was just emerging as a person in her own right, and needed more energy for herself. After Lucy had been in therapy a few months, and began to ask her mother questions about the trouble between them in the past, she was able to talk honestly about her earlier behavior, in ways that Lucy could understand and that reassured her that the beatings would not recur. By the time the divorce became final, about eight months after the mother came out of the hospital, their relationship had improved greatly. Custody was granted to the mother, but Lucy continued to spend weekends, or a week a month, with her father and grandparents. Though eager to go on these visits, she continued to need reassurances that mother would not get "sick" and disappear into the hospital again.

Bart Walsh came to discuss his daughter's treatment, as well as the story of the marriage, which had been heartbreaking for him. The Walsh's courtship had been brief, and Bart did not believe in "going too far" with a nice girl. Hilary had looked like someone out of *House Beautiful* magazine to him, and was fun to be with. He felt it was "love at first sight" and told her she was the right person to be his wife and mother of his children. He was shocked by the discrepancy between her behavior after marriage and his picture of an ideal wife. In addition, when Lucy was born, he felt he needed constantly to intervene in Hilary's anger at Lucy, and thought of himself as having to become both mother and father of the child. This further angered Hilary, who felt father and infant were ganging up on her to criticize and exclude her.

He now intended to ask for custody of Lucy, feeling that Hilary would not be stable enough to bring her up, nor provide for the proper education and manners, as he and his parents would do. In addition it became clear that he was very lonely. Although he saw a good deal of his parents, he did not feel it was right for him to "date" before the divorce was final. He missed Lucy sorely, even though he was also aware of the practical difficulties of providing her with care if he did have custody.

Mr. Walsh felt Hilary's behavior before hospitalization was sufficient to prove her unfit. He indicated that if custody were taken from her it would make clear to her that he had been right, rather than "prudish" (as she had accused him of being), about the nature of proper conduct. He felt rejected, and his pride and self-confidence had been severely shaken: We attempted to separate this issue from the notion that being awarded custody would prove anything about either of them as a person. The potentially destructive effects of a custody suit were discussed in terms of Lucy's later understanding of the situation, and her need to be free to identify with "good" and "fit" aspects of both parents. By the time the divorce came to court, some months later, he was willing to drop pursuit of custody. By this time he had begun cautiously to date again.

When I first saw Lucy, her nursery school teacher had described her to me
as an anxious little girl, who wanted to leave class whenever the room got
noisy. She repeatedly told her teacher that she thought the children who don't
say "please" and "thank you" should get punished, but seemed relieved when
the teacher refused to do this. Her mother reported that she was still waking at
night or "moaning and groaning" in her sleep and eating poorly, but she had
not punished Lucy for either of these since coming out of the hospital.

Lucy was a thin wisp of a four-year-old whose huge blue eyes spoke a
contrast to her matter-of-fact leaving of mother to come into the therapy play
room. She walked to the doll house as soon as she saw it, and picking up the
mother and girl dolls, said:

"Is it too big to hold them? Which is the mother and which is the daughter?"

"Maybe both of them can be held; can you show me about the mother and
daughter?"

Lucy, softly: "I don't want to. Can you be the little girl so I can look in your
ears and everything?"

t: "Sure."

Lucy pulled down the doctor's kit and looked into my ears and mouth.

Lucy: "You feel fine now, no more medicine."

t:: "I think you want the little girl and the mother both to feel fine and not to
be sick."

Lucy: "Mommy was sick at the hospital and I went to see her. But now you
better eat all your milk and potatoes like a good girl."

She was letting me know she needed more time before she could dwell for
long on the frightening aspects of having been her mother's little girl; but she
could show me some of what she experienced by switching to the role of the
doctor or mother who was in control of what happened. Just before she left
that day she told me she had had a bad dream and there was no good fairy to
make it better. She then asked me if the toy gun was real, "Can I shoot you and
you shoot me?" I told her "No, we won't hurt each other here, not now or
ever". Reportedly she was eager for her next appointment, impatient for the
week to pass. Lucy had given me the clue to her problem in the first sentence
she had spoken that hour: "Is it too big to hold them? Which is the mother and
which is the daughter?" Her wish to be the held little girl was as clear as it had
been during her night crying in babyhood, but that wish was associated in her
mind with hurting and being hurt. I did not verbalize that wish of hers, not
only because of her anxiety about it, but also because I did not yet know
whether her mother would be ready to fulfill those needs when Lucy expressed
them, and wanted to be sure that an awareness of her yearning, when
translated into action, would not be met by rebuff. However, luckily, mother's
tenderness toward her child was growing.

The second session Lucy ran into the therapy room and put the little girl doll into the dollhouse bed. She came over to me and said, "Now write down cookie monster," pointing to the page where I was taking notes on our session. I did so and she told me:

"If the cookie monster comes I'll get it right out. When the cookie monster comes to shiver me and gets mad at me, I get mad at the cookie monster."

t: "It comes to shiver you?"

Lucy: "To shiver and shake me at night. Grandma says there's a fairy godmother who zips off her magic wand and leaves it on your pillow. But in the morning, I think of a witch under my pillow."

t: "Is that the bad dream you told me about last week?"

Lucy: "Yes and I still have it."

I could then talk with her about the bad dream as the picture that was left in her mind of something that really happened to her, and how frightened and sad it made her. Perhaps she got shaken and it made her shiver. Although I don't usually approach children's dreams in this manner, Lucy's actual experience needed to be brought to the fore. As in other situations in which an actual trauma has been suffered (e.g., "shell shock") her dream recapitulated the drama of her anxiety. She was then able to tell me about the nights "a long time ago, before mommy got sick." She said "Every time I moaned and "growed" mommy screamed at me. She only hit some of me. Then I don't know what happened and when she came home from the hospital she said 'no more hitting and screaming' and she didn't any more."

We talked for a long time about how confused and upset mommy had been before she went to the hospital. It had not been Lucy's fault, though; mommy had really been mad at bigger people, and sometimes she got scared and mixed up so that she hit Lucy instead; Mommy knows she shouldn't have done that, and is learning now not to mix up who she's mad at anymore. Lucy walked to the dollhouse, said "time to wake up" to the girl doll and fed pieces of candy to girl, mother, father doll, a stuffed dog, and to herself. At home the week following that session mother reported that Lucy still woke crying at night, but if mother approached she would say "get away, don't stand there anymore." One night she added "I'm mad at you, I don't want to talk to you." Mother assured her during the day that Lucy could be angry at her and "get out" her feelings, and that if she was angry at Lucy she would tell her that too, and not hit.

During the next few weeks she continued to use her therapy sessions to play out concerns about her relationship to mother, father, and Adam, mother's new friend. Meanwhile she began to use various "supplies," such as candy, water, paint, and paper, voraciously, as though she could not count on their remaining available to her. I took up her feeling that she needed a lot now; that might mean she thought it wouldn't be there anymore after a while. She said "If I don't share with Tommy (boy at nursery school) he won't be my friend any more." This led to a discussion of her father, with whom she lived while mother was in the hospital and who just saw her on weekends now. Was that like not being her friend anymore? She told me that she wanted mommy to share Lucy so that mommy and daddy would be friends, but she wanted to live with mommy now. She also told me that daddy's voice sounded funny when he talked about mommy and maybe he would not be her daddy anymore. I let her know I would be talking with her daddy, that we wanted to work things out so that Lucy could be sure of always having daddy be her daddy and mommy her mommy even though they would not be living in the same house and be married anymore. She said:

"And my grandpa can put me over his shoulder like a hippopotamus—and my mommy can do it too now, I'm teaching her."

t: "And did you used to worry when Mommy was in the hospital that she wouldn't be your mommy anymore?"

Lucy: "Yes, I used to always think that."

t: "Did nobody tell you she'd be back?"

Lucy: "Yes, but I never believed them."

In her play with the puppets and dolls she repeatedly demonstrated her conflict between the wish for the loving, holding, or feeding parent and her fear of unpredictable anger between them. E.g., one day she came in saying:

"I didn't have a dream last night. I just slept by myself. Mommy and Adam are getting finer every day. What is this baby (picking up large baby doll)? She has the biggest mouth, I don't know if I like her,"

t: "Maybe she just needs a lot, Lucy."

Lucy: "Okay, the baby wants its mommy—mommy is a bear (picks up furry bear puppet) and we need a daddy too. I don't like the mommy, can we have a different mommy? (is looking through the puppet pile, picks out the mother and girl puppet).

Lucy then has the mother throw the child on the floor. She runs to find "a different mother" puppet, and has her pick up the child and hug it tenderly. She picks up the alligator puppet: "The alligator eats the baby up. I like the alligator because it won't eat me." (The alligator is reminiscent of the cookie monster in her earlier dream.) She puts them down, picks up mother and girl and has them alternately hug and hit each other.

t: "What are they doing?"

Lucy: "They are crying at each other."

t: "Tell me about it."

Lucy: "This one (mother) was hitting this one (girl)." She picks up the nurse puppet and has her hug the girl and then uses a yarn needle to take the mother's temperature.

t: "Maybe you are trying to show me that when you needed mommy to hug and feed you, she hadn't learned about that yet and hit you instead. Then you wished for a different mommy, and that made it even harder for you to believe she was coming back—you wanted the hitting mommy to go away and you wanted her back too, but different."

Lucy had made valiant use of an ingenious mental mechanism to maintain her belief in a loving mother; in her play she first split the mother into two people, one who throws the child down and the other who consoles it; however, then she combined them into one ambivalent figure who alternately hugs and hits and coped with the reality of her experience. References to her early and chronic difficulties in establishing a comfortable oral and tactile relationship to the mother were still extruded or projected in her play. That is, she expressed "not liking" the baby with the big mouth, but then projected the oral impulse on to the alligator who ate the baby "but not me." The baby first "wants" a "furry bear" mommy, with tactile softness, but then rejected it in favor of a different one. Meanwhile in her therapy relationship she often sought bodily contact by leaning against my lap, and also maintained a steady consumption of cookies or candy, usually in the midst of some doll-feeding play. At home she was reportedly trying some new foods, introduced by Adam, for the first time, and eating larger amounts. At night her mother still sometimes heard brief "moaning," but no longer went to her as Lucy did not wake at these times.

The following weeks Lucy had the large baby doll emit intermittent crying sounds which were disconnected from her other play or verbalizations. These occurred throughout the hour. When I mentioned it, she denied it was happening at all. At this time she became intensely attached to a stuffed angora kitten in the therapy room, wanting very much to have it and telling me that her own toys were not cuddly so she had no one to cuddle her at home. I decided to give her a close duplicate of the kitten for her birthday; she was disappointed in this and wanted the one "that comes from *our* room." I agreed that maybe she needs "ours," that she could take her cuddly feelings from here to keep at home. I gave her the one she had wanted first. I should have realized a substitute would not do. Reportedly she took the kitten to bed with her nightly and for the first time that week there were no reports of night "moaning." Mother was delighted with undisturbed nights.

The next session crying appeared in a dream. She told me: "Mommy doesn't punish me anymore when I don't know about it" and then stated "Something scary happened at night. I woke up and wanted water and thought there might not be any more water and so I couldn't breathe and so I cried instead: it was still my dream but I knowed I was doing it." We discussed this in terms of her fear of no one being there when she was thirsty or hungry; when she couldn't count on the people it seemed like all the drinks in the world might be gone too. She said, "It's lucky I came today because this candy has a lot of water in it." The next session her mother was ill, and Adam brought

Lucy. She asked for lots of paint water, then brought it all to the baby doll. She told me, "When the baby is thirsty and has no mommy she is sad, she doesn't know if mommy is coming back, see?"

t: "I see how sad that must be."

Lucy: "It makes me cry for the baby and mommy." Later that hour she informed me, "I have to go home to take care of mommy, she lets me bring her things now."

Another day she told me: "I wish Mommy and Adam would get married, but they can't."

t: "Why?"

Lucy: "Well, because they would fall out of love."

t: "Like mommy and daddy did?"

Lucy: "Yes." Two days earlier she had told her mother "I cried for daddy last night," and her mother had explained that daddy and she were still friends, but they did not make each other happy any more, so that it was best for both of them to part. Lucy was able to discuss wanting to be with both mommy and daddy and Adam too. She thought "taking turns" (between parents) was better than before, because mommy played with her more than she used to and so did Adam. Once she described with a twinkle in her eye two girlfriends, playing at her house, who fought with each other, "so I have to stop them."

t: "How come *you* have to be the one to stop them?"

Lucy (laughs): "No, mommy does that now."

t: "Yes, her job is to be the mommy and that way you can be the child."

That week she made a request of her mother "Can you like daddy just a little, just for me?" Her insistence at nursery school that others be punished had ceased. Things continued to go well between Lucy and her mother. Setting limits on Lucy's behavior became increasingly easy for her as her rage and guilt decreased. Adam took an active, helpful role in this too. Mrs. Walsh had felt enormously gratified when she was granted custody, feeling that for the first time in her life there was proof that she was trusted to be competent at an adult role, that is, being a mother. Some time after this she became increasingly conflicted about her feeling that caring for Lucy tied her down in her efforts to develop herself more fully in a number of directions. She was eager to pursue a talent in dancing; she had always wanted to do this, but had felt in adolescence that it was selfish and frivolous and had renounced it. She was also trying to work out with Adam a more mature and less dependent love relationship than she had previously experienced; she knew she had short-circuited her growing up by fleeing into a neurotic marriage so early. Feeling "fit" to be a mother, she decided to offer custody to the father legally and to work out a "sharing" of Lucy's care with him in future years.

Lucy's future confidence about being securely and permanently wanted by her parents is still at stake, and ideally her early experience with loss needed restitution, in the form of a permanent home and love commitment. Realistically, however, the parents, in also meeting their own needs, drastically reduced their ambivalence toward her, and did indeed love her in a responsible way. A custody suit, as had been threatened, would have compromised Lucy's chance to make peace with her mother, first by experiencing tenderness instead of hostility between them, and secondly by being able to identify with the mother as a "fit" and happy person. When I last heard about Lucy, two years after termination, she was reportedly flourishing, but I had no glimpse into her inner life at the time.

I had admiration for the parents, for subordinating an initial need to prove superiority to the spouse with whom they were bitterly disillusioned, to Lucy's long-range needs to continue caring about both of them. In addition, I found it necessary to take a clear stand with the mother's lawyer, at a time when a custody suit was contemplated, and he wished me to testify. I let him know that I did not wish to testify because I felt custody proceedings would be destructive to the child and both parents in the long run. Hence it would not be in his client's interest to subpoena me. The details of their earlier relationship would not be helpful in court and I could not easily withhold them. Several months later, when the divorce was about to come to court, I made clear, verbally and in writing, that Hilary Walsh had become capable of being a good mother and was working out her earlier problems. I saw no grounds for denying her custody, in fact felt it was important for her self-esteem, and urged that he help work out the situation peacefully between the parents. The lawyers and parents did the rest, and were instrumental as well in the later shifting of legal custody to the father, while both parents remained responsible for the actual care of the child.

This case, with a less than ideal solution, has been presented particularly because the early history is one which could easily lead to a custody suit. What would have been undermined was Lucy's glowing perseverance in facing her fears and tears in order to discover the "good" mother she knew she was searching for all along, and whom she needed in order to accept herself, even with a "big mouth" (as she had called it) as the expression of her need for comfort and nurturance, and to feel she was someone worth loving.

Custody Renounced and Parenting Regained:
Four Sets of Circumstances

The social climate which surrounds the woman who renounces custody of her children is still an arid one. Of the women I have known who have renounced custody out of willingness or inner necessity there is none who did not feel to some extent shunned by her previous social circle, relegated to a social isolation that magnified the already existing guilt and self-condemnation. Men in similar circumstances are not treated the same way.

It is not clear to me how far unconscious ambivalence toward children underlies the need to avoid a mother who actually leaves her children, as though her behavior might be contagious; or whether such behavior stirs up old fears of being abandoned oneself, fears the adult may prefer to leave dormant. In either case, the social shunning affects not only the woman's self-regard, but also her children's need to come to terms with this process, without making the assumption that something is wrong either with her or with themselves.

I have seen four kinds of circumstances under which women willingly forego the custody of their children. In all these circumstances the woman may carry with her a poignant fantasy of being reunited with her children at some time in the future, this time recognized and appreciated for her "real" self.

FAMILY TIMES FELT AS AN IMPEDIMENT TO
SELF-DEVELOPMENT: RACHEL GLADE

First is the woman who has come to feel that her role as wife and mother is deeply incompatible with her need to develop her full human potential, while her husband may be eager to maintain the parenting role.

Rachel Glade by mutual agreement left her two young children in the custody of her exhusband, while she pursued a career in science. She was an ambitious person. Having tried to "split" herself between the highly demanding expectations of her career, in which she felt a full-time commitment was prerequisite to advancement, and the emotional demands of the family, she had felt increasingly irritable and inadequate in both her roles. Her husband was a particularly nurturant man, happy to stop thinking about his professional commitments at five o'clock in order to devote himself to the children, and later to his search for a less career-oriented wife. His children after a period of some regression and tearfulness, with a sleep disturbance in the younger, were spontaneous and outgoing. They were insistently demanding about his evening time, in a way which made it difficult for him to have enough moments alone to become acquainted with new women. Whenever he did become interested in a woman, the children were quick to spot whether or not she had a receptive lap. Equally quickly they raised questions about whether she would be coming back or how long she would stay.

Each of the children expressed some grief and longing for the missing mother in a different way, reminiscent of aspects of their differing earlier relationship with her. The reactions of three-and-a-half-year-old Peter are described in a vignette, in chapter 2.

The second circumstance occurs when a woman feels desperately trapped in a bad marriage, but for one reason or another cannot simultaneously dissolve the marriage and keep her children.

Mrs. Greenwall

Mrs. Greenwall, for example, for years found all her attempts to establish a social life within the context of her marriage frustrated by her husband's particular style of life. Although the spouses had been chronically and increasingly estranged emotionally, her husband would not agree to a divorce or separation. As she neared the point at which she identified herself as middle-aged, and her children were adolescent, she felt increasingly desperate to establish herself as a person in her own right. She especially yearned for her children to know and appreciate the fun-loving and vibrant side of her personality, which she felt had been subdued throughout her unhappy marriage. For many years she had attempted to "cover up" both her unhappiness and her sense of being neglected by her husband, in order to preserve the facade of a happy family. She finally recognized that this was not only futile, but was also extracting a high psychic cost from her own and her children's development. She decided her only hope for a fuller life lay in a separation.

Finally, about three years after first asking for a divorce, she made it clear that she was leaving home. She bought a house with room for herself and her children and moved into it. Her husband made it equally clear that she was thereby forfeiting all "right" to be a mother. She reported that threats of violence, of burning her house down, etc., hung in the air. As in a number of other cases, the reaction to separation as though it might involve a death had an echo in the husband's past. His mother had died when he was a child. After his wife left home Mr. Greenwall made a number of rules about the children. For example, if they were to bring a friend into their mother's house, that friend would henceforth never again be welcome in father's house, in which they lived.

By the time she came to see me, Mrs. Greenwall felt acutely cut off from her children and perceived a hostile wall between herself and most of the adults in the limited social network in which she had previously functioned and contributed a good deal (members of the PTA, etc.). Feeling uninvited and without social support, she had not had the energy to shake the wall of avoidance by clarifying the circumstances surrounding her very limited contact with the children. She did not know what others assumed about it. The process of trying to resolve the separation between her husband and herself in a way which would not do damage to either, was an extremely slow one, fraught with setbacks and continued frustration in relation to the children. She worried about the children's care and development, knowing they were having problems, and feeling her hands were tied.

Some fragments of a dream during this time portray her sense of loss about the "vanishing" children, and about the missing network of human support which in fact did not hear her cries of distress.

"My parents and my aunt are talking in the hallway of a house. They are serene and happy and have shut me out. I see Jill (one of her children)—she is both a small baby and a teenager. She is close to another, older child, maybe Claire (another of her children). I realize the baby hasn't been bathed for a long time and that nobody has washed the towels for months. I put her in the tub. An interlude passes, after which I go back to get her and she has vanished. I try to tell my mother but she can't hear me and neither can my father. I scream and scream but nobody comes to help me. I look down a drain of some sort, clogged with leaves and twigs, and I see a small baby's hands imploring me. I reach down and find the baby, the Jill person, who has tiny hands like those of a doll. The hands are warm but the head is cold and in fact has turned into a doll's head. I am in despair and try again to attract my parents' attention, but can't. They are behind a glass wall now and can't hear anything."

She commented, "In the dream my father is very young and fresh and intent and it is a shock to see him undiminished and powerful. He doesn't communicate with me at all. My mother does a bit but I don't get my message through to her. Everyone is detached from me—like a picture I can see that doesn't care whether I'm watching it or not, and in which I have no place."

The baby Jill is, of course, not only the child for whom she cannot now provide needed care, but also herself, pleading for help before her life and "warmth" go down the drain. It is clear, too, that feeling herself an outsider to a charmed circle of unreachable others is not new to her. However, it is at just the point in her life where she had risked shedding the "doll-like" facade, the "cover-up" she felt necessary to hide a failing marriage, that the human support network had gaping holes. It indeed was behaving "like a picture I can see that doesn't care whether I'm watching it or not, and in which I have no place."

Estelle Phillips and George

Estelle Phillips consulted me about the multiple emotional problems of her thirteen-year-old son, George. She appeared guilt-ridden about his problems and told me the story of her first marriage. Describing her parents as cold— "not touching me or each other"—she said she was desperate enough for love to marry the first man who touched and seemed to want her. The couple had two children. She discovered quickly that her husband was violently abusive to her and the children, and increasingly alcoholic. He resisted separation and threatened to hurt her and the children if she tried to leave. In desperation one day she fled with a month's household money in her pocketbook. She established herself in a job, fearful of his finding her. Months later she made what she called "half-hearted attempts" at getting custody of the children, then aged two and four, but they remained in the care of the father and the paternal grandmother, with whom he now lived. About three years later, when mother had just remarried, father was sent to prison after being found guilty of sexually molesting children. Mrs. Phillips's children, then aged five and seven, were returned to her custody. The boy in particular had clearly suffered from malnutrition and dental decay, and was covered with bruises. She and the stepfather patiently and steadfastly tried to deal with the variety of the children's physical and emotional problems, but she never forgave herself for having left them in the first place. She blamed herself for her "selfishness," which, she felt, was still a characteristic, giving as evidence the fact that she insisted on keeping her own name, rather than changing it to her current husband's name—an act which hurt his feelings. I said that it sounded to me like she had to do what she did for self-preservation's sake and that it must have taken considerable courage to strike out on her own and then to take the children back when she felt up to it.

I added that if she had not left them at the time, she might not have become capable of becoming a real mother to them, as she was trying to be now, by now facing her own and her children's problems. She seemed relieved at this and then added that she knew that though she had made some feeble attempts at getting custody "there was something in me that was glad I couldn't take the children." She still found their clinging, dependent moments especially difficult. As she put it "I was feeling very helpless and the world around me was doing things to me." She let me know that she had made a suicide attempt, followed by some psychiatric care at the time. However, she felt the psychiatrist had not sustained an interest in her. She had indeed needed to learn to care enough about herself to be able to attempt the by then complicated job of caring for her children.

After a diagnostic evaluation of George, he was referred for individual therapy in addition to the recommendation of family therapy for all four individuals. Treatment had to take into account the mother's conflicting needs to be assured of sustained attention to her own dependency needs while simultaneously resisting encroachment on her autonomy and sense of control over herself and her fate. She could function well as a mother when she was not "trapped" by the feeling that her freedom was at stake, that she could not, as she put it "keep my own name."

George, a rotund thirteen-year-old, explained to me right away that "my mother had to leave me with my father when I was little—she couldn't help it."

He detailed many ways in which "my sister was pampered and I was mistreated." What he remembered most was getting strapped with the belt about twenty times regularly, and the fact that he was thin as a stick, while she was fat; she never seemed to get punished. When he was little and scared he turned to his grandmother, in whose bed he slept, while father slept with Jean, his sister. Grandmother had sympathy for him, though she was "kind of cuckoo too." Later "she went out of her mind because my old father hurt her a lot." When he was younger George wished he were a girl like Jean. George said that once he started living with his mother and new father he started "getting fatter" although his teeth were still ground down from being so nervous. His new father was much better, although George was scared of him too.

George had nightmares. He was not sure whether they were real and even in the daytime he constantly felt that something could happen to him. He said, "this guy haunts me from grade to grade." The "guy" was "like a green-eyed monster who might come in the window any time" and his eyes followed George wherever he went. He told me: At school "They don't like me because I'm so different and I'm scared to death all the time that I'll get hurt." Asked in what way he felt most different, he said, "I think I'm having a nervous breakdown. When I'm in class I start thinking that the guys will beat up on me after school. Then I think they are doing it right that minute and I will have to scream, but I can't get a sound out." After school was especially lonesome. Once he arrived home he felt safer, but often spent the afternoon crying or just biting his nails. He felt he could not express himself to anyone about how scared he was when no one was there. I talked with him about agreeing on his need for help in separating the awful, scary things that happened to him in the past from what he can expect from people now; that we wanted to plan for such help for him and his family. After he further described his panic states when in classes with certain boys, I also asked his permission to talk with the school to see if we could arrange his having a safe "time out" when he could leave class for a few minutes and go to the guidance department until he felt okay enough to return to class. He thought that would help, but did not believe it could be accomplished.

A phone call to the school established that they too were concerned about him. He was described as an extremely withdrawn boy who visibly shook with fear when the "tougher guys" were around. This had made him an object of scapegoating, and indeed he had been recently knocked down by a bunch of older boys. He was teased, about being "weird" and fat and often had books pushed out of his hands. He would not ever speak out in class in front of others, although he was willing to write. An attempt had been made by a guidance counselor to "draw him out" by including him in a small group of kids who all had trouble communicating. The group involved learning "trust and relaxation" and included some physical contact (e.g., the boys leading each other by the hand and feeling each others' faces). The guidance counselor had realized that George seemed more withdrawn and frightened after this. Recently he had shown obsessive interest in and admiration of the Nazi movement and the use of ammunition. This too was worrisome.

I indicated to the school counselor that for this particular boy physical stimulation from other boys or adult males was definitely counterindicated, while an "activity group" could be quite helpful to him. It was agreed that George should have "emergency egress" during panic states; and that attempts be made to protect him from beatings by building up a known friendship group, even if this only consisted of a couple of other boys. A few days later George reported surprise that the school and I had actually talked with each other, and some initial arrangements to help him feel safe had been made. Such surprise at helpful collaboration between two adults is frequently expressed by children who have experienced their parents as being primarily at odds with each other. At times a child will try to "split" two helping agencies, by playing one against the other, and it is important not to be drawn into such attempts.

In his second interview George appeared less panicky and began to discuss in detail his relationship with various boys at school, particularly one who would hit him and then blame it on George. He now tried not to show him how upset and scared he was. He complained actively today about his mother and stepfather ignoring him so that if they were home when he came home from school, nobody said "hi"; it was as though he was not there, "it's like I don't exist." It was then he stayed in his room and cried. We began to tie up his current need not to be ignored, his wish to be seen in order to feel he "was somebody," with his fantasies of being attacked and followed by eyes wherever he went. He had the right to work out other ways of getting the attention he needed than through being teased in the way he expected, but then bothered him so much. He discussed a boy, Ned, who was nice to him in the neighborhood but spurned him at school. He wondered if he should try to play with him in the afternoon.

Two weeks later he had discovered that Ned also thought other kids didn't like him. Most of the boys did not treat George differently at school from the way they did before but he had decided he would be less afraid if he walked to school rather than taking the bus with the other kids, and had done this for the past few days. He resented being called names by them, but this was different from the "nervous breakdown feelings." Asked about the difference, he said that he did not feel haunted when they were not actually there.

He and Ned had made up a creature like "a cute ball of fur," called the "Millis Power." Millis used to copy things in his master's voice and at night always imitated his master's voice, when his master was away. If things got too bad, Millis could go and start colonizing Mars, but meanwhile he was able to go to school. George and Ned wanted to form a "Millis Club" by taping and playing back all kinds of things about him that they could keep. George commented "Adolph Hitler was tensed exactly like I was—but I don't want to turn out a thing like him." In fact, he informed me, there are two opposites: there is "rotten Hitler power" and "Millis good power." "Hitler really only wanted power to exterminate others . . . Millis is different." He loved candy and in fact was about as big as George's own stomach after he had been eating a lot. Millis looked like a dumb animal and did what he was told; actually he did have a mind of his own, but sometimes he did not use it. Many people couldn't tell he had a mind of his own, because he would not tell anyone who teased him. I showed a lot of interest in Millis and the fact that he knew he had a mind of his own once he escaped from the teasing. I did not comment on Millis's need to copy his master's voice and imitate it at night, when his master was away. The latter had to do with George's methods of attempting to identify with an absent father figure, an issue which, in view of his experiences, was highly complex and anxiety-provoking for him. Knowing I would soon need to refer him to someone else for long-term therapy, I did not want to delve into areas that would best be recalled and reworked within a long-term, sustaining relationship. I let him know that I would be seeing his mother and stepfather the following week, and was going to suggest that he should have someone to see regularly, in addition to family therapy. He was in favor of family therapy especially "if I get to say my side too."

The following session George brought up several problems he was afraid to mention in front of the family and I supported the notion that in the planned family therapy meetings it would be safe for him to do so. He reported that he had one friend who, he felt, was loyal to him at present, but Ned was very restricted about what he was allowed to do and could only play with him once a week. George spent much of the hour putting on a puppet play involving mostly authority figures (policemen, teachers, etc.) who tried to get rid of the bear child puppet in various ways, such as defining him as a dirty animal that was not allowed on the sidewalk or teasing that he was really a girl disguised as a boy. George added, "I'm like the bear because I'm big and fat and roly-poly." He knew this was our last hour. We discussed his feeling of rejection and anger about being seen only "once a week," and how these feelings turned into ideas of not being liked or gotten rid of for one reason or another, such as "being fat or dirty or sometimes wanting to be a girl" as he had shown me with the puppets. When parents had left him in the past, it had been because of *their* problems and not because of him. I let him know that our saying goodbye wasn't because of anything he had said or done either. It was because he needed someone he could count on to see him regularly for a long period of time, and as that wasn't possible in this clinic, I wanted him and his family to be seen in the child-guidance clinic, where he could count on time for himself and more time for his family too.

George was seen in our clinic until his acute panic states subsided, while plans for more long-term treatment were being made. Like other children who have had shattering experiences with loss in the past, transfer to another person and setting does not occur without some feelings of rebuff. Ideally one would have had him begin with a therapist who could remain with him. However the urgency of his panic states called for an immediate evaluation, on which treatment recommendations could then be based. George's family, unlike a number of others who get "lost" between agencies when attempts at transfer are made, did follow through with the recommendations and George made a good therapeutic alliance with his therapist.

George was well aware that his mother couldn't help but leave him with his father when he was little. Her later care of him assuaged the sense of abandonment. However, he was still "haunted" by his earlier experiences, and the identity conflicts they led to. In his behavior, George expressed the need to feel victimized, which then led to states of homosexual panic, during which his reality testing was shaky. In his fantasy life he first alternated between identification with someone who was attacked by a male, and perhaps was a girl, and identification with the attacker, that is, the Nazi who has the ammunition and wanted to kill others. These identifications were in his case a direct outgrowth of his relationship with his father, and functioned to preserve that tie in its absence. Children like George sometimes become either lifelong victims, or withdrawn and "quiet" people who are prone, when they fall prey to the fantasy of being followed or attacked, to protect themselves by doing sudden violence to others, perhaps strangers. As anxiety-provoking as either of these identities were for George, they were preferable to the greater danger of feeling totally abandoned—e.g., George stated that when people did not greet him, it was as though he did not exist. His sense of self was highly dependent on being able to maintain an interaction with others. In this context the "following eyes" or "man coming in the window" served another function, that is, it constituted a defense against the terror of being alone and unseen and therefore not existing.

We see in George a fairly rapid emergence of another identification figure, the embodiment of his unmet childhood needs. "Millis power," the "cute little ball of fur," which is "about the size of my stomach" is presented as an opposite of Hitler, in wanting "good power" instead of "rotten power." He does not want to exterminate others, but, like George, "loves candy a lot." Millis is shared between George and a new friend. George began the process of testing out in his play to what extent those with childish needs (the "bear child" puppet, furry like Millis) might be accepted or rebuffed (told to get off the sidewalk for being a dirty animal, teased that he was really a girl). By this time he felt he had one friend who was loyal to him, and that the "nervous breakdown" feelings were gone because he did not feel "haunted by attackers when they were not really there."

I believe that the speed with which George was able to consider shifting his identification images, at least in an initial and very tentative way, had to do with the presence of his mother, who had needed to renounce, but then regained her parenting role. As real and terrifying as his experiences in father's household had been, the possibilities for care and acceptance from his mother and stepfather had reached him in time to be equally real. By the time he reached his mother's home George had multiple problems. I believe that she (along with her new husband) deserved considerable credit for stretching her endurance, tautened by her own deprived childhood, in trying to reestablish a loving relationship with the children who wanted, needed, and would continue for a very long time to need so much of her.

CHANGE OF CUSTODY BY MUTUAL AGREEMENT: ERNST MARTINIQUE

A change of custody is frequently appropriate in a third kind of situation, in which all participants are in agreement because of changing circumstances in the lives of the parents, as well as the child's changing needs—because, for instance, he grows older. In such a situation the child is apt to have free access to both parents and make the transition with a minimum of conflict.

Ernst's parents were divorced when he was six, and his father remarried three years later. Though Ernst's mother retained custody of the boy, he regularly stayed with father over weekends. Mother was warm and loving with the boy; simultaneously she continued to spend much of her time and emotional energy within the circle of her large, extended family and their friends from another country, resisting the boy's effort, once he entered school, to interest her in various aspects of American culture. Throughout Ernst's childhood, his father helped the boy deal with issues revolving around school and dentist, friends, hobbies, and lessons, etc. After father's remarriage, Ernst also developed a positive and solid relationship to his stepmother, who in turn enjoyed him. Increasingly mother turned over various responsibilities regarding Ernst to the father, expressing her wish not to have to cope with them directly. Ernst continued to feel he loved his mother, but became more and more restive about spending so much time with her and her relatives, rather than with his friends and other interests.

When Ernst was twelve, father suggested that he take legal custody of the boy, who would come to live with him, his wife, and new baby, while visiting mother whenever he wanted. She agreed with apparent relief. Ernst was told that both parents had agreed to this plan, but if he did not like it he should say so. He seemed excited at the prospect.

These parents had carefully presented the option to him in a way which both minimized his sense of guilt about "choosing" and any feeling of rejection by either parent. Both parents seemed to recognize that Ernst's approaching adolescence was an additional factor in making him feel more comfortable living with father and his family than alone, as the "man of the house," with mother. Mother, in turn, had felt that the boy increasingly interfered with her attachment to her extended family and friends, and resented his attempts to take her interest away from them. Father and stepmother made plans to preserve the boy's sense of continuity in a variety of ways. He was to finish the school year in his neighborhood school, while at the same time becoming acquainted with kids in his new neighborhood through various group activities with which father was willing to involve himself (such as mountain-climbing, etc.) Father and stepmother were aware of his need to work out the issues that his cultural heritage raised for his identity at his own pace. Having wanted the boy for some years, but having waited until they felt the move would not be disruptive to him or his mother, they took him into their home joyously and with minor trepidations.

CUSTODY CHANGE NECESSITATED BY EMOTIONAL INCAPACITY OF ONE PARENT: GERARDO AND LUCRETIA CASTILLO

The fourth kind of situation in which a mother willingly turns custody over to the father is when she knows she does not have the emotional resources to take care of the children. Both child and father are likely to feel bereft and helpless in this situation, and have a difficult time separating a mother's current incapacity from their own personal sense of failure and rejection. Often a fantasy that one should have been able to surmount whatever obstacles there were continues to affect father and children. After this discrepancy is faced it seems to become more possible for the remaining family to mourn their loss and deal with the reality of a parent who, they feel, has failed them, rather than introjecting the sense of failure in the form of symptoms which signify an identification with that parent to ameliorate the sense of loss. The parent may be tempted to project the failure onto a child. Positive and tender memories of the emotionally ill parent often remain after the mourning as a valid component of the past relationship, and can form a nucleus for reengagement with the parent if and when he or she is ready for this.

Gerardo Castillo

Jose Castillo had had custody of his son Gerardo, fourteen, and daughter Lucretia, eleven, for a year. His wife, who lived at a distance, in South Carolina, had seemed depressed throughout the marriage, but the depression increased in severity after the parents' divorce seven years before. She had tried a variety of forms of treatment, going to several psychiatrists and having had chemotherapy and shock treatment as well. However, she had continued to become more housebound, obese, and withdrawn from the children. A year before she had phoned father that she could no longer cope with the children, and sent them to live with him.

Mr. Castillo could not bring himself to tell the children why mother had given them up and helped promulgate her explanation about not having enough money to keep them. He told me "the idea of having a good mother was so important in getting me through my childhood, that I can't bear to think of the children as going without that." Meanwhile he feared that fourteen-year-old Gerardo was indeed becoming more and more like his mother. Mr. Castillo admitted and was ashamed of the fact that he yelled at his son in moments of anger: "Wait and see—you will be a failure just like your mother." We discussed the situation from the point of view that the children would eventually need an understanding of their mother's inability to care for them in terms of her limitations in the past and at present, rather than viewing it as their own failure.

Gerardo was referred to me after his school became concerned about his depressed demeanor, lack of concentration in school, inability to make any friends and increasing tendency to spend whole days in school without talking to anyone.

Gerardo was a soft-voiced, masculine-appearing boy with large, expressive eyes. When I asked what troubled him, he said "getting along at school and with my dad. Mom and dad got divorced a long time ago." Gerardo told me he used to live with his mother and see his father on weekends, but for the past year he had lived with father while mother was "all the way across the country." He gave a number of slightly different versions of why he was now living with father instead of mother; obviously this was a painful area for him. He finally said that the court had decided he should be with father and that the trouble was about alimony. Gerardo felt that his father and the kids at school looked down on him. He then told me of another "private" symptom. Whereas he used to be good at playing ball, throwing rocks at rabbits—or oranges at cars—along with his friends, since he had "left home" and come to live with father he could not throw anymore. He could not even catch a ball thrown to him. He believed his muscles were becoming soft. He was ashamed of this. It made him afraid of getting picked on by the boys at school, and he had been avoiding contact with them as much as he could. Meanwhile he felt very much alone and different from others.

I asked Gerardo what "home and mother" were like, and he said "My mother's like free and my father is strict." However, as he continued to describe his life at "home" it turned out that she had had increasingly little to do with the children. She locked her door and went into the room and watched TV most of the time. He finally said "I guess she doesn't want to be with us or eat with us." He then immediately defended her, in contrast to the woman father had been living with when Gerardo came to live with him. He was relieved to find father was not married to her, and she soon moved out. "She didn't like anything—not children or snakes—she didn't like my age and thought I would get wild—so then she moved out and I'm glad." However, father lost his temper easily, blamed Gerardo for the girlfriend's leaving and was especially furious about Gerardo doing so poorly in school. When he was really mad he yelled and hit and Gerardo was afraid of him.

I asked Gerardo what he thought would help most. He made it clear that he had a fantasy of returning to live with mother. He stated, "I think my mother thinks it's natural for boys to live with their mothers and for my sister to be with my father—I mean I hope my sister will because otherwise my father would be all alone." Nevertheless, he discussed last summer's visit to his mother and how actually it didn't work out. They were fighting all the time, it seemed. I said that it sounded sad to me—the difference between how he wished things would go between mother and himself and his actual experience last summer when he tried it again.

Gerardo's eyes filled with tears as he said, "I guess I try to put up a bluff—I think she is depressed—that's what people said . . . and she keeps us out like she didn't care . . . don't care about us really. All my life I try to think she cared for us and just now lately I'm beginning to think she doesn't." We discussed the fact that if what he said were so, that she was depressed, she might want to care but couldn't—at least not the way he wanted—being too tied up in her own problems to know how to take care of Gerardo and Lucretia at this point. Gerardo said that he had been so discouraged about a lot of things, he did not know if it was worth trying any more. For example, he loved reading science fiction, but knew no one else who did. And in school a boy attacked him so fast in karate "that I got terribly disappointed about the whole thing" and gave up trying. I reminded him that he used to be good at using his muscles and that those talents were still a part of him, even though he had "given up" on them at the moment. We would have to try and understand what the idea of "muscles going soft" meant to him. Meanwhile we could plan about other things he might find of help. We talked about my being talking with the school about finding some kids who shared Gerardo's interests, maybe through a science fiction club. Secondly, as he was afraid to let father know how scared he was of him, we discussed the possibility of his either talking with father himself, or of our all talking together after Gerardo's second visit. Finally, the whole question of "who am I going to live with, and who can I depend on, and in what way" should be discussed, because it obviously worried him. Before he left that day he told me that he didn't think he could live with his father till he grew up because father was "too strict and primitive." He added, sadly "A lot of times I think I'm a failure and my father says I am, just like my mom."

Gerardo was the kind of boy with whom one aches. I felt it was important to begin to strengthen a human-support network, including school and father, around him. This would be needed to help contain his distress over facing the painful feelings associated with a sense of failure about being shut out by his mother.

Mr. Castillo was willing to cooperate in his son's therapy. Having been brought up in a family in which pride and achievement were important cornerstones of success, he was ashamed whenever will-power did not overcome obstacles. He was hurt both by the "failure" of his marriage, and by what he called "laziness" on the part of his son, who was bright, but unable to achieve in school. We worked on separating these issues from his personal sense of failure. He was also quite frightened of Gerardo's moroseness, seeing it as the forerunner of the kind of depression from which his exwife suffered. I said that it was going to be important, both for Gerardo's and Mr. Castillo's sake, to tease apart the sources of Gerardo's depressed moods from his mother's case, because they were different states with different origins and solutions to them. In Gerardo's next interview I let him know that I was bothered by the degree to which he felt a failure at things; and that from where I sat I could see all kinds of good qualities about him; so that it didn't make sense from "looking at what was really true." So, we had to look at what he had expected of himself and why, to understand what the sense of failure was really about. Gerardo said, "I'd like to change my life and have friends and go places and stuff. But neither I nor my father think I ever can, not after everything that's happened."

t: "Like about your mother?"

Gerardo: "Yea, I think she probably had a hard time because she is so fat, and a woman, and different herself—but I think he made her worse because one simply can't talk to him or win his arguments no matter who one is."

t: "And did you think having you and Lucretia made things better or worse for mother and father in their trouble with each other?"

Gerardo: "I guess it made it a lot worse . . . she was so tired she would go to her bed and lie down; she didn't want to see us or *move a muscle*. We always wanted attention, like to show her something and she was always too tired and went to her room and locked the door. She'd put some food out for us and then lock the door."

t: "How lonely and lousy that must have been for you!"

He became tearful and said, "I felt sort of like she did—I mean we'd have these big fights and I would go climb a mountain or something and stay by myself a long time and then go back."

t: "And what did you feel then?"

Gerardo: "I know I failed her . . . because a lot of times we didn't do the dishes and we didn't do all the work we should have. Sometimes we were messy, especially my sister—we had this dog and cat and we didn't clean up all the times we should have. We should have taken care of everything better."

t: "But sometimes you didn't feel like moving a muscle either?"

Gerardo: "She said her parents never gave her any love and that my father wasn't nice to her either. Last summer when I went out there, when I tried staying with her she said that she wants me not to need anyone, she wants me to be like her. But ... this summer I wanted ... I think I needed her or someone." Tears were rolling down his cheeks.

t: "Gerardo, people need people. Anybody would. Needing people is okay."

After a while I could ask him about his thoughts when he needed his mother, and this brought into focus the symptom about "my muscles going soft." His mother didn't want to "move a muscle" in her depression, and had let him know that he should be like her, in not needing anyone. Increasingly rebuffed in other kinds of interactions with her, his only way of holding onto the relationship was to attempt to be like her, to be depressed and not use his muscles. Father's later identification of him with his mother confirmed his self-image at the time. He associated soft muscles with "being flabby like my mother."

This passive stance however, contained important elements of inhibition, accompanied by the sense of failure on his part. He felt his presence as a burden to mother, he wished to overcome this by being the active caretaker, successful where father had "failed." As a child, with dependency needs of his own, he could not of course do this. In addition, as a pubescent boy, the only male in the house, he had had fantasies he told me about, involving his mother e.g., once when he had been "jerking off" on the lonely mountainside after a fight with her. He now let me know that his description during the first interview of his "private" symptom, referred not only to the muscles in his arms, but fears about his "privates" also. In this context it became possible to discuss this fear.

I also talked at some length with him about the fact that he was not responsible for his mother's difficulties, that the job of taking care of things at home and trying to make her happy was too big a job for kids, like him and Lucretia. That definitely did not mean he was a failure. I added "I think you've been in a spot of feeling that your Dad is critical of you while mother wants you to be like her; that's an impossible spot to be in and feel okay." He said that if he could tell father some of the way he felt about having trouble studying, and grades, it would be different, but he was still afraid of his reaction. Father was still stronger than he. I told him I wouldn't mind letting his father know that the business of grades was not just a matter of will-power, and that I did not think Gerardo was a failure if his grades this semester didn't show what he was able to do. That might take a while; he would not really know what he could do until he felt better. However, it was also important for

Gerardo to be able to live with father now without having to be so afraid of his reaction, to be able to say what he thought. He asked to bring father with him next time, "to let him hear that."

The following session Mr. Castillo and Gerardo appeared together. Father reported that Gerardo seemed to have "perked up. He has begun to talk back and argue with me and I think that came from his sessions here." I asked what he meant and Mr. Castillo said that they had been discussing school grades and "I came on very strong." Suddenly Gerardo had cried and then said straight to his father, "Daddy, we have a problem not communicating with each other—but I'm going to tell you what I think even if you hit me for it." Father was taken aback that Gerardo had been thinking his father would hit him. He did "hit" a lot when Gerardo was little, but didn't think the boy would remember so much. Gerardo said with a smile that he thought his father had "improved" too, that he had not hit him and they had had a long talk instead. Meanwhile it had been Gerardo's fifteenth birthday and Gerardo had asked for a phone call to mother to see if he could visit her. Both father and son heard mother reply that she would take Gerardo if it were an emergency, but not under normal circumstances. They faced this together.

Mr. Castillo: "I want to be at peace about it, and am willing to do a lot for that." In front of Gerardo, with encouragement, he spoke about his helplessness in being able to alter anything in her condition. He now told Gerardo of the many times treatment had been begun and broken off by mother. He said that at the time of the divorce "I felt a little like Gerardo in how discouraged I was." This was extremely important for Gerardo to hear. It opened an empathic link between father and son, and meant that one could be depressed and still be a man like father.

As father and son talked, the fantasy of somehow returning to make mother happy enough so that she could forgive them or act in a friendly or welcoming fashion to them, emerged again. We talked a fair amount about their sense of responsibility for doing something for her; the interplay of their needs, wishes, and their guilt; and how these were related to feelings of depression and failure. Gerardo was able to examine this process in relation to the father rather than exclusively picturing himself as a failure "like mother." We did some planning about ways of being as supportive as possible to the mother. From many examples it sounded likely that people perceived her withdrawal as arrogance, and she was cut off from her former culture and family. How to reestablish such links was discussed, however, there might still be limits to the way she would respond. Meanwhile, it was important to work out their own problems with each other, so that they could make the most of their own abilities for getting something out of life.

As I saw Gerardo over the next few months, he did indeed begin to "perk up." The third month he stated that he had been doing a lot of thinking about himself, feeling that he no longer agreed with his father's harsh judgment of him. He reported improving grades, with A's in some subjects, though others were still poor. However, father thought that anything less than "all A's is being lazy" and now, when angry, threatened to send him away, or to work in the coal mines.

We discussed Gerardo's temptations to provoke various people, now especially those he wanted to focus on him and give him special attention. He described various ways of being provocative, and his own excited feelings, particularly toward young female teachers. He bought reading matter in line with his sexual fantasies and was aware of how angry he was at girls who rejected him. He had the impulse to mess up their desks, and hide their chairs at school and knew this was also related to his underlying anger at his mother. Having resumed karate and weight-lifting practice, he felt more able to hold his own with the boys, but was conflicted about whether to join one of the gangs at school. In a communication with the school (with permission from Gerardo) the principal told me that the boy seemed increasingly more relaxed, and that one even saw him smile or make jokes sometimes these days. Some months before he had spent whole days without talking to anyone, looking morose and turning down any overtures by other kids. I let him know in turn that it was likely that while Gerardo was becoming less depressed he would dare to be more spunky, easy to anger, and provocative, and would be apt to test out adults' reactions to this. He was just beginning to stand up to his father. The principal assured me he would be willing to have some defiance directed toward him if it came, and would be aware of Gerardo's need not be be "clobbered" for it, as he feared.

Gerardo had a period in which he revealed his rich fantasy life. In a science fiction scenario he shared secret violent fantasies, which he had experienced during the last year of living with, and being shut out by his mother, and which had contributed heavily to his guilt. "I'm getting savage in my head," he told me, as we discussed controlling his anger and expressing it in areas where it would not backfire on him. When the part-time housekeeper told him to go to his room for "talking fresh," he threw a tomato at her (knowing it would not hurt her like a rock would), saying "I've got pride. I'm going to hurt the ones who hurt me!" He also told me, "I was daydreaming about beating the guys in karate and even beating the master. I think I didn't used to let myself daydream like that, because what I really wanted then was to kill them." He used sticks and pencils to demonstrate to me how he was left standing after the master had been flattened. Gerardo's muscles were no longer soft. Among other things, he related the difference to his changed perception of himself and his father. "When I thought things were really all my fault and that my father hated me, I secretly wanted to kill him. Now I know he has a hot temper because he's frustrated too and when he's mad it doesn't mean I'm no good".

In another joint session with father, Gerardo complained about how praising and affectionate father was with Lucretia, while he still criticized Gerardo for being "less than perfect." Mr. Castillo became aware of the fact that while he often told Lucretia that he loved her, he had never told Gerardo this; yet it was in fact true, despite their arguments. He told Gerardo that no matter what he had said about sending him to the coal mines when he was angry, he in fact wanted Gerardo to live with him until he was grown. Gerardo asked his father why he treated Lucretia so differently. "You never show you feel sorry for me, without a mother—but you say 'poor Lucretia, not having a mother' when you talk to people." Mr. Castillo flinched only a little, before we recognized together that this was a matter of his "pride" about what men and boys should feel; and that maybe sadness or tenderness between them, which he almost automatically covered with anger, would not take away from being manly.

One day, in his fifth month of sessions, Gerardo and I both laughed at something funny he reported saying to the group of boys with whom he now often played along the railroad tracks. Then he was quiet.

t: "What are you thinking about now?"

Gerardo: "Moving along . . ." He sweeps his arm in a wide motion.

t: "What do you mean?"

Gerardo: "About us moving along . . . like we can talk about a lot of things, more and more you and I can . . . like people who get me mad and girl problems. I can even say here about how fat my mother is and it doesn't bother anyone . . . that's what I mean, like we're moving along together, like we're moving free . . ."

We explored his idea of our "moving along together." Gerardo first thought of dancing with a girl (there was a dance coming up at school, the first one he wanted to attend); then he recalled the feeling of "moving along" as something he had had when he was still happy while living with his mother long ago, before she was depressed. I reminded him that the first day he saw me he had described his mother as "free" (he had said, "like we're moving free") and then felt like crying when he remembered how she locked herself up in her room and shut him out.

Gerardo: "Yea, that's how she used to be . . . moving and free . . . she'd be in a good mood and like she didn't mind having us around . . . and then everything stopped . . . like time stopped . . . and she didn't want to move a muscle anymore, just lie in bed all day."

t: "And you thought your muscles shouldn't be moving free anymore either."

Gerardo: "And that my living shouldn't be moving ahead of her, with her just lying there. But I feel different now, like no matter what I did, maybe she wouldn't notice a lot anyway, I mean I can't change her anyway."

t: "Yea, I think there was a good feeling you shared with her when she was still moving along, and you were little. Then she stopped, and you thought you lost that feeling, and felt very sad and helpless and angry with her and yourself. But you know, you haven't lost it all . . . because that good feeling is *in* you still . . . it's yours and will stay with you, ready to share with people when you want."

Gerardo laughs again: "I know that now . . . and when someone is mean to me I don't like brood about it like I used to . . . I get mad like at Mary Jane. When she told Margie she'd be a dope to go to the dance with me I just wanted to mess up her desk, I didn't want to mess up myself anymore."

Gerardo still had an ordeal to face. When summer came plans were worked out for him and Lucretia to visit their mother for periods short enough for her to tolerate. They were to stay with an aunt and uncle near by, and just visit during the days. Although previously she had been closer to Gerardo, the elder and more helpful, than to Lucretia, mother now developed a special affinity for her daughter, asking her to return sooner and longer than her son. No matter how sensible Gerardo thought he should be about it all, it still hurt immensely. A long struggle ensued between his ready anger and the lyrical "moving free" feelings he had found within himself as a remnant from their better days.

Comments and Conclusions

Goldstein, Freud, and Solnit (1973) discussed guidelines for establishing custody. They stressed the overwhelming importance of continuity with a centrally loved individual in the child's life, and the damage which can be done by the capricious shifting of custody to someone other than the person to whom the child is emotionally attached. They pointed out that the lack of finality in legal child placement, which stems from the court's retention of jurisdiction over its decision, invites challenges by disappointed parties and is in conflict with the child's need for continuity. Hence a final choice between contending parents should be made. They recommended that the right of visitation should never be legally enforced, but maintained only where there is mutual consent by parent and child. The orientation is primarily based on custody disputes between a biologic parent and the parent figures who have actually been caring for the child. When parents divorce, the child has usually lived with both, and the consequences are perhaps different.

From clinical experience in dealing with children pressed into embodying their divorced parents' conflicts in custody suits or legally enforced visitation, I heartily concur with all these recommendations except one. It seems to me that the finality of custody decisions must be weighted very individually in accordance with the child's attachments and parents' motivation, as well as their sometimes changing capacity for parenting.

The children's material suggests that a parent, once loved, remains as a profound component of the child's later identity, even after permanent loss, affecting his identification patterns, sense of worth, and way of experiencing later emotional attachments. Traumas not dealt with are apt to be acted out in his own future relationships. Thus it may be in the child's best interest to preserve the possibility of contact with both parents, when he is ready for this and the associated reality testing.

For many of the parents the custody suit is a desperate weapon to fend off a catastrophic sense of loss, occasioned by the separation or divorce, but frequently recapitulating catastrophic losses and disappointments suffered in childhood. Although agreeing to separate, often at least one of the partners has a strong need to cling to the marital interaction by fighting. It is most helpful to both parents and child when the social system, including courts, lawyers, mental-health professionals and friends can form a supportive human network, aware of the underlying dynamics and the destructive aspects of attempting to solve them through the child, and prepared when possible not to abandon the parent during this period of stress.

A number of cases have come to my attention in which a child is told by one parent that the other parent wants to kill the child or the ex-spouse. I believe children are unable to cope with this idea, and that immediate intervention and clarification about what this means are essential. In one such case, an adolescent, after repeatedly hearing such allegations, reacted by killing someone himself. More often the children protect themselves vehemently from contact either with that parent or from the parent who has made the allegations. In doing this, they may be cruel to the parent. However, the sense of urgent dread remains, can lead to catastrophe, and must be dealt with. Legal visitation rights do not always take this into account.

One cannot underestimate the pain of the parent whose custody has been taken away and whose children are rejecting. One mother so longed for her children that she slept in a sleeping bag in the woods near their summer home in order just to catch a glimpse of them. Another mother described the anguish of finding the scene set for her court-ordered weekend visitations by the children's hammering two-by-fours to block her entrance to the door, stealing her key and refusing to eat any food she cooked. A third parent was stunned to hear on the phone from his children, "You're not my father any more—the court said so!" In many custody suits, everybody loses.

A growing number of court systems, in various kinds of liaisons with mental-health services, have in fact established a practice of interventions. These seem most helpful when the intervention is an a priori, sometimes mandatory procedure, attempting to resolve custody disputes before they come to court, and involving all concerned parties. Because these are usually both urgent and complicated situations, inadequate funding or too meager allotment of staff time can undermine their effectiveness.

When a child is chronically exposed to the need of one parent to bolster the self by damaging the other parent, as is often the case in the custody suit, his ability to value himself in relation to identification figures cannot help but suffer. In contrast, in those situations where the child is helped to see each parent's need more realistically, he is allowed some support for grief and resentment about the divergence of needs that have led to his losses, and appears less locked into the kind of guilt that prevents him from investing in new relationships.

Chapter 7

"THE TRUTH IS A HIT ON THE HEAD WITH A HAMMER": IMAGES OF THE PARTING PARENT AND THE SELF IN PUBESCENCE AND ADOLESCENCE

> In a universe divested of illusions
> and lights,
> Man feels an alien, a stranger.
>
> —Albert Camus

The Issues

"I used to get pleasure in school when all of a sudden I understood something," said adolescent Abbey nostalgically, "but now the truth is like a hit on the head with a hammer." Her sense of painful assault by what she now knew as "truth" about herself and her world was expressed not only through her words, but also by an unbearable tension in her head, the temptation to jump off a bridge, a severe loss of appetite, inability to concentrate in school, and only an occasional sense of relief in promiscuity. The snowballing of her symptoms had been precipitated some time earlier, when a phone call informed her that her brilliant, but alcoholic and promiscuous mother had been arrested and jailed for out-of-control, drunken driving, during which she had hit another car. Although Abbey's parents had long been divorced, and she had not lived with her mother since father had won custody of her when Abbey was eleven, she thought a great deal about her mother now.

This chapter deals with the experience of adolescence in a context of parental parting.

Material will be drawn both from adolescents for whom parental parting was complicated by a social stigma attached to the behavior of one of the parents, and from those for whom this was not the case. For a considerable proportion of the individuals discussed here, there were besides the trauma of partial or total loss of a parent figure, sudden changes in that parent, or disturbing revelations about him—such as alcoholism, psychosis, or suicide—with which the adolescent had to grapple, not only in terms of their psychic significance for him, but of the associated social stigma. In these cases, of course, parental difficulties had also affected the child's development prior to the period of parting. For other adolescents a major hurdle was the parental parting in itself, coinciding as it did with a period of development when new pubescent awareness and questioning about the meaning of their parents' inevitable disaffection for each other was closely linked with a new phase of identifications, now pictured in terms of adult roles and troubled expectations about their own future life. Some varieties of disruption in adolescent development will be described; the remarkable coping mechanisms and working through of conflict in some of the adolescents will be explored. Reference will also be made to youngsters who did not experience parental divorce as a major trauma, but who nevertheless reacted intensely at times of concentrated stress, e.g., when a parent remarried.

Adolescent development in identifications, cognition, and value systems was discussed in chapter 2. We might summarize the alterations in relationship to previously loved parents as follows:

The displacement of libidinal energy from childhood attachments to persons newly meaningful in the life of the individual has, in much of Western culture, been considered a prerequisite to the capacity for mature love relationships and to the attainment of a realistic and principled conscience. Although this process is probably never totally accomplished, Anny Katan (1937) has named it "object removal," to differentiate it from the kind of displacement where the new love object is a primarily symbolic representation of the old. Anna Freud has indicated that this has implications for psychoanalytic work with persons whose primary attachment is still to the parents, suggesting that true "transference" cannot be expected in working with the child prior to adolescence. Instead, the analyst or therapist becomes like an additional parent figure whose "educational" efforts are also internalized by the child, and other such parent figures have continued potential importance for the developing young person.

The decathexis of parent figures has been discussed in detail as one of the central tasks of adolescence (Blos, 1962; Deutsch, 1944; Erikson, 1950; Fraiberg, 1969). Normally in our culture this is said to occur in a series of steps, which include a period of disillusionment with the parent as a figure previously seen as wise and powerful; fluctuating periods of narcissistic withdrawal or urgent object-seeking; and the eventual capacity fully to invest new objects with libidinal energy. This is usually not accomplished until ego identity has been solidified to a certain extent, and the old attachment to parent figures appears in the form of identification with personality traits, either integrated into or rejected as part of the self. How this transformation takes place (if it does), what its timing is (e.g., does it normatively begin earlier these days, or for some social groups is it deferred until after adolescence—or forever?) and what features of the child's personality and/or previous social relationships promote such growth are still very much open to question.

In recent years, these questions have also compelled our attention toward the gaping discontinuities between the world of one generation and the next, or between the values and life styles of different cultural groups. Because of the galloping rate of cultural and technologic change, traits that were useful to living for the parent may not be so for his child. What becomes of the process of object-removal and the "selective" identification with aspects of the parent figures may be more complicated than before; we may have to ask ourselves what enduring human characteristics will remain as assets or important links between one generation and the next, regardless of the changes in the tasks of "external" life. What do the adolescents of parting parents, in focus here, pick out as identificatory links in various inner experiences and external situations?

Many of the adolescents experienced an exaggerated example of "discontinuity" in the image of a parent and I shall try to describe some of the correlated features of their reactions. Other adolescents also suffered the loss of one parent through divorce or separation, but without an externally imposed "discontinuity" in the image of that parent. The first series of adolescents discussed, had each suffered a particular kind of "traumatic" family disruption that involved not only separation of parents (the parents of two had separated earlier), but had been shocked by a new kind of "label" applied by family or wider social context to the behavior of one parent. Although earlier disturbance probably had major effects on many of the children's development prior to pubescence, each had found a way of coping with or to some degree denying its impact until a new level of awareness in the youngster or extreme of behavior in the parent seemed to coincide. They were then forced to deal with a different reality within themselves and in their social network. For example, fourteen-year-old Eddy, whose family had denied the extent of the mother's alcoholism until she died of cirrhosis of the liver, said, "I always thought of her smiling and sunning herself by the swimming pool." Thirteen-year-old James felt so vulnerable about the ridicule he expected from classmates that he kept the unsavory truths about his parents' separation entirely a secret for the first ten months, making up stories about the whereabouts of his missing parent. He could not allow himself to feel close to anyone who might discover the shameful secrets occurring at his house. When he finally did make a friend to whom he felt close enough to confide, he was relieved to find that he was not rejected because of his parents' behavior.

These young people had in common the fact that during the period when it is usual to struggle with an *internally* altered image of the parents, they were forced to face an actual change in one or both parents, of proportions so major that they lost the reality of their previous image of or relationship to that parent. This raises the question whether reality-based disillusionment at this age interfered with the process of internal decathexis and disillusionment with a more stable reality image, to which the relationship becomes changed but, eventually, not lost. Under the threat of actual loss of one of the identification figures, awareness of the disillusionment becomes too threatening. Most frequently, these young people attempted to idealize their version of the parent. In those who were forced to acknowledge the unpleasant features of the parent, particularly when this included a "social" label, a severe depression tended to appear.

Characteristics of the Group

THE ADOLESCENTS

Material will focus on twenty-six adolescents, involving twenty families. Additional adolescents, more peripherally known, will also be quoted or mentioned. These adolescents range from those for whom the changed image of the parent, including the associated social implications, became an intrinsic and major part of the trauma of loss, to those for whom the trauma was ameliorated by continued support and the possibility of reality testing of the image of the parent. The loss of a parent in the context of acute marital strife was most disruptive for adolescent development in those cases in which the absent parent suffered serious changes in well being, which also involved social devaluation. Such changes included suicide, alcoholism or promiscuity, when this was not part of the culturally accepted milieu; hospitalization for parental psychosis; or other drastic changes in the mother's life which removed her from care of the children. In the majority of these cases either the death (in the context of divorce), or the divorce itself, preceded the child's acute clinical disturbance. In three cases, the separation of the parents had occurred earlier, but the disturbing news about the parent did not become fully known until adolescence. For example, Angela became acutely redisturbed, in pubescence, after finding out who her "real" father was; Abbey, quoted earlier, had to integrate some shattering news into her image of her mother; Jane did not know, until she was fifteen, why her parents had separated.

As indicated in the appendix, the proportion of parents suffering from a period of emotional incapacitation was larger in this sample than for those in the younger generation of parents. This does *not* mean that they are necessarily higher in the population at large, but does suggest a relationship with the severity of distress in some of the adolescents.

It was also more difficult for parents to give the emotional, financial, or practical support (e.g., transportation) to adolescents in therapy than to the younger children. The adolescent in therapy often was in the process of defiant independence from the parent or reacting with a hostility which made life harder for the parent. In contrast, parents of the younger children more often took it for granted that transportation must be provided, that the parent was still needed and would also reap some benefit from the child's treatment. When hostility emerged, the parent tended to be much less threatened by this from the young child than from the adolescent.

In about one-fourth of the cases, the adolescents had continued free access to both parents (Eva, Christopher, Carole, Erika, Julia, Josie); in a somewhat larger number (Heather, Linda, Karen, Sara, James, Ralph, Abbey, Nick, Connie, Andy, Kerry, Roberta), the child's continued contacts with one spouse were perceived by the adolescent as disloyalty to the other; in about another fourth the absent parent either withdrew totally, or had nothing to do with the child unless the latter initiated contact (Angela, Jane, Randolph, Donna, Judy). Among the remaining cases are those in which marital discord had culminated in a death (Eileen, Shirley, Eddy).

Diagnostically, the adolescents varied greatly, but did share a number of clinical features. The great majority had either lost a previous enjoyment of learning or were, increasingly, cutting and failing classes (77 percent). Most of the adolescents were overtly depressed, with or without somatic components (69 percent). Many had conscious suicidal thoughts. A minority showed increased acting out with self-destructive components, but without conscious depression (31 percent) (e.g., one girl cut classes to "drag-race" at what she knew to be dangerous speeds). A number had run away for a time. One child, with an encapsulated psychosis, began to show strongly depressive features, once the psychosis subsided. Phobias and generalized withdrawal were symptoms in other cases. There was a great range in the degree to which difficulties were transient, or lasted over years.

An area of special focus in this chapter will be the meaning of "truth" for the self, the parents, and the rest of the world. In many cases in this group, one of the parent's presenting complaints about the referred adolescent was "lying," "playing with the truth," "untrustworthiness," "deviousness" etc. (62 percent). One parent, without complaint, just assumed that the child "makes up things" about the truth. In other cases (e.g., Julia, Heather, Eva, Christopher, Sarah, Randolph) the child's truthfulness was not in question.

Another common presenting difficulty was that the adolescent felt unable to make or maintain friendships, and complained of being "unconnected" to peers (58 percent). Among these were adolescents who described having had a best friend at some earlier time, but not now.

Most of the adolescents, with some exception, (e.g. Heather, Julia, and Karen) initially idealized their childhood relationship to the lost parent. The one child who had not known who her father was until adolescence (Angela) invented an idealized version of the parent.

In those cases in which a parent was lost in a way associated with dramatic change in status, identification with the "fallen" parent tended to be uppermost when the adolescent was initially seen. According to the parents, the adolescents were much more apt to behave like the absent parent than they had been before the loss. When this took the form of behavior which was associated with the lost parent's disturbance, a number of the adolescents were aware of feeling that they were "ruining" themselves, but did not know why.

The adolescents discussed in this chapter are more often girls than boys. There is a fairly simple explanation. When an adolescent boy is suffering from the absence of a father in the home, I tend to refer him to a male therapist who can function as a needed identification figure in addition to dealing with other relevant issues. I am more apt to see adolescent boys in therapy when there is a father or stepfather in the home, or when initial homosexual panic makes for difficulties in beginning with a male therapist.

The question of prognosis, in terms of the diagnosis of the adolescents discussed, will not be further pursued here. I believe that it may be heavily influenced by the consideration that many of the youngsters were suffering from a reactive disorder, in the sense that the acute disturbance was precipitated by a disruptive loss. The resultant clinical picture may have different meaning and prognosis than it would if it had occurred in adulthood or under other conditions. Specifically, I mean that the child's disturbance was often magnified by a partly unconscious identification with a devalued, depressed, or disturbed parent figure. Accessibility to change was still linked to external happenings, that is, to better opportunities for identification (sometimes with the same parent when he or she became less depressed or disturbed) when the adolescent and the human support network were ready for this.

For example, Angela suffered from a period of psychotic ideation first when a father figure left when she was five, and again, when she discovered the "truth" of her real father's identity. Yet she maintained adequate functioning in most areas of her life during these periods, and the psychotic episodes themselves were brief. When Linda's loss of her father was recapitulated by the simultaneous emotional loss of a close girlfriend and boyfriend, whose sexual interaction she had to witness while excluded herself, she responded with a suicidal and paranoid reaction during which she became consciously aware of an identification with her father, who had been hospitalized for a paranoid episode at the time of the divorce. The psychosis subsided, with daily therapy sessions and support by the mother, without hospitalization, after a week.

In other cases, much less severe difficulties, such as an underlying affective theme of sadness that was based on a fatalistic conviction that people cannot love each other in a sustained fashion persisted well beyond the loneliness and periods of despair which are usually intensified during adolescence. The future of this aspect of the personality is not yet clear.

The seriousness of the clinical disturbance when the adolescent was first seen cannot be assumed to correlate in any simple way with its impact on the person's future life. There were numbers of adolescents seen whose problems, were for various reasons, only partially resolved before treatment ended, and indications were that they should obtain further therapy in early adulthood, after actual separation from the parent had occurred, and at a time when the decision to enter or to end treatment would be their own.

The majority of the adolescents discussed were seen because they suffered from intense distress, with clinical symptoms, or exhibited behavior which was intolerable to their parent or school. Sometimes early distress signals went unnoticed, perhaps because the parents were preoccupied with their own problems, until the child's condition became acute. Referral occurred most often between six months to two-and-a-half years after parental separation. Some adolescents were seen only for an evaluation, to help them and their families make whatever plans appeared indicated. Parents sometimes came for brief or intermittent consultations about their wishes to work out their changing relationship to their adolescent children. Several adolescents came on their own at the end of adolescence to work out problems which they had managed to "postpone" after their parents' separation in an adaptive fashion that allowed them to continue their growth, but which were crippling their current relationships. A small number that I had seen during adolescence after their parents' divorce, returned in their early twenties. One eighteen-year-old came for help about the problems of a younger sibling, now left at home alone with her separated, but still warring, parents.

Because no attempt was made to "select" cases, other than by the similarity of events they had endured, and no comparison was made with a population which had no clinical contacts at all, any comment about the proportions of the population exhibiting one or another pattern must be taken as purely descriptive, and cannot be generalized to the proportions of similar patterns in other populations. The relevance of the patterns derives, not from the numbers involved, but from the content of the adolescents' experiences, which they may share with an unknown number of others in the population undergoing similar experiences.

THE PARENTS

Many of the parents had suffered chronic emotional deprivation in their relationships with each other. In those instances in which it was possible to listen to both parents, and to hear the discrepancy between the characteristics they had wished for in their spouses and the way they actually experienced them, I was often struck by a feeling that both partners were the victims of hopes and beliefs about the person they had married—dreams which they had managed to keep isolated from their real daily interactions. In their initial descriptions, parents most often veered back and forth between doubts about their own adequacy and embittered attacks on those characteristics of the spouse that they saw as having brought about the rift.

There were some differences, in family structure and involvement in work, from the sample of parents described in the chapter on multiple parent figures. Mothers were the absent parent in 42 percent of cases; fathers in 58 percent. Fathers had remarried (before or during my contact with the family) in 50 percent of cases, were living with women in 12 percent and had nonpermanent relationships with women in 23 percent. Two of the remarriages had again ended in divorce, and death parted a third. In contrast, only 19 percent of the mothers were remarried, none were living with a man, while 46 percent had intermittent male friends.

A smaller proportion of women than in chapter 5 had been involved in work or career development during their twenties or when their children were young (19 percent when child under five, 27 percent by the time child was ten). Although dissatisfied in various ways with their roles as wife or mother during the child's early years, they felt unable at the time to move outside these roles. The women's liberation movement and the associated social support for women, who combine child-rearing with work was in a less advanced stage, and its effects less available to the women.

Of the mothers, 35 percent either made a definitive turn toward work and career development or returned for advanced education in a new field around the time of the divorce. In some cases the final impetus for divorce was associated with the wish to do this. However, getting a start or getting the recognition they sought in their fields of work tended to be much more difficult than for the younger women of chapter 5. Once the women came to a realization of what they felt they had missed, they experienced a good deal of bitterness about "wasted" years. Similarly, they more often experienced, in new relationships to men, the wish to establish new permanent alliances, but an inability to do so. Two mothers experimented with dating much younger men, but then felt "used" in these relationships. More often than the younger group, they tended to end the marriage, to feel elated at the vision of a career, and then to experience a period of depression when work and love disappointments coincided.

All in all, it seemed to take many of the mothers a longer time to re-establish themselves in a new life-course associated with a sense of well-being, and the obstacles were often great.

FURTHER REACTIONS OF ADOLESCENTS AND PARENTS

The adolescents seen differed from one another in their reactions. For many, the externally imposed loss interfered with the process of time-modulated grief for childhood relationships, occurring in a fashion which was too abrupt and catastrophic to the adolescent to be bearable without being overwhelming. A number of them indeed suffered deeply from a depressive reaction, which went beyond the mourning for the lost parent, and "childhood," and involved severe self devaluation, suicidal thoughts, inability to eat, etc (e.g., Abbey). Others, though aware of their "shock" and "disbelief" about the situations which they were experiencing, tended to deny and negate its extent, only to come face to face with their grief in the form of acting out, which led them to experience identification with the lost parent (Shirley and Eddy). Angela, in a more extreme denial of reality, fantasied about her "left father." A number of others allied themselves with the remaining parent, at the cost of considerable constriction of their own emotional growth, and appeared to "postpone" dealing with the attachment to the lost parent until after they had gotten through their chronological adolescence (Heather, Linda, and Karen did this to varying degrees). Some adolescents seemed only briefly traumatized by the sudden change in their perception of the parents and themselves, and then reconstituted their relationships with both parents, simultaneously renewing their interest in life goals for themselves (Carol).

For a number of boys, and fewer girls, a move from the mother's to the father's home was constructive when it occurred because of the boy's wish rather than because of rejection by the mother. A number of other adolescents turned away from parents who were still locked in an untenable degree of conflict with each other. This was a self-preservative or "holding action," without which they might have been less able to function. It worked well for children who had already achieved a degree of inner autonomy, like Julia, but not for those whose sudden "self-sufficiency" was more heavily based on defenses against dependency, which was denied. Thus, thirteen-year-old James was aloof toward his mother, father, and school, and would admit to no difficulty, although he was flunking. Although two years had passed since his mother had left the household, his father, who had custody, clung to the legal remnants of a marriage that did not exist, still did not agree to proceed with the divorce, and required the children to ask his permission each time they wished to visit their mother. James exhibited a similar pattern of denial: at school, he would leave an exam in an exalted mood, telling the teacher he thought he had done brilliantly, only to be faced repeatedly with the crushing news that he had failed.

In general, unlike the younger children, a number of the adolescents attempted to take sides vigorously, expressing their disapproval, fighting or running away from the parents they blamed for involving them in their problems. Jane confided in neither mother nor stepfather, but ran away for a week after battles in which she accused her mother of neglecting her in favor of her stepfather. She was referred for treatment after pregnancy and abortion were followed by school failure. It was not uncommon for an adolescent to refuse to have anything to do with one or the other parent for a period, and then to reverse this stance. Similarly, a stepparent would be welcomed as a friend at one moment and become a bitter rival, or a person secretly longed for but openly rejected, the next.

It was common for the adolescent to express bitter jealousy about either a father's or mother's new spouse, particularly when witnessing their own parent's devotion to this person. Descriptions of a parent's "indifference" or criticism of the adolescent were painfully coupled with disdainful references to the "idiotic, gooey" looks which passed between the parent and new or prospective spouse. Donna, at thirteen, having exhausted her vilification of her stepfather, asked her mother to make a final choice between him and herself, vowing to witness no more. This process seemed to be most intense for those adolescents who were in the midst of attempting to renounce their own intense dependent or regressive wishes for closeness to a parent at the time when the parent was involved in previously unseen loving intimacy with a new partner. In contrast, a number of older adolescents who had already achieved some genuine independence were delighted and sometimes relieved to find a parent "in love and happy again." Still other adolescents, often after a period of coming to terms with the limitations in the support they could expect from their parents, turned toward a substitute family among other adults, or their peers (Eileen, Linda, Josie, and Angela).

Finally, there were a number of adolescents who underwent the prolonged and painful work of "mourning" not only for their childhood ideal of what parental love toward children and toward each other should be like, but also for the real unhappiness in their parents' lives. Most difficult to deal with were those identificatory links, experienced as closeness, which meant for the child that his or her own life was thus also fated to be unhappy. The personality strength needed to endure this in the service of personal development and crystalization of future goals will be described in some detail in the case of Eva. Again, the awareness that both parents cared about her, in spite of periods of mutual devaluation and bitterness, made it possible for her to integrate into her life a flexible living arrangement and continued contact with both parents. Similarly, Julia managed to grapple directly and progressively with the sad truths she had experienced about her parents' relationship to each other, in part because she and her older brother Scott provided each other with considerable emotional support and perspective on the parents' behavior. In other cases, too, siblings now more often became sustaining rather than rival figures. Erika, also highly aware of the islands of distress in each of her parents, had the time and support for "trial alliances" with each parent before her father's remarriage and a chance to experience a view of a happier relationship. In spite of this, there were periods of intense conflict about the shifting relationships, which will be described.

The parents, too, reacted in a somewhat different way to the adolescents than they did to their younger children. Since the adolescents were often articulate and accurately perceptive about the parents' behavior, their opinions were often felt as those of another adult, more difficult to "shrug off" than a temper tantrum from a four-year-old. In a number of cases, the adolescent felt pressure to become an ally, confidant, and emotional support to the parents at least as strongly as the younger children did. Most often a mother would share with her daughter many personal details—often derogatory—of her disappointment in her efforts at intimacy with the father. Fathers too, particularly those who wanted to maintain custody of their children in opposition to the mother's wishes, went to similar extremes. Twelve-year-old Kerry was told by her father that mother was a "lesbian whore" (neither of which she happened to be, and Kerry was confused), while thirteen-year-old James was regaled with stories of his mother's "bitchiness" and the notion that she was seeking a divorce only because of her selfishness and wish to bring frustration into their lives. A number of parents tried, but were unable to tolerate, direct expression of their anger and grief about the separation toward each other, in order to spare the children. For many, it was still agony to be in the same room with each other, or hear the voice of the former spouse on the phone to deal with some necessary arrangement. At the same time, they tended to create incidents which would require them to contact the spouse. In other cases, the child was the intermediary—e.g., Karen had been sent for years to collect the family's monthly money from the father, who would not send it through the mail. Nick was asked by his father to kick mother in the shins if she tried to enter the house and collect her belongings when it was not her visiting day. When he did so and she hit him in turn, father accused the mother of "child abuse." But more frequently, the degrading of the former spouse was through subtle innuendos, which often also reflected on the personality of the adolescent. Thus, Linda's mother, who had told the child about her father's psychotic episode but tried "not to blame him for leaving us," at the same time pointed out how much Linda looked like her father and used to want to do everything that he did. Eva's mother, bothered by the father's use of logical arguments when she wanted an emotional response, was easily angered by her daughter's rationality, which she likened to the father's. Heather's mother, who was concerned about whether her exhusband had psychotic and suicidal potential, looked anxiously for signs of Mona's being paranoid or "suicidal."

Many of the parents were aware that their divorce added stress to their adolescent children's lives, but might also provide an opportunity for more peaceful relationships with them. For most, the separation had not been sought lightly, but was a result of many years of discouragement about the possibilities of improving the marriage. Some had sought individual therapy, analysis, or marital counseling, and had come to the conclusion that it was not possible to work out the marital problems. In this way, they differed from some of the parents of the younger children, whose marriages had lasted only briefly and in several cases just into the babyhood of the first child. Others had not sought help, but problems had worsened to the point of catastrophic response on the part of at least one spouse; for example, Eileen's mother committed suicide on the evening following a bitter argument about whether divorce was impossible because religious convictions made it "immoral."

In spite of major readjustments in their own lives, for better or for worse, numbers of parents remained deeply tied to their childrens' welfare, willing to provide, when possible, the mixture of support and autonomy that would allow the adolescent to function at his or her best, and to grow. It was often not easy, and parents were surprised and sometimes ashamed at the intensity of their reaction to the adolescent who disappointed, criticized, or ignored the parent for reasons of his own. The adolescent appeared to need some degree of withdrawal from parental conflict in order to keep a foothold on a future with personal goals and hopes. At times this seemed like callousness to the parent, who often experienced simultaneously a mixture of fury at the child who criticized him or who no longer allowed himself to be controlled, and an intense sense of loss about the former relationship to the child. Though this is a common phenomenon in parents of adolescents, it was complicated by the parent's increased need for emotional support and validation from the child.

The child's emerging sexuality often focuses this anger and distress on a preoccupation with the sexual provocativeness of the child. For example, daughters sometimes dressed more seductively in the apartments of their single fathers than before. Several divorced fathers found their daughters' bralessness difficult to endure. The parent may be unaware of how much his or her own dating simultaneously stimulates sexual fantasies in the adolescent who is exposed to it, or expected to listen to descriptions. Again, the period just before a remarriage may be particularly difficult for both parent and child: it may symbolize a definitive turning away from each other, often with conscious anger and unconscious sorrow. For example, Erika's father, shortly after a happy remarriage, became tearful at the memory of his former close relationship with his daughter, who had become more aloof and rejecting of him. He, after all, had divorced his wife and not his child. The remarriage was to a woman much younger than his previous wife, a woman who had become a friend, companion, and advisor to the daughter, at times a refuge from battles with her mother. However, when the remarriage approached, it restimulated the girl's sense of being excluded rather than chosen by the father, and she reacted with anger, as well as a healthy, self-protective, but rebellious insistence that she be allowed to wear the old clothes in which she felt "like myself" instead of the new dress provided especially for the wedding.

Linda's father, who had ignored her when he was involved with his new wife and baby in a fashion extremely painful to Linda, became intensely involved again once Linda went on dates. After finding out that she had been picked up by a boy while hitchhiking, when she was seventeen, he beat her one hundred times with his belt; he then added that she didn't seem interested in him anymore. He told her at this moment that he had objected to her going to a child guidance clinic when she was eight years old because he had been told there were "incestuous desires" involved. (If this was really said, it should not have been!) He now asked her outright whether it was true or not that she had had such desires for him. This whole encounter was extraordinarily traumatic for Linda, undermining the much-needed defenses she had been able to build up over a period of years.

Among the adolescents, heterosexual interests were often loaded with more than the usual guilt toward their parents, almost as though they were abandoning an implicitly agreed-on philosophy that men and women are fated not to make each other happy. There were different implications for adolescents who saw their heterosexual interests in terms of succeeding or having pleasures unavailable to the parent, and for those who viewed their own activity as a form of "revenge" toward the parent who had forsaken them for someone new. Often, there was a double, contradictory message involved. Both parent and child engaged in flaunting, hiding, and expecting disapproval for such activity.

Linda's mother, for example, was at first careful about male visitors, then allowed them to stay overnight on the downstairs couch, while Linda felt grounded in her bedroom, so as not to interrupt anything. She felt highly threatened when a male friend of mother's came to her room to talk, put an arm around her, or sought any physical contact. Linda knew that her mother felt sexually undesirable, and wished to be proven wrong about this. Similar conflicts occured in other girls whose mothers were dating much younger men, who in turn also showed interest in the daughters.

Shirley's and Eddie's father, who had a constant stream of girlfriends, took an intense dislike to Shirley's steady boyfriend, and tried to convince her to go out with a lot of different boys on vacation, though she preferred not to. He had not been able to resist challenging each of Shirley's boyfriends to a motor-bike race by the time of the second date. Although he usually won, when the time came to race her new, steady boyfriend, he ran his motor bike into a tree.

Karen kept her sexual activities a secret, particularly since they involved someone close to her mother, but was preoccupied with mother "finding out" and felt she probably knew anyway.

A number of parents gave their children more than the usual amount of independence in their dealings with the world. Eva and Julia, for instance, had to fend for themselves from the age of thirteen in a variety of ways and were fairly unrestricted in what they were allowed to do. Both girls attributed some of their strength to this freedom, not granted more "protected" peers. With other children, the precocious independence was more clearly linked to loss and deprivation; and sometimes arbitarily countered by simultaneous restrictions, or by criticisms of the child's deportment. For example, Angela was effectively with her mother only during meal times, and was left to her friends on the street the remainder of the time. Shirley was catapulted, from a situation where she was closely watched and cared for by her mother, into a role as the mother in the household; then, rapidly, she was replaced as a focus of interest in the father's life. Similarly, Eileen for six months took care of father and household after mother's death and then was relegated to a position where her father no longer needed her. Both girls were simultaneous-ly pushed into and criticized for interest in a steady boyfriend, and had to conceal their activities in this area. Both, after having lost their mothers through death, were progressively abandoned by their fathers, whose own needs to replace their spouses without having mourned them were great. Neither father could tolerate "reminders" of his dead spouse. Neither stepmother in these cases was able to support closeness between father and daughter, nor able to provide it herself.

In some cases an adolescent demonstrated remarkable resilience and personal development in spite of a crushing history of family conflicts, repeated trial separations, and suicidal attempts on the part of at least one parent, until a final separation took place in the child's midadolescence. When I asked Julia how she had managed to cope so well in the midst of such a difficult situation, the answer was first in terms of an older sibling, close in age, with shom she had had a continuing strong bond and shared perspectives about the family problems; she then added, "It's been going on all my life and I got used to it, so it's no change." In cases with other kinds of family history, adolescents attributed the strength of their motivation to make sense out of their lives to the fact that while their parents might have been depressed and in conflict with one another, they both respected the adolescents' need for autonomy, and trusted them. In such cases, a parental complaint about the child's "untruthfulness" was *not* part of the referral picture.

Some of the implications of the themes discussed above will be briefly revisited before I illustrate them with excerpts from encounters with the adolescents:

I have referred to the adolescents discussed here as experiencing a disruptive, "traumatic" loss—"trauma," in the sense of an overwhelming or sudden onslaught for which the ego is unprepared. The adolescents' responses were determined by the interaction of multiple factors. These included:

1. The suddenness of the loss, (which affected the adolescent's opportunity to prepare himself for what was going to happen).

2. The importance of the particular lost parent in the previous maintenance of the child's self-esteem.

3. The familial and individual patterns for coping with stress.

4. Individual, family, and social interpretations of culpability for the loss.

5. The degree of family and social devaluation or "shame" connected with identification with, or longing for, the lost parent. At times the child not only had to deal with the complicated methods of extrusion used by one parent of the other, but also with the social image of the parent as "crazy," "selfish for killing themselves," "out of control," "hopeless," etc. At the other end of the continuum was the degree of support available for continued integration of identification with and/or longing for the absent parent.

6. Those aspects of personal development in the adolescent which were on the verge of emerging at the time of loss: the quality of relationship and of beginning disengagement with each parent (e.g., whether based on genuine beginning individuation or on "pseudo-independence"); the soundness of developing ego identity, partially based on identification patterns with the parents in childhood, prior to the loss; and the organization of cognitive development (e.g., as this relates to the capacity for relativism and for various "moral" postures or attitudes.)

7. The inner psychic resources brought to bear on the mental mechanisms, imagery, associated affects, and search for transformations in the image of the parent, the loss, and the self.

A brief recapitulation of some of the converging aspects of the adolescents' reactions follows.

Initial reactions tended to include many features of a "stress" response, expected as a way for dealing with trauma (Horowitz, 1976). Denial of the trauma alternated with breakthroughs of frightening or distressing affects and imagery. In many cases the struggle against what the adolescent now perceived as the "truth" about his parents continued, affecting the adolescent's experience of reality in regard to images of himself and his parents. Irreconcilable discrepancies in such images were most often associated with depression.

In those families where denial continued to be used as a major mechanism past the first months, during which it is common, the symptomatology in the adolescent was more apt to appear in the form of acting out in such a fashion that the ego-alien images reappeared in frightening and overwhelming form. Such acting out tended to diminish once the mourning process was begun, but to be reactivated when reminders or restimulation of the trauma occurred in a fashion faster than the adolescent could assimilate, or in the context of an inadequate human support network.

The adolescent's natural reactions to loss converged with a period of development when cognitive and moral issues are ordinarily considered in a new way, increasingly separated from infantile parental prohibitions, and becoming more relativistic. Interference with cognitive functioning especially in school work was the most common referral symptom (with depression the second most common), but it occurred in quite different forms, with different implications. I shall give some brief examples (these cases are later discussed in detail).

Numbers of adolescents avoided thinking by cutting classes: For Eddy and Shirley, the act of cutting classes in effect preceded the thought, while Jane was aware of being unable to tolerate the feeling of being "alone" associated with thinking while in class. She knew she could find a group—it did not matter whom—to hang around with outside. Carol struggled against the breakthrough of "horrible thoughts" when she allowed her mind to wander in class, as she needed to do for the creative writing she had previously enjoyed. She, too, defended herself against the associated pain by deciding to leave class to have fun with a friend. The search for gratification, another component of cutting classes which is often linked to notions about the missing parent, is discussed elsewhere (chapter 3).

Different defenses against painful thoughts were invoked by other adolescents. Eva experienced interference in the form of attempted isolation and numbing of painful affects, with a withdrawal from both sensory and ideational contact with stimulating people and ideas. This resulted in a feeling of confusion, inability to concentrate or to organize time. Heather needed to maintain an ideational vigilance against damaging self-perceptions. She had to withdraw from ideational areas in which she did not feel in complete control, lest a damaging "truth" be revealed (as through the ridicule in parental interactions). Eventually she withdrew from school entirely.

Most of the adolescents when first seen had in common loss of life goals and ability to visualize the future. The extent of this varied. It was most extreme in the case of Angela, who said she knew she would die while still fourteen. Energy was often needed to cling to the past, in the hope thereby of preventing future catastrophic losses. With one exception, each adolescent expressed at some time the wish to be a child again, at a time *before* the events had taken place; the childhood view of their future, which had been partly evolved with the absent parent, was incongruent with their current situation. This expressed wish usually included a mourning for what the adolescent had been deprived of in childhood—and which could now never be made up because of the absence of the parent; and a wish for freedom from the responsibility of the demands of the current life situation. Some sense of continuity of the self often began to re-emerge at times when the adolescent went over old letters, photo albums, etc., dating from the period prior to disruption. I tended to encourage the adolescents' recovering of their past self-images in this and other ways, to be integrated rather than extruded from the current sense of traumatically changed reality.

Adolescents who effectively lost both parents (e.g., Shirley, Eddy, Eileen) could decathect them, to an extent, over a prolonged period of time. Eddy, who had been most dependent on his mother, was the most vulnerable of the three. Shirley and Eileen felt repeatedly assaulted by the rejection of the remaining parent. By the time they were young adults, they had re-established themselves in lives of their own, integrating some valued features of the dead parent into their own lives and interests. However, Eileen continued to suffer intensely at times of loss.

Eva, Erica, and Carole exemplify adolescents who continued to have an important role in their parents' lives and affections, but were not drawn into a sense of major responsibility for fulfilling parental needs. Though they had difficulty modulating their identification with the needy components of their parents, and picturing themselves as having the potential for a happy future, the continued possibility of testing out parental reactions allowed for a slow, though at times volatile, shift between closeness to and individuation from their parents.

Illustrations from the adolescent's material are chosen to highlight the following commonly encountered issues: the wish for external stability at the time of inner change; the relation of the images of the self and the parting parents to the experience of the nature of truth and illusion; and relationships to others, outside the family, during the period of stress. Finally, more detailed therapy material is presented to exemplify three varieties of parental styles for coping with stress and the loss, and the associated experience of the adolescent.

Encounters with Adolescents

THE WISH FOR EXTERNAL STABILITY DURING TIMES OF
INNER CHANGE TOWARD AUTONOMY: ERIKA

A number of adolescents described how disturbing they found it that changes within them, even their unhappiness, could not be "private," but became swept up in the parents' own concerns. Particularly during pubescence, they felt that this encroached on their need to feel they could have a life and psyche of their own, uncontrolled by the parent, from whom they were just beginning to attempt independence. Fraiberg (1955) has discussed this issue in some detail in relation to the difficulties of involving girls of this age in psychotherapy. With the influx of new instinctual tensions, the girl struggles to resist the temptation of being regressively drawn toward the mother, which would involve putting herself, once again, into the position of feeling her childhood dependence, now sexually tinged. The maintenance of ego boundaries becomes a major priority, and may be manifested by a mixture of attitudes which include defending oneself stringently against establishing a dependent relationship with any adult female, while at the same time maintaining the feared assumption that mother figures can magically read one's thoughts anyway. The right to some psychic privacy is important for the girl of this age, as is some support for her own mastery of inner tensions, without active intervention (or "influence", as the girl usually puts it) by the mother. A stable image of the parent figure appears to be an important background for this accomplishment. For example, both pubescent boys and girls commonly complain when they perceive their mothers as "trying to act younger" and "not wanting to be her age"; they find it irritating and confusing, fearing that she wants to take part in the life of their generation, rather than her own.

I saw Erika, an intelligent, perceptive girl who had just turned fourteen, two years after her parents had separated. She saw them both regularly, and they each sustained a high level of interest in her and her well-being. Erika was an example of someone who had *not* been suddenly traumatized by the discovery of a disillusioning "truth."

Erika initially glowered at me, but allowed curiosity to enter her eyes when I did not look directly into her face. I asked if she had wanted to come, or been dragged in by the heels. She said that it certainly had not been her idea, that she definitely did not want to come in the future. I told her she would not be forced. She told me that there were times she had great "self-pity." She was unhappy, but she really hated it when her mother asked her a "million questions" about it, and would much rather cry in private when she felt like crying. She felt less upset about her parents' separating, because that had happened a while ago and she had gotten "used" to it, but their continued inability to agree about things bothered her. She described the changes in her mother (which were actually of a highly positive nature, involving preparation for a professional degree and a greater sense of independence and broadened horizons than previously). She said that the trouble was that "mother is in-between in life, and doesn't really belong anywhere now." The other day, her mother asked Erika whether it didn't make adolescence easier to have a mother who was changing, too. Erika answered vehemently, "Definitely not, *something has to stay the same!*" She explained, "I can change for myself, but I don't want to change *with* her, not *through her medium.*" She then discussed her friendships in a way reminiscent of her description of her mother. She was "between groups," and didn't "belong anywhere." She used to have a best friend, but this girl deserted her for the popular group. She felt that she could "handle my parents," but was most unhappy about having no friends.

She went back to discussing difficulties with her mother, especially her desire to know everything that Erika thought, and her "acting hurt" in response to Erika's refusal to tell her. She described a tug-of-war with her mother about minor decisions in other areas. I commented that maybe some of her trouble with her mother was about Erika's trying to sort out in what ways she wanted to be like her mother, and in what ways she wanted her own life to go very differently. If her mother's feelings got hurt about that, the tug-of-war was an especially tough one. The "tug-of-war" aptly pictured the pull toward her mother Erika sometimes felt. Erika described how free she had felt the year before, when her mother both worked and went to school, and was not home in the afternoons. Then she felt she could relax and be herself because "right now, I need my friends more than I need a mommy." Erika clearly made the point that she was seeking some distance from her mother in order to experience herself as a separate individual carrying the burden of her own unhappiness, rather than sharing that of her mother. The pull in the other direction is demonstrated by her description of her own problems of "not belonging anywhere" socially in the same words in which she described her mother. Her parents' separation was a gradual rather than abrupt and "traumatic" one, but she viewed herself correctly as a long-range bone of contention between the two, and was troubled by her guilt about this over a period of time. She seemed ready to face this and other problems, but was waiting for the parents to "settle down" into a stable life pattern first.

THE EXPERIENCE OF "TRUTH" ABOUT THE SELF AND PARENTS AND ITS RELATION TO FUTURE GOALS

The process of experiencing the "truth" about themselves and their parents had a prominent place in initial interviews with most of the adolescents seen. Both the current sense of reality and ideas about the future were affected. Attempts to fend off the painful nature of the new knowledge were at times desperate. Idealization of the absent parent was commonly combined with devaluation of the self.

The adolescent's view of "truth" and reality impinge on the process of identity formation. When the "truth" about a major identification figure, a parent, is experienced as an "assault" on the adolescent's identity, it tends at first to preclude further reality testing. Mastery through reality testing and slow assimilation of the "realities" may be particularly hampered if the "assault" is confirmed by the attitudes of those who constitute the youngster's major measure of available "truths."

The sudden loss of the "value" of a parent figure (in addition to partial or total loss of the actual parent) results in a suddenly changed image of the parent in reality. This may block the gradual deinvestment of childish images of the parent.

Adolescent questioning "and the parallel discovery or search for a new self" have been very generally associated. Kohlberg (1971) and others point out that these changes are in part related to the changing cognitive capacities of the adolescent, who is dealing with the problem of relativity of truth and value and its impingement on the development of morality and moral judgments about one's self and others (this has been discussed in more detail in chapter2).

Examples from initial interviews illustrate the adolescents' experience with the dawning of "truth," the images of self and parents associated with this, and its relation to learning more about life in the future. Differing ego mechanisms are utilized to cope with this issue.

Truth and Idealization

Abbey. Abbey, whose comment "The truth is a hit on the head with a hammer" begins this chapter, explained further, "Usually I love to read and think, but now thinking really scares me. I'm afraid of some sort of evil spirit that's part of me—that would make me do what I don't want to. I'm afraid I'll jump off a bridge just to get away from that. But there is no place to go anymore—my aunt and uncle hate my father now—my uncle sort of convinced me that my father is kind of an ogre. When I heard about my mother, I got this pressure in my head—I can't seem to eat anything, and I really just want to die. My mother could have died in that accident, but she was the one who hit the other car."

t: "And you said *you* were hit by the truth?"

Abbey: "Yea, the only time I'm happy is when I'm asleep . . . but now I wake up every twenty minutes and have these horrible dreams.

"All the things I've been told about my mother, I know they are true, but I also know they can't be that way. You should meet my mother—I wish you really could. She is really fantastic. She is beautiful and sparkling and charming and smart and my friends really always want to meet her when they hear about her from me." Tears well up in her eyes. "I think I miss her."

t: "I think you do too, and what's happening with her, all the trouble she is having, needn't make you feel ashamed about missing her. What do you think it means to you, the things you feel about mother now?"

Abbey: "I know I have to get my father to support me—and he can't be friends with me if I still think about my mother a lot. I think he thinks I'm like her, but my brother never has trouble. So I seem like I'm lying to myself all the time. I mean no one has really wanted to see how it is with me; I can be at the point of suicide and no one would want to see it. Once my aunt tried to tell me that there's a lot of good in me; that I'm really fantastic, but it was somehow like she didn't really believe it".

t: "What did you believe?"

Abbey: "I mean, if I'm fantastic, how come I failed with my mother when I was still living with her. I remember I used to try to pour the liquor down the sink, but she would just get mad at that and get some more. But I didn't think it would come to this. Maybe she is just a thirty-nine-year old baby, but she's wonderful, too. Nobody likes to see the truth because then they have to do something about it . . . like at boarding school, when I was gone for two weeks living at that boy's dorm . . . all the administrators really knew about it, but they all pretended it wasn't happening because that way they didn't have to do anything about it."

Abbey was capable of seeing the "truth" with a complexity she could not share with those around her. She knew that her mother was deeply upset and dangerously out of control, yet could be wonderful and lovable as well. Suicidal despair was something she had also seen in her mother during earlier periods in her life. However, the truth involved not only her mother's condition, but also the web of family disappointments and animosities, which meant to her at that moment that she could find no refuge there with her own truth intact. Wisely, she linked facing the "truth" with a sense of responsibility for doing something about it, and thus with danger to those for whom the consequences would be a sense of helplessness or failure. At a time in life when an investment in valued life goals marks a turning from more passive dependence on to active mastery of the wider world, the "truth," in Abbey's eyes, would render her and the human network on which she depended helpless rather than "free."

Carole. Carole was seen for a few sessions only, after her parents divorced and her mother remarried, and then felt she no longer needed to come. In spite of her intelligence and previous creativity, she was doing poorly in school, cutting classes, and she relentlessly devalued her own productions as "no good." She had previously been especially close to her father, also a creative person, sharing many interests with him. Referral followed after she confided tearfully to her mother one evening, "I just can't do anything any more." She told me the following.

Carole: "I used to love to write a lot of stuff—my father does too. But lately I haven't wanted to do anything like that—I just don't enjoy it any more at all."

t: "What is it like for you when you try it?"

Carole: "Now, if I try, only horrible things come out, so I just don't do it anymore. . . . When the divorce came, my sympathy was with my father. I guess I kind of associate him with my childhood . . . and then came eighth grade, I mean changing from junior high to high school—I think that was a big jump for me . . . and I remember that day . . . my father wasn't there like he used to be . . . I think I didn't *want* to learn anything in high school . . . I kind of feel incompetent now to do even the simplest thing . . . I don't know why . . . I know the more I cut classes the worse it gets, but that's better than sitting in school."

t: "What do you think of when you sit in school?"

Carole: "I guess it's like when I try to write—only awful thoughts come out—about how everything has changed."

t: "Can you tell me about it?"

Carole then described being caught "completely unaware" by the news that her parents were planning to divorce, and dwelt on ideal versions of family fun, as well as the parents' feelings toward each other when she was a child. Now, all of that had changed. Even her beloved dog, Linus, who had taken part in all the family camping trips, "I think from their honeymoon on, he feels old and useless now, he is almost paralyzed. The only solution is to put him to sleep, he is so unhappy."

t: "But putting your energies to sleep isn't the solution to your unhappiness, I know! You mention Linus feeling useless and that reminded me of your saying how incompetent you feel these days. Sometimes, people feel useless when they figure they ought to be able to make someone else happy; they wish they could, and feel horrible about not being able to do that, even though that isn't a kid's job, even someone your age."

Carole: "Well, you see, my father is unhappy, too—I know that, and he's been that way ever since they broke up and there is nothing he can do about it. He is just not like himself any more."

t: "It sounds like you feel you've lost what he used to be like, and are trying to find him again by sharing what he feels like. . . . When you think of your father, how do you picture him?"

Carole: "Well, he looks much younger than his age, and is always very, very handsome looking. He kind of looks like Mr. Clean in those TV ads."

t: "You mean, the ad where he whooshes in the house 'when the honeymoon is over' and helps the bride straighten everything out?"

Carole (laughs): "Yea, I guess I used to count on him to straighten things out for me, and now I can't anymore . . . and I can't even do anything for him. I don't know if he cares how much I visit or not. It's been three weeks since I've seen him."

t: "Even though he's unhappy in himself right now, I know that you are still terribly important to him. I think that once he gets to feeling less lonely in himself, he'll be able to show you more clearly again that you are connected with joy for him. But you can't do that job all by yourself. Meanwhile, what bothers me is that you are taking it out on yourself—I mean about being disappointed in yourself and in him. It's natural to be sad and angry about that, and not 'horrible' of you."

Carole then talks warmly of her father and the interests they have shared in natural things like hiking and camping, etc. She compares this with the different array of interests which she "can't stand" about her new stepfather. In contrast to Carole's description of her parents' idyllic relationship before her sudden shock when she was informed of the divorce, her mother told me that arguments between the parents had become chronic and not hidden from the children for some years before the divorce. She felt that Carole clung to the memories of the few good times "through rose-colored glasses." In the second interview, Carole reported having started to write again; she dealt more with issues of nurturance from, versus rivalry with mother. She talked about her pets, and the lively family of a girlfriend. She had called her father and was planning to spend the whole weekend with him. I took care to let the "honeymoon" fantasy of the previous interview lie without further comment.

In Carole's case, it was possible to assure her of her value in her father's eyes, because I knew both parents to be extraordinarily caring about her, in spite of her father's currently unfinished reaction to the meaning of the divorce. With less motivated parents, this cannot be done. Through a variety of circumstances, Carole regained her interest in school, life, and a future for herself. Her mother reported that she seemed more confident in herself and more accepting of her stepfather. She continued to spend a solid amount of time in both parental households, and in late adolescence lived for a year with her father, who was considerably happier with his own life by then. Later, she again chose writing as her prospective career, maintaining her "home base" in father's house, and a good relationship with her mother.

Eva. Eva, also aged fifteen when referred by a school counselor because of increasing depression, difficulties in concentrating, social isolation, and a "lost and blank" look in her eyes, was capable of exquisitely sensitive perceptions of herself and her environment. Her development will be described later in some detail. Here are excerpts from her initial description of the link between her parents' separation, her own cognitive development, and "disillusionment."

t: "When did most of the trouble start?"

Eva: "I think the trouble began in the seventh and eighth grade when I first began to question things in school. I mean like the dress code. It was then I realized about women's roles and everything."

t: "Can you tell me about that?"

Eva: "I mean it was then my mother told us that she wasted twelve years taking care of children when she could have been getting ahead in her career! And it's only lately that I've realized that my mother and father are a failure with each other. Mother thinks that father is a failure in relation to her, that she needs love and he doesn't, and my father thinks that mother is irrational. I don't have any clear feelings myself anymore . . . about school or anything."

t: "Is that like a kind of numbness, or do you think you avoid getting involved in feelings just now, or how is it?"

Eva: "Yes, I used to like to go into things deeply, and that worked out well in grade school. I got curious and excited and wanted to know things. But this year—my grades have never been as low in my life . . . like there is a lot of stuff that I don't understand in math that I used to really like a lot. My father understands it."

t: "Do you think that has something to do with it?"

Eva: "Well, when my mother is mad at me she sometimes calls me a 'totally rational being' like my father, but actually I can't really seem to think anymore. It's like a few years ago everything seemed so clear . . . like when I learned certain things at school there was that feeling of . . . well, suddenly everything fell into place . . . and now I'm not sure of anything any more. . . .

"I think this last year or maybe longer ago I became disillusioned about everything and I saw a lot of things I just didn't see before. I mean like about mother and father being such a complete failure with each other that they just want to get away from each other. That seems so sad now . . . I've been feeling a kind of blankness, as though nothing is coming into me and I feel like I'm wandering around in a daze . . . where I used to feel all invigorated and interested in things, now I've become all lazy and tired. I feel like I've lost, well, . . . like my drive to do anything. It's like everything around me is meaningless and the future just isn't going to come to anything good . . . whatever that is."

t: "What are you most disillusioned about?"

Eva: "I guess I'm most disillusioned about *them* . . . I never thought they were happy . . . now I think I should have *known* they weren't happy . . . but I never really knew it, and if I think of it it's still like a shock . . . even though if I make myself think about it, I remember that if they ever acted fondly, like if my Dad put his arm around my mother a long time ago . . . *that* was a shock to me . . . unsettling and unnatural, not like it was real. Now nothing seems real and I know I shy away from people . . . I have certain suspicions of people . . ."

t: "Like what?"

Eva: "I guess that they'll hurt me or I'll hurt them."

In another early session, Eva described how each parent perceived the situation in entirely different terms. Mother blamed father for being "cold," while father thought that she was not a good mother, because she put her work before her children.

t: "And where does that leave you?"

Eva: "I admire her for going after what she wants, I think she's right to do that, but I don't have any more clear feelings myself. It's like I don't expect anything special to happen ever, and don't make any plans because I don't have any clear convictions any more. I've even given up sports this year and I'm scared to get to know people of my own age . . . I'm really kind of critical of them. My father has the feeling that the whole day slips away from him and he can't get any work done either. He only does routine things—even his apartment reflects that and I get a cold feeling about it. He always welcomes me, but that doesn't seem real either, because he doesn't have to live with me the rest of the time. Mostly, I push people away and just feel like resting, sleeping—I only wish I could rest my mind and have a complete blank."

t: "And what do you find interrupting the blank?"

Here Eva came up with the first contradiction in the previously consistent picture of disillusionment: "the funny thing is that now they are separated, they seem much more to be going in the directions they want to . . . but I don't any more, I think I've given up."

In the long run, that contradiction stood Eva in good stead.

Initial Acceptance of the Devaluation of an Absent Parent

Karen and Heather had in common conscious acceptance of their mothers' bitter views about their fathers, and both allied themselves closely with their mothers throughout adolescence. For each of them, this was at a high psychic cost, in terms of establishing a sense of identity that they could value outside their mothers' domains.

Both girls spoke of being glad about the divorce, having egged mother on to take this action. Both of them postponed dealing with their positive feelings toward their fathers until the end of adolescence and experienced this first in the form of being severely traumatized by the breakup of a heterosexual relationship which mirrored many aspects of their concepts of father, but of which they demanded a total devotion reminiscent of their exclusive earlier bond with their mothers. In their early twenties, Heather abruptly and Karen gradually severed their ties with their mothers, and viewed their parents' motivation toward themselves in terms very different from those of midadolescence.

Karen. Karen entered therapy during her college years because she could fall in love only with men who had a close connection with her mother and who mistreated her. These relationships were her first secrets from mother, with whom both she and her sister had maintained an overclose relationship. She was in the process of choosing a profession allied with her mother's, in which she felt she would never be a success without the "entrance tickets" of her mother's previous successes. Since she was clearly a talented person, this perception was open to question. She told me, "It was always us against my father and I felt sometimes that our closeness was false—just to save ourselves from father."

Karen: "Things got worse between my parents until my father finally moved out when I was in the tenth grade. My mother kept telling me that my father was a sick, miserable man and very violent. As a child, I'd get in the middle, trying to protect my mother, while my sister stayed out of the fights. Mother kept telling me more about him and I would stay away from him, except when she sent me to pick up the money once a month after they separated. My goal is still that I want nothing to do with him, don't want him to phone me or anything. When he called my mother after they separated, I would be the one to take the phone off the hook." Yet Karen, too, lost her interest in school in the period following the divorce.

Karen: "It turned out that the year after the divorce I was flunking in school suddenly; my mother and father had to go to school together about it, but I cared nothing about school anymore. I started to become a go-go dancer and we were hired in a nightclub. I felt grownup in a way, like there was nothing left in school for me. I kept telling mother how thrilled I was that father left. Mother and I felt so good together because there was no more fear of fights. What was new was that I sort of took on the role of mother. I made mother call in to know when she was out with a man and what time she would be back and she would tell me a lot about him just to make me feel good. I found out later that she didn't really like them so much, and didn't know what to believe."

In a reversal of roles, the mother at this point acted like a young adolescent who seeks continued closeness to her mother by "sharing" a glorified version of her adventures on dates. Karen had some awareness of the "false" nature of closeness built on such sands.

After two months in therapy, Karen began to deal more directly with her intense, underlying feelings about her father. She felt tempted to respond to him at that time, but with the fear that she would again be disillusioned by him, specifically that his invitations were deceptive, his promises could not be counted on as "real." She reported, "The last time he wrote a letter, he sounded like he felt so rejected. He wrote, 'When you want a father, I'm here with open arms.' and I want to say, 'you're not there with open arms, it's all a big tease. You broke a promise and I can't ever trust you again. . . .' Then I found myself in the shower, crying and beating my fists against the wall. For the first time, I didn't know why I was crying. I kept saying, 'I hate you I hate you—to my father—and then from out of nowhere I was saying I love you—but I wasn't frightened . . . not like in the past when I've been afraid of going crazy."

In a later section of this chapter, Karen's further reality testing about her actual father will be described.

Prolonged Denial and Negation

Prolonged denial and negation about a family catastrophe occurred most often with adolescents whose families also had considerable difficulties tolerating anxiety or depression. This proclivity was associated with a general pattern of acting out of tensions, and specifically of aspects of the "forgotten" trauma associated with the loss. Eddy and Shirley and their family will be discussed in greater detail later. Here, however, are the perceptions they initially brought to therapy. Unlike the majority of the referred adolescents, neither of them was described as overtly depressed or unhappy.

Shirley and Eddy. Eddy's and Shirley's mother had died of cirrhosis of the liver after a number of years of increasing alcoholism. As the story later unwound, it became clear that the alcoholism followed a period when the fathers' business success brought him ownership of a larger operation; simultaneously the family moved to a wealthy neighborhood. Although they entertained lavishly at cocktail parties, Shirley, Eddy, and their mother felt out of place socially, and could not re-establish a group of friends with whose values and vocabulary they felt at home, as they had in their former simpler neighborhood. The children became used to seeing their mother always with a glass in her hand, but she and the family colluded to deny to themselves the extent of her drinking. When she became ill and instead of recovering became increasingly weak and yellowish-looking, she still maintained that she did not want a doctor, but probably just had a persisting bout of the flu. No one in the family insisted that she get medical care; by the time she was hospitalized, her condition was irreversible and shortly thereafter she died.

Untruthfulness was a family pattern. Where mother used "lying" as a defensive denial about her increasing drinking, it was clear to both children that father had admiration for those who were clever enough to lie without getting caught, and contempt for those who failed in attempted concealment. Father complained bitterly about the children's "lying," while simultaneously the school was at wit's end as to how to deal with the father's own tendency to falsify. The family was characterized both by a low tolerance for painful realities and a shared family ego ideal that emphasized "outsmarting" those who were seemingly more smart (i.e., more educated) as a measure of adequacy and strength. This extensive denial of the limits of reality in matters of health was associated first with the death of the mother, and, within a few years, with the death of the father as well.

Shirley put her sense of rude awakening this way in her first session with me: "Before mother died I always thought I'd never grow up and everything would be the same."

Eddy, aged fourteen, was referred to me after repeated urging by the school because he had failing grades, was cutting most of his classes, and was so provocative of the male teachers the rest of the time that he had been "suspended" from school repeatedly. The school staff felt helpless in dealing with the father, who was described as hot-tempered, blaming the school and "constantly being caught in lies," e.g., about the boy's whereabouts, etc. Although he had earlier agreed to have a tutor for the boy, and said he would get "the best that money can buy," he hired and fired a series of tutors in quick succession, asserting each time that the tutor had not carried out his wishes.

Mr. Winger first contrasted Shirley "who is upset because the family is not like a family any more, and is having a bad year at school, repeating the grade for the first time in her life" with Eddy, "who is a liar beyond belief . . . the trouble is, he is an extremely convincing liar." He had almost made a "sucker" out of his father that morning by saying he had a fever and couldn't go to school. Then his father caught him sticking the thermometer under hot water to make it go up. In view of the initial family picture, it was surprising to me that Eddy came willingly to therapy appointments, and eventually took considerable initiative in this; e.g., when both his father and the chauffeur overslept in the morning, he tramped through a couple of miles of snow to keep his appointments on time.

In initial interviews, Eddy spoke with great hostility about his father's girlfriend. "She's too young for him, she's a real pain in the ass; he spends a lot of money on her—he treats her much better than me—she gets mad if he don't."

t: "Treats her better than you?"

Eddy: "Yea, like a couple of weeks ago, my father forgot my birthday . . . he was spending the weekend with her . . . I wish he wouldn't treat his girlfriend over us, he tells us we're his family but he don't mean anything by that. With my father, if I try to stick up for myself, he yells at me, 'Don't yell at me or I'll ground you.' Anyway, I like him more when he's away because I think he's really out to get me. He mixes me up so much I try to get back at him, but he only cares what they say at school. He'll believe school but he won't believe me. Why should I tell lies?"

t: "Maybe a lot of things have *happened* to you lately that are hard to believe like your father paying attention to his girlfriend and forgetting your birthday—and like about your mother dying."

Eddy: "I don't think about that, about her dying I mean."

t: "Do you think of her in some other way?"

Eddy: "Yea, see, she used to always like to get a tan—so I always think of her by the swimming pool and she's looking happy and smiling."

t: "And you don't think of what happened after that?"

Eddy: "Well, after then, when she got sicker, she was always lying down anyway—so I just think of her lying down by the swimming pool instead, I mean I can really *see* her there."

t: "And do you see yourself, too, with her?"

Eddy: "Well, sometimes when I'm at school, like if I'm trying to get a rise out of someone—like my stupid gym teacher—and I see him raising his arm . . . except by school rules he's not allowed to hit me . . . so I know he can't do anything to me . . . then I want to have a good laugh . . . and I see her and want to run and tell her. We liked to laugh together."

When Eddy was younger, his mother frequently intervened to protect him from father's punishments. Father had said she overprotected Eddy in whatever scrapes he got into, and that he "kept trying to pry them apart."

In the second session, Eddy reported, "Things are a little better. I mean, my dad is not as mad at me and anyway he's in Texas for the weekend."

t: "Did he blow his top less generally when your mother was still alive?"

Eddy: "Yea, I think that's part of the trouble, since she died he never relaxes, he's always on the move. Like he can't stand to stay in two nights in a row or have only one girl at a time. And after his heart attack, he was told to slow down; it's not good for his heart. Anyway, it's not fair that he can get away with stuff that we can't."

He is beginning to consider that "part of the trouble" may be the handling of grief through frantic restlessness and the search for ever-changing companions. With the lack of current emotional support from the father, as well as Eddy's own need at this time to protect himself from painful affects, it seemed premature to approach his grief over his mother's death directly; the solace of picturing her comforting presence, unmarred by the "ugliness" he was later able to describe in her face and in his own thoughts appeared crucial until he had solidified his relationship to me, an array of "big brother" and tutor combinations recruited for him, and eventually the staff of a boarding school which attempted to provide consistent supports and limits for him. Within a few weeks, it became apparent that Shirley had also been cutting classes increasingly, and father had ignored the notices he had received from school. However, he brought her to see me also after she had an accident while "drag-racing" at more than her usual speed. She had been taken to the emergency ward of the same hospital in which her mother had died, and was clearly upset. Father seemed more shaken up and less angry at Shirley's difficulties than at Eddy's, and at this time accepted a referral for help for himself in dealing with the kids and his own reactions, which he had previously refused vehemently. Although he was seen by a highly skilled and flexible psychiatrist, he could tolerate treatment for only a few sessions before quitting.

Shirley also began her first hour by complaints about the father's girlfriends, and connected her "cutting classes" with "nobody noticing" any more.

Shirley: "I've been cutting classes a lot; it's not really helping . . . I mean I know I'm ruining myself."

t: "What would make you want to ruin yourself?"

Shirley: "Well, I don't think I was really close to my mother . . . I was closer to Dad and he runs away from everything . . . but if my mother was still around, she probably would be waiting, I wouldn't be cutting classes all the time. I just get away with murder now."

t: "You get away with *murder* now?"

Shirley: "Yea, my father doesn't check on me; I can get away with anything I want . . . I can spend money a lot . . . the only things I can't do is things as a *family* . . . like when my mother was still alive, we went to nightclubs a lot."

Later in the hour, we returned to the theme of "getting away with murder," as connected in her mind with loss of mother. She stated first that she did not know what to believe about her mother's death. She wouldn't go to the doctor when she was sick and had been looking yellower all the time. Shirley knew how much she drank, but Shirley had done nothing about it. In fact, she just hadn't thought about it. Mother's stay in the hospital was very short before her death. She said, "That hospital murdered my mother," by not paying attention to her fast enough. She then confided that she had premonitory powers and somehow knew her mother would die that night, although she still could not really believe that she was dead. Eventually, she revealed some guilt about her "premonition" about her mother's death "because the things I think come true in a spooky way." When I asked her "what else" she said that she told a kid he would have a car accident within two weeks and he did. This brought up her own identification with her mother at the time that she was in the same hospital where her mother died.

Shirley: "My accident really scared me. I thought I was doomed dying. I hate the hospital—I really blame that hospital and staff about mother dying; she had started to get better and they let her get worse again. When I was there with my back—I really smashed the car up good—had smashed into a lady, but she wasn't hurt. I was so scared in the emergency ward, but waited two hours to get X-rayed—if someone was dying, would you want to wait two hours? I'm scared now when I'm driving with my father—he kept saying I would be dead before I slow down, but he's playing with his own life right now, he never slows down."

Father was furious about the delay and planned to sue the hospital. I asked if Shirley had had any "premonition" about something like that happening to her. She said, "That's the funny part of it, I'd had this weird feeling for days that I might *die* but I couldn't figure what made me scared of dying. I didn't tell anybody that, you know I'm the kind who's loudmouthed and not scared of anything but now I don't tell anybody stuff. And then I went faster than ever dragging—you know, like the kid who I told was gonna have an accident—and I knew that was a lousy road for dragging anyway."

For Shirley, guilt and anger toward her mother, stemming from the period prior to the latter's death, complicated the remembering and experiencing of grief. She worked on this over a period of time, during which she was able to demystify her "premonitions" as a way of making sense out of her feelings without facing them as such. It became apparent that she felt she should have done something about her mother's condition—or persuaded her father to do so; at some level she recognized this in spite of negating responsibility for her premonition. Her anger at mother over the years had to do with her feeling that mother had chosen Eddy as her favorite, and with her subsequent rivalry with her mother—which in some sense she felt she had won—for displays of affection from father. She needed to differentiate her angry fantasies at mother, which also had been mixed with love, from the pattern which actually led to her death. She eventually recognized her premonition that she would die herself both as a form of self-punishment for "getting away with murder" and as a way of re-experiencing her mother's presence without having to tolerate grieving or longing for her presence. Although she was increasingly testing and defying her father and incurring his wrath, the self-destructive acting out ceased at this point.

Shirley: "Of course I knew both my parents liked drinking at parties a lot, but that was different, before they were fighting so much. But then she started looking funny during the day—sort of yellow and ugly and she kept saying it was just the flu again. *She just didn't look like my mother any more, so I think I just stopped looking at her. I was waiting for my mother . . . the way she used to look . . . to come back.* I just never figured my mother would die . . . it's like I'd hear of kids killed in accidents but I never thought it would happen to me. I never figured it would end with my having trouble in school and seeing a psychologist, like I couldn't get through the week without that. I figured my life really different—that things would be perfect—that I'd go to high school and have a boyfriend and not worry about anything. I guess the biggest difference is that mother died and my father has all that responsibility and is mad all the time.

"After mother died people said, 'You really should go on a trip and forget it' and I tried to. I hate to go to the cemetery. I can't stand to think that she is really dead, so last year I didn't go to the cemetery at all."

The first time that Shirley could bring up grieving directly was in relation to the family dog: "Before she died we also had a dog . . . and that dog felt like empty . . . it had followed her around . . . that dog was really mental . . . I mean really retarded . . . he ran around mental after she died and took a piece out of the gas man. She used to dress him up too for a party, like she liked buying clothes for all of us. We got rid of him last year when Dad wanted a white wall-to-wall carpet and he was still not really housebroken since she died, he never got housebroken again."

In this way, she revealed the intensity of the regressive feelings she feared were she fully to experience her loss and her lack of assurance that her environment could support rather than discard her, like the grieving dog, during such stress.

Pseudologia and Consoling Fantasy

Pseudologia has been discussed in chapter 3 as a phenomenon which belongs midway between fantasy, clearly distinguished from reality, and an occurrance which the individual believes to be real. When used by the adolescents encountered here, pseudologias, rather than emanating from conflict about awareness of an inner impulse, often in part brought to light an aspect of previously experienced reality the truth of which had been nullified by the current life, especially in the form of the relationship to one parent. Thus simultaneously they covered and betrayed the truth. The "truth" might involve belief in something which the adolescent had construed as an earlier promise, implicit or explicit, by a parent.

Consoling fantasies functioned very much like pseudologia when they were believed sufficiently to become part of the sense of reality of the individual. In both cases, the fantasy is only partly believed and is dropped when the individual is confronted with contradictory evidence. In this sense, it differs greatly from the kind of disturbance in reality sense associated with delusions or hallucinations.

A number of the adolescents ameliorated traumatic perceptions of the parent whom they lost, and about whom they were disillusioned, by clinging to happier fantasies instead. The degree to which this was protective consolation, as compared to a serious interference with reality testing, varied according to the personality of the adolescent, and the reality on which it was based.

Eileen. Eileen used pseudologia as a momentary intermission during a painful prcess that involved coming to terms with an increasingly rejecting father and stepmother while simultaneously grappling with unfinished mourning for her mother, who had committed suicide when Eileen was fourteen. When I first saw her at age sixteen, she was strongly protective of an idealized image of her mother, making clear to me in her first interview, "My aunt tries to tell me that my mother was sick and selfish to have done such a thing, but I know better. I don't like people to cut my mother down and I'm always ready to fight back." For some years the fantasy of still being loved by both parents resurfaced, and was expressed in the form of pseudologia to others.

Eileen had spent the birthday after her mother's suicide without the usual celebration. There was no birthday cake, nor gifts from her father. Her mother had always been lavish with gifts and loving notes. That evening she went to a party, but said she was "absent-minded" as her mother was on her mind; she toppled down the stairs, had to be taken to a hospital for a sprained ankle and cut on her head. It was a depressing birthday, except for the moments when she realized her friends cared about her, since they picked her up and took her to the hospital.

The following year a lavish arrangment of flowers with a loving note arrived at her place of work on Eileen's birthday. She proudly displayed them to her fellow workers. She did not mention that she had been the sender.

At a still later time, she needed an explanation about a period of absence from work in order to have an abortion, which she kept secret. She told her boss and colleagues that she was going "on a trip to Paris with my mother and father," a piece of fantasy based on a promise which had been made to her during the six months after her mother's death, and then broken by her father, who took her stepmother instead, leaving Eileen home to watch over her younger brothers.

Linda. Linda tried to protect herself by countering unhappy experiences with happier versions of both the present and the future. Although plagued by suicidal impulses and a conscious longing for death at various times throughout her adolescence, she managed to stop short of such self-destructiveness with the hope, fortunately persistent at such moments, that there could be a happier life in the future.

Linda was eleven when her father left home; he was hospitalized shortly thereafter for a paranoid episode. He had been Jewish, but after the hospitalization converted to Catholicism, and asked his three children to be converted with him. Linda, the middle child, had always been closest to her father, who in turn, had been responsible for more physical care of the child than the mother, or than for his other two daughters. Her babyhood years were complicated by severe eczema, to be followed by asthma. Linda's first skirmish with reality was apparent at nursery school, where (like Heather) she refused ever to wear a dress (like the other girls did in those days) or take off her fireman's hat, insistently saying that she was really a boy. This was different from the behavior of many young girls who play at being a boy, but can stop and know they are not.

At home, Linda followed her father around devotedly, trying to participate in whatever he did. Her treatment, at age eight, after referral to a child guidance clinic for "poor school work, enuresis, asthma, lying, stealing, and a lack of friends," was discontinued as earlier noted, after a social worker implied, that there were incestuous elements in the father-daughter attachment.

When father left the family, Linda first blamed herself, asking mother what she had done wrong to make father leave. The following two years, she openly blamed her mother and saw as much of father as possible. He was by then remarried to a Catholic woman and had a new baby.

Linda was referred.to me when she was fourteen, deeply depressed and friendless, and having difficulty with school work. She was at that time struggling to negate and "undo" some perceptions of the father's behavior by clinging desperately to memories of the positive relationship they had had. For example, she described an incident she had witnessed while visiting father and his new family "but I just don't believe it." After some angry words to his wife, father threw the little family poodle, whimpering, on the bed and beat her repeatedly with a belt. Linda countered this hastily with the memory of his gentle touch when he used to bathe her, insisting that her father could not be cruel. Being cradled in water and gentled by loving skin contact turned out to have a special central significance to her in view of the early eczema and asthma, and her feeling that she was physically disgusting to her mother as a child. Suicidal fantasies were cast most persistently in the image of being swept up in the arms of the sea.

In a similar way, Linda tried to dispel some of her reaction to the religious conversion. She made clear that the change from "being Jews" must have meant that father did not like himself or his children the way they were before. She was confused in her own identity about this, feeling neither "really" Jewish nor Catholic, but was hurt by the fact that a Jewish boy from school was not asking her out, telling her that his family allowed him to date only Jewish girls. She felt cut off from her childhood self, as though "no one knows I am the same person." She vividly and repeatedly recalled the donning of her communion dress in a beautiful ceremony when her father had asked her to convert, so beautiful that it made her feel that now everything would be wonderful. Needless to say, this promise was not fulfilled.

For the next three years, she grappled slowly with pieces of the "truth" about her parents' complicated conflicts and reactions to her, while she improved in her ability to relate to friends and do her school work, and in her general confidence in herself, in spite of recurrent depressive affect when she felt rejected by a peer. She became more independent of both parents, and especially found her visits to her father too disappointing to use her weekends that way, other than a few times a year. She "postponed" coming to terms with the still overwhelmingly intense attachment to the father until her last year in high school, when, because of needs of his own, he forcefully broke through her necessary defenses by a prolonged beating with a belt, and asking her directly if she felt attracted to him. This period is taken up elsewhere, along with a follow-up on the "postponement" of grieving, into her mid-twenties.

Restitutive Hallucination and Consoling Fantasy

Angela. Angela took more extreme measures to prevent the loss of a necessary image of the father in order to preserve her sense of identity as real in childhood. She dated the onset of restitutive auditory hallucinations and certain compulsive rituals ("feeding" her left arm with lotions and burning her right arm to punish it for evil powers) to the period after the loss of her first father figure, at age five, when she was told he had not actually been her father. These symptoms abated during a period in childhood between ages seven and twelve when she made up a satisfying fantasy about her real father. The discovery of and disillusionment about the discrepancy between this fantasy and the reality, coinciding with pubescence, ushered in new symptom formation, which brought her to treatment at the age of fourteen. She had been asking her mother to take her to a psychiatrist or psychologist ever since she was twelve, but was remarkable in having been able to keep the content of her symptoms secret, both from mother and from peers. She assumed, probably correctly, they would think her "crazy" if they knew, and that this would interfere with their relationship to her. In spite of her disturbance, she did not withdraw from peers nor cease to function in school although she was considered an "underachiever." She lived an astounding "double life," and was a richly endowed person with complicated ways of preserving her personal integrity. At this point, I shall only describe her reaction to the discovery of the "truth') about her father:

Angela: "My biggest shock in my life was to find out about my real father. Mother told me finally—after I'd been bugging her for years about it—that it was Jerry Green . . . and I had known him for a long time. He lives just a few blocks away and so does his wife and six kids. Some of them are older than me and some younger. I just couldn't think of him as my father when I first met him, and it was a while before I really went up to him. With his drinking and all, I didn't know ahead if he would recognize me anyway."

"I remember when I first found out that my 'left father' (who left when she was five and was the father of her younger brother, Mick) hadn't belonged to me at all, that he was just my brother's. It was after that I first heard the lotion bottles talking to me in the bathroom and the shaving bottles. (She had liked watching her "left" father shave.) And that was the first time I wasn't sure I existed; I thought I might not be real at all . . . and then I would hear the bottles talking to me, so I figured I must be there. Then after we moved to Chicago, I didn't hear voices anymore, and I stopped feeding my left arm with lotion, and burning my right arm with the iron and all that."

(The "left arm" turned out to stand for her "left father" as well as for the "good" part of herself.)

t: "What did you do different in Chicago?"

Angela: "I used to make up stories a lot of times about how my real father was and I knew that he would be a big film producer in Hollywood and that he was just waiting for me to be grown up enough to go to Hollywood all by myself to meet him. So when I found out it was Jerry Green, everything in my life changed again; I didn't feel like me anymore. I wasn't even sure I could be an actress anymore. Then the voices started again last year, only this time, I'm so scared of them. You see, they've been telling me I will die when I'm still fourteen."

Transitory Disbelief and Negation

Transitory belief about the reality of a separation was also characteristic of a number of adolescents whose parents were divorced in an "untraumatic" fashion, while the parents did their best to both inform and support their children. Eventually, confirmation of the reality of the divorce, especially when done in a "no-fault" fashion, tended to be followed by some relief of anxiety or inhibition in the adolescent.

Christopher. Christopher's parents informed their children that father was moving to an apartment of his own for a "trial separation" because they were as yet undecided about whether they felt able to solve their marital problems, or would each be happier building separate lives. Long after the announced decision that the separation would be permanent, and while the divorce was proceeding, Christopher still referred to it as a "trial separation." Though he frequently visited his father in his apartment, and saw evidence of the presence of other women (curtains made, cakes baked, etc.) he remained quite unbelieving that father was dating others for several months. When his father finally pushed him to face that he might become more involved with another woman, at the same time trying to tell him the facts of life, Christopher responded with an outpouring of mixed admiration and disgust at the idea of father's interest in sex. However, for the first time, he allowed himself to identify more openly with father than mother. His final acceptance of this possibility in his father coincided with the development of the more active components in his own personality, previously submerged by an inhibition of initiative in learning and a need to be a loser in sports. Though he liked to wrestle, he had compulsively allowed others to come out on top, while he ended pinned down flat on his back. He now produced a profusion of sexualized fantasies and "active" symbols, usually in joking form, and dealt with his conflicting sexual feelings. Sometime he called them "ugly" feelings but could now imagine that girls might not find him ugly. E.g. after excusing himself for "bombing into the room" so that he almost knocked down the previous patient (a female), he asked "What flies through the air, is green and long, weighs two hundred pounds and is the ugliest thing you ever saw?" The answer was "Super Pickle!"

He associated jokingly to a fantasy of penises flying and then to bombers trying to stake out a territory of their own. Staying with the fantasy, we talked about his anxiety over the aggression—bombing or getting bombed—which he connected with getting a territory or girl of his own. He felt he "could take it now—that I can be up there with the other guys". It became clear that it was not the separation, father's sexuality or the "facts of life" discussion in themselves which were associated with the changes in the boy, but also what Christopher felt as a change of attitude in his father. Christopher had seen his father as hypercritical of his mother and himself; he felt that no matter how hard they tried to please him together they would fail in meeting his expectations. Being passive and not trying were the safest expedients. After finally accepting that the parents' separate lives were associated for each with the possibility of increased self-esteem, he felt he could also be treated "separately" by his father, and could attempt to become more "manly" without being automatically consigned to failure. Simultaneously, his mother had not only gained in understanding of him, but was in addition more able to enjoy and "like" the more boisterous and assertive sides of his nature.

Protective Disengagement

Some adolescents reacted to the emotional pressures they experienced around their parents' separation by a kind of protective disengagement from the parents' problems. To the degree that it was successful, it allowed them to continue their own development. Since I am most apt to see adolescents in distress, there is probably a much larger proportion of such adolescent children of divorced parents in the general population than I came to know. It is more apt to be workable in late rather than early adolescence.

Ralph. Ralph's parents had separated when he was sixteen, but bitter conflicts involving the children's loyalties continued. When I met him he was eighteen, and told me, "I finally just decided to stop tearing myself to pieces with guilt trips about my parents. I love both my parents, and who I live with doesn't prove anything. At first, I tried to make everything come out equal, because they would put a guilt trip on me that made me feel like a pile of shit. Then I figured I couldn't be that bad, and I let them both know I won't take sides. When it first happened . . . for the first six months I just about told nobody . . . I was careful especially about a girl I kind of liked. I was always afraid if I told I would cry . . . and then she would see what a mess I was, and I didn't want that."

"If I had it to do over again, I guess I would tell someone. I kept wishing for a shoulder to cry on, but there wasn't any. I guess I wanted to be sure that I could pull myself together first. Later, when I did tell, I found out a lot of kids had the same situation, and we rapped about it at sailing club."

Julia. Julia came to see me at age seventeen because she was concerned about the welfare of her little sister, whom she had had to leave at home, between her separated, but still warring parents, while she went to college. She was a bright, warm, perceptive person with an obvious capacity for good relationships with people. She had a boyfriend, described as "quiet, kind and strong," but at present she liked "to have a lot of different friends and not be exclusive." She added, "The important thing to me about my boyfriend is that it's very mutual, we each listen to each other, stand by each other...and I think we are both secure in that."

The trouble between Julia's parents had been a part of her life as long as she could remember. She and her older brother Scott "stood by each other and did a lot of things together." When she was born, her parents separated for a year and then lived together again. Mother made some suicidal attempts. About four years ago, final separation procedures began, "but my father is still stalling." She described her father as having bad relationships to people. "He argues with you, till you can't think of anything to say, wears you to the nub, and then he suddenly forgives you. . . . I think the worst part is not knowing what is going to happen next. Mother is finally becoming more liberated, but for a long time she just denied herself everything she wanted. Sometimes she played the role of the martyr, thinking she was doing it for us and sometimes she thought it was better for all of us if she died and weren't around. My sister is the 'baby in the family' and I took care of her a lot when I was home; I was there for her, like Scott was for me."

Julia said that when she was little her father would shake her mother. "I remember hearing the noises and being scared—but I love my father . . . and it hurt me all so much . . . lately here I've been crying a lot just thinking about it, while I'm trying to write papers. In high school, I had my first big fight with my father. He said I lied, and I got furious. I played his game . . . he ridiculed me and screamed and yelled he was going to kill me. I ran to my room and locked it and he came and broke down the door. I didn't speak to him for two weeks after that . . . I lost twenty pounds meanwhile. But I think I kind of decided something during that time. I told him, 'I'm not forgiving you. I'm just making an agreement.' My little sister Kerry doesn't know how to do that yet. When either of them promises her a lot of things and then asks if she wouldn't rather live with them, she tells each of them yes. She doesn't dare say no. Then she gets upset and calls me on the phone. She is being torn right in half. I remember I used to think that it was somehow up to me, that if I couldn't do the right thing for them, I was failing. I don't feel that any more. I know I have to live my own life and that I can't solve their problems for them. When I was still living at home, I never wanted to bring my friends there because I could never be sure what they would witness. You know, the worst part of the fights were really not the great big happenings, but the constant tension . . . the little nitty gritty things that keep happening. It's like you are always sitting at the dinner table thinking, 'Is tonight the night something big and terrible will happen?' And that way, you can never relax."

RELATIONSHIPS TO OTHERS DURING THE PERIOD OF INTENSE STRESS

A majority of these adolescents encountered problems in investing adolescent friendships with affective energy, and in seeing them as valued representations of self and others in the process of identity formation. This was often experienced as one aspect of the depression and withdrawal from immediate or long-range life goals; and was described as a sense of not being "connected" to anyone, including peers. Difficulty in making friends was one of the four most common reasons given for referral (the others being school difficulties, depression, and "untrustworthiness.")

Friendships

In childhood, the parent figures are graced by the child with the power to nurture or diminish his self-esteem. Ordinarily, a gradual deinvestment of these childhood parent figures is accompanied by wide vacillations between a sense of emptiness and loss, including depressive moods, and an active seeking for new attachments through which the adolescent can validate his new self-perceptions, as well as reinvest the love he is to withdraw from parent figures in actual relationships. Although such relationships have been called "narcissistic" and "fickle" because they reflect different and changing aspects of the adolescent's ideal self and are often disrupted by the very intensity of wishes attached to them, they function as a major bridge between childhood attachments and a more adult capacity to love. The need to avoid emotional intimacy in adulthood is often associated with a history of an absence of the kind of communication and emotional interchange possible with a "best friend" in adolescence.

Thomas Wolfe (1946) describes the adolescent's urgent need for a peer group to help deal with a sense of emptiness, which has been discussed here (chapter 4) in relation to the "normal mourning" of adolescent development:

> He cannot endure to be alone
> He lives in a crowd, thinks with the crowd,
> Is afraid to be marked off from his fellows
> By an eccentricity.
> He joins clubs and is afraid of ridicule
> He is bored and unhappy
> And wretched most of the time
> For there is a great cavity in him.

The majority of adolescents described here also felt they could "not endure to be alone," but when initially seen often felt they had no choice but to be so. For a number of them, this was less connected to any long-standing personality difficulty, than to a jolting sense of recognition that their parents, who had been engaged in a relationship with each other, had "failed" in this engagement, and also felt alone. A fatalistic view about the permanence of this condition was often expressed.

There were exceptions to the initial pattern of friendlessness, e.g., in the cases of Carole and Julia. In these cases, the early presence of one or several best friends was correlated with the rapidity with which intense self-devaluation lifted to allow experiences in which the self could be appreciated to enter. Others, like Eva, had important intermittant friendships.

Another variation characterized the children who were not referred for any symptoms of overt depression, but tended to act out their grief in masked or self-destructive fashion; e.g., Shirley and Eddy both tended to "hang out" with a group or gang, characterized in treatment hours more in terms of their activities than individual characteristics. Jane gave similar descriptions. There was a high turnover of the population involved, but their availability was important.

The quality of friendships was a good barometer of changing images of the self. Making a new friend often heralded the possibility of feeling liked again. And the characteristics of the friends chosen often either mirrored the self-image, or constituted complementary counterparts. When an adolescent began to see himself as less deprived or excluded, the choice of friends broadened; he no longer chose only those who were also deprived and excluded. Similarly, when antisocial conduct changed, the adolescent was apt to switch the peer group with which he spent the most time, to one in which antisocial activities were less valued. Changing friends sometimes, but not always, occasioned guilt.

Jane. Jane was referred when, at age seventeen, she developed a pattern of increasing school difficulties and class-cutting that jeopardized her high school graduation. Jane's mother despaired about a daughter who "is th exact opposite of everything I've tried to teach her," and "has a way of not telling the truth, even when confronted with it." Her difficulties had increased since an abortion two years previously. Sexual activity began not long after her mother told her the "truth," that divorce between her parents had been precipitated by father's having an affair. Jane told me about this, "I just couldn't believe it . . . I couldn't believe he would do such a thing. I mean, I think that's morally wrong and I just didn't want to see him after that—then I didn't answer his letter and never heard from him again."

She then identified herself as a person who, mother always thought, did "wrong things". She slowly became aware of a self-rejection in her image of herself that paralleled her attempted rejection of her father. Father had always described himself as "too restless" for marriage. Although Jane had handled her fear of further abandonment in childhood by an adaptive pseudo-independence, she had needed the constant reassurance of having a "group" of friends. The important thing about the group was the interchangeability of available members, which prevented the sense of loss and pain associated for her with dependence on father or mother or any single person.

Jane described the best part of her life as the time during which mother worked, before she remarried—a time when Jane would come home after school to be "free." Being "free" meant bringing her friends home with her and going out with the kids to the park near where they lived. Much later in the session, she was able to say that she thought she had a problem in that "I can't stand to be alone" and therefore needed to be with friends rather than studying. This was one reason she had cut classes so much last year. Sitting through class made her feel alone and restless for others. She did not ever have a "real" friend until she went steady and got pregnant. However, she always had a group who could be counted on.

t: "Counted on like how?"

Jane: "Well, if one person isn't around, there is always another to do things with."

Friendships played a somewhat different role in the lives of those adolescents, who were initially overtly depressed, feeling "unconnected" to peers. After the initial preoccupation with depression, self-devaluation, and intense conscious or unconscious identification with the more traumatized of the two parents, shifts in friendship patterns began to emerge in a variety of ways. Some adolescents, like Heather, formed such a close alliance with the mother that peer friendships were effectively excluded and delayed until very late in adolescence. Although Heather had some avid interests, such as Shakespearean theatre, she would not attempt to make plans to attend such activities with a peer, but preferred to go with her mother only. Eva continued to feel she was basically a "loner" for a number of years, and described her father to be one as well. For a long time she assumed that valued relationships would inevitably be disrupted. However, she had intermittent periods of intimacy in relationships with both boys and girls, and to these her unparalleled directness, honesty, and appreciation of genuineness gave a jewel-like clarity and importance.

For Linda, close friendships began and continued in her high school years, coinciding with a period of revived development, when her learning and school involvement were optimal, she generally felt good about herself, and got along more easily with her mother, etc. But her best friends changed, usually because she became disappointed in their availability to her when she needed them. Her fantasy of finding an all-satisfying relationship imbued some relationships with a kind of intensity which led to their disruption, and a resurgence of depression in her. In therapy, attempts to understand and modify her wish for the all-gratifying love relationship became central. The stimulation of her fantasies and breakdown of her defenses occurred during her last year in high school and work on her postponed identification with the past psychosis of the father occurred later. It was after this that she became a member of a "substitute family" in junior college.

Among adolescents who tried protectively to disengage themselves to some extent from their parents' problems, peer relationships suffered less. However, the quality of the relationships tended to be heavily imbued with characteristics of the child's own pattern of coping. For example, thirteen-year-old James and fifteen-year-old Connie spent considerable time away from home and with friends, but had to provide "cover-up" explanations for many aspects of family interactions which the parents also needed to conceal from the rest of their community. This made the friendships less important and supportive to them than they might have otherwise been. In contrast, Julia and her brother Scott, who had lived with intense parental discord for as long as they could remember, made use throughout adolescence of warm and sustaining relationships, apparently modeled to some extent on their strong and trustful relationship to each other.

Often, those youngsters whose sense of "aloneness" was overwhelming when they first entered treatment, and was usually associated with a loss of interest in life goals, signaled an important turning point in treatment by making one or more new, real friends, or, later in adolescence, by entering into a love relationship. Often this was associated with a revitalization of goals and development, some increased distance from parental problems and the recapturing of initiative, sensual acuity, and vigor about the options open to them for shaping their lives. In a number of cases (e.g., Heather, Linda, and Karen) it was not possible for the adolescent to work out the postponed, but still crucial, elements of primitive identification and grief about a parent figure until after this step had been taken and the adolescent, in a sense, had at least a foothold on a life of his or her own.

The "Substitute Family"

An additional human support network, created by a number of adolescents after a period of time, was a "substitute family," including adults or totally composed of peers. Increased involvement with another family is common and constructive for adolescents in general. It allows not only for a broader choice of identification figures, but also removes continued interaction with adults from the degree of ambivalence the adolescent associates with current closeness to the parents. However, the substitute family appeared to have more than the usual importance for the adolescents encountered here. The adaptive use of the "substitute family" tended to occur during the period when the adolescent was coming to terms with the limitations in the emotional support he/she would receive from his/her own family. Among the adolescents who came for treatment, none except Carole had adopted this resource at the time they were first seen, but sought it out after periods ranging from a month to several years. The nature of the "substitute family" varied. What was common to all of them was that the child referred to these relationships by actually calling them the new "family" ties. In some cases, the adolescent became so much a part of the life of an actual, other family that he/she was treated and spoken of like another family member. In other cases, the structure of the "family" was in the form of communal living. In one case, it was clustered around a particular recreational facility that involved both adults and adolescents, e.g., Josie chose a roller-skating rink as "my second home," where she spent all her free time with her boy friend and his father, the manager "who can tell me how to act right without blowing his top like my father does."

It should be noted that living with a substitute family is often not helpful to those adolescents who utilize extensive acting out in either aggressive or sexual behavior to deal with inner tensions or externally stimulated disappointments. A warm family life usually stimulates dependency wishes that are intolerable to them, and hence are defended against by provoking a negative interaction with the adults, which is then apt to result in the child being ousted, further confirming his image of himself as rejected. Group placements, though also tumultuous, are usually more suitable.

Eileen. After some initial months in therapy, Eileen, like many adolescents, occasionally brought along a friend to her therapy hour. It did not take long to see that different friends brought into focus different aspects of her emotional functioning and that it was useful for her to be able to "show" me this, as well as to have some help in dealing with her relationships to them. During her first year of treatment, her closest friend, Polly, had been cutting more classes than Eileen, and was almost certain not to be able to graduate. Since she regularly intercepted the mail, her parents had not received school requests for conferences about this. Eileen brought Polly to her therapy session. Polly let me know that she felt nobody cared about her and that it did not matter anyway. She often toyed with the idea of driving her car off a bridge. With Polly demonstrating what Eileen had been feeling during her most despairing moments, the two had commiserated. Polly was becoming quite dependent on

Eileen to keep her company in cutting classes. Both girls dated the time at which they finally were completely "turned off" by school to the departure of their former principal. He had known them all by name, and although strict, was always willing to kid around with them as well. In contrast, the new principal didn't know them and "wouldn't care if we lived or died." We clarified that they were leaving school behind, like they felt the principal had left them, that in fact they were still mad at him about that. Among other things I suggested getting to know the new principal.

In spite of some initial protest on Polly's part, she was relieved to have her need for help clarified during the hour, and for Eileen and me to take some active steps toward this end. Eileen, who by that time was determined to give up cutting classes and wanted to graduate in order to retain the option of college at some later time, took the initiative in going to talk with the principal about her own and Polly's previous pattern of cutting classes and her view that Polly had not been able to "help it" before this, since she was too unhappy at home. Eileen tried to bargain for a return to school which would not penalize the girls for past classes missed to a greater extent than they were capable of making up. This was her way of preparing to leave her close friendship with Polly without overwhelming guilt. Her own needs had changed sufficiently for her to wish to seek out less disturbed companions. Leaving Polly behind was a difficult process for her, since it reinvoked her guilt about her neglected mother, who had committed suicide.

Over the next few months, I heard increasingly about Ethel and her warm and bustling household. Eileen began to spend most of her free time with Ethel's family. Ethel's mother always welcomed "setting another place" for her, and Ethel's father came to speak of her, affectionately, as "my other daughter"—a joke between them, because Eileen looked so different physically from the rest of the family. Eileen responded by calling him "my other father." When she brought Ethel along to therapy, the latter talked in glowing terms of how fond the younger children were of Eileen; the five-year-old, for instance, insisted that Eileen be the one to put him to bed. In this family setting she could feel appreciated rather than criticized. During this period, Eileen was no longer cutting classes, and, in spite of bitter and painful conflict with both her father and stepmother (described elsewhere) managed to finish high school.

Linda. Linda's brief psychotic decompensation, previously mentioned, occurred when, in her last year in high school, a small class in "communication" spent a week at a class member's house, where she was simultaneously exposed to and excluded from, sexual activity between two class members with whom she was emotionally involved. Just prior to this incident, the traumatic beating by her divorced father had occurred.

When she went to college, she left her dormitory after a few months and became part of a commune of three men and three women. The commune was simply called the "family." She described "feeling accepted no matter what I do" by the "family." A standard part of their greeting each other after any absence of a member was mutual hugging and kissing by all six members in a welcoming embrace. This was especially important to Linda. Needless to say, interpersonal complications also developed, but the "family" remained together for close to a year. Linda was aware that at the end of that school year, while the individual members made lavish promises to return to each other the next year, swearing they would never forget each other, they all really knew that they had "outgrown" their need for the "family." Indeed, Linda and several of the others found themselves in different cities the following year, and she had established a love relationship with an individual, rather than the family group.

Angela. The most complex substitute family structure encountered was created in the life of Angela, a resourceful, bright, and imaginative fourteen-year-old black girl. This family structure involved a whole community of peers, many of whom, like Angela, lived with only one parent, or with a mother and grandmother. When Angela, at age twelve, was finally told about her father, he welcomed her, and made it clear that he still considered her his daughter, although he could not actively involve himself in fathering her. When they accidentally met on the street, some time later, he took no initiative in attempting to maintain contact with her. Although Angela described this as "just natural" and in no way blamed him, she had lost interest in school the year after she found out who her father was, and then developed (among other symptoms) a number of fears about what a man might do to her. For example, when she was once riding in a cab with her grandmother and others, the cab driver offered to take them home, even though they had just a few cents less than the total cab fare. Angela assumed this meant that he would want to rape her, jumped out of the car while it was still in motion and made her way home through a snowstorm on foot—a two-hour trek. Shortly after this, she was unable to eat a hamburger at Burger King's, because she thought it would be poisoned. Although she had had a boyfriend when she was eleven and twelve, like many of her peers, she had broken up with him at that time because she wanted to have nothing to do with males. She suffered from nightmares that an ice pick was being jammed down her throat, so that she would wake up gagging and convinced she was going to die. In early months of therapy, she began to differentiate her sexual fears and fantasies from her feelings about the loss of her father in the household and the way these related to her terror that something dangerous would enter her mouth to kill her. Her mother, gifted in a field of art, had endured considerable hardships with resilience and continued love for her children. However, she had suffered from a period of immobilizing depression when Angela was a baby. At this time, the man living with her had taken an active role in feeding and caring for little Angela, until the birth of a new baby brother, Mick, when Angela was two. Three years later, he left the household, and Angela was cared for by a grandmother during the day. At that time, she was too young to be allowed the freedom of the streets and remembered it later as feeling "all alone." In therapy, she dwelt on this theme after her initial fears had subsided, and had times of feeling sad and tearful, allowing herself to "feel sorry for myself." These moods had a bittersweet quality to them; she would extend their duration by keeping a stack of records with sad lyrics. When her mother was out in the evening, she would play them, crying by the hour. During this time, she had fantasies of giving her father something he liked a lot, maybe better than the woman with whom he was living.

Here are some of the things she stated early in therapy:

Angela: "Ever since I was twelve, I knew I would die when I was fourteen, because fourteen is really being a teenager . . . I used to dream of growing up and mother would tell me that one doesn't need to depend on any one then. Then, I kept thinking a man was following us . . . that was the year after I found out about my father living with Joy and like I told you, I wouldn't get in a cab with anyone, not even my grandfather—only if my mother was there. I thought he would rape me."

t: "Were you missing your father those days?"

Angela: "I think I still feel closest to my father now—I held it against my mother that she never told me which one was my father—and let me think it was Mick's father when he lived with us. I mean she had differences with my real father, but I didn't. After a while I got scared, shy of asking her any more about him. I remember one time, when I liked him a lot and he wasn't living with us then; he took me by the hand and gave me five dollars. I didn't know anything then, so I didn't know why. He has a lot of kids and I don't blame him for being alcoholic now—I mean he had a job with his father and then his father died and he hasn't had any work since then. After mother did tell me, when I told him that I thought he was my father, he said, 'Yes, I'm your father and I love you,' and I forgave him everything."

"And the dude my mother went out with, I just don't like him in the same way, and I don't think she wanted to live with him either. She tells me not to have a boyfriend now, but she doesn't tell me about what happened with hers. Like, well one day me and Mick walked in the house and her clothes was on the floor and they was in the bedroom—and then they broke up, that's all. I think my mother doesn't want to depend on anyone any more."

Angela held steadfastly to the idea of some day having a house big enough to hold a "whole family," which was pictured as including an ever-changing number of aunts and uncles, nieces and nephews, and grandparents. She resisted early sexual activity, which many of her peers had already experienced, in line with her view that if she became pregnant this would foreclose her chance of finishing her education and would put her in the same position as her mother—having a baby (namely, herself) when she was too young to want to take care of it. Angela was convinced that her mother had not wanted her, though she had wanted Mick. "Mama ran away after she had me, and Gramma had to bring her back by force to take care of me. When Mick was born, she was nineteen already and everybody was happy and had a party."

Interviews with the mother revealed that she had actually been pleased with her pregnancy with Angela, once her own mother accepted it, but had suffered from severe depression during Angela's first year of life; she remembered the little girl's gurgling as the one thing that had made it worth opening her eyes in the morning. She had periods of staying in bed silently for much of the day, but remembered listening to the sound of the child gratefully, even though she felt unable to respond in kind. This image of the mother, immobilized and appearing lifeless in her depression, someone whom Angela wanted to wake to life, underlay some of Angela's own fantasies of helplessness and death.

Toward the end of the first year of therapy, as Angela dealt with these issues about her parents, she progressively solidified relationships with what she called her "play family." The "play family" was headed by a mother and father, aged sixteen and seventeen, who provided affection, reprimands, advice, protection from external threats and turmoil within the "real family," as well as a sense of being "trustworthy." Angela was the first daughter, and then other family members were added. Eventually, she had her own "play children" too, and felt some responsibility for them. There were fluid shifts between her play family and actual family members in her accounts. Here are some excerpts from her descriptions:

Angela: "In my play family, I have a daughter now too . . . I have three kids, a ten-year-old girl, ten-year-old boy, and eleven-year-old boy. I made my boy stop setting firecrackers yesterday."

"My father's mother called me to wish me a happy birthday—he's away now, but I think he has a job again. If I had money, I would buy my father a car and one for my play father and play uncle and one for me. I would build a house for my play family to all live and we would need fifteen rooms for all of us and my three children, too, of course. My play grandfather likes me and keeps trying to kiss me, you know, not like a grandfather, and I like him but not that way. But my play mother and father have been having trouble and that bothers me more. If they got a divorce, she said I would live with her and the boys would live with him. But in a way, I'm closer to him than to her, because she's so spoiled that he keeps having to do everything to make up with her."

The next session, she reports, "They broke up—and she's so crazy and greedy she's got another dude already—it's her fault they broke up. She said, 'Angie, you call your father to come back,' but she wouldn't talk to him and he said he loved her, but not unless she talks to him. I felt sorry for him and bad for her. When they broke up, my play brother ran away from home; his real father hit him, so he ran away and decided to stay with my play father. Now I have talked him into going back home again, making up with his real father."

t: "I know that their breaking up makes you feel deserted again, like when your mother broke up with Mick's father and told you he wasn't really yours anyway, and that you usually try to *do* something to see if you can stop it. What did you feel like *doing* this time?"

Angela: "Well, my boyfriend still wants to have sex, and I know I'm not ready, I try to tell him that, but he says he would take care of everything. But he told me he made this other girl have an abortion, because she is too young, and I would never want that."

She was aware of the temptation to have sex not only as part of her need for the security she derived from feeling taken care of, but also as a way of making a family in the face of her "play family's" disruption. She was in addition conflicted about a conscious wish to "give" her boyfriend a baby— particularly a baby boy—to prove that she cared about him. "I really want a son, a little boy to bring up—I hope I don't get a girl." Although a plan to have a child while single is now more often considered openly by girls who may be either white or black, among black people it is often shared by the boy, who sees it as the ultimate way of demonstrating his manhood. In contrast to the situation in the white culture, the adolescent black father often does not abdicate his responsiblity but often proudly acknowledges his baby and assumes some responsiblity for "taking care of" the girl and child, providing steady attention, and financial support when possible, etc. When he does not do this, the girl may consider herself unfairly deserted. However, sometimes she is the one who chooses not to continue the relationship or has another one that she prefers by the time the baby is born. Although the girl wants assurance that she will be "taken care of," I have seen little pressure toward marriage associated with the pregnancy. At times, the girl expresses reluctance to tie her future to the boy's through marriage, particularly if her own aspirations for a job or education in the long run exceed what she thinks is likely to be the boy's opportunity for education or employment. This was true of Angela, who like several of her peers, looked forward to having a baby as an important part of becoming a grown woman, though she was conflicted about when it should take place. She and her peers expected that a baby would always be welcomed without stigma in their family, and others' ideas about contraception and abortion were first treated with repugnance. Moreover, the girls were also aware of an ideological component (during the late 1960s and early 1970s). There was a strong feeling that the future of black people would be enhanced by increased black population, and that preventing the birth of a black baby would be against their racial self-interest. Some of these patterns have been perceptively described and illustrated by Ladner (1972). The increasing number of women in their twenties who opt to have a child without marriage present a somewhat different constellation of wishes and expectations.

On a personal level, it became apparent that Angela was reacting to the threatened loss of her "play family" with increased temptation to become a mother herself. She made plain her sense of loss that her "play father" was pushing her in a direction for which she had recently decided she wasn't ready, and said, "Even if they break up I'll still go to him sometimes. I mean if I'm his daughter, he'll just say 'that's my daughter,' and he'll tell me whenever he thinks I'm doing the wrong thing. Maybe I would know that he thinks that would be wrong for me, even without asking him. You know when my grandfather died, I had ESP, so I stayed in touch with him after that." By expecting to know the play father's values even without asking him, she was describing the manner in which they were becoming internalized.

Angela's relationships to her "play parents" remained stable and important to her for a long period of time, and any threatened changes in their roles were associated for her with a sense of loss of care. E.g., when her play father suggested that she become his girlfriend, even though he had been separated from her "play mother" for a while, her response included an implicit "incest taboo.": One day Angela came to her hour in tears and told me, "I'm afraid I'm losing my best friend, Kip—because he asked me to go with him. I told him I couldn't because I knew him too well—you know, it would be like going with my own father—he is more than a friend to me and I need him, Without him, I'm like by myself—I mean I've told him things I've told nobody else but you—things I could never tell my mother. If I went with him, he couldn't feel sympathy, it wouldn't be like that anymore. It was like he was made for me when I first knew him. Remember once, when I wanted to shoot up and he talked me out of it and stayed with me for a long time? He used to introduce me to his girlfriends and see first if I liked them and said I would have to approve of them, 'since you are my daughter.'" In other material, Angela made clear that while she could look to the image of a "father" for a protective, guiding and comforting support, in a boyfriend-girlfriend relationship she must be more cautious in her trust, and expected as a likely outcome that she would have to be the "strong" partner in the pair, and so no longer entitled to "sympathy."

Involvement in Fulfilling Parental Needs

The majority of adolescents seen were keenly aware of the unmet emotional needs of one or both parents. In some cases, the child felt both compassionate and in conflict over sympathy for both parents' positions, and slowly untangled his or her own sense of identity from those aspects of the parent which had led to their unhappiness (e.g., Eva. In others, the children took a firm stance about the extent to which they would involve themselves in their parents' difficulties, usually declaring that they did not want to "hear" any more of the parents' troubles than absolutely necessary. In some cases, the adolescent managed well under these circumstances, while in others a variety of symptoms, such as school failure and "lying," made their appearance (e.g., James and Connie).

When a child became definitely allied with one parent, there tended to be strong emotional pressures from that parent to maintain the intimacy. When this occurred with the parent of the opposite sex, either some symptoms of inhibition, e.g., phobias, tended to appear, or sexual expression, involving fantasies or some emotional link to the absent parent, were an aspect of development. Sarah exemplifies the inhibitions and phobias, Randolph the sexual relationship as a disguised quest for the absent parent.

Randolph. When Randolph was fifteen, a sudden disruption in father-son camaraderie occurred when father revealed his love affair with a young woman and left home. Both mother and son felt openly reproachful and angry with the father, while the boy suppressed his grief and longing for his relationship with the man he had previously emulated. Both deeply hurt beneath their bravado, they consoled each other with assurances that they preferred each other's company to his. His mother now turned to him in an intimate way, making him aware of her emotional frustration, and her expectation that Randolph would be nicer to her than his father. She seemed upset when Randolph went out with his friends, letting him know how lonely she was. She hinted that father perhaps disdained Randolph, as he disdained her. At a time in his development when Randolph needed to avoid awareness of sexual feelings in regard to his mother, as well as needing a supportive male identification figure, he was in an intolerable position. During this time he expressed, in a social studies class in school, his belief that men always hurt women and that women asked the impossible of men. Randolph appeared to deal with his dilemma by increasing his identification with the mother: she and he were in the same boat of needing love from a male. Secretly, however, he would succeed where she failed, thereby also revenging himself for the high cost of harmony which he felt his mother had extracted from him—namely that he would no longer seek out or love his father.

After almost a year, Randolph began a homosexual relationship with an older boy, the son of his father's best friend. His lover's father, not knowing the sexual nature of the relationship, befriended Randolph also, and was the chief source of news about the father's current well-being, as well as of nostalgic details of the two men's adventures together when they were Randolph's age. To this man, Randolph revealed his longing to have had such adventures, too. The man and his son assuaged Randolph's uncertainty about being rejected by his father for a time, but did not solve his problems. Randolph abhorred girls as being too dominating and aggressive, and felt deeply inadequate in their presence. However, he established a special friendship with two girls who were not romantically interested in him, but aroused his sympathy by telling him of their misfortunes with men. It was one of these girls, aware of his unhappiness, who brought him to therapy.

*Sarah.** Sarah differs from most of the sample of adolescents discussed here in detail, in that her parents had separated before she was ten years old. However, her father's move to an apartment of his own constituted a "trauma" for her in pubescence: it had strong symbolic meaning.

Sarah came for therapy at age twelve and a half: she had not eaten for five days and had also developed a fear of school. She had refused to be examined by the family doctor, a man, but was willing to talk with a woman therapist. The acute symptoms had followed a week's visit to her divorced father. Her parents had been divorced when Sarah was six, after the father had had a psychotic depression for which he was briefly hospitalized. The father reported that Sarah was the only one in the family who had shown affection at that time, and that it was she who kept him from killing himself. After the divorce, Sarah visited him every other weekend, and at these times, he had slept with her, until she was twelve. After the divorce, father had occupied the downstairs of his own mother's house. Before Sarah's outbreak of symptoms, he had suddenly decided to move out of his mother's house, and now had an apartment of his own. He celebrated this act of independence from his mother by buying and eating, for the first time in his life, a whole pound of bacon, which would have been strictly taboo in his mother's kosher household. The bacon made him sick and he vomited it, losing his appetite thereafter. In the next few days he repeatedly tried to gag himself, to vomit further. He told Sarah, who was visiting at this time, that now he was living alone he could marry a widow he knew, but that he really had a better time with Sarah. It was clear that for Sarah the taboo act of eating the bacon stood for other taboo things one might do away from mother. Sarah described how, as her parents were not on speaking terms, father would let her out of the car a block away, and she would "sneak into the house like a criminal." Characteristically, after visits to the father, Sarah would accuse her mother of not loving her, because

*Case material regarding Sarah has been previously presented in Tessman and Kaufman, 1969.

she would not take her out to dinner as father did. She would follow mother around, demanding more attention or complaining of various aches and pains. She would play with girls who came to her house, but was afraid to go to their houses lest she meet boys or big dogs on the street.

During the first interview it was possible to point out to Sarah that she seemed to be punishing herself for her split loyalties to her father and mother by suffering like the father and losing her appetite. She had complained that mother was mean to her by not buying her dinner. Now she was doing this to herself by not eating. I said that we would talk about the reasons she thought that she did not deserve food, so that she would not have to be so cruel to herself, and intentionally did not at this time touch on the various sexual and pregnancy fantasies underlying the eating disturbance. Sarah went home and ate. Within two weeks she also returned to school.

During the year and a half of treatment that followed, a history of childhood phobias and repetitive nightmares from ages six to ten emerged. Sarah had repeatedly dreamed of a man climbing in her window and carrying her away in his sack, attached to a big stick. Particularly in situations that represented a forbidden temptation or rivalrous victory over mother, she had had recurrent fantasies that some harm would come to her mother, who would leave her or die.

She had clung to mother throughout childhood, demanding reassurance about being loved. When Sarah was ten, mother remarried and Sarah bitterly resented her stepfather for "taking mother away from me." After the first year in treatment, she began attending church socials in spite of the presence of boys, but was always ready for retreat. For example, she excitedly looked forward to a hayride but managed to fall off the hay, causing the whole group to turn around and bring her home bruised. Thus she played out her fantasy of being the disgraced and fallen woman, not to be forgiven by her mother. By fourteen and a half she terminated therapy symptom-free, and was a happier, less inhibited person.

When she was in her early twenties, I heard from Sarah again. Her father had remarried some years previously and she saw him infrequently. She had been living "on my own" and apparently functioning well since graduation from high school, and tended to avoid spending much time at home where she still felt "criticized by mother, like a child." She came because of her indecision about whether to marry the man with whom she had fallen in love; he had just accepted a job in Colorado. Her description was of a mature love relationship. However, it seemed as though she wanted "permission" to commit herself to a heterosexual relationship and put distance between herself and home. She did decide to move with him, and married, informing her mother only afterwards in a long letter in which she detailed for the first time both her positive and negative feelings about each parent and the unnecessary burden of "guilt" she felt she had carried as the cost of her mother's approval. A short note to me a year later indicated that she felt she had made the right decision and was happy with her life and marriage.

Heather, Karen. In a number of cases, a pubescent daughter became closely allied with her mother's attitude toward the divorced father. Several courses of development could be discerned.

Continued mutual closeness short-circuited adolescent ego differentiation from the mother. These girls clung to an overpowerful image of the mother throughout adolescence, and were convinced that they could not become effective adults without her actual or symbolic protection. In spite of prepubescent periods of conflict with mother, they could not risk conflict or competition with her in adolescence. The issue of ego differentiation must be separated from identifications, as related to ego identity; in several of these cases a strong unconscious or conscious identification with the father existed and was fostered by the mother, and the girl became aware of needing to avoid a repetition of the parental interaction between herself and her mother (e.g., Heather and Karen). Both these girls postponed an emotional separation from the mother until after adolescence. Heather became symptomatic, but Karen appeared to function reasonably well, except for a one- or two-year period of school failure and cutting classes. At the end of adolescence, a reworking of their previous image of the father occurred in both cases. This happened after both girls at first transferred the need for an intense, exclusive devotion between themselves and their love partner from the quality of their earlier relationships to their mothers. For both, the threat of desertion by their love partners was associated with suicidal preoccupations or attempts in this context. They could not picture living without him.

As reality testing of the actual nature of the father progressed—this was, fortunately, possible in both cases—there were transformations in the quality of the love relationships the young women established. For a time (for Heather when she married and for Karen when she became committed to a career and to a man who treated her well), both girls made rather abrupt breaks with the mothers who had been so indispensable to them in adolescence. A more detailed description of aspects of the individuation process in both girls will be given in later excerpts.

SOME FAMILY STYLES OF COPING WITH STRESS, AND THEIR RELATIONSHIP TO THE ADOLESCENT'S DEVELOPMENT

The human support network most immediately relevant to the adolescent's ability to cope with the traumatic loss of a parent figure, or of the value previously attributed to that figure, was that provided by the remaining parent's own responses. The adolescent not only re-experienced his identifications with various "traits" of each parent—emulated, loved, or de-graded—but also identified with the processes used by the parents in assimilating identifications and in coping with stress. Thus, various family styles in the use of ego modes for tension discharge made their appearance in the ways of coping with losses and became part of the adolescent's character structure. After a period of time, often conflicts about the value of various ego modes in the life of the adolescent were tied to conflicts about the earlier identifications with one or both parents.

Impulsive Acting Out: The Wingers

The Wingers have been described previously as the family who jointly denied the mother's increasing illness from alcoholism, resulting in death from cirrhosis of the liver. The father reported that after her death all family members, at the advice of friends, tried to "get their minds off it" by traveling, remodeling the house, engaging in sports, etc. They tried to continue thinking of her as she had been before she changed from "happy and smiling" to unhappy and ill. Grief was something to be feared. The only described "grieving" member of the family, the dog, was removed. Grief would have been further complicated for the family by their unconscious guilt about their failure to intervene in her demise.

The oldest daughter, after about six months during which she "took care of" as many of the mother's functions as she could, saw herself as no longer needed by father or the family. Father involved himself in a frenetic array of activities which had the counterphobic quality of assuring him of his virility physical prowess, and aliveness. He simultaneously dated many women, although he declared himself serious about one of them, and involved himself in intensive sports, ranging from scuba diving and skiing to snowmobile and motorcycle racing. In a major remodelling of his house, he was impatient for materials, fired workmen, threatened law suits and cancelled orders if they were at all delayed. In the midst of this, he suffered a heart attack and was given orders to "slow down" in various areas of his life. He was so unable to tolerate the implications of this that, apparently, the day after his heart attack he sat propped up in his hospital bed, making managerial decisions about his business over two different telephones and drinking liquor, forbidden by his doctors, which a friend had smuggled into the hospital for him. When I first met with him about his children's problems a year later, he implied that he was afraid of death only by indicating that he had had a hard time believing the heart attack could have happened to him, and by continuing his death-defy-ing activities at an undiminished pace. In a similar way, when he talked of his wife's death, he alluded to her increasing dissatisfaction with activities which took him away from her, her "jealousy" over his flirtations and her implications that he was sexually inadequate. He countered this by saying that the women he has been seeing since her death could have told her she was wrong in this. They had, he said, been on the verge of divorce for two years. At the time of her death, he felt the most important thing was for "the rest of us to go on living," and acted accordingly.

When his daughter got into difficulty, he finally entered therapy himself with a skilled psychiatrist, but after a few sessions he quit. Over the next few months, he was increasingly away from home, and when he was home, was either out in the evening, asking his children to lie about his whereabouts if his fiancee called, or was home drinking too much. By this time, the children's need for a more stable and supportive human network was evident, and they both changed (after I recommended this) from a public to a private school which had flexible boarding facilities. Before his remarriage, Mr. Winger took the children out of treatment.

A year and a half after the marriage (he never slowed down), Mr. Winger died of a heart attack. When the boarding school contacted me about this, I was given the phone number of the stepmother, who had already sold the house and moved to another state, but was visiting that weekend. I called her to ask how she and the children were. She had not seen Eddy for some months, except at the funeral, and told me that Shirley was leading "a good life of her own," that over the past year she had had very little to do with the family. "She cut herself off," she said, " 'Cause for Shirley, it's Shirley first." Mrs. Winger could not talk long, since she had a date who did not like to be kept waiting.

Shirley, previously referred to, connected her mother's death to her own guilty premonitions and her "being able to get away with murder now." Although she at first described herself as "not close to my mother at all—I was closer to Dad," she was also aware that if mother were alive she would not be cutting classes and thereby "ruining herself." Her accident while speeding had finally brought her identification with the dead mother to the fore, and early interviews were taken up with her fear of letting herself react to her mother's death, with some clarification and amelioration of her guilt about her own role, and some support and admiration for the way she had coped with the family's needs after her mother died. We discussed ways of dealing with her need to make up stories about why her mother had died in order that the other kids would not look down on her "as loud and stupid and doing crazy things." Shirley had experienced peers and their families shying away from her already, before mother's death, when they "guessed" the problem with alcoholism.

With Shirley's cooperation, a program was set up with the school counselor, so that Shirley's class-cutting would be "noticed," and she would be called in to discuss it whenever it occurred. The third week, Shirley came in furious after the guidance counselor talked with her about the matter. "She said that she thought I was looking for attention, like I can't be on my own.

That really got me steamed!" She was then able to discuss how much she despised dependency in herself; we related this to the abrupt way she had had to change from being "a kid with a mother waiting at home" to acting, literally, as though she were all on her own. She mentioned her fondness for the teachers of her freshman year.

Shirley: "The class was very small and the teacher good; she explained everything. She wasn't a softy ... I mean, you couldn't get away with everything; she would notice if you weren't there. I wasn't afraid to speak up in class then either. Now I always think the kids will know I'm stupid or too loud ... You know ... the kids are not friendly any more. That started, like, before mother died ... they look me up and down ... I don't think I ever really depended on my mother, I mean, like I couldn't talk to her."

t: "How come?"

Shirley: "Well, Eddy was my mother's favorite and he depended on her. I ran to mother if I was hurt though, I knew she would always be around or would leave someone else to be. Then after she died, I had to grow up real fast. People would say, 'you're a big girl now,' and call me 'little mother.' I kind of liked that, with my father depending on me a lot ... till I found out how hard it was doing the work and the cooking. Then my father got a couple to be the housekeepers, but he was out most of the time then."

t: "So you felt invited to be the 'little mother' and you felt good about being needed like that ... although I bet it also felt strange about it being *you* and not your mother there ... but then you got left behind in a different way ... this time by your father."

Shirley: "Yea, my father really looked like he was having a good time after a while ... and it was most of the time without me or Eddy."

The next week she reported: "I only skipped a couple of classes this week, that's less than any time this year." She commented on her fear of her father's reckless driving, and revealed: "You know what I said about never being close to my mother isn't really true."

t: "I thought from the way you talked about the little dog who followed her around and felt so empty afterwards, that sometimes you must have felt close to her, too."

Shirley: "Well, I used to go to the beauty parlor with her all the time and go shopping; she used to buy clothes for me and dress us nice, Eddy too. If something went wrong with me and she was alive, I know I could go to her."

t: "But she is not alive any more! You hate to picture that, but then some of the things you do ... the things that make you scared of dying, remind you of it in other ways. So maybe letting yourself think of it is better instead of having to do ..."

Shirley: "Stuff like the night I crashed into that lady and thought I was dead, punished for life."

t: "Somewhere in you, you must have thought that you ought to be dead and punished for life for what happened to your mother. You know, Shirley, you didn't make your mother die."

Shirley: "When I thought about it most, was that night *before* she actually died. I kept thinking about whether I would wear black, and I kept thinking of each of my teachers coming up and saying how sorry they were and maybe putting their arms around me . . . being let out of school the day of the funeral and everybody being extra nice to me. And then I thought, but if she were alive I would get a big birthday party—she always loved big parties and she always made me a cake—that was stupid because I'm too old to care about stuff like cakes and I can always buy one."

t: "But it's not stupid or bad to want to daydream about people being nice to you and comforting, or birthday cakes . . . it's just human."

Shirley: "Before she died . . . my mother used to always love cooking . . . and then she started not even doing that . . . and complaining about my father all the time . . . and I didn't want to hear. I just wanted to be off with my friends."

t: "So you're telling me that somehow you *knew* something was wrong and ran away from it because it made you angry . . . the way you said your father runs away from everything. You picture her as someone you could always run to when something was wrong, and you feel bad about not doing the same for her."

Shirley put her head in her hands and for the first time I heard her cry.

Shirley: "Before we moved here when I was eleven, things were different. We were like a family then."

The next session, Shirley reported she had not cut any classes, but was so far behind that she wouldn't catch up. There was nothing at home to make her want to study. She was thinking of going to New York because her boyfriend was there. She asked her father if she could go for his birthday, but he said no. The he took off on a flight to see his girlfriend.

Shirley: "I wanted so much to leave on the next flight to see my boyfriend, but I didn't have the money and couldn't charge it. I kept seeing myself getting hijacked or something."

Her father, she said, did not want her to keep the same boyfriend for a long time. When they had gone on a trip to California last New Year's, father kept pushing her to go out with other boys, but she did not want to; she and her boyfriend had decided not to go out with others while he was away at junior college this year. When her brothers had parties, her father let them have three or four girls in the bedroom at the same time. He told them there was "safety in numbers." She was aware that he, too, might find "safety" in numbers of girlfriends at present, but did not want to imitate his way. She said, "I'm more like my mother that way." This was her first reference to a positive likeness to mother, rather than to being like her in being "ruined."

We talked about her wish for "safety" from things she might want to do, but would be sorry she did afterwards. How could we build this into her life, now that she could not look to mother for this any more?

Shirley: "When he goes away for the weekend, he says not to use his car; so I tell him to take it to the airport and leave it so . . . I know that's the only way I won't be tempted."

Her attitude toward school was similar: "It would be a lot better not to have open campus, so I won't get tempted to cut. I really still hate it; I don't care what the teachers think of me, except my sewing teacher. I mean, they're not interested in a person."

t: "As a matter of fact, we should keep that an open question, about what school would be best for you now . . . you need people who are interested in what happens to you. Is your feeling about the teachers not caring at all like when your dad goes off for the weekend without the family?"

Shirley: "Well, there's this thing I noticed, that I thought about since last week. See, I've been promised a new car in the spring, 'cause of my other one being wrecked and I've been driving very careful now. I noticed after the accident that my father never told me to drive careful with my car, he just doesn't let me use *his* anymore. *He is afraid the car will get wrecked more than about me.* With my mother it was the same thing . . . she had the car I'm using till my new one comes and that was okay to mess up, but his car would be spotless and he wouldn't let anyone touch it, he never let her touch it."

t: "And you don't want to be treated like she was by him; you're wondering how much he is able to care about who gets wrecked. Maybe he sometimes gets so busy having to prove that nothing will happen to him, that he has a hard time seeing and caring about others when they need him."

Shirley: "Yea, and there's something else too. . . . I don't want to lie for him anymore."

She revealed that for years she had cooperated not only in "telling lies for him" to others, such as customers, but had had a counterpart in her own relationship to him. She would do something forbidden, and wait in excited expectation that, no matter how hard she tried to hide the truth, he would find her out and "get mad." If he didn't bother to find out, it was a sign to her that he didn't care; this usually led to intensified efforts. He forgave her easily, in contrast to his anger at the boys, and she savored this difference. After forgiving her he usually gave her extra spending money. As Shirley put it, "I'd feel guilty and leave clues for dad to find out. A lot of things I get away with, a lot not." This was her own style of courting danger.

As Shirley reviewed some of these events she came to the conclusion that his anger at finding his rules broken had to do with his need to feel approved by her rather than with her welfare per se. When the three adolescents had a party during one of her father's absences, they raided his liquor cabinets. Shirley was "scared of drinking" and stuck to ginger ale; but Eddy was drunk. When father discovered this, he was furious, and "grounded" the kids until they and their friends had paid him back the full amount needed to replace the liquor. However, he did not ask them not to drink.

I had a conference with father at this point, hoping that he might return to his psychiatrist, and to plan with him about more external supports for the children. He liked the idea of a particular private school as being helpful to both his children, in having sufficient staff to enable them to catch up with their grade level and to involve them in after-school activities as well. I was outspoken about the childrens' need to be honest with themselves and the school (this had been his chief complaint about them originally); I pointed out that this was connected with the freedom not to have to make up excuses for him to his girlfriends or customers. I was clear about his continued importance to his children, and said that, although the feelings about his wife's death were unpleasant enough that I was not surprised he wanted to get away from it all, for the children this also meant he was getting away from them; this was one reason that they were reacting with hurt and anger. Surprisingly, he told Shirley that I had talked with him about her no longer needing to make up excuses to Rita; he was, he said, at the point of considering marriage to Rita. A private school visit was arranged; Shirley liked it, and planned to transfer shortly. Eddy followed suit the following autumn.

In therapy, Shirley for the first time discussed her future interests in detail. She was interested in designing clothes and wanted to take as many art and sewing courses as she could. Both she and her mother always loved clothes, and she had a flair for design. She added, "And I asked Dad for a tutor in vocabulary for the next few weeks . . . I know I'm not a reader because I really can't sit still long enough . . . but at my house my friends use words that I've never heard before, and I finally want to do something about that. I think I can learn something now."

She described herself as "not so bothered" when father "blows his stack, I take it less personal."

A few weeks later, after having transferred to the other school, she reported, "I'm doing so much better it's not even funny! I like the kids and the teachers. I'm already all caught up in classes except in science. It's not open classroom, so there's really no way to cut. The kids aren't snobby like I was afraid they would be in a private school, some of them are having extra tutoring too. The teachers don't mind sticking around after school if you have trouble with anything." In the same hour:

"I told my father he should get married to Rita already. At least that would be another person to take care of things, but he says he's afraid his life would be monotonous. Eddy and Clyde and I all agree about Rita. When she's up for the weekend, he's calmer and she doesn't try to tell us what to do. None of us could stand Gail (an earlier girlfriend both children had complained about); she was just after his money anyway; she thought she was such a hot ticket."

Shirley's relationship to her own boyfriend solidified as his return home for the summer approached. She reviewed all the "fun" they had had together, but, interestingly, began to wonder whether they would be able to "talk to each other" enough to stay serious. As the phone bills from their conversations mounted, father suddenly forbade her to make any more calls to him. She developed her own system of calling by giving a false credit card number. When the phone company finally traced the calls and her father was informed, "he really blew his stack at me, screaming at me, 'you dumb broad, why did you have to make those calls from where they can trace them; if you'd done it from a phone booth you could have gotten away with it.'" She reviewed his style of morality and its consequences.

Shirley: "The way he figures, something is wrong if you get caught at it, and not otherwise. That's how I must have been figuring for a long time too, like about cutting in school and a lot of stuff I've done to see if I could get away with it or if he would catch me. And remember, I kind of wanted to get caught all the time. Maybe my mother went the same way, wanting somebody to stop her, to *make* her go to the doctor . . . and it did her no good not to decide for herself what was good for her."

The next session, Shirley reported: "I would feel so much better if I didn't have to sneak for my father. He's weird; he's like playing with my mind. Sometimes he's so liberal and we get away with everything and there's no one around to watch us since mother died . . . and then all of a sudden he cracks down like mental—everything goes back and forth so drastically, you can never figure ahead. I think he's got to make himself out like he's better than me to shut me up. Now when he threatens me I say as soon as I get away from him I'm on my own and will be deciding for myself. He's always got a threat for us, but next year I'm eighteen and could leave the house.

"He and Rita are going to get married this summer, but he's still having other dates. Things have been lousy with him and he's constantly at me. He fights with everyone; he fired the housekeeper and the tutor Eddy likes. I've been going to science every day after school to catch up and when I come home he yells at me, 'You're never around any more when things need to be done.'"

t: "It sounds like he is having a rough time, too, about the changes since your mother died. He may be feeling he's losing you in some way now, too; now that you're not influenced so much by what he thinks and now that he is getting married to Rita . . . except that he doesn't know how to express that sense of loss . . . I wish he could, and that's why the school and I tried to get him to see Dr. X . . . it might have made it better for him, as well as for you and Eddy."

Shirley: "Well, I want to work this summer to make some money, so I won't have to depend on my father for everything . . . right now I want to have as little to do with my father as possible. I think I don't want to end up like either my mother or father."

Eddy. Eddy has been previously described as holding onto the image of his mother as smiling and happy. Where his sister, Shirley, eventually brought up considerable guilt about the death of the mother, Eddy felt more responsible for the father's first heart attack.

Eddy: "My father's heart attack—it was caused by the birthday party he gave for me last year. I didn't want one; I'd rather have just had the family do something—but he wanted me to have it and he had to order all the catered stuff at the last minute and really worked himself up. It happened the next day. The day after the heart attack, nobody could tell he was sick. There he was with the radio and TV on at the same time, with a couple of phones and a bar in his room."

t: "Where did you get the idea that the heart attack was caused by that party?"

Eddy: "I'm not sure but my father says I'm the one who always makes for extra trouble in the house. He's always said that, but my mother used to stand up for me." We discussed the causes of heart attacks, trying to separate the cause from the "timing" of the attack, the day after Eddy's birthday. A long-standing antagonism between the two was evident, particularly when Eddy chafed against his father's expectations of him. Since some of father's ambitions for Eddy were unrealistic, at least in terms of the boy's past functioning and psychological test data, Eddy's image of his future self also reflected his struggle over what was "fake" versus what was "real," with an undertone which characterized the family ideology: it seemed that whatever won was, ultimately, what was real; however, for Eddy, not only power but the quality of "treating each other right" was emerging as a wish and value, still expressed in monetary terms. Such ends justified "fake" means.

Eddy: "I might be a wrestler, even though it's fake. You get $400 a match. I mentioned that to my father and he made fun of me. 'That's for a bum,' he says, 'you'll turn out to be a bum.' But I know a wrestler who is not a bum, I mean they really treat each other right. There's this one I know who won and then gave a $200 jacket to the other. I consider a bum a guy who comes out of a bar all drunk; a wrestler is probably a lot cleaner than my father."

About school, he said: "I don't want to get suspended any more. If I try to explain to Dad how it is there he acts like I'm trying to take over his business. He thinks a lot of what I do is stupid or crazy. Like he wants me to be a big genius and I'm not. I'm not going to sit around or have a business, all I'm trying to do in school is win my rights. If I didn't stick up for my rights with the gym teacher, he'd really make a sucker out of me. Maybe boarding school is a good idea because my father and I fight so much. I think the school is afraid of him too . . . The guidance counselor can talk to him, but I don't think she can bring up things like he says you did, about the stuff about my mother and him and how it still affects us and that he should be talking to someone too. I don't know why you weren't scared of him. With me, if I say one word wrong, he goes mental, like crazy."

A few weeks later:

t: "And does your Dad pay attention when you are not in trouble?"

Eddy: "I don't know, not much. I mean I wonder what the hell he'll do if I get new friends. My friend Dick and I decided yesterday not to hang around with the other guys any more, to find new friends who get in trouble less. If he doesn't notice in two weeks I've changed then I'm getting in trouble again and I don't care if I get kicked out of school."

t: "What are the new guys like?"

Eddy: "They're the ones who play ice hockey most of the time and a couple of them are gonna help me fix up my motor scooter. They don't just sit around drinking beer and smoking grass or getting into fights."

About possible boarding-school plans, he said: "Yea, I'd like a school where I can have some friends and not walk around like a total stranger all day."

As he improved his grades the following months, with the aid of a tutor, he said: "Things are so-so; my father is always in a lousy mood. He's always had this big thing about grades, now I'm getting good grades and he's still mad. About my tutor—I like him, but my father thinks he's a jerk and wants to get rid of him. He teaches me more than school, he is a patient guy. I mean I know he will still be sitting there when I finish the problem."

t: "And that's one of the things you wish about your father?"

Eddy (laughs): "Yea, but I couldn't see him being like that."

t: "I think you're right that being patient is a big problem for him; he seems to feel that he has to get on top of a situation in a hurry, even though he may be scared underneath."

Eddy: "Two weeks after my mother died, he said he would be married again in two years, he would take a bet on that."

t: "How did you feel about that?"

Eddy: "I don't know. I thought of my mother, she used to go skating with us sometimes, I couldn't see someone else doing that."

t: "You must have missed her so terribly!"

A silent nod. It was not the time to push further about this. I only said: "It must be awful for you to face your pain about that, while at the same time things at home are still in such a tangle."

The following session, he reported an interesting change in the connection he was able to make between "thinking" and "doing". Consistent with this was the fact that his acting-out rather than goal-oriented activity had diminished, as reflected in his interest in changing his group of friends. The image of the "patient" tutor from whom he was learning, as opposed to the "impatient" father whom he was beginning to identify as having difficulty delaying action, related to this change also. Subsequent to this change, his capacity to tolerate memories rose.

Eddy: "It's funny, it's different when I feel tempted to skip class. For some reason, I'm not ever skipping right now ... I think first of getting caught ... I mean the thought comes in my head first and I tell myself 'forget it.'"

t: "And how did it used to be?"

Eddy: "I used to be on my way already without ever thinking about it."

After this, Eddy began to recover some early memories about being "deceived" by his older brother, who always outsmarted him.

Eddy: "When we would get two bags of candy from my mother we would put them together ... We would eat half and then Clyde would say, 'We ate your half, so now get out of here,' and I would believe him!" From this, he went to his early relationship with father, whom he had always believed was the smartest and most powerful man there was. Sadism was a part of this picture: one either participated or became a victim. He described past summers at camp, "My brother and I were known as the trouble makers and we'd find out who squealed and bash them over the head. We killed frogs and put them in guys' beds, took down the flag pole and hid it. Last summer, we caused the most trouble. We beat up a lot of guys without any reason ... and the counselors and we had a couple of fights. A kid was noisy, so I smacked him, hit him over the head with a tennis racket. They hated us. When my father came, all the kids were afraid he would come in there with a gun—they thought he would beat them up, but he just kind of walked around. ... They should have thrown us out when we got there, but they were afraid to lose their reputation. We were trying to get thrown out since we got there."

t: "The stuff about your father with a gun and beating guys up ... was that ever something you thought ... that he could do it to you ... so you always had to be prepared ... you'd rather beat up someone else first than have it happen to you?"

Eddy: "If we did the beating up, I think he was prouder of us."

t: "And you wanted so much to have him be proud of you?"

Eddy: "Well, Clyde and I won over some of his counselors because they thought my father would pick a fight."

t: "You mean that he would be like you, or that he would defend you?"

Eddy: "That he would be like us. Clyde and I tied a kid to a tree and left him there. He thought it was a joke and that we would let him go, but we didn't because he was just a pain in the ass. Dad thought that was really funny; he liked that."

t: "Tell me about the kid who was a pain in the ass."

Eddy: "Actually, the counselors really hated the kids so they didn't care what we did to them . . . The kids were a pain, yelling and crying and stuff like that."

I said quietly, "And how about yourself as a kid, when you were little?"

He blushed, an unusual response for him.

Eddy: "I know my parents had it with us, they would send us to our rooms when we did stuff like that. But they picked on Clyde and me more. I remember once my mother said to the baby sitter, 'The boys go to bed at nine and Shirley goes at ten.' Then she whispered to the sitter that Shirley really goes at eleven. So we *caught* her at it." (This was the first negative memory of mother he had brought up.)

t: "You mean putting one over on you, too? That must have hurt your feelings, because you kind of expected it from Clyde and your father but you counted on your mother in a different way."

Eddy: "My father probably got frustrated with my mother because she drank so much that she couldn't remember anything. I mean sometimes she was smiling, but *she wasn't looking at anybody, if you know what I mean.*"

He sought my eyes desperately at this point, and there was suffering in his face.

t: "So there were moments when you walked around like a stranger, as you've put it . . . even before your mother died."

We sat together in silence.

The next few months were dominated by a number of themes. He now recalled that:

Eddy: "My mother drank heavy all day I think, I mean she had to have a cocktail before coffee in the morning . . . It's funny that I never knew till last fall about my mother, even when you told me and father then told me it was true, it's like I knew she was always holding a glass, but I still never thought of her that way. I made up stuff about her looking happy, but that was really when we were little, before we even had the swimming pool."

t: "It wasn't *all* made up because you remember her loving you and being nice and your loving her back when you were little and you'll always be able to keep that feeling because it really happened; it was later when she got unhappy and had too much trouble drinking to be able to keep things that way, that you felt so lonely you wanted to kid yourself about everything being okay still."

He came to differentiate "kidding himself" from "putting one over on somebody" and from "lying" out of fear of punishment. "Kidding myself" he most vehemently rejected: he saw it leading to frightening consequences. He talked of a friend of his father who had just died "of the same thing as mother," yet "my father is still kidding himself that it can't happen to him." A number of times, he "kidded himself" about his school work. He would get a B in a quiz and then be very surprised when he later flunked the course because he did not continue to keep up with it. Regular meetings with the guidance counselor were set up so that they could jointly keep track of his actual situation in each course.

Eddy's relationship with his father did not show much change, and the two continued to lock horns over a variety of issues. He told of a friend who had been to jail a couple of times, whose mother was blind, and whose "father just took off" without trying to get his son out of jail. We took this up, in terms both of his feelings about his father leaving his mother in the lurch when she needed him, and his wondering whether father would come and get him out of jail if necessary. He decided that it was not worth trying to find out; that it wouldn't prove anything anyway. Father needed to have things his own way; he reported, "so my father says, 'you're going to have your hair cut the way I like it,' and I say 'I'll get out of my chair,' and he says, 'I'll flatten you if you do.'"

One of the factors making it possible for Eddy to loosen his investment in a provocative interaction with his father was the improvement in his relationships at school. For example, he described the gym teacher:

Eddy: "Remember the coach who used to give me all that trouble? Well, we're friends now. He shows me a lot of good moves, how to get out of a hold with another kid."

t: "I've noticed that you're friends now with a bunch of people, where things started as a fight."

Eddy: "Yea, I think I'm figuring now that if I keep at it, then they will start acting different too...like Mr. Steel (the gym teacher)."

t: "You used to feel that either they would smash you or you would have to smash them; now you are letting them help you get strong, like you want in wrestling."

Eddy: "Yea, that's what I found out. If you start working, then they help you work hard and everything goes along pretty good. It's not like they have to trick you to show you they're better. I mean they kid around and tease, but not to make you feel lousy. It isn't like that with my father maybe, but Mr. Steel's a different sort of guy, I found out. With my father, I still feel helpless, because if he hits me and I hit him back, he'll put me out of the house. If I ever work with my dad in his company, I just have to figure for that ahead of time, figure whether it'll be worth it. I don't think Rita will calm him out of that when they get married because my mother really never could either."

Grieving had not been possible in this family. The pattern for both parents had been toward immediate gratification, avoiding pain, and denying things they feared, with counterphobic reactions. This pattern was most clearly seen in the father. The family morality, which included chronic lying and manipulation, was in accordance with Kohlberg's (1971) "preconventional" stage, and involved an early stage of images of human relationships, based on a power versus weakness model. The constriction of personal growth to this level was accompanied, in the father, by an inability to empathize with and to care for the needs of the children, in spite of the fact that he was involved with and attached to them.

Shirley avoided thinking about her mother's death until her own driving accident, which had meaning in the context of her prediction to a boy that he would "kill himself" if he drove so fast. In that sense, her fast driving was an acting out with unconscious suicidal meanings. When Shirley landed in the hospital where her mother had died, she first blamed the hospital for "murderous" neglect, and then herself. Eventually, once she was able to admit her sense of guilt and to grieve, she was also able to consider the contribution of each parent's personality to what had happened. In addition, she had to deal with the social "shame" connected with her mother's death.

Aware that no effort had been made to stop her mother by external intervention, Shirley knew that she herself needed external controls (of driving, cutting classes, doing homework) to keep from "ruining herself." She interpreted the absence of these as a lack of caring; neither she nor her father, she felt, had cared enough about mother to override her veto about the need for medical or psychiatric care, and the denial.

Her correct "premonitions" about both her mother's death and a boy's accident, and her wishful fantasies of people being nice to her after the death, were based on negated perceptions available in the preconscious. The angry aspect of such fantasies (the image that "someone else would be nicer to me than you are") had to do with the preference she felt for her father, who "spoiled" her, and her anger at mother for "spoiling" and preferring Eddy. She pictured their relationship as one in which she could "do things," but not "talk to" her mother. In view of this image, it was interesting that one of the first areas in which she initiated seeking change was the wish for a "vocabulary tutor," to help her become a person more capable of verbal interchange.

When Shirley was able to mourn (more briefly than most of the adolescents seen), this was both for her mother and for the loss of her own previously envisioned future, ruined by mother's desertion of her. After this, she considered the ways in which she was really also deserted by her father, e.g., when he forbade her the use of his car but showed no concern for her driving safely in her own, and scolded her, not for doing wrong, but for being caught. She began to feel he could not care for her as a person, and became more reluctant to tie her own well-being to his.

Both children tried to improve their grades (poor school performance had been one of father's presenting complaints) and found that this gained them nothing with him. When they copied his style of delinquency, they were made to feel inferior, rather than guilty when they got caught, unlike him.

Once Shirley's changed school situation allowed for more protective and supportive surroundings, and she had begun to deal with the loss of her mother, she built her aspirations on what she and her mother had shared in their most positive moments together: mother loved to dress her up and Shirley wanted to become a dress designer. At the same time, her desire to communicate better with friends, with the help of a tutor, meant a change in relation to a shared, but unspoken, family feeling of educational inferiority, which seemed to contribute to their difficulties in a new neighborhood which they could now, financially, afford but where the educational level was, on the average, higher than the one they had shared with their neighbors previously. With "success," the whole family had lost a previously supportive human network. In picking a school for Shirley, care was taken not to place her again in an environment which might extrude her on this basis. It is interesting that although her relationship with her boyfriend continued into the summer, she did not wish to "rush things" and became ambivalent when they had "little to say to each other."

Eddy needed to hold on to the image of the "smiling, happy mother" until he could begin to extricate himself from his comfortless reality. For many years, he had tried to emulate the sadomasochistic view of human relationships that he perceived in his father. Although effectively this mirrored his real experience with his father, who was deeply ambivalent toward him, his concrete and exaggerated visions of violence—such as that of his father coming to camp with a gun, and his own aggressiveness at camp, were efforts to shield his own dependency and sense of aloneness with a veneer of anger. He assumed, it is clear, that such dependency would render him helpless to the parents' rejection. Once he had faced what he had experienced as parental rejection, he could bring up his ideas about the way each parent had, in a sense, deserted the other in need, as well as deserting him. He was then able to focus on what had "really" happened, and to differentiate various ways of manipulating the "truth" from the mechanism of "kidding myself" which had led both him and his parents into considerable difficulty with themselves.

Because the home continued to remain essentially unsupportive to the development of ego mechanisms through which he could continue to grow, and because he was both improving at school and showing sporadic signs of utilizing new male identification figures (his gym teacher at school) in a constructive way, a shift to a boarding school was planned for him in the fall. His own observation that he gave up cutting classes when he came to a point of cognitive change—that is, when he "thought about it before doing it"—was an interesting one, and heralded his increasing tolerance for emerging memories, affects and a reworking of past cognitive foreclosure.

The fact that both Eddy and Shirley attended therapy sessions without ever "cutting" them was probably related to their great need for a reliable and supportive female in their lives. Their mother had actually filled this role during their early childhood, thus making it possible for them to utilize such a relationship without great initial distrust.

Neither adolescent remained in therapy long enough for the negative aspects of the transference to emerge fully and for them to come to terms with their remaining anger at their mother. It was not long before the father's continued headlong flight from fear and grief, apparently inaccessible to interruption, ended in the further tragedy of his death, another loss for the children, difficult to bear. I continue to feel concern for their future well-being.

The Consoling Alliance:
Postponement of Grief and of Individuation

In a number of cases, divorce was followed by the formation of a consoling protective alliance between mother and adolescent daughter. Although this provided the pair with some emotional support for dealing with the painful feelings associated with disappointment in the man, there were major disadvantages for the daughter's development, in three major areas:

1. The daughter became overdependent on the mother for emotional sustenance, and did not risk adolescent individuation because it would endanger closeness to mother. This resulted in continued feelings of incompleteness and inadequacy without the mother.

2. To maintain the alliance, positive features of the father had to be denied, while negative features with which the daughter identified became a deeply degraded aspect of her self-image.

3. Growth in the areas of reality sense, associated with reality testing, was stymied by the need to maintain the stereotyped image of the father. The daughters experienced this in the form of a certain falsity about some aspects of their situation, or an exclusion from the reality of "what is really going on." In addition, the sexualization of the adolescent girl's relationship to mother became a complication.

Illustrations of this pattern will be taken from Heather and Karen. Both girls postponed their grief and longing for the father until the end of adolescence. At that time, and in their early twenties, they lived out components of their grief in their love relationships with men, and put a sudden forceful distance between themselves and their mothers. It must be said that in neither case did the mother foresee what difficulties would be associated with the alliance for their daughters. They tended to see the daughters' situations vis-a-vis the fathers as being like their own, and assumed that they were offering the kind of support and comfort they, too, wished to have.

Heather. I first met Heather after she had been absent from high school for six weeks during her senior year and was sleeping at least fourteen hours a day. When not sleeping she still felt fatigued, depressed, and not sure there was anything worthwhile to live for. Medical findings were negative. High school reports described her as isolated, contemptuous of others, and needing always to get the highest grade. Since she was very bright, this had usually been easy for her. Her parents had separated a year before, and she and her brothers had moved with their mother to an apartment. She and mother shared a room and she liked it that way. The summer before I saw her, she had gone to camp, but had to be brought home within a week. She feared crowds. Heather told me in the first interview that she hated the city and would like to live alone in the country. Her horse was still with her father and she went to visit him (the horse) there, often leaving the barn without seeing father. Her horse was used to being alone. However, this week, there was another horse in the barn and her horse might get attached to him. That would be bad, because he had always been so independent. Initial descriptions of threats experienced currently, that is, "this week," are often good clues to transference fears; she was warning me that emotional involvement was a threat to her.

t: "Would it lead to trouble, this getting attached?"

Heather "Yes, it's much better to be independent. For instance, I know I never want to get married because I want to live away from people."

t: "What happens when you are with people?"

Heather "It's very *disgusting* . . . last week I went to a folk dance festival . . . my mother thought I should do something . . . girls gave way to primitive impulses . . . yelling and everything . . . I wasn't sure what. But I don't want to be around such things."

t: "You get disgusted when others look like they are out of control; being able to control yourself must be important to you."

Heather: "It is."

She described her pride and pleasure in exacting obedience from her horse. She did not tell me that riding was the one important activity she had engaged in with her father. She did tell me that two years before she used to pretend to be a horse herself and was able to get another girl to take turns being horse and rider with her. They played this by the hour.

Heather: "Now everyone at high school is different, and I think they are despicable."

t: "Are there times in your life now that seem good to you?" I asked about what was good in her life, because, knowing how depressed she was, I wanted both of us to have a sense of what positives we could build on before further opening up her problems.

Heather: "The only good times are when mother and I talk. Mother tells me a lot about father, how aloof he is and how lonely she was while they were married."

t: "How did *you* feel about your parents separating?"

Heather: "Happy. I wanted it ever since mother thought of it—things had been getting worse for years with the tension. Mother seemed unhappy ever since I was born. I used to think it was my fault, when she was tired or not as understanding as I wanted. Once at the breakfast table we were naughty and she threw down a plate crying. I followed her to her room and asked, 'What's the matter?' but she wouldn't tell me. More often, she tried to help me. But now she tells me a lot, I mean about how unhappy my father made her. We make fun of him together; she told me he was just like a dried-up mushroom more than a man. She said I didn't get a response from my father because he covers his feelings so, that he is not unhappy at all."

This was not true. I met with the father and found that although he was a highly intellectual and controlled person, he was in fact desperately unhappy, and for a time had the notion that if he just continued to live in the family house, his wife and children would somehow return to him. Eventually, he gave up this idea and after some years remarried. Heather's mother, in spite of her assertions to the daughter that her father did not feel unhappy, was meanwhile concerned enough that he might be suicidal to attempt to arrange psychiatric care for him. Heather's awareness that she was being made privy to less than the whole truth had been with her for some time, but expressed itself in a sense of inadequacy. For example, when she was younger, she had started to join the Campfire Girls. She said, "But at the meeting, I felt left out . . . I thought there were spies who looked like me but were really much more able . . . and they didn't tell me what they knew . . . like what to do in Campfire Girls, what was really going on." She withdrew after the second meeting. Much later, in her twenties, and just before a second period of therapy she had similar feelings after being absent one session in a lab course in college, that "they all seemed to know what they were doing and looking at me as though I were an idiot." She dropped the course in spite of her superior grades.

In relation to these perceptions of herself, we were eventually, during the second period of therapy able to look at the role of disdain and contempt in her life. Disdain was a way to maintain a needed distance from others and their impulses (lest they arouse her own); it was also a mechanism she and mother used in talking about father. By ridiculing him, they took revenge, protecting themselves from the feelings associated with what they perceived as his rejection of them. However, beneath this lurked Heather's contempt for herself, associated with the expectation that she too would be a victim of derision and ridicule by others. In this and other characteristics (her "aloofness" and self-controlled nature) her identification with mother's view of the father came to the fore. Having truly felt ignored by her father, in contrast to her brothers, she clung to her mother, fearing that if she was like father, mother would discard her as well.

Although Heather paid little attention to her father during her adolescence, a telltale sign of her attachment remained in the form of the horse, who was still stabled at his home. Although varieties of love for horses are almost ubiquitous in adolescent girls who have access to horses, the pretense of actually being the horse occurs in only a small minority at this age. Initially, she stressed the importance to her of strict control of the horse and its self-sufficiency, but eventually became aware of her wish for father to care more for the horse (he had promised to build a better stall and hadn't done so), and for him to be its rider.

Discussion of further work with Heather during high school will be omitted in order to focus on her later development. Therapy was difficult for her initially because she expected to feel exposed as inadequate and ridiculed, and because her dependency feelings, saved exclusively for her mother, were so dangerous to her. I was cautious, knowing that her defense structure must not be undermined while she still was so afraid of her impulses. Although she rapidly returned to school and stayed in therapy until graduation, both mother and daughter resisted changes in their exclusive relationship, e.g., they ignored the recommendation that Heather sleep in a room of her own, for which space was available.

She left therapy when she finished high school, now wanting to try living independently from mother. She and I agreed that she ought to avail herself of further therapy wherever she lived if unfinished problems interfered with her life.

I saw Heather again about five years later, when she was a college senior. She had made a suicidal attempt, following a weekend of "encounter therapy" which she and her boyfriend had attended together. There was strong group pressure to "reveal everything about myself, and I felt like all my fears were under a floodlight. They wanted to break me down before they would accept me." She told me that her boyfriend, Anton, had wanted to break up with her because "I'm too possessive; I want all his attention. Last weekend we broke up, thinking maybe we are not right for each other. I just want to die, I have no other interest in life now—if I died I would stop being a burden to him." While interested in Anton, Heather had gotten behind in her course work, then "felt like an idiot" and stopped going to classes. She was afraid she would "fail" "and I've never taken a course in which I couldn't succeed if I wanted to." While she was briefly in hospital, both her boyfriend and her father visited, each showing care and concern. She had described Anton to me as "an aloof kind of person who doesn't show his feelings."

She talked about herself as "failing with Anton. I have been thinking for a while that either he or I should be dead. I could go on living if he were dead. But if he were alive and rejected me or showed interest in another woman . . . I would know I failed . . . I realized before I did it (suicidal attempt) that I was the one in the wrong, that I was demanding too much of him."

t: "There are two parts to what you are saying . . . wanting love and attention in an intimate relationship is not wrong; it's human and nothing to blame yourself for. But your need to feel on top of the situation by needing constant reassurance that you haven't failed—making Anton's devotion a *test* of not failing and then feeling like an 'idiot' when you are not sure of that—that is a kind of burden that strains your relationships and that you ought to do some work on."

Heather (tearfully): "I guess so".

t: "You know, your thought of only one of you living and the way you handled it by deciding to try to kill yourself—was a kind of way of protecting him." Because her anger at Anton had been so overwhelmingly frightening to Heather, it was important for her to know that that was not all she felt toward him, that is, that she had also cared enough about him to want to save his life. It would then be easier to face the anger too.

Heather: "I know I didn't want to hurt him, I didn't know what else to do . . . I used to rely on my mother for everything, but now I've cut myself off from my mother. I think I was attracted to Anton because of his aloofness. He wasn't pressing me for a relationship like other guys do. I'm always attracted when I get no response."

t: "And then?"

Heather: "And then I'm enraged by it."

t: "Isn't that a pattern worth working on too?"

In the following months, as she re-established contact with both Anton and her course work, she examined her images of men and women.

Heather: "There is the degraded housewife . . . used by a man and then left high and dry and trapped into being depressed, like my mother. Or there's being independent and competent but not needing anyone. Being intellectual is the only honorable life I know, yet I hate working at desks, hate classes and study, while everyone around me seems so competent."

"I was dependent on mother much longer than most people. If anything came up I always went to her. Everything else seemed superfluous because I always had her. But I think that's part of why I've always been afraid of being an idiot. I think I knew I was missing something or else I would have known what others did. So I kept my mother as my favorite companion, I was scared of groups. When a school group went to a play I was angry to sit with them instead of my mother; I didn't want to be associated with them or what they did. Then when I started college, I acted the opposite. With mother I used to flaunt my racy life in her face, or, I would think about telling my father all about it. But it was all more like a fencing match than love-making . . . until I got involved with Anton and everything changed; I gave up everything to be with him."

Anton was still very much interested in Heather, as she was in him, though understandably he had been frightened off by feeling that she was making him responsible for her welfare. That was why they had sought out the encounter group. Heather and Anton began to see each other on a less intensive basis, and were both willing to work on the problems in their relationship. Some initial therapy time was focussed on what they might expect of each other. Meanwhile, Heather became able to review her earlier relationships to each of her parents.

Heather: "I guess when I was little I wanted her to favor me over the boys . . . and everything outside was kind of a threat and that continued for a long time, especially after the divorce. The boys shared interests with my father and mother and I shared interests. I guess I don't like the idea of being female any more than I ever did. My father just didn't notice me. I remember watching in the basement where he was building a coaster with my brother, and wishing that the tools and the ability to do that were mine, or that I was them."

t: "So you thought you had to be someone different like a boy to be worthy of your father's attention. That goal was impossible—even when you got good at fencing. No wonder you felt nothing you ever did was quite good enough. Meanwhile you had to miss a lot of fun in enjoying being yourself."

Heather: "Yes, and last year there was a man I worked for and he was harsh and critical of me, and I think I was attracted to him for that. Last year when I went home for the summer, I didn't like the idea of sharing a room with my mother anymore. I remember you thought long ago that wasn't a good idea, but I was too afraid of anyone coming between my mother and me."

Some months later, when she and Anton were engaged, she discussed her experience with the encounter group that led to the suicidal attempt. The group had insisted that they would have to break down her "stubbornness" and "resistance" to revealing her feelings, and that she would have to "grow up" and get used to sharing Anton's attention with others. They picked another woman for him to be "sympathetic" to. He was to embrace her, while Heather told the group what she felt. Heather felt both destroyed, and destructive, but justly punished for her "selfishness."

Heather: "It was so hard for me when I was hurt—there was only a feeling of wanting to destroy—to hurt him physically or myself. I've done a lot of things in the past I felt bad and guilty about so I felt I deserved whatever I got."

This kind of confronting encounter group, with its strong social pressure toward the dissolution of needed defenses, can be disastrous for many people, not only those with Heather's character structure.

Heather: "When I think about that weekend—it won't lie down and be forgotten, and when it comes up it is like everything is a pretense and it is real . . . like anything I do . . . that experience can laugh at me pretending that I'm another person—that I'm like normal now and enjoying myself. Also because I know what really goes on at that place, while other people think it's a perfectly okay place to send people to, they don't realize it can destroy them . . . what it does to them."

t: "I don't think it's ok to send people there. You know, that's the other side of the coin of what you've described about situations—like the lab and the Campfire girls—where you felt everyone was in the know and withholding the truth from you. You knew something about that place that nobody else was admitting to, nor would let you admit to. And at home you knew some things too."

Heather: "Yes, that mother and father hated each other, even when they were sounding polite; mother always was 'explaining' my father but really made him sound like an idiot."

t: "Do you recognize that word in your picture of yourself?"

Heather laughed, then broke down in tears.

For several individuals described a moment of laughter preceded tears. Both require a loosening of emotional controls. For Heather the shift echoed her ability to now move from contempt for the "idiot" to sympathy for the "idiot," who had, after all, not been such an idiot.

t: "Perhaps that's part of the reality you are talking about, that won't lie down . . . the part of you that wanted desperately to be close to your father, even when you and mother were busy picking him apart . . . that made you feel you were viewed like your father . . . an 'idiot' who wasn't told what you and mother were saying about him. But now you know that he was not an idiot, in fact, he's made a pretty happy life for himself too."

She cried for all the years she has been angry at father and ignoring him as he had ignored her.

Heather: "I don't trust my mother at this point at all . . . I feel like she had insidious motives . . . like an emissary of a dreadful place . . . she goes on as though nothing happened, when all the time she was part of this violation of anyone's integrity, like in the encounter group. Telling her I want to be away from her isn't easy. I know that all along my hatred of school was tied up with my lack of confidence and wanting to be with her. After my father was gone, it was like an unspoken deal with mother, that she would share her experience and talents and that way kept me close. But meanwhile, I always had to feel insecure and incomplete . . . the way we've talked about. Then she would get mad at my jealousy when I was a teenager. She called it pathological and paranoid . . . and that's what she called my father. Sometimes I think of her now as the witch coming to Sleeping Beauty's birthday party to spoil it."

t: "Do you think that is part of why you were so ready for punishment about wanting Anton?"

Heather: "Well, it still seems incredible and surprising to me constantly that Anton is really expressing all this affection for me, and that we are really going to be married. It's becoming much more real than the past. I mean I was aware of his affection on an intellectual level, but now I am also letting myself feel it. I've stopped trying to make him prove it or being afraid of losing him. There are things we have accepted about each other just as we are—almost like trying to catch up on childhood and be adults too—I mean like not working so hard and letting ourselves be playful and light hearted too. There aren't any rigid roles—and I've discovered I don't mind being a woman after all."

t: "Yes, I think you've changed about what you see as possible and okay for a woman."

Heather: "Mother kept accusing my father of being an emotional recluse. Part of the reason I think now is that she was at fault and that's because I know it takes two to have it be that way . . . for instance, with Anton I don't let that happen now and neither does he . . . so mother made herself indispensable to me. She says now it isn't fair that I reject her because of what she did, that she was trying to do good. I wished she had pushed me into the world sooner, instead of always paving the way, making me feel I couldn't do anything myself. Like writing excuses for me to stay out of school. She let me do anything except want a boyfriend or think that my father was a decent guy."

Heather frequently brought Anton on visits to her father's house, but kept her distance from her mother until after she and Anton were married. She and Anton continued to delight in what she called "our hedonistic phase" of happiness with each other. Nevertheless, she remained in therapy for a time after her marriage, to deal with whatever might still "haunt" her from the past, so that she could feel more secure in calling her future her own.

A hidden factor in Heather's situation was the degree of futility her mother had felt during her marriage, and the absence of a human support network to ameliorate her helplessness and guilt. She had, in fact, had extensive contact with a child guidance clinic about one of her other children. According to her, she had been advised by those she had asked there to remain with the marriage. When eventually she sought some therapy for herself, she became aware of how guilty she had felt about divorce, and was then able to proceed with it. Feeling as resentful and guilty as she did at the time, understandably she had a strong need to justify her actions by convincing her daughter with all the evidence she could muster. Among the children, Heather, was the most receptive to this. However, mother should not have needed such proof that she was doing the right thing and was therefore blameless in separating. An acknowledgment that it was best for all of them should have been enough.

Perhaps if these events had taken place in today's social climate she might have dealt with it differently.

Heather's degree of hostility toward her mother became exaggerated by her need to put enough distance between them to enable her to function independently. At first, some aspects of her relationship to Anton mirrored the "exclusiveness" she had maintained with her mother, and brought her to grief. She needed to work out aspects of her own sexual identification, in the sense of learning that men don't have to be indifferent to women. She brought up images tied to her past—forbidden yearnings for her father—and grieved about their past alienation. She then felt able, progressively, to separate her self-image and relationship to her new husband from the images of self and parents she experienced in childhood.

Karen. Karen is mentioned because her reality testing took the direct form of re-exploring the nature of her father, whom she had avoided for years. As she was an outgoing person, the extent of her problems did not become apparent until the end of adolescence, when she could get involved only with men who were closely linked with her mother. Psychic separation from the family was not something she could picture. As she once, said, in regard to a man who was interested in her, "Well, I can't imagine sleeping with a *stranger, who has nothing to do with the family!* My mother is lucky having my cousin Grant, it's like having a family and a husband at the same time." Clearly she needed to resolve her family attachments before feeling she could have a life of her own.

Karen's initial acceptance of her mother's devaluation of father has been described earlier in the chapter, along with the first breakthrough of positive feelings for her father. When she first came to therapy she had told me her goal was to have nothing to do with father. But after two months, during a crying spell of "I hate you, I hate you" about father, she found that "out of nowhere I was saying I love you."

She was now ready to examine the quality of her attachment to her mother. In her dreams, the possibility—as well as the dangers—of separating from mother began to emerge.

Here is an example.

Karen: "I dreamt about my mother. The first part of it is like my childhood dreams. Some killer is loose and I'm really scared, sure he would really come into the house . . . I wanted to sleep in my mother's bed. Then mother and I are on the bus and at one point, my mother fell on her face on the bus and she was OK; then I felt the liquid coming down over my legs . . . I didn't know if it came from me or her because she and I had been in contact . . . so I don't know if it was from her period or my period. I looked down and saw clear liquid running down instead, and I yelled, 'It's happening, it's happening' and I had in mind something breaking and liquid . . . like childbirth . . . out of the womb . . . like separating from her." Though associations to the dream are omitted here, the fluidity of ego boundaries are portrayed graphically. The "killer" had to do with a fused image of her father and herself.

However, the following month she was able to say: "I can't stand just being Madeleine Platten's daughter any more. I have something in *me,* too."

In a phone conversation with her mother she said, "Mother, look what you are doing, how dare you put a negative thing on every male."

Mother, according to Karen, replied, "Yes, I know I'm overprotective, but that's better than letting you get hurt and be foolish."

Karen: "I started crying over the phone. I think I realized that she's been setting up this thing with a man . . . and then tearing it down. It's like if I'm seeing a man, it's a betrayal of her. I'm so used to not separating from them, I can't imagine my sister and mother except together. Everything I do they are always a part of me; they are really like my *skin*; I couldn't survive without them."

t: "And in return for having them, you renounced certain things, like the right to have a man care reliably about you . . . and now you are afraid that you can't love a man in a sustained way. In all of that you still underrate yourself and overrate the power of your mother."

Thereafter, Karen reviewed her ways of holding on to the image of her father by repeating the negative parts of the relationship as she pictured it with her lovers. She had always picked someone who cut her down and deserted her, and then felt traumatized. I told her:

t: "That means it must be unfinished business from the past. You must have cared about your father in some way to want to keep repeating it like that. Maybe there are some things about him that you haven't told either me or yourself about.

Karen: "I realize that I don't really remember my father very much before the divorce. When mother started her career, I didn't like it much, being left alone with him. If he told me to turn off the TV and go to bed, I would write in my diary that he's been screaming at me. I made it sound worse. Actually, it was mother who always said he's been screaming at her because he resents her career. After the divorce, when I had to meet him to get the money, that was torture for me. I think we were both mad then."

t: "Mad that that's what things had come to between you, just an exchange of money? You say you don't remember much about him in the early years. Maybe you will want to find out more for yourself, so you can make up your own mind about what he is really like and how you feel about him."

Karen began the process of such "reality testing" in a safer arena. She decided to look up the first boyfriend, whose departure had so devastated her, in order to understand what had "really happened." As her artistic talents would suggest, she was a person who approached life by watching her experiences take shape, and then coming to terms with what she saw "out there" as well as within herself. When she returned from this encounter, she reported feeling "older" and pleased about it. She now knew there were many things Brian liked about her, and saw her own role in pushing the relationship to its conclusion. She felt "older," in the sense that "it really freaks me out now to think that I was so paralyzed, like if he threw me out I'd die. It wasn't just feeling empty, more like I had no substance at all."

Over the next year, Karen made some important decisions about her career, risky in the sense of not having her mother's support, but challenging and satisfying to Karen. Her career choice involved a move to another state, but she continued to come for a session about twice a year, or to write a note about important happenings in her life. Here is a recent communication:

"I'd like to write you a longer letter than this, or even talk to you by phone— or maybe even take a trip to Boston. Let me just say here that shortly after seeing you last time, I contacted my father—and so, have been spending time with him over the past few months. It is extraordinary. He is not a demon! Not perfect, of course, but the man is human with many sides to him, just like the rest of us. Our relationship is still new and so it will take awhile to settle into whatever relationship we are going to have. He is presently thrilled that I have given him a chance to be my father. I am, too. Of course, I'm still wary of him, but even if he does 'turn on me' I'll be facing it for real instead of in my head. I am greatly relieved. Also, I am *not* back with Ned. Also a relief. And, have been seeing a new person—not an intense passionate affair—and he is wonderful to me; a whole, sweet, good person and I love it."

Hope and Despair in the Search for Truth:
Images of a New Civilization

Eva. Excerpts from Eva's description of her experience in relation to parental separation will be given in some detail. First, she is an example of those adolescents who persevere through difficult times of self-examination and change with considerable courage. Secondly, her situation illustrates the subtle infusion of ideologic change into pre-existing parental conflict, with more than subtle results. That is, the liberation of women was pictured as being accomplished through freedom to pursue a career, but at the cost of devaluing previous components of the self, which had included caring for children. Progressive demeaning of the quality of energy involved in childrearing, occurring in parts of the population in our country, can be as constricting to the full development of women as giving it priority.

The continued impact of changing customs and ideology on the human relationship network has implications for the therapy process when working with children of divorce. Modifications involves periods of deviation from the restriction of one's focus primarily to the psychic reactions of the individual. It becomes important with adolescents who are attuned to ideologic issues actively to introduce the role of social perceptions and meanings insofar as they affect real changes in the parents, in order to lay the groundwork for a reinterpretation of the personal catastrophes. That is, implicit and explicit assumptions of the parents about the meaning of the changes frequently had to be addressed in order to relieve enough initial guilt or resignation in the adolescent so that the inner reactions might then be dealt with.

In Eva's case, this involved actively challenging her assumptions about what had made her mother's past life so unhappy. Had mother been "forced" into her role by father? or Eva? or her own expectations, derived from the human relationship network of her past? What options for change had been overlooked and what was available now? How would it all affect what Eva could hope for in relationships? Did the baby have to be thrown out with the bathwater? Did Eva need to continue simultaneously to view herself as a burden when she needed a mother, and to defend herself against making "attachments" which had come to naught between her parents? On an individual level continued tension between the parents over a long period of time is accurately reflected in Eva's internalization of each parent's attitude toward the other, transformed into sefl-criticism and inhibition. Simultaneously she retained the capacity for pleasure and intermittent intimacy, for she had not nullified any of the good moments. Like many of the adolescents she asked, "Which reality is real?" I attempted, in dealing with Eva's guilt and resignation, not only to deal with inner conflict but actively to convey: "The failure of your parent's illusions made a bad reality for you. In self-defense you erected a wall of anger in order not to be so hurt. There are other ways of not being hurt, because relationships between people don't inevitably have to be that way." Like many of the other adolescents, Eva suffered from depression and loneliness, difficulties in concentration, a sense of being "disconnected" from meaningful relationships and "fated" to be unhappy. But when not incapacitated by constricting depression, she functioned in a highly creative fashion, presenting exquisitely correct perceptions of what went on between people, including her parents, as well as within herself. Her drive toward "honesty," at times excruciatingly self-critical, was associated with isolation of affect and intellectualization, and, occasionally, a sense of depersonalization. When affect was available to her, however, it was rich and intense.

Both of Eva's parents underwent a prolonged period of distress during their separation and the rebuilding of their own life directions. Although mother had initiated the divorce, certain by then that her needs could not be met within the marriage, and never regretted it, she was forced within the years after separation to make major revisions in her expectations of fulfillment and recognition from an independent career, as well as in what she could expect in new heterosexual relationships. A variety of disappointments in each of these areas quickly changed the heady sense of freedom she first felt after the decision to separate. Although she then no longer felt victimized by her marriage, she was beset by a variety of new problems by which she felt victimized in different ways.

Eva's father reacted to the initial separation with shock and depression, and a sense of failure about having been "ousted" by his wife. Feelings of inadequacy briefly became generalized to his profession, in which he had been extraordinarily competent, but for a time felt as though his accomplishments were "fake." An idealized image of his mother, who had died when he was a young boy, shadowed the wished-for image of his wife. Anger and criticism toward each other were particularly difficult for either partner to tolerate without serious loss of self-esteem. In their different ways, each had been the victim of illusions about each other and their life together. It was unfortunate that neither parent had felt entitled or able to grapple with their differences before they became magnified beyond repair. But by the time Eva was seventeen, father in particular was feeling much better about himself and an enthusiastic, creative involvement in his work had been rekindled.

Both of Eva's parents remained deeply interested in her throughout adolescence. She had free and flexible access to them both, and was allowed considerable autonomy in decision-making. In fact, with which parent she stayed overnight was so much left up to her that Eva had difficulty feeling she "belonged" to either home. Both parents talked openly with her about aspects of their own life and attitudes.

Eva was able to sustain the process of reality testing about each parent and herself; as yet, she sees none of them as "happy." She is an arrestingly likeable person, whose potential for a rich adult humanity surfaces continually, just beneath a still present shimmer of despair.

Excerpts begin from her first interview and continue—with major omissions, of course—over a period of two years. Additional quotes from Eva's initial sessions are in section 2a of this chapter.

First Six Months of Treatment
      t: "Come in—what troubles you?"
      Eva: "Lately I guess I'm depressed all the time . . . I'm friendly with people for a little while, but don't have any real friends . . . like I put a *wall* between myself and them . . . I don't know whether people think I'm odd or sort of snooty. My mother is off on her own most of the time lately . . . so I'm alone a lot since my parents separated a little over a year ago. They haven't gotten

along for a long time; they get on each other's backs; they couldn't communicate at all."

t: "There was a *'wall'* between them that way?"

Eva: "Yes, so it was a good thing they separated. My mother is very independent and gets done what she wants—she goes off to San Francisco a lot and is aggressive and outgoing. She says her work is the most important thing in her life and she'll do whatever it takes to carry it through."

t: "So how do you and Carl manage with her away so much?"

Eva: "We usually have most of the housework done by the time she comes home at night . . . we take turns cooking, but get in fights about that. Like the other night, Carl just cooked himself some chicken and ate it and didn't make any for anybody else."

"When I visit my father, he does everything for us and suddenly it is a very warm atmosphere, but it just doesn't seem real after the weekend, because then he goes off and doesn't know what the rest of us go through during the week. For twelve years, my mother stayed home and didn't work, then she got so mad that she decided she would never let father force her to do that anymore, she had just been wasting her life."

t: "He forced her?"

Eva: "She says so."

Later in the hour:

t: "Your mother must have felt desperate about changing things . . . but I don't understand yet about wasting her life! Has that part been bothering you, too, what she meant about that?"

Eva: "My mother told me I had a temper when I was little, that I tried to dominate everyone; she said I was kind of overwhelming when I wanted something—she sounded like she felt *forced* . . . like with my father. But in a way, I have a lot of sympathy for her, more than for my father, about what has always been expected of her as a woman. I agree with her and admire her for going after what she wants now."

Early in Eva's therapy, we spent much time discussing sex roles, making an attempt to differentiate whether her father alone or a combination of cultural pressures and mother's own conflicts had "forced" her into a role within which she had found it impossible to make her needs known earlier either to father or herself. This seemed like necessary groundwork for two reasons: To enable Eva to experience what she clearly felt was a degree of rejection by her mother for Eva's also "forcing" her into a different perspective—not merely as the embodiment of "wasted years"—and to allow her to feel more comfortable with me before having to deal with this painful issue. As it later emerged, the nucleus of Eva's depression revolved around her reaction to her mother's mood swings early in her life. At times, when mother had felt overwhelmed by her and depressed, Eva had been left in her crib or playpen for long periods of time. At other times, there had been considerable pleasurable mutual activity, such as mother reading to daughter, going to the park, etc. All in all, she had spent a lot of individual time with Eva. But she considered her a very demanding child, and found Carl, born two years later, to be an "easier" and "more adaptable" baby; she did not express the same annoyance about his "demands," and the relationship was a smoother one.

In the third month of therapy, Eva talked more openly about being angry at mother because she made her feel like a "bad" person.

Eva: "Mother has always told me how nice Carl was to be with, and meanwhile she says I am never satisfied, she and I are arguing constantly, I guess she hates to be pushed around."

t: "It feels lousy to be told someone else is nicer to be with—that must have been hurting you for a long time . . . you've told me how much you admire the way your mom is . . . did you figure the arguments were your fault then, or what? And what actually goes on?"

Eva: "Well, now if I think about it, there are some funny things that don't come out even . . . like she swears at us all the time, but acts like it hurts her feelings terribly if I ever do it back."

Eva was then able to consider the possibility that her mother had had a need to feel "victimized" to justify her own dissatisfactions; thus she would apparently goad Eva and her father into what was described as "being dominating" (e.g., swearing and then feeling attacked by the reply).

The following week, Eva reported having met a nice new girl at school, but she did not expect much to come of it. Again, the sense of distance created by anger and the underlying question of her adolescence—"Can people really love each other?"—came to the fore.

Eva: "I get a kind of resentment that's hard to overcome, a kind of cold feeling, a feeling of anger, of just not caring, an unresponsiveness. Sometimes I still have good times with Carl. But I don't think my mother or brother have been very close to me, and sometimes I don't think I feel any real love for either of them. Mostly, it's a feeling of not caring—I wish I didn't have all this school work . . . I feel like it's not worth it . . . like nothing is. Getting to know people is such a great effort . . . I tell myself I don't have the time, but it's really that I'm just not involved. I wish I didn't have a million obligations, that I keep feeling bad and guilty about. Sometimes I think I could start with a new group of people, but I got back to the same me, so what's the use?"

Shortly after that she reported meeting a boy she liked at a party and having a good long talk. She realized that this was the first such talk she had had with anyone her age for a long time. However, she found she was looking for something to be angry about, looking to see if he was "even the least little bit chauvinistic." At the party, the slow dancing was depressing to her because of the boys' "possessive kind of holding," but then she was not really feeling friendly. Rock dancing she enjoyed, "but it's like being in your own world."

t: "How would you like it to be?"

Eva: "Well, all this week I've been watching couples with their arms around each other . . . it kept crossing my mind . . . that it would be enjoyable for me just holding someone . . . but I would have to feel like a friend first."

She returned to this theme the following week: "I know I've just been scared of people this whole year and kept them off. At first, I'm not scared, I might seem friendly but then I get very uncomfortable."

t: "Is it when you start to *feel* something about them, like wanting them to like you or something like that?"

Eva: "I think so, I start being very suspicious of whether they really like me or I really like them . . . or whether it's all worth paying attention to, or just a waste of time."

The phrase had meaning, in the context of mother's attitudes to Eva's needs, both as a baby, and now.

t: "'A waste of time,'—There you are using your mother's phrase again, the one you felt hurt by, as though time with you was wasted. And maybe she is still trying to protect herself from getting re-involved with anything that takes her from her work. But there are other ways of protecting one's interests that don't shut out the people one cares about—that she's had a hard time learning so far."

Eva (in a small voice): "Today I asked her for a ride to the doctors' to get the splint off my arm, and she said she couldn't waste her time doing that, that I could call up and find out how to get there on my own. Actually, it wasn't all that hard, but I had to wait for the bus for a long time."

t: "With wet snow coming down."

Eva (laughs but tears come to her eyes): "With wet snow coming down . . . sometimes I try to put myself in someone else's role to see how they would see me."

t: "Tell me about it."

Eva: "Well, sometimes when I'm here with you I see myself as a different person . . . than I am the rest of the week, and I wonder which is 'real.'"

Later that session we talked some about the depression and loneliness, the self-doubts, the periods of irritability, not only with the ex-spouse but everyone else in the family as well, that beset parents who have decided to break up. People who have just separated feel more vulnerable about many things, and looking for somebody else to blame is part of the picture. I made clear that these feelings don't usually last forever, that eventually her parents were apt to find new energies in themselves to get on with their own life goals. Even if things stayed glum for them, Eva did not have to make it her fate too.

Soon after this, Eva reported:

Eva: "The last few weeks, I can get along with my mother much better—but there is always this conflict in me . . . about still not understanding about my parents."

t: "What do you feel as the conflict?"

Eva: "Well, I've been very defensive with my mother and my father, too. It's because I know each parent dislikes something in the other—and it's like I'm not the same person when I'm with my father than when I'm with my mother. But all in all, I have to accept my mother more than my father, because she was pushed into the background when she was married to him. Maybe I see my parents as both failures in making attachments. I think my father is still hoping they'll somehow get together again. He doesn't see how things really are. I mean I think he wanted security and a house and a family and the feeling of being with other people through my mother . . . because he's more of a loner. So he idealized her, he wanted her to be something she wasn't. When my mother used to have parties, she didn't plan things. Some people don't like her rushing around and forgetfulness and quick reactions and always counting her chickens before they are hatched."

t: "And you?"

Eva: "For me, I guess it meant getting blamed a lot of times before she knew what was going on . . . she would have a reaction before I ever tell her why I did something. I realized all those things affected me, but it doesn't help me to be different . . . like at school, I'm feeling bad because I'm still not doing well at all . . . partly because I'm nervous all the time and partly I make careless mistakes because I can't get my mind on it. I've never gotten C's like this in my life before."

t: "I hope you know that it's not a test of what you can do when you're not feeling depressed."

Eva: "Actually, this week I haven't been depressed . . . I started enjoying the piano again, I could listen to what I was playing again. But there are a lot of other things I just don't see anymore."

t: "Like what?"

Eva: "I don't mean about my parents now, but things around me . . . I don't get *images* about things any more and I used to. And I don't think I've ever lately been with kids and felt any real attachment with them. I'm just with myself observing things."

The following session, Eva says: "suddenly I'm interested in really soaking up piano again . . . like I do feel it's leading someplace. I didn't tell you last week that I started volunteering in the settlement house . . . tutoring and helping kids design projects they want to build . . . I really enjoyed it. I think I've gotten over the first hurdle with one boy . . . that he was really cranky at first when he didn't know if I would be able to get the equipment he needs. I've been taking notes about those afternoons, like you do at our sessions, I find I notice a lot more that way and *things don't just slip away."*

Still in her "normal days" she feels that maybe it all isn't real, that it doesn't have any meaning.

t: "That seems tied up for you with the issue of whether people can really care about each other, the way they are really."

Eva: "I'm all confused about that. Often I feel my father doesn't really care, but I know he cares, he's wise in a sense, but I just can't understand his way of looking at things. Meanwhile, mother is telling me that he is being vicious about the divorce, because he doesn't think her capable of being a good mother. He thinks he shouldn't have to support her career in addition to us, to buy all those tools for archaeology she wants now, and she thinks he ought to give her backpay for the years when she stayed home and worked as a housewife. And it gets all confused in me whenever *I* want to do something . . . like she wants me to take archaeology courses and go on a dig (mother's interest) and he wanted me to take that class in medical engineering and for a minute I wanted to do *both*."

t: "Like you want *both* your parents rather than having to choose between them—and you needn't actually choose between them that way."

Eva: "But I knew each one thought the other's idea was not as good . . . so I didn't sign up for either one."

We discussed how the criticism of each parent about the other's interest went on inside Eva, until neither interest seemed worthwhile to her . . . and that immobilized her. She picked up the work "immobilize," commenting that often she felt that way all over, that she used to have much more spontaneous reactions, even sadness and anger . . . and not the kind of blankness from this past year. She said: "It's like all my senses are not as sharp; seeing and hearing and everything—I think I've just begun to hear music again."

t: "Senses like seeing and hearing also make contact and connections with people and things around you and it is this connection you haven't trusted yourself with lately."

Eva: "I think I've been trying to see the truth and also not to see it. If I let myself, I'm afraid I might do something silly—like run around wild and shouting, instead of thinking everything out—I realized I felt like doing that in gym . . . I used to be very competitive in rowing. So I didn't take rowing at all this year . . . people used to think I got out of hand in that. The other thing is what I told you last time . . . if I see lovers, I kind of envy them . . . and try to push it out of my mind . . . and then I avoid that person if I can because I hate the feeling . . . *because I really think they never loved each other and that it can't happen to me."*

t: "That's still your feeling about your parents you are talking about."

Eva: "Sometimes I wish I was still a kid, that I wouldn't have to think things out, that I wouldn't know about people."

t: "It's not so dangerous to let yourself feel like a kid once in a while."

As she left that hour she laughed spontaneously after the first of the double doors of the office is opened (doors are double for sound proofing, to assure privacy). She commented how funny it was about the double door, "You usually imagine being 'out' after the door opens, and it turns out there is really another one and I'm still here." I added, "In fact, you aren't forgotten once you leave, either." This feeling, of a sense of contact during the therapy hours, which was then disrupted at the end of the hour, after which she felt "disconnected" or "lost" and questioned whether it was worth it at all became a repetitive theme she brought up, reminiscent of the disruption of the relationships she felt with her parents and peers.

Another day:

Eva: "I still can't get to know people—I'm annoyed at them, I don't want to know them—like I don't feel connections inside—it's not *continuous* to feel connected to anyone. Sometimes I look forward to the next day at school, but when I get there the wall of anger is there and it will be there forever—I don't *want* it to come down—if it does, they'll feel me to be inconsistent and unsophisticated, too embarrassed and unhappy and they would want somebody who is not always serious like me."

t: "I think you don't want it to come down because you figure if they know how you *feel*, underneath how reasonable and self-controlled you act, that they would reject you . . . your wall of anger . . . it's there to protect you from feeling rejected, it *about* your fear of being rejected and all the pain you would feel about taking that risk again. You must be plenty mad at me too a lot of times when it feels to you like we've just gotten started here and then you're surprised that time is up already."

She agrees gingerly, but adds that it's not reasonable to get mad at me, she just feels disconnected and strange. It seemed time to bridge the chasm between her "reasonable" self and her anger at me, for she converted anger into feeling "disconnected," which left her helpless and depressed. So, I added, "And don't you ever think to yourself at that time 'here I am walking by myself in this freezing wind and weather while that damn old so and so Tessman is sitting in the house with her car in the driveway . . . not even giving me a ride?"

Her mother's difficulty in providing Eva with transportation when she needed it was one form of emotional abandonment she had adjusted to. Keeping therapy appointments involved several bus changes, followed by a considerable walk, weighed down with an armload of school books.

Rough gasps of laughter break from her body, and turn into quiet tears. "I hadn't thought of swearing at you." She wept as stoically as she lived, with shoulders held straight. I wanted to comfort her directly but knew that would interfere and distract her from the need to accept herself with her anger in the long run. She said, as though ashamed of it, that sometimes the words we said here didn't mean much of anything, but she was aware that eye contact meant a lot to her. This was true not only here but with others too. She now expressed both her longing, and her frustration with me that we only talked in therapy, rather than doing things together.

Over the following year, she frequently referred to feeling "safe" here, no matter what she felt because she "trusted" that I would share my reactions with her without becoming "involved" or wanting something from her in turn. Nevertheless, the limitations on direct emotional gratification within the relationship, continued to be frustrating to Eva who had, from an early age, developed a protective self-control against the expression of her wish for nonverbal contacts. Occasionally I could give her a ride to the bus, and for a time, during this period we had two-hour sessions every other week instead of the weekly hour. I sometimes switch to double sessions with those individuals for whom the sense of emotional contact, which is risked only gradually during each session, becomes quickly transformed into a feeling of vulnerability to abandonment.

In the following weeks, we could take a fresh look, from various vantage points, at her continued experience of feeling lost, disconnected, and "dazed" right after she left the sessions. The ending of sessions symbolized to her the ending of her childhood "innocence"—her belief that the parents would stay together, rather than be parted—and her related loss of self-esteem; at a deeper level it was a reflection of the alternations in early childhood between her mother's involvement with her and prolonged isolation in the playpen. Since relegation to the playpen, especially after she was too old for it, often coincided with mother's periods of disenchantment with her, these disruptions were associated, for her, with aggression. A hunger for eye contact, not uncommon as a human desire, served to reconstitute a disrupted relationship. It remains in the realm of speculation whether her use of visual contact, which she numbed during periods of depression ("I don't get images any more;" "My senses are dull this year;" as well as feeling "dazed") contributed to her later gift for symbolizing emotional experiences in terms of visual imagery. Her struggle about whether to absorb and use or to cast out her sensory impressions and their meanings was reflected in a range of cognitive functioning, which had bearing on her difficulties with school work. By her last year of high school, she was much more actively involved in school and came to be viewed as an impressive thinker by her teachers.

Finally, a consideration of her "lost" reactions to the end of therapy sessions also led to a turning point in her sense that she did have options in what happened to her. Where first she had experienced these feelings as an expression of her helplessness about her fate when she was "cast out", she came to see that it was she who "disconnected" herself from the sessions by her anger about "rejection"; she actively cast out the content of the session so that she could not take it with her, in the form of "remembering." For a time, some self-acceptance about her anger regarding the deprivations she had experienced was a theme; this coincided with a description of past relationships with people for whom she had simultaneously longed and defended herself from longing by "making herself find fault" with them.

Eva reported a number of changes in herself:

Eva: "I'm really getting along much better with mother these days ... It's like we understand and accept each other ... like about her being angry at everything when she comes home and acting unreasonably ... I just don't lash out at her anymore ... I notice that when I start a subject that annoys her, I just drop it for the time being."

t: "What do you think makes for the difference?"

Eva: "I think I don't take everything like that so personally anymore; I don't react like it's a criticism of me, that something is wrong with me."

Over the next few months, during which Eva brought dreams and writings from her journal into therapy, work proceeded through these. The following fall, Eva made efforts to regain a sense of control over her life and relationships and would openly reject with her parents, peers, and teachers whatever she felt to be a devalued role. For instance, she stated, "I like doing things for my mother these days ... but I also let her know that the kind of job like 'go get my slippers—or get me a pack of cigarettes'... well, I would never ask that of anyone, because it puts us on a different plane, so I told her that."

One of her dreams involves a detail in which she was attempting to bury a little animal and "each time I buried it, I wasn't satisfied."

t: "Do you have some notions about what it means to you?"

Eva: "I guess I feel that I've lost my childhood, maybe I was always too tense ... but there are other things that I've tried to bury completely, to get rid of them and now I'm not sure I want to do that."

t: "Tell me about it."

Eva: "Well, I was clearing up my room, and wanted to get rid of all my old things. I went through all the old costumes I had ... and I wish I could wear them again ... Kings and queens and wild animals ... I used to like to write plays and put them on for my brothers' birthday parties. And I remember running free as a child, but ... but ... I don't know."

t: "You've talked about being afraid if you let yourself go you would 'run wild' and giving up sports this year because of how involved you got ... letting your body have a go at people during the game."

Eva: "Yea, I think that's the part, because I never saw my parents being playful with each other or spontaneous, I always think people will think I'm too wild."

She went on to describe the process of cleaning out her room.

Eva: "Last week in my room, I started looking a long time at that crack I always liked on the ceiling—I used to lie in bed and see it. Then the next day, I tried visiting grammar school and for some reason went to see my kindergarten teacher. I wanted to see if she would recognize me if she saw me. I used to like her a lot . . . when I was in school some of the teachers felt like they were like a mother to me . . . and I looked up to them a lot too."

She was working at accepting her childhood self, as reflected in the eyes of the actual teachers who had been fond of her, bridging instead of cutting off her adolescent yearnings from their earlier roots. No longer was she satisfied to bury her childhood along with her parents' marriage.

At this time, she was aware of the struggle between a renewed interest in the use of her energies and her shifting moods and relationships, as these affected her sense of herself. As she said, "I want to use time in a quality way now—not just mindlessly. But I have trouble organizing anything—and my mood is constantly changing from euphoric to really depressed to just sadness . . . one moment I feel warm toward somebody, and the next like an icicle. When I am happy, I feel a kind of airiness in mind and body. When I am tense, I am afraid to breathe deeply, like my heart will stop." She began, over the next few months, to have her first love relationship with a boy who was as cautious about emotional commitment as she. Frequently and unpredictably, he acted in an aloof fashion, leaving her to experience painful longing and fantasizing about his presence. As her earlier depression had interfered with sensory acuity and enjoyment, the sense of disruptive desertion now spoiled her pleasure in activities previously associated with him. This time, however, unlike when first seen, she took the initiative in clarifying to herself and in a conversation with him that she could not tolerate affection which was so intermittent that it could not become part of her sense of continuing reality. As she said, "It destroys me when I think about it . . . I feel so separated from him . . . and that's why I can't interpret the Bach inventions on the piano anymore . . . that he liked to hear me play . . . I think my needs are different than his . . . I like whatever I'm doing to be a part of me. If he embraces or kisses me, I don't want to act like it never happened afterwards."

In her sessions with me, she is also more able to express, in a focussed way, her anger at "ending," rather than in the experience of feeling lost and dazed. As she tells me, "I can always count on things being the same here, because I'm here to talk about things. It's a very controlled situation that way . . . no matter what I say I feel I can trust you because you're not trying to force anything out of me and I don't feel threatened like that you would be shocked . . . The anger I somewhat feel is just before I begin talking, like I have to put something in words . . . even though I know you've told me I don't. But harder than that is at the end when I have to find a way to say goodbye . . . it's still like the situation has now suddenly changed, and you're no longer open to me. I know no other way to deal with leaving; I feel cold and forced and impersonal afterwards . . . like there is only a small eye in my head for the world around me."

One day, Eva was working on an essay, picturing a society which might be formed by a group of adolescents, who find themselves suddenly without adults. Particularly interesting features of the proposed society were her provisions for productive work and intimacy; the respect accorded to individual differences; the use of space in allowances for separateness and togetherness; and finally, a proposed "day of mourning" each year for the mutual remembering of the first day when the community members were lost and abandoned.

Eva discussed the society: "There will be about 50-75 people in each town, sharing 100 acres. But each is connected to other cities . . . once they are old enough, like maybe fifteen, children would go to various communities who share an interest, like music or writing or science. Then there are central places for people to meet and give performances or share information. Some would want to stay in the middle because they haven't decided where they wanted to go. All people participate in work that they choose, but the "dirty" work would be equally shared by everyone. If somebody had a kid they would have time off for that. If somebody didn't do any job, they might have to go elsewhere to try and see if they can set up a community of their own. But if something was wrong with somebody, I mean, if somebody killed someone or if somebody went crazy they would stay in the central community and would be watched and given a job and therapy. Everybody would have a place."

"I don't know what to do about getting married or not—or who would take care of children. When children are older they would be in contact with various skills, how to make things and how to ask questions—like kids usually ask questions till school pressures them not to. Parents could choose if they leave you in the central community or take you to their village. Maybe there shouldn't be marriages and no certificates that say somebody is yours."

t: "How would you want it for yourself."

Eva: "I think I would want a relationship to one person, I don't know if promiscuity would be so good. If they are married, it ties them together and makes their children more secure, but maybe that should be only if two people loved each other and wanted a stronger than usual bond—but not if the two people change."

"The only illegal thing would be harming others, promiscuity would not be illegal. But if you try to commit suicide . . . people who commit suicide like they see no alternative . . . nothing to look forward to . . . I remember feeling that way . . . they would be seen by somebody in time. People would be allowed to move around if they don't like the roles and attitudes of one community, so they can go to another."

"I don't know what one would do about attitudes in the community like competitiveness, fear of each other, disgust and envy, hate and lack of responsibility or nonacceptance of others. I know there is a lot of tension in me when somebody expects me to do a certain job . . . or puts me in a certain role . . . and I don't always volunteer either, like when I'm tired."

The children would leave the subcommunity when old enough so that they might be exposed to "people with different common interests. The teachers in the central communities will be workers from all the subcommunities who will come to the farm once or twice a week to demonstrate some skill. Aside from voting on various issues, the members of the different subcoms will have many other contacts and forms of communications. The transportation from one town to another will be free and frequent. In the central community, there will be several public institutions. One will be a library, containing all the books that were originally in the house, plus new writings contributed by professionals and writers from all the subcoms. Children caan also submit stories of their own."

"Entertainment provided by people from all the subcoms will take place on the farm. There will be performances, participatory events, like dances, kite festivals, and general *celebrations.* After harvest there could be a day like Thanksgiving. In winter, there could be a snow celebration and in spring a celebration of the rebirth of nature. People would also have birthday parties. *The most important celebration would be in memory of the first day of our isolation. This occasion would last for two days. On the first, there would be a ritual re-enactment of the day of initial shock. Groups would walk around the barn, in the woods, and down to the old site of the town of Greenwood, looking for all the other people in the world. But of course, they wouldn't find them. The reactions would be remembered. The surprise, the disbelief, the sadness, and happiness.* Then the wanderers would return to the farm and talk about the old world and how it was. During the first day the only foods eaten would be berries and wild plants from the forest. That evening, there would be a meeting to decide on *one community project which everyone can participate in.* The second day, the project would be carried out. *Afterwards, there would be lots of eating and enjoyment; a celebration.*

Eva's civilization epitomized the presence of an optimal human support network. I was struck by her respect for individuality; her way of combining work with intimacy. The communities of those who shared work and interests were small, but they also had "free" and frequent connections to others, and reflected her care not to desert those in emotional distress, while still providing options for them, and her continued struggle about the permanence of love relationships and care of children. Meanwhile, continuity of identity was assured through the centralized collection of history and "new writings," including the perceptions of children. Finally, I was struck by her bringing into focus the role of mourning over the lost adults, and the remembering of that mourning as a way of revitalizing future goals and valued, joyful current celebrations. It was the quintessance of her reply to her feeling of being lost.

Eva is an example of those adolescents who were able to continue testing the reality of their changing inner images of the parent figures, to make criticisms that were not confirmed as catastrophes, and thereby did not foreclose the possibility of being able to live with the "truth" about their parents and themselves.

Chapter 8

"WHEN DEATH DID US PART": THE IMPACT OF
THE DECEASED—A COMPARISON

Eleanor Roosevelt's parents were separated when she was eight, and a year later her mother died of diptheria. Eleanor then lived with her grandmother. She wrote: My father explained to me that my mother was gone and she had been all the world to him and now he had only my brothers and myself, that my brothers were very young, and he and I must keep close together. Someday, I would make a home for him again, we would travel together, and do many things which he painted as interesting and pleasant, to be looked forward to, in the future together. Somehow, it was always he and I. I did not understand whether my brothers were to be our children or whether he felt that they would be at school and college and later independent. There started that day a feeling which never left me—that he and I were very close together, and someday would have a life of our own together. He told me to write, often, to be a good girl, not to give any trouble, to grow up into a woman be could be proud of, and he would come to see me whenever it was possible. When he left, I was all alone to keep our secret of mutual understanding and to adjust myself to my new existence.

Though he was so little with us, my father dominated all this period of my life. Subconsciously, I must have been waiting always for his visits.

Within the year, her father too was killed, in a riding accident: Just before I was ten years old, word came that my father had died. My aunts told me, but I simply refused to believe it, and while I wept long and went to bed still weeping, I finally went to sleep and began the next day living my dream world as usual. My grandmother decided that we children should not go to the funeral, and so I had no tangible thing to make death real to me. From that time on, I knew in my mind that my father was dead, and yet I lived with him more closely, probably, than I had when he was alive . . . They always tried to talk to me, and I wished to be left alone to live in a dream world in which I was the heroine and my father the hero. Into this world, I retired as soon as I went to bed and as soon as I woke in the morning, and all the time I was walking or when anyone bored me.

—Eleanor Roosevelt, quoted in Erikson (1964)

The death of a parent during childhood puts a more complete and final end to a relationship than does the loss of a parent who, though partially absent because of divorce or separation, still exists in the real world. In this chapter, I want to focus on children's ways of coping with loss by death as compared with the losses resulting from divorce, discussed in the previous three chapters. Illustrative material is taken from a child and two adolescents shortly after the death of a parent; and from a series of adults who were in various ways still unfinished with the death of a parent in childhood when they were seen. As has also been true in previous chapters, no attempt is made to select cases "representative" of those who have suffered such losses. Instead, the attempt is to catch "in vivo" the mental processes involved in the work of mourning, or the result of the absence of mourning. Some comparative comments on loss by death and loss by divorce are focused on the role of the human support network; the reality sense of the bereaved; the quest for the lost wanted parent; and the role of identification processes.

THE HUMAN SUPPORT NETWORK

A network of supportive human relationships appears to have been essential for the children of the deceased and the divorced: it makes possible constructive coping with the loss, and eventually with the associated grief. In both cases, the child needed to know that his basic needs for care would continue to be met in spite of his loss, before it was possible to face the affects associated with the loss. In addition, the child's ability to mourn was greatly affected by the presence of a figure whom he cared about, and who could sustain him, or symbolically help contain or "hold" him in his grief.

However, there were also some persistent differences in the role of the human support network for the bereaved. Interventions by others, however well-meaning, were often at first viewed as disturbing intrusions rather than as supportive unless the person was particularly attuned to the needs of the child. There seemed to be a number of reasons for this. In the first place, the human support network tended to foster the idealization of the dead person, making other views of him highly guilt-inducing for the child. Particularly in public, any negative feeling toward the dead had to be suppressed, one way or another. For example, those children who felt unable to cry for the parent or to cry for the parent in public (at the funeral) felt definitely blamed for this. The idealized public version of the parent tended to interfere with the resolution of the child's ambivalence, unless someone, preferably the remaining parent, was able to accept, with the child, the memories of both positive and negative features of the dead.

Secondly, some of the feelings of the child about his dead parent seemed deeply private to him, based on the treasuring of memories. The dead parent, unlike the divorced parent, was no longer in existence in a way in which he could be experienced by others. Strangers who were unable to share the child's perceptions and hadn't known the dead person were, in this context, also often viewed as an intrusion rather than a support. For example, when a stranger grabbed Wendy to express sympathy about "your dear dead father," the child's impulse was to laugh, with the thought, "why, she never even knew my father!" She was, of course, chided for her laughter and felt guilty about that. In a similar way, the well-meaning attempts at "rallying" a substitute figure to accompany the child at later "father-daughter" dinners, etc., may mean to the child that the fact that the dead parent cannot really be replaced is not acknowledged by others.

Thirdly, there appears to be a period, if the child manages to grieve for the dead parent, when some withdrawal from social relationships is appropriate. There are times when the image of the dead parent and the associated grief underlie the child's reality sense, and make superficial social contacts incongruous; he experiences them as an unreasonable demand on him. In one family, this was expressed as "just wanting to be alone together" with one another after the death. In another, in which the whole bereaved family was invited for dinner at the house of friends, the child could not tolerate the interactions which were occurring as "though nothing had happened," and ran from the house to be by herself in the car.

If one accepts, however, that the human support network in the case of the bereaved must be particularly attuned to the nuances involved, the presence of other, supportive individuals remains a crucial factor in whether the child can cope with the loss in ways which might foster rather than impede further development. Several adults mentioned the two or three years following the death of their parent as the most lonely and despairing in their lives. In these cases, the death was accompanied by other major changes in their living arrangements, and particularly by a feeling that they lacked support from the remaining parent.

Indeed, the role of the remaining parent was often at the heart of the matter. One helpful way in which the situation of the bereaved child differed from that of the child of divorce was that the longing of the child for the lost parent did not tend to represent disloyalty to the remaining parent, and could be more easily expressed. At a later time, however, when the remaining parent was attempting to make a new adjustment (e.g., to remarry), he or she might not want reminders of the past, and might attempt to extrude those aspects of the child which were linked to memories of the dead parent. There were enormous differences in the degree to which the remaining parent was able to support the grieving of the child, or allowed himself to feel sad in the child's presence. In Tod's and Peggy's family, shared grief brought the family close together; Michael was all alone with his feelings, unable even to ask for explanations and offered none; Natasha, though reprimanded for not crying, was in the midst of a social and political structure which now suddenly despised a father who had been previously admired; Amy's mother, though caring and supportive, could not let her see that she felt sad too.

REALITY SENSE

Reality sense must be differentiated from "reality testing." The child's reality sense includes what he knows to be true from his own experiences, and the way these experiences felt to him. This has been discussed in the previous chapter, in regard to the experience of "truth." One's reality sense may be contradicted by later "reality testing," or by the perceptions of others around one. If it is so contradicted the child either loses trust in his own perceptions, or attempts to validate those perceptions in reality, by recreating an experience which he hopes will prove them to be true.

In most of the bereaved individuals discussed here, reality testing was unimpaired; yet the reality sense did not fit the current situation. Part of this reality sense had been built around the interaction between the self and the wanted, lost parent. When loss through death occurs, mourning, decathexis, grappling with guilt, the overcoming of fears of a similar fate through identification, etc., may all occur. Still, there is something else left: the reality sense includes the experience of past, affective sharing with a beloved. The affectively experienced early love continues as a strongly motivating force, pushing for validation in later perceptions. Such validations may be obstructed by either internal (ambivalence) or external forces. However, if a loved parent is now dead, the child seems to need continued validation of his earlier experiences, through sustaining perceptions from the other parent, or from others. Thus he needs not only the usual help in dealing with the factual realities of the death, but a recognition that there is something that still exists of the relationship for him: that is, the affectively shared experience. In order to complete mourning and be able to invest in other relationships, the child must know that this was a reality, rather than just existing in his imagination. Case material regarding Amy will illustrate this issue.

The child survivor of a dead parent seems to live with a dual knowledge. Consciously, he knows his parent is dead. This fact may have been made more or less real to him by the explanations of the remaining parent, the possibility of attending the funeral and seeing that the parent is dead, etc. In fact, explanations about the reality of death, its causes and circumstances, its uncontagious nature, and especially clear explanations that the child is not to blame, are extremely helpful for the necessary reality testing, and for his need to differentiate himself and his fate from that of the dead parent. In a number of the cases described, this aspect was neglected, was insufficient, or went unheard by the child because of disturbing features in his remaining relationships. Few had been told simply and directly that they were not to blame; that their own fate did not have to be the same; that all people experience sadness and anger, and usually guilt when a person dies. Learning in general may be impeded if the child is prevented from "learning" about the death. He may experience this as not wanting to know, assuming that knowing will be bad news. This may mean to him the bad news that he might have been at fault (Michael is an example of this).

Even in the presence of such knowledge, however, there is a contradiction: in the unconscious, in dreams and fantasies, a permanent absence cannot be pictured, and thus does not exist. Hence. through dreams, fantasies, or visions, the child knows the parent is still present in some form. This leads us to a consideration of the quest for the lost, wanted parent.

THE QUEST FOR THE LOST, WANTED PARENT

The quest to validate both the perception that the parent is still present in some way and the affects associated with it may appear in the form of a ceaseless search, or of a waiting for the dead beloved to reappear. The "normality" and commonness of such an expectation has been well documented for recently bereaved adults by Parkes (1972), and for long-bereaved adults by Jacobson (1971) and others. For the still developing child, defenses are vulnerable, and the impact of overwhelming grief can be catastrophic. Grieving must take place slowly, and with the sustaining presence of others who also love the child. When grieving is aborted because either the external or internal supports cannot bear it, the developing child remains in some way haunted. Because of the definitely experienced but "irrational" duality of the presence of the lost, wanted parent, much that is felt about him remains private in the child and cannot be easily shared with others. This is true not only of negative or feared images, but also of the distillations of love, which fuel the continued quest.

Aspects of the quest for the wanted parent are reflected in the case material in a variety of phenomena, which include:

1. *Literal clinging to the dead.* This is a denial of the reality that death has occurred and that one must part. It occurs rarely.

2. *Searching.* The bereaved finds himself searching faces in the street, supermarket, or crowd, expecting finally to catch a glimpse of the wanted parent.

3. *Presences.* The bereaved experiences a sense of the lost parent's presence. Although he cannot be seen, he is felt to be in the room, watching from above, feeling hurt if his former wife or child is disloyal, being within spitting distance, smiling approval, etc. The presence is felt in a way quite different from that of an internalized conscience that approves or disapproves of the actions of the child. Such presences were transiently reinvoked by adults in the midst of grief work.

4. *Transitional objects and transitional phenomena.* Aspects of previously shared, gratifying, sensual and affective experiences with the dead parent were perpetuated in transitional objects or transitional phenomena unconsciously linked with that parent. During grief work the links may become conscious.

5. *Expectations of communication.* Some bereaved individuals had a constant or intermittent unconscious anticipation of receiving a message (such as a letter) from the deceased.

6. *Recreation of painful affects.* In this mode, the individual sought to preserve the interaction with the lost one by repetitively experiencing (with someone else) the sequence of affects last shared, followed by a painful sense of disruption or loss.

7. *Recreation of unconscious components of the shared relationship.* Perpetuating unconscious components of the shared relationship could have highly positive or negative effects. It was constructive, for example, when it involved living up to treasured aspects of an ego ideal shared with the dead person. It was then seen in terms of a tribute or gift to that person.

8. *Memories.* The degree to which the dead parent was represented in the memory of the bereaved differed greatly. A paucity of memories, particularly in adults whose parents had died when they were already old enough to retain memories (e.g., age ten), was often associated with a pathologic overidentification with the dead parent which made grieving difficult. A richness of memory tended more often to coincide with a parallel richness of available affects, and the capacity to tolerate grieving. The grieving process in itself frequently stirred previously inaccessible memories. During grieving the affective tone of memories frequently changed (e.g., from happy to disappointing, or the opposite).

9. *The painful awareness of the absence of the presence.* A shift in reality sense sometimes accompanied the grieving process in such a way that the bereaved person eventually came to face the absence of the previously cherished presence. This moment was intensely painful, but tended to be

followed by a reshuffling of the gratifications sought from current relationships, through an attempt to come to terms with the fact that the love expected from the lost parent would not be forthcoming, and hence might have to be sought in different ways from current relationships when the quest is renounced. Symbolic rather than literal fidelity might then remain.

IDENTIFICATION PROCESSES

Identification with the deceased parent has been one aspect of the child's relationship to him prior to death. After death, identification becomes in addition a favored defense, a way of "keeping" the wanted person by internalizing his image and becoming more like him oneself. The sense of closeness is achieved through likeness.

Aspects of identification with the dead person occurred in all the cases, but there were major differences in the impact of the identification upon the developing personality. These differences appeared to depend partly on the developmental level of the ego processes available to the child, but were also heavily influenced by the quality of the relationship prior to the parent's death, and the nature of the supportive relationships available in the environment. When a modicum of grieving was possible, there appeared to be less likelihood of pathologic overidentification with the dead. One of the complications that differentiates the bereaved from the children of divorce is that aggression can no longer be directed outward at the person, as it can at an absent but existing parent. When such aggression has no outlet and also prevents grieving, there is a greater likelihood that it will be directed against the self, and that the individual will identify with negatively viewed components of the deceased.

When closeness to the wanted, dead parent is achieved by an identification with his infirmity or deadness, it involves the numbing of impulses associated with aliveness. This can occur in the form of an individual's renunciation of growth, of feeling, or of pleasure. The consequently depressed person described himself as "unable to feel or enjoy life." Wishes to renounce life itself may be apparent. Guilt about survival while the parent is dead, especially given ambivalent attitudes about that parent that are unacceptable to the self, can solidify these identifications into a lifelong pattern of renunciations. Such identifications are extremely threatening and usually unconscious.

A different source of the wish for deadness, often expressed in suicidal fantasies or attempts, is the early, loving closeness to the parent, which remains within the child's reality sense as an experience of unity, of the merging of ego boundaries in order to feel cozily united. In the cases discussed here, this form of wished-for merger was associated with aspects of the quest for the parent (transitional object phenomena, presences, fantasied communication, etc.) and much less heavily imbued with prior deprivation or consequent overwhelming hostility.

Identification processes occurred along a range of developmental levels. These are not merely a matter of age: for example, a number of cases presented widely varying reactions, although the children were all around the age of ten when the parent died (Vicky, Mary Ann, Michael, Alex, Wendy). In some cases, identifications centered upon the child's perception of physical or sex-linked attributes or images of exaggerated power versus helplessness, while in others there was a much heavier emphasis on attitudes and personality traits. In all of them, affects in interaction with the deceased were a leitmotiv within their sense of reality about the lost parent and themselves. In cases where a rich, loving, and growth-enhancing relationship existed for the child before the death of the parent, identifications with the positive features of the parent immortalized the evidence of his past presence.

At the end of the chapter I shall comment briefly on the case material in connection with these issues. The degree to which the impact of the deceased shone through or shadowed the life of the bereaved becomes evident in the material itself. More subtle perhaps is the question of the other aspects of the personality affected by the process of grieving. It appeared that those individuals who were able to experience their loss and grieving were able better to communicate and tolerate their affect in general, to review their reality testing about current relationships, and to accept both love and modulated hate toward the same individual as cohabiting within them.

Encounters with Children, Adolescents and Adults

A CHILD: GUILT, FEAR AND TRANSFIGURATION—VICKY

Vicky, a ten-year-old, was in therapy when her mother died. A progressive illness had confined her mother to a wheelchair since the little girl was eight. Vicky suffered much guilt, especially over her sexual curiosities and fondness for her permissive father. She saw her mother as the disciplinarian in the household, well able to wield the hairbrush to punish her children in spite of her confined movements. Actually, Vicky's adolescent brothers were more often spanked with the brush than Vicky. Shortly before the mother's death, Vicky had been severely reprimanded by her mother for undressing without pulling down the shades. She had had some fantasies about the college boy who lived across the way and sometimes played ball with her: she thought he looked like the prince in the Cinderella book she had, and wondered how she looked to him. Wanting to exhibit herself was not spurred by romantic fantasies alone, but included Vicky's wish for assurance that her body was undamaged and not like her mother's.

After the mother's death, Vicky experienced terror before she felt grief. She became frightened at night, insisting that locks be put on her windows. She told me she was unsure that her mother would really stay put in her grave, and expected that she might climb through the window when Vicky was asleep in order to punish her. As she worked out some of the meaning of this, it became clear that the fantasy represented a complicated condensation of her libidinous wishes and her guilt. She had been conscious of her wish to be seen and admired by the "prince," who had already given her some attention. She had been told that it was "bad" to do this and was punished by her mother; during this time she had talked about the Cinderella story in which the mean stepmother did not want the young girl to have any fun, and she had associated this with being angry at her mother for ordering people around from her wheelchair. When father and she were giggling together, mother interrupted and ordered both around, saying they were too "irresponsible." In reality, mother was concerned about father's ability to provide guidance in the family after her death, and recognized "giggling" as sometimes meaning that he had had too much to drink.

However, in an earlier period of childhood, Vicky had been especially dependent on her mother, and had been praised for her compliance and prettiness. Appearances had always been important in the family. Mother then was still well. In her fantasy, Vicky was first aware of fearing the punitive mother, who now had no life or "fun," in contrast to Vicky. Vicky, in fact, felt she might have usurped her mother's pleasures and that she deserved punishment for doing so. Later, she became aware of the grief that was centered in the same fantasy: that she wished her mother would come back, freed from the shackles of her wheelchair, and able to climb or fly into the window to be with her daughter again. She imagined mother in a Peter Pan fantasy, in which Vickie would never grow up and, with her mother, would have children, whom they would treat with the loving kindness that her own mother had more often shown before her illness. She came to identify the mobile mother as her "real mother," rejecting the more harsh, ill, and incapacitated "stepmother" of the wheelchair. Her loss had begun with mother's illness; not her death.

TWO ADOLESCENTS: SUPPORTED GRIEVING—TOD AND PEGGY

Tod was fifteen and Peggy thirteen when their mother died. Mother had intuitively and supportively prepared for her continuity with the children by putting special care into those shared activities which the children could carry on after her death. Father was able not only to share some of his grieving for mother with his son and daughter, and to support theirs, but also made extra time available to each. During the first year after her death, special occasions, such as Christmas, that were expected to evoke painful memories, were spent in the comforting presence of grandparents. Tod and Peggy mourned their mother deeply and constructively without forfeiting aspects of their own development. The references they made to their quest for mother after her death, their guilt and longing to "make up" for past ambivalence; and their identification with mother, through experiencing her role in still-valued activities and attitudes which they continued, are all usual components of working through a grief reaction under optimal internal and external conditions.

Tod and Peggy saw me about six months after their mother had died. They were both appealing individuals, personable, thoughtful and articulate. Peggy came first; Tod next.

Peggy

Peggy: "My mother was sick for about two years before she died . . . that was six months ago. That last year, I helped her around the house a lot, and at the end, my grandmother came out to help too. Mother and I made up a cookbook together and I've got that and cook from it a lot. She showed me how to sew too. She was a wonderful mother . . . she was very smart . . . but she was happy to stay home, so she was always there when we needed her."

t: "Did you know she was going to die?"

Peggy: "Yea, I knew she might die for a while when we went to the hospital to see her, at least my father let us know it was a possibility. After she died, we just felt like staying home together for several days, being with each other and not outsiders.

t: "And what do you feel about it now?"

Peggy: "I know my mother is dead, but I still sometimes just can't believe it." (Tears had started while she talked.) "Like shopping in a crowd . . . somebody will turn their head . . . and for a moment I expect it to be my mother."

t: "Yes, and when it turns out to be someone else, that must shake you up still . . . do you picture her other ways, too?"

Peggy: "I talk to her in my head a lot, like I imagine what mother would say about different things I'm doing, or Dad does."

t: "Like what?"

Peggy: "Well, I especially think she wouldn't like his going out with Rhonda. She is so different from my mother, like opposites. I don't think she would mind if he went out with my aunt, because she liked the same things as my mother and I know she wouldn't want him to just stay lonely."

t: "And you?"

Peggy: "I would rather have it by my aunt too, not anyone so different."

t: "You've been telling me what a great mother she was, and from everything you said and your own feelings about it, I'm convinced she was too. Still, I have never seen a kid yet who didn't feel like really getting mad at their mothers sometimes, too, who didn't have times that were not quite so great between them . . . and often those are times that bother them a lot still after a parent dies. . . ."

Peggy: "Well, she used to get pretty mad at us about cleaning our rooms. We used to tease her about nagging us, but that would make her even madder. She liked everything to be correct, like table manners. The once I was maddest at her I remember—when she wouldn't let me go out because I had to finish my homework and when the kids came by to pick me up I mimicked her in a real sarcastic voice like this . . . (Peggy now demonstrated the sarcastic voice and then found herself weeping.) I could see she was really hurt."

I waited till she had finished crying.

t: "The idea of hurting her bothers you a lot still."

Peggy: "Yea, I wish I would have told her I was sorry after, but I never did."

t: "And now it bothers you because you can't tell her anymore that you were sorry, and make it up with her."

She nodded.

t: "That's one of the big troubles people usually have when somebody they love dies . . . that whatever they want to make up still, the chance is gone . . . and in their mind they keep picturing it going differently. I would bet from what you've told me about your mother that she pretty solidly knew you loved her; and when you got mad at her a lot like most kids do . . . and that she forgave you for that . . . and probably for other stuff you *haven't* told me about . . . a long time ago."

Peggy: "I think she really knew we were with her by all the help we gave her around the house and everything. After she died, first I thought I could do everything around the house . . . or that we could . . . and then I found out that it was more work than I'd thought and I guess my father thought too, it was too much responsibility for us. . . ."

t: "I would agree with him."

Peggy: "So anyway, then we got a housekeeper and I was glad. She is really nice. I mean she wouldn't ever tell me what to do, but she's around when we come home from school . . . and likes to play cards and stuff."

Peggy now described her antipathy to women whom her father might like and who would try to tell her what to do. That role was reserved for mother.

We talked for a while about how she had been managing without her mother. We discussed times when kids usually expect to find their mother on deck: how it was when she had her first period, her birthday, telling someone about a boy she liked. She then mentioned that Christmas was not so bad, because they went to their grandparents' house, as usual.

Peggy: "You know what we found out?"

t: "What?"

Peggy: "That all the things we *wished* could happen . . . *could happen now* when she wasn't there . . . and we found out that they weren't so great!"

t: "Like what?"

Peggy: "Well, she was pretty strict about the number of cookies after school and before dinner . . . so a couple of months after she died, Tod and I would come home and absolutely stuff ourselves with whole boxes of cookies . . . and it just wasn't great at all . . . I was just never hungry enough for dinner, even if dinner was something especially good. So now I just discipline myself about that, and about a lot of the things she used to say that I didn't want to accept when she said them."

Thus Peggy had internalized and identified with some of her mother's values. She had previously viewed them as prohibitions, but now saw them as suiting her self-interest as well. Although there had been some conflict between mother and Peggy, she felt now she "agrees" with mother more. She told me she missed being able to tell mother that, for it would have made mother happy.

Peggy talked warmly of her father and the fact that "he does a lot with me." She was more ambivalent, however, about the time and energy he might spend with someone outside the family, who was "different" from mother, and might not be good for any of them. Her concern about further change and the loss of support that such a possibility might involve predominated the rest of the session.

Tod

Tod's description of the mutual support within the family was in many ways similar to Peggy's and need not be repeated here. However, there were some differences, too. Tod had actually had fewer areas of disagreement with his mother, but had perhaps been more dependent on her to uphold his rights and opinions at times of rivalry with the persuasive Peggy. Although, like the rest of the family, he had mourned openly, he was now at a point of wanting to "pull myself together" and to cry no more.

Tod: "Things have been kind of hard . . . about my mother . . . a lot of times when my father wasn't home and had to work. Well . . . I think I really took my mother for granted."

t: "Like how?"

Tod: "Like she would always help me with my homework . . . and now nobody does that . . . and she saw to it that Peggy didn't get away with a lot more than I did. . . . My father is forgetful sometimes . . . I mean he tries to be fair and everything, but I discovered the other day that my sister's allowance is higher than mine, even though she's younger. Mother was great at keeping track of things like that, she wouldn't have let that happen. And if Peggy started yelling about something, my mother would listen to reason. I mean, it wasn't like she was the boss . . . I can't think of a word to describe it. . . ."

t: "Yes, it must be hard to describe her in words . . . do you picture her in your mind . . . how?"

Tod: "I used to do that a lot at first after she died . . . now I try to put her out of my mind sometimes . . . I don't want to start crying and everything again."

t: "There's nothing to be ashamed of about crying . . . I mean a lot of grown guys do it, even if they don't talk about it. But maybe you have other reasons too, for wanting to get over that part, and getting on with the rest of your life."

Tod: "I have to pull myself together . . . my grades have kind of dropped . . . I don't know if I'm doing all I could."

t: "It's natural to feel depressed for a while . . . and like doing less too . . . while you're missing someone you lost . . . and who meant so much to you. But maybe you have some other thoughts, too, about when you said you don't know if you're doing all you could. Are you wishing you did something . . . that you *could* have done?"

Tod: "Well, my father—he went to visit my mother in the hospital every day, of course, and I did too, most of the time. But a lot of times, I didn't talk to her, I just turned my back and sat and watched the ballgame on TV. I didn't know what to say; I don't know if she minded . . . but at least I could have paid more attention and talked to her."

t: "Just having you with her must have meant a lot to her . . . I would think all your mixed feelings about her getting sick . . . and sort of leaving you in the lurch like that would have made it extra hard to talk and even might have made you feel like turning your back on her a bit." (Father told me later that mother had been too weak at the time for conversation anyway. Since she did not look physically changed, except for weight loss, this may not have been clear to the boy.) "It sounds like she was the one who made sure that you got the attention you needed at home, and you started feeling bad about not doing the same for her. But maybe her needs were really different from yours."

Tod went on from this to discuss Rhonda, whom his father was seeing. He saw her differently than Peggy did, and looked to her to be helpful, as mother had been. He added: "She would probably get along as well with my father as mother did . . . and she could take care of us while Dad is off working. Also, I think my Dad would be happier than without her . . . I mean he does a bunch of stuff with me now, but he doesn't have the time for things like a lot of basketball, and she would remind him not to be absent-minded about it. Most of the afternoons, I call up my friend, even to check homework. I think if she were around, I would run up the phone bill less."

Tod's thoughts of his mother offered less consolation than Peggy's did; he was trying to stop feeling the pain and tears. He was readier to turn toward a substitute, whom he pictured as caring for him much as his mother had, while simultaneously assuring his father's availability to him. His view of Rhonda had less to do with her as a person than with his wish to fill the void mother had left. In contrast, Peggy viewed the women her father might like in a very selective fashion, and feared their interference in her relationship with her father. Although she, too, wished for someone like mother (e.g., her aunt), she felt strongly that a woman who seemed to embody some of the unconscious components of her conflicts with mother (rivalry and control) without the redeeming, strongly positive features would be an unwelcome intrusion and would lead, for her, to further loss. These differences probably had to do with the different sexes and needs of the two adolescents, the actual differences in their parents' relationships to them, and the actual characteristics of the woman father father was beginning to see steadily.

Both adolescents, as well as their father, had a strong and continuing sense of their mother's positive influence in their lives. Since only a single interview (dealing with an upcoming family decision) had been planned, I did not deem it advisable to attempt to uncover possible unconscious fantasies about surviving while the mother had died. Any work with guilt remained at the level at which Peggy and Tod presented it; that is, it was concerned with misdeeds or inadequacies they believed they had displayed toward their mother, and with the possibility of forgiveness for these.

ADULTS BEREAVED IN CHILDHOOD

Literal Clinging to the Dead: Mary Ann

Mary Ann is the mother of Lou Ann, described at length in chapter 5. Mary Ann's mother, also named Lou Ann, had borne her at age fourteen, and the two of them first lived in the household of Mary Ann's grandmother. Lou Ann then married an older man, left Mary Ann with grandmother, but was in and out of the household. In contrast to grandmother, Lou Ann was nice to Mary Ann and the child was very attached to her. When Mary Ann was eleven, her mother died. Mary Ann recalled that she threw herself into the grave with her mother, clung to her, and refused to be "pulled off her"; in her memory, when they were finally "pried apart" by force, by several adult men, her ankles were broken. She was "in shock" for two weeks and couldn't move. The memory may be distorted. Severe difficulties in the next year of life with her grandmother resulted in Mary Ann's placement in a home for neglected children by age twelve.

Mary Ann continued a desperate search for a mother much of her life. She felt she married because she liked her husband's mother so much. When after a stormy period the marriage broke up, she moved in with her mother-in-law, and reacted with homicidal and suicidal urges toward anyone who "might come between us" (between her ex-mother-in-law and herself). She named her oldest daughter Lou Ann, after her mother, and delegated to her many maternal responsibilities, e.g., housework, the care and feeding of the younger siblings, guardianship of the money, and the role of the sexual adult, etc. She told Lou Ann many times that she was replacing the other Lou Ann, Mary Ann's lost mother. Mary Ann saw the world as primarily populated by mothers and babies. As Lou Ann became pubescent, she made clear to her daughter that she wished and expected her to have a baby, thereby attempting to recreate the lost, wanted interaction of "Lou Ann and her baby" (her mother and herself). In this reversal of mother-daughter roles, there was a strong push toward incest between Lou Ann and her father (Mary Ann's ex-husband). Although consciously furious at this idea, she made her daughter promise to "give the little rascal to me" should she become pregnant. She pictured the new baby, who was never conceived, as a boy and felt she would have had an easier life herself as a male.

Additional problems related to her continued need for mothering were her extreme obesity and alcoholism. The quest for the lost wanted parent is usually carried on in more symbolic and less concrete, extreme forms than in the case of Mary Ann. Her deprivations had been too severe for too long to make it possible for her to face the loss of her mother. Intervention was necessary not only for her sake, but for the development of her children as well.

Identification in the Absence of Memory: Michael

Michael was a forty-six-year-old married man, the father of three children. He came to see me in a severely depressed state, shortly after he was offered an office promotion which he had turned down. He did clerical work which did not make full use of the training he had received in college. He had always been considered a "good guy" and devoted family man by others, and by his wife. The degree of his distress initially overshadowed many positive features of his personality.

When first seen, he was suffering from a cluster of difficulties which included frequent crying spells, early morning waking accompanied by frightening thoughts of impending doom, fear of being alone in the house, inability to enjoy anything (dysphoria), exhaustion, memory and concentration impairment, etc. Each morning, he worried about whether he would be able to get through another day, but tried his best to hide his depressed state from others. He had tried heroically to manage to make himself better by following remedies he had heard of from past friends, or read about, but could not do so any longer. His wife, who in the past had cheered him up when necessary, now had some problems of her own and he could no longer count on her in the same way. His overriding thought now was, "It's all downhill, my life is over."

He had had two years of psychotherapy in his late thirties, around problems with his son. He told me that he had experienced the psychiatrist as "my torturer" because "something was demanded of me" and "he wouldn't tell me what to do." During this time, however, he had never thought of himself as depressed and his own symptoms had not been severe.

Michael's mother had become terminally ill when she was forty-six and he was six. She died when he was eleven. In therapy, the paucity of memories regarding his relationship to his mother was striking, and persisted for a long time. His reactions to her illness and death had to be reconstructed and worked through in connection with a series of symbolic equivalents: e.g., his reactions to the death of a friend, changes in his relationship with his wife, and his view of me, of the therapy process, and of medication. As he suffered from a syndrome of difficulties which is often helped in this way, medication, administered by someone else, was added to psychotherapy as a part of the treatment program. Although there was an amelioration of the most distressing symptoms during the initial year of treatment, milder recurrences of depression continued into the third year, when he went through a period of intense mourning. This occurred when his own assertiveness and individuation had progressed enough that he wanted to feel like an equal partner with his wife, rather than depending on her chiefly for mothering. He was anguished at the temporary conflict that this change caused between them (sobbing rather than quietly weeping about the expected desertion) and was plagued by the thought that their relationship might not survive (it did).

The offer of promotion for Michael, at the expense of a fellow worker, had stirred up overwhelming guilt about the possibility of succeeding over someone else and facing the retaliation of the unpromoted fellow worker. He saw his own success as intrinsically connected to someone else's downfall. Coincidentally, it occurred when he was forty-six, the age at which his mother's illness had begun. These issues strengthened a lifelong unconscious identification with the mother. It was really she who went "downhill" from that age on, and whose life was soon over, but he was initially unaware of that connection. He had taken over from his mother the expected loss of life and loss of life's enjoyments.

These are some of the things Michael told me at the beginning of the first interview:

Michael: "I'm afraid I'm going to cry."

t: "That's okay."

Michael did cry intermittently throughout the interview, "I have a fear of everything, undertaking anything."

t: "What sort of fear?"

Michael: "I wake every morning at two or three, knowing something terrible is going to happen. I don't know what. Like the house we have in Vermont, that if we go up there the wood will have rotted and animals destroyed the inside. So I don't want to go up weekends. There's nothing I enjoy doing anymore, I don't like it when my wife leaves the house. I don't know how I will go through the day. I dread it if somebody calls because I don't want them to know. *I keep thinking it's all downhill, my life is over."*

t: "When did you start feeling like that?"

Michael: "I don't know. To some extent my wife used to help me, encourage me when I needed it. She is always an optimist and I'm not. And my daughter had a sunny disposition as a small child and I needed that. I needed somebody to smile at me. Now she and my son are almost grown, they're both more hostile. Could you call me by my first name?"

A little later, I commented that he was telling me he felt he had lost the smiles and encouragement he needed. Had there been other losses in his life?

Michael: "There was a lot of sickness and death in my family; my parents died. I mean, my mother died when I was eleven. I lived with my older sister and father until college. Then my father died. My mother was forty when I was born; *I can't remember her at all.* I think I felt responsible for trying to make my father happy after she was gone, and not to be a burden to my sister."

t: "Your mother, was she sick long before she died?"

Michael: "She was in bed about the last five years . . . I was about six, I guess."

t: "That would make her about forty-six when she got sick, yes? How old are you now yourself?"

Michael: "I'm forty-six."

The following issues emerged in therapy over a period of time and I shall comment on them individually:

a. Dread of the dead body and the contagion of deadness
b. Deprivation, the paucity of memories, and difficulties in "taking in" relationships; the hope for magic rescue
c. Awareness of relief when someone went away or died
d. Fear of change and of abandonment
e. The bargain, "I'll be good if you'll take care of me"
f. Remaining dependent and resentful, but not close
g. Crisis and grief associated with growth of individuality and the awareness of death wishes: a turning point

a. *Dread of the dead body and the contagion of deadness.* One of the few memories Michael eventually had of his mother was the sight of her body in the casket at the memorial service.

Michael: "There was the body all cold and waxy-looking and strange. I was in terror that someone would ask me to touch or to kiss her. I was revolted and didn't want anyone to know that. I wasn't sure what she had had and if it might be contagious. I don't think I even knew that her breasts had been taken off. I never asked any questions."

He had not found out if closeness to her might make him die, too. The revulsion and fear covered an underlying longing to be close to a mother, a longing which had long been unfulfilled.

b. *Deprivation, the paucity of memories, and difficulties in "taking in" in relationships: the hope for magic rescue.* Michael had experienced maternal deprivation in his childhood in a number of ways. As he perceived it, he was an unwanted "accident," born when his mother was forty, over ten years after his siblings were born. For whatever reason, (we do not know if she was depressed) she turned much of his care over to the older sibs, who tolerated, but also teased him. He had a single memory of her in early childhood. Once when he was in the first grade, she came to school to pick him up and took him to lunch. When he was six, she became ill and increasingly bedridden. Her door was usually closed to him. She went to the hospital for months at a time. Shortly before her death, he remembered, "a big, black bed day after day—it was awesome-looking. Something sticks in my mind, maybe the day she died. It was Memorial Day and the newspaper said something about 'dead.' Memorial Day was a holiday and I wondered why people were so happy."

This was the first clue that he felt guilty about feeling "happy" himself that it was she and not he who had died. He then also remembered that during those years, she had fought with Michael's older sister about wearing lipstick and going out with boys. Mother had told Marie, his sister, "You'll be the death of me yet." Michael watched but did not remember ever "fighting with mother" himself. His father he described as "very quiet, reading his newspaper," but not actively supportive to the lonely little boy.

Michael tried to "take" the nurturant gratification which was denied him in early childhood, in a number of ways which symbolize, but do not directly involve, relationships to others. He remembered these one session which he began by the statement, "I'm an unbelievably self-centered and selfish person." He first said that the statement referred to his annoyance at being interrupted by his wife when he wanted to watch the baseball game on TV. I asked what else he wanted for himself, when he was little, that he felt "selfish" about. He remembered that when he was nine or ten he began taking money out of mother's pocketbook. Also, she used to hide some candy in the house for guests, and he would search it out and eat it all by himself. He added, "I still play that same game in our house. I do the same thing, but I hide it from myself so I won't gain more weight. But I still sneak. Usually, I kept my mouth shut at the hospital and at home. Often no word was spoken between us. I'm not sure I ever knew her breasts were removed. I didn't ask my sisters things either . . . I don't know why none of the family seemed to communicate with each other . . . much later in adolescence, I asked Marie about sex, I mean, sperm. She said it was fish. I don't know if I told you that I sucked my thumb until I got married."

There had been attempts to "break" him of the habit of thumb sucking by putting his hands into what he remembered as "metal mitts," which took away the softness. This did not work, and he resumed sucking his thumb, secretly. His search for oral gratification emphasized obtaining it alone, (thumb, candy hidden from him by mother) without connected images of a wanted person (he kept his mouth shut at the hospital, no words were spoken, her breasts were gone). Thumbsucking normally begins before the tendency to use transitional objects, which represent a combination of the wanted parent and the self. Transitional objects were not relied on by Michael, as far as is known.

Michael made many references to the lack of communication—verbal or affective interchange—between family members. He did not seek, nor was he given explanations or support during his mother's illness. As an adult, he and his sister saw each other occasionally, but "have nothing to say to each other." When, later in therapy, he made more active attempts to recapture a sense of what his mother had been like, he found out extremely little from his sister, even though she was in her early twenties when their mother died. He did, however, unearth a letter from her, written before her death to the sister. It was a brave and stilted, carefully lettered, self-controlled message. It conveyed to the daughter that she would now have the responsibility of the family, that she should be "brave" and inspire the rest of the family to be so, too, and that she should make sure that the father would not be "too unhappy." There was no specific mention of, or message to, Michael and no provision for anyone's grief. There was no expression of her own suffering, or sadness, or indignation about having to leave her family.

Associated with Michael's deprivation in oral gratification and emotional contact in childhood (we do not really know what his babyhood was like, except that he had not been wanted) and his feeling that gratification was forbidden or stolen (the candy and the thumb) was a difficulty in the process of "taking in" both within relationships and from the world at large. Most importantly, he had not internalized the image of a loving mother who could supply him with memories and self-esteem in her absence. "Taking in" was affected in a number of ways. He remembered that in college he would frequently fall asleep during lectures (not taking them in) and later, at work, while reading, although he had had plenty of sleep. He said of this time, "I just went through the motions in college, I never involved myself." This was an unrecognized forerunner of later depression. While severely depressed later, he could not watch or retain anything he saw on TV or read in magazines and suffered from a general impairment of memory. Remembering conversations was most difficult of all. He often complained about sessions with me, "When I leave here, I lose what I got here, so what good can it do me?" He would come saying he had forgotten everything he was going to tell me. Eventually, we agreed that he should write down his thoughts when he had them, and he began to see that he could still think. He often insisted that he knew he could not be helped—it would take the "impossible." This comment had several meanings. At one level, he was right; what he believed would make him better was "impossible": no one could give him back a live mother.

Early in therapy, this particular belief expressed itself in his wishes in a form we came to refer to as his "magic rescue." He said, "I grew up believing everything comes to him who waits." If he just waited long enough, somehow, probably with luck, everything would turn out all right. His wife's optimism used to assure him that he was right, but his serious problems with his sons and daughters, during adolescence, and in his work-setting had destroyed his belief in this. At the beginning, medication also had great significance for him in this context. The evening after his initial dose (long before, as he had been informed, a physiological effect was possible) he became elated with the conviction that the pills had made him well. His depression then worsened for weeks, while he felt that his last hope for cure, the "magic pills," were not helping him. A recurrence of hope, followed by despair, followed each adjustment in dose and type of medication during the first year of therapy. "I think of them as magic pills and then it turns out they haven't changed me."

After a few months, Michael still professed a lack of memory for our sessions, but began to use them to be less harsh with himself. During this time, for example, he would say,

Michael: "I can't remember what we talked about here last time, but that afternoon I kept telling myself that I must not feel guilty all the time. I did not cause mother to die. Still, it is such a struggle to get through each thing during the day. I must get a grip on life . . . I feel like I can unburden myself here, but I can't remember what we said afterwards. I still have no ability to enjoy anything."

Slowly, he became aware that both his wishes for magic help and his furious disappointments were also directed at me. He began to be able to contain his ambivalence, to direct both at the same person. For example, one day he said:

"I think of the medication as good or bad. How can it be in between?"

t: "Your view of a mother is also as either 'all good and rescuing you' or 'all bad and deserting you', not as a real person with some lousy things and some things you might have liked about her."

Michael: "I always think of people that way, good or bad, but they can change from one to the other. My mother-in-law, I used to think of as all good and lately as all bad. When she dies, I don't know if I'll be able to be sorry or just feel relief. But I think my mother didn't treat herself too well either. I always assume that I'll be a loser, myself." (Relief at the death of others is something we shall return to.)

The following week, he commented:

Michael: "I feel so empty, I just wish I would feel good, I am aware of how other people can handle things. Do you know how mad I am at you? You recommended that I see Dr. Z. about medication. I thought that would make it all right and it hasn't. Contact is so difficult, I can't ever express myself."

t: "You've let me know how mad you are at me; that expresses some of what you are feeling, that Dr. Tessman is a bitch for not having made you feel better. That doesn't have to cut off contact."

Michael: "But I'm scared alone. I try to be cheery; not to let anyone else know how lousy I feel. I thought about depending on you and that frightens me. The first vacation, I never missed you. It was like you didn't exist for me when you were gone. I never thought of you. I know from other people in therapy I thought maybe I'm supposed to miss you. But now...I though of something today...that I needed you to pull me up from the quicksand by the hand ... that you would be the one to pull me up."

c. *Awareness of relief when someone went away or died.* The secret experience of relief when someone went away or died was a major source of guilt for Michael. He said, "Ever since my mother died, it's a relief when people leave me." In milder form, it occurred when his wife or guests left the room and he knew no further demand would be made on him at the moment. He was more ashamed of his distress when his grown children visited, and of his enormous relief when they left. When they were home, he was reminded of their problems, and felt himself a failure when he could not do something about these. Once they left again, he simply did not think of them, their problems, or how their problems reflected on him as a "failure." After he had been some months in therapy, a friend to whom he had formerly been closer died. He had been helpful to this friend in the past, but had recently turned down a request for a loan from him. Michael's first reaction was a feeling of relief; only later did some components of grieving come to the fore.

Michael: "I felt numbed by it but not mournful. At the funeral, I was uncomfortable that I was happy and relieved that it wasn't me. There was that feeling of revulsion and disgust at the dead body again."

t: "That's the *natural* feeling we have been talking about that happens when someone else dies. Of *course* you are glad it isn't you. You defend yourself from feeling close to the dead person by reminding yourself how different you are at that moment, how alive. You don't want to touch or get near the dead body. One problem about your mother was how guilty you felt about all that; so guilty about naturally wanting to be alive, and trying to make up for being mad at her and having wanted closeness when you were little that you made yourself 'take in' her deadness and no longer enjoying anything till now you are afraid you're doomed to be a loser too. You're *not* your mother, you know."

Michael: "For so many years I didn't even know what my mother died of. I don't want to know too much because it might be bad news, so I never asked. That reminds me of something. I looked at the mirror yesterday and thought 'God, but you're ugly!'"

t: "So you looked at yourself and thought you saw bad news: I'm ugly. Ugly, how so?"

Michael: "Just ugly. I do remember that sometime during those years I exposed myself to the girls in the neighborhood. When I realized what I had done by the time I was about thirteen, I felt it was horrible; there was no way to atone. I was ill-informed about sex, my education was neglected."

t: "You must have wanted some reassurance about your penis and being a boy. Some reassurance, too, that you were different from your mother; that the same things would not happen to you."

Michael: "I think so. It's like being different or thinking different than people expect—it's like arguing. But when you say it like that it doesn't sound so bad. Maybe I don't have to be ashamed about it. About my mother-in-law. I managed to argue with my wife about her; because I don't want her to visit on Mother's Day. I thought 'what if she were to die; how will people know I'm mourning when I detest her so!'"

t: "What does that bring to mind?"

Michael: "My always thinking, what if something terrible happened and it were my fault." I mean with my mother-in-law a lot of times I just want to be rid of her."

t: "That won't kill her."

This, of course, allowed us to discuss, not for the first time, his fear of being blamed for mother's death. Especially when he felt aggressive (as being offered promotion over his fellow worker at the office had made him feel, or "arguing") he ended up feeling worthless, blaming himself for things he had not even done. Slowly, we could bring into focus his dependence, passivity, and feelings of worthlessness as not only reflecting his past deprivations but also his way of attempting to convince himself that others were responsible for what happened in the world, and that therefore it could not be his "fault." The evidence that his attempt did not work for him, that it did not after all make him feel blamefree, was seen in the self-punishment by which he took over from his mother the burden of feeling ill, that "life was over."

Michael: "I grew up with the feeling that I was powerless; things just occurred; I have no effect on what happens. I was passive and never struggled. I was grateful to my sister for taking care of me and just tagged along. Her friends teased me about being ugly. My initial adjustment to my marriage played into my feelings that someone would take care of me . . . I let my wife make the decisions. I still instinctively feel that way."

t: "If things just happen, nobody is responsible; certainly *you* can't be held responsible."

Michael: "I was always afraid in a relationship if it made any demand on me, if I was responsible for something. When I had questions and doubts, my wife reassured me, made me feel it would be all right. I must have been very naive and unrealistic about marriage. It was such a shock when the children got older and *weren't* all right. I didn't want to face that. I think I was attracted to my wife and married so early because she seemed so self-confident. I knew if I married I wouldn't have to face the world alone."

d. Fear of change and of abandonment. For many years, Michael had been afraid of change and abandonment, what he referred to above as "facing the world alone." He hated vacations and trips. He was terrified when a neighbor told his wife they were moving out of the suburbs into the city now that their children were grown. He dreaded the idea of ever leaving his home, although he felt that he had no "friends" in the neighborhood. In his relationships, he was constricted partly because he didn't "risk" unpredictable reactions to more spontaneity.

t: "Change means loss to you?"

Michael: "Yes. And I fulfill that prophecy because when I get something new and make a change like that, I have to devalue it. I choose between two things; and turn down the one I want." He brought up an incident when he had gone with an office mate to pick out new cameras.

He was excited because it was the first time in many months he had wanted anything new; not long ago he had refused to accept even birthday presents from his wife. At the camera shop there was only one of the kind he thought best and he convinced his peer to take it, leaving him with the lesser one. The camera was an important symbol, connected with his new wish to retain images. He became aware that he was jealous now that his friend had the better camera because "he has so much and I have so little anyway." "The one .I want" stood for the mother he felt he never had, and would always lose, unless he countered that by identifying with her "losing."

e. The Bargain: "I'll be good if you'll take care of me." Michael and his family were not religious and had never attended church. However, he remembered that sometime during early adolescence he began to pray. This was his promise to God: "I'll be good if you'll take care of me." The same bargain characterized his adolescence with his sister and father. He was often teased and called ugly, but this was worth the security. The other side of this assumption was, of course, that if he were *not* good, he would not be taken care of.

f. Remaining dependent and resentful, but not close. Progressively, Michael became clearer that much resentment colored those relationships in which he felt dependent. He compared himself unfavorably with his wife and office mates who seemed more independent and effective to him. In addition, they had "real friends," while he felt that people always had to remain distant for him. He began to test who would reject him, and about what.

Michael: "I see how much fun Roberta (his wife) has, and I'm so envious."

t: "You're entitled to have fun, too . . . it won't take hers away."

Michael: "My sister once said she would be proud of me for going to college. But when I didn't get accepted at my first choice, I think she gloated over my getting rejected. You know, I keep feeling I must be a disappointment to you; that I'm not well yet. I feel nothing fails like failure and that I might fail here too."

t: "You won't be disappointing or hurting me that way, but you might hurt yourself if you continue to *have to* think of yourself as a failure. You must think it's the only way you have of holding on to your past and your mother, and not to risk having anyone you need—like your sister—be envious".

This statement was *not* meant to be reassuring on my part. On the contrary, it was meant to confront him with the possibility that he might remain in an impasse if he clung forever to the role of the "loser." In this role, he was assured that he would not be envied (for instance, by his sister, whose rejection he did not risk). This role also implied an angry reproach at others for allowing him to suffer, and an attempt to make them feel guilty about him (as he had been made to feel guilty about his mother's suffering). Such guilt was meant to hurt me (he would be a disappointment to me) and to negate any "effectiveness"—a quality he admired and of which he was now envious—that I might have. I let him know that he could not hurt me in this way, and that he would not need to atone. Continued progress depended in part on his also becoming an active advocate of himself. I wanted to continue the mobilization of his own ego resources.

Michael: "I feel so threatened by the idea that one of us could say 'This is a waste of time; let's forget it.' I have some understanding now, but I still have to work to apply it."

t: "That would be good work, more power to you!"

g. Crisis and grief associated with the growth of individuality and the awareness of previously repressed death wishes. During the third year of therapy, Michael underwent a crisis of mourning associated with the growth of his individuality vis-a-vis his wife. This represented a turning point, in the sense that shortly thereafter he reported "feeling better than anytime in the last ten years." Therapy, however, was not yet discontinued.

Michael's wife, Roberta, had been extremely supportive, though dominating, during the early years of the marriage, until the children left. She then developed some interests of her own which made her less supportive to

Michael. She was also less "optimistic" and hence less available to counteract his pessimism and anxiety, though she was still quite attentive to him. She truly cared for him and about him.

Michael began to become increasingly assertive with her about his opinions and plans—a change from his previous demanding dependency. He now had strong views about the choice of vacation spots, coping with children and finances, etc., not always congruent with her views. He felt himself to be irrationally angry with her sometimes. For example, it became an obsession with him to win over her at cards, and not be the "loser." He needed this as a proof that he had a mind as good as hers. When he did lose, he would become so enraged he had to leave the room speechless. He could not tolerate signs of domination now, feeling these as condescension.

Michael: "I should be grateful because without her I would have nothing, but I want to hurt her, for her ability to think clearly and to shove me around. I've always waited for her to initiate sex so she won't think me aggressive; I just wait for her."

t: "and when you want to hurt her, how do you feel?"

As he talked of the wish to hurt her, he was crying.

Michael: "It feels awful, it's like something is pushing down on my head, not allowing anything to move around. I tell myself, 'If you get up smiling, you'll be okay,' but the terrible feeling is pushing down on me."

Michael and I now knew that this was the repetitive theme of much of his life: the angry thoughts about being deprived by someone he wanted; the wish to hurt; the intense fear of being responsible for loss and death, followed by his immobilizing himself as the "loser" and the dead one, too. He felt these things somatically.

In this and the following session, Michael was wracked with sobs, much different from the quiet weeping during many of his earlier sessions.

Michael: "I have never been in such pain in my life. I couldn't wait to get here today. What if I lose her? I couldn't bear to lose Roberta, how can she want me the way I am? I tried to tell her how I felt; she couldn't see why it's so important to me whether I win at cards or where we go to dinner. She says she has her worries too, but I can't believe that. Her life is good, she has brought it about by her own strength and persistence and all of yesterday *I wished her ill and dead.* I couldn't tell her that."

t: "You don't have to; it's more important that you work out what that means to you . . . and then what you want and can expect of each other. What did you feel just before you wished her dead?"

Michael (Sobbing): "I felt, 'but you promised what happens to you will happen to me; you promised you'll always be there.'"

This then, was finally the delayed grieving of a lonely boy for the mother he secretly felt had promised to take him along. It could not happen until his unconscious identification with her was given up enough for him to picture her as someone outside of himself, to want and to mourn. Michael's marriage survived, and he began to allow himself to enjoy it and to enjoy living again, while tolerating a certain degree of conflict within himself, his marriage, and his other relationships.

The Displaced Beckoning of a Lost, Loved Mother: Alex

Alex was not in extended therapy and the material about him is sketchy. He was a successful architect, a bachelor with a winning manner, and a ready capacity for candidness and introspection. He came because of some conflicts with his colleagues, who, he felt, did not appreciate his innovative style in his desire to design a structure which would maximize opportunities for communal living. He was at a point in his life where he wanted more free and intimate social and sexual involvements than those which had been part of his previous lifestyle. His fiancee of long standing was appalled by these changes in him, while he, in turn, had begun to feel that she was too controlling and restrictive of him.

When he was ten, his mother had died rather suddenly of an infectious disease after a few days in the hospital. He described the event:

Alex: "I knew things didn't look good for her in the hospital, but I didn't really believe anything would happen. The things that stick in my mind: they used to send a telegram in those days when you didn't live near the hospital. It just said, 'Your wife has passed away.' I didn't cry. My brother said, 'Why aren't you crying?' I did a few days later when it all seemed more real. I remember my father acting very, very sad, looking out the window as though he wanted to jump. I must have been surprised that he cared that much . . . I had always figured that they didn't really like each other much; the atmosphere was tense most of the time because my mother would yell and fight and my father listened. She yelled and screamed and he just sat there watching. That was painful for me. If I was in trouble, I always ran to mother, like once when I stole a fountain pen. Mother was always proud of what I did."

t: "And after she died, how did you picture her?"

Alex: "I looked for her. I thought I could see her in the street afterwards when I was going to school (tears in his eyes). I must have been looked at as strange. She always considered me very bright; she had been married before to an artist who left her . . . I think she saw some of that in me. Before she died, she had already put away the money for me to go to college."

t: "What else was she like?"

Alex: "She was considered very good-looking, although a little heavy. She was dramatic, extroverted, and very warm . . . especially with me. For some reason, I have this image of her—she was always welcoming everybody—of opening a window in the middle of the night and reaching out her arm to let some guy climb in the window at a party we had. We lived on the ground floor. We were pretty poor then.

"My father was very different; very nonaggressive. He was never harsh, but a critical guy. He would nag at me, 'You don't work hard enough.' After mother died there was nobody to run to. He and I lived alone for a while after she died. He didn't appreciate me like my mother did."

t: "What are your thoughts?"

Alex: "One is that he got pushed around and yelled at by my mother and the other was that I was kind of ashamed of him. I would get bothered when he helped clear the table. He was sort of soft, heavy around the nipples. Once when I was about thirteen, I got mad at him and said, 'You're just like a woman; you practically have tits.' I got very irritated with him, didn't think of him as proud enough. I didn't want to be like that."

In this and another session, we pulled together some of the threads he had spun out. These included his mother's pride in him and the way this probably contributed to his self-confidence in his work and his inner sense that he could create something valuable. We discussed his image of his mother as warm, welcoming, and volatile, but somehow favoring him over the father at whom she yelled. Alex had an antipathy to being "controlled" by his colleagues or his fiancee, and this seemed to involve a notion of being like the father or others at whom mother might get angry. He himself made the connection between the architectural planning which left room for communal living and the fantasy that "that's just what mother would have liked."

The quest for the dead mother (among the faces on the street) is a common one for the recently bereaved, and occurred in various ways for a number of the individuals described in this chapter and chapter 7. In addition, the idea of father having "tits," that is, in effect, that the remaining parent possessed features of both mother and father, occurred in several cases (e.g., Amy), after the death of a parent in childhood. It is partly a wish for replacement of what has been lost. In this case, however, the "softness" in father was identified with lack of pride, and Alex in adolescence attempted not to identify with it.

In another session, Alex brought up some complications in his love life. He had had a long and solid relationship to the woman he expected to marry, but simultaneously as well as before knowing her, had had a series of what he called "infatuations." The girl was always warm and open, responsive and appreciative of his talents, but usually involved in a relationship with someone else. He would become friends and would long for her intensely, but until recently, had not carried the longing into further action. Recently, he had tried to make a loving foursome involving himself and his financee and the other couple. It was distressing to his fiancee and was not working out for the other girl either. The girl had, in fact, told him she must end the relationship, and her nearness now aroused intense pain followed by depression and feelings of sexual inadequacy. He discussed similar infatuations in the past and it became clear to both of us that the qualities of the girls mirrored those he saw in his mother as directed toward him. They contrasted with the "controlling" features of his fiancee, about which he was touchy, and which were reminiscent of those aspects of his mother he thought were directed, in a devaluing manner, at father. It was hard for him to picture the positive side of mother's and father's relationship to each other.

We left open the question of the connection between the disrupted relationship to his mother, and the current quest and longing. He commented, "I don't feel life would be settled by just going ahead and marrying Janice, not like I thought four years ago. There is still some underlying dissatisfaction and anger in me about that idea. You know, I *never* give up."

In his next appointment, he took the initiative in identifying a pattern which was troubling to him:

Alex: "I have a feeling of progress here, after the last session when we talked about my mother and how her dying interrupted . . . left me frustrated. I realize that when I get involved in these infatuations I always have the same experience. I feel appreciated, like there is a lot between us, and then as I get more directly sexual about it, the woman always cuts me off, there is a change in her vibrations. It is always very painful for me, takes me a long time to get over. It's like I'm compulsive in my behavior toward some women and then have to get frustrated. It's always followed by a piece of frustration. The ultimate test is the sexual one, and so I end up feeling sexually rejected and inadequate somehow. I don't have the same confidence there that I do in my work. I thought about how my mother might fit into that picture. I should add to what I told you that she was very good-looking, but quite heavy, not erotic that I can remember. What I did dig up in myself after the last session was someone a little different, a little before mother died. I had a very intense experience with intense feelings."

t: "Can you tell me about it?"

Alex: "My fourth-grade teacher disliked me. I was a good student but she gave me poor marks, for some reason she kind of had it in for me. The next year, about two to three weeks into the semester she left and another teacher took her place. She was very slim . . . I mean lithe but with breasts . . . her figure was important . . . she had a lot of influence on me. It was almost like a love affair. I was her favorite clearly, my marks were tops, she made me editor of the paper and I felt there was clearly something between us. I think it was really the happiest year of my whole life . . . I guess I felt loved without any conflicts between us at all . . . and somehow special. Then I was sick and out of school a couple of weeks and when I came back she was gone and the old teacher back again. It was as though everything that had happened between us had never existed. I ended up with B's, although I had gotten straight A's all the time she was there, but all that was lost."

t: "Did you ever try to find out why she left, or to be in touch with her?"

Alex: "No, I never thought of that. No explanations were given so I never knew what happened. Right after that was when my mother died."

t: "So you lost both at the same time! You must have felt terribly deserted."

He described his life with father during the following years.

Alex: "Ages twelve and thirteen were terribly unhappy, probably the worst of my life. I had daydreams of sex fantasies all the time and was very withdrawn from other kids. At fourteen, some friend told me about a girl, twelve years old, whom they thought I would like. I thought about *her* for a whole year before she even came to town the next summer. The first time I met her, my friend said afterwards that she liked me and I was like in heaven, super high . . . then when she dated others I was shattered."

t: "In the daydreams you mentioned, what were your fantasies like?"

Alex: "They were *not* about my mother. When I was eleven, I stopped thinking about my mother and kept daydreaming about the teacher. I kept just admiring her; that year in school had really been heavenly."

t: "In your fantasies you admired her . . . like how?"

Alex: "I'm a little embarassed about it for some reason . . . the way I pictured her, well, she had a long, long penis like a snake . . . kind of playful . . . and she would beckon me or someone with it, and playfully wrap it around them . . . we would enjoy wrapping it around each other."

This innovative, tender fantasy had a number of meanings. We discussed what it might have meant to him. The snake was pictured as a charming and playful instrument of temptation, beckoning, and embracing him (much like Eve tempting Adam, but taking matters into her own hands rather than blaming the snake.). He had actually often had his mother's arms around him in a tender embrace. He thought it likely that the teacher and he may also have fondly embraced, but did not remember this clearly. In this sense, the fantasy was the embodiment of his wish to be lovingly held again, especially now, to make his grief and loneliness more bearable. Elsewhere in this book, I have discussed the role of the supportive human network, preferably in the form of a deeply loved person, such as the remaining parent, in the expression and working through of grief. Since Alex and his father apparently could not console each other, Alex dreamt up the penis-arms around him on his own.

Secondly, in his fantasy, there is a shift from the quest for his mother ("I looked for her face on the street," "There was no one to run to after mother died," "When I was eleven I stopped thinking about her") to the teacher he also loved, and for whom he had also been special. Unlike his mother, she was still alive and not irretrievably lost ("I never give up"). In addition, the conscious sexualization of his fantasies during pubescence would have made such desires toward mother taboo to him, so that it was necessary to displace them to someone else. Finally, the affection between him and the teacher was a *real* experience on which fantasies fed. Like his relationship with his mother, it was suddenly disrupted, leaving him feeling "cut off." The pain of such a sequence has been an intrinsic part of his later longed-for relationships (penis-snakes are the opposite of being "cut off". They have grown long.)

The attribution of the snakelike penis to the loved woman is in itself of interest. He is generally attracted to "lithe and slim-bodied" women, rather than heavy women, like his mother. Pubescent boys normally attempt to shed or distance themselves from past components of identification with their mothers, and body features symbolizing them. The "controlling" aspects of the mother are also feared and rejected with more vehemence by the pubescent boys than either before or later, when their own sexual identification is on firmer ground. For Alex, being controlled was also like being put into the less admired role of his father. The general tendency to respond to loss with some identification must have strengthened the regressive pull in this direction at the time when Alex's mother died. However, their earlier relationship had enough security, tenderness, and exuberance, so that less energy was involved in identification than in the continued quest, expressed in his fantasies, for someone who embodied her best and least threatening qualities. He needed to negate the possibility that the person who excited him has no penis or could "cut me off" if they were to be alive. Meanwhile, the feared "softness" is attributed to father. That is, in pubescence, his passion was stirred by someone fantasied as like himself, with a penis for playful delights. However, the affective content of the interaction was modeled on what he experienced with his mother, which was then disrupted. Ironically, the woman with the beckoning snake was reminiscent of an image of mother that he had retained: through the open window her arms beckoned a welcome to a man who comes to a party in the middle of the night. He painted a touching picture of the impact of his loss, and the sequence of his feelings and self-images, as he recreated them painfully in current longings:

"Those few years after my mother died were the most despairing and empty ... I don't remember doing anything other than daydreaming. Finally, at age fourteen or fifteen, I started talking to people and making friends again. But often my moodiness, tendency to be morose returned.

"The odd thing is that with that teacher, I was a completely different person; a lively kid, a hot-shot personality ... and just a few years later a recluse, feeling like an outcast."

He knew he had a joyous "hot-shot" self when vitalized by the appreciation of a loving beckoner; this knowledge he had to lose and find, and lose and find.

Fidelity: "The Words 'I Love You Forever' Make Me Cry": Amy

Amy combined in an ingenious fashion aspects of identification with her father which were mostly unconscious with a poignant attempt to continue her relationship with him in fantasy, through an imaginary companion and in the form of transitional object phenomena. She felt a fierce loyalty to him and his memory, and renounced any commitment of herself to relationships which would have betrayed the unconscious promise between herself and her father to be true to each other forever. Amy was a creative, charming person, in her early thirties, treasured by her friends for her delightful companionship, quick and intuitive wit, and reliable loyalty. She was highly intelligent and able in her profession, though often she felt inadequate. She had been in analysis for a period of years before I saw her for psychotherapy. A brief synopsis of relevant life events and her reactions to them, as she told them to me, precedes the excerpts from interviews.

Amy was the only child of two devoted parents, her father a music teacher and mother a writer of short stories. When she was five, the death of her father in hospital in a distant city while on a business trip brought about many changes in her life. Her mother wanted to spare the little girl from pain, and did not take her to the funeral service.

Amy could not conjure up a mental image of her father as dead. Numbers of times the little girl asked her mother to cry for "daddy" and was upset when her mother did not do so. Her mother, a deeply empathic person, was struggling to maintain her own self-control. She had cried on the train, on the way home from the hospital, but would not do so in front of Amy. When mother remarried five years later, Amy insisted on keeping her father's last name herself, and did so into adulthood. In her twenties, Amy entered analysis with a male analyst and recalled some difficulties in establishing a relationship with him. Her first thought when she was asked to lie on the couch was "I'm in a coffin." Throughout her analysis, she felt her analyst to be "like a ghost." Thus, death entered her image of both analyst and self. She fantasied that even if she got so angry that she would reach back to hit him, her hand would go right through his head, as he could not be "real." Therefore, she decided that it was futile to express her anger. She made, and survived, a suicidal attempt while breaking up with a boyfriend during the analysis. Eventually, she ended analysis and sought out a woman therapist to deal with remaining problems. A theme of "belonging together" with the dead father was persistent. For example, she was angry with her mother that the latter had not bought a space adjacent to her father's in the cemetery for Amy to be buried in when she died. She was, however, very attached to her mother and valued the affection between them, and had been quite gingerly in adult life about risking conflict or competition with her.

During her latency years, after the father's death, Amy had a number of fears. One of these involved the fantasy that her mother had Hitler or an alligator inside her, or was herself Hitler in disguise. She thought an operation might have changed the mother's sex. In her twenties, she established a passionate love relationship, not sexually consummated at the time, with a man who was unavailable as a steady lover or husband, and who lived in a distant country. She had many fantasies that although separated by time, space and circumstances, the two of them somehow "belonged together." She felt that they looked so similar that it was "like we have the same genes." When there was a possibility of circumstances changing, so that the romance might become more real, she experienced intense anxiety at the prospect. For this young woman, the recovery of memories of the father and the solidification of her image of him as real, based on the reality of their past feelings for each other, was an elusive, painful process, less accessible than the readily available fantasies of reunion. At the beginning of therapy, she commented that she could "feel nothing" about her father's death, though she knew it had affected her, and had never been able to cry in analysis.

The following excerpts are from a three-month period during her second year of therapy. Much is, of course, omitted. Current reality crises, as well as issues in her relationship with her mother, were more prominent during the first year. In the first session quoted, she was making clear her constant anticipatory elation at the prospect of receiving a message from far away, and consequent disappointment.

She has been talking about a "let-down feeling" about a letter that did not come. The mailbox was empty.

t: "Do you have other 'mailbox feelings?'"

Amy (laughs): "Funny . . . nobody ever asked me that before . . . I do! They used to be about letters from Sven basically, but they started long before Sven . . . in correspondence with people in the past . . . I've always looked through the hole of the mail box for red and blue edges of air mail letters. It's always letters from far away . . . white envelopes just don't turn me on, even if they are nice long letters from friends from home. The funny thing is that the anticipation is greater than the *real thing. The pleasure is in anticipating . . .* once I receive the letter I don't care that much."

t: "You want a letter from a distance, like from Sven . . . but you want to hold on to the feeling of anticipation . . . not the 'real thing.'"

Amy: "I sometimes think if my father came back the joy of having him would be less than the joy of anticipation. I used to think that if you didn't write to somebody it was like letting the person die. Other people *know* that people are out there. I guess I've needed proof."

She was discussing her fears about three years after her father died. She was never afraid of her mother, but only of what might be in her, Hitler or the alligator.

t: "Did you think of what Hitler or the alligator might do?"

Amy: "Hitler would torture me, take off my skin; I guess the alligator would chew me, and then eat me. I was eight, I remember that apartment."

t: "Skin and chewing ... what are your thoughts—any about you and chewing?" (Chewing had come up earlier that session.)

Amy: "At night I would do two things...I would do something...with putting the sheet around my mouth...rubbing the edge around my lips, and pushing some in...and oh...I would rock my head from side to side and sing...I made up a song about my father" (begins to hum).

t: "Song about your father?"

Amy: "Once upon a time
   my father died
   I was so sad
   I couldn't have replied
   then we moved to the lagoon
   I learned to eat with a fork and spoon"

(Amy was surprised she knew it still.) "I used to sing it loudly to make my mother furious when she was going out. Then my mother met this monster, I thought, this creep, Alfred (her stepfather) and he's torturing me ... I used to think that he would like to kill me, too ... that he would have a car accident with me just to get rid of me, so he could have my mother to himself."

Amy's thoughts of being eaten or having her skin taken off, both of which involve a loss of ego boundaries associated with the experiencing of closeness as a merging process, occurred after her father had died. She pictured the impulses involved as located within her mother, but in masculine (Hitler), aggressive form. From this she associated to a more consoling contact, using a transitional object, the sheet, to soothe the skin around her mouth, while singing about her father. In her song, she moved from silent sorrow ("I was so sad I couldn't have replied.") back to the wish to take something in or eat. The reference to this is now in a modulated, "civilized" form ("I learned to eat with a fork and spoon"). Experiencing mother and father as literally "rolled into one" now, all her needs and fear of retaliation were attached to her mother, and she wanted to get rid of any man who intruded. In addition she was the reminder to mother and her future stepfather of the father's existence and wanted her mother to feel reproached for not remaining true to him. In all its overdetermination, her song was a complicated accomplishment. I did not yet know that her father used to sing to her before she went to sleep.

The following session, she said:

"There's a melody in my mind ..."

t: "Can you catch it?"

Amy: " 'Where have all the flowers gone ... a long time ago ... gone to the graveyards' ... I can't remember the rest."

t: "Flowers . . . to the graveyard?"

Amy: "I wanted to *do* that; I did want to put flowers on my father's grave. I had lots of plays I made up . . . I wanted to bring him flowers on his birthday. Now I know what I haven't thought of in years. I would ask my mother to take me to the grave and she would say, 'It's too far away.' . . . I would pretend myself putting flowers on his grave and was very concerned about flowers. She told me someone else would take care of that. That was all during the same time I thought Hitler and the alligator in her. I couldn't have gone there alone, and she didn't want to go. Now suddenly I am thinking that once she went there without me."

t: "But you wanted to bring him flowers yourself . . ."

Amy: "He would *have known* somehow that I brought flowers . . . now I picture Professor Maenchen (an elderly, helpful, live professor). I just imagined my father would know."

t: "That you and the flowers came to him . . . and then?"

Amy: "And then the flowers were . . . that it would keep something alive . . . that's a spooky thought . . . flowers coming out of the grave . . . fertilized . . . I try to imagine what the body would look like . . . (tears in her eyes) . . . I want to know if there is *anything* there . . . no skin maybe, but something still there . . ."

t: "Your feelings for him are still there."

Amy's song fragments covered rich imagery and affect, in some ways analogous (though different in construction) to dream material. That she reserved this for her songs was important, because singing was tied to her relationship with father. This session, she had presented a touching fantasy, that of bringing her flower to be fertilized by the father's body, and thereby "keeping something alive." Sexual fantasies underlying this wish, which was to take place on his birthday, were not yet clear to her. She felt her mother discouraged her from this symbolic revitalization, that she considered it too "far away" for Amy, but perhaps did it herself. Maintaining contact with those who are "far away" remained a persistent theme, but she was frustrated in her efforts to deal with it more directly. She considered whether something might be "still there," even if without the "skin" which had come up previously. One of her fears about Hitler had been that he would take off her skin.

Amy: "Did I ever tell you I had a make-believe brother?"
t: "Nope."
Amy: "His name was Terry and his father was a policeman. We talked and I remember his father. It was after my father died . . . we talked on the intercom . . . at a distance. It didn't bother me that we had two different fathers. I wonder how long he lasted. I don't remember his leaving. That was before we

moved, so it was before the alligator and Hitler, I guess I was six or seven."

t: "Do you remember how he began?"

Amy: "No, I do remember it was after the summer at camp . . . the first time I remember seeing a penis . . . Nicky and I undressing each other at camp . . . I thought it looked so big, like a baseball bat with a ring around it."

t: "And . . ."

Amy: "I was afraid of airplane crashes all that year. I would hide my head when a newsreel came on . . . and of fires. Do you think there's a connection between sex and death?"

These fears were related to sexual excitement, and will not be further elaborated here. The size of the penis makes it likely that her memory of sex play with a little boy is a screen memory about a view of an adult's penis. Its size and potential power makes it frightening, yet it is meant to be played with (baseball bat). The creation of an imaginary brother who still had a father was remembered after she recalled the fantasy of growing fertilized flowers on father's birthday and wondering if there were anything still there. For Amy, as for several individuals I have known who had a parent die in childhood (e.g., Alex in this chapter), both the self *and* the remaining parent had fantasied counterparts of the same sex as the dead parent.

Amy began talking about a friend who called her in a crisis, thinking she was going to die from having eaten contaminated fish. The friend's husband had just gone on a trip, and though she had fantasied having an affair, now that he was gone she realized how completely dependent on him she had been. Amy said, "Now that he is gone, she will have to find out who she is. I wonder why I am so attached to her, that I feel it in my stomach when she is upset—I feel that way about some friends. I remember how miserable I was when she got married. I was terribly jealous; angry that she had another best friend and was getting married; I felt like I was a kid and she was a grownup." This led her to discuss feelings about her mother's remarriage and the birth of her half-sister when Amy was thirteen. Amy thought, when she would wheel the carriage down the street, people probably believed she was the mother of the baby. She remembered that when she was a little girl, she wheeled around a doll carriage containing not a doll but a heart-shaped pillow, which said on it "I love you." She could not remember who gave it to her, but remembered wheeling it on the day she went to say goodbye to the neighbors when she and mother were moving, after father's death.

Amy: "Tuesday was Hitler's birthday . . ."

t: "But no flowers for Hitler. . . . When did Hitler go *out* of your mother?"

Amy: "I was still afraid when we were living in Philadelphia, then it stopped, when she got married again. I was also afraid of being kidnapped at the same time. There was a story of a boy who got kidnapped and his fingers were all cut off by a mean nasty man. About the alligator, I don't *remember* the thought that it would eat me; that just came up lately. I had a friend who had a cute little alligator . . . she adored it and I hated it . . . I had heard about people throwing alligators in the toilet and then they would get huge and live inside the toilet."

t: "Like the alligators living in your mother . . . they returned after they had been gotten rid of . . . what else might do that?"

She returned to talking about her father:

Amy: "I pictured my father in heaven . . . I thought of him as being someplace . . . definitely around . . . I felt his presence and knew he was watching . . . I had a lot of little conversations with him. Once this girl said sarcastically, 'Oh, I forgot to say my prayers up to God,' and then she spat up to the sky . . . and I felt awful because I thought she might have missed God and spat at my father . . . even though all the time I was definitely an atheist."

t: "What do you think he would have minded most?"

Amy: "I'm sure that he was hurt when mother got married again . . . that she could forget him so quickly . . . How weird death is . . . I mean they disappear and just leave others' lives all fucked up."

t: "You *feel* his leaving you now?"

Amy: "It's so weird how powerful absence is. When we talked about him before I remembered talking to him . . . and I didn't feel like crying, because we were talking about his *presence* . . . now it's his *absence* and that hurts."

She is tearful. A little later, she adds softly,

Amy: "What kept me from being sad at six and seven was that he was present for me—I was pretending all the time he was still there. When airplanes went overhead, I would sing the National Anthem . . . no, something else, it was 'Our father gave to thee, anchor of liberty, to thee I sing'; later it had something about 'land where my father died.'"

It is hardly necessary to comment on Amy's thoughts of fidelity to his presence. She expressed it so clearly. Her experience of his presence, and the need to face the grief-laden possibility of his absence constitute the issue discussed in chapters 3 and 10.

Amy: "Once while I was in college, I went back to look at the old house where we lived with my father. I expected all kinds of memories, but it seemed like there was nothing there. It was like the past didn't want to open itself up for me, it mocked my efforts . . . and then I was aware of having deceived my father in some way . . . it was a blank . . . empty search . . . the street was deserted, the house solitary . . . the only thing that struck me was the lack of rapport between me and the house . . . I tried to catch images of a complete family in it and couldn't."

t: "Part of why you have had to be so faithful to him is because you were afraid unless you worked hard at it you *might* forget, and he would feel deceived. But he is not alive any more, so to stay true you have had to deaden your own longing for love from a man who might really return it without leaving you."

Amy: "Whenever I went to the airport, I wondered if I was near him . . . I knew his grave was in ——— somewhere . . . I kept thinking of visiting him. I think he felt unappreciated."

t: "What do you mean?"

Amy: "When mother was with Alfred . . . I never deceived him. But the real difference was that my mother knew he was gone—she accepted the loss and I didn't. I still don't know to this day how she felt. When Derrick died at camp—I think I loved him after my father died, he was kind of a substitute father—I would sing every single song that he taught me . . . for at least six months . . . it was like a promise not to forget him. The reason I did that is that *I wanted the songs to go on* . . . you see, he had made some of them up, some had nonsense syllables . . . and *if I didn't keep singing them I might forget.*"

t: "After your father died you kept singing too . . . not to forget."

Amy: "With my father, I had that feeling with the flute. I always thought if there was a fire in the house the first thing I would save is his flute. But when I try to play it, I am disappointed."

t: "How should it sound?"

Amy: "You know, he used to sing to me before I went to sleep every night."

T: "Now it's getting clearer—how you carried on something that had been precious between you."

Amy: "I remember some of them." (She recalls three different songs.)

t: "The three songs you remember all deal with partings."

Amy: "What I want to know, was there any skin left, bones left or only dust."

t: "What do you really want to know?"

Amy: "Is he alone in his grave . . . *he isn't* . . . I mean he isn't there any more . . . none of him is left." (Sobs.)

She now had let us know that the transitional phenomenon of singing before sleep indeed derived from her actual relationship with father, and thus preserved that relationship. She continued to face the loss.

Amy: "My mother said the day I found out about his death I kept riding my tricycle around in the backyard. I remember telling myself, 'I'll never see him again,' because that's what she explained that death meant . . . like a broken record I said it over and over. Also, I went to the neighbors and told them they would have to find another music teacher. I was there with all of them and my mother couldn't get me to come home, I wanted to stay there. Somehow, I don't remember living there with my mother alone at all, not until we moved. I wonder where that pillow is that said 'I love you,' that I used to wheel around."

t: "Going home with mother must have meant facing his 'absence,' that you'll 'never see him again' . . . I think the pain about that would have been overwhelming for you at the time. So you put a lot of energy into all kinds of ways trying not to have that be true . . . and some of your good energy has stayed there, making you give up on other possibilities."

Amy: "And then I had the idea of deceiving my father by spying on his ghost."

t: "Like how?"

Amy: "To check if he were there all the time . . . I pictured someone like Casper the Ghost . . . you know, the friendly one who is made out of a *sheet* . . . I like that idea."

t: "And you used to like sheets."

Amy: "God, what a memory you have, doesn't anything disappear? With the sheet it was my middle finger doing it, this finger was up in my mouth and the sheet was around my mouth . . . sheets . . . my father's clothes . . . what a thought! Maybe that's how the concept of ghosts came in the first place . . . people didn't want people to die."

t: "I wouldn't be surprised."

Amy: "I always thought Dr. A. (her former analyst) was like a ghost or machine . . . he knew that I thought that but he still stayed that way."

t: "You wanted contact with a ghost . . . his skin, your skin and something in your mouth. You have wondered if there is anything left of his *skin* in the grave."

This took us from father to mother, and to coverings of the skin, that is, clothes. Her capacity to console herself about separation from father had its origins in her dependence on her mother as a comforting person. She remembered that the cut of her dresses in high school was different from her friends', because she would only wear clothes her mother made for her. When complimented, she would automatically reply, "Thank you, my mother made it." In later years, she liked the sound of the sewing machine or typewriter while going to sleep. This transitional phenomenon replaced the earlier sounds of the father's singing, and later her own voice.

Amy: "Can one person be right for more than one? In my guts, I probably think there is only *one* person . . . my father . . . or I thought Sven. There's this picture of my father and mother . . . my father was a lot older, so she looks like a little girl. I can't picture their married life together . . . I never think of her that way with him, having a nice life together."

t: "You've thought of him and you?"

Amy: "I would have been nicer to him if I wouldn't have gotten removed."

This allows us to discuss her rivalry with her mother, her guilt about the yearning for her father, and her fear that over this issue she might lose mother as well.

Amy: "About my father . . . what I discovered this weekend is *that he loved* me. It all started here the week we talked about what he was really like. I went home and rummaged around the drawers some more and I found an envelope of paintings and drawings. You know, my imaginary brother, Terry . . . he wore glasses . . . and in the drawings my father made of himself he always had his glasses on. I found a four-page letter he wrote me when I was four. There was a picture of him with his glasses and then an arrow and a kiss . . . *he was blowing me a kiss across the distance.* In the letter, he called me 'my little angel' like he often did. He made a great big heart on it, with an arrow and the words 'It's all yours!' There were four pages of love. My God, he knew I was alive and cared about me! It's not fair . . . the words he wrote me . . . *the words 'I love you forever' made me cry* . . . forever was only for a year and then he was dead. My mother and Alfred said that my father was very possessive, a jealous person about my mother and me, maybe he passed that on to me."

Amy had finally arrived at the feeling that she was loved in reality by her father. This could not be lost, and therefore left her feeling less under the burden of recreating the love relationship on her own.

Amy: "I'm not awake yet this morning" (closes her eyes).

t: "What would you like to hear in your sleep?"

Amy: "My father singing mostly . . . I wish you'd entertain me, or something."

Later in the session:

Amy: "My father was a lively person, the opposite of deadly, that's full of death. So it didn't make sense."

t: "That he was really dead?"

Amy: "Hmm . . . The weird thing about the letter . . . I keep thinking that I never knew before that he had a relationship . . . *I mean real relationship to me, not just in my mind.* The letters are different than the old photos that way. Anybody can take a picture, but the letters he wrote were what he was feeling . . . I keep feeling that my mother is annoyed about all the questions about my father. I wonder whether when I thought of him in heaven I was there as a little angel too. I don't know. I had a funny thought right now of my biology teacher, the one who made a pass at me, he is the same age as my father would be now . . . and that's the same number of dollars my phone bill is this month."

t: "Keeping communication going at long distance costs you something too?"

Amy: "I always like long distance calls, communication from afar."

t: "Sven was at a long distance too . . . is it also a safe distance?"

Amy: "Sex . . . and distance . . . and father. I've always thought that sex and death have something to do with each other."

t: "You've been afraid of your own excitement in sex . . . afraid to let yourself just be overcome by it and lose control . . . like the fires you were afraid of."

Amy: "I think of Zeus coming down and raping . . . did he change himself into a woman or rape a swan? Now Victor Hugo comes to mind. Have you seen the movie *Adele H?* She was unhappy that her father didn't love her. He wrote about the dead daughter he did love. In the book, he talks about going to the grave and bringing flowers and notices nothing but her and he talks to her. Adele feels left out because he loves somebody else. Back to Zeus and changing . . . did my father turn himself into mother? Actually a swan would have been a little nicer than Hitler. Why didn't he get inside me . . . instead of my mother?

t: "I think you wished that sometimes. But the angry part of your feelings toward him for leaving you, and for being with mother, moments of hating him, you turned those into a punishing, scary image of him inside your mother . . . Hitler and the alligator . . . who had been gotten rid of, like your friend's alligator thrown down the toilet but growing still. You tried to get rid of those feelings and couldn't. I think you tried to preserve your father that way, by not remembering your own angry feelings. Meanwhile, you kept the good part and the good feelings and have been trying to stay true to them all your life . . . longing for a loving message from him across the distance. But your fantasies about it started from a reality; you saw that now in his letters. In the midst of your love and excitement . . . perhaps wishing he'd get inside of you like you said . . . came death. That was a frightening coincidence, but your excitement didn't bring it about."

Amy: "I have been thinking about what it would be like to be dead. Thinking about life and death is not new to me, but what's new is that *I don't want to be dead.* That thought is scary, too, because death used to be a comforting thought, kind of appealing. I thought about how I used to feel about suicide when I tried it. Nobody understood. I kept saying, 'When you don't like being someplace, you move out!"

Amy now talked about a friend who called her psychiatrist by his first name, although he was a "very distant person."

Amy: "I think it's people who can't stand the distance who use first names like that . . . I guess you need some sense of familiarity and acceptance and when you don't feel it, patients pretend it's there by using a first name. Maybe I don't have to do that with you because you don't act high and mighty about things. I don't feel that sort of distance here."

She was talking about distance in relationships and real vs. pretended communication.

Amy: "When I tried to commit suicide I thought I was perfectly sane all the way through. I never lost contact with reality and felt very lucidly that I was moving somewhere . . . maybe joining my father . . . at least getting out."

t: "There are different kinds of reality. If you thought one moves away if one doesn't like someplace . . . and your father . . ."

Amy: "He was forced to move away. I guess that's what I thought when I was five."

t: "Forced . . . because?"

Amy: "Maybe it was more fun . . . to be an angel . . . I used to imagine he was a great big angel, flying around through the air."

t: "Air male?" (A frivolous remark on my part; a needless interruption of her mood. My associations had led to her love of airmail letters and from there to her father's actual letter of blowing kisses to her across the distance; addressing her as "little angel." But it had not come from her that session. The verbalizations perhaps met my need for play at that moment more than hers. This sometimes happens, and I regretted it. However, she caught my meaning and laughed about the role of airmail letters in her life.)

Amy: "I am thinking of existentialism . . . I mean something in my philosophy is changing."

t: "Like what?"

Amy: "I've always kept an idea in reserve . . . that if things get too bad in this world . . . I'll just disappear. And now, it would be scary to be dead. Somewhere along the line, my concept of being dead has changed."

Discontinuity in the Image of a Parent:
The Strength to Survive and Be Whole: Natasha

Natasha's life story, as told to me over a period of time, is a tribute to the strength of human endurance, hope, and vitality. She survived devastating horrors in a war and the loss of a much loved father. In addition, the discontinuity in the image of her father, both in herself and in the human network surrounding her, was a severe trauma. Nevertheless, she was able to uproot herself in such a way that eventually, and with painful work and surprising capacity for insight, she became a whole, feeling, and thinking person, whose ethical human relationships, ability to grapple with difficult philosophical issues, and capacity for affection are all a part of her appeal. She had never been, and is still not easy on herself; she is apt to and has had to shoulder a lion's share of responsibility for a successful outcome in various life situations, and particularly in the face of adversity. This attitude was evident in her therapy as well. Ordinarily, when I see someone with her life experience, I do not probe to uncover memories and losses which are so extreme. Reviving such overwhelming traumas can seriously undermine the individual's capacity to function in the present. However, Natasha's urge—and her need—to make peace with her past were so great that she often took the initiative in probing more deeply into the meaning of her reactions in adolescence, the time of her greatest trauma. We jointly kept an eye on the level of anxiety involved for her. At times she said about memories, "I'm not ready to open that gate yet," but would soon be restive to go ahead. I believe that some of the capacity to surmount painful obstacles derived from an ego mode identified with and associated by Natasha with her loving childhood relationship with her father.

Natasha's father had been a high-level government official with considerable power. During her childhood, Natasha's family was admired and respected in her community, and she saw that many people looked to her father for advice and help. Although he was busy with political meetings and other duties much of the time, and hence less available to Natasha than she wished, he was seen as a kind and just leader by her and others. It was during wartime. When Natasha was fourteen, the political situation in the country changed, occupation forces were about to take over, and her father suddenly was viewed as a traitor rather than a hero. He was arrested and dragged out of the house during the middle of one night, and within a year the remaining family heard that he had died in a prison camp. The family, now despised by neighbors, managed to escape to live with relatives, in another part of the country, still in fear of being captured by enemy soldiers. Friends close in the past did not dare make contact lest they be discovered and imprisoned too. During that terrible year, Natasha also came to know, with shock, that father's idology included a sense of superiority to other people, a superiority which he believed it was important to immortalize, even at the cost of exterminating other people who might be traitors. She felt a previously unknown hardness in herself toward him, could not forgive him, and did not cry at the news of his death. For close to thirty years, she tried not to allow herself really to "feel" anything. She was eager to leave Europe and did so in late adolescence.

After managing to come to America on her own, she met and married a man who had also escaped from her country, with an equally harrowing past. For over twenty years, she accepted whatever suffering she felt emanated from her difficult marriage as though it were deserved; she expected, and sometimes seemed to invite, punishment. When family circumstances made it necessary for her to earn a living, she rapidly sought out higher education, mastering demanding requirements, with her extraordinary intelligence, in record time. For as long as possible, however, she avoided the required "philosophy" course, knowing it would deeply attract and disturb her, as, in thinking about such things, her own feelings might emerge. She did indeed become deeply involved in the course, but in a way which stirred up the conflicts left behind in adolescence. In the midst of what she felt to be an insoluble philosophical dilemma, she became preoccupied with suicide, and even began to make a suicidal attempt. In the midst of this, it occurred to her that another way of dealing with what she felt at that moment as the "evil" within herself might be to attempt to make peace with God. She and her family had never been religious. Instead of killing herself, she sought out a minister who was extremely helpful to her.

I saw her a few years later. Much material relating to her current life situation will be omitted, both for the preservation of privacy and in order to focus on the issues related to the death of her father. The initial interview included the following:

Natasha: "If I were clear what is making my life so miserable, I wouldn't be here. Currently, my life is so miserable I don't see the point of going on with it. I don't feel good about myself and my life is awful. I don't even believe in a good afterlife. I grew up in Russia, during World War II. I stopped school at age fifteen, at the end of the war, and worked as a teacher. Then I managed to get away to America . . . and quickly ended up getting married. Ivan is also Russian; he escaped too. My question is if I should have a divorce?"

t: "What troubles you most of all?"

Natasha: "I don't feel I have a capacity to love people and I feel very unlovable."

t: "Can you tell me about that?"

Natasha: "Basically, I feel guilty for not having been able to love my mother. She is a very cold woman who I never could please. Mother was given to unreasonable punishments and nothing I did ever seemed to please her. I just couldn't get along with her. My father was a government official . . . and I loved him very much. After the war, he was arrested as a traitor. He was taken to prison camp and I never saw him again. We had news that he died there. I feel guilty because I know I would have been a Communist too, if he had lived."

t: "Guilty?"

Natasha: "I hadn't realized everything that would involve . . . feeling superior . . . and agreeing to the extermination of traitors. When I found out after he was gone that he must have believed those things, I felt horrified and betrayed because I had always believed when he taught me."

t: "It sounds like you had *two* images of him . . . and they didn't fit together."

Natasha: "Yes, during the war everyone admired him. He was kind to everyone and kinder to me than my mother. All kinds of people turned to him for help, and he never let them down."

t: "So whatever else it turned out he thought, you had the experience of some good in him and between you and him."

With depressed people who are devastated by the negative components of their introjects or identification figures, it becomes important, when possible, to prepare the groundwork for facing negative feelings by also establishing with them that these at one time did not constitute the whole of their reality sense. Natasha had said that her most disturbing trouble was the feeling of being unloving and unlovable. I wanted to clarify with her between us that a loving relationship had once existed for her (and hence could exist again) even if it was now lost, before allowing her to delve further into her sense of guilt and desolation.

Natasha: "At home, my parents hardly ever talked to each other. Now Ivan and I don't, or at least we can't communicate. My mother was also an active party member. After my father was arrested, we first didn't dare flee because we thought it might be harder for him to find us. But when we heard of other whole families getting arrested we fled to my mother's relatives."

t: "And then?"

Natasha: "Some other people lived with us too, in hiding. A man and his wife; he got interested in me. I was fifteen then, and I think I kind of fell in love with him. But I felt it was wrong, we had some—some sex play—and I thought I might go insane. At sixteen, I went off on my own."

She now had brought up another area of guilt, this time for positive, sexual feelings. Previously she had mentioned feeling betrayed; did she also see herself as the "betrayer" at whom anger is justified? In the long run, traitors get killed.

She discussed her husband and the lack of respect and emotional support she felt from him. If she tried to talk to him, he answered "Don't bother me, I have enough troubles of my own." She added, "Maybe if I felt things were under my control more, I could straighten out."

t: "During the war, the things that happened to you and your family weren't under your control at all and you must have felt terribly helpless. When you were a child, your father seemed to be a person in control and you admired that . . . and then that image came crashing down too. You've had to manage a lot, and it seems to me in many ways remarkably well."

Natasha: "I do have an excellent job. I've gotten promoted several times so I administer a department now. I think I'm well liked by the people there, and the people work well together as a group. I finished college in night school, when Ivan had no job for a while and somebody in the family had to have a stable job.

(I had wanted to know if somewhere, at work or church or elsewhere, she had some network of human support. As it turned out, she was in fact respected as a leader in certain situations, such as at work, like her father.)

t: "So you've kept things under control in that way, but within you now?"

Natasha: "I wish I was dead, but I'm not happy at that prospect either. All week I was aware of the feeling of worth that I did *not* have. But this week, I've started to question whether I always needed to be the victim."

t: "Let's try to understand what being a victim means to you from your past life and why you've had to lend yourself to that role for so long."

Natasha: "When I grew up I grew up very unreligious. My father agreed, said it would be pure hypocrisy. But after all the disaster happened and my father was lost, I began to feel a need for religion. With each religion, I found an obstacle because I couldn't believe all of it; I felt I would be dishonest joining a church. I was struggling about free will vs. determinism. I kept asking 'If there is so much misery how could a good God create it?' "

t: "That was much like what troubled you about your father . . . *if* he were in control like he seemed to be, how could a good father let such disasters happen . . . and turn out to believe something different than he showed you?"

Natasha: "It was after I took that philosophy course that was required . . . it stirred up . . . I started thinking about it . . . then when I became desolate and suicidal. Then I thought the fact that I was unable to believe in God might be what's wrong with me. I felt out of grace and belonged that way. When the minister talked on 'disbelief' like it was all right, I felt included and better again. This whole business of failure of faith is free of . . . is out of normal logical reality. My framework of reality can't be put in any conventional one . . . but it includes two sides of a question, perhaps it means living with both."

t: "There are many kinds of reality . . . and living with both sides of a question . . . or a feeling . . . may be very important."

Natasha: "You asked about being a victim. For many years after we were first married if we had an argument, Ivan would hit me, push me against the wall and I was full of bruises, but never questioned it. I would try to appease him or blame myself, thinking I'm so unattractive. He constantly called me stupid and still does. Last week, I realized I was angry about it."

t: "Why do you think you have been blaming yourself for so long?"

Natasha: "My whole adolescence undermined my confidence. I believed in the whole Communist ideology and when I found out what it really involved it shook me up very badly. I couldn't trust my judgment about anything anymore."

t: "When you found out more about what your father had believed?"

Natasha: "Where he died in prison . . . a lot of people died there . . . later we heard that my father was given a lot of credit for lifting morale there. My father had a lot of charisma, he was a leader type. I am ashamed to say my feelings for him were wiped out . . . I was angry at him for having been a believer and for staying where we were . . . we could have left earlier . . . we had options to do that, we knew we were likely to get occupied. During the occupation, he talked of 'going down with the flag flying.' It was awful. I didn't get raped but my mother almost did. When they arrested him in the middle of the night he went elegantly dressed and dignified still. He said, 'I would like to say goodbye first,' and then he went."

t: "I don't believe your feelings about him have been wiped out . . . I think they've been in limbo . . . because they've needed to be."

Natasha now talked about her husband and his inability to stay around whenever she was in the hospital having a baby. At the birth of each of their children, he had ignored her, and the moment she was home from the hospital expected her to get up and do everything exactly as usual. He could not tolerate any sign of illness or weakness in her, though he had told her she would be criminal to consider leaving him because he was a sick man.

t: "So you haven't been able to count on anybody but yourself."

Natasha: "That's right, somebody has to keep going. It's like death and dying is a part of life, but the worst is being expected to live on."

Both she and I by this time knew that she was suffering, among other things, from aspects of what has been called the "survivor syndrome," involving terrible guilt about surviving while others around one have died. Such guilt is often so huge it is insurmountable. As her father was the most important of the many dead who were around her, understanding and recapturing her relationship to him further would, I hoped, precede her facing this component of his death and her guilt.

Several weeks later, Natasha came in and showed me some beautiful embroidery she was doing; we admired it together. She told me of the pressures of a harrowing week, which would have tried the patience of a saint, but she did not complain. By now, she was comfortable enough with me so that I could say,

t: "What are you trying to make up for, to have to be such a superwoman all the time?"

Natasha: "I guess it's an attempt to be like the God I look for . . . the best I can come up with is the evil and incompleteness in the world that I . . . this striving in me to be more perfect. Not only does it not make sense, but it is a sin to be . . . to try to be without sin . . . just to justify yourself. It is really arrogant. Because of my inability to believe anything I was totally alienated from everything . . . society. I couldn't be a part of anything and always felt like an outsider. You know how when my husband gets sick I expect that everyone will get angry at me!"

t: "By now I know." (We laughed). (Her life has been so grim. Some moments of laughter are important, even in the midst of serious work. In the context here its aim is to shift attitudes toward her readiness to take blame.)

Natasha: "Now that I'm coming here I feel supported and protected by society. My big quarrel has been 'who let all this misery happen?' . . . it's the huge discrepancies I can't remember that I bitterly resent."

t: "Discrepancies in you, too?"

Natasha: "Yes, because I totally feel anger at being betrayed and deserted. I remember my mother and others were very angry at me because I didn't show any feeling of loss or grief about my father. I couldn't cry. I felt betrayed because I believed whatever he told me, and he told me that discipline and suffering were justified in the cause of the national good, that we had to go on no matter what; that that's what the whole war was about."

t: "You felt betrayed but I think you tried *not to betray him*. You tried staying true to the idea that you have to be the strong one, no matter what. That way, you wanted to stay in touch with him and the ideas you'd shared."

Natasha: "My first suicidal attempt—it seems to me now that that's what it was—was when my mother sent me to the store for some milk. There was an air raid warning and everyone took cover. I didn't, but just stood there watching the planes, thinking, 'Gee, I wish I were there in that airplane.' It shot at me, right close by. I remember being aware 'I could have been dead, there is blood on me' . . . *That was me shooting at me!* . . . like an attempt by myself to commit suicide . . . a part of me I have known about, that would come at me sometime."

t: "I'm glad it missed you."

Natasha: "Thanks."

Natasha brought in to show me a small picture of herself with her father, on a brooch.

t: "There you are together!"

Natasha: "I feel there are a lot of good things and bad things to work on now. I wonder if I'm not casting Ivan in the role of the bully because he is really not as strong as I would like him to be. I must have been afraid that if I married someone as strong as my father I would be . . . my own strength would be reinforced and I would end up like my father. I always wanted to end up like my father when I was a child, but never after he was arrested. My mother thought as a female I was a total flop . . . I didn't have boyfriends from age eleven to fifteen . . . I matured late, with my first period at fourteen and that made me look like a freak in her eyes. This week, I've been able to think more about my father. He was very absorbed in his work, seldom at home in the evening. But when he was there he was easy to talk to, we went on a lot of walks and we always admired the same things. He had a telescope. We used to go out and look into the sky and he would explain stars and how marvelous everything in the distance was."

t: "So your looking up at the sky, wishing you were in the airplane . . . like you mentioned last week . . . didn't come out of nowhere . . . it was connected to the kind of image you had had *with* your father . . . when things were harmonious between you."

Natasha: "That hadn't occurred to me, but yes, we looked at the sky a lot. And vacations were happy, we sat and loafed and picked flowers. I think vacations were the most supportive part of my childhood. I never saw my father angry because my parents didn't quarrel in front of me."

t: "You said they didn't talk to each other either . . . but you and he?"

Natasha: "We talked . . . he liked to talk. My father used to give a lot of parties. People would drop in for supper and much of the time somebody would be living with us, friends or relatives in trouble. My father was always willing to help. There would be grand parties for New Year's Eve and he would make up a box full of sayings, supposed to be prophetic for the year to come."

t: "Like what?"

Natasha: "Like . . . I think one was about *'Memories are the only Paradise from which you cannot be evicted.'*"

t: *"Memories are the only Paradise from which you cannot be evicted!"*

Natasha: "He made me aware of the importance of things, made everything more alive. (She allowed herself some tears for the first time.) I see him as an equal now and he would respond and know how I felt."

Natasha now put her head into her hands and wept. I was deeply moved at her grief—her having retrieved words about "memory" as the "Paradise" from which she was no longer evicted.

Natasha: "Now I see myself in an embrace with him." She wrapped her own arms around her shoulders. "We are both saying, 'It's all right.' I am very much like him, not only thinking in terms of genetic influence but through his guidance and passing on of his values."

t: (after a while) "You are forgiving each other . . . and now you feel he would have liked you again."

Natasha: "Yes, I think he would have been proud of me too. There is an awareness I have from him of the capacity for evil. I have to, I want to accept that as a part of myself too."

t: "What you talk of as 'evil' is tied up with your anger. Anger isn't evil in itself; anger usually has grown out of fear. You had reason for terror in your abandonment. The question is what one does with it."

Natasha: "I have always been afraid of it; but it is probably a great gift because it has made me feel more related to a collective humanism, so that I can participate in the achievement of that humanity as well as in the evil. That's important to me. I mean if you feel tied into the awareness of evil, you have a right to be tied into the achievements as well."

t: "You've always done your part in that . . . and then some."

Natasha: "What I don't want is his participation in the idea of greatness, and his enjoyment of power. I will fight those things in myself. But I can see how maybe he wasn't aware of what was really going on in the country. He never mentioned the idea of eliminating traitors. It was more like if you have a gift given to you like will power or moral fiber, you have to develop it to the fullest and share it with a collective entity."

t: "You are not shutting your father out anymore; you are letting yourself know about the gift you felt he passed on to you. I think you are really ready now to look more closely at what you really felt toward him and your mother, and what they were really like for you."

Natasha: "I wish the suffering in my marriage would end—that *it* would end—but divorce is like death and destruction, and it is like an existential statement that I am now against death."

She discussed an incident involving her affection for her youngest child. The child had wondered how much Natasha and I were alike and she felt pleased about this idea. She reported realizing that week that she had been making an intense effort for years "to keep the evil in me at bay." It occurred to her "that I do not really need to be afraid of my subconscious because maybe I'm not that bad."

t: "What comes to your mind?"

Natasha: "After the war, I had not gone back to school. Instead, I worked for a year with refugee children. I remember being on duty by myself with thirty kids and twelve sick with whooping cough. I was exhausted. There was some Lysol next to the cough medicine and I was so exhausted I started to give the wrong thing . . . the kid spit it out and was all right. Why couldn't I have just said, 'I'm too darn tired,' and let someone else do it? Somehow, that was like when I stood in front of the airplane. I'm beginning to know what my problem is . . . in many situations I can't tell what is good and what not."

In describing the near accident with the child, she was moving closer to her potential role in contributing to death. It was connected with the image of herself as strong enough to do anything, an image which combined her identification with the father of her childhood with a necessary defense against the helplessness he experienced when death and disaster had actually surrounded her.

Natasha discussed the sex play with Boris, the married man who, with his wife, lived with mother and her relatives after the father's arrest. "I think my real anger is at my mother about that. She was totally dependent on our relatives to keep us, and wasn't willing to risk any trouble. It was like she sold me in order to be allowed to stay. I don't think she is capable of sympathy. When my younger brother tried to commit suicide and was sent to a sanatorium a few years ago, she just wrote me that it was proof of how 'weak' he is."

Natasha was dealing with the problem of the lack of rapport she felt between herself and her mother and her expectation of criticism rather than protection from her. She expected me to be critical too.

Natasha: "Last time, after I told you the incident about the Lysol, I thought you might be so appalled by me that you wouldn't want to see me anymore; that you would see me as a potential murderess."

t: "No, I wasn't appalled by you. But I think *you* have been . . . you have been in the face of death . . . and at a time when you were terribly deserted and angry . . . feeling as though you might have a part in the killing. But you *haven't* damaged or killed anyone and *there's no way you could have stopped it.* You weren't that powerful and guilty as you felt."

Natasha: "You know, the trouble with my marriage now is that I'm not acting like a robot; I'm beginning to feel free to be me. And I don't know if Ivan can take that or not. Making peace with my father here was terribly powerful for me. I was sitting under a tree the other day thinking about it . . . till I realized . . . I was taken aback when I thought that forgiveness to my father is also forgiveness to myself. I had been wishing I was dead, but couldn't face that because the idea of life after death . . . in my mind before that would be a picture of a kind of hell. . . I know you know I don't believe that literally . . . but still, and it had the idea of meeting my father in it."

"With my mother it is different. My guilt is not that I hate her, but that I just don't care. She suffered a great deal. My antagonism toward her didn't stem from early childhood, but more later. I would think about 'what if there is a disaster and one died,' and I would have rather had father and me be left. Toward the end of the war, we were all unreasonable. Near the time when I almost got killed by the bomb, there were also great periods of joy. We didn't know what would happen next, so there was no real reason not to pick all the daisies there were . . . I picked them and made garlands for me and many of our friends . . . we got used to the sound of gunshots at night. Sometimes people were returning from prison camp, musicians would be at the window celebrating . . . At that point, I didn't yet feel betrayed by father, or the country . . . I didn't realize what we had done to people till a year later.

"I always take it for granted that I won't get helped and am surprised and touched when I do."

t: "Like when you wanted help from your mother and didn't get it?"

Natasha: "I had a nightmare last night . . . I was lost, looking for the person who can help me out. Do you think that I put myself in that position? Ivan last night actually tried . . . I was very touched when he did it. I was taking down my hair and he said, 'Let me brush it for you.' He has never done that before."

t: "Was there anyone you turned to when you were little—other than your father?"

Natasha: "I think I had a real attachment to my maid and then she left when my brother was born. Then I was punished for things I didn't know what it was. Mother would put me in the cellar with the coal and the potatoes. Once I broke one of the slats."

t: "What were your thoughts about mother then?"

Natasha: "For a long time, I even thought I wasn't my mother's child! I remember a story she once told at the dinner table. She told about watching a merry-go-round one day and there was an accident—and the man had his hand torn off—and that's what brought me!"

t: "Is there more?"

Natasha: "I interpreted that he couldn't take care of me and handed me to my mother, and that that's how she got me. For the longest time, I thought I was a foster child."

t: "So you felt you had really been the man's before your mother took you. Maybe we can find out more about what that meant to you. I would guess it involved a remarkable effort on your part to explain to yourself why you and your mother didn't feel closer like you wished for. You tried hard not to blame anybody, so you decided for a while that the distance between you was because that wasn't your *real* mother. You must have wanted to preserve an image of her you wanted to love, to split her up like that."

Natasha: "Last week, I left here feeling enormously elated. I had an image of my own subconscious that I can trust myself and not fear so much. If what you said came out of my mind, the strength in me to explain the trouble between myself and mother like that ... I must have a strong will to live! I visualized the man with the bleeding stump crying out and holding me cradled and saying, 'Will someone take care of my baby?'" (Her own arms form a cradling position as she talks.)

t: "That kind of cradling, embracing, is what you pictured between yourself and your father when you were forgiving each other."

Natasha: "The time before my father died, I guess I still felt secure. I expected I would finish high school and probably study physics or philosophy. I would get married and have twelve children and the servants would help take care of the house. My father wouldn't have interfered with what I wanted. At the same time, I also saw that my mother was often crying, she must have been left alone without my father too much. I imagined my mother pleading with my father to stay home more and father saying no to her, but I never saw that.

The months before they took my father ... I remember I was busy dreaming up a storm about boyfriends which I didn't have yet. And then I went through a state of shock ... months of shock when I didn't look at the future at all ... the past and the future were a black wall and there was only the terrible present. I didn't even want to think of my father because by then he had betrayed me. First he was a hero and then he was a criminal and so I was a criminal too."

t: "You didn't want to think of him, but in your mind you shared his fate."

Natasha: "People would say, 'Here comes that traitor's brat.' When the invasion came, the enemy soldiers had us do all kinds of *ugly* work, they said, 'Let them clean up the mess, they did the damage.' My mother was too weak, so she sent me as the substitute ... all the other women were adults. One day ... we were shoveling bodies ... the ground was hardened blood ... we didn't know if there was another layer of bodies underneath or not . . . maggots were all over crawling up my legs. Everyone else vomited and couldn't go on, but I was still digging. One of the soldiers finally felt sorry for me and brought me a can of liverwurst and I took it home to my relatives."

I found I couldn't say anything, but I think she knew I was with her.

Natasha: "That last session was hard, but I think it was valuable.' I think through the week I was able to carry a thread and define one area of tension in me. We talked about it here. The question of what values I discarded and what I kept."

She discussed her increasing awareness of the enormous underlying resentment she felt whenever she needed to maintain the role of the strong and invulnerable one, while others abandoned their tasks or leaned on her. The strength, of course, was associated with her early image of her father. This session she described a young girl at work who was goofing off while "I am responsible and get blamed. For the first time, I took the attitude, 'It's tough beans if she has to miss a party, it's not fair for her to go around bitching while I do all the work.' "

We related this to the last session in which she had described her endurance in substituting for her mother by continuing to bury the bodies, while other vomited and gave up.

The following session, she brought in, for the first time, an erotic dream of a doctor she liked.

Natasha: "We were sitting together and he was slowly and in a loving way starting to undress me. This probing and dragging things up and laying things bare may be doing me some good. In the dream, he got slightly undressed too."

Consciously, she had felt betrayed by this doctor, because she had assumed that he believed the unpleasant things her husband had told him about her, and expected him to feel critical of her. When she realized the discrepancy between the dream and her expectation, I pointed out that in fact I happened to know that this doctor did not feel critical of her. He thought she was a nice person.

Natasha: "That would fit with . . . well, lately I feel I don't have to defend and justify myself all the time. One thing I'm really pleased about . . . to tell you an idea that is a risk because it is entirely irrational. I take an idea and like to experience it from all angles, which is why it is important to me . . . why can I tell you serenely? If it comes to my integrity about my ideas . . . I would go to a mental hospital before giving them up."

t: "You won't have to . . ."

Natasha: "I feel I'm not really as threatened as I thought I was. One of the most wonderful experiences is when I suddenly see things can fall into place and make sense. If I can use symbols, I feel like I have finally gotten to the innermost part of my being and . . . and it is light . . . of which I was afraid . . . like a combination of my feeling and my being . . . what I want to be and what I am. There has always been a tension of being capable and powerful . . . and then of being evil. There has been a continued effort on my part not to have the evil use of power. You have said it is just anger about not having my needs met. What I am getting to is that I can rely on the good . . . that that is almost as reliable as my breathing . . . I don't know if it would be true under all circumstances. At least, I know I'm a hell of a lot more critical of myself than other people . . . except Ivan . . . and it doesn't seem fair to me any more. One good thing after we talked about that last session: I rethought my relationship with Boris and I agree that I overrate my guilt. He had enormous charisma and power over me. My preoccupation with it is really a kind of arrogance, as though we were equal. Under the circumstances, I was really much more vulnerable, and might as well not pretend otherwise."

t: "Vulnerability vs. power has had so many meanings for you that have affected your life. I'm glad you have preserved what it takes to make you able to unravel some of them now. Among other things, having power is tied up with an image of your father which you loved, and we have to raise the question whether you are afraid that if you want to give some of that up, whether you feel you would be getting rid of your father at the same time."

Natasha: "I think I am finally making some progress. What you said last time made me think, 'How much of my parents is in me; and how much I'm afraid I would kill them off if I threw some of those notions of power out.' It feels like that is a gate I'm afraid to open right now, but I feel like I have it now anytime to tell myself, 'Do I want to look at that?' and feel reasonably happy about it. One phrase comes to mind, 'love endures all,' but maybe that's a childish thought and I have to put it away to become more capable of love.

"My feelings about my mother when I was little—I really see myself more with the maid. But with mother I was mainly afraid I would hurt her and that I had. People would say, 'Don't get Matka (Russian word for mother) upset.' She suffered from migraines, so it would be 'You'll bring on one of Matka's headaches.' Mother would say, 'When you are naughty I can't love you.' It would be things like break a dish, stain a dress, or not being nice to grandma. I think I was already afraid of being accused of things I didn't do to an extraordinary degree."

Natasha: "I'm feeling somewhat low—started thinking about my parents with an unexpected result: it took the form of feeling sorry for myself and my present situation."

t: "That's not so surprising, so don't be mean to yourself about that."

Natasha: "That brings up how I feel about pain generally—I would say I haven't felt, I have wanted to discard it. But I realized that much of what bothered me at fifteen has still been going on in my present life. I have had the assumption that I have to continue it, no matter what. But I'm beginning to question that. There is no doubt about it, my satisfaction has been in being the Rock of Gibraltar and having people lean on me. There is still a fantastic wish of salvaging the whole thing. Last week I left here partly angry at you and partly elated."

t: "You let yourself get angry at me! Congratulations!"

Natasha (laughs): "You raised the question of when Ivan hurts me, whether I somehow welcome it as a punishment, and then feel more justified . . . or something like that. First, that hurt my feelings and I was angry with you. Then I realized that what there is, is that if suddenly I was very happy I would have to pay for it with a big disaster."

t: "That was a sequence in your life that you didn't bring about. Happiness and then disaster. You know, we've come to the conclusion that you're not that powerful after all, and don't need to be. Maybe questioning that power makes you angry too."

Natasha: "I was so proud of myself last week—I actually started an argument with Ivan and didn't even short-circuit it like usually. I stuck it out. Even if I've messed things up in the past, my mother messed things up for me and I can see now it didn't destroy me. I'm not so apprehensive about making a mistake. I think I'm beginning to feel a little bit healthier than I did. Do you remember the fantasy of the genie in the bottle I had . . . that I was afraid to let it out, that I thought it might kill me?"

t: "Yes, the genie seemed to be something within yourself you were afraid to let out."

Natasha: "I realized that the genie was about my being power-hungry, to arrange and have everything my way, so that I won't have to suffer. It would be not to depend on anybody who is unreliable and who will let me down. It has a lot of anger in it at my father for having trusted him to be in the picture . . . instead of in prison, leaving us unprotected about any of the horrible things they did to us, like the nights of freezing in cattle cars."

t: "Once you thought *him* powerful enough."

Natasha: "I think of my father as a powerful man and think of myself as powerful and I am proud that I am like my father; but maybe really good parents are *not* those like my father. His power failed him and I'm afraid my power will fail me—I'm not as powerful as I want to be . . . and now I realize that has its benefits."

Natasha: "Last week, you asked me about the moment I first remember feeling unprotected—and I have been thinking of the duality in me. What I was afraid of was not only my power . . . but what happened when I felt unprotected by my father ... the first moment must have really been my attempt to revenge myself on my father."

t: "And how did you do that?"

Natasha: "With Boris ... no one protected me. He was always putting my father down ... he said he would never have gotten caught and dragged to prison while his family was deserted. Of course, all that time Boris was fiddling around with me and ignored his own family. I identified very much with my father, but I never *defended* my father to Boris. I betrayed him like that."

t: "So that added to your guilt, and somewhere in you, you defined yourself as a 'traitor' too. Before your father was taken, when you were thirteen and fourteen already, how were things between you then?"

Natasha: "This is how close I was to my father and yet wasn't: The night that ——— (Russian city) went up in flames ... I was on duty putting out incendiary bombs. It meant being up on the roof with my father and I thought it was neat. That night dad and I were standing on the factory roof. He said, 'I think tonight this city is going to be destroyed ... it is too dangerous ... I want you to go downstairs.' I was terribly, terribly hurt."

t: "You felt sent away and could not share that with him. You must have felt he didn't trust you to be able to do it ... though you know he was really protecting you ... he must have cared about what would happen to you."

Natasha: "I felt like he didn't love me like before. I remember thinking, 'I'll show my father somebody loves me,' and I was really ready for Boris then. But then, I also thought, 'My father is a criminal so I am a criminal so I will be as bad as I can.' I ended up admiring Boris enormously and felt I was being disloyal to my father. My father knew Boris and didn't approve of him as a person. Boris had a sparkling personality and introduced me to the enjoyment of intellectual and artistic things. My father was much more spiritual in a way. Boris was practical—work and pleasure. My father was work- and duty-oriented. Both were serene in what they represented—and having the wonderful illusion they were always right. My father would have suffered about the way Boris lived it up. Both were quite oblivious to the damage they might leave in their wake."

t: "In relationship to Boris you ended up feeling rebuffed too."

Natasha: "Yes, when that was over I cried for two weeks and then was relieved it was over. Funny, I let myself cry for him and not for my father."

t: "You didn't care as much; it wasn't as overwhelming a loss."

Natasha: "I guess I was lucky to have known two splendid men. After that, the run-of-the-mill guy doesn't look so good. Maybe I can't have the splendid feeling of participating in building the country that my ancestors did. But the guilt I have is well balanced by the facet that I am able to enjoy beautiful and good things."

t: "I agree."

Natasha: "I still have been feeling miserable, thinking of my parents and Boris and how I've adapted my whole identity toward them. I feel sorry for me."

t: "You have had a great deal to cause you sadness in your life. But you still have choices now."

Natasha: "I tried so hard not to be sad after my father was taken, I think in order not to be bitter. I don't want to be a drag for everyone. Maybe I was even the Rock of Gibraltar for my father. Then there is the admission of the fact that I'm not as powerful as I want. There's a tremendous relief that I wasn't able to do something about what happened to me and my father. Maybe some of the feelings of fear, punishment, and false accusation were unnecessary, but I have always been ready for that. I always felt that if Ivan tells lies about me, he will be believed and not I."

t: "With Boris you had a real experience and a lot of feeling about it. But it was secret and you felt guilty. You knew it existed, but there was no validation in reality. In front of others, he acted as though it wasn't happening."

Natasha: "When I was naughty, my mother and father talked of needing to break my will—both of them?"

t: "Both of them?"

Natasha: "No, it is not both of them! I always knew my father admired someone with a strong will. He told me one of the things he liked about me was having a strong will. That that was necessary to survive and live a meaningful life. But it was mother's and father's expressed policy that any disagreements have to be concealed. It was his great striving for harmony."

t: "Boris and you had a secret that made you feel guilty—but excluded when his wife was there. Your father and you shared an admiration for will power, but he talked of 'breaking your will' when he was with your mother?"

Natasha: "I remember once, a kid who lived on the block . . . and I went for an adventure walk without telling. My father was upset with me, and I felt very betrayed. I thought he would like that. I felt, 'You are acting like my mother, how could you do that to me?' Father had treated me as a kid, with respect. Mother expected me to act only like a girl."

During the next few sessions, Natasha brought up a number of new perspectives on her mother:

Natasha: "I think during my early childhood she was a very lonely and scared and unhappy woman—and to some extent, dad treated her with the same unresponsiveness that Ivan treats me. I am sort of seeing her from the outside in now; it hadn't occurred to me to think from her point of view."

She became aware of the many restrictions on the role her mother felt allowed to play, and the degree to which she felt devalued as a person herself. She began to see how mother's inhibitions limited the possibility for warmth toward her little daughter; Natasha had sorely missed this and assumed it was caused by her own naughtiness. She recovered some early memories of a warmhearted grandmother with whom she felt more free to be herself and accepted.

At about this time, a minor skirmish in which her adolescent son was involved brought a police car to her door late at night. After the police left, Natasha made an emergency call to me; something she resorted to only in crises. The following session:

t: "Did the police liner strike terror into you?"

Natasha: "Yes, I had the image of when they came to arrest my father. I've had a terror of anyone in uniform. I used to not be able to buy a postage stamp because they have uniforms in the post office."

We now talked at some length about recognizing the terrifying realities of her past life and the remaining vulnerability associated with any reminders of those realities (such as the police). We needed to differentiate these from the conflicts in her childhood and the complicated feelings about her father which had given rise to so much guilt and sadness in her. The effects of her wishes for power, and her anger after disappointment in father had to be separated from the guilt she felt about what happened in her country, so that she could choose to let herself have some happiness without being followed by the "disaster" which she had said earlier that she expected. She talked of her past fears of "being put away" in a mental institution, seeing it now as her way of joining her father. We linked her first suicidal impulse (to stand up to the airplane to be shot at, instead of seeking shelter) to a mixed act of love and self-punishment. She knew her father admired her will power in standing up to adversity; she and father had stood on duty together on the roof the night of the bombings. He had talked of "going down with flags flying" but he had sent her downstairs for safety and she felt hurt, as though she had failed him. The next time, she would not go down to the shelter and "fail" him again, even if it cost her her life. One day she stated:

"Only lately have I been able to see my father as one man, with both good and evil. So much time has passed and so much else has colored things. I've come to the painful conclusion that I'm kidding myself with all my fancy talk of moral responsibility for Ivan. I no longer think it is my moral responsibility to stay together no matter what, resenting it all the time. I may be more free to work out my problems with him now that I don't think I *have* to stay with him, that it is like a punishment I deserve. In fact, I could say in a way that I have been using him, by having him use me to assuage my own guilt. Actually, that protected me from facing myself and my feelings. I couldn't have risked being rejected by anyone. Do you know that all my married life I have been trying to feel nothing. When he and I married, I don't think I would have been ready for real intimacy anyway . . . but now that's different. Also, I don't know whether

I would be capable and would want to uproot myself from my past again. The first time that happened—when my father was taken—and I was cut off from my past and everything I believed, it was as though I and everyone around me had died.

What's been of value to me lately . . . is that extraordinary impulse . . . that I can trust my integrity . . . that it would stand by me . . . I think that is what has finally achieved peace with the memory of my father."

Integration of an Enriching Identification with the Quest for Affects Shared with a Loved Father: Wendy

Wendy was a married mother of three children, in her late twenties, talented in her career in the field of communications. Her husband was an internist. One liked her quickly. An exceptional ability to come to the heart of a matter without detours, to exude a love of life, and to behave in a warm and forthright manner, made being with her refreshing.

She sought treatment in part to gain greater understanding of herself, and the conflicting pulls of family and career; and in part because she felt there was something "unfinished" for her about the death of her father when she was ten. The impulse toward tears was close at the first mention of her father. I felt this to be a good sign that her feelings were accessible to her, in the context of her excellent functioning in her work, and as a wife and mother.

Wendy had experienced a warm and vibrant relationship to her father, although she tended to repress any negative aspects. After his death she had been instrumental in holding together the family of younger children, and helping her mother to cope with her life. Her strength and straightforwardness combined to foster the family's reliance on her direction, and at times control. She maintained this role willingly, at times using empathy to ward off her anger at those who disappointed her.

Wendy was aware of maintaining fragments of her interaction with her father. For example, she bought a chair identical to the one he had sat in to hold her on his lap while he read to her. She married a man who both cared about personal relationships and loved mountain-climbing like her father had.

Some years after the father's death, during Wendy's adolescence, her mother remarried a man who, in her eyes, was overconcerned with material values and could not tolerate the emotional honesty she had associated with her father. The vibrancy in the family was slowly replaced by a different style of life, which appeared hypocritical to the young woman. She was aware that her mother's occasional references to her father now had a distant quality, "as though she were talking about the mailman." In therapy, Wendy became increasingly aware of her disappointment and sense of loss about the changes in her family after her father died. This included the inability of her mother and stepfather to recognize her particular talents, or respond to her needs.

The particular qualities she had identified with her father, his vibrancy and emotional directness, and which she herself carried into her own emotional relationships, had now been ambivalently extruded by her mother, and to a lesser degree by some of her younger siblings. While others in her profession and during her college years both liked and admired her, letting her know that she had something special to offer, she felt repeatedly about her family that "they cannot recognize who I really am." Early in therapy, she had glaring examples of her mother's responses to siblings' achievements, in contrast to hers—a change from her childhood life. In this sense, the family treated her in part as the ghost of her father, reminding them of past life values and principles on which they had turned their backs in order to make a remarriage work, leaving her to carry them on alone.

Wendy's identification with her father coexisted with memories of the affective interaction between them, and a quest for similar affects in new relationships. The identification was at a high level of ego differentiation, involving personal attributes, traits, and values. Since she was neither fixated at, nor regressed to, earlier levels of identification expressed in wishes to merge identities, or to have and share sex-linked characteristics, her feminine identification was in no way compromised.

The excerpts from sessions described here are fragments related to the loss of her father, omitting the rich array of other issues. One of these, mentioned above, was the emergence of a pattern in her interaction during visits to her mother, siblings, and stepfather. She would bring up reminders of her father, in the form of conversation or by living out his style of approaching life, including achievements he would have valued. She felt that these reminders were not perceived or appreciated, but instead were cancelled out by the family's focus on new and different values, taken on after the mother's remarriage. This material will not be detailed further here.

Wendy: "My mother greatly relied on me after my father died. She went back to school and eventually remarried. I think she is very competitive with me, never really treated me as a daughter after he died. I guess I've been a daughter, sister and mother to her. People have always told me, 'You have something special to offer,' but mother could never recognize anything like that. Otherwise, she is a loving, giving person; she used to be great with children."

She talks of her younger siblings and sense of responsibility for the well-being of each.

t: "And what was your dad like?"

Wendy: "My father had a fine sense of humor and a lot of energy . . . and yet he was able to understand what people needed. Like on the first day of kindergarten, he packed me a stick of gum in my pocketbook . . . and then I was able to be on my way. It was like he added a friendly touch to each event."

t: "That was before he got sick?"

Wendy: "His illness started for me one rainy day when mother announced that dad had to go into L.A. I sensed something was wrong. I said that night, 'Dad. have I ever been to a hospital?' he laughed and said that he should have explained to me that he had a lump growing and would be going to the hospital to make sure what it was."

t: "He laughed?"

Wendy: "Not really to make light of it, more at my having guessed. That Thanksgiving and Christmas went with the knowledge of his terminal illness. He was very sick and couldn't eat. He started to cook, just for the smell of it. I can't keep the facts straight in my head. The summer he died we were in the house in the woods. I was sleeping in my mother's room for some reason. I got up and looked out the window . . . and saw the moon making a path from the sky into the water. Then my mother rounded up all the kids and told us gently, 'Daddy just died.'

"After my father died, there is a whole year missing I can't remember. Mother had problems with being overwhelmed and having too many kids, so I took over and whipped everyone into action.

"Other things happened after my father's death. We never went to his funeral. I resented that. Mother tried to protect us from grieving. So I somatized instead. I thought I had a lump growing and got taken to the doctor and of course it turned out to be nothing. Also, I had a hard time catching my breath. I think to breathe deeply would have been to relax. That started while he was still in the hospital.

"After he died, my mother was overwhelmed. She would either act very helpless or get angry at everything, lose control . . . like break a dish. Once she leveled everything, swept everything off the table. I was frightened by the change in her. During my adolescence, she would enrage me . . . and then we would make up and hug and be close."

t: "What got to you most about her then?"

Wendy: "That she was demanding all the time. Also, when someone puts on a helpless act it always makes me mad."

t: "You didn't let yourself do that, act helpless?"

Wendy: "I still don't. The other thing is that mother's relationship to Gus (step-father) is so different; their life is so different."

t: "What was it like when you were little?"

Wendy: "I remember mother and father having fun together, her giggling and his chasing her around the house, around the dining room table. I remember only one real fight. My father was effective in communication, both his affection and his anger were predictable. Gus is a lot different, there is great formality and a need to be impressive. The house we moved into was elegant and appearances became much more important to my mother. I remember the moment when I realized she was seriously considering marrying Gus."

t: "Tell me about it."

Wendy: "Every Sunday we would have a leg of lamb with garlic . . . all of us loved garlic. One Sunday, no garlic. I asked her why and she said, 'Mr. Kant (Gus) doesn't like garlic'; from then on we never had it with garlic again."

t: "The flavor everyone loved got traded in for Mr. Kant?"

Wendy: "I had a great conversation with my mother. I feel things are settling with my family in important ways for me. with our buying a house of our own. (Wendy and her family had been living in a rented house.) We were talking about my sense of entitlement here the other day, what it's okay for me to have for myself without taking care of everyone else first. Mother now has a sense of entitlement too, with her oriental art course, and that makes it easier for me. I think it allows her to sense the world in a variety of levels of getting pleasures out of it. Yet her attitude has been for so long, 'I am so artistic and the real world is too full of suffering . . . how misunderstood I am.' Now, I am less caught up in it. I simply told her 'I care about you, but I also need you as a mother, you have to cope with where that leaves you.' I was able to tell her that her helplessness makes trouble between us. I felt in closer contact with the family again." (Silence.)

t: "What are you thinking now?"

Wendy: "I find it gratifying here, I never had a chance for interest in just my own thoughts and actions; I guess it makes me feel appreciated."

t: "At your mother's house too you are trying to get through now, about what you need."

Wendy: "I always wanted to be the one to my mother who was strong and capable."

t: "And what does that mean about what you've kept under cover, so as not to rock the boat . . . here and at home?"

We arrive at the conclusion that she is afraid of letting fleeting impulses of anger or dependency toward me show, though she is becoming more aware of these. When I had to be away for a session, she pictured "Dr. Tessman goofing off, romping around with her husband and children." It was a time when neither vacation nor romping was available to her, so she was envious. The family in her childhood had romped. We discussed her use of empathy, evident in many of her responses, as an adaptive way (a strong asset in her career in communications) that she dealt with anger and prevented a sense of loss.

Wendy: "I had a rough week and an odd dream about you. You were writing in your notebook . . . you looked away from me and I felt neglected by you. I said, 'It's the same thing happening again.' About therapy, I know that it's something I want for *myself.* I don't want to have to justify it to be entitled to it."

t: "In your dream it was 'the same thing happening *again.*' So it has happened before."

Wendy: "I don't know when . . . the first time I remember kind of falling apart was after I went with the guy I told you about. After he left to go to grad school and we broke up it really hit me hard. I had to say 'Someone I loved left me.' "

t: "And where does that thought take you?"

Wendy: "My problem is that I idealize my relationship to my father. I have my favorite images and I cannot remember the rest. There is that letter he wrote to all of us before he died. He sounded so confident. preparing for his death, almost as though he was proud of the way he was handling it." (She had brought, in the previous session, a copy of the letter for me to read.)

t: "And what was missing that you wanted to hear?"

Wendy: "I guess it was really not about *us* in any way . . . *there was no direct objection to his leaving us.*"

t: "I felt like you do when I read the letter . . . it was beautifully put about his own reactions . . . but he was no longer able to reach out to you . . . to let you take part in the anger and grief about having to die."

Wendy: "I think he made it imperative that we accept his death—and he called on us all to carry on and I got caught up in his wishes, against my own needs. I dreamt about him too this week—his death—there was a boardwalk and bicycles and a wagon in the place where we spend summers. A hearse, but in a wagon, casketlike—it went away from me and then came back again." *then came back again.*"

t: "Wagons and bicycles were part of your life together. His death was final . . . *but like the wagon you wanted him to come back again.*"

Wendy (in tears): "I never cry in front of my mother . . . I resented that, about not being allowed to go to the funeral."

Wendy: "I had another dream about my father. He came back but he came back sick. There were a lot of people from the office and they were all in bed . . . they were trying to get close to him and fighting this woman . . . I was so mad at her . . . this woman was kicked in the ass and I kicked at her too . . . I belonged there and couldn't get any closer."

t: "What are your thoughts?"

Wendy: "I remember once I was disappointed in him . . . when he was sick . . . I asked him some question about school work and he said 'leave me alone.' "

t: "So you felt deserted by the change in him before he died . . . and must have felt furious with him about that."

Wendy: "Also I have to face now that there was another side to him, less honest and direct and more ready to cover his own feelings . . . that's what I've been thinking after we talked about his letter."

We also talked about her rivalry and anger at the "others" who were there when she wanted to be alone with father. It was not clear to what extent they were sibs or mother. The woman in the dream was someone at work she *did* want to "kick in the ass" for her dependence on others.

Wendy: "I went to ask my mother whether she ever misses my father still. She said, 'Wendy, it's been twenty years!' It was an enormous relief to me that she's not sitting around waiting for him to return. I felt very much more peaceful . . . to think that she didn't need me to remind her of him."

Wendy: "I dreamt about a girl friend, whose first husband actually died. In the dream, she had two kids and told me Jim (her second husband) was in the hospital. Then she called back and said, 'Jim just died; a mirror fell and cut his lip and he bled to death.' I packed my bags to go and help take care of things."

t: "What do you make of it?"

Wendy: "My initial thought is, 'Her loss and my loss gives us something in common.' I've always been fond of Jim. Lately, he has shown himself to be more narcissistic and self-absorbed than I thought in his writings. I think of my father's operation and his dried and cracked lips. My father was very much concerned with a production of a piece of work; by the end, I think he saw his dying as a piece of work like that . In his letter, it is almost as though he embraced death to be cherished and looked forward to. He isolated his feelings, and that was the opposite of one of the things I had loved about him. I used to worry about mother dying too and then I would have to take care of all the kids . . . that's in the dream too, I guess. I realize at this point that I have less anxiety about losing my husband, that that's happening while I'm giving up the notion of his being like my father. I thought of something else about the other dream, where my father was in the wagon. One of my most vivid memories of my father is walking downtown with him hand in hand to buy a little red wagon for Ginger's (sister) birthday. I was so envious of her, a red wagon of her own!"

t: "In your dream, a mirror fell on him and cut him . . . so he was looking at himself when he died . . . not at you . . . he bled then. In an earlier dream you felt neglected when I didn't look at you."

Wendy: "About my father, I've felt lately that I have been doing his work for him—that there was an unreal quality of his facing his death. He wrote everything down, but he left our feelings out of it. I wonder if he had difficulty facing a death because he never really faced a loss; that he just couldn't imagine it."

t: "That's very likely a correct intuition on your part."

Wendy: "After my father died, I remember being very nervous thinking of what extra attention I would get. There was this awful lady who came up to me and put her hands on my shoulders and said, 'Oh Wendy, I'm so sorry about your dear father.' I think I laughed because she didn't even know my father and then felt horrible and my mother chided me for being rude. You asked the other day what else it meant to me to have my father die. I've been thinking that it makes one different, it makes one have to give explanations to other people all the time. Like a father-daughter dinner at school. I tried to get my mother to go, but attempts were made to get someone else, some man to go in place of my father. And once there was a dance for fathers . . . and some man was borrowed."

t: "What did you feel?"

Wendy: *"That they were trying to make up for something that I knew nobody could ever make up for."*

t: "It sounds like after your father died, outsiders felt to you like intruders; acting as though your relationship to your father was no longer important or a part of you; as though you should turn to someone new when you still were busy with thoughts of your father. You said once that the whole year after his death you can't remember . . . has some of that come back to you?"

Wendy: "It's odd, something reminded me of that period last week. I was at that medical cocktail party I hated, everybody was so stuffy and status-oriented. I know I overreact to those because they symbolize my mother and Gus being so formal and trying to make an impression, instead of natural and fun, like it used to be with my father. But anyway, in the middle of the party I was very uncomfortable—just couldn't seem to cope with it; and I had the impulse just to leave. Of course, I couldn't with all of Stan's colleagues there. But anyway, it reminded me of the period after my father's dying. I had a great fear that people would treat me differently . . . that they would make me talk about it. For instance, there was a whole family who asked us all over for dinner—I didn't want to be treated like a bereft child—in the same way that I don't want to be treated like an appendage of Stan's when I go to a medical party, I want to go as myself. If we were asked someplace after my father died, I sometimes just left and ran to the car and stayed by myself. I just wanted to withdraw and hoped that nobody would notice."

t: "At the cocktail party you want to go as yourself . . . and when you ran to the car, you didn't want to be pressured by someone else's expectations, you wanted to be yourself. What did you feel by yourself?"

Wendy: "I could be sad."

t: "And you've said you never let your mother see your cry!"

Having faced some of the ambivalence toward her father, and thus allowed the sadness to emerge, Wendy now filled in some of the details of the lovely relationship she had with her father and its effect on her subsequent self.

Wendy described an argument with an indecisive colleague about an upcoming decision. She needed his agreement before action could be taken. She had the thought, "When I was on my own I could always make decisions because my father really trusted me."

t: "Tell me about it."

Wendy: "Once he had gone to rent a boat and he told me 'You can run the boat today.' Then for some reason a friend came too and was wary about getting in if I was going to run it. But my father said, 'That's okay, Wend, I have confidence in you, and wouldn't do it any other way.' Also, my father and I loved kiteflying, he would teach me tricks, but then let me do it myself. I remember once I won a kiteflying contest . . . I must have been seven or eight. It's not just that I wanted to do it on my own, but also that he let me. He had a certain trust and confidence that I've thought of as a part of myself . . . that I don't seem to need that constant checking back about what people think . . . like at work, people have asked me how come I can keep coping under the stress of everybody else's opinion being divided.

"I guess what I remember about mother is that she didn't interfere with that . . . and I suddenly appreciate that about her. Father and I took walks, looked at birds, and shared a lot. I remember one birthday when I was little and driving her up the wall asking every two minutes when the party would start and what games we would play, etc. She asked my father 'Oh please, take her for a walk' and he did, like he enjoyed it, not just to get me out of the way. I had the chance to see them work together like that. With Stan and our kids it doesn't always work that way.

"He had a facility with all things at once . . . while mother gets more overwhelmed . . . but he had a high tolerance for confusion, in a way more patience. There was a repetitive dream I had as a child I think of now: I was walking down the middle of the road in my ballet costume—the dream has a Degas-like perspective—I was pintsized, in a tutu and slippers tied Spanish style—there were women at the sides not interfering in any way . . . and I have this visceral sensation about the feeling . . . that I was kind of contained . . . not restricted, but very secure . . . like I was solitary in walking, but not alone. Now as I think of the dream, it reminds me of our buying the house to have another baby—a rich environment which has room for creativity and independent strivings too—both moving on and being safe—in the dream I felt surrounded, but don't know by what."

In beautiful dream imagery, she had described not only her body image, but also the kind of "contained—not restricted but secure" rapport she felt with her father and which was supported by mother. It is this kind of environment which is fertile for the rich development of feelings and capacity for grief. Her father's active participation in her care, including the "containing" tenderness, was probably especially important in view of the fact that another sibling was born just before she was two, an age when she still needed sustained attention in caring.

Father's relationships, as Wendy saw them, were cooperative in nature not only with her mother, but also with friends or assistants in his work.

Wendy: "My father was never too busy to fix my dolls—if he had his hands full, his assistant would put down his tools and do it. I had an elaborate game when I was very little, probably to get attention away from others. I would get myself locked into the bathroom by mistake and he would have to come and take the hinges off . . . and he never left me long alone by myself in there. Then every night I would be on his lap while I listened to the news and had to practice being quiet. But I knew he would read me a story after. I told you I found a chair exactly like that for our new house.

"I think he would have liked the person I am. He is in his absence still an incredibly important part of my life. So much of who I am developed from him. It's funny, after my hour here a few weeks ago I left feeling that I had developed a kind of aggressive survival instinct in regard to my brothers and sisters and coping with everything at home when mother needed me to do that. Today with the things we've said about my father, I feel different about myself when I see how *it came from him too, how it's a continuation of one of his strengths."*

Wendy makes clear that the self-esteem associated with aspects of her self-image changes in accordance with her awareness of the associated identification figures. In this case, she can value herself more when she realizes she had identified with father. Such a shift in self-esteem is the crucial reason to explore the relationship between images of self and parents. The unconscious aspects of such identifications may contain the most valued or most despised components of the self, but often cannot be either evaluated realistically, nor given up, until the underlying identificatory links become clear.

Wendy: "I am trying to remember if I thought my father treated me differently. He did seem to see me as a person somehow."

t: "That's always been an important issue for you, with your mother and with Stan's and your colleagues and friends."

Wendy: "I mean he didn't see me just as a 'first-born female child', which might have been disappointing to some. I was never infantilized by him even though he was a very loving person. Loving like . . . I remember when mother and father went out and we had a sitter, my sister and I slept in their bed till they came home and they would carry us asleep into our bed . . . I would act extra sleepy and made sure he carried us. There was something about the way he did simple things that was very nurturant—or maybe gracious is the word, rather than out of duty. On Saturdays, he would make a big omelet for lunch—very carefully—I do mine too fast and they don't come out as well— and the painter who helped around the house would be invited and they were good friends with each other and I loved listening to them. Everything he did was done with pride and like it was meant to last."

t: *"And you expected that he would last too."*

Wendy: *"I guess I am fighting all the time against feeling abandoned (tears)."*

t (a little later): "The kind of response you got from him has lasted inside you and become a part of how vibrant, direct and caring you are all at the same time. Yet I think you resent it terribly, you are always disappointed when you don't get that kind of appreciation from Stan or others, or when your family gets threatened by those very qualities in you."

Wendy: "I guess one reason I can't ask people for support is because of exactly that . . . I know my mother doesn't respond that way . . . but it backfires because when I can't show my wanting it, everyone just assumes I don't need any support and I louse up my chances even more. By not asking for support I shut it off . . . *but to let go of the possibility that my father will somehow reappear . . . in some one else (tears)* . . . I guess I have to realize it's not the same relationship with Stan before I can get taken care of too. In that way, sometimes the things I loved most about my father now get in my way."

Comments

The psychic mechanisms evoked in the bereaved child to cope with the overwhelming trauma of the death of a parent are again conjured up in the process of beginning or completing grief. Some become a focus of therapy in themselves, while others are like guideposts along the trail.

When identification replaces memory (as in the case of Michael), the image of the dead must be reconstructed to some extent in order to be dealt with as someone outside the self.

Identification, in fantasy and in action (lived out), may have features which are both positive and negative for the individual, and both their origin and current value to the person must be distinguished. Thus, Wendy decided that much as she loved her father, his need for mastery, with which she identified and which was an asset to her, also hindered others from seeing her need to be dependent when she wanted support.

In therapy, the transitional objects, phenomena, presences, communications with the dead, etc., are noticed, but not initially questioned. Like dreams, they are a fruitful route to clues about the former relationship, and perhaps a hint that ego differentiation has not been securely completed, or may become vulnerable under stress. Eventually they are explored in terms of the underlying magic thinking belonging to the time when they were first constructed.

The recreation of painful affects preserves a tie to the wanted parent, but may hamper the individual's chance for current, fulfilling relationships. In milder form (the repetition of feeling painfully cut off in the midst of an intense libidinal attachment), this occurred in one of the cases illustrated here (Alex). In much more extreme form (die or kill) it surfaces in those cases, not often initially applicants for psychotherapy, in which a spouse's wish for a separation or divorce is greeted with suicidal or homicidal threats. As mentioned elsewhere in this book, a disproportionate number of such cases, often involved in custody disputes, turn out to have had a parent die before the age of ten. In these cases, painful affects equated with "death" have been stirred up by later threat of loss or separation. In contrast, other individuals who experienced such loss remained attuned to painful affects in ways which helped them be empathic with the losses of others, such as their children (e.g., the father of Eva, in chapter 7).

Comments about the case material follow.

Vicky illustrates simultaneous awareness of the parent's being dead (and in her grave) and an expectation of the return of her presence. Although the return of the mother was linked with fears of retaliation for Vicky's "badness," an underlying longing for the return of the lost, loved mother emerged as well. Perhaps it is better to be haunted and punished, than never to be haunted at all. In restitutive fantasy, Vicky, like many other bereaved children, erased the disfiguring signs of the illness which had diminished the love between mother and daughter, and restored her to being the well mother of their earlier life together.

Tod and Peggy are discussed as an example of constructive, supported grieving. The human support network was in evidence. Both mother and father had prepared them for the death and made provisions for the continuity of the children's lives. Father and children were close in their grief and did not want any intrusion. Later the wider network of grandparents, other relatives, old friends, and the housekeeper were available when wanted. Both Tod and Peggy were preoccupied with the image of their mother after death, and Peggy told of the familiar "searching" for mother's face in supermarkets. Both had a fund of memories about her, and a sense of continuity attached to particular activities and values she shared with them (the cookbook for Peggy; school work for Tod). As is usual, both experienced some guilt. This is perceived in terms of a past "failure" in interaction with her, especially burdensome because they could now no longer change the event or "make up" with mother about it. The finality of death often faces individuals with the helplessness of no longer being able to fulfill past promises of improving the relationship. The particular events mentioned differed, in accordance with the differences in the adolescents' own personalities and relationships to mother. Peggy's incident was more of rivalry, in the form of a "put-down" (mimicking mother sarcastically for restricting her fun with peers). Tod felt guilty about having failed to give her attention, like the supportive attention she offered him when he sought or needed it. Similarly, Tod and Peggy had different attitudes about the possibility of accepting father's involvement with another woman, with or without "mothering." Again Peggy felt more selective and critical about who might be acceptable, but also more "loyal" to the image of mother, while Tod was ready for maternal attention, as long as this made his father happy, too. Neither father, Tod or Peggy had short-circuited their mourning nor had they forfeited their continued growth.

For Michael, the evocation of memory was especially difficult, and had to be accomplished in the form of reconstruction through what was experienced in current relationships. In this case, lacunae in the actual opportunities for shared experiences with the mother, accompanied by a lack of communication in the family, made for a paucity of positive images and affected about his interactions with the mother. His identification was with his mother's deadness, suffering, and dysphoria, and the major trade-off was that one would be taken care of while in this state. The identification was, of course, frightening, and he was not conscious of it. Search for her image in either literal searching, memory, "presences," or in the formal of transitional objects was minimal. He did, however, have a precursor to the transitional object—his own thumb—to comfort him. He sucked his thumb until he married. His own development appeared disrupted, in the sense that he did not progress in the usual strides toward independence and sexual initiative in adolescence; analogously, he was upset by his children when they became adolescent. His happiest period in life had been when he had transferred his dependency to his wife, who was able to support him emotionally without reminders of the unhappy past. Michael portrays what is often described as a "classical" depression with enormous guilt, sense of helplessness, and fear of being held responsible for bad happenings. Like others who are vulnerable to suffering from such depression, it is likely that he never was assured of a focussed, unambivalent welcome by either parent.

In Alex, the same age as Michael at the death of his mother, we see a different array of ego mechanisms. He had experienced a stimulating, confidence-inducing boyhood as his mother's favorite, though this made him feel uncomfortable with the less favored father. Identification with the mother, that is, being like her, as a defense against loss is only hinted at by two fragments of material. One is that he and the object of his fantasies were both alike in having penises; secondly, that he fought against being like the father, whom he accused of being like a woman. Guilt about mother's death did not, at least in these early sessions, appear as a prominent feature, but the quest for her did, at a number of levels: (1) searching—after her death he searched the faces ont he street, expecting her presence; (2) memories of her fondness for him, which brought tears to his eyes; (3) fantasy—a preoccupation with her image, which was then displaced onto a teacher who was with him the last year of his mother's life, and also had its own reality. With the teacher, he felt he had "practically a love affair" and centered his sexual fantasies around her for several years. Yet the fantasy of the loving embrace of the snakes has strong derivatives of both the imagery and affective content of the relationship to his mother. The quest for the intensely desired woman who is first a source of joy, but then inevitably disrupts the relationship by changing her "vibes" and cutting him off, leaving him to experience grief and pain, became a repeated theme in his life. He held onto the relationship by perpetuating the painful sequence of affects in such loss. (4) a living-out of an aspect of the ego ideal between him and his mother: that he would achieve, be creative and successful as she always knew he would. She had not saved the family money to sent him to college in vain.

Amy had experienced a tender, loving relationship with her father. We see a range of modes of dealing with his death, which include various aspects of identification and of the quest for him, based on the conviction that he must still exist for her somehow. Since she was only five when he died, her impulse life, ego modes, and actual interactions with him differed from those potentially available to children whose parents die later in their development. Amy's mother well-meaningly tried to protect the little girl from grieving, and she was not exposed to the reality of seeing his dead body, visiting his grave or watching her mother mourn. The reality sense invested in believing in his existence remained as strong as her knowledge that he was dead. Her grief reaction unfolded over a period of time in her early thirties in an intricate combination of identification and quest. Eventually, those aspects of the identification which were expressed in the wish to merge with him in death (suicidal wishes) when she felt deserted by others, were replaced by memories which proved the reality of her father's loving relationship to her, without the necessity for such regression. Aspects of identification also occurred in her love for a man "who has the same genes." In Amy's case, the quest for the wanted parent appeared during childhood in a number of the forms discussed previously:

1. Presences—she frequently felt his presence or his watching her, and had conversations with him.

2. Imaginary companion—she created a male imaginary companion with a living father, with whom she communicated over distances.

3. Airmail messages—she carried a sense of elated anticipation about a message from a beloved, far enough away so that it has to come by airmail. This fantasy had its origins in the real letters the father sent the four-year-old daughter, blowing kisses across distances.

4. Transitional objects and transitional phenomena—indications are that at the time when Amy's father died, she was stimulated by exciting (firelike) sexual wishes as a part of her tenderness toward him. She was guilty and afraid about these, particularly since they coincided with the period of her father's death. It seems likely (though this is unclear) that she retreated from these wishes in her imagery about him to the preceding "safer" period, when affectionate contact between them consisted of tender cuddling, but at an earlier stage of development, a time when transitional objects and transitional phenomena are created to deal with separations. She used the transitional object of the sheet, as a comforting contact with her mouth, a contact which in her mind was associated with closeness to the father's skin and clothes. The capacity to use this transitional object probably grew out of an earlier tender relationship with her mother. The fantasy of the consoling skin contact also was used restitutionally as a defense against the fantasy of incorporating or eating the father in order to have him back (and being eaten in return). The defended-against part of the fantasy was projected onto the mother: it was she who had incorporated a man, "Hitler," and an orally aggressive animal—the "alligator." In this complicated fashion she tried to make sure that no part of the father was lost. Another transitional phenomenon which immortalized her actual relationship to the father was her singing at night, before sleeping. She sang as he used to sing to her. This was a rich avenue of expression for her, a pathway to preconscious and unconscious links between imagery, affects, and words. Her song fragments (e.g., in therapy) always said what she meant, and were as much a communication as an expression of fantasy.

5. Fantasy—as she proceeded with reality testing about her real father and his real relationship to her (through fragments of evidence from the past, such as his letter, and her mother's explanations), she was progressively able to grieve for his absence and to relinquish the wish to join him in death.

Natasha's identification with various aspects of her father bound their relationship before, rather than only after, she lost him through death. He was both loved and admired by her and others in her community. By age fifteen, a distant relationship with her mother combined with the strong, mutually enhancing camaraderie with father shaped her self-esteem around the ideals father and daughter shared. Although after his death she attempted to reject him and extrude his values from hers, this would have killed off valued components in herself. In a death sentence to herself, she first sought to join him instead. The human support network crashed down around her, simultaneously with the loss of her father. Emulated before, he was now devalued by all. Even mother did not protect Natasha from sexual advances by a man who now looked down on father, in order not to risk her security. Around her the war was a nightmare come true.

A revitalization of her strength and ability to feel was associated with her urgent need to be reconciled with him in order to want to live. This involved forgiving him by accepting his death but remembering his presence. Memories were available as soon as she was ready. This sense of his presence was strong particularly during her grief work. Transitional objects or phenomena related to the father as far as I know, did not make an appearance. However, certain qualities in herself, which she identified with the father, were experienced in fantasied, reanimated form, while being worked through. For example, the genie who pleaded to be let out of the bottle where she had been keeping him captive, was, in her words, the "power-hungry" aspect of her father that she wanted now to fight within herself. The strength of Natasha's continuing tie with her father was attested to by the strength of her motivation to face the disasters in her life in order to put them behind her and construct something alive and good. Where her father had taught her never to give up ("Go down with the flags flying") Natasha eventually could fly her flags, but not go down.

Wendy illustrates a highly effective integration of her identification with the dead father with a continued quest for the vibrant affects shared with the father. The combination allowed her very rich relationships. There is a parallel richness to the quality of her memories of the dead father and the role he played in her life. Again, the groundwork for this identification had been laid prior to his death, and defense against loss was not its primary function. Her identification was primarily with treasured ego modes and attitudes, rather than with bodily attributes, and in no way disturbed her femininity. In addition, the fact that her mother seemed not to be threatened by the mutual affection between father and daughter—that she gave some evidence of a joyous relationship to him herself with which Wendy could also identify—and that her father was nurturant as well as invigorating, made it easier for identification and her use of his style of relating to others to cohabit.

An identification with a concrete symptom of the father occurred in Wendy transiently, shortly after his death, (the fear she had a lump growing) and was attributed by her to the need to control, rather than grieve fully at the time. Transitional objects connected with the father were not in evidence. But at a more ego-integrated level, Wendy quite purposefully chose a chair for her new house which was like the one she had shared with her father.

For Wendy, grief for the father was accompanied by two ideas previously held at bay. She faced the fact that there was a negative side to his assets, and that she had negative feelings about it. That is, her father's need for mastery extended to include his way of coping with his own death—a way which excluded Wendy and made her feel that she, too, must always master, rather than grieve. Secondly, she (like Amy) faced the powerful impact of the idea of the father's *absence,* in contrast to the previously long-cherished, unconscious hope that someday, somewhere or with someone like him, she would again find herself in his *presence.*

Numbers of children who, like Vicky, had lived with a long or debilitating illness in a parent before death made clear that their losses began at the time of the change in relationships caused by the combination of the parent's incapacity, and other family members' stressed reactions. The child's guilt about feeling angry during this time further complicated grieving. As twelve-year-old Joshua blurted out tearfully while recalling visits to his dying father, "My father couldn't do anything anymore, and he couldn't even take the blame!" Such children tended to manifest a special feature in their fantasies of reunion: In their image they were apt to repair the body of a parent who had changed through illness before death, so that the image of their quest was that of the parent before such troubles began. For example, seven-year-old Dennis, referred because of stomach aches six months after his mother died, complained of having to sit on the couch with Mommy who now "covered herself with a blanket because her stomach and everything under it was being eaten away". She had had cancer of the colon. While talking, Dennis offered to draw a picture of a mermaid, which he said he always drew now, but threw away if she "doesn't come out right". In his drawing the mermaid had long hair like his mother used to have and her lower half was a strong, beautiful fish tail. Dennis explained that the mermaid's stomach used to be human, but now it was better than that. Whenever she said goodbye she never died; she just swam away and then, when you least expect it, she came back.

Frequently the child of the parent with a prolonged illness feels uncomfortable not only about the threatened identification with the damaged body, but also suffers the guilt and sadness of feeling that he cannot love this "different" parent like the "whole" parent he loved before. Children who avoid talk about the deceased parent with the remaining parent may be most reluctant to admit this part of their reaction, a reaction which also fends off further grief.

An interesting component of the image of the dead parent is that some individuals eventually manage to bring it under their control, using it in the service of the ego. For example a man whose much loved mother died when he was eleven, had always suffered from a sense of sexual inadequacy and inhibition. However, when he was near fifty, and wanted to prolong his "staying power" in intercourse with his wife in order to satisfy her, he would, at will, conjure up the image of his mother dying, knowing that this would immediately diminish his sexual excitement, thereby enabling him to prolong intercourse.

For other individuals the image of the lost parent resurfaced particularly during periods of inner renewal and became integrated with gratifying hopes and expectations. For example, Wendy was surprised when, after much grief work about her father, tears again sprang to her eyes as she realized her longing for his presence and response at the moment when she had announced her pregnancy. Alternately with her tears, she mused gladly about the possible echoes of her father's personality which she might recognize or experience in different ways with her expected baby. She had described him as "a person who added a friendly touch to each event." Though her current event would not be blessed with his friendly touch, she endeavored, and was well endowed to bring the flavor of friendliness into her child's life.

For the children of the divorced, continued reality testing was usually possible, to some extent. Continued contacts that provided information about what the parent was really like could help transform the magical image of childhood to one of less fearsome and less magnetic proportions. This process was not available to some, either because of the absent parent had withdrawn or the remaining parent was hostile. It seemed most difficult in some of the cases in which divorce not only coincided with the pubescence of the child, but also with devaluation of the parent in the human network surrounding the child. For numbers of children the process of grieving was prolonged and complicated by repeated sequences of raised hopes, glimpses of fulfillment of these hopes, followed by frustration and despair. Promises made and broken were the prototype of this; the sequence tended to be lived out in other relationships at the end of adolescence.

For the children of the deceased, the drama took place between themselves and the image of the lost parent, who was not available in reality for testing the transformations of one's image or trying new modes of interaction. Nevertheless, one had to make peace with the image in order to have energies fully available to invest in new relationships. In some sense, coming to terms with the meaning of the past and grieving were tasks that could be finished.

Part III

Toward a Conclusion

Chapter 9

WAYS OF COPING WITH PARENTAL PARTING:
SOME RELEVANT FACTORS

He is mad about being small when you
were big, but no, that's not it, he is mad
about being helpless when you were
powerful, but no, not that either, he is mad
about being contingent when you were
necessary, not quite it, he is insane because
when he loved you, you didn't notice.

—Donald Barthelme,
from *The Dead Father*

This chapter briefly summarizes some of the factors found to be related to
the child's ways of coping with parental divorce or death. The case material
will not be repeated here, but can be found in the preceding chapters under the
names of the children mentioned. In order to make tentative generalizations
from the material, I have omitted or simplified complex and individual
dynamics, which can also be found in the previous chapters. The tentative
generalizations made here concern the particular children and parents
encountered; they may differ for other kinds of populations of children of the
divorced or deceased.

Age

The age of the child at the time of parental parting affected the meaning of the loss to the child, the quality of his distress, and the range of ego mechanisms available to him for coping with it. Nevertheless, age in itself appeared to be less prognostic of the degree to which the child worked through the loss than were several other factors, such as the home parent's eventual well-being; the child's relationships to the parents before the loss and their manner of coping with stress; and the availability of appropriately supportive relationships during the period of stress. Frequently the maturity of ego mechanisms brought to bear on dealing with the trauma differed significantly from what would be expected from a developmental schema according to age. For example, quite young children (between the ages of two and four) could express complicated perceptions and fantasies about the disrupted relationships, and could grieve to some extent in a constructive fashion when emotionally supported to do so.

UNDER TWO

Children who were under two when parents separated showed a range of reactions. It happened that within the sample all maintained regular contact with both parents. Several children between one and two showed intensive searching for the absent parent, accompanied by crying and a transient increase in general separation anxiety. One child showed no distress and rapidly accepted a substitute mother. Examples of three kinds of reactions follow:

Nicky at seventeen months engaged in intensive searching for father, in every crevice of the new apartment he and his mother shared, and cried while doing so. This pattern was repeated at each parting during the first week of separation. Later, visits were arranged so that father brought him to the sitter, where mother picked him up. He continued for some months to be clinging, whining, and cried a lot, but then began to ask for his father, and to verbalize as well as play out with doll house figures his questions and wishes about father. In play with doll house figures, he reunited his parents. One cannot be certain what he was thinking while crying during his search, but it is likely that the crying expressed his longing and fear of loss more than representing mourning, which would follow the confirmation of loss. Father had been his primary caretaker during his first year of life.

Melissa at eighteen months was turned over to her father for custody, but remained in her own home. Although she went for visits with mother readily, she did not express grief for her during the rest of the week. Ten days after mother's departure from the house, Melissa was in good spirits, eating well and had an active affectionate interchange with father. For example, she called for her father by singing "Dad, Dad, Dad", and made up a game in which she laughingly grabbed his glasses, giving him a kiss whenever she managed to get them off. An unusually caring housekeeper and later stepmother were available to her, and she became readily attached to them. Regressive behavior was not prominent until a year or two later, when visits to her mother occasioned considerable anxiety; the next day she would cling tightly to her stepmother. Her mother had always been highly ambivalent toward Melissa; while father was unusually nurturant.

When Mark's parents initially separated he was under a year. Within a few months regular weekends and then weeks with father were established. The little boy was described as a depressed, clinging, and insecure child throughout his second and third year of life. Transitional objects were important and he carried his favorite blanket everywhere until he was four. He developed an ego-alien symptom of identification with aspects of his relationship with father in the form of encopresis (fantasies underlying the symptom are in chapter 4). This was simultaneously a transitional object with which he comforted himself when he felt lonely. Although he fantasied a lot about his father, he did not openly grieve for him during this time. He too, had a supportive, additional father figure available.

AGE 2-5

At age two and three affecto-motor identifications with the absent parent were prominent reactions to separation. Periods of distress and crying before or after visits to the absent parent were common, along with periods of separation anxiety about the home parent. Sometimes there were repeated questions about the separation if the home parent was receptive to this, but the answers often did not satisfy the child. When emotional support was not available, defenses against dependency and painful feelings associated with loss began to make their appearance in the form of pseudomaturity, hyperactivity, or vigilance; these influenced later character structure. By age four and five, initial affecto-motor identifications sometimes changed, while the child manifested complex ideas and fantasies about the separation, its causes, and its future. Compassionate caring about what the parent was feeling, guilt, and the beginnings of recognition that the relationship was permanently lost or altered, with concomitant mourning, all made their appearance in some children of this age. Examples of reactions in this age group follow.

Jeremy, aged two years and eleven months, who never knew his father and hence had no memory of him, began to wish to find him at this age. He had lively reunion fantasies and a need to know whether his father would have liked him. However, he had no loss, no mourning.

Daniel, at two and a half, reacted to separation with expressed longing for his father, accompanied by repeated periods of prolonged crying and distress. He simultaneously first identified with him by sitting in his chair and keeping away other contenders. By age four he expressed grieving both for his father, and for the new father figure, an important, though ambivalent relationship in his life for over a year before he too left. He expressed this both in motor expressions of restless searching, verbalizations of visiting and wishing to "keep" those he cared about, but displayed an awareness of the painful missing of the parent which would beset him in the future, in contrast to his mother.

Lucy began her symptom of night crying and moaning when she was two, through a period of six months' separation while her mother was in the hospital at age three (and she lived with father and his parents) and continuing while she lived with mother after hospitalization; father had moved away, but saw her on visits. The moaning and crying at night shifted when she had a dream of herself "crying" and could bring its meaning into therapy. Lucy had repeated losses of mother's affection, when mother could not help but hit her at night for crying. Her material suggests that genuine grieving for her affectionate mother, which she contrasted in her mind with her "angry" mother, occurred at the age of two, that it was increased by her fear that mother would never come back from the hospital during their long separation at the age of three; and continued in ego-alien symptom form (only during sleep) until Lucy could remember her earlier overwhelming sense of loss, and begin to accept her own sadness and dependency wishes in therapy and her actual relationship to mother. She continued to feel great sadness at the rift between her parents at age four, at that time grieving also for her absent father. Her night crying is reminiscent of two children in the Furman (1974) series, who were between one and two when a parent died. Both had periods of sobbing in their sleep only. Only some days later did they allow the remaining parent to hold and comfort them, talking of the dead parent. They were then able to shift to daytime weeping, leaving their sleep undisturbed. Some degree of precocious ego development, common in children who early in life become vigilant about changes in their emotional environment, was noticeable in Lucy and had served to master the dependency needs she feared. However, when she was four she grieved for the absent father.

Peter showed signs of identification, searching for, and then grieving for the mother who left him when he was three. Like mourning in older people, sadness would overcome him at the point at which he realized his searching had been fruitless.

Pam, in therapy many years later (at age twelve), eventually remembered a period of intense grieving, with crying and screaming for her father during the week after he left. Simultaneously, she clung to a whirling horse on a merrygoround, a motor activity which recapitulated her favorite times with her father. Grieving and emotional catharsis were not supported. Pam's character structure evolved around a series of defenses against affects and trustful relationships. Motor restlessness, aggressive defenses, and impulsivity made for difficulties in learning and in relationships. Much delayed mourning occurred during therapy after the character problems had been to some degree ameliorated. During this period of mourning she recovered the memories of her three-year-old, grieving self.

Lou Ann's reactions to the first loss of her mother (who gave her to father at age three) are not known. Though she remembers crying in the closet while living with father, there was current cause for distress since she was left hungry in the closet while stepmother engaged in sexual activities with a number of men. Lou Ann's deprivations were multiple and severe. She developed problems in reality testing and ego integration. Yet she was a remarkably competent child in coping with the multiple problems which beset her family. Her main way of coping with loss was to attempt to make restitution through the creation of a mother-child unit. When she identified with her father, it was also in this respect, that is, she saw her father as an abandoned child like Lou Ann. At each early developmental stage, Lou Ann's unmet needs were too overwhelming not to be the most pressing of anxieties, though her capacity for tolerating affect was considerable. Her reactions to her past losses had been in the direction of mastery rather than grief.

Children aged four and five when they lost a parent all already had a complicated set of fantasies about "why" it happened, and at one time or another all except two expressed conscious wishes for parental reunion. A number of these children developed symptoms which represented an ego-alien identification with the parent. In each case, conflict between the parents was still present, and the children felt to some extent disloyal, both about the longing for the absent parent, and the pleasures they might accept from a new parent substitute. Once the symptom was linked to the absent parent, the child could bring his grief into the open. Mourning did not have a sustained or anguished quality, but occurred in the form of tender fantasies, sadly remembered. This was especially true of Jenny and Cheryl. Both these children were afraid enough of losing their mothers also, so they had not dared express their feelings openly. Both eventually expressed anger at the mother about the separation. Both were concerned about the absent father and wanted to care for him. Sean and Susan showed more elements of guilt about the welfare of the absent father, while making an attachment to a new parent figure. Sean identified with his father's crying and "not wanting to see" the new man in mother's life, while Susan was often not eager to visit her father, but so concerned about "not hurting his feelings" that she made many excuses rather than tell him directly she sometimes wanted to stay with mother and later with stepfather too. Her presenting symptom at age seven (school phobia) was associated with separation anxiety and the unconscious fantasies about "hurting each other dead" with which she first struggled at the time her parents separated.

Amy, whose father died, was unable to continue to test the reality of her feelings for him. For a long time, she continued in fidelity to his image, being convinced that he was somewhere where he could see her and know what she was doing. Other aspects of her quest for him were expressed in her choice of transitional objects (after his death), and her use of the transitional phenomenon of singing herself to sleep, which was a continuation of her father's songs to her. Later suicidal fantasies were linked to the idea of joining him. In addition, she projected feared qualities of the father onto her mother, and experienced some regression from the highly stimulating sexual fantasies she had by the time of his death. Intermittent grieving did occur, in the form of crying for her father during latency years. During this time, when playing dramatic games which involved sad endings, Amy knew she could get herself to cry by thinking of her father. Nevertheless, in adulthood, grief, like anxiety and libidinous excitement, was enormously feared as traumatically overwhelming to the ego, and had to be resolved slowly.

The five-year-olds already had a complex notion of each of their parents' needs, a compassionate temptation to fill them, and a capacity for sadness about the future without the parent, as well as the current loss.

LATENCY

For children who were in the latency period at the time of their parents' separation, the different roles they had played in the family and the nature of the continuing relationship to the parents, greatly affected their reactions. Two children were seriously depressed. In one seven-year-old boy, Tim, suicidal preoccupations became evident after repeated separations and attempts at reunion had failed, and the father had once more left, this time "finally." In the other case, the boy was clear about feeling himself an extra burden to his family, and identified with the extruded father. Others in this age group, e.g., Kenny, also expressed the notion that no one needed them, no one cared if they lived or died. Two of the girls became phobic—either at the time or in pubescence (Sarah—but not openly depressed, in the context of a close, tempting relationship with the father. Both girls increased their dependent and angry demands on the mother, accusing her of caring less for them than father did. Others, like Betsy, were able to see themselves as still valued by both parents, and mustered highly effective means of coping with their situation, while still expressing their wish that things had gone differently. They were able to see more readily than the younger children that the absent parent had needed to leave the spouse rather than the child.

Children who had little or no contact with the absent parent at this age were also often able to cope well when they were secure with the home parent. Some boys were hyperaggressive, attempting to fulfill what they pictured as a male role, in the absence of a sustaining, constructive model.

Other children of this age tried to devise ways of juggling their loyalties to both parents, while being aware of considerable guilt. Eight-year-old Nicole had asked her father to take her to a psychologist after she heard from a friend that psychologists keep secrets. She told me her secret: she felt she could not tell either parent how "yucky" she felt because she had assented to each parent's question about preferring to live with them. "When Daddy and I are plotting to live on the farm he's going to buy, and have baby animals and everything, it feels like I'm plotting against my best bosom buddy." She responded with relief to being told that she should not have to keep her secret because the adults would end up making the decision about where she would live, although her wishes and feelings about it were important in working out what would be best.

With encouragement, many of the children of this age were quite open about their wishes, e.g., to see their absent parent more, or refusing to visit his apartment while his girlfriend was there. They could be similarly open about their sadness and indignation, but expressed a sense of vulnerability about how to stop being overwhelmed by their feelings. For example, Craig's sadness pervaded all his waking moments, Nellie complained that her pillow was still wet in the morning because she could not stop herself from crying herself to sleep.

Reactions to death often included determined denial. The day after seven-year-old Margie's father died, she crayoned posters which she put in each window of the house, saying "Please come again." Jackie, nine, and Brian, seven, avoided all discussion of their mother the year before she died, and hid the pictures they had of her.

Around age ten, complicated grief reactions were prominent in children of both the divorced and the deceased. They often clearly perceived their parents as individuals and tried actively to integrate these perceptions with their reality. Gwen and Noah, Wendy and Alex would be examples. Prolonged periods of painful sadness were tolerated either within therapy, or within a supportive family setting after the death of a parent. Some children who could not share their grieving with the remaining parent, and at this age often not with their peer group, nevertheless experienced it as grief secretly, e.g., crying alone in bed at night, feeling acutely lonely and despairing, withdrawing from social relationships. The degree of guilt associated with the death of a parent varied with the prior relationship. For example, Alex had primarily lonely, libidinous fantasies and daydreams about his mother and lost teacher, without evidence of great guilt or ambivalence. Angry feelings were centered on the father instead. In contrast, Vicky had to deal with guilt in the form of fantasied punishment from her mother before grieving was possible. Michael handled enormous guilt through identification with the dead mother; he lacked the internal confidence in his resources and external supports to make grief tolerable. Wendy, in contrast, experienced intense grief and then turned to a pattern of identification with positive aspects of her father, especially his proclivity for constructive mastery of stress.

Rick, rejected by his father, who had first sought custody, had expressed his sense of hurt and longing, but eventually and slowly, to some extent decathected the father. Support from his mother and older brothers enabled him to turn toward new identification figures. In such cases clear evidence of rejection by an absent parent was sometimes necessary before the child could withdraw his investment in the parent in turn and could fully involve himself in other relationships. However, it remained important to resolve the "why" of the rejection.

ADOLESCENCE

Adolescents reacted in a great variety of ways. Reunion fantasies were not as openly expressed, though when a visit between parents was devoid of its former hostilities, they too tended to think in terms of how it "might have been."

The adolescents under sixteen whose parent had died (Eddie, Shirley, Eileen, Natasha, Peggy, and Tod) either experienced a period of mourning, or utilized extensive defenses against this. All except Peggy and Tod, who had mourned without intervention in the context of a supportive home, experienced intense grief during therapy. The nature of the mourning varied according to the personality structure and family situations, with Eddy and Shirley mourning most briefly, Eileen involving herself in slow and repeated mourning for her mother. She coped with the loss of her father, who withdrew emotional support from her as soon as he had a new partner, in a different way; that is, in acting out the rejection, desertion, and painful anger over a series of years in relationships to other men. Long after therapy had ended and she was living elsewhere, she would call me at times of such crisis. Natasha, amid the holocaust, delayed her mourning for her father, identifying with both positive and negative features of him. The suicidal fantasies were heavily colored with guilt, both because she felt she had emotionally abandoned him after he abandoned her and because she had loved a man with whose ideology she later could not make peace.

For some children, e.g., Gerardo and Angela, the hope for much sustenance from their living but absent parent was small, and they too faced the task of mourning. Gerardo had developed maladaptive symptoms of identification with the mother (muscles "going soft," motor retardation, depression, and withdrawal), which had many components of depression together with an idealized but wavering image of her. It was difficult, but necessary, to separate the degree to which his depression was an identification with mother or a reaction to his mother's rejection. When his depression lifted, he became much more aware of the underlying hostility.

Angela's symptoms initially included an encapsulated psychosis, together with the conviction that she would die at age fourteen. It was an unusual clinical picture because the psychotic ideation did not pervade the rest of functioning; because auditory hallucinations are still rare during psychoses at her age; and because a number of her symptoms, e.g., temporary paralyses of her left arm, had a less disturbed "hysterical" quality. After Angela's psychosis receded, she underwent a period of grief, characterized by a great sadness which she said at first she could hardly bear, but eventually found consoling, for instance, playing sad records and weeping. Angela's grieving was split in two different ways. One was for the image of the glamorous father whose future was linked to hers (he was a movie producer, she would act); however, this defensive version of the father had been built up after she had lost her "left father" in actuality and in fantasy at age five. The second period of actual symptoms (ages five and twelve) which involved her "left" arm and the hearing of voices was precipitated by events which recapitulated some of the earlier loss by depriving her of her consoling fantasy about who her father was.

A number of the other adolescents under fifteen when their parents parted developed a depressive reaction when confronted with both the separation and a devalued image of the absent parent. This was most often first handled with a conscious or unconscious idealized version of the absent parent, but according to their personality structures, some adolescents acted out what they thought of as the less savory aspects of the parent in their own lives, and others directed criticisms toward themselves. Suicidal preoccupations were present in many, and the inability to picture a satisfying future in many others. Although such orientation toward the future does not usually develop till midadolescence, for these individuals it had a more dramatic quality, in denying that a happy future might even be a possibility. Various impairments in concentration, or the active avoidance of school in the form of cutting classes, occurred frequently. The adolescents evinced a continued tie to the parent figures in their descriptions of various activities which they perceived as forbidden, and in which they engaged with the image of the parents' reaction in mind. This is, of course, usual for young adolescents, but for these individuals it continued into late adolescence and sometimes their twenties.

Older adolescents tended to be more able to make some emotional disengagement which protected them from the disruption of their own development. Ralph is an example of this pattern. Simultaneously, there was clear evidence in him of a period of desolate grieving, feeling like crying, and wishing for a nonexistent shoulder to cry on. Julia grieved, but did not function as a depressed person.

Some adolescents postponed their grieving. A number of girls displayed a conscious hostility toward the absent parent but unconsciously identified with aspects of him, and thus devalued themselves, in order to maintain an alliance with the remaining parent. At the end of adolescence, when separation from the remaining parent was necessary in order to pursue their own goals in life, the grief for the absent parent made its appearance first in the form of acting out, by clinging to a compulsory role of either deserted or deserting love partner (depending on their defense structure), which was unconsciously linked to their view of parental interaction. The end of such relationship was apt to usher in both current and past, defended-against mourning. After this they established more positive love relationships and also reestablished the long-dormant, positive relationship to their absent parent, when possible.

A number of other adolescents, each with some parental support seemed to have a volatile relationship to each parent, testing out in action the various transformations in the image of themselves and their parents. Among them too, depressive affect made its appearance, being particularly strong either the first two years after separation, or at the time of a planned remarriage by one of the parents. Sometimes the depression was tied to a notion that adult men and women simply could not make each other happy and that there was nothing for them to look forward to, or at least count on, in that area. The ordinary process of adolescent differentiation from the parent figures, as loving as the parents might be, was particularly important in helping the adolescents define their future hopes for themselves.

Information About the Causes and Effects
of the Divorce or Death

Misinformation or misunderstandings regarding the real causes and effects of the death or separation frequently surfaced as a component of the child's difficulties.

Explanations without experience did not have much meaning for the children under age two. Children between the ages of two and a half and seventeen, however, had a great need for enough information to help make sense out of their current situation and to allay anxieties about the future. Conveying such information often seemed to be an extraordinarily difficult task for the parent. Some parents consciously veered between telling their children "everything" or "nothing." The most frequent early misrepresentation was that the permanently separating parent was away for only a short time, e.g., "a couple of weeks." This occurred not only with very young children but also with well-supported ten-year-olds, like Noah, and frequently fueled the child's expectations of reunion.

There seem to be a number of obstacles in the way of answering the child's questions, spoken or unspoken. First, the parent is often in intense distress him- or herself, and may not "trust" himself to share too much of this feeling with the child, lest it overwhelm them both. Secondly, the parent under stress often assumes that the child's feelings are similar to his, and that perhaps there is nothing further that would be helpful to explain. Conveying information to the child in a constructive fashion requires of the parent that he or she differentiate himself and his feelings sufficiently from those of the child that the child's concerns can be pictured, and his questions answered. For those parents who are aware that the child has a very different reaction from their own (e.g., that the child does not have the same reasons for bitterness as the spouse, and wants to continue to love the absent parent) there is often a conscious, laudable attempt to protect the child from hearing the hostility the parent has felt toward the spouse. Finally, the emotional impact of the child's questions, once allowed, is often such as to be disturbing to the parent, who is already coping with a great deal, and fears being pushed beyond his or her endurance. This is most clear in some cases of death of a spouse. Tolerance for one's own grief is necessary before one can support the child in grief. More often, the parent, whose own struggles over loss are usually stimulated even by separations he has wanted, has a hard time facing with equanimity those questions asked coolly by the young child, when he is allowed to do so. E.g., a four-year-old whose father had just left home asked her mother, "And who will fix my hair in ponytails when you die?" In other cases, the parent fears that the child will blame him or her for not being able to "keep" the spouse (and the child indeed often does this) and explanations become heavily imbued with the need to justify rather than inform about the situation. Other parents are astounding in their capacity to empathize with the child's distress, even when this has a quite different quality from their own, and to extend themselves during this vital time in such a way that they can both hear and answer the child's concerns as they emerge. Nothing should ever be said that is not so; but not everything that is so should be said.

For all the young children (two to five) and for about half the children aged six to nine, a first and immediate area of concern was "Who will take care of things now?" They needed detailed, mundane answers about routines or activities previously shared with each parent, visiting arrangements, etc.. In addition, they needed the spoken reassurance that they would not be sent away like the absent parent. This was particularly essential in those cases where separation was accompanied by other major changes in the child's life, e.g., mother going to work, or a move to a different house or school. Even though it is often impossible to tell the child that his needs will be met in the same ways as before, he is made secure and can better exercise a sense of mastery when he knows what is most likely to happen in the immediate future and that the parents plan to continue to work out what is best for all concerned.

Adolescents, too, needed a chance to bring up the question of future eventualities, e.g., "If the parent I live with gets sick or dies, will my other parent take me to live with him (or her) or not?" Because the adolescent senses that such ideas are imbued with his fearful fantasies, he often has even a harder time bringing such questions up than the younger children.

Next to concerns about immediate future care, all children (over two and a half) and adolescents needed to make sense out of "why" the parents separated. This is a topic that opens many wounds—feelings of rejection, failure, blame, unlovability, etc.—not surprisingly, it is often painful for parents to discuss honestly but simply, in a way that does not assault the reality sense of the child (in that he has experienced the "why" at various levels in the form of pre-existing tension at home, but may have come to the wrong conclusions), and yet is not used to assuage the parent's feeling of having to "justify" the action. In fact, it is important for both parent and child to know that it is all right to divorce when continuing to live together is making the partners very unhappy and their chance for building a better life requires their living separate lives.

The information available to the children of the deceased encountered in this book is clouded by being retrospective in the cases of those who were not adults. The studies of Nagy (chapter 2) suggest that a realistic conception of death does not evolve until ages six to nine, but the Furmans (1964a, 1974) have shown that much younger children can be helped to understand the realities of death. Reconstructed material suggests that there were many differences in the amount of information available to the child even of ten years, within the sample here, and with different effects on his later functioning. For example, in Michael's family, noncommunication about important issues was usual. He did not know the exact nature of the illness his mother suffered for five years, or whether "she still had her breasts" or not. When she died, he could not ask whether her illness was contagious. He retreated to an identification with her illness which constricted his later possibilities for independence and enjoyment of life. Alex, who was surprised by the news of his mother's death by telegram, witnessed his father's sadness, which was like his own. However, he was also surprised by that, since his father (according to the boy's perception) had never made clear his positive attachment to the mother. No one shared Alex's lonely, erotic fantasies and despair over the next few years. The lack of information he focussed on was displaced onto a teacher he also had loved: "*Why* was the teacher suddenly gone in a way which changed his life?"

At the other extreme, Wendy, Tod, and Peggy were all prepared for the death, although, of course, the bereaved is never prepared for his actual reaction. As Wendy's father had written a long description of his own experience while dying, she had an unusual amount of information available to her. Eventually this helped her to deal with a secret area of hurt about her father—that he seemed emotionally more "disengaged" from the family and more absorbed in himself near the time of his death.

Five-year-old Amy "knew" about her father's death in the sense that she had a conscious conviction, denied unconsciously, that death means, "I will never see him again," a conviction she believed her mother must have explained to her. Yet she may have been hampered in her belief in the reality of his death by the lack of evidence. He died in a distant city, she never saw the dead body, attended the funeral, or visited his grave until adulthood. She inferred her mother's sadness but could not see her cry.

Fourteen-year-old Natasha, prevented from grieving for the father who died in prison camp, also did not see the "evidence" of his death, but believed the news of it. While postponing mourning, she maintained a conviction, based on identification with him as well as with others who were killed around her, that sooner or later she too, would be "dragged off in the middle of the night like a criminal and killed."

Most of the young children of divorce, by the time I saw them, already knew that their parents "fought a lot" and "couldn't get along" and therefore separated. In fact, reunion fantasies were often present in the bittersweet imagery of wishing the parents could be together again without fighting, but knowing that they "can't stop." Although this constituted part of a meaningful explanation to the child, it turned out to be insufficient, because it led to other unanswered questions, associated with intense anxiety. The children often assumed that if they "fought" with their remaining parent this too would be followed by separation.

It was usually helpful for the parent actively to assure the child that they would remain together either until he grew up, or as long as he needed or wished to, and that that was the home parent's wish. In addition, it was helpful to clarify that the absent parent had decided to separate from the spouse, rather than the children themselves, even though the effect was that he would be with the children less, too. In those cases in which a child, or disputes about that child, had actually contributed heavily to the rift between the parents, it was useless to deny this (for the child had overheard it many times, even with parents who apparently had made firm rules for themselves not to "discuss in front of the children"). Denial about disputes over the child would offend his reality sense and undermine his capacity to trust his own perception or judgment. It was, however, helpful to clarify in such cases that "The fighting about you—that you probably heard—was a kind of sign that daddy and I couldn't agree on enough things to make each other happy, but it doesn't mean that it was *because* of you, so it doesn't make it your fault or doing."

In other cases, the limitations on the parents' relationship to the child were less transient, less likely to change (e.g., in the case of Gerardo, whose mother wishes or fantasies, it was also important to clarify the reasons. Failure to do so tended to produce an increasing gap between the child's hopeful fantasies and denial of loss and the constant frustration and disappointment he was exposed to if the parent forgot visits, broke promises, or simply neglected the child. Such behavior may be a temporary phenomenon. For example, one father seemed to neglect his daughter by repeatedly forgetting visits during the time his exwife was living with another man, because he could not tolerate the feelings this situation stirred up in him. When the relationship broke up after two years, he became attentive to the little girl again. In such a case visitation arrangements should take complicated feelings between exspouses into account. For example, a "neglectful" parent may be able to become involved if he can pick up the child in neutral territory, such as school, rather than at home. More often the pattern was the opposite. That is, the absent parent was attentive for a time after the divorce, but increasingly less so once his own life went in a different direction, e.g., once he remarried.

In other cases, the limitations on the parents' relationship to the child were less transient, less likely to change (e.g., in the case of Gerardo, whose mother had been seriously depressed for many years.) In such cases, the child had to be helped to see the realistic limitations of the parent, perhaps with compassion, but not in such a way that the burden of the failure of the relationship rested with the child.

Two other types of information for the child: what role he is expected to have toward the home parent; and what feeling states are "usual and expected" both in himself and his parents.

It was useful for the parent to make it clear what household tasks would now have to be shared and distributed within the family, and what role the child had in this. Such explanations tended to make the child feel good (in spite of much haggling and complaining over chores) and helped mobilize his resourcefulness and sense of mastery about the current situation. In cases where there was an enormous difference in what was required of him "before" and "after" the divorce, it often also contributed to a sense of loss, including the loss of childhood pleasures. It seemed important to clarify, however—and often the child perceived the opposite message—that the child was not expected to take the place of the other parent.

This could be put in such terms as, "You know, I don't expect you to make up for daddy (or mother) or to take over for daddy (or mother) now that he (she) is away. I will still make all the grownup decisions, too, though I'll talk them over with you when I can."

This particular issue came up for the children of the deceased as well as the children of the divorced. For instance, both Shirley and Eileen took over the household chores after their mothers died and both were referred to by their fathers and outsiders as "little mothers," or heard similar innuendoes during that time. Both girls were then abruptly ousted from this role when their fathers chose new partners, a time when neither father nor partner wanted to be reminded of the dead spouse. In contrast, Peggy, whose mother also died during her mid-adolescence, had the fantasy that she "could do everything" her mother had done around the house, but her father wisely decided that this was undue responsibility for her, that she needed to be an adolescent, rather than filling her mother's shoes.

Another area of information that frequently came up during the therapy process, but that was also useful for parents to handle on their own, in different terms depending on the age of the child, was that of emotion. First, the child needed to know that his own feelings of sadness and hurt, anger and anxiety were to be expected, because this was what children almost always felt when there was a divorce or separation. Expressing some of these feelings was necessary, and not a sign of either weakness or hatefulness. The child was feeling that way because of the things that had happened to him, and he was not alone in feeling that way. Bit by bit, the family would try to straighten out what the feelings were about, and what would make things as good as possible for everyone, and he (the child) would have a part in this too.

In an analogous way, the child knew that the parents were distressed, either more volatile, sad, withdrawn, or irritable with him. It was also helpful to tell the child this simply: adults usually are upset at this time, too. The other half of the message, perhaps the information most often omitted, is the fact that both the parents' and the child's distress are unlikely to be permanent. That is, it was helpful for the child to know that these problems usually take quite a while to work out, but that ordinarily people begin to feel a lot better again after a year or two. Of course, individual circumstances grossly affect the course of what happens, and again what is told the child must be only what is likely to be true. However, many children and adolescents can profit from the expectation that they haven't lost their happy parent or happy self forever, even though there is not instant cure (other than denial) for what ails them all. This is a very different message from the pressure sometimes conveyed to the child, that he should "forget" the absent parent, or "get his mind off his troubles" by keeping busy in order to feel better again, or should immediately like a substitute.

One of the factors most highly correlated with the child's well-being a few years after the divorce was the well-being of the remaining parent; the expectation that the parent will not remain unhappy forever is, then, enormously anxiety-relieving to the child, and guilt-relieving to the adolescent.

The reality of the parents' well-being and their feelings toward each other continue to change for years following the divorce. For the child, a continued appraisal of those realities in the form of information needed to explain them as they impinged on him had a more active place in therapy material than usual with other children and adolescents. This will be explored further in the section on the role of the relationship to each parent and in the chapter on therapy (10).

The Personality of the Child at the Time of Parental Parting

Differences in the personality structure of the children were indissolubly related to their ways of coping with the divorce or death. Such differences were instrumental in determining the developmental level of wishes and fears experienced by the child at the time of loss; the range of ego mechanisms available to help him cope with the loss; his perception of various components of the image attributed to each parent (which ranged from that of a being magically imbued with immense powers to gratify or punish, to fairly realistic views); his perception of the causes for loss and of ways of making restitution; and the degree to which he experienced the parting—how overwhelmed by uncontrollable forces he felt. Variations in personality affected the complicated interplay between the developing child's individuality and the satisfactions and deprivations he had experienced in relationships and sense of mastery before the period of loss. A full examination of the relationship between individual variations in personality and the handling of loss would be too exhaustive here, and its implications are better dealt with in discussions reserved for that purpose.

Character structure, of course, had a major bearing on the choice of treatment modes. E.g., a child with symptoms of psychosis, such as Angela, invoked different treatment modalities from Pam, who needed to be more secure in her use of ego controls and capacity to utilize identifications before her grief could be expected to be manageable. Treatment of both was different from that of Noah, Eva, Wendy, Mark, or others whose existing personality structure had the ready resources for recognizing and coping with the impact of their losses on their current functioning. This issue is further discussed in chapter 10.

It is difficult to evaluate the success of attempts to cope with loss in terms of pre-existing personality, partly because the children's personality styles, lives, and goals were truly so different from each other. For example, Eva, with a capacity for complex perception and affective integration, maintained some underlying degree of affective sadness for years, though this was less intense and more intermittent than previously, and did not prevent her from seeking active engagement in learning and personal relationships. Perhaps she remained sad partly because she had cared a lot when first she cared, and her emotional commitments as well as her disappointments were deep. Shirley, quoted as an example of an adolescent favoring tension discharge through impulsive action—ego mechanisms which tend to bar the tolerance for grief—went through a period of brief but focussed mourning for both parents, and then seemed to reinvest herself rather independently in a set of new relationships. These two examples are perhaps mentioned as a paradox, in that on the whole ego modes like Eva's favored the eventual resolution of feelings about loss, while children more totally involved in denial, negation, or living out their fantasies rather than remembering the past had greater difficulty tolerating the anxiety and affective experience of mourning when this was necessary.

One might also question the reverse impact: that is, what was the effect of parental divorce or death on the further development of the child?

In those children whose losses were multiple and were accompanied by other, severe deprivations the effect of the loss cannot be separated from those other factors that fostered the later disturbance.

In no child encountered here did the loss result in a massive regression of ego functions (walking, talking, perception, etc.), but since the youngest children were around eighteen months, this would not be expected.

The array of symptoms among the younger children, including nightmares, separation anxiety, symptoms around urination or defecation, temper tantrums, clinging, touching phobias, food refusals, school phobias, chronic restlessness or irritability did not differentiate this group from other children in this age group whose symptoms have brought referral. Perhaps exceptions to this are night sobbing, and prolonged periods of crying and searching for the absent parent. What did distinguish the symptoms this group displayed was the frequently direct but often disguised connection between the symptom and the loss. Some of these symptoms seemed to disappear more rapidly than usually expected, once the missing connections were made.

Among the younger group of children particularly, further personality development did not appear impeded, and many of them seemed to flourish again rather rapidly. At the time they were seen, none had developed any tendency to deinvest in relationships, or to make these on a shallow basis only. Some children touchingly took the lead (like Daniel) in clarifying with their parent that their emotional investment in two different father figures still was meaningful to them, even if the mother needed to experience this differently herself. The development of some of the children could be complicated if the child sees himself as the first choice of the mother, if he "outlasts" a series of relationships she has to others. I do not know whether this will interfere with their freedom in later love choices, perhaps resulting in some inhibition in adulthood.

As mentioned previously, the child's experience of at least one solidly good relationship to build on augured well for the capacity needed to deal with loss. In addition, a certain degree of tolerance for anxiety and for affects, albeit mixed with its fair share of denial and other necessary defensive and adaptive ego mechanisms, appeared helpful in allowing the child to cope with the loss without forfeiting either his own growth or the future willingness to be open to new relationships and identification figures that was necessary to complete his development.

The adolescent's situation differs, in that initial identifications have usually been solidified and he is less dependent on new parent figures for the continued development of ego functions. However, the divorce or death often seriously disrupted or vilified the internalized identification figure, drastically lowering the adolescent's self-esteem simultaneously with his reality loss. Such adolescents often urgently needed a process allowing for the inner transformation of the suddenly degraded internalized parent figure, lest loss of all life goals threaten.

Once the adolescents had dealt with this component of their identifications, both peer and adult figures (most often including the parents) were reinvested with emotional energy of a different kind. For some adolescents, there was a long period of living out ego-alien aspects either of their identification with the absent parent, or the painful aspects of the experienced relationships. For those adolescents who had difficulty differentiating their identity from their mother's during adolescence such "living out", as well as their mourning, was postponed until they had achieved sufficient independence from the mother.

Some adolescents were much happier and functioned better after moving from the home of one parent to the other, or living for a time with an alternate family.

A number of other adolescents had coped with the loss by a certain amount of "disengagement" from the parents' problems. When this was based on a pseudo-independence, they tended to run into difficulties, e.g., in making judgments, in other situations. Others who were to some degree genuinely independent made the most of other available substitute relationship and tended to do extremely well.

No specific consequences of the death of a parent for the further personality development of the child can be detailed here either, other than to say that those in therapy reacted to current situations involving separations or potential losses with an awareness that they were "sensitive" to what it entailed. As mentioned elsewhere, a number of other adults who did not seek therapy but were divorcing parents of children I saw had themselves been bereaved in childhood. Some of them were particularly attuned to a sense of loss and able to be especially empathic with their children's plight. Eva's father would be an example. Some others, unaware of any direct connections to the past, reacted to the separation or divorce as though it must involve a death. Suicidal or homicidal threats or preoccupations sometimes surfaced in this context.

None of the children of the deceased whom I have described (other than Mary Ann, who was just too deprived) failed to make meaningful, individual relationships to other people, though several withheld from these relationships the quintessence of their desire, which they reserved with fidelity for images displaced from their memory of the loved parent. This pattern was based more on their libidinal investment than on deep-seated ambivalence or guilt.

Overidentification with a dead parent was more apt to occur in a context in which guilt was considerable. A strongly loving relationship may have preceded this (e.g., Natasha), prior to the period of anger and guilt. In other cases, e.g., Michael, the prior relationship was characterized by meager interchange.

Numbers of children of the bereaved grew into richly endowed adults.

The Meeting of Needs for Sustained Caring

The child's needs for sustained caring had to be provided for before the child could deal with the anxiety about what was happening to him. Although in some cases the reality made it easy to assure the child of this, in others change brought by divorce or death involved enough emotional and economic upheaval to make such assurances difficult or inconsistent with the facts. In such cases, it was important for the parents to have immediate help with their real circumstances, including budgets, child care during a parent's working hours, ways of staying in the same house or neighborhood if possible, or the child's finishing the year in the same school or nursery school if a move had to be made, even though this would involve extra transportation, etc. When the parent was in acute emotional distress, immediately available help was important not only for him, but to also make it possible for him to remain invested in the child's well-being. Most situations encountered were not at one extreme or the other in the ability to meet the child's basic needs, but somewhere in between. In such cases most usually a period of time was required, and a kind of cost-benefit analysis of what the effects of various changes would be for everyone involved, e.g., the mother's beginning to work. For both young and older children it was usually best if continuity in other important relationships (like school, or with babysitter) could be maintained while the parents parted. When the relationships were sustained, children sometimes showed surprising capacity for adapting to other changes which they and their families had expected to be quite traumatic for them. (e.g., both seventeen-month-old Nicky and eleven-year-old Noah at first reacted with intense anxiety to moving away from their home, but then adapted very rapidly to this change when concomitant relationships were not lost).

In the long run, meeting the child's needs for sustained care involved at least one parent (or parent substitute) spending a great deal of time in the physical and affectional care of the young child; less time and energy was involved for the adolescents, but intense, volatile reactions resulted if the child felt suddenly neglected.

Parental Modes of Coping with Stress

Favored parental modes of coping with stress usually affected both the context in which the separation or divorce occurred, and the ways of coping with the incurred stress. For children of the deceased, such family modes were also reflected in the preparation for death when this was expected; they could of course have no bearing on unexpected death.

I was repeatedly impressed by the numbers of parents who cared intensely about providing as much support as possible for the child in his coping with the stress of the upcoming separation and divorce. This was sometimes true of both parents, though they often disagreed about how to go about it. The parent who cared was as likely to be the "absent" parent as the one with whom the child remained. Either mother or father could be remarkably good at the essentials of parenting. Although often the parents were puzzled by aspects of the child's behavior, (such as phobias which were not obviously connected to the trauma, or an adolescent's illicit activities, not in the realm of family values) they expressed concern about various areas of his future well-being: that he grow up feeling loved; that he be able to feel independent; that she not be "soured" on men forever; that she regain self-confidence, etc. In these families, affectional needs, the capacity for feelings and the development of individuality were consciously valued both for the child and the self.

In many of these families, the child was given considerable support and "permission" for experiencing his own reactions, talking them out with others and experimenting with his own behavior to some degree. Not surprisingly, however, when the family modes were supposedly based on such a value system, both parent and child were often sensitively attuned to the unspoken contradictions. That is, the child might know perfectly well that it was okay to say anything, as long as he didn't praise Daddy, at which point a curtain of steel would descend between him and his mother. A child might know of the parents' secret disdain for those who weep, although he had verbal permission to do so. Such children were often able to be extremely articulate, both about the basically secure, empathic relationship they had with a parent, and the limitations in the current, unspoken contract with that parent about what should or should not be felt or revealed. As the parents were empathic with the needs of the child (though the most common distortion was to confuse the child's needs with their own), so the child tended to be empathic with the parent. This meant that they sometimes did not dare risk conflict, which would have been easier with less "understanding" parents. Among this group of parents and children there were many subtle variations, not further differentiated here. On the whole, the parents tried to foster the child's cognitive and emotional tools for coping with loss.

Many other kinds of family modes existed. Of course, the two parents often developed increasingly different perceptions, values, and ways of handling stress, differences which at times reflected the growth of one parent and not another, or their simultaneous development in different directions, and affected the decision to divorce. Such differences were often emphasized or even caricatured at the time of the divorce. Among the families of the younger children, separation, once, decided upon, tended to be accomplished fairly quickly. In contrast, a majority of the adolescents had experienced some years of agonizing by their parents over the decision to separate accompanied by increased or intermittent strife.

Numbers of the adolescents could date the onset of their perception of increased strife. Frequently, in initial interviews, the adolescent pictured this as much more recent than he did in later interviews, when memories of the parents' past interaction came into focus for him.

A number of the families consciously favored the denial or negation of feelings: troubles are best handled by "forgetting," "getting your mind off it," "keeping busy," "keeping cheerful thoughts," etc. In some of these families, the result was a massive kind of noncommunication, in which the child felt isolated, keeping his anguish secret, not daring to bring it to the attention of others. Feelings were simply not talked about, but hidden. Michael would be an example. In other families, at least some family members combined this with fairly frantic and constant activity, a need never to be alone or relax, and a constantly changing panorama of personal or sexual interactions. Shirley's and Eddy's family are an example of this. Along with this pattern sometimes went repeated acting out rather than facing of stress, an acting out sometimes intermittently disrupted by the breakthrough of highly disturbing thoughts.

Lou Ann and Mary Ann represent another kind of pattern. Losses were so overwhelmingly feared that a constant quest for restitution by establishing mother-baby relationships was lived out. As it was believed that one could not count on tomorrow, gratification and impulse expression were urgent. For example, in this family a celebration atmosphere prevailed at times: money was spent freely not only for festive food (desserts) and drink, but to clip several dogs' ears in fashionable style, and to buy a large new refrigerator which cheered everyone up because it was brightly colored (the old white one was not broken). Meanwhile, money was not available for regular meals, rent, or winter clothing for the children. Ego differentiation between various family members was fluid. Mother often called one child by the name of another, and had called her eldest after her own dead mother, Lou Ann. Most, but not all family members slept in one large bed, together with an assortment of animals, though other beds were in an adjacent room. In this case, it was necessary to meet the child's basic needs in a sustained fashion over a long period to begin the ego differentiation necessary to a sense of identity separate from that of the mother. Only after this could the child begin to give up the compulsive need to recreate a mother-baby relationship in which, in fantasy, she could nurture and be nurtured, protect and be protected. Identification with the father as another neglected child then came to the fore, and was eventually mourned and deinvested.

The above three descriptions of different family "modes" are only examples, and much oversimplified. Most family modes encountered were less extreme. The importance of such modes lies in the fact that the child during development identifies not only with each parent as an individual, but also with the processes of problem-solving in which he has watched the parent engage. To a greater or lesser extent, the processes or ego modes are integrated into his own attempts to solve problems and cope with stress.

Children seemed to benefit when they could perceive and select from a variety of ego modes utilized by their two different parent figures. The sense of potential mastery was often further enriched when the child had a meaningful contact, eventually also experienced as an identification, with an additional parent figure, who almost invariably was described by the child as "doing things differently." If the child could see and identify with ego modes which were collaborative rather than adversary, as his parents had been, this aided synthesis. The important role of parental modes of dealing with stress is suggested by the fact that children, of widely differing ages within the same family, tended to resume growth to the same degree much more often than children of the same age but of different families. A notable exception to this trend occurred in families in which one child, usually the most vulnerable, was clearly identified as being more like the absent parent than the rest.

The Relationship With the Absent Parent

The nature of the relationship to the wanted, absent person has not often been considered as an important determinant of reactions to loss. In the children encountered here, it appeared as a central feature, affecting the child's efforts to cope. When the relationship had major significance for the child's ability to maintain self-esteem and rewarding relatedness, both the mourning and the subsequent ability to identify selectively with the absent parent were also greater.

Surprisingly, this meaning was not simply determined by which parent had been the primary caretaker of the child. For example, eighteen-month-old Melissa shifted, along with the rest of her family, from mother's to father's care and custody with noticeable growth rather than regression in various areas of ego development. On the other hand, Lucy, who had experienced alternate periods of care from mother and father with grandparents, reserved deep mourning for the disrupted components of her relationship to her mother, though she also grieved for the father.

One of the questions raised throughout this book has been the balance in the child's use of identification vs. continued quest, as a way to preserve the tie to the absent person. Here the nature of the previous relationship seemed to play an intricate role.

This was perhaps more evident in the children of the deceased. Where overidentification with the illness or deadness of the parent occurred in more than transient form, it seemed to be in the context of a prior period of deprivation in that relationship, associated with considerable resentment and guilt in the child. The child tended to remember few experiences of other ways of being together or feeling close. At the other end of the continuum, in cases where the quest was intensely continued in a variety of guises, though identification was also secondarily present, there was clear evidence of a pre-existing relationship which had been affectively and libidinally treasured, and then rather suddenly disrupted by death. In cases where selective, enriching identification was combined with a quest for affective aspects of the previous relationship, that relationship had provided the child both affectional gratification and a model for adaptive ego modes. There were persons who suffered the death of a parent in childhood and grew up to be superbly developed and vibrant adults.

In the children of the divorced one more often saw a split into areas of identification with the absent parent and areas of quest for him. The two sides of this split might be simultaneous—the child, for instance, constantly visualizing the loving absent mother while identifying with her perceived alcoholism or promiscuity. Or they might occur as a split over time—identifications with the absent parent combined with overt rejection of him during adolescence, then followed by an intense quest, acted out in other relationships in postadolescence. The necessity for such a split was often found in the relationship to the home parent, who could not like the child when he longed for the other parent.

As mentioned above, almost all children, except those who were "allied" with one parent, at first wished for reunion of their parents, and fragments of this wish often remained in attenuated form over a period of years. By age ten, the child usually firmly "knew" it could not come true. However, within a year or two, if a child became part of a new family constellation, he also often expressed great gladness that things had turned out as they did. The new lesson that mothers and fathers could really like and love each other was never lost on the child, and had major implications for his ability to picture his own future relationships in a positive way.

Among adolescents fewer than half openly expressed a fantasy of reunion between parents, though the great majority at some time expressed grief for the period of childhood, before they consciously faced that the parents were in such strife. For the children whose relationship to the absent parent had been a deep and rewarding one, grief and longing to be with that parent again tended to be expressed directly, when the home parent allowed it. Though these children might feel deeply rejected and transiently wish to reject the parent in turn, on the whole their attachment persisted in a way which could be made known to the absent parent, and in fact often reassured him that he was still needed by the child. Such absent parents usually cared about their children in turn, but visits had to be planned in such a way that unnecessary confrontations with the former spouse, which often neither could tolerate, did not totally spoil their postdivorce relationship to the child. These children, mostly aged four to ten, in turn cared a great deal about the well-being, loneliness, or happiness of their parents.

Other children were given simultaneously to greater withdrawal from the absent parent and a greater degree of denial, in fantasy, of the rejection they felt. Some became "pseudo-independent" from relationships generally, others were seriously depressed and apathetic. In these cases more real withdrawal from the child had occurred prior to the separation, or for significant periods of time. In one such case, the child was described as largely "neglected" between the ages of two and five because of the intensity of the preseparation turmoil in the parents' relationship to each other. In another, several turbulent separations and unsuccessful reunions had occurred when the child was between the ages of five and eight, though the father had long periods of absence from home even before this time. The absences were always longer than the reunions. During reunions too much was promised. After a "final" separation when the boy was eight, he became seriously depressed and preoccupied with suicide.

Among the very young children (two to five) a somewhat different pattern prevailed. When the relationship had been close and caring, the child, again, seemed able to express his intense "missing" of the absent parent and to continue to be eager to see him. There were already powerful loyalties, expressed in refusal to let anyone take the absent parent's place, e.g., a two-and-a-half-year-old occupied his father's chair whenever visitors came, making sure that no one else could sit in it. Like the somewhat older children, the child was preoccupied with whether, or how much, he and the absent parent still liked each other. When such a relationship was not sustained in reality, however, the very young child had a greater need to hold on to a fantasy of the absent parent not only as a loved person, but also as someone big and good and strong to identify with.

When such fantasies persisted in the absence of actual parenting from the absent person, the child was sometimes able to transfer them after a period of time to a new, more appropriately parenting figure, without the period of real grief. Thus five-year-old Susan accepted attention from her new father substitute, though she wanted to be sure this would not hurt her father's feelings. Absence of grief for the real relationship also occurred in cases where there had been no "real" loss, cases of adopted children or those who had never known the absent parent, e.g., Jeremy and Emily. However, reunion fantasies persisted, serving the young child's need to know whether the parent liked him (or would have liked him) and his interest in how like the parent he might be. Because the young child needs these fantasies to grow on, it is not wise to disturb them unless an adequate parent substitute is available to supply what is missing.

For adolescents, the relationship before the loss seemed more prognostic of the long-range rather than immediate solution. Many adolescents temporarily turned against a previously much loved parent figure during the aftermath of the divorce. There own need to disengage themselves, to some extent, from their past affections at this time of their lives played into the volatility of reactions. When a father remarried, girls particularly were apt to hide their feelings of rejection behind hostility, as an open expression of hurt would betray the strength of their remaining affection, by which they were bewildered, and which, in fact, they needed to cope with in other ways. In the long run, however, they often made peace with the same father.

I have mentioned, identification with those aspects of the absent parent that were devalued by the remaining parent was one way of coping that was particularly disruptive of adolescent development. A fair number of other adolescents were able, after experiencing a period of greater or less distress, to resume a constructive relationship with both parents, each now seen more individually. Others, as I have noted, utilized a kind of protective disengagement. For some adolescents whose relationship to the absent parent had contained the quintessence of loving interchange, "making peace" with that parent was prerequisite to the resumption of life goals.

The absent parent often felt in a particularly difficult situation vis-a-vis his continued role in the children's lives. As the home parent, involved with the child on a day-to-day basis, took an increasing amount of responsibility for decision-making, the absent parent frequently felt that he was no longer centrally needed, that his own role was at the fringe of the child's life. Because time and parental authority were now felt to be so limited, he frequently tried to cram visits full of good times and felt greater than usual reluctance to discipline the child. Secretly both he and the child after a while may resent the artificial quality of eternally trying to put their best foot forward with each other, and long for the more natural rough-and-tumble communication and activities which are usual in parent-child relationships. Another difficulty for the absent parent is that he had more often been uprooted from all the social supports and continuity which still existed for the child and home parent. Acute bouts of loneliness and feelings of exclusion often undermined the self-confidence of the recently separated absent parent, standing in the way of more active parenting during visits. It was often hard work to establish natural settings and activities between fathers and visiting children, but in the long run rewarding to both. Absent fathers or mothers who felt they were no longer needed by their children were simply wrong. Whatever else took place in the life of the child did not substitute for the meaning of his relationship to his real, absent father or mother, a relationship which, in the long run, inevitably affected his sense of worth and identity.

The Relationship With the Home Parent

When one parent was absent because of divorce or death, the relationship to the home parent became imbued with an extra charge of both positive and negative affects, and seemed inevitably complicated.

Of all factors related to the child's way of coping with loss, the role of the home parent seemed most central. Some years after the divorce or death, the well-being of the child appeared closely related to the well-being of the parent. There were important exceptions to this. Sometimes the remaining parent became so involved in his or her own life goals that the child was effectively excluded, and had suffered because of it. In other cases, e.g., Jane, the remaining parent had to cope with life on her own for a number of years, in ways which taxed her emotional resources so heavily that the child adapted with a period of pseudo-independence, associated with problems in ego synthesis and stringent defenses against dependency. By the time the mother remarried and a happy family setting was available, the child's period of openness to parental identifications had passed. In contrast, Robin also used a resourceful independence to cope with many changes in relationships. However, her mother did not emotionally withdraw from her, and Robin was just ten when mother remarried. We see in her a piquant, dramatic struggle between her conflicting needs to accept and to reject her stepfather, a debate about whether she can trust herself and others to love again.

From the point of view of the child, the most important aspects of the home parent's postdivorce life are these:

Is the parent depressed, deprived or angry most of the time, or is he or she living a satisfying life? This has importance both for the child's identifications, and for the emotional resources directly available to him. If the child or adolescent can see that the separation or death has not, in the long run, "ruined" the remaining parent's life, it is easier for him to see that his own does not have to be "ruined" either. Though children whose parents did remain pervasively distressed often eventually also made an inner decision to make the most of their own lives, problems of guilt and of identification with the unfulfilled parent represented an extra hurdle. This finding, that the well-being of the home parent is crucial, has been brought home to me repeatedly in questions parents ask about how much of their own goals they must "give up" for the sake of the child, or whether they should remain in an unchangeably, unhappy marriage for the sake of the child. One can usually answer honestly that the parent's own well-being is also "for the sake of the child," as long as the child does not get neglected in the interim. Although this balance is not always easy to maintain, if one is aware of the need one can seek to make provisions that do not compromise the possibilities of a full life for either parent or child. I was impressed with the great number of custodial parents who, after an initial period of distress following the separation or death, were able to move toward meaningful goals for themselves, with or without a new love or marriage partner, but without seriously withdrawing their emotional investment in their children.

Interaction with the child was exceedingly important prior to, during, and for some years after the parting, in a variety of ways. Inevitably, most children felt some heightened irritability and emotional withdrawal from them during the most friction-filled period before separation. This was also true for children of the deceased when a long or debilitating illness preceded the death. During such a period the child felt the relationship and the parents had "changed" and the loss already started. The treasured images of the desceased parent almost invariably were of a period before he was ill, when he and the relationship were still whole. This was not true in cases of sudden death, which sometimes resulted in a sense of sudden, traumatic disruption of the relationship to both parents.

There were great differences in the degree to which the remaining parent, in the midst of turmoil himself or herself, could communicate, empathize, or interact with the child. Even young children seemed highly attuned to the wish of the parent to be with him or to "get rid" of him, in his own necessary absorption in his own problems. As young children were apt to become more clinging, anxious, and irritable themselves during this time, their real demands on the home parent increased in a way which invited rejection or made it necessary for the parent to delimit the time spent with the child. Home parents were often surprised to find that some of the clinging and demanding could decrease rapidly if the parent was attuned to the meanings of the child's fears and could repeatedly provide him with information and reassurance, especially about further abandonment. Numbers of parents during this time expressed the notion that in fact the presence of the child provided the motivation to "pull myself together" and was a reminder that there were pleasures to be had in life. Frequently, these parents were able to feel a new serenity, freedom, and playfulness in their relationship to the child, now that it was "disentangled" from the tensions prior to the separation. The children who were enjoyed in this way seemed to know it, while others saw themselves clearly as an added, unwanted burden in their parents' current life.

From before age three, the child had a complicated set of ideas and feelings about the home parent's feelings about the absent spouse. These could be clearly verbalized or played out with puppets, family dolls, and doll houses, etc., by the child. Such play or comment generally represented a correct perception of the affective theme between the parents, distorted by or assimilated into the scenario of the child's current, developmentally influenced level of wishes and fears. Although they represented the interaction in quite different terms, children of this age had in common with older children and adolescents a clear awareness of the point at which longing or grief for the absent parent represented a form of disloyalty which could endanger their relationship to the home parent.

Such awareness in the children placed on the home parent the burden of giving the child emotional permission to continue caring about the absent parent, and to long or grieve for him. Numbers of symptoms in childhood, and extensive behavior patterns in adolescence, seemed to develop in reaction to the child's perception that he must no longer love, admire, or grieve for the absent parent. This perception assaulted the child's image of and loving investment in both parents, the adolescent's sense of reality and eventual identificatory synthesis that were prerequisites to a sound and valued adult ego identity.

In dealing with this difficult area of the relationship to the home parent, it was often useful to attempt to help the parent separate his/her own reaction to the spouse from that of the child. The parent usually had more than enough reason to feel deserted and angry, or bitter and vengeful, but his/her relationship to the spouse, and therefore needs, were different from those of the child. The parent should not "hide" the fact that he was angry at the spouse, for this was usually impossible, and anyway would not be real or believed by the child. However, he could actively encourage the child to talk about or remember the child's experiences with the absent parent, thereby giving him a chance to express his longing and come to terms with the current changes in the relationship. This was very, very difficult for some parents to carry through, while others were able to recognize its importance for the child sufficiently so that they had, spontaneously, already responded in this way. It was a process which could be most solidly counted on in those parents whose own lives were on the way to being happier already, and those whose emotional resources included an empathic understanding, but not overidentification, with their children.

In addition to permission still to care about the absent parent, many children needed an emotionally significant adult to help them grieve. For most children the home parent was of primary importance in this, although new parent figures and step-parents also often deepened their relationship to the child by being attuned to this need and helping to sustain him during this time.

Spouses of the deceased were in a different position from the divorced. The bereaved tended to be intensely involved in their own mourning. There were, however, great differences in the degree to which they needed to control this in themselves, for inner reasons, or in order to cope with the external demands of their changed life situation. There were also great differences, among parents who grieved deeply themselves, in the degree to which they trusted themselves to share grieving with the child without overwhelming him, and simultaneously to remain attuned to the doses of grief that the child could tolerate and would find relieving. Tod and Peggy's father is an example of a man who supported his adolescent children through shared grieving.

Divorcing parents more often were in a distress which included an inseparable mixture of mourning and bitterness. The mourning of the parent was sometimes as confusing to the child as the private areas of bitterness, since it was often in contradiction to the "rational" decision to divorce and resulted in behavior which was inconsistent in the eyes of the child. It propelled the divorcing parents simultaneously toward and away from each other, and often in each parent stimulated volatile mixtures of hatred, affection, and yearning. Sometimes parents, very determined to divorce, after all spent a night together. If the decision to divorce was an irrevocable one, the child often needed to have this clarified repeatedly, in order to accept that reunion would not occur, in spite of the mixed messages emanating from the parent's behavior.

Facing the child with the permanence of the altered relationship to the absent parent was difficult for many parents in itself; e.g., numbers of children had been told that their parent would be away for "a little while" or "two weeks". The permanence of the change usually brought grief to the fore, and it was then that the parent could be deeply helpful to the child if he was able to empathize with the child's loss (as distinct from his own) and symbolically to "hold" the child through his grief.

The image which the home parent had of the absent parent continued to affect children intensely through adolescence. Adolescents, in turn, made many judgments of their own. A variety of different patterns were discernable.

For the children of the deceased, there was usually no pressure toward devaluing the dead parent. There were exceptions to this. For example, in one case (Natasha) the whole human network turned against a previously admired political figure with hatred. In another (Rebecca) the mother who had hung herself was talked about as "crazy." However, in most cases, on the contrary, there was some pressure to maintain an idealized version of the dead. The home parent often had difficulty opening up lines of communication with the child that permitted the sharing of memories and feelings toward the dead that had elements of anger. During a period of actual mourning, whether immediate or delayed, for the dead, such images were sources of grief and guilt that compounded the grief for the longed-for relationship to the parent.

Among the divorced, some parents of adolescents were able, usually with considerable self-restraint, to avoid burdening the child with the degree of anger at the spouse which was necessary to accomplish the separation. In such cases the children still perceived some of the sources of the difficulty, as they must and should in order to understand the separation, but viewed this more in terms of the particular parents not being "right" for each other, than in terms of them having themselves to devalue either parent. It was then the child's task to sort out what about each was not "right" for him either—e.g., a father's critical attitudes. Christopher would be an example of this.

A common pattern included the adolescent's awareness of the components of character which one spouse most hated or devalued in the other. This awareness the adolescent often combined with the perception that, now that the spouse was away, he himself, whether he was of the same sex as the spouse or not, was viewed as behaving more like that spouse than previously. It was as though the spouse, having been deprived of his or her best enemy or source of disappointment, for a time, put the adolescent in that role. A strongly self-devaluing identification with the absent parent was frequently combined, in such cases, with a conscious idealization of that parent in order to preserve the positive components of the relationship. In cases where parental animosity was intense, this pattern was accompanied by depression, loss of life goals, learning difficulties, and often suicidal preoccupations (e.g., Abbey, Jane). Eva, whose parents both wanted to be highly supportive of her and tried not to use her in the service of their own needs, had a much milder dose of the same dynamics.

Another pattern which had emotional hazards for the adolescent was for one part to establish a close alliance with him or her, turning to the adolescent for fulfillment of the parent's emotional needs, amelioration of loneliness, etc. The nucleus on which such an alliance was predicated was the allied couple's rejection by the spouse, or their vehement rejection of him. In heterosexual alliances such adolescents had difficulties in dealing with the sexual seductiveness of the situation. Randolph and Sarah are examples. If the adolescent was of the same sex as the home parent, his differentiation from the parent could not proceed adequately (e.g., Heather, Karen). Because, to some extent, adolescent and parent were engaged in fulfilling each other's needs in mutual consolation, they tended to avoid intervention in this relationship until serious difficulties ensued.

In a few situations, with both younger children and adolescents, one of the parents continued to be psychologically disturbed in a way which resulted in highly traumatic interactions with the child. In these cases, the custodial parent had to protect the child or adolescent from contact with the other parent, and inability to do so exposed the child to psychological harm. In each of these few cases, the absent parent had either not sufficiently recovered from a previous psychosis—or not changed sufficiently from a previously known pattern of dangerous or violent behavior—to give assurance that the child would not be traumatized. This sometimes put the custodial parent in a very difficult position, in which he/she was sometimes blamed by both the former spouse and the child. In such cases it was necessary to help the child or adolescent gain some realistic understanding of the parent's disturbance and its consequences, as well as to differentiate the disturbed behavior from other components of that parent's past interaction with the child. Frequently, the child's secret, feared identification with the psychotic aspects of the parent came to the fore during this process. In contrast to these few cases, there were other parents who had suffered from a psychosis, but were able to relate constructively to their children. Manic-depressive illnesses in a parent rarely posed the problems for the children that were more often posed by a parent with a paranoid character or paranoid schizophrenic illnesses.

Finally, an important function for the home parent, especially of the adolescent, was to grant his child sufficient autonomy to continue his development. The adolescent's trust in his own inner resources and capacity for self-control is strengthened by the parent's trust, the image of the person the parent expects him to be. Such "trust" of course only works when appropriate to the adolescent's functioning, and not when its underpinnings are neglect. Frequently, adolescents could make excellent use of considerable independence, which allowed them to build emotional investments in other relationships and identification figures.

New Parent Figures and Step-Parents

New parent figures and step-parents can become either bitter rivals or enriching identification figures who are also valued by the child. Sometimes they are both. They do not, however, seem to take the place of the original, absent parent. In many cases it was a pleasure to watch the albeit faltering steps by which children and step-parents travelled toward warm, caring, and enduring relationships to each other.

For young children who have largely lost their interaction with the absent parent, a new parent figure is helpful in providing the identificatory model they still need badly in order to further their development. Usually the parent figure is perceived first as someone who provides additional attention for the bereft child, and who makes mother "happier" in a way which improves her relationship to him too. A highly significant, supportive role for the new parent figure or step-parent is to be available to the child while he is undergoing the painful experience of missing the absent parent and grieving for the changed relationship. The more the new parent figure shows interest in the other parent only, and the more transient he is, the less likely is it that the child will make an enduring emotional investment in turn. Even very young children, e.g., two-year-olds, sometimes maintain a deep loyalty to their absent parent, and initially resist all offers of a substitute relationship.

If the adult allows the child to take his time, and does not demand an emotional response from him, the child usually thaws out enough to begin accepting some interaction. It is not necessary and often is confusing to the child, however, to be brought a lot of "gifts" by the new adult. Interacting in an enjoyable activity, or simple readiness to be attentive to the child's needs when he allows this, are apt to be more helpful. Those young children who persistently rejected adult figures of the same sex as the absent parent were most often those who were struggling with unfinished, defended-against grief for the absent parent. Chapter 5 described many young children whose developing personalities and identifications were deeply enriched by the step-parent, while simultaneously they preserved their real, but altered relationship to their absent parent, often along with his or her spouse. These children seemed able selectively to maximize their identification with a variety of interests and ego modes embodied by their multiple parents, and eventually to choose the qualities they wished to make into their own. This was sustained, however, only with those parent figures who continued to have an individualized and meaningful interaction with the child. Children whose parents were intensely and primarily involved in seeking out suitable partners, and who experienced a rapid turnover of such partners, did not make these attachments, but instead tended to see the other adults as intruders who threatened to take the home parent's interest away from them. An interesting phenomenon observed in both boys and girls who experienced parental parting before the age of five, and then saw their parents choose new partners, was that the fantasy of being chosen (or rejected) as a love partner for a parent was not settled in the usual way, but often persisted into later years.

Children who were between the ages of six to nine when their parents remarried or were both dating varied between feeling increasingly bereft and even more of a "burden" to the home parent, who was showing more active interest in other adults than in them, and accepting the attention of the new adults with pleasure but without initial signs of deep attachment. One girl whose mother remarried when she was seven seemed to accept her step-father and increasingly made up excuses not to leave home to visit her father. At the same time, however, she insisted that certain new rituals be carried out by the teacher at school; these included addressing her by her full name (father's last name) before she was willing to enter the class. In interviews, she expressed great concern about her father's welfare, and guilt about leaving him "alone until he has someone too."

By age ten, numbers of children expressed fierce, open loyalty to the absent parent, divorced or deceased. Ten- and eleven-year-olds were apt to mobilize their talents for the construction of imaginative mental artillery to fend off intruding, potential step-parents; step-parents whom they later came to want as well. Noah, Robin, and Amy would be examples. Each also had considerable affective investment in their rich relationships with their mothers by that time, and were reluctant to risk change in this. Gwen, who had had a highly ambivalent relationship with her absent mother, initially complained about missing her mother, but soon became warmly attached to her stepmother, and quickly began to identify with her in a constructive way. In the same age group some children, both boys and girls, expressed vast indignation when the absent parent chose a new partner, and in effect asked him to choose between them and the partner. For example, they would not visit the absent parent while signs of the new partner, such as clothes, were in the apartment.

For the adolescents a new spouse or love partner for either parent was inevitably viewed with a mixture of feelings; such a partner for a time usually had to walk a tightrope, neither rushing in to win the child over before he was ready, or too ready to abdicate the role as spouse merely because the adolescent considered him or her a rival. Step-parents were sometimes put into a difficult position: they needed to show compassion for the adjustment the child had to make to a new parent figure; yet moments shared between the adolescent and his real parent brought home the strength of the tie between them, often leaving the step-parent feeling acutely displaced by the adolescent in the affections of the new spouse. Some step-parents felt richly rewarded when they had been able to wait out this storm and found themselves in the role of a loved confidant whom the adolescent could eventually trust in important matters.

Unconscious hostility toward the absent parent was often ready to be projected onto the step-parent as a means of protecting the positive ties to the absent, wanted parent. For example, Donna's father had neglected and rebuffed her since the divorce. Donna's presence reminded him too much of his former wife, and he could not cope with the memories. Donna defended her father's lack of interest in her and continued to idealize him, while expressing fury at her stepfather. She told me: "I was ready for him. Even before I met him I had this idea that stepfathers were people who threw people in the cellar and were psychotic or sadistic. But he's worse! I didn't imagine how selfish he turned out to be. Why should I do work in school when my mother is slaving just for him, waiting on him and everything? What's my payoff going to be?"

Several adolescents initially sought out their prospective stepmothers, progressively treating them as older friends and advisors. As their fathers came near to remarriage, hostilities and attempts to interrupt the relationship between the two adults began. Girls were apt to be highly critical but also often highly perceptive about their father's choices in love partners. Boys who had lost a mother more often looked for maternal qualities in the prospective stepmother.

It was often useful, both for the child and the prospective step-parent, to know that they could not be expected to love each other right away, or perhaps ever. Living within the same family, they would, however, have to recognize the legitimacy of each other's needs and make some adjustments. If they then came to love each other, as many step-parents and children do, that would be a bonus to look forward to. When this was initially made clear it tended to reduce the guilt both child and step-parent were prone to feel if the relationship was less than ideal. When guilt over negative feelings developed in the child, who knew that his home parent wanted him to be nice to the new spouse, the child was apt to provoke fights with the step-parent to make him or her mad, in order then to have a righteous cause to be angry with the step-parent in turn. With older children or adolescents I sometimes met with them, the parent, and prospective step-parent before the remarriage in order to air some of such upcoming issues.

Complex dynamics, with both positive and negative components for the older child or young adolescent, were involved when the parent's new choice of love partner differed drastically from the personality of the exspouse. One example: numbers of men had chosen in their young years a mate who strongly embodied maternal qualities to them and to the children. This was made evident by the quality of the relationships within the family even though it may not have been the wish of the wife. After the death or divorce from such a mate, the man, in a different phase of his own adulthood, now chose a woman, usually younger and with quite different qualities. She was apt to be viewed by him as either much more independent, erotic or stimulating than the former wife, or to have a kind of youthful vulnerability which made him feel protective and highly adequate and adventurous with her. The issues of mutual dependency, constriction, or domination with which he had struggled within the first marriage he was now ready to lay to rest, in order to pursue previously unfulfilled dreams which the fact of middle age made more urgent. This not so unusual pattern was sometimes at first extraordinarily painful for adolescent girls to witness, for the father's new love partner was simultaneously too much and too little like themselves. Reactions to this pattern tended to be volatile. The girls' most common complaints were "she's much too young for him" or "he's making a fool of himself over her and he never would have done that with mother. Even the people he works with won't respect him any more." It seemed crucial for the girl to have sources of self-esteem in her other relationships before feeling comfortable with the father's choice and benefitting from the potential for identification and companionship.

During mid and late adolescence both, some boys and girls seemed attuned to their parents' need for a fulfilling adult relationship, and at times expressed relief when the parent had a happy relationship. Some expressed the idea that the parent's happiness would then no longer worry them. Adolescents who felt so, even though they might criticize the particular choice, usually could picture the time when they themselves would lead desirable lives of their own.

The factors relevant to the child's way of coping with parental parting are many, complex and inter-related. A period of more or less intense distress is not only usual for the child, but, with emotional support to face and work it through, it may have a constructive component in helping him develop a tolerance for dealing with unavoidably painful feelings and realities in later life.

When a child deals with loss, age has a bearing on the range of ego mechanisms available to him; socioeconomic factors have bearing on the range of life circumstances available to the family: does mother have to work whether she likes it or not, or can she get education to pursue a desirable career? Can she stay home with her child if she chooses or pick the best among sitters or day-care centers if she doesn't? Parental modes of coping with stress have bearing on the range of ways for experiencing grief and problem solving with which the child can identify. New parent figures have important bearing on enriching life and identifications. However, the most crucial correlates of the child's later well-being appear to reside in the ways he experiences the quality of both the pre and postseparation relationships to each of the parents and his capacity to make peace within himself with their meaning. Of these, the well-being of the home parent with whom the child lives provides an especially sensitive barometer.

Chapter 10

REFLECTIONS ON THERAPY

The torment, formerly diffuse,
has acquired name and address.

—Ingmar Bergman, quoted in
the *New York Times Magazine*

Therapy cannot undo the absence of a wanted person, nor the associated pain. But it can help the person make peace with his loss, so that the capacity for loving does not depart with the beloved. The therapy process is a many-faceted topic, beyond the scope of this book. My comments pertain only to certain aspects of therapy interaction which the children of parting parents encountered here brought to the fore, and highlighted as intrinsic to their common experience. In addition brief reference is made to differences in treatment modalities evoked by differences in the personality organization of the children when initially encountered.

Parental parting is not a psychiatric problem, but an event which happened and had psychic consequences for all family members. Frequently a supportive human network is needed more than psychotherapy. Therapy does not take the place of friendship, nor is it useful when primarily sought for this. That is, when the need to build a supportive network of relationships which may include parents, teachers, peers, social-support groups for the adults, etc., attempts may be made to work this out with the adults, without instituting therapy with the child. However, although loss is not in itself a psychiatric problem, many times its emotional and social consequences brand the growing person and affect the social network within which he is growing. Both then need attention. When the child or adult suffers from the experience of the loss in a way he cannot or has not shared with others; when he presents a variety of substitutes for grief, either in the form of symptons, constriction of personality or life goals, or repetitive patterns of interactions which provoke rejection, continued painful affects, or the renunciation of important aspects of the self, brief or extensive therapy intervention is usually indicated.

Each situation that I have described here differed and none was approached in identical fashion. On many occasions there was a wide discrepancy between what one would ideally offer to a child and family, and what was feasible, given the real limitations either in the agency resources available, or the likelihood of the family being able to carry through recommendations which taxed their frustration tolerance and persistence at a time when they needed more support than usual. It was particularly difficult successfully to transfer families seen in initial clinic evaluation to another setting, without compounding the issues of loss and rejection. It eventually became my feeling that a person suffering from parental parting should not be seen for more than two evaluatory sessions if transfer to another person was to follow. When possible, it was better to have the evaluation done by the potential therapist.

Some people were helped greatly by the therapy process and others were not. The kinds of interventions utilized within therapy, varied more than usual. The extensiveness of involvement varied, from a minimum of clarification and support for the parent or parents, so that they might then support the child; to a single interview with the child, who made clear connections between a puzzling symptom and the meanings, either unconscious or secret, of the parental parting, meanings which could then with his permission be discussed with the parent or parents; to the extensive recovery of memories over a long period of time, with associated reworking of perceptions of the self, the wanted absent person, and the meaning of the loss or change. The extensiveness of the therapy process was not automatically correlated with the severity of disturbance, for some of the most disturbing phenomena could not be easily approached by psychotherapy (e.g., a considerable proportion of those involved in prolonged custody litigation). There were other particularly difficult situations: those in which the parent and child had formed a "consoling alliance" which was gratifying to both partners during the child's early and midadolescence. Generally, both partners feared disruption of this relationship through therapy, and sought therapy only when symptoms became disabling; in this situation, therapy proceeded more fruitfully at the end of adolescence. Another difficult, though by no means unapproachable, situation was one in which the defenses against loss had pervaded the character structure in such a way that there already were multiple secondary effects in the development of ego integration, usually with attendant learning problems, difficulties in impulse control, and other characterological constraints. In such cases, adaptations in therapy modalities aimed toward ego building were prerequisites for direct dealing with the underlying grief (see below). The degree of initial disturbance also could not be correlated in a simple way with the quality of the person's eventual sense of self; for example, some persons who underwent a psychotic period eventually reconstituted themselves and their lives in a highly positive fashion.

Many children and adults did deal with conflict by exploring in sustained psychotherapy the intrapsychic links, underlying assumptions about themselves and what happened with their parents, and the gamut of associated affects. However, this was feasible to attempt only with children who showed the emotional strength to undertake this process and who simultaneously had one or two parents expected to be sufficiently supportive throughout the process. In other families, such psychotherapy would have run counter to their immediate goals, or various practical considerations made it difficult or impossible.

Three issues affecting therapy with children of parting parents will be briefly considered: (1) work related to the human network surrounding the person; (2) the issue of the absence of the wanted person; and (3) the impact of personality organization on transference, countertransference and the therapy process.

Work Related to the Human Relationship Network Surrounding the Person

In evaluating a child's situation, a first step included the scanning of the human relationships around him with an eye toward maximizing resources for sustained emotional support. One quickly becomes aware that, for children of parting parents, working through the sense of loss and even the acceptance of new parent figures involve painful feelings made tolerable by consistent support in important relationships. In therapy, this often meant immediate work to strengthen that network, rather than waiting for trouble to manifest itself there. For example, while it is usual for therapists to be in touch with a child's teacher about problems that may provoke a negative reaction toward the child by the school, one sometimes hesitates to initiate such contact unless it seems necessary, for one must counterbalance positive results against the risk of the child's teacher unnecessarily viewing the child as "disturbed" and unconsciously altering expectations and attitudes toward him. However, the teacher is often a more important than usual figure for the child for parting parents, and early contact with the school or nursery school was much more often helpful than not. The kinds of collaboration set up with schools in regard to cutting classes (chapter 3), not allowing acting out of symptoms, the problem of getting "thrown out" (Noah, chapter 4), learning problems (Pam, chapter 5), special conditions of support (Susan chapter 9), etc., are described elsewhere in this book.

Similarly, talking with others who could provide supportive relationships to the child, such as housekeepers, babysitters, grandparents, scout leaders, etc., was more essential early in the treatment than usual. With adolescents, for whom the maintenance of relationships independent of the therapy may be important, in a way analogous to the maintenance of relationships independent of the parents, collaboration with the human support system is much more complicated. As mentioned elsewhere, however, the adolescent is frequently quite willing for the therapist to request an interview with the "absent" parent, or collaborate with other adults in dealing with such issues as cutting classes or generally, for them to remain in touch with each other. For example, an excellent teacher of a sixteen-year-old boy repeatedly called me over a period of a year, with the boy's consent. Although he very much liked the boy, who had sought him out after school (while being unable to concentrate in school), and enjoyed the discussion of precociously adult issues with him, he recognized the intensity of the boy's involvement and feared "getting in too deep." He had felt increasingly tense and emotionally drained by talks with the boy and had considered telling the boy he could not take time to see him anymore. We worked out ways of coping with the boy's intensity without the teacher's abandoning him. In addition, a special after-school project was planned with the teacher that involved the boy with two other adolescents in useful community action related to his interests hoping that this might ameliorate his social isolation. As in the example above, other adults had been made uncomfortable by recognizing sexual undercurrents in the intensity of adolescents' attachments to them. When the identificatory and restitutional needs of the adolescents underlying the sexualization could be made clear to the adult, frequently he or she could continue the relationship by responding to these issues directly and in a way which diminished the sexualization.

Adolescents were the ones most often bringing their friends along to therapy sessions, or asking directly for their parents to be seen about some particular issue. As self-image changed in the adolescent over time, so choice of friends also tended to change. Contact with both parents, when possible, was useful even when the parent was in individual therapy elsewhere himself. More often than is usual, parent and child were intermittently seen together, either with each other, only or with a prospective step-parent as well. This was usually followed by an individual session with the child. The joint sessions often centered upon the communication of particular feelings the child or parent had felt he needed to withhold from the other and with facing or establishing the realities of the relationship to the absent parent. Sometimes joint sessions occurred over the entry of a step-parent into the life of the child or adolescent.

More frequently than with most children referred for other kinds of issues, there was an early focus in the therapy on what had actually happened to them; a continuing "tracking" of the realities of their parents' divorce or plans for a new partner, as it related to them. Some realities about a parent who had been insufficiently able to care for the child, also needed to be brought into the child's perception when it was clearly affecting him, even if the child denied or did not offer this material. In most cases, the child himself quickly enough offered contradictory clues to such reality limitations, making it possible to begin this process through his own material. Confirming a rejecting parent's current limitations was central to the attempt to lift the burden of blame from shoulders too young to bear it.

There were other modalities used which I do not generally bring into children's therapy. For example, at times I stated quite flatfootedly that I knew the child must be struggling with anger, worry, and sadness about himself and a parent, because that is *always* present in some way or other when parents divorce. The child usually heard this with relief. The statement could be made because the child's problems, though individualized, were in part a reaction to what had actually happened to him, rather than the product of a totally internalized conflict. Whatever else was going on, and this varied greatly, some combination of anxiety, anger, and sadness seemed ubiquitous.

At other times, e.g., when a child or parent was being shunned by the human network around him, I had absolutely no hesitation in making moralistic-sounding statements that it was wrong for him to be subjected to this kind of social isolation, even though such behavior might be motivated by various fears in others. (fear of contagion, feelings of inadequacy about being useful, etc.). It was then often more possible for the child or adult to explore the meaning of his own reaction, which perhaps was still maintaining the alienation from others. It was important, however, for the therapist not to get trapped into a stalemate by ways in which the child or adult might have been "victimized" by those around him. Unless the focus eventually returned to the reactions and options for the child or adult, such a stalemate would reinforce the alienation and undermine ego resources needed for change.

Since many children went through a period of grief during which they particularly needed the home parent, the speed of work with the child had to be coordinated, to some extent, with the parents' ability to be emotionally supportive to him. If the child were to begin a grief process intolerable for the parent to witness, it would not help him grow. In a similar way, one had to gauge the family's usual methods for tension discharge, and the degree to which they were compatible with the child's need for extra support. As many of the parents were under an unusual amount of both inner and outer stress at the same time as the child, their need for a supportive human network was equally great.

The role of the human support network appeared different in those cases in which a parent was lost through death rather than divorce. Numbers of adults recalling their childhood bereavement had experienced the particular forms in which surrounding adults experienced their sympathy as a demand for an emotional response which they could not make at the time. At times these expressions were felt as garish, incongruous to, and intrusive upon their private feelings; a number felt especially chided for not crying about the death, when they could not cry at all, or at least not in public. Some children of deceased parents were highly selective about those whom they wanted to choose for sharing their grief. Ideally, it was often someone who, they felt, would not only understand them, but also have some similarity of personality or value system to the dead parent. For them, the timing of any intervention by a human support network was important—and it must not be too soon. Like the children of divorce, the children of the deceased experienced the remaining parent as the most important person. The degree to which that parent had been available and able to share the mourning varied widely, and the consequences therefore varied. When the child was ready, someone with whom to share the grief seemed to be an essential component of the ability to sustain it. Hence, in the therapy of bereaved children, looking for or attempting to build such availability is the first step.

The Absence of the Wanted Person

My own experience in working with some of those children, adults, and parents was deeply moving. Many times I sat in the presence of moments of such naked love and longing—later branded by fear, guilt and anger—that it made me ache with and for the child or adult. It was perhaps most difficult to restrain the temptation to comfort or respond directly, or to divert to a too easy substitute the memory that still haunted the person's life. One had repeatedly to remind oneself that the loss of a wanted person is real and cannot be undone, and yet can remain as a vitalizing force, whether the Cheshire Cat smiles on or no. This recurrent phenomenon in myself churned my thinking about the presence or absence of the wanted person, within the psyche and within the external world. Because problems centered upon the absence of the wanted person, it seemed that a needed person had to be present at the right time in order for this issue to be brought to the fore in a way which augured well for its reworking. Yet almost intrinsic to the nature of the issue were complications arising within the therapy and the therapist.

I shall discuss these complications in relation to the following issues: not undertaking or "promising" more than could be finished; being reliably present; countering magical thinking by clarifying one's nonpresence; resisting one's own impulse toward denial and restitution; confrontation of the absence; and the acceptance of the duality of the reality sense.

In some situations, the loss is not worked through within the therapy itself. The child who has lost a parent frequently turns quickly to the therapist as a kind of substitute. The combination of valiance and neediness so evident in many of the children naturally invites a warm emotional response. Yet in early encounters with children I saw, it seemed important not to be drawn into the role of substitute parent. In the first place, I was highly aware of my own role as "temporary" in the child's life. Loss had already been a trauma, one that it was preferable not to repeat during the developmental years. Of course, there was greater leeway with those children whom it would be possible to see for extended treatment if this was indicated, than with those who were being seen for an evaluation before other plans were made. Numbers of the children were particulary sensitive to the disruption of any interaction which they interpreted as involving a "promise" of continued contact. The notion of a "broken promise" that had affected them was brought up repeatedly by both children and adults, and usually related to the disruption of continuity, the "change" in their relationships. Unspoken promises by the absent person to "be there" were believed by children of both the divorced and the deceased. Hence it was particularly important to understate rather than overstate any "promise" about what therapy would offer allowing the problem of the "broken promise" to emerge by itself through the inevitable frustrations that occurred within treatment.

Secondly, many of the younger children, in particular, were in a state of transition between parent figures. Very brief therapy contacts in which the therapist did *not* become a central figure in their lives could sometimes establish the links between the symptoms and the hidden, distorted anxiety or grief for the absent parent. This material could then be shared with the home parent or with new parent figures, fostering the helpful aspects of their own parental roles. The child in these situations had much greater need to make a deep emotional investment in the parent figures who would stay with him than in a therapist. For example, Sean, Melissa, Susan, Jenny, Daniel, and Jeremy, were in this situation. Similarly, Gwen and Jeffrey, who were seen on a more intensive basis for some months, were then for several years given a monthly hour for the family, to be used by either of the children, the father, or the stepmother, or to be divided among them. Both Jeffrey's and Gwen's predominant need was the establishment of a deep relationship with their stepmother. As both she and they were capable of evolving this once the children's extreme comflicts of loyalties had been partially worked through, continued, intensive therapy was counterindicated, since it might possibly divert their energies from the relationship with each other.

When a child or adult was working through within therapy, facing the absence of the wanted person, attempting to avoid too quickly becoming a parent substitute was differently motivated: restitution would avert the necessary grief, depriving the child of the opportunity to find within himself the strength to tolerate the associated feelings about his reality. Although in this sense the relationship needed to proceed slowly, the child did, however, need a reliable enough relationship with sufficient sense of emotional contact to be able to risk his sadness. To some extent being reliable meant making an attempt to be available at times of crises, especially when the child's distress about feeling deserted was great. For example, many children continued to have a dread of abandonment at times when the separated or divorced parents resumed fighting (most often at times of child visitation, or over the phone). The child was given my phone number to use at such times if he needed it rather than wait out the rest of the week, although he also knew that he might not be able to reach me right away; that it might take several hours before I could reach him back. Related to this was the fact that most children were not only dealing with what had happened to them in the past, but were subjected to the still continuing trauma of parental distress. Eventually their parents would redirect their lives—usually after one or two years post parting, but sometimes not until much later, or never. Meanwhile, despite the best of intentions, and sometimes in the face of untenable promises to the child that the fighting would stop, bitter scenes or encounters between parents might still erupt unpredictably. Or, equally confusing to the child, the separated parents might spend a night together, then part again without explanation. The child was often helped if he could see that such parents were in conflict about the separation themselves; that missing each other and being furious could coexist. Other kinds of real, continued trauma occurred, in the form of other changes in the life of the child necessitated by the divorce or death. Frequently, the child, highly attuned to the distress of one parent or the other, also needed the relief of being assured that this parent would not be neglected, that the parent would be provided with someone reliable (other than the child) to turn to.

Simultaneous to the process of establishing a relationship in which one was reliably present, there had to be, paradoxically, its opposite: the clarification of one's absence in such a way that the person would eventually face whatever magical thinking was involved in the wish usually intensified after loss, for the ever-present parent. This will be further commented on in relation to termination. However, it is the issue of permanent absence, which, with its implications, lies at the heart of grieving within therapy. The painful implication, when total loss rather than change has occurred, is that the individual must make an internal decision to want to live life fully, even if he were forever "alone"—that is, without the wanted person. For when someone is still the person most wanted, all states without that person are aloneness. Later, when the capacity for loving someone else has been regained, new connections to others can become deeply meaningful again, and being by oneself for a time can also be tolerated or enjoyed. For example, such an internal decision to live fully emerged in Natasha (whose father died in prison camp) during a period of my absence, when she again felt the absence of her father. In a note written after our last session before a vacation, she implied that understanding our work together was valuable to her on her own in my absence. The unspoken reproach to me for leaving might be guessed from the fact that she mentioned the exact time of absence—four weeks—twice, but she will give fuller voice to that reproach when I safely return. She wrote:

It is a gift that today's session—the last before the 4-week break in continuity, probably was one of the central ones of the year. I finally faced the fact that my father did sacrifice himself in a way for his family (rather than escaping before being taken prisoner as some others had) and that I would have vastly preferred to die in chaos with him than to accept his death and its challenge to live through the chaos, *alone, without him,* and to succeed to a meaningful and happy life. It is both terrifying and releasing to me to accept the basic idea that what he did was freely given, without strings and obligations, just to be joyfully accepted even if one totally fails—sacrifices cannot be vindicated, do not have to be vindicated. They stand alone on the merit of the person who gave it. This may sound crazy to you, but the fact is, it is a very accelerated start on four plus weeks worth of some very valuable work on clarifying translating my individual experiences into harmony with basically valid experiences and truth—something I thoroughly enjoy doing, and virtually have been living for.

Confrontations concerned with "absences" were sometimes necessary and always painful. In most cases such confrontations were not needed. For example, for most children of divorce a drastic change in relationship rather than a total loss was being dealt with. For many others, such as children of the deceased, (e.g., Amy, Wendy, Natasha) the permanent absence was faced when grief work had progressed sufficiently. In contrast, confrontation was necessary in those cases in which it became clear that the wanted person would never again love the child as the child wished, yet the child's emotional resources were tied up in a debilitating denial of that truth. At times I came to recognize the need for such confrontations through an awareness of my own emotional reaction; e.g., if I were tempted either to join the child in upholding his blatant denial that he could be so unwanted or tempted to comfort him directly. Gerardo, for example, evoked such reactions with his simultaneous descriptions of his mother as wonderful and wanting him to live with her more than she wanted his sister (the reverse was true); while in reality she stayed increasingly locked in her room, only putting out food for the children, and had, in fact, sent the children to father because she could not manage to care for them anymore. Confrontation with such discrepancies tended to bring about a change in affect (in Gerardo's case, he began to cry) as a forerunner of changes in symptom and identification patterns.

Other therapists' reactions may differ, but they are apt to develop a system of cues from within to aid in the recognition of what is happening between the patient and themselves.

Confrontations with children of parting parents occurred primarily in two areas. One involved the "effort to unmask denial" which has been described by Weisman (1973) as the function of confrontation in psychotherapy. The particular area of denial, however, was less often one of inner impulse than it was the clinging to a psychic reality in which the child could still obtain the love of the absent parent just as he wished it, if only he could change himself, the world, the parents, or whatever. Giving up the denial also involved coping with the need for an omnipotent self- or parent-image that could make everything come out all right if only he or she were good enough and wished to do so.

A second kind of confrontation was of a different order, and more common with depressed adults than with children. When it occurred, it took place at much later stages of therapy, usually after the individual had begun to remember or reconstruct painful affects related to the absent, wanted person. At this time, he sometimes expressed the conviction that things were hopeless, that he or she could not possibly really change, in spite of new insights. This was sometimes couched in terms of fear or convictions of failing in therapy. This attitude, too, constituted a defense against abandoning the quest for the wanted, absent person, by perpetuating old patterns of interactions and fending off different possibilities. Provocative and angry feelings toward the therapist were a part of this picture, a "challenge" to him to do something about the stalemate, coupled with an assumption that this was impossible. Rather than reassurance—useless in such a situation—confrontations stirred up by the challenge that the therapist detected tended more often to clarify the interaction between the individual and the therapist, as well as to provide the individual with evidence that the therapist actively cared about his well-being, to the extent of getting angry about the possibility of his eternal suffering. Such confrontation might involve a recognition that the "hopelessness" was real, if "hope" was invested only in the notion of still being loved by the wanted, absent person, or by his "unique" form of love; this was impossible. In fact, the individual might indeed remain at a stalemate if his need to hold on to his painful feelings about the lost person continued to be so great that the idea of a happier life in the future entailed too great a risk for him to consider it.

In these particular cases the idea of "failing" in therapy was usually tied to the concept that the lost relationship had "failed" and to the dreaded conviction that either the self or the parent (or therapist) was the source of failure, doomed to be condemned forever. As such individuals were chronically vulnerable, prone to turn their anger against themselves, a confrontation with their own role in the process and the active presentation of alternatives seemed useful in mobilizing a perception of choices. The case of Michael (chapter 8) illustrates some of these issues.

The meanings of confrontation in therapy have been considered by Myerson (1973), who stated: "If we do examine the context in which we decide to confront or not to confront, we will frequently find that our decision is influenced in part by nonrational factors, in effect by our countertransference." Myerson referred to Bibring's (1954) delineation of the psychotherapeutic process, which started from the vantage point of the uninvolved therapist who, on the basis of his knowledge about how psychotherapy works and his clear notion of what he wants to accomplish, decides the appropriate intervention to produce the desired change in the patient, e.g., deciding whether at a given moment to use clarification or interpretation, with their differing effect on the defensive armor of the patient. Myerson, however, probed more deeply the therapist's choice of intervention, by making the affective connections between the inner states of patient and therapist. He commented that Bibring's frame of reference "puts us in the somewhat unreal position of the detached, basically uninvolved therapist rather than in that of the position of actual therapist trying to work with a resistant patient. Thus, his approach is not applicable if we are considering how far and in what ways our emotional reactions to our patients and their emotional reactions to our reactions actually influence, interfere with, and sometimes promote the therapeutic process." He suggested that irritation in the therapist, a natural reaction to a defensive patient, can, especially when recognized and tolerated by the therapist, lead to the choice of a kind of confrontation that combines evidence of caring about the patient with a confrontation that is partially stimulated by the irritation.

Myerson pointed out that "obviously the way the patient perceives or the meaning he ascribes to what the therapist is attempting to convey to him is the decisive factor in whether the therapist's response is appropriate. He stated that Bibring's concepts of the therapeutic process ignored "what I believe to be crucial, i.e., how the affective tone of the therapist affects the patient."

Myerson's approach is especially fertile, leading forward to recognition of an essential component of the therapeutic process, and backward to recapture the enduring component of the patient's past, lost relationships. It is precisely what he refers to as the "affective tone" that lies at the heart of the bereft person's yearning for the absent other, and hence at some point at the heart of the ambience with the therapist.

The nuances of affective tone within the therapy situation are most difficult to describe verbally; they do not emerge fully from the descriptions of encounters with children and parents in the preceding chapters. Yet they provide both the most valuable clues to the actual as well as wished-for relationship to the absent person, and the vitality of—or unifying direction within—the therapy process itself. For example, in Gerardo's case (chapter 6) the joyous feeling of "moving along together, moving free" which emerged in the therapy had been a leitmotiv of his early experience, a yearning for a particular kind of relationship with his mother that was later reversed by her immobilizing depression, itself mirrored in his own symptom of immobilized muscles. He had clung to both components of the traumatic change while, in his words, "everything stopped, time stopped." For Lucy (also chapter 6), the wish to be gently held added an equally compelling affective tone to the therapeutic interaction, and formed the nucleus of what she had to work out with her mother.

Amy (chapter 8), Linda, and Eileen (chapter 7) had in different ways been intensely stimulated to excitement by a wanted person, and then abandoned; this process had been re-enacted in their lives. The repetition of this sequence, as well as the question of rescue from such an intolerable state of tension, was the need that had to be confronted before an affective tone of trust in their own resources for growth was sought. In contrast, Wendy (chapter 8) came to speak of the combination of support, trust in her capacities, and freedom from constraint which she felt in the therapy relationship, and which she identified as missing painfully when revived in memories of her dead father.

Resolution of conflict with the absent, wanted person often involves renunciation of the wish for control of that person. Such control might be entirely in the thought and imagination of the individual who shapes the image of the beloved in accordance with his wishes; or it may result in attempted control over others, either in actual relationships or by avoiding such relationships (to maintain control over never again being controlled). Thus the child faces the fact that nothing he could have done, no matter how pleasing, could have kept the parent, and, conversely, that nothing he did actually drove the patient away. Ordinarily, both aspects of this interaction will be tried out in relation to the therapist: what will please? what will drive away? how one can protect oneself from the possibility of being hurt again? Beneath the wish to control the relationship resides the fear of helplessness, that was induced by the child's inability to have in actuality influenced events favorably. The fantasied control whether in acting out, in transitional object formation, etc., counters such feelings of helplessness adaptively for a time, but perhaps at the cost eventually of free internal development.

Renouncing such control means that the child or adult must risk something: he must give the wanted, absent person the freedom to "go away" if he so wishes. Often the attempt to picture and come to terms with the absence occurs simultaneously with being able to experience a loosening of resistance to transformations in the image of the absent parent. Occasionally, this risk results in total loss. For example, in cases where it must be faced that the parent was truly not capable of caring about the child, or has transferred all of his or her interest to a new person or family, the needed transformation in that case involves slowly abandoning the wish for love from that person, and eventually the discovery that there is no one one cannot live without.

More often the required transformation is one of risking allowing the absent, wanted person to be him or herself, being cognizant of the consequent reverberation on one's self-image. Such a risk is sometimes difficult for the person who has suffered and been traumatized by loss. As previously discussed, the traumatic or overwhelming aspects of such an experience, while the child was helpless, may promote a "fixation," not necessarily of a particular impulse or libidinal level, but rather of the interaction experienced, then painfully disrupted, and assimilated to the child's then current libidinous and cognitive development. Such a "fixation" resists change as a way of resisting further loss. In the adult, the fantasy that one needs a particular person to make one happy is part of feeling oneself to be in love and committed to another. It was, however, true in a different way in childhood, when all others paled in importance beside the parents, that there was only one (or two) persons one could love. The person who is bereft in the midst of intense loving, new or long-fulfilled, may feel he (or she) will never love again. This is usually simply not true.

Not only the affect of grieving may be postponed and displaced or distorted, but, simultaneously, the image of the wanted, other person and the self remain in limbo. For example, if a person had felt loved at the time loss occurred, he or she may cling to the image of themselves just as they were then, with the fantasy that only by so doing will they be loved again. If the loss culminated in a period during which the child felt rejected, sexually discarded, inadequate, etc., these qualities may remain actively present in the beginning of a new relationship, and the person may require various impossible, or, at best impractical "proofs" of love from the new partner. Such proofs put an extra strain on the relationship and lead to an unnecessary rejection of those aspects of the other person which turn out to be different from the original image. Many step-parents were first subjected to this kind of rejection by children. Many of the divorcing parents suffered from such discrepancies about each other themselves. Adolescents encountered them in their first love relationships when they neared adulthood. In grief work during therapy, transformations of the fixated, affect-laden images of the self and the wanted, missing person occur spontaneously when a free influx of memories is again allowed. Memories activate the establishment of crucial links between the image, affect, and reality sense which resulted in the meaning the person attributed to his own and others' feelings and behavior, a meaning which could now be re-examined in the light from new horizons.

Within the therapy process, and especially around termination, the issues of final loss and the forms of the relationship that persist come to the fore. In many cases the finality of termination is an issue important to resolve fully. However, with children of parting parents, I tend not to discourage follow-up contacts when the child or parent requests it. Usually, this is not introduced until after the child has had some time for venting anger at me over a coming termination which usually revives for him similar feelings toward the parent who left. Often he is aware of experiencing himself as less vulnerable now. In other cases, the child himself feels ready to terminate, with mixed feelings; again, though, I maintain more of an "open door" policy than usual.

Working out the magical component of the therapist's continued presence, when needed, often remains an important, but dormant problem. The person may appear ready to terminate, but with the unconscious proviso of continued contact. I prefer to be available for this, but caution myself to note whether the person *expects* me to be there if the need for rescue is felt. This is a position dangerous for the individual because one cannot and will not always be there; as well, it indicates that the fantasy of being able to make the therapist materialize at will has not been worked out. This issue must first be taken up directly, and then also as well through working out with the person to which he might turn to when necessary. For example, both Eileen and Karen (chapter 7) kept in touch with me for several years after ending therapy. Karen came for appointments from another state about twice a year, making productive use of the sessions. Eileen called during emergencies. Both young women tended to seek me out at times when they had lost a love partner. As Eileen once put it, "All I want is to make him love me again." (She had lost her mother through suicide; her father through his abrupt loss of interest and rejection of her when he remarried.) That one cannot force another person to love or stay with one is a painful reality that one must eventually assimilate. Karen was indignant one summer to find that I was away for a month when she felt she needed me. Thereafter we undertook a period of prolonged clarification of the differences between her image of me as "always there" and my real existence as a separate person with a life of my own, interested in her well-being but not always available. Simultaneously, we reviewed a list of reliable family members, friends, and therapists in the city where she now lived in terms of her access to them. With both Eileen and Karen, therapy had ended with the understanding that there were unfinished issues concerning which it was advisable for the young women to seek further therapy.

Renouncing one's wishes, or facing the fact that one will never again have a particular kind of pleasure sound familiarly like the giving up of all infantile wishes (Eileen could not make her friend love her again no matter how much she wished it). However, the implications of the child's renunciation of the quest for the absent parent in the form it was most intensely experienced are quite different. Infantile wishes are renounced at least partially because, once brought to light, they are really not all they were cracked up to be in childhood—at least, not in comparison to what one might now have instead; or their expression was forbidden and consequently led to anxiety over loss of love or pangs of guilt. These are internal reasons for renouncing them. There is no such compelling reason for giving up the pleasures of a lost relationship, other than that it is gone—that external reality does not comply with the wish. However, the compulsion to behave as though love might still be forthcoming from a lost relationship stifles the risk-taking decisions involved in growth.

Eventually, freedom from ways that the individual has seen as prescribed, if he is to love or be loved, is often felt by the bereft person as a great relief, or a freeing of energies. Sometimes the person will speak of being able to make choices himself rather than in order to please the absent person. At the same time, he may speak of his own gains in self-development in terms of a renewed emotional contact with the memory of the absent person: "I think (s)he might have liked the person that I've become."

What happes to the fantasy of the permanence of the beloved, which, as earlier mentioned, has its roots in the fact that the unconscious is unable to picture a "no" or an absence?

I believe such a fantasy may linger in some individuals, in accordance with an accepted duality in reality sense or a comfortable differentiation between psychic and external reality. That is, the individual "knows" that the absent, wanted person is not gone from his life, as surely as he also "knows" that he *is* gone. The paradox may surface in attenuated form, in dreams and reveries, or in isolated but flagrant bits of behavior. A flagrant example: a man in his forties functioned well in most areas of his life. He was not in therapy himself, but had brought his daughter for treatment. When this man's mother had died, he had planted berry bushes on her grave, and each year went to eat berries from her grave. He believed that his child showed traits which he referred to as a "reincarnation" of his mother. When he ate berries from his mother's grave, he felt happy rather than sad; a happy feeling that she was still providing him with food. Lewin (1950) discussed this kind of fantasy of being nurtured.

The majority of children and adults who had been children of parting parents did not need to cling as literally to the notion of an ongoing relationship with the wanted, absent parent. The degree of renunciation or grieving involved in giving up such an image varied enormously, in accordance with the degree of "absence" suffered, the quality of the lost relationship, and the availability, at the right time, of other caring adults. After the child or adult came to terms with the necessary degree of absence or change as well as the permanence of the impact of the past relationship, it was often possible for him to build on the positive components of the affective tone he had treasured in previous intimacy with the wanted person. In this way, memory, fantasy, affect, and remaining love still resided within him, ready to flourish again within his current life. Such an individual's psychic reality allowed for the possibility that the person was gone, but that love, once tied to that person, was not.

The Impact of Personality Organization on Transference, Countertransference, and the Therapy Process*

Not only the common experience of parental parting, but also the individual's personality organization had a major impact on the therapy process. The unfolding of interpersonal reactions and expectations in therapy provided the central opportunity for observing the child's or adult's perception of human relationships and the ego patterns he used to deal with them. In turn, the nature of this reaction had important bearing on the treatment process. Freud (1920) thought that the psychoses or the "narcissistic neuroses" were inaccessible to psychoanalytically oriented treatment because a transference relationship could not be developed.

Underlying this assumption was the concept that, in the psychotic patient, the relationship to the parent, from which the transference potential was evolved, was insufficiently developed. Others, such as Federn (1952) and Fromm-Reichmann (1939, 1952, 1959), responded to the difference in the type of relationship developed by the psychotic patient in therapy by modifications of technique that took that difference in object relationship into account.

Therapy proceeds not only through transference/countertransference, but also through the real relationship that emerges between people who have lived through affectively laden experience with one another. Although differences in transference and countertransference reactions and their relationship to character are beyond the scope or topic of this book, I do want to discuss very

*Some of the discussion to follow was presented in greater detail in Tessman and Kaufman, 1963. My thanks to Irving Kaufman for his collaboration in that paper.

briefly some of the differences in the therapy process that are determined by differences in personality organization in the child. Different modalities of interaction are appropriate with children who would ordinarily be described in standard diagnostic evaluation as suffering from either a (a) neurosis, (b) an impulse-ridden character disorder, or (c) a psychosis. It must be remembered that numbers of children and adults in this book do not belong, diagnostically, in any category of disturbed personality organization, but were either suffering from the reactions to a trauma, with resulting vulnerabilities, or were seeking help in planning their own and their children's well-being in the hope of minimizing the likelihood of later emotional problems. Although a variety of categories exist in the diagnostic nomenclature (e.g., adjustment reaction of childhood, etc.), I shall refer to them here as children or adults in reactive distress. Most frequently the distress was evident in either masked or open signs of depression, in reaction to the trauma of loss which rendered the child helpless in his wish to alter it. Among the depressed, more of the younger children showed the intensified clinging, partial regression, and wish for sustaining contact which character-izes anaclitic depressions; more of the adolescent depressions were of the introjective type, in which harsh self-judgments replicated identification with a devalued object. Characteristically this devaluation coexisted with an idealization of the absent parent. One dynamic component however, differentiated these cases from those more usually described in comparisons of anaclitic as opposed to introjective depressions (Blatt, 1974). The devalued attributes of the absent parent often did not derive from the internal relations between the child and that parent. Instead they evolved from the complicated partial identification also with the remaining parent, and the internalization of that parent's devaluation of the absent one—and were then compounded by the child's own anger about the loss. Frequently the devaluation could not be resolved in the usual course of therapeutic alleviation of depressive self-criticism, until either such devaluation was no longer necessary to maintain the love of the remaining parent, or until a rejection of, and independence from that remaining parent began. During this period, of course, this involved other disruptions in the integration of identifications.

The children and adults whose distress was manifested by a masked or open depressive reaction varied widely in the transience of the distress, and in their overall personality organization.

I mention this in particular because, for example, anti-social behavior, masking depression in a child of parting parents may have quite different diagnostic significance than usual. For purposes of discussion here, those children who suffered only from reactive distress, without signs of other disturbance in their personality organization, are grouped with neurotic children in terms of applicable treatment modalities, which would be inappropriate with the more severely disturbed. Some of the substantive issues common to the therapy of children of parting parents were discussed in an earlier section. We now consider the impact of the personality organization of the child, on transference, countertransference, and the therapy process. "Transference" denotes that for the child or adult, the relationship with the therapist becomes imbued with the infantile wishes and fear which were once directed toward the parent. Countertransference refers to the therapist's reaction to the transference. Glover (1955) stated, "Allowing for the differences in character, temperament and symptom-type between the analyst and his patient, the counter-resistances of the analyst in any given situation are similar and equal in intensity to the resistance of the patient in that situation." It seems, however, that countertransference may include a wide variety of other reactions.

The child's perception of the transference, and the ego patterns he utilizes to deal with that perception, tend to reflect the process of his particular symptom formation and the strengths and vulnerabilities of his personality organization. Frequently, personal relations and ego patterns, as expressed through the transference, can be further understood by an evaluation of the countertransference. In this sense, the nature of the transference and countertransference provide important diagnostic and prognostic clues.

Neurotic, impulse-ridden, and psychotic children can often be differentiated from each other by the predominant content of the anxiety brought to the transference. This is likely to appear in the form of annihilation anxiety for the psychotic child, anxiety associated with abandonment for the impulse-ridden child with a character disorder, and signal anxiety for the neurotic child. That is, the neurotic child is usually able to utilize anxiety as a barometer of his feelings of endangerment; in this sense, he can use the anxiety rather than being rendered helpless by it. In addition, there are important differences in the ego's way of perceiving and dealing with the transference phenomenon. These include the degree to which projection contributes to the image used; the degree to which the transference view is treated as fantasy or reality—that is, the concreteness of the thought process about it—and the extent to which the child can ally himself with the therapist to look at the transference, identifies with the therapist's attitude toward his impulses, or handles the feelings aroused by the transference by somatization, acting out, or delusion. The ego processes utilized to cope with the transference feelings are sometimes of more prognostic significance than the clinical picture and apparent severity of the disturbance at the beginning of therapy. Factors associated with the tolerance for emotional closeness as opposed to distance, with the delineation of ego boundaries, and with the intactness of identification processes in themselves, appear crucial. Thus, for example, some psychotic children or adolescents recover more fully than expected, when the psychosis has evolved from an identification with one or both psychotic parents, but the child has retained the capacity to utilize identification processes with nonpsychotic individuals as well. Conversely, when mild clinical symptomatology and psychological test data suggest a "neurotic" personality organization, indications in the transference of rapid loss of ego boundaries, e.g., of fantasies of being identical to the therapist, linked with the notion that only one of the two—patient or therapist—can survive, should alert the therapist to the possibility that not only concrete aspects of the thought process but also reactions to thought as though it were reality must be taken into consideration during treatment. Examples of such use of transference phenomena, which contrast to the presenting clinical picture, are given elsewhere (Tessman and Kaufman, 1963).

Several issues complicate the use of transference material for clarifying diagnosis and prognosis. First, in intensive psychotherapy the regression a neurotic patient normally undergoes is also expressed in the transference wishes and ways of coping with them. With a neurotic patient, the transference. Expectations of danger associated with taboo wishes are patient's energy may go into his attempt to compel the therapist to behave in accordance with the transference wishes—e.g., to give him some concrete evidence of "love"—or to become involved in a sado-masochistic struggle with him. Particularly the adolescent, whose normal needs are to displace his libidinal wishes away from his parents in order to establish new love objects and identification figures, may imbue the transference with a turbulent intensity and reality which frequently brings up the question of differential diagnosis (i.e., "adolescent turmoil" versus psychosis).

Secondly, in childhood the therapy relationship is only partially based on transference, expectations of danger associated with taboo wishes are expressed or defended against, and the child normally makes the attempt to manipulate the therapist in accordance with the particular content of the transference. However, as he has not yet fully internalized adult standards, he is still in reality highly dependent upon adults, and of necessity the therapist is perceived as an additional adult representative of reality. This is the "educational" role of the therapist Anna Freud (1946) has written about. Some of the more commonly encountered transference and countertransference phenomena that emerge in therapy are described below, differentiating between experience with children who are either neurotic or normal, but reactively distressed, children who are impulse ridden, and psychotic children.

THE NEUROTIC CHILD OR CHILD IN REACTIVE DISTRESS

Characteristically, in more or less disguised ways, the neurotic child or child in reactive distress is able to verbalize, play out, or draw his perception of the therapist-patient relationship. He experiences the impulse to express wishes he considers taboo, and will attempt to make the therapist behave in accordance with these wishes. He may express anxiety about the punishments that he fantasies will be a consequence of the forbidden wishes consciously, through dreams, or through symptom formation.

The normal or neurotic child can be helped to perceive the discrepancy between the transference image and the actual behavior of the therapist, and can make use of this awareness in his attempts to gain mastery over his conflicts. For example, the child may try to provoke the therapist into acting like a punishing superego or parent figure, and thereby attempt to alleviate his guilt feelings rather than deal with them. When the therapist refuses to be put into such a role, he can point out the pattern to the child, and ask why he might need to do this. Clarification of transference patterns frequently brings up associated memories of similar patterns with family members, making this material available for working through. The therapist can ally himself early in treatment with the ego of the child who is reactively distressed or neurotic rather than impulse-ridden or psychotic, observing and making therapeutic use of transference reactions. Both the impulse the child considers taboo, and his method of coping with it, can come under fruitful scrutiny. Ego patterns utilized to deal with the transference may often be approached early in therapy, before the child can easily tolerate dealing with the awareness that he has wishes which he considers taboo.

When a positive transference is expressed through the wish to identify with the therapist, the reactively distressed or the neurotic child is apt to identify with the therapist's attitudes toward his impulses and ways of treating people. This way of identifying, which is consistent with an advanced stage of ego development, is in contrast to that of the schizophrenic child, who would be apt to echo the posture, mannerisms, and actions of the therapist in a concrete, literal way, or the impulse-ridden, or "borderline" child, who would attempt to emulate the omnipotence which he fantasies his therapist has. Again, an exception to this occurs with the adolescent, whose search for identification figures other than parents may make his imitations of the therapist more concrete. Adolescent's postures or mannerisms are often a perceptive, unconscious caricature of the posture or mannerisms of an adult important to them.

will vary with the personality of the therapist and the particular neurosis and defense pattern of the child. The child's capacity to make a meaningful relationship and to use play and fantasy material imaginatively is usually gratifying to the therapist. The therapist may risk becoming so intrigued by the imaginative play that he loses sight of the need also to utilize the material for ego building. Such ego building can occur when the therapist supports the child's interest in genuine sublimations and potentially gratifying realities, rather than interpreting their underlying libidinal significance.

Negative countertransference feelings are often related to some defense pattern in the child. For example, the child with a learning problem may successfully frustrate all the therapist's efforts by a controlling defensiveness that is expressed in a willingness only to play checkers or build model airplanes, rather than bringing up meaningful material; the phobic child may become phobic of the therapist. The therapist may be irked by a particular personality characteristic of the child, e.g., feminine mannerisms in a boy, or a cloying sweetness veneering aggression. In such a case, he must ask himself why this characteristic bothers him personally or threatens him, before he can evaluate its meaning in the transference. However, countertransference rarely ends treatment with the neurotic child.

With neurotic children, a rapid "transference cure" based primarily on a positive relationship to the therapist and manifested by the disappearance of the symptoms occurs relatively often. In such a case, it is particularly important to evaluate whether without further work the child is apt to cling to his present level of adjustment, or whether he has gained enough inner freedom to be able to grow optimally at future developmental levels.

THE IMPULSE-RIDDEN CHILD

Although there is no classical transference neurosis with the child who has an impulse-ridden character disorder, certain patterns of reaction to the therapist tend to emerge.

The child is not at first able to use an observing ego to deal with the transference, but reacts to the therapist as though he actually were the parent who promises to fulfill his needs, but then is apt to disappoint and desert him. In line with his level of ego development, his view of the therapist is dominated by opposites—omnipotence versus weakness or helplessness—and he makes more use of acting out than of fantasy and verbalization to cope with the transference development. Anxiety about his wishes for restitution of a deserting or depriving parent figure and his fear of abandonment frequently leads the impulse-ridden child to act out by breaking appointments, stealing when feeling deprived by the therapist, being unresponsive during interviews, or avoiding involvement with the therapist in other ways. Frequently, his concept of human relations, which revolves around hurting or being hurt, is made clear in his transference reactions. In initial interviews, the child may be wary, sullen, or openly hostile, making clear that he has little reason to trust anyone. Or he may instead reveal his dependency in the transference immediately, often with considerable urgency. Pam and Lou Ann (chapter 5) exemplify children with such initially contrasting defense organizations. It often takes a long time to get through the initially hostile relationship, which then usually turns into a dependent one. The perceptions of the therapist are complex. Often these children at first react as though the therapist were a representative of the authority and hostility they anticipate from their environment. As treatment progresses, they allow the therapist to see that they also are looking for someone to meet their dependency needs. When the child brings his conflicting needs of deep dependency and overt hostility into treatment, he may create a negative interaction. The therapist is cast in the role of the depriving parent who has withheld the necessary supplies.

Repeatedly, the core issue revealed by the child's pattern of interaction with his therapist tends to revolve around separation, desertion, and abandonment, usually handled at first by some equivalent of running away, and hence rejection of the therapist.

The ego mechanisms of projection, denial, identification with the aggressor, and acting out are all used to cope with the transference feelings which cannot be tolerated by the child as a feeling or a fantasy. Dyadic relations are of primary importance, although the child may create "triangles" to deal with frustration in relation to the primary attachment figure. For example, the child who cannot tolerate feeling deprived by the mother quickly proves he can get gratification from someone else. Such motivation frequently propels young adolescent girls into sexual activity before they are emotionally ready for this. This level of functioning is not as deeply regressed as the schizophrenic child's, or as advanced as the conflicts about triadic relationships and the stage of ego development of the child whose disturbance is at the neurotic level.

When the impulse-ridden child begins to identify with his therapist, he attempts to partake of the omnipotence he has projected onto the therapist. This stems from the stage of ego development when the child wants to be part of the parent whom he considers omnipotent. It may result in some complications when acted out by the adolescent. For example, Eddy (chapter 7) repeatedly had courted danger to prove to himself that he was immune to it. A lack of judgment can turn courting danger into tragedy.

Such children stimulate a complicated reaction in the therapist. The child's impulsiveness may be either a threat to the therapist's controls or may give him vicarious gratification, leading to overpunitive or overpermissive reactions. At first there often is a fantasy of rescuing the child whose deprivation and needs are apparent. This early enthusiasm is frequently followed by disenchantment, a feeling of hopelessness, and frustration, with the child, who is viewed as unmotivated, hopeless, and untreatable. The therapist may react to the underlying depression of these children by a depressive reaction, and may react to their hostility with counterhostility. The therapist picks up these feelings and reacts as though he were rejected, as though the best he has to offer is not valued or appreciated. If the therapist can overcome his own negative reaction to this type of patient, he can often establish a relationship by giving the child the ego support of authority and structure to control the impulsiveness. The therapist initially relates by dealing with tangible, concrete issues, including clarifying consequences of actions, rather than making interpretations of feelings as with the neurotic child. The child can then often begin to accept that a pattern can be seen in his behavior—e.g., feeling compelled to break a rule as soon as he becomes aware of wanting to depend on someone; or feeling compelled to steal whenever he feels disappointed by a parent figure. In working with these children, the therapist, along with a social support network, has to supply the missing parenting through a restitutive experience. Ideally, this should result in a period of ego building which will give the child the emotional capacity to deal with his past losses and rejection, and diminish the fear of involvement; this is necessary before the impulse-ridden child can reach the point of sufficient trust to tolerate the implications of a transference relationship.

THE PSYCHOTIC CHILD

The psychotic child does not establish a "transference neurosis," but instead interacts with his therapist with an intense wish for closeness but a simultaneous fear that the closeness will lead to engulfment or destruction. The core anxiety which emerges is annihilation anxiety. The therapist may become for the psychotic child the embodiment of his symbolic thinking and may be reacted to as though he were the projected impulse rather than a person.

The therapist takes an active role in interpreting reality, demonstrating that it does not have to be destructive, by refusing to participate in the patient's distortion but presenting another, more positive alternative to the psychotic fears. In this way, he becomes a meaningful figure in the child's world. This is especially indicated when a child's behavior is self-destructive. The psychotic fears are accepted as fantasies which have important meanings, but will not come true.

Angela, for example, was convinced she would die at the age she came to therapy, fourteen. She heard voices telling her to do the opposite of what she wanted. This meant, to her, controlling the "evil" in her right arm, which might want to kill someone, by immobilizing it and burning it with an iron, while meanwhile feeding lotions to her "good" left arm (which stood for her "left" father as well as symbolizing one side of her impulse life). Whenever something bad happened—for instance, a house burning down blocks away—she knew it was her fault. She felt her arm had powers "worse than the whole human race." Although I did not initially dispute her "voices" I took an active role with Angela, commanding her authoritatively to be good to both her arms for the coming week, stating that we would have to find ways to help her control herself without hurting herself. She was able to comply with this enough to explore what her arms meant to her in the following sessions. The equation of the "left arm" with the "left father" emerged, together with the terror that the other arm either would or already had destroyed the "left one." She had not seen her "left father" since age five. However, before she gave up hearing voices, the voices changed character for some weeks. Instead of harsh, punitive voices, a voice now sometimes lovingly called her name when she felt all alone or unsure of existing. Such a shift in the voices mirrored the initial attempt in therapy to begin substituting a more benign voice of authority than the harsh and self-destructive one she had needed. As Angela had many personality strengths, her initial state of terror was responsive to a variety of interventions.

The therapeutic relationship to the child with a psychosis will at first be influenced by the form and severity of disturbance. If one perceives relationships as a particularly sore and sensitive area for the psychotic child, then the degree to which the child actively excludes the therapist is a useful barometer of anxiety. It sometimes takes a while to become aware of the underlying fear of closeness and the defenses erected as a barrier to it. The first signs may be apparent in the transference when the child, after an initial period of progress, suddenly becomes preoccupied and bizarre, in this way shutting out the relationship to the therapist. His response usually involves fears of destroying or being destroyed. In coping with this image of the self and therapist, the child tests out whether the therapist treats the impulse as reality.

The ego mechanisms which become manifest in the transference are regressive and restitutive patterns utilizing primary-process mechanisms, including massive withdrawal and delusional attitudes toward the transference. Primary-process ideation may be shown by the child's inability to distinguish the word from the thing itself. Symbol is treated as reality.

The psychotic child creates the widest range of countertransference patterns. These include the pleasure of watching a person emerge out of chaos; gratification at being able to understand the child's cryptic, symbolic communication; a sense of being actively excluded; a wish to nurture the child, who can accept it only slowly; fear, curiosity, or sometimes repulsion at the child's bizarre behavior; and a fear of being engulfed by the child's intense needs. Therapists often complain that they feel drained by psychotic children. Severely psychotic children's direct expression of primitive or infantile impulses and fantasies, e.g., smearing feces, screaming in terror, attacking the therapist bodily, or accusing him of biting them, etc., may stimulate regressive wishes and fears in the therapist. Unless a therapist has a certain degree of tolerance for undisguised impulse expression, some interest in symbolic communication, and a readiness to engage in decisive, protective action when called for, he is apt to be more comfortable treating children who are not severely psychotic. Changes in the interaction between therapist and psychotic children during progressive stages of treatment are described elsewhere (Tessman and Kaufman, 1967). However, once the child has made emotional contact with the therapist and feels at least partially understood, the therapist usually has enormous importance in his life, reviving the wish to overcome his isolation and withdrawal.

It behooves the therapist to remain attuned to the quality of defenses against anxiety manifested by the child, as well as to the congruence between the child's awareness of his need and the likelihood of his being emotionally supported by those in his environment. The intensity of the anxiety is not, however, a measure of its threat to the optimal functioning of the personality. For example, intense anxiety was often manifested and tolerated by young children in transient reactive distress, who in play therapy are quickly able to articulate and work through their concerns, allowing for a resumption of inner growth through restitution of relationships and identification figures.

As transference deepens, changes in the quality of expressed wishes and accompanying defenses are usual. However, regressive changes in ego modes utilized to cope with transference feelings (e.g., delusional, somatic, etc.) require changes in therapeutic modality, with a flexible use of active, restitutive support from the therapist.

Wishes brought to consciousness which are either overwhelmingly threatening or unfulfillable must eventually be renounced. It is most feasible to attempt this in psychotherapy when, for the duration, ways of channeling the attendant energy are on the horizon. For the child who has lost a parent the wish for reunion is not fulfillable in the way the child has pictured it. The therapist, then, must be prepared to absorb the combination of longing, fury, and sadness that attends this discovery on the part of the child, and then attempt to facilitate a supportive human relationships network within which he may continue his growth. In many children the memory of longing for an absent one was left behind, and yet remained. Linda, who had insisted on sleeping in her father's bed for a whole year after he had left her home when she was a child, wrote in her twenties:

> "My past is light years away
> but
> still a small sorrowful self
> is part of me forever"

Chapter 11

TOWARD A CONCLUSION

The main
thing in life
is
not to be afraid
to be human

—Pablo Casals

In formulating some tentative conclusions from the clinical material, I shall return to questions raised during the opening chapters of this book.

Identifications and the Quest

1. *What factors or patterns appear to be debilitating rather than enriching to the growth of the child of the divorced or deceased?*
The following conditions appear to be debilitating influences on the child:
   a. If he is neglected during the period prior to, during, and after the loss, i.e., if the loss of one parent is compounded by the loss of sustained caring by the remaining parent and other significant adults.
   b. If he is not allowed grief or longing for the absent parent.
   c. If he is unable to alter the distress of the home parent while aspiring to do so; if he sees himself as more of a burden than a joy.
   d. If he is identified with the absent parent by the home parent or by the

human relationship network, while that absent parent is devalued.

e. If he is used as a mediating weapon between the parents.

f. If he has no additional parent figure available when he is ready for it. The additional parent figure need not be a love partner of the home parent, or a step-parent, but must be an involved and caring other adult in the life of the child. The data are not clear if it is important that this person be of the same sex as the absent parent, so that the child has continued experience with adults of both sexes. However, both the verbalizations and symptoms of the younger children and the acting-out patterns of the adolescents who do not have such a figure available suggest that the sex is important.

g. If he has inadequate opportunities for reality testing about the absent parent. Such reality testing must include both the positive and the negative features of the real parent as the child experienced them and the child's own positive and negative feelings about this experience. Reality testing of the necessary degree of loss or change in the relationship, and progressive clarification of the real causes of the loss, are also crucial.

Enriching identifications seem to occur most easily when the following conditions are available to the child:

a. If he is supported in grief work in such a way that defensive identifications utilized to prevent loss can give way to more selective and less defensive identifications that capitalize on the positive qualities which have been experienced with the absent parent instead of focusing primarily on either the negative or the "suffering" aspects of that parent.

b. If he has continued access to the absent parent for reality testing, as well as a continued real, though altered, relationship. Such access is most desirable when planned around the needs of the child rather than primarily the parent. For example, when parted parents live far from each other, occasional visits usually meet the child's need better than "equal" time with each parent, which disrupts all other important continuities in the child's home life and human interaction network. If the divorced parents' proximity exposes the child to their continued bitterness toward each other, the child usually fares better if the parents live far apart, even though this may deprive him of frequency of visits with the absent parent. In a small minority of cases, in which it can be predicted that the current personality features or social situation of the absent parent will make contact highly traumatic for the child, access during the developmental years if counterindicated. When a parent has died, of course, access is not possible, but it is important that the child continue reality testing regarding the dead parent, through information and the sharing of memories, both positive and negative, with the home parent.

c. If he is allowed to validate the positive aspects of his quest for the absent parent, eventually to risk giving up the magical components of the remainder of the quest, or to convert the fervor for the quest into other rewarding aspects of life.

d. If he has other identification figures, preferably of the same sex as the absent parent. In order to constitute a significant identification figure the person must stay long enough and care about the child enough to make a difference. It is particularly helpful to the child of divorce if this person can also demonstrate a cooperative relationship to the home parent, so that the child sees that there can be pleasure between a man and a woman, and if the person happens to differ in those personal characteristics that contributed to the problems between the parents.

e. If he remains a member of valued groups during the period of distress. Extended family, such as grandparents or uncles and aunts as well as nursery school, babysitters, friendship groups, activity, church, or temple groups, may all, depending on the quality of their relationship to the child, be part of the necessary network of human support.

2. *What identifications became alien to the child's conscious concept of the self and yet made their appearance in distorted form (symptoms or negative identity)? How did they get pushed into this role within the child's inner reality?*

In all cases seen, ego-alien forms of identification had in common with ego-syntonic identifications at least a partial underpinning, in the form of a wish for a continued sense of emotional contact or closeness with the absent parent. In young children, disguised symptoms very commonly represented an aspect of the absent parent which they perceived as being disliked by the home parent, but felt compelled to perpetuate in a provocative form. For example, Mark's boisterousness, a quality he and father prized about each other, became partially converted into provocative "boom-booms," in the form of feces, presented to the mother where he was sure they would disturb her.

A second form of ego-alien identification occurred in the context of punishment for taboo wishes that might alienate the absent parent or that made the child feel disloyal to him. Sean's expressed wish to be blind constituted such an identification with a father who had cried because he did not want "to see" mother with a new love partner. In a similar vein, both Noah and Craig acted out being ejected from the house, just as their absent father had been.

A third form of ego-alien, negative identification occurred during adolescence, when unresolved identity issues more frequently came to the fore. The adolescent frequently perceived the combination of parental fears of or preoccupation with his "turning out" like the absent parent with his own fantasies about what that parent may have been like. In particular, untested fantasies about that parent having been sexually fickle, a prostitute, deserting, "delinquent" or irresponsible in some other way, violent, or psychotic lent themselves to such identifications. When acted out by the adolescent they could have serious consequences for his future life, making it especially important that they be recognized and linked, with the adolescent, to their origin and function in his or her current development. Pam, for instance, exemplifies a prostitute fantasy about her biologic mother; as it turned out, this did not happen to be true.

For children of the deceased, identification with the illness, suffering, dysphoria or deadness of the lost parent tended both to have libidinous meanings and to serve as a defense against the guilt about having survived.

3. We raised a number of questions regarding the interplay of identifications and the quest for the absent parent: *Does the image of the wanted person as present in the external world fade, as identification with aspects of that person takes place? When does an active quest for the wanted person coexist, if it does, with an identification which preserves components of the real relationship, or is utilized as a defense against loss? And, eventually, where does the image of the absent, wanted person go?*

To begin with the ending: the clinical material suggests that the image of the absent, wanted person does not disappear within the psychic reality of the individual. Affectively colored aspects of the image remain available in dream, fantasy life, and memories. Derivatives of the image, when the individual was once intensely involved with it, may continue to enhance the individual's reality sense, his identity, his choice and motivation in love and in work.

We have previously asked whether a final renunciation of loved persons occurs even in the adult, or whether the lost, wanted person is still eternally sought in disguised forms. It seems that the ego ideal in particular is tied either to unconscious percepts of once treasured moments of intimacy with a wanted person, or to defenses against frightening moments of distress within such intimacy. This affective component of the ego ideal appears to seek its reality counterpart in lasting images of the external world and in new relationships. It may contribute to quite divergent expressions—for example, emerging as an ebullient force, an elan de vie, or as a drive toward creative construction in thought or deed—or make its appearance in a fatalistic conviction about eventual disappointment or despair.

In some cases transformations in the ego ideal occurred in tandem with the achievement of a developmentally higher level of ego mechanisms utilized for identification with the absent person. In such cases the treasured ambience of the ego ideal remained, but the degree of perfection or omnipotence aspired to was relaxed. For example, Noah (chapter 5) often functioned as a leader with family members, as well as others, a role which was congruent with both father's and mother's wishes toward him since his early childhood. As he allowed himself slowly to shed the sense of almost total responsibility for, and identification with father, evolving a selectively positive identification with him instead, he also struggled to shed his ego ideal of the wished-for omnipotence and the demand for exclusive allegiance which had been troublesome for him in the past. At age thirteen, he was talking about views of God, rejecting both omniscience and possessiveness:

Noah: "Actually I think everybody would have their own personal god, just like having their own personality. Probably the reason people believe in God is to make them feel better, like if something went wrong, that he'd help you. But the God in the Bible I don't believe in that . . . the God in the Bible is very *conceited*—about 'I have spoken and that makes it so' and that stuff about 'you shall have no other gods before me'—that's really not right, because people

t: "And you seem to be letting yourself do that now too, when you admire something Steve does or even a stranger without feeling like you're letting your father down. You mention God in people's minds as helping, do you ever picture a god getting mad?" (He had told me earlier of an angry episode between him and stepfather that week, after which they had made up.)

Noah: "I wouldn't want one who gets mad, my god wouldn't get angry. If I did something really bad though he would help me not do it anymore."

t: "Is that kind of god connected with any person in your mind?"

Noah (laughs): "I guess I really said what I would like someone to be, how I would like to be myself."

This, then is part of his current ego ideal. He next jokes about his old heroes out of *Mad Magazine*. His humor too is part of his valued self, but the "mad" or angry feelings, e.g., in episodes between him and his stepfather Steve, are banished from his image of God, and trouble him still.

At times, a sense of hopelessness about the individual's approximation to his ego ideal indicated that components of the ideal were invested in a relationship which was permanently gone and not at first remembered as such. It was, for example, encountered in those depressed individuals who repeatedly expressed the conviction that nothing could help—a statement that could mean that the lost, wanted person could not be found to help them feel as they wished.

For each individual, one must ask to what degree preoccupation with the quest is paid for in inhibitions about investing fully in new and potentially satisfying relationships. The clinical material suggests that the quest and these identifications do exist side by side.

A review of the case material indicates that constriction of further growth is most clearly associated with situations in which the quest emerged predominantly as a defense against loss, unbolstered by sufficiently positive realities in the previous relationship and by an adequate human support network at the time of loss. Such quests may function as a repudiation of a distressing reality (e.g., Mary Ann, deal with overwhelming guilt (e.g., Michael), or defend against a devalued identification (e.g., Pam, Heather, Linda). When, in contrast, the quest emerges primarily as a validation of the positive features of the relationship that the child has previously experienced, and has in part warded off the painful aspects of unrestrained grieving, personality development can continue to reap its benefits. The case of Wendy is an example.

When conditions are favorable, both identifications and the images of the wanted person are transformed during the process of grieving or longing so as no longer to preclude an emotional investment in newly wanted persons, or, more simply, the capacity to love again. It seems, however, that when such grieving does not or cannot occur for inner reasons (e.g., immaturity) or external reasons (e.g., lack of support in family members; identification with other modes of dealing with tensions in the family; or active fear of and prohibition of mourning and longing), images of the self and the wanted, absent person may remain "fixed" in the form in which they were experienced at the time of parting. At that time, they were shaped not only by the child's developmental level of wishes and fears, which may imbue them with more or less magical powers to punish or gratify, but also by the trauma of the parting itself and by the associated, often misunderstood or distorted feelings about the causes of the loss.

The Human Interaction Network and the Quest

The quest occurs when the loved one is known in a manner that is contradicted by logical reality. It is an outgrowth of the reality sense, associated with the individual's integrity and identity, standing up to reality testing. Although the quest always involves some degree of denial, it is also based on a particular reality. To varying degrees, in cases seen here, that reality consisted of the affective tone of the relationship with the absent person.

Perceptions that emerge from the quest can be made known to members of the human relationship network. If the reality component of the quest is lifted from the unconscious and this perception can be validated, it is often possible to see and deal with the magical component. I have seen no versions of the quest that grew entirely in the imagination of the quester; instead, it has always represented the assimilation of a fragment of reality into the current libidinal strivings and forms of ideation. Such fragments can begin with a comment made by someone about the absent person, a fact misinterpreted, or with a correct reading of a wish or fantasy in the home parent about the absent one (e.g., in the cases of Jeremy, Emily, Linda, Pam). Such a quest, as a way of being true to the self, of preserving one's integrity by defining oneself partially in terms of those one loves, is evident in adolescents who invent a pseudologic lie out of something they know to be true.

When one considers that reality has different levels, the paradox melts. However, when the wanted parent is absent, the child is forced to rely more heavily on the way in which the surrounding human relationship network perceives the parent. Legal or social definitions of a parent as "unfit," "immoral," or simply at fault in the parting, become integral components of the remembered relationship between the parent and the self, and hence of aspects of the self-image, even though they may be defended against or denied. A person who actually knew the parent, with his positive and negative impact on the child, can be constructively influential in helping the child integrate this aspect of his loss.

For each individual the effect of the human support network on eventual identification patterns and associated self-esteem will vary, depending on his perception of that network and the extent to which those perceptions are related to his most fundamental conflicts.

Let me cite examples of such complex, unpredictable interplay:

1. *Natasha* (chapter 8) had lost her human support network at the same time as she lost her father, at age fourteen. Previously, father had been a government official who was generally viewed as a hero. During wartime, a change in political regime resulted in his being defined as a traitor, dragged off to prison camp and to death. Here is a small incident that throws light on the relationship between self-esteem, identification, and social acceptance. She first described her reactions to feeling accused, an issue which had its roots in criticisms she experienced in early childhood, but which came in ghastly fashion to a head with the fate of her father, and his ideology abandoned by his former social supports. Both she and he were suddenly deviants. In the second, contrasting excerpt from the same session, she again described her sense of worth, this time in the context of a supportive social group. In either situation she is committed to the integrity in her values (the material quoted occurred about a month after the material quoted in chapter 8). Natasha was discussing expectations that were laid down for her in childhood, and which she had not fulfilled:

Natasha: "If you don't fulfill expectations, the trouble is thinking that something is wrong with you instead of the expectations."

t: "Yes, that's been a trouble to you for many years. What did you think about yourself?"

Natasha: "In the past, you know that I've always had a low opinion of myself . . . because I just hadn't fulfilled expectations. I am always afraid that someone will get a completely wrong picture of me."

t: "Like?"

Natasha: "Like Ivan's boss last year, when I knew that Ivan was telling lies about me . . . during the time when he was so suicidal himself. But his boss believed them and had a completely wrong picture of me, and I had no opportunity to set them right. I was afraid if he believed all that Ivan said, Ivan might really get me committed to a mental hospital. I remember being disillusioned . . . because first my illusion had been that a head of a department would know when somebody is lying."

t: "This business about lies . . . that would be believed by others and lead to your downfall, with you helpless . . . has come up time and again. It must have some special meaning to you . . . You act like you are convinced it is something which has already *happened* in some way."

Natasha: "Yes, my father was *wrongly accused* . . . no matter what he said or any of us said he wouldn't have been believed . . . it was official policy that now they (father and others in his position) were traitors . . . so he was completely helpless to change anything and so was I."

t: "But you knew from your own experience that his 'traitorship' involved some 'lie' somewhere."

Natasha: "Yes, the irony of it all was that before that his whole ideology about the factories he owned was dedicated to bringing profits back to the consumers; he had their interests at heart, I knew that from how he treated people. Then when ——— took over, they changed the system and he agreed to things he didn't believe in; and that was when he was imprisoned . . . and he felt that he could not leave his responsibility there, while the owners of the other factories around all fled; part of why I was so mad at him is that he would not flee, while others did—he might still be alive now."

Later in the hour, she was talking about a weekend she had shared with a church social group whose values she expected would be different from her own very individual beliefs. She felt that she could ignore the differences without rejection. To her surprise, she found that she shared a philosophic viewpoint with members of this group. She described this as a "wonderful experience":

Natasha: "That I do not stand alone and outside . . . I am tied in and supported . . . by a structure that I thought would not support me. A community type of feeling that is necessary for me to have."

t: "To be supported like that—feels like . . ."

Natasha: "That I am in tune . . . that I can accept things I consider valuable and am accepted and acceptable; it increases my feelings of my own value to find myself in tune with things I admire. I know I can never do that now without taking some risks too . . . the risk of being rejected . . . and that's a risk I might not have taken a while ago. I was too threatened to even think of that idea, instead I made escape plans . . . not to be alive if I had to live forever with an alien dogma."

Thus she experienced some restitution for her earlier trauma. Like her father she could not live with a dogma alien to her beliefs. *Unlike* him she could bring a view into a divergent social group and feel supported rather than dead.

2. Excerpts from *Noah's* material allow a glimpse of the role of two different kinds of human interaction networks in his life: his view of the extended family of grandparents, and of religious or cultural heritage. Both have bearing on the way he attempted to synthesize his current identity. The degree to which people are alike, the same, or different were central conflicts during his therapy, in his attempts to maintain different varieties of closeness to his two parent figures. After a period of overidentification, particularly

with his father's suffering, he was able to maintain a positive, sharing tie with him in reality, but to disengage himself from the idea of having to be identical. In his vision of the human support network, permission for individuality or deviance without extrusion was important.

Noah's Jewish identity was a strongly affective link, not only with father and mother (more with father) but also with the two sets of grandparents with whom he had shared many holidays. As the oldest grandson of his paternal grandparents, he had had a special place in their pride and affection. After his parents' divorce, he was for a time much distressed at the animosity between his mother and paternal grandparents, and in the two sets of grandparents' relationship to each other. He then made a relationship to his stepfather's Christian parents, to find he liked them too, and shared different things with them (e.g., love of pets). He developed a persistent wish that all three sets of grandparents (minus maternal grandfather, who died) make peace with each other at the time of his bar mitzvah. At the same time, the new grandparents were seen in a special, but different light. "My new grandparents . . . they are not like grandparents to me . . . they are just like people, just like my friends. It's the same with all of Steve's relatives. Sometimes, Steve's sister-in-law will say, 'Where's your father?' when she means Steve, and I just say to her 'He's Steve, to me, not my father, but it's really just as good that way.' I have to keep reminding people about that." He added that his concept of being different in religion did not preclude support: "I sure wouldn't want Steve to change his religion just for us . . . to be like us . . . because I wouldn't want to do that either if I didn't believe in it. I don't think it's important to feel the same as each other about that, there are other things we can share."

Noah's identification of Steve's family as being "like friends" is significant because his friends constituted a sustaining network for him during times when he was grieved about parental dissent. For example, during a brief period of acute depression when he could not manage the change to junior high school, full of unfamiliar faces, a quick shift of assignment to a classroom containing some of his old friends made it possible for him to return to school. However, consistently with his age, it was the group of peers from whose standards he could not stray too far. At age ten, like many ten-year-olds, he managed not to let them see that he wanted to cry. At age twelve and a half, he stated, "I got all A's except one B—in shop—I'd be really embarrassed in front of the other kids if I got all A's!" At the same time, he was able, at this age, to help other children with their feelings about parental divorce, saying that he could do this because he remembered how it felt to him—especially the urgent need to blame somebody—and how that had changed. Noah's home and friendship became a steadying refuge for friends whose parents were divorcing.

Noah and Natasha, though they, their conflicts, and their human support networks were very different, both experienced self-esteem in the context of a sense of affective contact expressed through identification with similarities in the surrounding human network that did not oblige them to forego deviance or individuality.

3. A woman in her early fifties spent two years dealing with the emotional aftermath of twenty-five years of marriage, which had culminated in a bitter, litiginous divorce. During that tumultuous two years, she found some comfort in past friendships, but needed most of her emotional energy to deal with her depression, with continued barbs from her husband, with a job, and with constructive, emotional availability to her growing children. She availed herself of various support and "singles" groups, finding some of them demoralizing, but meeting people she liked in others. With a man she met in such a group, she discovered, for the first time in her life, that she needed and was capable of responsive sexuality. He was, however, not permanent in her life. Her pleasure in such intimacy became a part of her new image of herself, leading her to a conflict previously not experienced. As she said, "I know that the feelings for sex are a part of me now, and I'm not willing to do without them any more . . . I might have never known that if I'd stayed married to Harry." In line with this, she made a painful decision to forego a companionable, platonic relationship with another man who was not interested in her sexually, risking a sense of aloneness that would have frightened her earlier in life. The outcome is not yet clear. However, the kind of human support network she needed and found worthwhile clearly differed at different phases of her life after her divorce.

4. When a child or adult needs to grieve, the human support network can, symbolically, function like a human hammock, cradling the person to make grief bearable. Such cradling is akin to Winnicott's (1970) concept of the "holding" environment. Three-year-old Peter (chapter 1) exemplified the need for this. Each time he recognized that the woman he ran toward was not his absent mother, he ran sobbing into the arms of his father. Lucy (chapter 6) was able to convert her night groaning after her mother became able to express tenderness and hold her. She heralded this development by needing to be given a cuddly toy from the therapy room, to take home to hold at night. Furman (1974) describes two children under the age of two, whose parent had died. For them, too, sobbing spells which disrupted their sleep changed to weeping while awake (with undisturbed nights) once the babies allowed the remaining parent to hold and console them. Numbers of adults during grief work became conscious of a wish to be held, or symbolically supplied this themselves. For example, Natasha hugged herself as she pictured a forgiving embrace with her dead father. Such real or symbolic holding, in the form of some expression of caring, may be needed from the parent, substitute parent, teacher, therapist, or other person especially "chosen" by the individual to share his grief. If that person is actually the parent he, in turn, must have the support to be able to

carry this through. This has been discussed earlier. When such support has been unavailable and grieving has been deflected, delayed, or distorted in symptoms, therapy may be useful.

Contingencies in the Human Support Network

The human support network is not useful unless it is there in the eyes of the beholder; this occurs only when it is mediated by individuals in some way significant to the person. It is not enough that somebody cares; it matters who. Support is effective either when there develops a personal attachment, or the individual values the opinion of those in the network enough that his self-perception is affected. Such value may be attached to groups who are seen as being in authority: courts, schools, teachers, church members, doctors, the neighborhood gossips, etc. This suggests that there are no universal prescriptions for the choice of human support networks. What is supportive for one person may not be for another; the needs of the children of divorce may differ from those of the bereaved; the needs of the individual may change drastically over a period of time.

In a minority of cases the nature of the individual makes it particularly difficult for him to experience the human support network; the difficulty may be transient or more intractable. For example, transient difficulty is felt by the child who feels that accepting a positive opinion of one parent is a form of disloyalty to the other; by the person in grief who is not ready for renewed sociability; by the person who cannot accept a substitute parent or love relationship yet because this threatens the attachment to the absent parent; by the late latency or young adolescent child who cannot confide in peers without shame and needs to put his best foot forward; or by the man who, caught in personal-cultural attitudes that equate sadness with weakness, cannot confide in colleagues, though he may be able to tolerate grief internally. Solace from new relationships is frequently complicated by the fact that a new, tender relationship inevitably arouses memories and comparisons with the old. For example, several people divorced with "good reason" after long marriages, found years later that new, otherwise satisfactory, sexual and affectionate relationships were initially "spoiled" through the absence of a particular sense of humor felt as uniquely shared with the previous spouse. One such person, who later remarried, by then had built up a pleasurable habit of different witty repartees with the new spouse, also felt to be unique to their relationship.

More enduring difficulties in making use of appropriate and adequate support are experienced by individuals with a paranoid or schizoid character structure or by persons usually described as having a narcissistic character disorder. However, individuals in the latter group often are greatly dependent on the human interaction network. A severe fall in self-esteem results from withdrawal of respect or admiration by others. Frequently, the model of human relations is such that people are readily divided into "friends" and "foes." Often there are "secret" tests for the person from whom support is sought, and if he does not pass them in the exact manner prescribed by the individual to prove he is cared about, then he is not "for" him, and must be against him.

A compulsive need to drop this person as a potential ally ensues; he is, basically, never forgiven. The tendency to seek out the powerful, measuring them in terms of what they can do for one, results in the rejection of many interactions which would be acceptable to other people. An enormous fear that they will be exposed as potentially weak or vulnerable makes it difficult for such people to seek out supportive networks. Similarly, chronic experience with loss may lead to defenses integrated into a character structure which inhibits the use of support.

Following loss, an increased need for human support coincides, in individuals with the kinds of character structure enumerated above, with defenses against an intimacy which has been experienced as destructive to the self, in one way or another. Closeness which too rapidly stimulates dependence or libidinal strivings is apt to undermine the defense structure, leading to increased personal disturbance. Those who wish to be supportive of such individuals must be prepared to respect their need for dignity and their sensitivity to rejection or perceived criticism from others, at the same time maintaining enough leeway in emotional closeness so that the individual does not experience unmanageable anxiety. The implication of these issues for the therapy relationship are beyond the scope of this book.

Comments

The clinical material suggests that a parental parting because of divorce or death creeps into every crevice of a child's life for a time, seen or unseen by himself and others. The quest for the wanted, absent parent and its counterpart in renunciation, grief, and acceptance of change, though often at first disguised, without doubt continues to affect the particular balance that the child may hold between acquaintance with despair and a renewal of growth, vitality, or joy.

What can we say about the role of the human interaction network and about the parent figures available to the child throughout the period of upheaval and loss in particular? Given all the complex realities of his parents' ending their relationship to each other, are there still ways of enhancing the chance for a constructive resolution of the necessary loss? Much of the clinical material in this book attempts to illustrate variations on the theme of coping with loss, with differences in outcome. Some tentative generalizations about factors that may promote favorable outcomes were put forth in chapter 9 and the previous section of this chapter. Many questions remain unanswered, however.

The effect of current social change, for example, is wide open to speculation. In an earlier chapter we found reasons for optimism, especially insofar as the relationships between men and women are concerned. But there are also many signs of strain. One of the most common I see in women in their twenties or early thirties, by now deeply affected by the women's liberation movement, is the terrible pressure of an impossible ideal of liberated womanhood, gliding effortlessly through the roles of professional or "equal" worker, wife, mother, supportive friend to other women, etc. The tyranny of such an ideal especially when social planning and resources to support it are only available to few, can be as harsh as was the earlier tyranny, thirty years ago, of the ideal of the perfect wife and supermother.

There are other disquieting signs of side effects of the changes which took place in the sixties. Hendin (1975) painted a picture of a generation oriented toward instant gratification, fearing the emotional risks of long-lasting and intimate relationships, of genuine feeling and commitment. As he put it, "What distinguishes this generation is its active pursuit of disengagement, detachment, fragmentation, and emotional numbness." Elsewhere he states that joylessness marks most of the lives of the young people he encountered.

Rothchild and Wolf (1976) explored the lives of children in a great variety of communes. They included communal living arrangements sought by the young people of the sixties as a part of a more "liberated" life, political communes, urban and rural communes, as well as the highly structured communal environments of Synanon and the religious commune of the Hare Krishna. Some were still new, labile, and faltering experiments, while others operated on as established a stability and ideology as the kibbutzim. The book is frightening, in two ways: first, one witnesses the translation of widely divergent, but equally dogmatically believed ideologies, into varieties of skewed child-rearing practices. Extremes of either neglect or control are perpetrated in the name of finding freedom or peace.

There are striking contrasts in the descriptions of children whose parents wished to free them from all sexual and social role constraints, but who strike one as having experienced little real interaction with adults. By age nine or ten they are described as listless and apathetic; and as though there is nothing worth involving oneself in. There are poignant descriptions of parents who cannot say "no" to their children because control is against their ideology, and find themselves with distraught, impulse-ridden children with whom they cannot cope and whom they in many ways reject. In contrast, the Hare Krishna children are supervised relentlessly and taught early that they must renounce all impulse and independent thought in order to belong totally to Hare Krishna.

Some more hopeful descriptions are given of certain rural communes in which the children are helpful participants in the community, but with the proviso that intellectuality and the free exchange of feelings are discouraged as probably disruptive to the group purpose. Most of the children described have one thing in common: adaptation to the adults' practices appears so complete as to leave them grossly unprepared to deal with the problems and pleasures of living outside their childhood environment. Thus, paradoxically, though the wish to have freedom of choice in life style may have motivated the parents, the children no longer appear to have such a choice. How they will actually fare as adults remains to be seen. However, the book reminds one rudely to ward off sentimentality, to bear in mind that idealism is not enough.

Other kinds of disturbing reminders continue to underline the tie between culturally shared practices and children's personalities, regardless of whether one attributes the similarity of behavior to imitative learning or identifications. I earlier mentioned Bellak and Antell's (1974) intercultural study of aggressive behavior on children's playgrounds clearly demonstrated the vastly greater incidence of sadism from adult to child, and between children, on German playgrounds, than on Italian or Danish playgrounds. There is no way to avert the conclusion that the child passes onto others what he himself has experienced.

The optimal role of man and woman toward each other and toward their children will remain a complex issue, eternally unsettled and varying widely in accordance with individual needs and proclivities. How the woman's role is perceived within the social network varies widely too, and continues to affect high-level planning, even when the observers are astute individuals looking at identical data. For example, in 1974, Conway and Parsons both scrutinized patterns of women's functioning in academia. Conway asked, "Why has almost a century of access to higher education for women in the United States not apparently had some impact on the general pattern of female employment in industrializing society?" She noted that women's colleges produce twice as many women achievers per thousand women enrolled as do coeducational institutions, and suggested that "in the area of motivation, levels of aspiration, and the achievement of identity as an intellectual worker there may be many negative aspects of admission to predominantly male-oriented institutions of higher education for women students." She traced the historical impetus for coeducation as well as the maintenance of intellectually demeaning role expectations for women in academia, commenting especially on their exclusion from research and intellectual initiative.

Parsons, whose forte has always been his conceptual clarity, spoke within the same collection of studies, of a correlation as though it were causation. Parsons stated that evidence from his studies suggests that the participation of women at faculty levels tends to involve a role pattern which is different from that of men. It is our hunch, which we hope to examine carefully in the near future, that this is not a simple matter of sexism, that is, of discrimination on grounds of sex, but that it may very well turn out to be at least partly a matter of sex-typed differences of preference and inclination. Two contexts illustrate such differences. In the first case, we find that women faculty members are by and large less concerned with commitments to research than their male counterparts of comparable training and appointment status, and correspondingly more concerned with teaching. Second, as between the two primary grades of teaching performed by members of faculties of arts and sciences, women faculty members are more concerned with undergraduate training than with graduate teaching. They tend to assume a kind of "caring" role vis-a-vis their students to a higher degree than their male counterparts.

He opined that "if there is to be a major change in the sex composition of the academic profession, these differences and others comparable to them may in the long run bring about considerable changes. It could turn out that undergraduate teaching would become a particularly feminine prerogative, but we cannot be sure." Thus, the social interaction network was described by Conway as molding women's academic role to a considerable degree, while Parsons sketched its form as a likely outcome of women's nature. Such conflicting views will inevitably be repeated in multiple ways within the family and social milieu of the individual, impinging on self-image as well as opportunity.

Were we as a culture to come to the point of true social options for the individual, however, it is likely that inner conflict between the simultaneous pulls of emotional involvement in infant and child care and other aspects of functioning would continue to exist for many women even under the optimal opportunities for part-time work during child-rearing years. A parent may find that he or she may want to evolve a way to shift from a dispassionate, rationally organized mode required at work to an intuitively responsive mode, sometimes more emotionally focused, sometimes "hanging loose," sometimes mobilizing decisiveness and self-critical modes stimulated by the care of young children which may be necessary to allow oneself fully to enjoy them. Many men and women suffer from conflict between such potentially coexisting cognitive and emotional orientations. Such conflict would be difficult to deny, for example, for any nursing mother who, during the hours of a stimulating, exacting job, allows her mind to wander for a moment to that baby, to find that as a result, embarrassingly, her milk has suddenly flooded through the nursing pads to her blouse. Perhaps not only society, but each individual, might profit from coming to know and tolerate within themselves the range of emotional and intellectual orientations, enjoyable and productive in different situations and relationships. Notman (1964) wisely wrote over a decade ago about the very individual combination of strains and advantages and the necessity for flexible shifts of emotional orientation in combining the roles of wife, mother, and woman psychiatrist. Such an individual adjustment of the conflicting pulls inherent in parents' roles is, of course, conceivable only in the context of a social and economic framework which makes it possible, and which recognizes that, in the long run, men, women, and children would benefit.

Many questions remain unanswered. What is the role of the culture in making possible lasting, caring relationships, with room for both intimacy and autonomy for the individual and for participation in the community of others about whom one cares?

Can agencies be set up specifically geared to the needs of people rendered potentially vulnerable by loss of parent or spouse? Comparison of the children of the deceased and children of the divorced suggests that there are differences in what is needed. The intervention program which Wallerstein and Kelly (1976b) offered to families during early stages of parental separation, prior to the time of final decisions about visitation, custody, etc., appears particularly promising. One hopes that in the long run such services will also be expanded beyond the middle-class population, and will not exclude children who were known to have prior psychological difficulty. Similarly, support groups described by Weiss (1975a,b, 1976) for both the recently bereaved and separated sound extraordinarily helpful. A variety of other resources organized by professionals or entirely by participants (e.g., widow-to-widow groups) are now mushrooming throughout the country, making the need evident.

In contrast, many court-associated services though recently much improved still suffer from such attrition of staff and funds that the urgent issues which emerge in custody suits and often demand intensive care and attention worsen by default or time lag. Social resources at the time they are needed have never been easily available to those who experience losses most chronically—the poor. Among this group, the interaction with social agencies is frequently experienced and sometimes correctly perceived as a demeaning process in which the individuals feel judged or are offered "advice" about their way of life which is not only condescending but also runs counter to the individual's sense of integrity and attachment to his own cultural values.

We have focused on identification processes and their relation to the human interaction network during two periods in the life of the child of the divorced or deceased. One period encompasses all the years of development, but affects the child in concentrated form during early formative years. The second period is before, during, and following the divorce or death of the parent. During the early years of development, the value put on any group of individual characteristics by the human relationship network, first the family and then the increasingly expanded world of other people who have meaning in the child's life—the degree of tolerance for deviance, the degree to which the child has a role which is wanted, needed, or enjoyed rather than seen a burden to others—all of these will be reflected in aspects of the individual's valuation of himself. In men's and women's relationships to each other and to their children, those issues which affected the parents' sense of value, themselves are apt to be repeated. Thus, for example, it turns out that one of the most difficult facets of women's self-devaluation to deal with is not that which is visible in the form of overt discrimination, but the more subtle history of criticism by their own mothers, who were caught in the social value system of their time. And so, the dog keeps barking at his own echo.

During the second period discussed, when the individual is undergoing the loss of a wanted parent, the role of the human relationship network in affecting future identifications is complicated by the individual's need to come to terms with the loss. However, when the child has experienced appropriate support during this time, he appears more able eventually to trust his capacity for loving and for widening his choice of enriching identification again.

Where does this account of the children of parting parents leave us? Although greater resources for help are an obvious first step, caring for the individual in distress over loss can never be made into a routine process. Essentially, the person who has suffered the partial or total loss of a wanted parent is not a patient in the usual sense, who "simply" needs treatment. He is someone who needs a human interaction to revitalize growth that has been discouraged. For example, we might hypothetically postulate that all little girls who grow up fatherless between the ages of three and twelve will first try their unspent passions in relationships which must come to grief unless there is permission in childhood for some kind of attachment to a responsive adult man. We would still be unable to provide a routine, ideal solution. The solution is dependent in part on the fact that the substitute experience must be a *real* relationship, which cannot be easily legislated or funded. However, providing for resources which might maximize opportunities for such relationships to develop are indeed in the realm of social planning. For example, the increased number of men on the staffs of nursery and elementary schools will have an impact on fatherless young children.

Hendin (1975), Rothchild and Wolf (1976), and a host of earlier studies are in consensus about the suggestion that when there is eternal transience in relationships something vital in life is missed. The children of the divorced and the deceased encountered here have not yet, with a few exceptions, sought transience as an avoidance of commitment. But, to be worthwhile means, literally, to be worth someone's while. Children of transience do not feel they are worth anyone's while, and risk suffering all the consequences of this.

Most of the children encountered here made amply clear that having once loved, they were willing to love again if given the chance. That chance can be undermined if loving departs with the beloved; if the necessary grieving, with its associated transformations in image of the self and wanted, absent person, has not been risked; if no substitute relationship is available in time, with enough persistence to overcome the initial mistrust and displaced, negative feelings from the absent parent; or if the relationship to either the first or second such person is forbidden or devalued by the home parent or human interaction network.

Adults have some options about the qualities that are conveyed to the young as important. Amitai (1976) reminds us that teaching must be by example and not exhortation. He described school systems that have adapted Kohlberg's (1971) concepts of morality in the form of including "moral-dilemma" discussions in their teaching. Yet the children responded to the "hidden curriculum," a concept aptly introduced by Snyder (1971) to denote the impact of value discrepancies in a college setting. They knew that the school fostered a model of competitiveness leading to only selected signs of "success," while the discussion tried to negate this.

It is perhaps necessary, and might be a great relief to both men and women, to look toward becoming more of a caring culture. Is the "taboo on tenderness," about which Suthie (1935) wrote many years ago still equally strong, or can we look forward to a time when men and women have fewer qualms in extending themselves to others when they are moved to do so? Has this been a part of the exhilarating work of life omitted from our education, isolated as part of "women's work," or considered too distracting to our need for control over our technologically complicated future? Do we have a real choice except to accept that we cannot control our own or our children's future beyond a point anyway, that new, as yet unimagined variables will sway our ships of state-of-mind? Won't sustained caring strengthen rather than weaken us in dealing with life?

The children of the divorced and the deceased have lost a previously wanted image of caring. The image cannot be duplicated; often, indeed, the loss was necessary or in the best interests of parents or child.

There appears to be no doubt that discontinuity and change in life problems and in the means available for solutions are now constant, perhaps still accelerating. Such constant change may have contributed heavily to various factors promoting inconstancy in relationships among the current generation of children and parents. Some such shifts have clearly grown out of positive forces—the courage to leave a bad marriage, or unwillingness to forego self-development for empty security. Others are the byproduct of constraining anxieties—the fear of deep emotional commitment. It becomes important to separate the flexibilities required by a chaotically transient world from those involved in making, maintaining, and enjoying human relationships. Love, after all, does not make the world go round, just the people within it. We have no indications that the nature of longing, shared laughter or passion, grief or desolation affects individuals more or less strongly than it did a thousand years ago.

Some of the children of parting parents highlight the essence of a paradox. They gained from their losses. Once knowing or feeling what they had lost, they explored what they had wanted. Sometimes cautious, impatient with pretext and wise before their time, they set out to rediscover what could be between people. Their search was most easily marked by confidence or joy when their parent too felt him- or herself to be worthwhile.

Noah (chapter 5) made this prediction: "I think my generation is going to have less divorce; there are so many kids with divorced parents now . . . who know what it's like, that they'll be more careful."

t: "Like how?"

Noah: "Like about both things—that getting married at the time is what they really want—and that that's the very person they will want to be with."

t: "And you think they'll be better at feeling sure?"

Noah: "Yea, maybe because they won't be able to pretend so much. When they decide to get married they'll have to go through thinking, 'How would this relationship end . . . how would I feel?' I mean they can't pretend to themselves that it can't happen, so, knowing that, they might care less about who would be to blame, and care more about how they feel."

Appendix

SOME FAMILIAL CIRCUMSTANCES COMPARED

A numerical description of some familial circumstances for the children of parting parents, discussed in different chapters, follows. As variables affecting the samples were in no way controlled, differences between the age groups of children cannot be generalized to other populations. Some differences do, however, appear consistent with recent changes in life styles, as discussed in chapter 1 and may be consistent with phenomena associated with the different average age of the parents. In the interests of the preservation of privacy, no individual listing of the association between the child's presenting symptomatology, problems, or state of well-being in relation to familial circumstances is included, as such data might make the family more identifiable.

The relevance of the differences in familial circumstances for the child's attempt to deal with parental parting is discussed in a general way in the appropriate chapters. Most noticeably in the younger sample of parents, more mothers were either working or going to school while their children were young, but also often re-establishing stable, new heterosexual relationships fairly rapidly after divorce or separation. In the older generation of parents, mothers had been much less apt to work while the children were young. There was a marked discrepancy between the relatively high rate of remarriages of fathers, while mothers were, so far, frequently without new stable heterosexual relationships. In this sample, mothers were more often the absent parent than for the younger children. Differences in the periods of incapacitation of parenting occur between the two samples but are less than the proportion among those for whom custody disputes were not amenable to mediation prior to jurisdiction by the court.

Because circumstances sometimes differed for two children from the same family, (e.g., one child might live with mother, the other with father) data are listed from the point of view of the child, rather than the family. Data regarding other children not included in the sample, but within the same family, are not tabulated. As these are not research samples with variables controlled through selection or treatment of the population, computation of statistical significance or difference would be misleading and is not included.

Children of Divorce: Some Familial Circumstances

	Children age 1-11 (chapter 5)		Adolescents (chapter 7)	
	No.	%	No.	%
1. Numbers in Sample				
No. of children	24		26	
No. of families	18		20	
2. Living Arrangement				
Child lived with mother following divorce (includes cases with mother absent 4 months or less before divorce)	19	79	15	58
Child lived with father following divorce	5	21	11	42
Home parent shifted within 2 years of divorce; or child spent equal time with each parent	4	17	7	27
3. Maternal Employment				
Mother working full- or part-time; or in training, college, etc.:				
When child under age 5	20	83	5	19
When child under age 10	22	92	7	27
When child adolescent, or starting around period of separation	—	—	16	62

	Children age 1-11 (chapter 5)		Adolescents (chapter 7)	
	No.	%	No.	%
4. No. of children in family				
Child known is only child	8	33	4	15
One of two children	11	46	10	38
Three or more children	5	21	12	46
5. Parents' adult love relationships at time child was seen				
Mothers				
Remarried	6	25	5	19
Stabilized living with man	4	17	0	0
New parent figure in home: Total		42		19
Serial relationships	5	21	2	8
Transient relationships or "dating" several people or occasional date	5	21	10	38
No known heterosexual relationship	4	17	5	19
Lesbian relationship			1	4
(Mother dead)			3	
No information			1	
Fathers				
Remarried	3	13	13	50
Stabilized living with woman	2	8	3	12
New parent figure in home: Total		21		62
Serial relationships	5	17	2	8
Transient relationships, "dating" several people or occasional date	12	50	4	15

	Children age 1-11 (chapter 5)		Adolescents (chapter 7)	
	No.	%	No.	%
No known heterosexual relationships	2	8	4	15

6. Period of emotional incapacitation for parenting

Mothers

Mother emotionally incapacitated, e.g., during psychosis, suicidal attempt with psychiatric hospitalization, imprisonment, incapacitating alcoholism	5	21	8	31

Fathers

Father emotionally incapacitated, e.g., during psychosis, suicidal attempt with psychiatric hospitalization, imprisonment, incapacitating alcoholism	3	13	7	27
Emotional incapacitation of one parent: Total		34		58

7. Home parent's support of child in dealing with feelings about absent parent

Home parent able or partially able to give constructive emotional support to child in child's expression of feelings about absent parent	10*	42	4*	15
	5**	21	8**	23
Total		63		38
Home parent intensely threatened by child's feeling for absent parent	9	37	16	62

* yes
** partially

Children of the Deceased (chapter 8):
Summary of Familial Circumstances

Material is based on 19 individuals, aged 6 to 54, who lost a parent through death by the time they were 15 years old. Mother had died in 13 cases, father in 6. The parents' marriage had been intact in 18 cases, prior to the death of a parent; 16 of the children livd with the remaining parent after the death; 2 were "boarded out," 1 lived with grandmother prior to multiple foster placements. In 10 cases the remaining parent remarried. In one case the remaining parent was never known (the child was placed in an agency). In two cases the remaining parent died within three years of the other parent's death. Four mothers had worked while the child was younger than 10.

Children in Custody Disputes (chapter 6):
Summary of Familial Circumstances

Thirteen families were involved. This does not include cases in which a parent willingly renounced custody (also discussed in chapter 6). Children were in the custody of father in six cases, of mother in seven cases. In two cases custody eventually shifted from mother to father, in one from father to mother, and in two shared or joint custody was established. The proportion of families in which one or both parents suffered a period of emotional incapacitation for parenting was highest in this group.

REFERENCES

Abraham, K. (1924). A short study of the development of the libido in the light of mental disorders. In his *Selected Papers in Psychoanalysis.* London: Hogarth Press, 1927.

Adams, M. (1971). A single woman in today's society: a re-appraisal. *American Journal of Orthopsychiatry* 41:776-786.

Adams, W. (1972). Drop out wife. *Life Magazine,* March 17.

Adelson, J. (1971). The political imagination of the young adolescent. *Daedalus* 100:1013-1050.

Alpert, A. (1964). A brief communication on children's reaction to the assassination of the president. *Psychoanalytic Study of the Child* 19.

Altman, L. (1975). *The Dream in Psychoanalysis.* New York: International Universities Press.

Amitai, E. (1976). Do as I say, not as I do. *New York Times Magazine,* September 26.

Anthony, E. J., and Benedek, T., eds. (1970). *Parenthood: Its Psychology and Psychopathology.* Boston: Little, Brown and Co.

Apolloni, T., and Cooke, T. P. (1975). Peer behavior conceptualized as a variable influencing infant and toddler development. *American Journal of Orthopsychiatry* 45:4-17.

Bakwin, H. (1949). Emotional deprivation in infants. *Journal of Pediatrics* 35:512-521.

Bandura, A., and Walters, R. (1963). *Social Learning and Personality Development.* New York: Holt, Rinehart and Winston.

Barnes, M. J. (1964). Reactions to the death of a mother. *Psychoanalytic Study of the Child* 19.

Barthelme, D. (1975). *The Dead Father.* New York: Farrar, Straus, and Giroux.

Bateson, G., and Mead, M. (1949). *Balinese Character.* New York, New York Academy of Science.

Baum, C. (1976). The best of both parents. *New York Times Magazine,* October 31.

Beels, C. (1976). The case of the vanishing Mommy. *New York Times magazine,* July 4.

Belin, H. (1976). Dropping out of motherhood. *Radcliffe Quarterly* 62 (June).

Bellak, L., and Antell M.(1974). An intercultural study of aggressive behavior on a children's playground. *American Journal of Orthopsychiatry* 34:503-511.

Benedek, T. (1959). Parenthood as a developmental phase. *Journal of the American Psychoanalytic Association* 7:389-417.

——— (1970). The psychologic approach to parenthood. Part II Anthony and Benedek, 1970.

Beres, D., and Obers, S. (1950). The effects of extreme deprivation in infancy on psychic structure in adolescence: a study in ego development. *Psychoanalytic Study of the Child* 5.

Bettelheim, B. (1969). *The Children of the Dream.* London: Collier-Macmillan.

Bibring, E. (1953). The mechanism of depression. In *Affective Disorders,* ed. P. Greenacre. New York: International Universities Press.

——— (1954). Psychoanalysis and the dynamic psychotherapies. *Journal of the American Psychoanalytic Association* 2.

Bibring, G. L. (1964). Some considerations regarding the ego ideal in the psychoanalytic process. *Journal of the American Psychoanalytic Association* 12:517-521.

Blatt, S. J. (1974). Anaclitic and introjective depression. *Psychoanalytic Study of the Child* 29. New Haven: Yale University Press.

Blos, P. (1941). *The Adolescent Personality.* New York: Appleton-Century-Crofts.

——— (1962). *On Adolescence: A Psychoanalytic Interpretation.* New York: The Free Press of Glencoe.

——— (1963). Female delinquency: three typical constellations. Paper presented at the Annual Conference of the *American Orthopsychiatric Association* March.

——— (1968). Character formation in adolescence. *Psychoanalytic Study of the Child* 23.

———— (1971). The child analyst looks at the young adolescent. *Daedalus* 100(4):961–978.

———— (1974). The genealogy of the ego ideal. *Psychoanalytic Study of the Child.* 29.

Bowlby, J. (1946). *Forty-four Juvenile Thieves: Their Character and Home Life.* London: Ballière, Tindall and Cox.

———— (1951) Maternal care and mental health. *Geneva World Health Organization Monograph* No. 2. New York: Columbia University Press.

———— (1960). Grief and mourning in infancy and early childhood. *Psychoanalytic Study of the Child* 15.

———— (1963). Pathological mourning and childhood mourning. *Journal of the American Psychoanalytic Association* 11:500–541.

————, Robertson, J., and Rosenbluth, D. (1952). A two year old goes to the hospital. *Psychoanalytic Study of the Child* 7.

Bralove, M. (1975). Runaway wives. *Wall Street Journal,* October 1.

Brazelton, T. B. (1974). *Toddlers and Parents.* New York: Delacorte Press.

Brewster, H. E. (1952). Separation reaction in psychosomatic disease and neurosis. *Psychosomatic Medicine* 14:154–160.

Broadbeck, A. J. and Irwin, O. C. (1946). Speech behavior of infants without families. *Child Development* 17:145–156.

Brody, S. (1956). *Patterns of Mothering.* New York: International Universities Press.

Bronfenbrenner, U. (1958). Socialization and social class through time and space. In *Readings in Social Psychology,* ed. E. E. Maccoby, T. M. Newcomb, and E. L. Hartley. New York: Holt, Rinehart and Winston.

———— (1970). *Two Worlds of Childhood: US and USSR.* New York: Russell Sage Foundation.

Buhler, C. (1930). *The First Year of Life.* New York: John Day.

Busch, F. (1974). Dimensions of the first transitional object. *Psychoanalytic Study of the Child* 29.

Caldwell, B. (1973). What does research teach us about day care of children under three? In *Annual Progress in Child Psychiatry and Child Development,* ed. S. Chess and A. Thomas. New York: Brunner-Mazel.

Cath, S. H. (1965). Some dynamics of middle and later years. In *Geriatric Psychiatry: Grief, Loss and Emotional Disorders in the Aging Process.* New York: International Universities Press.

Conway, J. (1974). Coeducation and women's studies: two approaches to the question of woman's place in the contemporary university. *Daedalus* 103(4):239–249.

David, M., Nicolas, J., Roudinesco, J., Robertson, J. and Bowlby, J. (1952).

Responses of young children to separation from their mothers. *Courrier,* vol. II (2:66–78; 3:131–142).

Davis, A., and Havighurst, R. J. (1946). Social class and color differences in child rearing. *American Sociological Reivew* 11:698–710.

—— (1947). *Father of the Man.* Boston: Houghton Mifflin.

Derdeyn, A. P. (1975). Child custody consultation. *American Journal of Orthopsychiatry* 45:791–801.

Despert, J. L. (1962). *Children of Divorce.* New York: Doubleday.

Deutsch, H. (1937). Absence of grief. *Psychoanalytic Quarterly* 6:12–22.

—— (1944). *The Psychology of Women: A Psychoanalytic Interpretation,* vol. 1. New York: Grune and Stratton.

—— (1965). A two year old boy's first love comes to grief. In *her Neuroses and Character Types.* New York: International Universities Press.

Douvan, E., and Adelson, J. (1966). *The Adolescent Experience.* New York: John Wiley.

Eisenberg, L. (1972). The *human* nature of human nature. *Science* 176:123–128.

—— (1975). Caring for children and working: dilemmas of contemporary womanhood. *Pediatrics* 56:24–28.

Erikson, E. (1950). *Childhood and Society.* New York: Norton.

—— (1956). The problem of ego identity. *Journal of the American Psychoanalytic Association,* vol. 4. Reprinted in *Psychological Issues,* vol. 1. New York: International Universities Press, 1959.

—— (1956). Reflections on Dr. Borg's life cycle. *Daedalus* 85(2):1–28.

—— (1959). Identity and the life cycle. *Psychological Issues,* vol. 1. New York: International Universities Press.

Erikson, J. (1964). Nothing to fear: notes on the life of Eleanor Roosevelt. *Daedalus,* 93(2):781–801.

Federn, P. (1952). *Ego Psychology and the Psychoses.* New York: Basic Books.

Fenichel, O. (1945). *The Psychoanalytic Theory of Neurosis.* New York: Norton.

Ferenczi, S. (1913). Stages in the development of the sense of reality. *Selected Papers of Sandor Ferenczi.* Vol. 1, *Sex in Psychoanalysis.* New York: Basic Books, 1950.

—— (1926). Sensations of giddiness at the end of the psychoanalytic session. In *Further Contributions to the Theory and Technique of Psychoanalysis,* Chapter 23. London: Institute of Psychoanalysis and Hogarth Press.

Finkelstein, H. (1975). quoted in: Fathers and divorce, a matter of custody. *Boston Globe, Nov.*

Fisher, L. (1952). Hospitalism in a six-month old infant. *American Journal of Orthopsychiatry* 22:522–533.

Flugel, J. C. (1950). *The Psychoanalytic Study of the Family.* London: Hogarth Press.

Fraiberg, S. (1955). Some considerations in the introduction of therapy in puberty. *Psychoanalytic Study of the Child* 10.

―― (1969). Libidinal object constancy and mental representations. *Psychoanalytic Study of the Child.* 24.

Freed, D. J. (1974). Grounds for divorce in the American jurisdictions (as of June 1, 1974). *Family Law Quarterly* 8:401–423.

French, T. (1929). Psychogenic material related to the function of the semicircular canals. *International Journal of Psycho-Analysis* 10:498–510.

Freud, A. (1926). *The Psychoanalytic Treatment of Children.* London: Imago, 1946.

―― (1937). *The Ego and the Mechanisms of Defense.* New York: International Universities Press, 1946.

―― (1952). Influences in the development of ego and id. *Psychoanalytic Study of the Child* 7.

――(1960). Discussion of Bowlby (1960). *Psychoanalytic Study of the Child* 15.

―― (1967). About losing and being lost. *Psychoanalytic Study of the Child* 22.

――, and Burlingham, D. (1939–45). Infants without families: report on the Hampstead nurseries. *The Writings of Anna Freud,* vol. 3. New York: International Universities Press.

――, and Burlingham, D. (1943). *War and Children.* New York: International Universities Press.

Freud, S. (1910). Three contributions to the theory of sex: II. Infantile sexuality. In *The Basic Writings of Sigmund Frued,* ed. A. A. Brill. New York: Modern Library, 1938.

―― (1914). On narcissism: an introduction. *Collected Papers,* vol. 4. London: Hogarth, 1950.

―― (1917). Mourning and melancholia. *Collected Papers,* vol. 4. London: Hogarth, 1950.

―― (1920). Beyond the pleasure principle. In *The Standard Edition of the Complete Psychological Works of Sigmund Freud,* vol. 18, ed. J. Strachey. London: Hogarth, 1955.

―― (1920b). *Introductory Lectures to Psychoanalysis.* New York: Boni and Liveright.

————(1925). Negation. In *Collected Papers,* vol. 5. London: Hogarth, 1950.

———— (1930). *Civilization and Its Discontents.* London: Hogarth, 1946.

———— (1927). *The Ego and the Id.* London: Hogarth Press, 1949.

———— (1933). *New Introductory Lectures on Psychoanalysis.* New York: Norton.

———— (1940). *An Outline of Psychoanalysis.* New York: Norton, 1949.

Fromm-Reichmann, F. (1939). Transference problems in schizophrenia. *Psychoanalytic Quarterly* 8(4):412–426.

———— (1952). Some aspects of psychoanalytic psychotherapy with schizophrenics. In *Psychotherapy with Schizophrenics,* E. Body and F. Redlich. New York: International Universities Press.

———— (1959). *Psychoanalysis and Psychotherapy: selected papers of Frieda Fromm Reichmann.* Chicago: University of Chicago Press.

Furman, E. (1974). *A Child's Parent Dies: Studies in Childhood Bereavement.* New Haven: Yale University Press.

Furman, R. (1964a). Death and the young child: some preliminary considerations. *Psychoanalytic Study of the Child* 19.

————(1964b). A death of a six year old's mother during his analysis. *Psychoanalytic Study of the Child* 19.

Gardner, R. (1976). *Psychotherapy with Children of Divorce.* New York: Jason Aronson.

Gauthier, Y. (1965). The mourning reaction of a ten and a half year old boy. *Psychoanalytic Study of the Child* 20.

Geleerd, E. R. (1967). *The Child Analyst at Work.* New York: International Universities Press.

Gitelson, M. (1948). Character synthesis: the psychotherapeutic problems of adolescence. *American Journal of Orthopsychiatry* 18:423–432.

Glover, E. (1955). *The Technique of Psychoanalysis.* New York: International Universities Press.

Goldfarb, W. (1943). Infant rearing and problem behavior. *American Journal of Orthopsychiatry* 13:249–265.

Goldstein, J., Freud, A., and Solnit, A. (1973). *Beyond the Best Interests of the Child.* New York: Macmillan.

Greenacre, P. (1941). The predisposition to anxiety. In her *Trauma, Growth, and Personality.* London: Hogarth Press, 1969.

————(1957). The childhood of the artist. *Psychoanalytic Study of the Child.*

————(1959). Play and creative imagination. *Psychoanalytic Study of the Child.*

Greenberg, M., and Morris, N. (1974). Engrossment: the newborn's impact upon the father. *American Journal of Orthopsychiatry* 34:520–531.

Handel, G. (1970). Sociological aspects of parenthood. In *Parenthood, Its Pathology and Its Psychopathology,* ed. J. Anthony and T. Benedek. Boston: Little, Brown.

Handel, G., and Rainwater, L. (1964). Persistence and change in working class life style. In *Blue Collar World,* ed. A. Shostak and W. Gromberg. Englewood Cliffs, New Jersey: Prentice Hall.

Harnick, J. (1932). Introjection and projection in the mechanism of depression. *International Journal of Psycho-Analysis* 13:424–430.

Hartmann, H. (1952). The mutual influences in the development of ego and id. *Psychoanaltic Study of the Child* 7.

———, Kris, E., and Loewenstein, R. M. (1946). Comments on the formation of psychic structure. *Psychoanalytic Study of the Child* 2.

———, and Loewenstein, R. M. (1962). Notes on the Super-Ego. *Psychoanalytic Study of the Child,* 17.

Heinicke, C., Friedman, D., Prescott, E., Puncel, C., and Sale, J. S. (1973). The organization of day care: considerations relating to the mental health of child and family. *American Journal of Orthopsychiatry* 43:8–22.

———, and Westheimer, I. (1965). *Brief Separations.* New York: International Universities Press.

Hendin, H. (1975). *The Age of Sensation.* New York: Norton.

Hoffer, W. (1953). The mutual influences in the development of ego and id: earliest stages. *Psychoanalytic Study of the Child* 7.

Hooker, D. (1942). Fetal reflexes and instinctual reflexes. *Psychosomatic Medicine* 4:199–206.

Hopkins, N. (1976). The high price of success in science. *Radcliffe Quarterly,* June.

Horowitz, M. J. (1976). *Stress Response Syndromes.* New York: Jason Aronson.

Inhelder, B., and Piaget, J. (1958). *The Growth of Logical Thinking from Childhood to Adolescence.* New York: Basic Books.

Isakower, O. (1938). A contribution to the psychopathology of phenomena associated with falling asleep. *International Journal of Psycho-Analysis* 19:331–345.

Jacobson, E. (1953). On the metapsychology of cyclothmic depression. In *Affective Disorders,* ed. P. Greenacre. New York: International Universities Press.

——— (1954). The self and the object world: vicissitudes of infantile cathexis and their influence on ideational and affective development. *Psychoanalytic Study of the Child* 9.

———— (1957). Normal and pathological moods: their nature and function. *Psychoanalytic Study of the Child* 12.

Jacobson, E. (1961). Adolescent moods and the remodeling of psychic structures in adolescence. *Psychoanalytic Study of the Child* 16.

———— (1964). *The Self and the Object World.* New York: International Universities Press.

———— (1971). A special response to early object loss. In her *Depression, Comparative Studies of Normal, Neurotic and Psychotic Conditions.* New York: International Universities Press.

Joffe, W. G., and Sandler, J. (1965). Notes on pain, depression, and individuation. *Psychoanalytic Study of the Child* 20.

Johnson, A. (1949). Sanctions for superego lacunae of adolescents. In *Searchlights on Delinquency,* ed. K. R. Eissler. New York: International Universities Press.

Jones, E. (1913). The phantasy of the reversal of generations. In *Papers on Psychoanalysis.* Boston: Beacon Press, 1961.

Jones, M. (1948). Adolescent friendships. *American Psychologist* 3:352.

Jung, C. G. (1961). *Memories, Dreams, Reflections.* New York: Random House.

Kahne, H. (1976). *The Future of Marriage, Family, and Children, with a Postscript on Sexuality.* A Report to WNET/13, New York City. Radcliffe Institute, Cambridge, Mass.

Kahne, M. (1967). On the persistence of transitional phenomena into adult life. *International Journal of Psycho-Analysis* 48:247–258.

———— (1976). Cultural differences: whose trouble are we talking about? *Exchange* 11(4):36–40.

Katan, A. (1937). The role of displacement in agoraphobia. *International Journal of Psycho-Analysis* 32:41–50.

Katz, D. (1976). We're slowing down, marrying less, living longer. A report based on National Center for Health Statistics. *Boston Globe,* July 22.

Kaufman, I., and Heims, L. (1958). The body image of the juvenile delinquent. *American Journal of Orthopsychiatry* 28:146–159.

Kelly, J. B., and Wallerstein, J. S. (1976). The effects of divorce: experiences of the child in early latency. *American Journal of Orthopsyicatry* 46:20–32.

Klein, M. (1940). Mourning and its relation to manic depressive states. *International Journal of Psycho-Analysis* 21:125–153.

———— (1950). *The Psychoanalysis of Children.* London: Hogarth Press.

Kohlberg, L. (1966). A cognitive-developmental analysis of children's sex role concepts and attitudes. In *The Development of Sex Differences,* ed. E. Maccoby. Stanford, Cal. Stanford University Press.

————, and Gilligan, C. (1971). The adolescent as a philosopher: the discovery of the self in a postconventional world. *Daedalus,* 100(4):1051–1086.

————, and Kramer, R. (1969). Continuities and discontinuities in childhood and adult moral development. *Human Development* 12:93–120.

Kohn, M. L. (1963). Social class and parent-child relationships: an interpretation. *American Journal of Sociology* 68:471–480.

Krech, D., and Crutchfield, R. (1948). *Theory and Problems in Social Psychology.* New York: McGraw-Hill.

Kris, E. (1950). On pre-conscious mental processes. *Psychoanalytic Quarterly* 19:540–560.

———— (1955). Neutralization and sublimation: observations on young children. *Psychoanalytic Study of the Child* 10.

Kristol, I. (1976). The poverty of equality. *New York Times,* July 12.

Kubie, L. (1953). The distortion of the symbolic process in neurosis and psychosis. *Journal of the American Psycho-Analytic Association* 1:59–86.

Ladner, J. A. (1972). *Tomorrow's Tomorrow: The Black Woman.* New York: Doubleday.

Lampl-De Groot, J. (1962). Ego ideal and superego. *Psychoanalytic Study of the Child* 17.

Landis, J. T. (1960). The trauma of children when parents divorce. *Marriage and Family Living* 22:7-13.

Lasch, C. (1975). The family and history parts 1 and 2. *New York Review of Books,* Nov. 13, Dec. 11.

Laufer, M. (1966). Object loss and mourning during adolescence. *Psychoanalytic Study of the Child* 21.

Levine, J. (1976). *Who Will Raise the Children? New Options for Fathers (and Mothers).* Philadelphia: Lippincott.

Levinson, D., Darrow, C., Klein, E., Levinson, M., and McKee, B. (1972). The psychosocial development of men in early adulthood and the mid-life transition. *Preprint,* Research Unit for Social Psychology and Psychiatry, Connecticut Mental Health Center and Department of Psychiatry, Yale University.

Lewin, B. (1937). A type of neurotic hypomanic reaction. *Archives of Neurology and Psychiatry* 37:868–873.

———— (1950). *The Psychoanalysis of Elation.* New York: Norton.

Lifton, R. J. (1976). Talk given at the Education Research Center, Massachusetts Institute of Technology, Spring.

Light, P. (1976). Counseling two-career couples at the Harvard Business School. *Radcliffe Quarterly,* December.

Lindemann, E. (1944). The symptomatology and management of acute grief. *American Journal of Psychiatry* 101:141–148.

Linner, B. (1971). What does equality between the sexes imply? *American Journal of Orthopsychiatry* 41:747–756.

Loewenstein, R. (1954). Discussion of E. Kris, Problems of infantile neurosis. *Psychoanalytic Study of the Child* 9.

Loomie, L. S., Rosen, V. H., and Stein, M. H. (1958). Ernst Kris and the gifted adolescent project. *Psychoanalytic Study of the Child* 13.

Lynn, D. B. (1974). *The Father—His Role in Child Development*. Monterey, Cal: Brooks, Cole.

Lynd, H. M. (1958). *On Shame and the Search for Identity*. New York: Harcourt Brace.

MacKinnon, D. (1949). The unconscious. Course given in Psychology Department, University of California, Berkeley.

Maccoby, E. (1966). Sex differences in intellectual functioning. In E. Maccoby and C. Jacklin, *The Development of Sex Differences*. Stanford, Cal.: Stanford University Press.

————, and Jacklin, C. (1974). *The Psychology of Sex Differences*. Stanford, Cal.: Stanford University Press.

Market Opinion Research (1975). Commissioned by the President's Commission on the Observation of International Women's Year. Reported in *Boston Globe*, December 7, 1975.

Matte, B. I. (1941). On introjection and the process of psychic metabolism. *International Journal of Psycho-Analysis* 22:17–60.

McKee, J. P., and Sheriffs, A. C. (1960). Men's and women's beliefs, ideals, and self-concepts. In *The Adolescent: A Book of Readings*, ed. J. M. Seidman. New York:Holt, Rinehart, and Winston.

Miller, J. B. (1973). New issues, new approaches. In *Psychoanalysis and Women*, ed. J. B. Miller. New York: Brunner-Mazel.

———— (1976). *Toward a New Psychology of Women*. Boston: Beacon Press.

Modell, A. (1968). *Object Love and Reality*. New York: International Universities Press.

Mouton, R. (1973). A survey and re-evaluation of the concept of penis envy. In *Psychoanalysis and Women*, ed. J. B. Miller. New York: Brunner-Mazel.

Myerson, P. G. (1963). Assimilation of unconscious material. *International Journal of Psycho-Analysis* 44:317–327.

———— (1973). The meanings of confrontation. In *Confrontations in Psychotherapy*, ed. G. Adler and P. Myerson. New York: Jason Aronson.

Nagera, H. (1969). The imaginary companion: its significance for ego development and conflict solution. *Psychoanalytic Study of the Child* 24.

————— (1970). Children's reactions to the death of important objects: a developmental approach. *Psychoanalytic Study of the Child* 25.

Nagy, M. (1948). The child's theories concerning death. *Journal of Genetic Psychology* 73:3–4, 26–27.

Neubauer, P. B. (1960). The one parent child and his oedipal development. *Psychoanalytic Study of the Child* 15.

Notman, M. (1964). Twelve years later: a woman psychiatrist. *Psychiatric Opinion,* Fall, p. 27.

Nunberg, H. (1932). *Principles of Psychoanalysis.* New York: International Universities Press.

Nyquist, E. B. (1975). New York State education commissioner, quoted in the *New York Times.*

O'Brien, P. (1976). Midlife crisis—women who walk out. *Boston Globe,* April 31.

Parkes, C. M. (1972). *Bereavement: Studies of Grief in Adult Life.* New York: International Universities Press.

Parsons, T. (1974). Stability and change in the American university. *Daedalus* 103(4):269–277.

————— and Bales, R. (1965). *Family, Socialization and Interaction Process.* New York: Free Press of Glencoe.

Pavenstedt, E., ed. (1967). *The Drifters.* Boston: Little, Brown and Co.

Peterson, C. (1976). The divorce boom keeps booming. Boston Globe, October 26.

Piaget, J. (1932), *The Moral Judgment of the Child.* London: Kegan Paul

————— (1954). The development of object constancy. In *The Construction of Reality in the Child.* New York: Basic Books.

————— (1969). The intellectual development of the adolescent. In *Adolescence: Psychosocial Perspectives,* ed. G. Caplan and S. Lebovici. New York: Basic Books.

Piers, G. and Singer, M. (1953). *Shame and Guilt.* Springfield, Ill.: Thomas.

Rainwater, L., Coleman, R., and Handel, G. (1959). *Workingman's Wife: Her Personality, World and Life Style.* New York: Oceana.

Rapaport, D., ed. (1951). *Organization and Pathology of Thought.* New York: Columbia University Press.

Rapoport, R.; and Rapoport, R. N. (1969). The dual career family. *Human Relations* 22:3–30.

Reich, A. (1954). Early identifications as archaic elements in the superego. In *Psychoanalytic Contributions.* New York: International Universities Press, 1973.

————— (1958). Discussion of S. Loonie, V. Rosen, and M. Stein. Report of the gifted adolescent project. *Psychoanalytic Study of the Child* 13.

Reik, T. (1936). *Surprise and the Psychoanalyst.* London: Kegan Paul.

Ritvo, S., and Solnit, A. (1958). Influences of early mother-child interaction on identification processes. *Psychoanalytic Study of the Child* 13.

Rivers, Caryl (1975). Can a woman be liberated and married? *New York Times Magazine,* Nov. 2.

Robertson, J. (1953). Some responses of young children to loss of maternal care. *Nursing Times* 49:382–386.

———— and Robertson, J. (1971). Young children in brief separation: a fresh look. *Psychoanalytic Study of the Child* 26.

Rochlin, G. (1953). Loss and restitution. *Psychoanalytic Study of the Child* 8.

———— (1965). *Griefs and Discontents: The Forces of Change.* Boston: Little, Brown.

Rohlen, T. (1976). The promise of adulthood in Japanese spiritualism. *Daedulus* 105(2):125–143.

Root, N. (1957). A neurosis in adolescence. *Psychoanalytic Study of the Child* 12.

Roszak, T. (1968). *The Making of a Counter Culture.* New York: Doubleday.

Rothchild, J., and Wolf, S. (1976). *The Children of the Counterculture.* New York: Doubleday.

Rowe, M. (1976). Child care for the 1980s; traditional sex roles or androgeny. Massachusetts Institute of Technology, Cambridge, Mass. Mimeo.

Rubin, J. Z., Provenzano, F. J., and Luria, Z. (1974). The eye of the beholder: parents' views on sex of newborns. *American Journal of Orthopsychiatry* 44:512–519.

Rutter, M. (1972). *Maternal Deprivation Reassessed.* Harmondsworth: Penguin Books.

———— (1973). Maternal deprivation reconsidered. In *Annual Progress in Child Psychiatry,* ed. S. Chess and A. Thomas. New York: Brunner-Mazel.

Sandler, J., Holder, A., and Meers, D. (1963). The ego ideal and the ideal self. *Psychoanalytic Study of the Child* 18.

Sanford, N. (1971). Authoritarianism and social destructivness. In *Sanctions for Evil,* ed. N. Sanford and C. Comstock. San Francisco: Jossey-Bass.

————, Adkins, M.M., Miller, R. B., Cobb, E. A., and others (1943). *Physique, personality and scholarship. Monographs of the Society for Research in Child Development,* vol. 8(1). Washington, D.C., National Research Council.

Schafer, R. (1960). The loving and beloved superego in Freud's structural theory. *Psychoanalytic Study of the Child* 15.

———— (1968). *Aspects of Internalization.* New York: International Universities Press.

Scharl, A. E. (1961). Regression and restitution in object loss: clinical observations. *Psychoanalytic Study of the Child* 16.

Schilder, P. (1951). Manic depressive psychosis. In his *Introduction to a Psychoanalytic Psychiatry*. New York: International Universities Press.

Schneider, P. (1975). Report planned and coordinated by P. Schneider in the Census Bureau, Population Division.

Schur, M. (1953). The ego. In *Anxiety in Drives, Affects, Behavior,* ed. R. M. Loewenstein. New York: International Universities Press.

———(1955), Comments on the metapsychology of somatization. *Psychoanalytic Study of the Child* 10.

Sears, R. R. (1965). Development of gender role. In *Sex and Behavior,* ed. F. A. Beach. New York: Wiley.

Sechehaye, M. (1951). *Autobiography of a Schizophrenic Girl.* New York: Grune and Stratton.

Seidenberg, R. (1973). (1) Is anatomy destiny? (2) For the future—equity? (3) The trauma of eventlessness. In *Psychoanalysis and Women,* ed. J. B. Miller. New York: Brunner-Mazel.

Shilder, P. (1935). *The Image and Appearance of the Human Body.* London: Kegan, Paul.

Skard, A. G. (1965). Maternal deprivation: the research and its implications. *Journal of Marriage and Family Living* 27:333–343.

Skeels, H. M. (1940). Some Iowa studies of the mental growth of children in relation to differentials of environment: a summary. *39th Yearbook, National Society for the Study of Education,* Part 2.

——— (1942). A study of the effects of differential stimulation on mentally retarded children: a follow-up report. *American Journal of Mental Deficiency* 46:340–350.

Sklar, A. (1976). *Runaway Wives.* New York: Coward, McCann and Geoghegan.

Smith, M. (1976). Knocking down bars. *Radcliffe Quarterly.* 62:(Sept.)2.

Snyder, B. (1971). *The Hidden Curriculum.* New York: Knopf.

Snyder, B. R., and Tessman, L. H. (1965). Creativity in gifted students and scientists. In *Creativity in Childhood and Adolescense,* ed. H. H. Anderson. Palo Alto, Cal.: Science and Behavior Books.

Sollenberger, R. (1940). Some relationships between the urinary excretion of male hormone by maturing boys and their expressed interest and activities. *Journal of Psychology* 9:179–190.

Sperling, O. E. (1954). An imaginary companion, representing a pre-stage of the superego. *Psychoanalytic Study of the Child* 9.

Spitz, R. (1945). Hospitalism: an inquiry into the genesis of psychiatric conditions in early childhood. *Psychoanalytic Study of the Child* 1.

——— (1946). Hospitalism: a follow-up study. *Psychoanalytic Study of the Child* 2.

——— (1955). The primal cavity: a contribution to the genesis of perception and its role for psychoanalytic theory. *Psychoanalytic Study of the Child* 10.

——— (1962). Autoerotism re-examined: the role of early sexual behavior patterns in personality formation. *Psychoanalytic Study of the Child* 17.

——— (1965). *The First Year of Life: A Psychoanalytic Study of Normal and Deviant Development of Object Relations.* New York: International Universities Press.

——— and Wolf, K. M. (1946). Anaclitic depression: an inquriy into the genesis of psychiatric conditions in early childhood, II. *Psychoanalytic Study of the Child* 2.

——— and Wolf, K. (1949). Autoerotism, some empirical findings and hypotheses on three of its manifestations in the first year of life. *Psychoanalytic Study of the Child* 4.

Steinman, A. (1963). A study of the concept of feminine role of 51 middleclass American families. *Genetic Psychology Monographs,* vol. 67.

Stengel, E. (1939). Studies on the psychopathology of compulsive wandering. *British Journal of Medical Psychology* 18:250–254.

——— (1943). Further studies on pathological wandering. *Journal of Mental Science* 89:224–241.

Stevenson, O. (1954). The first treasured possession: a study of the part played by a specially loved object and toys in the lives of certain children. *Psychoanalytic Study of the Child* 9.

Stoltz, L. M. (1960). Effect of maternal employment on children. *Child Development* 31:749–782.

Stone, C. P. and Barker, R. G. (1939). The attitudes and interests of pre-menarchal and post-menarchal girls. *Journal of Genetic Psychology* 57:393–414.

Stutsman, R. (1931). *Mental Measurement of Pre-school Children.* New York: World.

Sullivan, E. (1975). The marriage boom: a nationwide report. *Redbook,* February. (1965).

Sullivan, H. S. (1965). *Personal Psychopathology: Early Formulations (1929-1933).* New York: Norton.

Suthie, I. (1935). *The Origins of Love and Hate.* London: Kegan Pual, Trench, Trabney and Co.

Symonds, A. (1973). Phobias after marriage: women's declaration of dependence. In *Psychoanalysis and Women,* ed. J. B. Miller. New York: Brunner-Mazel.

Symonds, P. M. (1945). Inventory of themes in adolescent fantasy. *American Journal of Orthopsychiatry* 15:318–328.

Tait, K. (1975). *My Father, Bertrand Russell.* New York: Harcourt Brace Jovanovich.

Tartakoff, H. (1966). The normal personality in our culture and the Nobel prize complex. In *Psychoanalysis—A General Psychology: Essays in Honor of Heinz Hartmann,* ed. R. M. Loewenstein. New York: International Universities Press.

Tessman, L. H. (1969). The care and feeding of the transitional object. Paper presented at the Meeting of the American Orthopsychiatric Association.

———, and Kaufman, I. (1963). Transference and countertransference in the treatment of neurotic, character disordered, and psychotic children. Paper presented at the Meeting of the American Orthopsychiatric Association.

———, and Kaufman, I. (1967). Treatment techniques, the primary process, and ego development in schizophrenic children. *Journal of the American Academy of Child Psychiatry* 6:98–115.

———, and Kaufman, I. (1969). Variations on a theme of incest. In *Family Dynamics and Female Sexual Delinquency,* ed. O. Pollak and A. Friedman. Palo Alto, Cal.: Science and Behavior Books.

Tolpin, M. (1971). On the beginnings of a cohesive self: an application of the concept of transmuting internalization to the study of the transitional object and signal anxiety. *Psychoanalytic Study of the Child* 26.

Tooley, K. (1976). Antisocial behavior and social alienation post divorce: the "man of the house" and his mother. *American Journal of Orthopsychiatry* 46:33–42.

Torgerson, D. (1973). *Daily Times* (Mamaroneck, New York). Feb. 20, p. 4.

Tryon, C. M. (1944). Adolescent peer culture. In *Adolescence: Forty-third Yearbook, National Society for the Study of Education.* Chicago: University of Chicago Press.

United Nations Demographic Yearbook (1969).

Wallerstein, J. S., and Kelly, J. B. (1976a). The effects of parental divorce: experiences of the child in later latency. *American Journal of Orthopsychiatry* 46:256–269.

——— (1976b). Divorce counseling: a community service for families in the midst of divorce. Paper presented at the Meeting of the American Orthopsychiatric Association, 1976.

Wallston, B. (1974). The effect of maternal employment on children. In *Annual Progress in Child Psychiatry and Child Development,* ed. S. Chess and A. Thomas. New York: Brunner-Mazel.

Watson, J. B. (1929). *Behavior: An Introduction to Comparative Psychology.* New York: Holt.

Weisman, A. (1973). Confrontation, countertransference and contest. In *Confrontation in Psychotherapy,* ed. A. Adler and P. G. Myerson. New York: Jason Aronson.

Weiss, E. (1944). Clinical aspects of depression. *Psychoanalytic Quarterly* 13:445–461.

Weiss, R. S. (1975a). *Marital Separation.* New York: Basic Books.

———(1975b). The provisions of social relationships. In *Doing unto Others,* ed. Z. Rubin. Cambridge: Harvard University Press.

——— (1976). Transition states and other stressful situations: their nature, and programs for their management. In *Support Systems and Mutual Help,* ed. G. Caplan and Killilea. In press.

Wheeler, M. (1975). *No fault divorce.* quoted by Levey R., *Boston Globe, Dec. 31.*

Willoughby, R. R. (1937). Sexuality in the second decade. *Monograph of the Society for Research in Child Development,* vol. 2. no. 3 Washington, D.C.: National Research Council.

Winnicott, D. W. (1953). Transitional objects and transitional phenomena. *International Journal of Psycho-Analysis* 34: 89-97.

———(1970). The mother-infant experience of mutuality. In *Parenthood, its Psychology and Psychopathology,* ed. E. J. Anthony and T. Benedek. Boston: Little, Brown and Co.

——— (1971). *Playing and Reality.* New York: Basic Books.

Wolfenstein, M. (1966). How is mourning possible? *Psychoanalytic Study of the Child* 21.

——— (1969). Loss, rage, and repetition. *Psychoanalytic Study of the Child* 24.

Yarrow, M. R. (1961). Maternal employment and child rearing. *Children* 8:223–228.

———, Scott, P., DeLeeus, L., and Heinig, C. (1962). Child-rearing in families of working and non-working mothers. *Sociometry* 25:122–140.

Zachrey, C.B. (1940). Emotional problems of adolesence. *Bulletin of the Menninger Clinic,* May 1940.

Zetzel, E. (1949). Anxiety and the capacity to bear it. In *The Capacity or Emotional Growth.* New York: International Universities Press. 1970

———(1965). On the incapacity to bear depression. In her *The Capacity for Emotional Growth.* New York International Universities Press.

Ziferstein, I. (1968). Speaking prose without knowing it: critical evaluation of G. Heim, "Social Psychiatric Treatment of Schizophrenia in The Soviet Union." *International Journal of Psychiatry* 6:366-370

INDEX

Abraham, K., 105
acting out, impulsive, coping with stress and, 376-390
Adams, M., 13
Adams, W., 28
Adelson, J., 58, 62
adolescence
    development, family styles of coping with stress and, 375-414
    development, identification as process in, 60-70
    grieving as component of, analogous to mourning, 140-141
    See also images of parting parent and self
adulthood
    development, identification as process in, 70-80
    capacity to bear painful affects, grieving and, 141-146
affects, capacity to bear painful, adult life, grieving and, 141-146

age, as factor in coping with parental parting, 492-500
Alpert, A., 136
Amitai, E. 570
Antell, M., 57, 566
Anthony, E. J., 74
Apolloni, T., 21
attitudes, toward childrearing, changing, 14-22
autonomy, inner change toward, wish for external stability during times of, 339-341

Bakwin, H., 16
Barker, R. G., 66
Barnes, M. J., 132, 139
Barthelme, D., 491
Bateson, G., 105
Baum, C., 29
beckoning, of lost, loved mother, displaced, 440-445
Beeles, C., 28
Belin, H., 28

Bellak, L., 57, 566
Benedek, T., 44, 49, 74, 75
Beres, D., 17
Bergman, Ingmar, 10
Bettelheim, B., 19
Bibring, E., 144, 537
Blatt, S. J., 543
Blos, P., 49, 61, 62, 63, 64, 70, 86, 93, 140, 324
Bowlby, J., 121, 122, 123, 125, 127, 132, 137
Bralove, M., 28
Brazelton, B., 15
Brewster, H. E., 106
Brody, S., 43, 50
Bronfenbrenner, U., 15, 19
Buhler, C., 51
Burlingham, D. 121, 122
Busch, F., 115

Caldwell, B., 19
caring, sustained, meeting needs of, 509-510
Cath, S. H., 49, 79
child care, ideology and customs concerning, changes in, 24-30
childhood, grief in, 132-140
childrearing, changing attitudes toward, 14-22
clinging to dead, literal, impact of deceased and, 428-479
cognitive model, early, of what makes objects appear and disappear, 99-102
Conway, J., 566, 567
Cooke, T. P., 21
coping with parental parting, 490-525
    absent parent, relationship with, 512-516

age, 492-500
causes and effects of divorce or death, 500-506
home parent, relationship with, 516-521
new parent figures and stepparents, 521-525
parental modes of coping with stress, 510-512
personality of child at time of parental parting, 506-509
sustained caring, meeting needs of, 509-510
See also stress

countertransference, impact of personality organization on, 542-551
Crutchfield, R., 66, 126
Cummings, E. E., 149
custody suit, child in, 277-321
averted, 292-301
comments and conclusions, 319-321
enemy, child transformed into, 281-288
father's conflict, child in service of, 288-292
renounced and regained, 301-319
    abandonment, reluctant, 303-310
    emotional incapacity of one parent, custody change necessitated by, 311-319
    family ties as felt impediment, 301-303
    mutual agreement, change of custody by, 310-311
customs, concerning marriage, divorce and child care, changes in, 24-30

David, M., 122, 124

Davis, A., 15

deceased, impact of, 415-488
  adults bereaved in childhood, 428-481
    discontinuity in image of parent, 455-472
    displaced beckoning of lost, loved mother, 440-445
    fidelity, 445-455
    identification in absence of memories, 429-440
    integration of enriching identification with quest for affects shared with loved father, 472-481
    literal clinging to dead, 428-429
  causes and effects, 500-506
  comments, 481-488
  fear and transfiguration, in child, 422-423
  human support network, 416-418
  ideas about, developmental study of, 102-104
  identification processes and, 421-422
  and quest for lost, wanted parent, 419-421
  reality sense, 418-419
  supported grieving, in adolescents, 423-428

defenses, against loss, 268-271

denial
  prolonged, experience of "truth" about self and parents and, 349-354
  in service of quest, 118-120

Derdeyn, A. P., 278, 279

despair, in search for truth, coping with stress and, 400-414

Deutsch, H., 63, 77, 81, 90, 116, 132, 133, 324

devaluation of absent parent, initial acceptance of, 347-349

development, identification as process in, 50-80
  in adolescence, 60-70
  in early childhood, 50-60
  in post-adolescence and childhood, 70-80

disbelief, transitory, experience of "truth" about self and parents and, 358-359

discontinuity in image of parent, impact of deceased and, 455-472

disengagement, protective, experience of "truth" about self and parents and, 359-361

divorce
  causes and effects, 500-506
  ideology and customs concerning changes in, 24-30

Douvan, E., 62

early childhood, development, identification as process in, 50-60

ego ideal, role of identification processes and, 84-87

Eisenberg, L., 6, 9, 11, 22, 26

emotional incapacity of one parent, custody change necessitated by, 311-319

empathy, magical gestures of imitation vs. trial identification for purpose of, in service of quest, 120

enemy, child transformed into, custody suit and, 281-288

Erikson, E., 42, 48, 49, 61, 80, 324, 416

family
    characteristics of, multiple parent
        figures on identifications of
        child and, 149-155
    in history, changing role of, 22-23
    styles of coping with stress, adoles-
        cent development and, 375-
        414
    "substitute," during period of
        intense stress, 364-371
    ties, as felt impediment, custody
        suit and, 301-303
fantasy
    consoling, experience of "truth"
        about self and parents and,
        354-358
    reunion, in absence of actual loss,
        162-171
    in service of quest, 120-121
father
    conflict of, child in service of,
        custody suit and, 288-292
    integration of enriching identifica-
        tion with quest for affects
        shared with loved, 472-481
fear and transfiguration, in child,
    impact of deceased and, 420-
    423
Federn, P., 542
Fenichel, O., 51, 116, 118, 119
Ferenczi, S., 106, 111, 118
fidelity, impact of deceased and, 445-
    455
Finkelstein, H., 29
Fraiberg, S., 49, 99, 324, 340
Freed, D. J., 27
French, T., 106
Freud, A., 29, 49, 63, 77, 99, 100, 118,
    121, 122, 123, 132, 138, 140,
    319, 545
Freud, S., 63, 80, 81, 82, 119, 133,
    226, 542

friendships during period of intense
    stress, 361-364
Fromm-Reichmann, F. 542
Furman, E., 132, 139, 562
Furman, R., 132, 139, 140

Gardner, R., 142
Gauthier, Y., 139
gestures, magical, in service of quest,
    111
    vs. trial identification for purpose
        of empathy, 120
Gilligan, C., 49, 66, 67, 68, 70
Gitelson, M., 65
Glover, E., 544
Goldfarb, W., 16
Goldstein, J., 29, 319
Greenacre, P., 77, 105, 142
Greenberg, M., 20
grieving, 131-146
    as adolescence component, analo-
        gous to mourning, 140-141
    capacity to bear painful affects,
        and adult life, 141-146
    in childhood, 132-140
    postponement of, coping with
        stress and, 390-400
    supported, in adolescents, impact
        of deceased and, 423-428
    transient disguised symptoms of
        grief, working through, 193-
        204

hallucinations, restitutive, expe-
        rience of "truth" about self
        and parents and, 354-358
Harnick, J., 105
Hartmann, H., 61, 85, 100
Havighurst, R. J., 15
Heims, L., 94

Heinicke, C., 123
Hendin, H., 565, 569
Hoffer, W., 100
home parent, relationships with, 512-516
Hooker, D., 104
hope, in search for truth, coping with stress and, 400-414
Hopkins, N., 13, 25
Horowitz, M. J., 118, 337

idealization, in experience of "truth" about self and parents, and future goals, 342-347
identification processes, role of, 41-87
deceased and, impact of, 421-422
development, identification as process in, 50-80
in adolescence, 60-70
in early childhood, 50-60
in post-adolescence and adulthood, 70-80
ego ideal and, 84-87
mixtures of identification and quest for wanted person, 45-48
mode for coping with loss, identification as, 80-84
questions regarding role of identification, 48-50
identifications of child, multiple parent figures on, 149-277
characteristics of family, 149-155
encounters with children and parents, 162-171
defenses against loss and mistrust of remarriage, 268-271
early identity crisis and incompatible identifications, 226-233

early loss, two retrospective views on effects of, 233-268
grief, transient disguised symptoms of, working through, 193-204
initial reactions to separation, 171-184
reunion fantasy in absence of actual loss, 162-171
shifts in identification processes over period of time, 204-226
enrichment of identifications, 271-277
psychic factors and human support system, 149-155
ideology, concerning marriage, divorce and child care, changes in, 24-30
images of parting parent and self in pubescence and adolescence, 323-414
characteristics of group, 326-339
adolescents, 326-330
parents, 330-331
reactions, further, 331-339
encounters with adolescents, 339-414
coping with stress, family styles of, 375-414
adolescent's development and, 375-414
experience of "truth" about self and parents, and future goals, 341-361
relationships to others during period of intense stress, 361-375
imitation, magical gestures of, vs. trial identification, for purpose of empathy, in service of quest, 120
impulse-ridden child, therapy and, 547-549

individuation, postponement of, coping with stress and, 390-400
Inhelder, B., 67
interactions
between men and women, changes in, 6-14
early experienced, and their later re-emergence in nonverbal forms of quest, 104-106
introjection in service of quest, 107
involvement in fulfilling parental needs, during period of intense stress, 371-375
Isakower, O., 105

Jacklin, C., 11, 12
Jacobson, E., 49, 50, 51, 52, 53, 66, 77, 81, 86, 90, 105, 121, 125, 132, 145, 146, 419
Johnson, A., 57, 65
Jones, E., 66, 98
Jung, C. G., 64

Kahne, M., 5, 29, 26, 27, 28, 29, 30, 112, 113
Katan, A., 324
Katz, D., 26, 28
Kaufman, I., 57, 94, 373, 542, 545, 551
Kelley, J. B., 33, 34, 90, 568
Klein, M., 133
Kohlberg, L., 49, 62, 67, 68, 70, 342, 388, 570
Kohn, M. L., 16
Kramer, R., 62
Krech, D., 66, 126
Kris, E., 61, 77
Kubie, L., 102

Lampl-deGroot, J., 86
Landis, J. T., 13
Lasch, C., 22, 23
Laufer, M., 141
Levinson, D., 49, 78, 79, 86
Lewin, B., 104, 105, 107, 121, 126, 234, 541
Lifton, R. J., 82
Light, P., 26
Lindemann, E., 82, 108
Linner, B., 11
Loomie, L. S., 76, 77
loss
absence of actual, reunion fantasy in, 162-171
early, retrospective views on effects of, 233-268
identification as mode for coping with, 80-84
See also coping with parental parting; deceased; quest
Lowenstein, R., 51, 61, 85
Luckert, R., 57
Luria, Z., 21
"lying," in service of quest, 116-118
Lynn, D. B., 13

Maccoby, E., 11, 12
McKee, J. P., 12
MacKinnon, D., 85
magical gestures of imitation, vs. trial identification for purpose of empathy, in service of quest, 120
magic re-creation of person through gesture and thought in service of quest, 111
marriage, relationship network impact on parents during, 5-30
attitudes toward childrearing, changing, 14-22

family in history, changing role of, 22-23

ideology and customs concerning marriage, divorce and child care, change in, 24-30

interaction between men and women, changes in, 6-14

Matte, B. I., 105

Mead, M., 105

memories, identification in absence of, 429-440

men, changes in interaction between women and, 6-14

Miller, J. B., 10, 11, 12, 26, 49, 76, 81

Modell, A., 113

Morris, N., 20

mother, lost, loved, displaced beckoning of, 440-445

mourning. *See* grieving

Myerson, P. G., 55, 57, 537, 538

Nagera, H., 132, 133

Nagy, M., 94, 102

negation

experience of "truth" about self and parents and, 349-354, 358-359

in service of quest, 118-120

Neubauer, P. B., 135

neurotic child, therapy and, 545-547

new parent figures, 521-525

Nicolas, J., 122

Notman, M., 568

Nunberg, H., 86

Nyquist, E. B., 13

Obers, S., 17

O'Brien, P., 28

Parkes, C. M., 90, 121, 126, 127, 145, 419

Parsons, T., 566, 567

parting period, relationship network during, 30-39

children, supports and lacunae for, 35-37

parents, supports and lacunae for, 30-35

summary, 37-39

See also coping with parental parting; images of parting parent

Pavenstedt, E., 16, 17

personality

of child at time of parental parting, 506-509

organization, impact of, on transference, counter-transference, and therapy process, 542-551

Piaget, J., 49, 66, 67, 68, 70, 94, 99, 100, 101, 107, 110

post-adolescence development, identification as process in, 70-80

presences in service of quest, 110-111

Provenzano, F. J., 21

pseudologia

experience of "truth" about self and parents and, 349-354

in service of quest, 116-118

psychotic child, therapy and, 549-551

pubescence, images of self in. *See* images of parting parent and self

quest for wanted person, 90-129

comments, 128-129

and deceased, impact of, 419-421

empirical findings regarding, 121-128

mixtures of identification and, 45, 48
nature and function of, 90-94
psychic and behavioral mechanisms in service of, and their development, 94-121
basis for quest in unconscious, 97-99
developmental study of ideas about death, 102-104
early cognitive models of what makes objects appear and disappear, 99-102
early experienced interactions and their later re-emergence in nonverbal forms of quest, 104-106
forms of psychic mechanisms in service of quest, 106-121

Rainwater, L., 15, 16
Rapaport, D., 102
Rapoport, R., 20, 26
Rapoport, R. N., 20, 26
reactive distress, child in, therapy and, 545-547
reality sense, impact of deceased and, 418-419
Reich, A., 77, 85
Reik, T., 120
relationships, child's, to others, during period of intense stress, 361-375
friendships, 361-364
involvement in fulfilling parental needs, 371-375
"substitute family," 364-371
remarriage, mistrust of, 268-271
remembering in service of quest, 108-110

reunion fantasy, in absence of actual loss, 162-171
Rivers, C., 26
Robertson, J., 122, 124, 129, 138
Robertson, Joyce, 124, 125, 129, 138
Rochlin, G., 90, 121, 126, 132, 138
Rohlen, T., 70
Root, N., 140
Rosen, V. H., 76, 77
Rothchild, J., 27, 565, 569
Roudinesco, J., 122
Rowe, M., 26
Rubin, J. Z., 21
Rutter, M., 19

searching in service of quest, 107-108
Sears, R. R., 63
Sechehaye, M., 100
Schafer, R., 49, 53, 55, 56, 97, 98, 102, 109, 110, 120
Scharl, A. E., 132, 135
Schilder, P., 100, 185
Schneider, P., 27
Schur, M., 105, 142
self image. See images of parting parent and self
separation, initial reactions to, 171-184
Sheriffs, A. C., 12
Skard, A. G., 20
Skeels, H. M., 19
Sklar, A., 28
Smith, M., 25
Snyder, B. R., 76, 570
Sollenberger, R., 66
Solnit, A., 29, 319
Spitz, R., 17, 18, 51, 104, 107, 121, 123
stability, external, wish for, during times of inner change toward autonomy, 339-341

Steichen, E., 41
Stein, M. H., 76, 77
Steinman, A., 12
Stengel, E., 126
step-parents, 521-525
Stevenson, O., 112
Stone, C. P., 66
stress, coping with, family styles of, adolescent's development and, 375-414, 510-512
  acting out, impulsive, 376-390
  hope and despair in search for truth, 400-414
  postponement of grief and of individuation, 390-400
Stutsman, R., 102
"substitute family," during period of intense stress, 364-371
Sullivan, E., 24, 27
Sullivan, H. S., 63
Suthie, I., 570
Symonds, A., 11
Symonds, P. M., 66

Tessman, L. H., 57, 76, 114, 373, 542, 545, 551
therapy, 527-551
  absence of wanted person, 532-542
  personality organization, impact of, on transference, countertransference, and therapy process, 542-551
  impulse-ridden child, 547-549
  neurotic child or child in reactive distress, 545-547
  psychotic child, 549-551
  work related to human relationship, 529-532
Tolpin, M., 114
transference, impact of personality organization on, 542-551

transfiguration, fear and, in child, impact of deceased and, 422-423
transitional object and transitional phenomena, in service of quest, 111-116
"truth," experience of, about self and parting parent, future goals and, 341-361
  initial acceptance of devaluation of absent parent, 347-349
  prolonged denial and negation, 349-354
  protective disengagement, 359-361
  pseudologica and consoling fantasy, 354-357
  restitutive hallucinations and consoling fantasies, 357-358
  transitory disbelief and negation, 358-359
  truth and idealization, 342-347

unconscious, basis for quest in, 97-99
U.S. Bureau of Census, 28
United States Children's Bureau, 15

Wallerstein, J. S., 33, 34, 90, 568
Wallston, B., 20
Watson, J. B., 15
Weisman, A., 536
Weiss, R. S., 27, 32, 33, 34, 90, 121, 127, 568
Wheeler, M., 27
Winnicott, D. W., 4, 111, 112, 562
Wolf, K., 17, 18, 27, 121, 565, 569
Wolfe, T., 361
Wolfenstein, M., 132, 135, 136
women, changes in interaction between men and, 6-14

Yarrow, M. R., 20

Zachrey, C. B., 65
Zetzel, E., 95, 142, 143